Theatre Arts on Acting

Books are to be return
the last date k

"The s ...ding players of today stand on an uneasy bridge between two extrem ...eatrical development. Behind us lie the glories of tradition, the grand manner, the star system [. . .] Before us lie the fear of convention and imitation, the demand for novelty, the restless, impatient craving for easy success [. . .]" John Gielgud

"I hate actors who bump into the furniture, or stand where they seem to be goosed by an armchair, or are frightened by tables, beds, lamps, doors and the surroundings in general." Hume Cronyn

During its fifty year run, *Theatre Arts Magazine* was a bustling forum for the foremost names in the performing arts. Renowned theatre historian **Laurence Senelick** has plundered its archives to assemble a stellar collection of articles on every aspect of the theatrical life.

Contributors include:

Konstantin Stanislavsky on Character Building; Stark Young on Illusion in Acting; Edith Isaacs on Typecasting; Lee Strasberg on Past Performances; Cedric Hardwicke on The Moribund Craft of Acting; as well as articles by and about Michael Chekhov, John Gielgud, Fred Astaire, Richard Boleslavsky, Shelley Winters, Laurence Olivier, Bette Davis, Alastair Cooke and Vivien Leigh

Laurence Senelick is Fletcher Professor of Drama and Oratory at Tufts University, and winner of the George Jean Nathan award for Dramatic Criticism. He is the author of over 20 books on theatre history and dramatic theory and a practising actor, director and translator.

Routledge Theatre Classics

The Routledge Theatre Classics series brings some of the theatrical world's seminal texts to a new generation. Drawn from Routledge's extensive archives, including the renowned Theatre Arts imprint, each volume has received expert editorial attention to update it for today's reader. This collection brings the theatre of the 20th Century into the spotlight of the 21st.

Titles include:

On the Art of the Theatre – by Edward Gordon Craig
Edited by Franc Chamberlain
A prescient vision of the state of theatre from one of its great modernisers, still bearing huge influence almost a century after it was written.

***Theatre Arts* on Acting** – edited by Laurence Senelick
A compendium of articles from the pages of Theatre Arts Magazine, with contributions from John Gielgud, Michael Chekhov, Konstantin Stanislavsky and Lee Strasberg among others.

Stanislavsky in Focus, 2nd Edition – by Sharon M. Carnicke
A crucial exploration of one of the theatre's towering figures. Dispels the misconceptions that dog his teachings and explains the truth behind the myth.

Theatre: The Rediscovery of Style, and other writings – by Michel Saint-Denis
Edited by Jane Baldwin
Combines Saint-Denis' two major works, moving seamlessly from theory to practice and addressing everything from actor training to the synergy of modern and classical theatre.

Theatre Arts on Acting

**Edited, with an Introduction, by
Laurence Senelick**

 Routledge
Taylor & Francis Group

LONDON AND NEW YORK

First published 2008
by Routledge
2 Park Squre, Milton Park, Abingdon, Oxon, OX14 4RN

Simultaneously published in the USA and Canada
by Routledge
270 Madison Avenue, New York, NY 10016

Routledge is an imprint of the Taylor & Francis Group, an informa business

Typeset in Baskerville by RefineCatch Limited, Bungay, Suffolk, UK
Printed and bound in Great Britain by
CPI Antony Rowe, Chippenham, Wiltshire

British Library Cataloguing in Publication Data
A catalogue record for this book is available from the British Library

Library of Congress Cataloging-in-Publication Data
Theatre arts on acting / edited and with an introduction by Laurence
Senelick.
      p. cm.
   Articles published in Theatre arts, 1916–1961.
   Includes bibliographical references.
   1. Acting. I. Senelick, Laurence.
   PN2061.T47 2008
   792.02′8–dc22   2008003041

ISBN10: 0–415–77492–6 (hb)
ISBN10: 0–415–77493–2 (pb)

ISBN13: 978–0–415–77492–5 (hb)
ISBN13: 978–0–415–77493–2 (pb)

For Darcy

Contents

Acknowledgments

The publishers would like to thank all of the relatives and rights holders whose generous and enthusiastic assistance has allowed this unique volume to take shape. These include David Ellis; David Pryce-Jones, Lina M. Granada, Prudence Faxon, Peter MacGowan, Marie J. Taylor, Lisa Dowdeswell, Cherrie Raimann, Kim Barrett, Susan Cooper Cronyn, Edward Hardwicke, Michael Houseman, Aimee Scheff, Maxime Mardoukhaev, Georgia Glover, Michael I. Adler, Samuel A. Bowman, Barry N. Malzberg. Special thanks goes to Julene Knox, for her indefatigable work in securing permission for the articles collected here.

"The Actor as Thinker" by Eric Bentley is copyright 1948, 1949, 1950, 1951, 1952, 1953, 1981 by Eric Bentley. Reprinted from *In Search Of Theater*, by Eric Bentley, by permission of Applause Theater Book Publishers.

"An actor must have three selves" (Michael Chekhov, Dec. 1952)
Used with permission of the Chekhov estate.

"A crux in English acting" (Alistair Cooke, Sept. 1932) © The Estate of Alistair Cooke

"Notes on film acting" (Hume Cronyn, June 1949) d.2003
"Dear Diary" (Hume Cronyn, July 1961)
Reprinted by kind permission of Susan Cooper Cronyn.

"The Gielgud MACBETH" (Ashley Dukes, Oct. 1942) d.1959
Reprinted by kind permission of David Ellis on behalf of The Estate of Ashley Dukes.

"Acting in my time" (St John Ervine, Aug. 1935) reproduced courtesy of The Society of Authors as the Literary Representatives of the Estate of St John Ervine.

"An actor prepares: a comment on Stanislavsky's method" (John Gielgud, Jan. 1937)
"An artist's apprenticeship" (John Gielgud, June–July 1937)
"Speak the speech, I pray you" (John Gielgud, Apr. 1951)
reprinted by kind permission of the Sir John Gielgud Charitable Trust.

"Comedienne from Radcliffe: Josephine Hull" (William Lindsay Gresham, June 1945). Reprinted by permission of Brandt & Hochman Literary Agents, Inc.

"The moribund craft of acting" (Cedric Hardwicke, Feb. 1939)
"An actor stakes his claim" (Cedric Hardwicke, Feb. 1958)
Reprinted by kind permission of Edward Hardwicke.

"Shakespeare and the American actor" (John Houseman, July 1956)
Reprinted by kind permission of Michael Houseman.

"The month of Duse" (Kenneth Macgowan, Jan. 1924)
Reprinted by kind permission of The Estate of Kenneth Macgowan.

"Sir Laurence and Larry" (Alan Pryce-Jones, Feb. 1961)
Reproduced by kind permission of the Estate of Alan Pryce-Jones

"Seven interviews in search of good acting" (Aimee Scheff, Mar. 1952)
Reprinted by kind permission of Aimee Scheff

"An actor prepares: comments on Stanislavsky's method" (Robert Sherwood, Harold Clurman, Norris Houghton, Feb. 1937)
Reprinted by permission of Brandt & Hochman Literary Agents, Inc.

"The Oliviers" (Sewell Stokes, Dec. 1945)
Reprinted by permission of David Higham Associates.

"Past performances" (Lee Strasberg, May 1950) © LS Library LLC.
Reprinted with permission.

"The voice in the theatre" (Stark Young, Oct. 1921)
"Giovanni Grasso" (Stark Young, Jan. 1922)
"Illusion in acting" (Stark Young, Feb. 1924)
"Billets doux" (Stark Young, Oct. 1929)
"Mei Lan-Fang" (Stark Young, Apr. 1930)
Reprinted by kind permission of Samuel A. Bowman.

"A study of the Actors Studio" (Maurice Zolotow, Aug., Sept. 1956)
Reprinted by permission of The Estate of Maurice Zolotow.

Introduction

When the first issue of *Theatre Arts* made its bow in Detroit in 1916, it entered a crowded field of American theatrical periodicals. The ordinary playgoer had access to such lavishly illustrated journals as *Theatre*, the *New York Dramatic Mirror* and the *Green Book Magazine*, which also covered opera, fashion and the newly emerging genre of film. The professional "show business" was served by the New York *Clipper*, *Variety* and *Billboard*. *The Drama* and *The Dramatic Magazine* concentrated on plays and playwrights, and other publications were devoted to vaudeville and burlesque. Given the competition, why did Stewart Cheney, the founder of *Theatre Arts*, think another magazine necessary?

As its later editors were to explain, it was meant to be "the mouthpiece, the forum of the young artist in revolt against the stale, the conventional, the stereotyped. It flaunted the word 'art' in the face of 'show business' and proclaimed in its first issue the intention to 'conserve and develop the creative impulse in the American theatre; to provide a permanent record of American dramatic art [. . .] to hasten the day when the speculator will step out of the established playhouse and let the artist come in." Performance and its criticism were to be practised not with the box office in mind; works were to be judged by a higher criterion. This disdain for the commercial theatre would be tempered in time, but at the inception the goals were distinctly utopian. Cheney, who had been serving as a paid dramatic critic for a mere six years, had his eyes and ears firmly fixed on Europe. He had heard the stirrings of the New Stagecraft and read what he could of the reforms and innovations of André Antoine, Adolphe Appia, Konstantin Stanislavsky, Gordon Craig, Max Reinhardt, and the Abbey Theatre. His ideal dramatists were Rostand, Maeterlinck, Shaw and Lady Gregory. His intention, stated in his inaugural editorial, was for *Theatre Arts Magazine* to "cover all those contributive arts that are working toward that wider synthetic art of the theatre which is yet to be realized." His magazine would therefore be less a record of the current theatre than a harbinger and champion of the theatre to come.

The European bias caused problems on the eve of the First World War. When *Theatre Arts* published a photograph of a German theatre, Detroit rose up in protest. Cheney's response was to take his quarterly to New York and a less provincial ambience. The move to the acknowledged Mecca of detested show business had significant consequences. It enabled Cheney to take on a wider circle of contributors and a supportive editorial board. Cheney had called the magazine the "organ of the progressives" (2, 1 December 1917, p1), so his new colleagues – Edith J. R. Isaacs, Kenneth Macgowan and Marion Tucker – were high-minded individuals who held advanced views, not only of reforming the theatre, but also of improving society at large.

Another effect of the move to New York was a less Puritanical approach to Broadway and its denizens. As the ideas of the reformers and revolutionaries became standard practice in the commercial theatre, *Theatre Arts* responded by becoming more catholic in its tastes. The magazine's idealism came to be leavened with a healthy acceptance of the practicalities of theatre, acknowledging the best of the "legit" without approving compromise or mediocrity. In addition to regular reporting on educational and community theatre, coverage was given to the popular arts and eventually to the rival artform, the movies. Still, a smack of the original principles never entirely disappeared from *Theatre Arts'* flavour.

The editors' ascetic aesthetics could be seen in the magazine's format. At the inception, its look and feel embodied Arts and Crafts principles of design and might have issued from the workshop of Elbert Hubbard. For the first few years, it was printed in heavy black ink on thick paper, bound in wrappers of dark colours or muted gray. In the 1920s and 1930s, it simply alternated its covers from red to green to orange to yellow, eventually settling on the latter two hues, without any graphic images. Cover photos and drawings appeared only in the late 1930s. Along with simple vignettes interspersed throughout the text, the main illustrations were full-page photographs printed on coated paper. Although glossy periodicals like *Stage* and *Theatre Magazine* carried lavish advertisements for luxury items such as cars, furs and cigarettes, the advertising admitted to *Theatre Arts* remained marginal, theatre-related, and relegated to the front and back matter.

Theatre Arts' reformist goals were personified by the two women who became its guiding lights for many years. Edith Isaacs, the college-educated and well-to-do wife of a New York lawyer and composer, had been drama critic for *Ainslee's Magazine* and a frequent contributor to the women's press before she joined the editorial board in 1919. She became the editor-in-chief in 1922 and two years later expanded *Theatre Arts* from a quarterly to a monthly, enlarging its physical size in the process. Isaacs was also a leading stockholder and donor. Even during the period of its broadest popularity, *Theatre Arts* was never financially independent, but stayed indebted to a number of wealthy patrons. These included the Elmhirsts, who founded the Dartington School for the Arts and were responsible for bringing Michael Chekhov to America. Private support enabled *Theatre Arts* to maintain its high standards, but the biases of the patrons could also be seen in its emphases.

Isaacs had a strong interest in the Little Theatre Movement, so both college and community theatres were allowed a good deal of space. One issue a year was devoted to the "Tributary Theatre," a telling term, which, more than "regional theatre", indicated that the hinterlands were what really nourished the big-city stages. She also took an active part in the Federal Theatre Project, having long supported the work of Hallie Flanagan. Like many white intellectuals of the time, she was fascinated by black culture, organizing the first New York exhibition of native African art and dedicating the August 1942 issue of *Theatre Arts* to "the Negro in the American theatre".

As editor, Isaacs opened out Cheney's focus on theatre of the future to cover the present and discover the past. She began running articles on theatre history, to record how what had been could inspire what was to come. Special issues were devoted to Adolphe Appia, Lope de Vega, musical comedy, Shakespeare and the modern stage, theatrical literature and a number of national theatres. She established Theatre Arts Books to put out collected articles and monographs. It published Richard Boleslavsky's lessons on acting, which have never gone out of print. In 1947 the press's editorial duties were invested in Robert Gottlieb, who oversaw the series of translations and adaptations of Stanislavsky's writings by Elizabeth Reynolds Hapgood.

Isaacs was on friendly terms with Eugene O'Neill, Thornton Wilder, Martha Graham, Robert Edmond Jones, Jo Mielziner, Donald Oenslager and John Mason Brown, all of whom frequently showed up in the magazine either as contributors or subjects. Her most fruitful association, however, was with Rosamond Gilder, daughter of the influential poet and journalist Richard Watson Gilder. Gilder began at *Theatre Arts* as a proofreader and joined the editorial staff in 1924. The two women worked as a team, with Isaacs often initiating a project which Gilder would execute. Gilder's own book *Enter the Actress* (1931) was a pioneering study of the emergence of women on the early modern stage.

Stewart Cheney's eagerness to advance the New Stagecraft had meant an emphasis on directors and designers, the visionaries who were to chart the course of twentieth-century theatre. The illustrations of their work, either drawings or photographs of productions, were among the valuable features of each issue, so much so that separate portfolios of them for classroom use were made available in compact boxes. Playwrights were also to the fore, since the American drama was viewed as immature, unengaged with ideas. Experimentation, fed by European trends and nativist traditions, was to be encouraged – hence the promotion of Eugene O'Neill. One-act plays often appeared in the early issues, among them Langston Hughes' translations of Garcia Lorca.

Isaacs and Gilder, however, never lost sight of the crews of these enterprises. Under their guidance, there began to be longer articles on individual players and, more importantly, approaches to acting. *Theatre Arts* raised the technique of the interview beyond mere celebrity worship to probing inquiries into the principles and practices of the working actor.

The American stage, when the first issue of *Theatre Arts* appeared, was still in thrall to the nineteenth-century star system. The actor-manager may have been succumbing in the monopolistic grip of the producer, but audiences continued to buy tickets to see players rather than plays. Throwbacks like Walter Hampden trouped the country in such romantic vehicles as *Cyrano* and *Richelieu*. Plays were written to showcase the talents and personalities of particular performers, and tended to the formulaic. The acting profession was unorganized, rehearsals were unpaid and managerial abuses rife. *Theatre Arts* never subscribed to Gordon

Craig's concept of the Übermarionette and the effacement of the actor, but it did insist on acting that went beyond the cult of personality and the routine. It hoped to raise the dignity and artistic aims of the actor. It looked to amateur performance, such as at Antoine's Théâtre Libre and community efforts, as well as the sophisticated professionalism of Reinhardt's and Granville-Barker's companies, responsive to a director's conceptions, to reinvigorate the American stage. The kinds of plays that were emerging from Professor Baker's laboratory at Harvard or chosen for performance by the Provincetown Players needed a more intimate type of performance.

The Theatre Guild was the first viable New York enterprise to embody these trends. It embraced the New Stagecraft in principle, although in reality it shuttled between idealism and the demands of the marketplace. Its favourite "highbrow" playwrights were O'Neill and Shaw, but it varied them with costume dramas and high comedies to keep its audience amused as well as enlightened. In some respects, it resembled the old-fashioned stock company, with a troupe of seasoned performers who appeared in multiple guises in the course of a season. Over time, however, some of its players, especially the Lunts, moved up to the glamorous headliner category, drawing in the public by their own charisma. They, in turn, became travelling stars in the traditional mould.

An important catalyst for change in American acting was the visits of the Moscow Art Theatre in 1923–4. One of the first American publications to recognize the significance of Stanislavsky, *Theatre Arts* had devoted an early issue to his work, and continued throughout its life to promote his ideas. What distinguished the effect of the Art Theatre from that of tours of earlier foreign stars was the tightness of the ensemble, the contribution of each element of the production to the desired impression. Salvini, Bernhardt and Duse had been surrounded by scratch companies and often played in fit-up scenery. Even though the Art Theatre had to recruit its crowd scenes locally, it held daily rehearsals and was dedicated to the idea of art as a surrogate religion.

After its departure, a number of defectors and emigrés with their thick accents inculcated their own versions of Stanislavskian concepts to avid Americans. The American Laboratory Theatre, run by Boleslavsky and Maria Ouspenskaya, in turn inspired the Group Theatre, a collective of primarily Jewish, left-wing New Yorkers. The Group aspired to the seamless ensembles of the Art Theatre, but it also wanted to change society in a radical way. Its founding coincided with the Depression and the strident proselytizing of the Communist Party. On the one hand, the Group worshipped Chekhov, the swansong of a dying empire, and, on the other, hoped to emulate the agitprop methods of Meyerhold and the Proletkult. In interpreting Stanislavsky, a schism arose, leading to the hard-shell variant, preached by Lee Strasberg, and soft-shell variant, promulgated by Stella Adler. A host of lesser sects pullulated in their wake.

Internecine squabbles contributed to the dissolution of the Group Theatre, but so did success. Many of its strongest actors, as well as its house dramatist Clifford Odets, were wooed away by Hollywood, "selling out" in the opinion of some. Before the advent of the talkies, the cinema had not been serious competition for the live theatre. The Wall Street crash of 1929 limited the amount of money available for stage productions, and the film studios needed actors who could read lines. The westward flow was unstaunchable. Actors from the Group reconstituted themselves in Los Angeles as the Actors' Lab; emigré acting teachers found new students and opportunities on the West Coast. A cross-fertilization between stage and film could be seen in a more psychologized, less flamboyant acting technique.

A brief proliferation of theatrical experiment occurred under the Federal Theatre Project of the National Recovery Act, but its funding was cut off, because Congress found it too left of center politically. The identification of advanced acting methods with left-wing political agitation was to have dire effects after the Second World War. The House Committee on Un-American Activities (HUAC) and Senator Joseph McCarthy were intent on winkling out Communists and their influence from every aspect of American life. The "entertainment industry" engaged their attention, and the movies, television and, to a lesser extent, the live theatre were to be purged of Reds and fellow travellers. A generation of talented actors and directors was suddenly blacklisted, and could find no work in their own country.

The breach was filled by those who had either remained apolitical or who had cooperated with HUAC. The new prominence of those former Group members, Elia Kazan and Lee Strasberg, is due in part to this factor. The Actors Studio in New York, founded by Kazan (who had named names) and dominated by Strasberg (who took no part in politics), inculcated a kind of acting which was internalized, agonized and intimate, drawn from one's own emotions. It was a type of performance ideal for the camera and the projection of personality, less effective for interpreting the classics and creating diverse characters. It was also, significantly, a medium for personal, rather than public, dramas. Symptomatic of the theatre's retreat from the political forum, it was not so effective in satire and social protest, elements which might offend the powers that be.

Theatre Arts remained above the fray, offering its pages to all manner of schools and opinions. In 1948 it was amalgamated with *Stage Magazine*, and its format and contents were adjusted to appeal to a wider public. Interviews and photo spreads became more common. Each issue published the text of a play currently on Broadway. Nevertheless, just as its earlier issues were able to include Jaques-Dalcroze and Fanny Brice between the same covers, so these later issues offered a forum to both proponents and detractors of Method acting. If its torch burned less brightly, that reflected the state of American theatre. No longer the foremost performance art as it had been in the early twentieth century, the stage now played second-fiddle to other media. The demise of the magazine in 1964 was a byblow of that decline. Even in its final numbers, however, it offered the American public close looks at new directions, with its presentations on Bertolt Brecht and his actors. To the very end, *Theatre Arts* kept its eye on the distant, rosy prospect.

Laurence Senelick

Part I

Acting in the American tradition

1 Acting and the New Stagecraft

Walter Prichard Eaton

November 1916

Theatre Arts was founded to propagate the New Stagecraft, which, born of the ideas of Adolphe Appia and Edward Gordon Craig, was concerned largely with scene design and the stage picture. The very first article in the very first issue, however, turned its attention to how these innovations affected acting and how, in turn, acting was to respond. Not so much a manifesto as a modest proposal, it was written by Walter Prichard Eaton (1878–1957), a Harvard-educated dramatic critic of long experience, who later became professor of playwriting at Yale. He would eventually write a chronicle of the first ten years of the Theatre Guild. In championing the New Stagecraft, he was careful not to turn professional and amateur, realism and conventionalism, commercial and experimental into opposing camps; rather, he argued that the best of all factions be preserved.

———————

THE new spirit of experimentation in the arts of the theatre has, so far at least, affected the American theatre but little, so little, indeed, that the result is almost negligible. By the American theatre I mean, of course, the professional theatre patronized by the great public, which sends its productions out through the land and is, when all is said, the stronghold which must be stormed and captured before Progress can claim a victory. Robert Jones and Joseph Urban and Livingston Platt, to be sure, have designed certain settings, some of them beautiful settings; and Maxfield Parrish is now being called in to give his talent to the theatre. Yet one would scarcely call the Ziegfeld "Follies" an experiment in the new stagecraft, though Mr. Urban did design the settings; while the ballet at the Hippodrome, devised by Bakst and Pavlowa, was, after the first night or two, so befuddled with Hippodrome chorus girls (who finally were hauled up on wires as a climax!) that it would hardly be distinguished from the Good Old Stuff. We must, I fear, face the fact that the experimental spirit in America is still an amateur spirit, and in the immediate future, at least, we must look for its flowering, for the results of genuine experiment, in the various "little theatres" and other refuges of the dissatisfied or the dilettantes. After all, there can be no progress without dissatisfaction, and it is often enough the dilettante with talent who becomes the professional with power.

But in my own observations of these experimental theatres, I have been struck with one odd fact. While the experimenters were eager to produce fresher and more vital drama, to create more illusive and effective lighting effects, to paint more suggestive and beautiful scenery, to get away from the dull rut of conventional "realism," at the same time they were, almost without exception, apparently quite neglectful of showing us fresher, more vital, more illusive *acting*, or at any rate ignorant of how to do it. In the case of such an organization as the Washington Square Players, say, we must of course be mindful of the fact that the scene-painters are frequently professional artists, the dramatists professional dramatists, while the actors have been for the most part amateurs. No amateur, however gifted, can walk out on the boards and give at once a performance without a flaw, can give a performance as illusive of character as any second-rate professional with intelligence. All the more reason, then, why the actors in the experimental theatres should be trained at least to do well what they can do well, and what the conventional professional actors do badly, while they are learning slowly in the hard school of practice to create the illusion of character.

What are some of the things they could be trained to do? In the first place, they could be trained to speak. The new stagecraft, so far as it has been practised here, seems to have forgotten that as long as it is dedicated to the spoken drama, part of its task will be to make that speech audible, and consequently to make it effective to the last degree. Ask yourself this question: if you were witnessing "Hamlet," which would you rather find, a glorious, illusive setting with a bad actor mumbling "To be or not to be . . . .", or a bare stage and Booth speaking those words as only he could speak them? Certainly, most people would choose Booth, and they would be quite right in so doing. Yet, under the influence of our bald, colloquial modern drama, beautiful speech, clean enunciation, a sense for rhythm, has almost perished from the professional stage. Let a modern author write a speech which he wants to hear delivered like music as well as human conversation — and he weeps bloody tears at each rehearsal. There are no actors to read it. It cannot be read properly without proper feeling for verbal felicities, and without practice. But a feeling for verbal felicities is just what genuine devotees of the new stagecraft should have, or their boasted devotion to beauty is a one-sided thing; and practice in correct, clean, felicitous utterance is just what the stages of our experimental theatres should afford. The rankest amateur ought to be able to pronounce correctly, and enunciate all the syllables of a polysyllabic word without swallowing the penult. If he cannot, he should be politely invited to become a professional and join Mr. Cohan's company. When you enter a little theatre you ought at least to be confident of hearing better speech than in any Broadway production.

Our experimental theatres are not dedicated to realism. They do not neglect it, but the new stagecraft needs the fanciful, the poetic, the suggestive, for its full expression. And the fanciful, the poetic, the suggestive in drama cannot be acted as the realistic drama is acted. The instinct which leads the opera singer to gesticulate like a windmill, which leads Lou-Tellegen to strike romantic attitudes, is a perfectly sound instinct. Convention has made the result grotesque, to be sure, but in their hatred of convention too many experimental theatres have quite lost sight of the rightness of the instinct, and as a result play a scene of romance or poetry, in a setting not of this world but of the abstract land of beauty, with actors who stand about as stiff as freshmen at the President's first reception, talking in the nasal, colloquial tones of the average American. This may be unconventional, but it isn't good art, and it is holding back the new stagecraft in popular regard. If the new stagecraft is to play fantasy and poetry, in imaginative, beautiful sets, it must train its actors to beauty and grace of carriage, to fluidity of pose, to expressive gesture (there is nothing poetic about keeping your hands in your pockets, as the mere public very well knows), to that general charm of romantic bearing which certain of the older actors even in our generation possessed, which is as old as histrionic art, indeed, and will always be as young as the latest lyric. To try to foster and develop this charm should be a task of the experimental theatres. If they cannot keep those who possess it from the affectations and absurdities of conventional romance, from the posturings of a Lou-Tellegen, that is merely a confession of weakness on their part. It is no sign of strength, certainly, to be so afraid of the excesses that you abolish the essentials.

Indeed, in the revolt from the conventions of the "commercial" theatre, it is rather to be feared that we have tended to throw overboard a good deal that is sound and necessary. Enough light to see the actors' faces is one thing. The downright force and predominant importance of good acting is another. When all is said, the spoken drama is brought to life for an audience by the actors, not the electrician nor the scene-painter, not the costume designer nor the orchestra conductor nor even the stage-manager, but *by the actors*. It is they the audience watches, recking not of the director who may have trained them; they who are, for three hours traffic, the protagonists of the play. It can be no better than they are, and with the great public its success will depend upon them.

Little theatres, experimental theatres of all sorts, may help the new stagecraft in a hundred ways, and bring various kinds of pleasure to us, but they will never ultimately persuade the public unless they can show illusive acting, unless they can train players to *impersonate*, to bring the characters of the drama to vivid life. Too many of our experimental theatres are weakest on this most important side; they have neglected the art of acting, the foundation stone of the dramatic structure, and the stone which changes least of all with the changing styles of architecture. They ask patronage to behold beautiful scenery, to hear brilliant "lines," to witness the play of magic lights; but what the public primarily pays for is a story, so well acted that it cheats them into belief. The new stagecraft has got to play the game. It has got to furnish the actors. Nor is that so impossible a task, if once we realize its necessity.

2 The place of the actor in "the new movement"

Claude King

July 1922

Claude King (1875–1941) was an English-born actor, who had played Dr. Watson in Conan Doyle's dramatization of his Sherlock Holmes story *The Speckled Band* (1910). He began appearing on Broadway in 1906, and had several roles in the Theatre Guild premiere of Shaw's *Back to Methusaleh* (1922), although his best part was the young playwright Tom Wrench in *Trelawney of the "Wells"* (1925). From 1923, he appeared in Hollywood films, many with Lon Chaney, usually typecast as an "English gentleman", and was one of the founding members of the Screen Actors Guild.

———————————

In all that has been written and said about the new movement in the theatre, I find so much about décor and lighting and so little about acting, that I am almost reduced to feeling that the actor has no place in the revolution or evolution, if the term is a better one, that is undoubtedly taking place. And since it is upon the shoulders of the actor that the final burden has to be carried, I think it is now due to him to find out just what his position is, or is going to be. For remember that when the curtain rises on the first night, the author may not be present, the artist responsible for the décor may be comfortably working in his studio on the models for his next production, the manager may be on his way to Europe, but the actor has to be there, on the spot, to interpret the living part of the accumulated efforts of all concerned.

Gordon Craig has released the current in the direction of the spiritual and the imaginative in the theatre, and the present trouble is that very often in the experimental theatre the scenery soars in the regions of the new movement, while the actor plays in something less than the good "old fashioned" way. If the actor can give the required quality to any scene the lighting and scenery should serve to accentuate and heighten that quality in some way, but the experiment must not be used as a compensation for the lack of the required quality in the actor. If the theatre is going to advance healthily it must keep near to, and conscious of its source. Then only will it become a vital part of the whole social organism.

And when I speak of the actor I mean the trained actor, the man who has served his apprenticeship at his craft, and has learned his technique sufficiently well to be able to forget it, or at any rate to hide its mechanics. Talma says that twenty years is the minimum period required to learn the art of acting, and both Irving and Forbes Robertson have agreed that he is right. But the mere term of years spent in the theatre is not necessarily important; they must have been years spent in the proper acquisition of the knowledge required to make the actor, in the fullest sense of the term, an interpreter of the play.

We so often see a brilliant young performer spoiled by too early success. It takes character and a very beautiful kind of humility for the young to realize the need of study, not book-lore necessarily, rather the study of the many and various phases of human nature, the cultivation of understanding, the appreciation of all the curious reactions and nuances which go to make up our individualities.

Perhaps one of the most necessary things for the actor of today to acquire is social perspective. We are, on the whole, rather inclined to think of our work in just terms of "theatre." I think this will disappear as we extend our human sympathies, intensify our human contacts, and cultivate a greater flexibility of mind in the direction of wonder and imagination. Automatically the actor who enlarges his vision will grow away from the traditional convention towards something which is truer, simpler, more modern, still retaining what is good in the older forms. A phrase of Gilbert Murray's haunts me, "Dominant emotion tempered by gentler thought." This phrase applied to the actor conveys to me the power of giving to each part the requisite emotion, fitting into a thoughtful conception of the whole play; but, mark you, the emotion must be dominant, projected; we want no intellectual meandering.

If the theatre of today is the theatre of the idea, that idea has to be embodied, and the actor needs not only to understand but to feel the significance of his role in relation to the governing idea of the play.

The value to the actor of the social drama is very interesting. Taking a long view of the playwrights from the eighties, their plays largely reflect the awakening of the people to political and social self-consciousness. Through these plays the actor establishes his identity with the social organism. Artists often anticipate the general acknowledgment of some new current, but artists are a rare species. The actor who still thinks in terms of the theatre apart from the social organism, or in terms of his own personality, may have a long road to travel before he attains to the simplicity, the integrity, or even the "groping sincerity" which characterize the real artist.

After all what is this thing which has come to be called the New Movement? Is it not as it affects the actor just another angle of approach, a development of the spirit of the time, a new vision by which we re-view all plays? Let us apply it to a classic, Shakespeare for example. Macbeth, instead of a mighty melodrama, becomes in the light of present day psychology the document of two human souls, exalted, illegitimately ambitious. Outraged Nature at the helm breaks them. The woman may not pervert her sex to the uses of "direst cruelty," the man may not wade to an empty form of power through the lovely life-blood of friends. Played perfectly in the spirit of the new movement, this play would uncover the whole canker of illegitimate personal ambition. Can you imagine it? Each actor in his right relation to the whole, those two splendid lovers disintegrating before our very eyes, in some wild vortex of ambition; here is this mighty problem told in language of such beauty as to give "balm to hurt minds."

Gordon Craig says in "The Art of The Theatre": "It is impossible for a work of art ever to be produced where more than one brain is permitted to direct; and if works of art are not seen in the theatre this one reason is a sufficient one, though there are plenty more. There must be one man capable of inventing and rehearsing a play; of designing and superintending the construction of both scenery and costume; of writing any necessary music; of inventing such machinery as is needed and the lighting that is to be used." Kenneth Macgowan describes this demand as the extravagance of the ideal, in his very excellent book "The Theatre of Tomorrow," and I entirely agree with him.

The influence of Craig seems to have moved towards the "theatric," that is, the thing to be seen, the sensuous appeal of the aesthetic, even to the substitution of the "über-marionette" for the actor, and thus he may succeed in producing a new form for the theatre in the same way as has been accomplished by the Russian Ballet with its characteristic mime and music. But we actors care for the spoken word, and what we look for is not the "über-marionette" but the "über-director."

My experience teaches me that the best direction is done when the director approaches his task in much the same manner as he would if he were a musical conductor preparing an orchestra for the playing of a symphony. That is, he must study his manuscript thoroughly before rehearsal so that he knows what results he is to get from his orchestra when the work is played; and the actor should be as well trained as are the musicians, as a matter of course; for remember that the director does not control each performance, like the conductor does, he has to rely upon the actor to retain interpretation, tone and tempo as rehearsed.

It is impossible to overestimate the importance of team work in the new movement. We recognize its importance in a football team or a racing boat, and it is just as essential in the theatre. In a novel, the name of which escapes me, there is a description of a boat race in which the hero is rowing stroke, and the authoress to emphasize the almost superhuman effort of the hero expresses herself thus, "All rowed fast in that boat, but none so fast as Bouncer." Imagine the result! We can all remember how plays have been upset by the use of this precise method, times without number.

Granville Barker says in his recently published book "The Exemplary Theatre," that a company that is playing well together as a team will produce a joint result that is 50 per cent better than the individual achievement of any one of its members, and this is absolutely true. My mind naturally goes back to the four years I spent with Granville Barker, which the World War interrupted, and he was such a man as I describe. He had a thoroughly contagious and beautifully informed enthusiasm. We did a great number of plays during that period, and the first rehearsal of each play was used for the exposition of his aim in that play, so that we all knew the goal in view and worked towards it. Not only the company, but Albert Rutherston, or Norman Wilkinson, or Arthur Ricketts, or whoever was doing the décor, worked with him just as the company did, and thus we achieved a real unity under his masterly control. I remember an interesting thing in connection with this enthusiasm which often struck me at the time, and that was the reverent attitude,—I don't know how else to describe it,—of everybody about the theatre during the rehearsal. We all spoke in whispers and moved about as silently as possible when not engaged in the scene in progress, we kept out of the line of sight as far as possible, and apart from the text of the play, the only sound ever heard was the voice of Barker giving directions: in short, the stage was a sanctuary. And this was not the result of an order, but just the normal tribute of us all to the interest of the work in progress. The result was that every minute spent at rehearsal was creative and fruitful, and we did more work in three hours in such an atmosphere than one usually does in six hours of the ordinary kind of rehearsal. I do not wish for one moment to suggest that this method is peculiar to Granville Barker, but I think most actors will agree with me that it is not the general rule to be privileged to work in such an atmosphere. With him there was no rigidity of method with the individual actor, I have known him to discard approach after approach until he found the one most suited to the personality of the actor concerned, to bring through his idea. I have even known him to discard his direction of an entire act, and after two or three days to come to it again from an entirely different angle, getting the result through an almost uncanny appreciation of the material in hand.

We look for other such groups in the Anglo-Saxon theatre; groups similar to those established by Stanislavsky, Reinhardt, Copeau, with companies and directors working constantly together instead of in haphazard agglomeration as they do now. It is in such an association that the new movement will take root and the theatre of tomorrow grow to its fullest possibility.

3   Billets doux

Stark Young

October 1929

One of the boons conferred by *Theatre Arts* was to provide a forum for Stark Young (1881–1963), arguably the most perceptive and poetic dramatic critic America has produced. The Mississippi-born aesthete had studied at Yale under the eminent critic Brander Mathews. A popular professor of literature, Young was eased out of his position at Amherst College because of his homosexuality, and moved to New York, where he became dramatic critic for the weekly *New Republic* from 1922 until his retirement in 1947, worked a stint as reviewer for the New York *Times* (1924–5) and was associate editor of *Theatre Arts* (1921–30). Throughout the 1920s, Young, an advocate of the New Stagecraft, published criticism and plays, lectured at the New School for Social Research, and worked at the Provincetown Playhouse. His criticism, expressed in a limpid prose, was sensitive to the technical, as well as the literary, aspects of theatre.

To a well-dressed wretched young lady

Your situation is only one out of many. I have seen your case paralleled in *Street Scene*, with Erin O'Brien Moore, in Claudette Colbert's *Dynamo* heroine, in Zita Johann's *Machinal*, and in other plays. This is it: there is a young lady who is, one way or another, in dire distress. She is poor, or ruined, or lives with hard parents near sweatshops; she is wretched or weary or horrified at her mother's murder and her father's arrest, and so on and so on. Meanwhile as far as her toilette goes, she is unruffled. Her little frock is the neatest and smartest, always in good taste. Her shoes fit beautifully, sit trimly on the ground, her hat is chic, her legs shine in perfect hosiery, made more perfect by the perfection of the ankles and the competence of the footlights. And all the time we are to believe in her poverty, her pathetic soul-starvation, her agony, seduction or what not, though it is quite plain to all that, as the advertisements say, you can't go wrong in any of these accoutrements.

You, I know, have explained to me how different it really is. I wrote this about you, you remember, and you sent me a pleasant little letter, giving me statistics of cost prices. This frock of yours, your three frocks which you change so engagingly as the tragedy progresses from curtain to curtain, you bought at a Forty-second Street sale for fifteen dollars each, a dollar less, a dollar more. The shoes came from a cheap general shop, at four dollars and a half.

Well now, what shall I say? In the first place that we have an example of our dear human habit of persuading ourselves into what we want to believe. Everybody knows that the profit on frocks and shoes is enormous and that the expensive shops are those in which we are supposed to pay for the taste provided. If we have the taste and confidence ourselves, we can often get the same things elsewhere at much less. We will let that pass. It is true that if you carry to the cheap sale the eye that is familiar with good style, good line, the price at which you get your costume has very little to do with it. Your taste is just the point, your line, effect.

But, you argue, this little wretched girl you portray might also go to these sales, since our American girls have a natural eye for effects. That, too, while it seems a piece of realism, has no point. The scene, the play, paints a dramatic misery, poverty, hardship, provincialism, what not. Art is forever a form of restatement. You have, therefore, to recreate these qualities in your appearance. Your mother has just been breathing her last, you neat little thing there on the stage; do you expect us to believe that your soul has been rumpled; no, not by a long shot. I remain comfortable, reassured that your inside is as smoothed and well pressed as your sleeve, as trim as your hair, and that like those stockings of yours, it will not run or ravel.

There is another point. In formal drama, where the statement is statuesque and remote, you would require a costume formal and grand. In the most tragic crisis, your appearance, your clothes, your gesture would, like the epoch and the whole dramatic style, remain formal and decorative. But you, dear personality child, have cast out all this from your theory. You are natural, you are yourself, you are like life. You give us straight stuff, you are willing to hit us in the face with your plain words; the names you call the ladies of the evening, the current sins and diverse human frailties, are a caution. At one point only do you break down, realism vanishes—in no grand far-off stylization of the Greek drama did a skirt ever hang better than yours or a face and headdress remain more stylish and attractive.

To an actress warming her hands

In your first scene, where you meet your sister's fiancé—whom you will later capture for yourself—you have a line where you say it is cold and turn to the fire to warm your hands. I can see you now. "It's cold today," you say, and turn toward the fire and hold out your pretty hands.

But that is all wrong; and in this moment lies one of the secrets of all acting. What really happens is that the feeling of cold is in your body. Indeed the idea of all actions arises first in the nerves and muscles of your body, and we should see your action promised there in your movement before the words are spoken at all. In this case even the hands held out do not come first. The inclination of your shoulders and whole mass indicates a turning toward the desired warmth, and from this movement the gesture of your hands derives, and from that the words.

There is another point: the proper timing and rhythm of movement in such instances helps to get the speech itself into its proper scale; what you have to say finds its right proportion within the whole scene. You do not lose time and proportion dwelling on what deserves only a limited amount of stress. In fact, if the audience saw the movement and heard the word *cold*, nothing else need concern you, your next speech might already begin or the other actor take up his cue, the life of the scene go on. More thought in this direction might rid American acting of a good deal of that spacing out of single speeches, that stupid gap between cues and that monotony of stress in the dialogue, that does so much to take the life out of plays.

To the victim of a long run

YOUR play has run a year and a half now, and you are beginning to pity yourself very hard. How can you be an artist and get no chance at diverse roles? How terrible it is to grow stale in a part, to be sick of it! You can hardly bear to go through it, you say; you have even come to the point where you can hardly remember the lines.

No doubt it would be better to enjoy the chance of many characters and many effects. You would like to do different kinds of things, to have a change, to create something fresh. There are theatres in Europe where this might be more likely; you are in America, however.

But search your heart. We live in the land of Success, you know that. Aren't you, when you come right down to it, thrilled to remember that you are a part of a phenomenal theatrical success, a year and a half in town and then two years on the road? And if you had these several chances you speak of, one role and then another and another, would you not want them on condition that you be as successful in each of them as you have been in this run and as well paid—speaking of Europe, for there you would earn far less—so that you could live like your friends in society? If, however, neither of these suppositions be true, the fact remains that you will not have these chances, you must go on with this role or drop out to God knows where, and so we must think out the case as best we can.

Why not learn to study this performance of yours constantly? Try it one way and then another. In single speeches try a change of the tone, take a line more slowly, take certain cues more closely on the heels of the preceding speech, delay the timing a few beats here, sharpen your consonants there. You can turn the part, with this opportunity of trying things over night after night, into a school for technique—that may be some comfort.

Or, why not take some of the vaudeville people and study them and watch the way they work? Take that Mr. Winfred and Mr. Mills in their Chinese act, which appears yearly in some review, and which I myself, though a poor theatregoer, have seen four times and always enjoyed and seen the audience enjoy. Watch these performers tackle each moment as it arrives. They have their eyes, not on what they are feeling themselves, but on making the moment go over with the audience. Moment by moment they turn the performance into an adventure, and relieve themselves through a wholesome technical excitement. By keeping their performance alive, they keep themselves going.

Your case is sad enough, looking at it from a human and artistic standpoint, but not so sad as you make it. You need to consider technical attack and execution as such; you need to develop a memory for what you do, and have done, and its effect, so that you may repeat it or study it as time goes on; you need to get yourself, your personal self, in a clearer relation to your performance and to the craft of acting; you need to clear your head of the notion that the business of art is to express you—the business of art is to express you, all right, but it is your business to create something in art. This something will not be merely you, it will create as well as exhibit.

To an actor who desires to act parts with a grand style

You have done very well and can have as much as any of the younger actors, but you are impatient, nobly enough, to do a hero that has style. There are great roles and you know it, great roles outside the realistic schools. Well, some day, if you become a very great star, with managers, for a few seasons, eating out of your hands, they will let you try a production of a Shakespeare play, or Cyrano, or a Tolstoi hero, provided, that is, you oblige them by making a good run lower down in drama or in some familiar realism, excellent, if you like, but also appealing. That day may come, but even then you will have players around you who know little of how such plays are to be acted, a director without any schooling in the dramatic style he must undertake, and audiences either not numerous or not very anxious to be delighted with stylish, complex, or poetic effects.

If you feel very strongly about this, you had better quit now, for you will never have much of this that you desire. The drama follows the epoch that it is written to express and entertain, and the quality or school of acting must always depend on the drama that it interprets. Of all the arts that go to make up the theatre art, acting comes last in independence. Our epoch lacks style in the sense you mean the word, something formal or elevated or elaborate or grand. Our long-run system, based on high costs of production and democratic necessities, cannot cater to the special few. Some day there may be a turn toward the other method and toward the style you dream of, or there may not. But not in your time. If you feel too strongly about this state of things, you had better quit.

To an actor on kidding

Even the stage hands speak of your habit of doing what they call kid the play. The line will be, "Not out there in the blazing sun, poor boy!" and you will add, half under your breath, the day being June in New York, "Yes, and it's hot in here, too." The line is, "I'm going home," and you say, as you turn your head away, "If I can get a taxi." Et cetera, et cetera. There is no pleasure in recalling these side remarks of yours.

You try this trick a few weeks after the play opens, when you are beginning to tire of it; and if the run is long, you grow quite outrageous with your kidding. The author may by then have quit dropping in to see the piece, or gone to Europe, or, if he does keep an eye on the performance, may register his objection gently or violently, according to the security of his position as a dramatist or his conscience as an artist.

Well, my child—you seem a child when you do this, though you are nearing forty—you are very wrong. This sort of thing descends from the old days when the play was nothing and people went to see acting, or when the plays were such stock affairs with such stock situations that the actor improvised or refreshed them according to the needs of the moment and threw sarcastic monkey wrenches into them if he happened to be great enough or his temperament enough off-key that day. With you the habit comes sometimes from boredom; sometimes from a childish vanity that wishes to amuse your fellow players on the stage with your nerve and waggishness; sometimes from contempt for the whole business; sometimes from mere caprice or vagrancy of mind. But whatever makes you do it, it is a foolish racket, shameful in sincere dramatic writing, frivolous in an artist, and sadly flat as wit. If you did it brilliantly enough, we might forgive you and let it pass as caricature, better than the thing in hand—but don't be very sure of that.

Once I heard Caruso sing a whole aria to a pin in the belt of the soprano's dress that had stuck him when he embraced her—*O—spilla crudele*—cruel pin. And once I heard Sarah Bernhardt in *Tosca*, standing over Scarpia's body, when she had stabbed him, break into invective against the scenery. A piece of the wings had swung on its hinges and flapped against her; *cette colonne va tomber*, she declaimed, in a rasping, tragic voice of hate and revenge, her eyes on her dead enemy, "this column is going to fall, these damned carpenters haven't got any sense." But these were artists who knew how to establish a current that swept the audience along, and who, moreover, were performing in foreign tongues to American audiences, with all the ironic possibilities involved in that situation. These were great impishnesses, as it were, even in such artists, and doubtful enough at that. You had best forget them and stick to your business.

If your spirits are high, they can capture ebullience for the lines written for you to speak; ebullience if the lines are gay; or the same teeming spirits and energy may darken and intensify the tragic places. If you are bored with the weeks of repetition, you had better—as Dorothy Dix or Cousin Marian would say in their correspondence columns—read our letter to the young player with the long-run problem. If you are in too great a despair, you had best reconsider your choice of a profession, and not try to eat your cake and have it too.

If nothing else will stop you, try to think of yourself in the dramatist's shoes, whose lines you are mistreating; as if, after your big scene or during it, one of the actors put in a comment, "You don't say!" or winked openly at somebody in the company or in the audience, or stole your moment by taking out his watch, catching the footlights in it and flashing it in somebody's eyes out in front—that old trick for spitefully rattling the audience and spoiling a rival's scene. If this happened to you, my dear—you take yourself very seriously, you know—what a pouting we should have!

To one who is apologetic

THERE are plenty of plays where the lines, motives and scenes are merely cheap and tricky, full of hokum and effects contrived to catch the cheaper audiences. The piece you are in now is less that than it is a case of sincere intention without sense enough or talent enough to carry through. But I have seen you in the other sort of play too, and seen your trouble and dilemma.

You are intelligent and educated and know people with intelligence and cultivation. In the face of them now you are quite hamstrung. You cannot bear to have these people think that you don't know what rot you are speaking or what tricky tosh it is that you are forced to pretend to feel; you are overcome with the irony of your situation. How shall I write you about it?

Well, in the first place, you illustrate the point that for many phases of the stage career it is perhaps a blessed thing to be riffraff, to be talent that came from the gutter or was born in the slums or in some hungry little village. You will not detect the rot so easily then, and even if you do, you will be so pleased at this chance to appear before the footlights and to wear good clothes that nothing else will matter. Or, failing that, you might fortunately be an egoist of such a passion of egotism and exhibitionism that the mere chance to show yourself would sweep you along in a Bacchic frenzy. Even—to take a summit in the theatre—Bernhardt could face any kind of rubbish with the aplomb and simplicity of a vain, spoiled child, so long as it glorified and exhibited her and allowed her overwhelming magnificence a chance. Such stage opportunity is the balm and medicine of this exhibiting ego that is so large a part of stage talent.

You have the ego and exhibitionism all right but not so openly. Education and association with cultivated people have made you less shameless about it; your desire to show and express yourself is there but it is driven further in. At any rate, here we have you in this play where obviously you feel absurd, uneasy lest you be thought the same sort of idiot as the dramatist, and all that. You are very nice and it would be pleasant to be useful to you. What about it?

Of course you are not obliged to act in this piece. But, if nothing else offers, you are, I think, right to take it; an actor should act; the acting psychology suffers from lack of exercise; it is not good for most actors, even great ones, not to be playing. Very well, the problem remains. At the start, then, note this: the basis of your problem consists in the actor's relation to the matter he acts, which amounts to saying that what he adds to it is his comment. He is an artist only in so far as he gives us, not something as it is, but as he recreates it in terms of his art—acting—gives us the thing he portrays plus his comment upon it. A picture of a landscape is not the landscape, plainly, but the painter's idea expressed by means of the landscape taken as subject-matter or material. The actor's case is the same. He necessarily expresses his own comment or idea—you in your role, for instance, are bound to give us your comment on it. But you must not let this analogy, or parallel in the arts, mix you up. Leaving aside more beautiful qualities, let us come down to the brass tacks of your persistent quandary. Say, then, the landscape is banal, and the painter chooses it because of that. What he does is to express banality in terms of this landscape. Banality is his intention.

You on your side know that for all their pious pretensions your scene and your lines are banal. Yes, but—and this is the point—the dramatist's intention was to express not banality but virtue and thrill. If we follow up the comparison with the painter, we should say that you are struggling not with the banality of the land-scape but with the poorness of the pigment. Your case is that of a sculptor working with poor marble, trying to shape it into a worthwhile statue. You are not to slight your scene and lines, letting us know one way or another that you recognize their trashiness, not at all. Your business is to force them so far as possible into something alive and good—provided always, that is, you are in the play at all.

How to do this is another matter. You must proceed not as if you turned your brains into a joke and really thought these scenes and lines good art; but must rather, in spite of their failure, discern their possible meanings and intentions, what they might have been in the hands of a good dramatist, and taking this as a start must try to restate them, force them forward, sublimate their dullness into a better essence, pour your own strong depths into their arid channels of life. Technically you can do some of this by striking, in your delivery, the living words and slighting the dead or cheap ones; by hurrying over one phrase and stressing another. You can freshen even the dullest dialogue by keying up your cues, throw-ing life and variety into your tempo, surprise into your phrase movement; and the flattest word sometimes will come alive by tone or by vitality of enunciation, the most vacuous scene by the beauty and power of your own vitality or by the truth of your gesture and pantomime.

If with all this on your part, your scene falls flat, it is not your fault, you have done what you could. If you make your scenes and lines go over the footlights, good; as a child of the theatre you are at your best.

If, when you have given so much of your art and your own spiritual, mental or emotional depths, to the scene and thereby made the moment a fine one, though by these very same means the play is shown up for the rot it is, that is good also; as an artist, stung by life and taking whatever opportunity arises for giving us your soul and the soul of things, you are worthy of yourself.

To an actress who wishes to get herself in place

You are doing well in your art and have a sincere desire to paint truly the thing you wish to convey. But you are mixed up with regard to yourself in relation to what you are acting. It might be of use to you if we established one point about the subjective and objective, what you might do with yourself when the end you are seeking is one or the other.

A subjective effect, which is the kind an artist like Duse very often sought, though she understood somewhat, of course, the more objective effects also, is one in which the scene is wrung from the actor's own inner feeling and quality. The ideal in this case is to bring into play the last quivering, intense life within you. You must try to breathe with the emotion in the scene, sway with it as a flame breathes and sways to the air it lives by. By this quivering and intense life the soul enacts itself, and is true and shining. In this sort of acting the success of every perform-ance will depend on the purity of the flame, on the quiver and immediacy, the echo of the still small voice within. When these fail, as they must in some per-formances, however good the intentions may be, all that remains is the memory of them in the actor's mind and manner, which is a good deal, and the things their presence and their divine havoc have wrought on the actor's mask. As Virgil led Dante, and was his guide and sweet master, so the life within guides the actor through the darkness and light of creation; and without this guide at any moment the track is perilous and without happiness to the artist himself.

The objective is exactly the opposite. It moves from the final line, the perman-ent expressive form, the containing ultimate body of the thought, and toward the central life of the thing that is to be expressed and conveyed. It begins far down in the personal self, what you feel about the dramatic moment, what your own intense response to it may be, what excitement and imagination it arouses in you. But through all this excitement, response and quivering intense life, you are to discover an external image, in movement and tone, that will render it. This is to be perfected and to remain; you have found the body that will convey the soul of the moment and that will remain expressive of it. In a sense, after this it will be independent of you, it has its own power, free of what you feel. You must keep clear this fact, and make yourself, not so much as in the subjective, a glass above your own inner life, through which it appears, but a substance from which this form is created, an instrument through which the full meaning is set forth.

These two aspects of the art of acting are not sharply separated, of course, but the presence of each in the other now and then will benefit either. Permanent forms in image, in movement or tone and stage effect, need to be present in the most subjective of performances, to give them finality at the right moment, to secure them against lapses in feeling and inspiration, to help subordinate the actor's personal quality to the right restatement that makes art. And in the more objective style of acting the pressure of the inner life of the artist will keep fresh the source from which the form arose and in this manner preserve its full life.

4   Paul Muni: A profile and a self-portrait

Morton Eustis

March 1940

The Yiddish theatres on New York's East Side were not only lively purveyors of entertainment and enlightenment to its immigrant audiences. They were also a breeding ground for some of the best actors on the English-speaking stage. Bertha Kalisch and Jacob Ben-Ami were plucked from their stages to star on Broadway. Stella and Luther Adler, progeny of the tragedian Jacob Adler, became active in the Group Theatre. Galicia-born Muni Weisenfreund (Meshilem Meier Weisenfreund, 1895–1967) had been on the Yiddish stage from childhood, usually disguised by a heavy old-age make-up, when the producer Sam Harris discovered him and gave him a leading role in *We Americans* (1924). A brief stint in Hollywood playing seven roles in *Seven Faces* (1929) earned him Lon Chaney's title "Man of 1,000 Faces", but sent him back to Broadway. His hit as the poor boy turned affluent lawyer in *Counsellor-at-Law* (1931) had film producers calling again, and he yielded to their blandishments. At first he tended to be cast as proles – criminals, labourers, self-made men (*Scarface, I Am a Fugitive from a Chain Gang*), but in the late 1930s became first choice for historical champions of progress: Zola, Pasteur, Juarez, roles which he researched assiduously. Late in life, he made a great comeback in the Clarence Darrow part in *Inherit the Wind* (1955).

Morton Eustis (1905–44), a former newspaperman, was the scion of an old Virginia family who grew up on a historic estate in Loudon County. On the editorial staff of *Theatre Arts* from 1933 to 1942 he launched several of its series, including those on the finances of show business, directing and the actor's work on his role. He also wrote six plays, before he was killed commanding a tank in the Colmar Pocket in France. A monument to him was erected in Normandy. Eustis' privately printed war letters to his mother served as the basis of a musical in 2002.

––––––––––

ASK THE theorist to describe the technique of a craft within his special orbit of knowledge and he is apt to wax eloquent. Make the same request of the man who has learned to apply that technique, a person really practised in his profession, and nine times out of ten he is unable to give a coherent response. He knows what he does. But how is another question.

The actor, of all technicians, seems least able to place a definitive finger on the practical aspects of his sphere of endeavor. He has, moreover, a curious reluctance to probe beneath the surface of a sound and fury that is at all times deeply personal. The painter, the sculptor, the poet or the composer uses his technique and his genius to fashion a work of art that is complete within itself. It may be a revelation of the artist — painful, extraordinary or sublime — but the appreciation it evokes has nothing to do with the artist as a man. Everything the actor does in performance, however, creative or interpretive, is related directly, in essence and accomplishment, to the actor's own person — to his physique, his physiognomy, his mentality, his nervous system, his storehouse of emotion and, above all, to that spark of personality which makes him a positive rather than a negative agent on the stage.

Disguise himself as he please, the actor is always himself. Do what he will, he is always the *deus ex machina* of his role. Almost all actors, in consequence, who are not exhibitionists or amateurs, become hesitant, uncertain, embarrassed, even, if they are asked to subject to analysis those facets of their work that reveal themselves. To evaluate the abc's of acting for the public 'is a little' — as Paul Muni puts it — 'like undressing in public'.

Paul Muni is not only, as he says, inarticulate about his technical approach to acting (though he is far more articulate than most actors) but he wishes to remain so, even to himself. He was brought up in the practical school where the actor learned to act by acting. He worked things out for himself and wants to continue to do so. He has never read a book about acting. He never intends to. He distrusts systems and theories of acting as he might apply them to himself.

'I don't want to give the impression for a moment,' he says, 'that I regard acting as something which is so sacred that you have to put it on some kind of pinnacle. That kind of talk makes me squirm. Acting is a job like any other. But you can't analyze it too much. The last thing I want to think about is *how* I achieve an effect.'

Muni looks up from his dressing-room table at the Ethel Barrymore Theatre and smiles as he picks up a jar of cold cream to remove his make-up. He is still King McCloud of *Key Largo* in all but facial expression. He wears the rough brown uniform of the deserter from Loyalist Spain. He has the character's black tousled hair, his dark flashing eyes with the tortured lines around them, the heavy expressive eyebrows, the finely molded forehead with the quizzical lines that seem to come to a point just over the bridge of his nose. There is a suggestion, too, of the same vibrancy and intensity that, a few moments earlier, were so deeply impregnated in the character who let himself be killed that he might at the last 'win, dying'. But all the contours are smoother now, the lines less taut, the body and face more relaxed. And the smile is definitely out of character. It has in it, rather, the gaiety and enthusiasm that must have been King McCloud's before disillusionment stalked him on the Spanish hilltop where Maxwell Anderson first presents him to us. And why not? The performance that evening was one of those when everything fused. The house was responsive and appreciative. What more could an actor ask, except to be spared another interview?

'Look,' says Muni, talking slowly, his head cocked to one side, 'I'm afraid this sounds precious — this not knowing much about my job and not wanting to talk about it. But think of it this way. You know how to roller skate, don't you? Well, if someone asks you: how do you do it, what is your answer? You don't know. You just do it. You've learned how. You can become more adept by practising. But if you try to think about what you are doing while you are actually rolling along in the park, if you look down at the wheels and attempt to puzzle out what's going on, you fall down. Well, that is a little how I feel. I'll try to answer any questions that I can. But I won't guarantee that I won't fall down or change my opinions later. There's no "last word", you know, about this business.'

Speaking of roller skates, the familiar — and, no doubt, inaccurate — legend comes to mind of a wizened old man with long, straggly hair and a flowing beard who was wont to terrify the street urchins playing in the alley back of the old Yiddish Theatre in the Bowery, by skating past them with wild agility. This outlandish creature was one of the most talented juveniles of the Yiddish troupe — by name, Paul Muni — taking his exercise between the acts of a brilliantly made-up characterization. Born in Lemberg, Austria, young Muni was brought to this country at the age of four by his parents. He received his official education in New York and Chicago while his mother and father were acting in Yiddish Repertory in those cities, but his educational baptism came at the age of twelve when the company was on tour. One night at Cleveland one of the troupe fell sick and Muni was pressed into service. The play was a stark social tragedy known as *Two Corpses at Breakfast*, the part that of a doddering old banker. The youth acquitted himself so well as an octogenarian that he soon renounced his intention of becoming the number one violinist in the pit, and was taken on as a regular member of the company. He played every kind of part but he was such a wizard at make-up that his most famous roles all through his teens were of a bearded variety. For eighteen years he played with the Art Theatre, and other Yiddish repertories, receiving a practical apprenticeship such as has been granted to few actors in our theatre. His first opportunity for a Broadway role was almost lost because of his age. One of Sam Harris' scouts had seen him in a Boston stock company and told Mr. Harris he was just the person to portray the old Jew in *We Americans*. Harris' comment as soon as Muni presented himself at his office was, 'Why, he's just a kid,' and the only way Muni could persuade him that he could portray the role was, so the story goes, to make up then and there. He was so warmly acclaimed in this character part that he had equal difficulty the next year in persuading the management of the prison drama, *Four Walls*, that he could play the part of a young man just as adroitly. He went to Hollywood the following season to play his first screen role in *The Valiant*, a movie which its sponsors wanted to shelve but which became a surprise success largely owing to his straightforward performance. Upon his return to New York, he appeared in a fairly unpromising vehicle known as *This One Man*, and the next year created two memorable stage portraits as the Middle-Western hero of *Rock Me Julie* and the hard-boiled lawyer of Elmer Rice's *Counsellor-at-Law*.

Those who had not seen young Muni in the Yiddish theatre, where his versatility had earned him the title of the man with many faces, had had, so far, no opportunity to judge the actor in a great part or even to measure his ability against a long series of impersonations, yet the quality that Muni brought to the stage was one that almost immediately catapulted him into stardom — 'that extra quality', as John Anderson expressed it in THEATRE ARTS in 1931, 'that goes beyond merely one performance and embraces a talent of quite obvious personal persuasion. . . . He leaves no blurred edges or any frayed outlines. They are sharp, clear, in full focus, because he sees them himself and commands the fluency and vitality to show what he is thinking about. There is power and richness of texture in his acting and a sort of personal violence that is carefully used for touches that are compelling and unforgettable.'

For the next eight years, Broadway was not to see the volatile personality in the flesh, but they were years which were not wasted, years which secured Academy Awards for his Zola and Louis Pasteur, and produced a gallery of such fine portrayals as those in *Scarface, I Am a Fugitive from a Chain Gang, Black Fury, The Good Earth, Juarez* and this year's *We Are Not Alone*. Muni was so convincing in each of these divergent roles that he earned the reputation on the coast of submerging himself and living a part for the duration of its screening. This ridiculous assumption undoubtedly sprang partly from the fact that the actor disliked the publicity mill of Hollywood and did not frequent the usual star-studded fronts, but the underlying reasons behind the myth were the seriousness with which he attacked each part and the persuasiveness of the performances themselves.

Muni has still to play his Hamlet (and may it come soon), to measure his talents against the great parts with great traditions, but his King McCloud in his triumphant return to Broadway in *Key Largo* shows no evidence that he will ever 'fall down' while on his acting roller skates. For that 'personal violence', tempered, carefully shaded, but ever present, continues to give to his portrayals on stage and screen the quality which, to quote Anderson, makes them 'unforgettable'.

'If I were to use a principle at all in acting,' says Muni, now seated in the far corner of a restaurant and looking thoughtfully and perhaps a bit dazedly at a typewritten list of questions, 'it would be that if the mind — the basic generator — functions alertly and sums up its impulses and conclusions to a correct result, it is possible for the actor to achieve something creative. Technique, which comes with practice, gives you the firm foundation on which to build your structure. But unless the mind sends out the sparks, the forces that stimulate the body to perform a series of actions that generate a spontaneous emotion, nothing creative can happen.' The actor first learns the abc's that all the actors of the past have bequeathed to him. These are the short cuts which can either, as in Muni's case, be self taught through long and grueling experience, or else be learned in a school. But acting, in Muni's opinion, only starts where these first essentials finish. From then on the actor must work out his own method — enlarging and enriching his technique — from his own head.

'If his apparatus up here is not functioning,' says Muni, touching his forehead, 'all the technique in the world won't save him; if it is, I'd almost say that the technique would take care of itself.'

It is interesting to find Muni dwelling so consistently on the importance of mind over matter, for 'thoughtful' is one of the first adjectives that spring to mind when you see him perform. He may pass over lightly the value of the so-called abc's because they come to him almost instinctively today, after training of a type which does not exist for most young actors, but his insistence on the fact that this layer of technique is only an undercurrent, that nothing creative can happen which does not emanate consciously from the brain, is an illuminating point of view on the art of acting. Yet Muni does not believe that the actor should reason too much about a performance. He treats each part as an entirely new problem, as if it were his first in the theatre or the movies, and makes no attempt to build it as a technical structure.

'I never think, in reading a script,' he says, 'that I will use such and such a gesture here, or that this is the point at which effect number twenty-two should be pulled out of the hat. If I were consciously to do certain things to attain certain effects, I'd become self-conscious and lose the ability to create a spontaneous impression.'

In life, Muni points out, people do not act, they react, adjusting themselves to other characters and different situations. The actor does much the same thing, except that he does it as a business. He reacts to the part out of something that is within himself. All the time he is playing he is exhibiting some facet of himself related to the character. That is why the actor must have some affinity, some kinship, spiritual or physical, however remote it may be, with the character. The mind has to relate that kinship always to the part while the actor is on the stage. One good reason why: 'the closer the role is to you, the more painful is the process of holding it up to public scrutiny.'

'Muni is never Muni on the stage or screen,' a columnist once wrote. An incorrect, but, on the whole, gratifying, statement. For Muni is always Muni or a part of him. If he were not, he would not, in his own estimation, be able to make the audience believe in the veracity of the character. As Muni puts it: 'I like to think that King McCloud is not Paul Muni, yet I know that there's a bit of Muni in McCloud, or, rather a bit of McCloud in Muni, that he is a kind of collaboration, part McCloud, part Muni, and of course part Maxwell Anderson, because Anderson could not have written the role if the character did not contain something of himself. My job is to see that the "part Muni" in McCloud is the part that belongs to him, not the part that had a fellowship with Zola or the English country doctor in *We Are Not Alone*. It is really very difficult to explain what I mean — as a matter of fact, I have never thought of this in quite this sense until tonight, and I may think quite differently tomorrow night — but I suppose that what an actor does, or should do, is to subjugate his own personality to those lines of the characterization that he understands because they are a part of him.'

When Muni first went to Hollywood, he found several aspects of film-making 'disconcerting' — the constant breaking up of scenes, the lack of continuity in shooting, the loss of an audience to which to key his performance. But gradually he worked his way through these difficulties as an inevitable part of the job and not only learned to make the best of them but, as should be evident, to let them make the best of him.

He soon discovered that the lack of an audience was an advantage rather than a disadvantage in the medium; that he had to concentrate so hard to play the same scene again and again with any spontaneity that non-routine interruptions would throw him completely off key. He found, too, that once he had resorted to certain mental contortions to keep from going stale in the repetitive sequences — the long, medium and close-up shots of the same action — he was no longer bothered by this factor.

Muni attacks a part for the screen in basically the same manner as for the stage, but with certain differences. As there is no long rehearsal period in the movies in which the actor can work out the details and accustom himself to the personalities he is working with, Muni thinks that it requires more effort, more imagination to work out a scene on the screen than on the stage. The actor has to imagine the cast he is playing with, as he does not see it until the shooting starts. He has to imagine how the others will react to him, key his performance accordingly, and then 'leave it to fate'. Always, too, there are last minute changes in the script or in the direction, so that the actor cannot work out his part in all its details at home, but must learn to adjust himself quickly and willingly to unforeseen developments.

Taking scenes out of continuity, starting in the middle or end of a picture instead of the beginning, is not too difficult a handicap for the actor 'if he absorbs the contents of the story and of the character so thoroughly that he can always keep himself in the frame of the character. You know what has happened before, even if you have not played it out. You know the reactions these events would have had on you and you carry this over vicariously with you — don't ask me how — so that you have a mental flow of the story and of your role always before you.'

The breaking up of scenes has its compensations for the actor as well as for the audience. If the rushes show that all the shorts are bad, it gives the actor a chance to do the scene again. It also makes it possible to choose the best scenes from the many taken, 'whereas in the theatre, a scene played is a scene played.'

Making pictures, as Muni sees it, is a much more 'interdependent process' than acting in the theatre, and the actors and technicians have to work together to the best advantage of the film. Muni does, however, insist on seeing a shooting script long enough ahead of time to enable him to assimilate the part and, in the case of Zola, according to a report from Hollywood, he first read five books on the character, then went over the complete script, read every part of it into a dicta-phone and played it back to hear it, after which he learned his lines.

Although Muni is the first to admit the importance of the role the director plays both in the theatre and on the Hollywood lot, he says that his performance has never been influenced very much by a director. He talks over his part with him, especially any points that seem to be cloudy, but once he has established the characterization in his mind, he works it out for himself. He is only too glad to have the director tell him that any part of his interpretation is wrong, to explain what he thinks it should be, but he is adamant on the point that he must work out the change for himself without the director's help.

Muni does not act a part — to get back to the boards on which he is now playing — in exactly the same style and tempo at each performance. The general pattern remains constant, but individual movements, gestures and intonations 'depend upon how I feel, how the audience is reacting, how the others are playing, how alert my mind is'. He does not like members of the cast ever to tell him that he has done a particular thing well at any special moment. 'If it is bad, yes, by all means, tell me; but if it is good, don't make me become conscious of it. I know obviously that I am acting a part on the stage but I don't want to think of it except in relation to my part.'

The less said about the actor's emotion in the theatre the better, according to almost every actor. Talking 'around the subject', Muni has this to say: 'If you are listening to music and are suddenly carried away, it is some chemistry in you that responds to the music. It is not the music, but something within you that has been released by the music. Similarly, in the theatre, if you are doing a scene which stimulates some feeling within you, the same kind of chemical reaction takes place. Naturally it is disciplined. You cannot lose yourself in the part but you can, and I think you should, let the part open in you the reservoirs of feeling which are dammed up. I don't think the actor simulates the emotion as much as he draws it out of himself and is stimulated by it. To illustrate: you see a child run over, crossing the street. You have an instinctive reaction of horror which is not simulated. An hour later, when you tell a friend about it, you can still evoke the feeling almost as acutely as when you were there. A year later you might not be able to feel the same physical shock but you could still recreate the emotion within you, and it would be natural and not simulated. When I say to the girl in *Key Largo:* "Must it be death?" knowing that there is a choice, I don't think of Paul Muni talking to Uta Hagen. I think that I have seen in the girl's eyes that expression which comes into everyone's eyes when there is a choice between life and death. I use my mind every second to make myself think of such images and to key my response accordingly. The mind is all important. Yet if I thought about Paul Muni, I could not give a performance. There you are!' The actor shrugs his shoulders. 'There *is* no conclusion. That's what makes it interesting.'

5   Margaret Sullavan

John Van Druten

May 1944

Margaret Sullavan (1911–60) was considered one of the freshest comic talents in the American theatre. She emerged on the Broadway stage in 1931 and two years later made her first Hollywood film. She and James Stewart were linked as a light-comedy couple in four movies, the best of which is Ernst Lubitsch's *The Shop Around the Corner* (1940). She returned to Broadway in the three-character war-time play *The Voice of the Turtle* (1943), which ran for over 1,500 performances and gave a boost to Ronald Reagan's career when he played in the 1947 film. Owing to a congenital hearing defect, Sullavan retired in 1950 but reappeared two years later on Broadway in *The Deep Blue Sea*. Her premature death (suicide by barbiturates) was a serious loss to American comic performance.

John Van Druten (1901–57), who had studied law at the University of London, had his first West End success with *Young Woodley* (1925), a play about a sensitive youth who fancies himself in love with an older woman. In America, Van Druten showed himself a skilled adapter of novels, with *Old Acquaintance* and *Leave Her to Heaven* (both 1940). After the success of *The Voice of the Turtle*, he returned to dramatizing prose works (*I Remember Mama*, 1944; *I Am a Camera*, 1951).

When Margaret Sullavan's name was announced for my play, *The Voice of the Turtle,* I was delighted by the enthusiasm that it evoked in almost everyone I talked to, professional or otherwise, even though, on investigation, it was hard to know just what this enthusiasm was based on. Margaret Sullavan's career, when you come to look at it in the pages of *Who's Who in the Theatre,* is so slender as to be quite astonishing. A handful of flops in the early thirties; a three-year gap, followed by *Stage Door,* her only real hit-show until now; and then another absence, this time of seven years, up to her present performance. Two plays only in the past ten years; the record was so meagre as to drive me to the conclusion that her popularity must be due to her screen, rather than her stage, career.

It was at this point that I began to examine myself and the basis of my own enthusiasm. When her name occurred to me half-way through the first act of my play, I paused with hands suspended over my typewriter in delight. I could not, from that moment onwards, think of anyone else for the part, and I did not stop to ask myself why I should have been so certain of her. Now, I began to wonder. I had seen her act twice only: in a play called *Chrysalis,* in which I remember her only very indistinctly, and in *Stage Door,* her performance in which, though I thought it good, I cannot in all honesty claim to recall in any detail. Her face, her bangs of hair, her stance and certain tricks of voice are all that remain with me; only the final curtain evokes a picture of an actual moment. Nor, in my case, had her screen career anything to do with it, for I realised suddenly that I have never seen a single picture in which she has appeared. A trailer of *Mortal Storm* is the whole extent of my acquaintance with her movie personality. Yet the response to her name which I found in all my friends was mine also. How to account for it?

In my own case, I think the answer lies in the fact that I had met Miss Sullavan personally. I did not know her well, but we had met once or twice at parties in Hollywood, and I had found her utterly unlike a movie star and utterly unlike an actress. To begin with, she has what Auriol Lee once described as the rarest and most attractive things in a woman: 'hair-colored hair and skin-colored skin'. She has a simplicity, an almost embarrassing directness and a friendliness that have nothing of the theatre's gush about them. She seems, in fact, as my mother would have put it, 'just like a real girl', which is, I think, the quality that has pervaded all her work and endeared her to the public, though it may have damaged her career in pictures, stopping her from reaching the topmost ranks of box-office stardom, where a certain artificiality of glamour and a larger-than-life stature of personality are the first requirements. Movie stars, like gods and goddesses, must be of another dimension, and what flows through their veins is not quite mortal blood. This was sometime true of the theatre, but the screen has made it less so. Thirty years ago, Margaret Sullavan might have found it harder to be a stage star than today.

For she has always been a star; that is another odd thing about her career. She has never played a small part on Broadway and very few outside it. Her smallest Broadway role was that of the daughter in *Dinner at Eight*, right in the middle of her career — a part which she took over late in the run, having refused it when it was first offered.

To go back to the beginning, Margaret Sullavan was born in Norfolk, Virginia, of parents who did not approve of the theatre. She studied interpretive dancing, and at the age of seventeen, while living in Cambridge, Massachusetts, went to see the Boston company of a New York musical success. The leading lady in that company was so bad that the young dancer in the audience said to herself, 'I could be better than that,' and straightway switched careers to the theatre, going down and enrolling next morning as a student member of the E. E. Clive Stock Company, known as the Copley Players, and paying money for her experience, which consisted in sitting around, watching, listening and very occasionally walking on as a super. From there she went to the group that still seems a little fabulous when its roster is told over. The University Players, acting each summer at Falmouth on Cape Cod, listed among their members the inexperienced names of James Stewart, Myron McCormick, Henry Fonda, Bretaigne Windust, Joshua Logan, Kent Smith, Mildred Natwick and Barbara O'Neill. It was there that Margaret Sullavan played her first parts, and began with big ones, such as the heroine in *A Kiss for Cinderella*, although the young Fonda told her she was not as good in it as a girl of thirteen with whom he had recently played it in Omaha. The young girl's name was Dorothy McGuire.

From Cape Cod, Margaret Sullavan went to New York to find a job. The offers that she encountered reduced themselves to two: to do ingenue leads for the Jitney Players, or to be an offstage voice for the Theatre Guild. The difficulty of making such a choice was solved for her by her parents, who dragged her back home, although soon after they allowed her to accept the job of understudying Elizabeth Love in the southern company of *Strictly Dishonorable*, figuring perhaps that under-studies seldom play and that it was not quite the same thing as acting. In this case, however, it turned out to be precisely the same thing, for Miss Love went down with appendicitis before the tour had been out three weeks, and the first city in which Margaret Sullavan found herself called upon to play the disrobing south-ern heroine was her own hometown of Norfolk, Virginia. Relations with the family were awkward after that.

When the tour ended, there was another summer engagement where a talent scout for the Shuberts saw her, reporting her as 'a promising, red-headed actress, in need of voice training'. Where the phrase 'red-headed' came from no one has ever known, for Miss Sullavan's hair was then, as it is now, a natural mid-blonde color; but the part about needing voice training was based on the fact that she was suffering from acute laryngitis at the time, a complaint which she continued to cultivate, finding her husky voice to be her most salable asset, earning her the description of a 'baby Barrymore'. For quite a time she deliberately tried to catch colds, for fear the huskiness should leave her. As audiences know, it never has. Throat doctors, called in when she has colds nowadays, are appalled at the treat-ment she has given her vocal chords and threaten her with permanent voiceless-ness unless she undertakes the training that the talent scout recommended back in 1931. She even talks of doing so, provided she can find someone who will teach her to produce the same sounds without strain, and not give her a new voice instead. For the most part, the one that she has serves her very well; when she is tired or has a cold, its middle register deserts her, leaving nothing between its low tones and a squeak, an effect that is sometimes criticized as being 'one of her tricks'. But the husky voice is there to stay.

The Shuberts listened to their scout, and offered her the lead in a piece called *A Modern Virgin*, together with a two-year contract. The play was of the kind hope-fully described as daring, and the husky leading lady had to speak such lines as 'I wish you'd tell me how one avoids having a baby.' It ran for fifty-three perform-ances, and Miss Sullavan's notices were spectacular. This was followed by two plays, also short-lived, entitled *If Love Were All* and *Happy Landing*, in both of which she played the lead, and then it was that the offer came to play the girl in *Dinner at Eight*, which she declined because she had also been offered the gangster-girl in *Chrysalis* and thought it would be more interesting to step out into a character role than to play another of her sex-adventuring Park Avenue young women. When *Chrysalis* came to rehearsal, however, the inevitable happened; parts were switched; June Walker played the moll, and Margaret Sullavan the society girl whose excursion into low life was the story of the play. Again there was only a short run, followed by an even shorter one in *Bad Manners*, which apparently had the same plot and part as all the others; and then, back to replace Marguerite Churchill in the rejected role in *Dinner at Eight*.

It was then that Hollywood raised its head, also with the offer of a star part, the heroine of *Only Yesterday*. Never believing that she would really play it, Miss Sullavan accepted the offer because of a twenty-five-hundred-dollar guarantee, and set off for the Coast in the firm conviction that she would not be used but would be allowed to sit around and collect her guarantee. The picture was almost her most successful one. She returned to New York when it was done and looked for work again, without finding anything she cared about. She would not play any more of the old parts and nothing else was offered her, so it was Hollywood again to play in *Little Man, What Now?*, and staying three years, though she stole back to do seasons of summer stock just for the love of it, returning to Broadway for *Stage Door*, her last play until now.

For the past seven years she has been a legend, the legend of someone who would never come back. Almost everyone in the theatre whom I told that Margaret Sullavan was going to do my play laughed and said, 'Don't you believe it. She may *talk* about doing it, but she'll never sign the contract.' When I reported that the contract was signed, they still were sceptical. 'If everything else fails,' they said, 'she'll have a baby. She'll never do the play.'

The reasons for these theories about her are, I think, first, the memory of the occasion when she terminated the run of *Stage Door* by having a baby (and paid a very large sum of money for doing so), and secondly, the number of times when, because she still loves the theatre, she has allowed herself to toy with offers to return, only to reject them in the end because they were not what she really wanted. What she really wanted was the right play, rightly done, and the fact that that one should have turned out to be mine is something that I find extremely flattering. The theatre had disappointed her; she had a standard of perfection for it and for what she wanted to do in it; she had not liked most of the parts she had been given; and too often the plays that she did were thrown on, rather than produced or directed, in a slipshod, 'Oh, it'll get by' manner. In California, she had made a life for herself with intermittent pictures, a husband, a home and three children, a life so attractive that when I saw her in it, I wondered whether there was anything good enough to persuade her to leave it. But she knew the hour when it struck, and from the moment when we had agreed on Elliott Nugent as her leading man and found him available, there was no more hesitation. A date was set for rehearsals, and on the morning of that date, refusing offers of escort, she was sitting on the bare stage of the Martin Beck Theatre, twenty minutes before the hour called for rehearsal.

I had been warned, too, that I should find her 'difficult', and that my experience as her director would not be an easy one. I can only say that I never hope for an easier or a pleasanter. Her major fault, actually, it seems to me, is an excessive self-mistrust. Direction, with Margaret Sullavan, is largely a matter of encouragement and of enhancing her self-confidence in what she is doing, although I found it fatal ever to praise her for a specific reading or a particular piece of business. Once told that she had played a certain passage really well, she would become self-conscious about it and incapable of recapturing it for perhaps a full week. But she is morbidly eager for criticism, digging it out of you in a desire for perfection. Whenever visitors went to her dressing-room during our out-of-town weeks with the play and started complimenting her on her performance, her invariable interruption was 'Yes, but what *didn't* you like? What did you think was *bad?*' And when I, a few days before our New York opening, went backstage after a performance with only three notes to give her, her comment, which was only half jesting, was: 'You don't care any more. You've lost interest.'

This desire for perfection is, actually, I think, the root of her whole attitude towards the theatre, for herself and others. I have been with her to plays, and watched respect wither in her as actors or directors displayed cheap wares; I sat beside her at *Othello* and *The Two Mrs. Carrolls*, and saw her as a young student in her eagerness to learn and admire. She has a passion for the theatre that is the equal of my own enlarged one, feeding my vanity and encouraging me in my favorite vice by listening to my theatrical memories, asking questions, and wanting descriptions of players she has never seen. Her point of view, it seems to me, is exactly that with which she joined the University Players fourteen years ago; the enthusiasm of the really intelligent amateur, polished now with the years of her experience.

Of the range and scope of her talents, I cannot yet speak with certainty. Her physical attributes, especially her tiny frame, must limit her to some extent. Her work, at the moment, is inclined to be miniature in its best effects; she dislikes having to project — a result of the movies, possibly — and her performance, seen from the fifth row, is infinitely more glowing than from the back of the theatre. She moves exquisitely, handling her whole body with plasticity and freedom. She never speaks on the stage without thinking, and she has the great gift of being able to listen, and reposefully. She works indefatigably, and during our rehearsals would never leave the theatre for the lunch-break, preferring to remain, checking lines and business with the stage-manager, and then curling up to sleep on a hard bench for the remainder of the hour. She has played no classic parts and would, I think, be doubtful of her ability to do so, though she would like nothing better than to try. If New York had been London, with its Sunday Societies, its Gate and Westminster Theatres, and Arts Theatre Club, she would by now have ventured some of them, as well as a number of interesting and new, but uncommercial, plays, and her own art, as well as our theatrical experience, would have benefited. She has been, perhaps more than anyone, the victim of the star system and of the bondage to expense and over-organization from which the New York theatre suffers; but if anyone can find a way of putting on *The Master Builder* for special performances, I think I can guarantee him a magnificent and more than eager Hilda Wangel.

6 Comedienne from Radcliffe: Josephine Hull

William Lindsay Gresham

June 1945

Stars, though known for glamour, come in all sizes and shapes. One of the unlikeli-est was Josephine Hull (Sherwood, 1886–1957) who first caught the public eye in *Craig's Wife* (1926). She created the *distraite* Penny Sycamore in *You Can't Take It With You* (1936), the homicidal biddy Abby Brewster in *Arsenic and Old Lace* (1941) and Elwood P. Dowd's interfering sister in *Harvey* (1945), winning an Oscar for the film version (she also repeated the last two roles on television). A diminutive and dumpy matron with a dithery manner, she embodied the well-upholstered club-women seen in Helen Hokinson's *New Yorker* cartoons. She collapsed during the run of *The Solid Gold Cadillac* (1954) and retired from the stage.

William Lindsay Gresham (1909–62) had a checkered career as folk singer, medic for the Loyalists during the Spanish Civil War, and a failed suicide, before he settled into writing pulp fiction. His most famous works are the *noir*ish sideshow novel *Nightmare Alley* (1946) and its non-fiction counterpart *Monster Midway* (1954). His final suicide attempt was successful.

'WHEN Duse came up to Radcliffe to see about entering her daughter a bunch of us gathered around, worshiping. One with more nerve than the rest asked her to write her name in chalk on the blackboard and she did, not smiling, knowing why we wanted it.

'When she was gone we drew a "frame" around the signature and wrote on all sides "DO NOT TOUCH." Duse's autograph stayed there for years. Then one summer a janitor or cleaning woman scrubbed it off. When we returned in the fall we were heartbroken. That name held magic. And we had lost it!'

Josephine Hull, now sharing the comedy honors with Frank Fay in Mary Chase's fantasy *Harvey*, was recalling her college days.

'I had opportunities that so many other young people in the theatre miss. I got so much out of college; we had George Lyman Kittredge for Chaucer and Shakespeare. And George Pierce Baker for drama history and stagecraft. And Charles Townsend Copeland — the famous "Copey" — for English "lit". Copey would have made a wonderful actor — he put so much life into anything he was talking about; he had the dramatic gift. Men like these gave me a groundwork for the theatre that I couldn't have gained in any other way. Everything they said made you want to go and find out more by yourself. I fell in love with the theatre. But theory can take you just so far. I knew that the only way to learn to act is to do it.

'In those days there were no experimental or "little" theatres — the beginner had to start in stock or try to get into one of the road companies. While I was still at Radcliffe I began to study acting with Mrs. Erving Winslow. As Kate Reignolds she had been leading woman in the old Boston Museum Company. Once she told me about a Mrs. Vincent, a famous old character actress, who had been with the Boston Museum, playing landladies and Dickens characters. Mrs. Vincent had a trotting walk which she used for comedy effects — in one scene she carried a full teakettle across the stage. At every step a little jet of water spouted from the kettle — bounced out by Mrs Vincent's walk. I never forgot that and years afterward, when I was working on the part of Abbie Brewster in *Arsenic and Old Lace*, I tried it out. Mr Bretaigne Windust liked it and I had the skirt of my dress shortened a little and wore white stockings so the audience could see my feet. They loved that walk of Abbie Brewster's — when Mrs. Vincent's trot came back to the boards.

'I went about getting into the theatre the practical way. It was a big advantage if a young actress could sing and play the piano and I studied both and that got me interested in musical theory and I studied harmony. I wrote two operettas — books and music — while I was still in school and we put them on. I wanted to learn everything.

'My first job was with the Castle Square players in Boston and then I went on tour with George Ober, doing the Broadhurst farces. The only job open when I applied was the soubrette. I got a ballet dancer to show me some steps in a hurry and I had a spangled costume from an amateur show, so I went on the road as the singing and dancing soubrette. I got thirty dollars a week and out of this I had to pay hotel bills and pullmans . . . this was a long time before Equity. Another girl and I teamed up and once a week we would take a room with a bath and do lots of bathing.

'The following summer I went up to Peak's Island, Maine, with the stock company there and the year after Wilton Lackaye gave me a part in *The Man and the Law* — a dramatized version of *Les Misérables* which he was taking on the road. I played a double role — Fantine and her daughter, Cosette.

'In those days an actress had to provide her own wigs and gowns. For Cosette I wore a blonde wig which alone cost fifty dollars. It would cost a couple of hundred today. And the costumes! I had to borrow three hundred dollars from Mother for my costumes.

'Those were wonderful times, touring with Wilton Lackaye. Mr. Lackaye had a bitter wit and his sarcasm could cut you like a whip. Only he never used it on anyone who was on the level and trying to learn and he had a sense of humor which made life interesting for the rest of us.

'I remember one scene where Jean Valjean is telling Cosette about her mother. It was one of the big tear-jerking scenes of the play — in a rose garden by moonlight. As the curtain went up I, as Cosette, was seated on a bench. Jean Valjean comes on and starts to tell me about Fantine and her sacrifices for me. Well, one evening a stagehand left a feather duster on the bench. It was behind me and I didn't see it in time to hide it.

'Mr. Lackaye came on, spotted the duster, and was furious. He picked it up and all during that emotional scene he proceeded to dust off the rose bushes! Not a soul in the audience noticed it. Maybe they were crying too hard to see very well. But I thought I would burst. Lackaye had his eye on me and I knew that if I blew up the results would be terrible. I kept my head and managed to get through the scene without laughing.

'I think my years at college helped me here — I knew what I was doing and where I was and I felt secure in my knowledge. It gave me poise. I knew then the value of thorough preparation for the theatre.

'Lackaye never said anything about it later but I think he respected my self-control. After that I had greater confidence. I knew that nothing that could happen onstage would make me blow up.'

In 1910 the young actress (she was then Josephine Sherwood) married Shelley Vaughn Hull, one of the most gifted actors of his time. After his death in the influenza epidemic of 1919 Josephine Hull left the stage. But the theatre was too strong an influence in her life and she returned to it to direct Jessie Bonstelle's Detroit stock company.

'I was terribly thrilled to get the job,' Mrs. Hull says, 'because I so wanted to stay in the theatre even though I felt that I couldn't act any more. We had a fine season in Detroit. Frank Morgan was with us and Ann Harding and Kenneth MacKenna. It was a splendid cast and we did *Smilin' Through*, *The Man Who Came Back* — the play in which Shelley's brother, Henry Hull, had starred on Broadway — *The Copperhead* and many others.

'I was invited back the second summer and I played one small character role myself. Miss Bonstelle advised me, "You are too good an actress not to act. Start now as a character woman while you're young — you'll be very wise." And what she said proved to be excellent advice.

'When I came back to New York the Equity Players were planning to do John Howard Lawson's *Roger Bloomer*. Augustin Duncan was directing. When he was suddenly taken ill they gave the job to me. Now there were a hundred and sixty-eight light cues in that show and Duncan had never written a lighting plot — he carried it all in his head. We had a hectic time but we opened and Duncan was well enough to see it. Afterward he said calmly, "It's fine — you had nothing to worry about." But I felt as if I had dropped ten years of my life getting the show into shape.

'My real comeback as an actress was in *Fata Morgana*. Alec Woollcott, who always told me I should keep on acting, suggested me for the part. I've never forgotten his kindness.

'After that I played the woman with the roses in *Craig's Wife* and then I had so many parts I can't remember them all. It was anything but plain sailing. So many shows opened and closed quickly that I began to wonder if I could actually afford to stay in the theatre. When I came to settle up my accounts at the end of a year I found that I was not making both ends meet. I was tempted to give it up and try to make my living by writing.

'Then George Kaufman sent me the script of a play and it had a character that

I fell completely in love with — Penny Sycamore. The play, of course, was *You Can't Take It With You.*

'I had never met our producer, Max Gordon, but just before we opened in Princeton, New Jersey, he had sent me a nice little note. I wanted to thank him. After the show we all crowded into cars to go to the station. There were not enough cars so a number of men, including Moss Hart, squeezed into the car with us and sat on our knees. I mentioned to Mr. Hart that Max Gordon had sent me this note and said I would like to thank him for it.

' "Now's your chance," Hart said dryly. "He's sitting on your lap!"'

'That show was grand fun. When we opened in Philadelphia we literally laid them in the aisles. One lady fell out of her seat and rolled in the aisle, laughing. At the same performance a man in the balcony laughed so hard that he hit his head on the balcony rail and knocked himself out.

'After *You Can't Take It With You* came *Arsenic and Old Lace* and that was when I used old Mrs. Vincent's trotting walk. That was something I got from another actress but usually I build up a character from things I've seen people do. For instance, I've played several New England parts in radio shows. I start such a character with memories of an old boardinghouse keeper I used to know. After she had served the pancakes she would walk from guest to guest with a pitcher, doling out maple syrup. And of each she would ask the same question: "Will ye hev it raound and raound or in a puddil in the middil?" Remembering that one line can put me right in the "middil" of a New England character.'

In recent years Mrs. Hull has developed a type of comedy which is hers alone—a sort of combination of Helen Hokinson and Lewis Carroll. This is her own distinctive gift; but of comedy in general she says: 'It is made up of detail; you have to have an eye for the comic — in others and in yourself, too. Some of my best bits of comedy have grown out of blunders I have made myself. They made me laugh afterward and I built them into good stage laughs.

'For instance, in *Harvey* I have a scene where Veta Simmons is talking to a society reporter on the telephone. One evening I absent-mindedly put down the telephone and went on talking as if the person on the other end of the wire could still hear me. This got a big laugh and I kept it in the show.

'Comedy has to have an underlying structure of drama. Burlesque and satire are different but true comedy needs pathos to shadow it and bring out the high-lights. When I started on the part of Veta I began to dig and dig into it to discover Veta's main emotional conflict. It is this: she is torn between a deep love for her genial, tippling brother, Elwood — who sees the invisible white rabbit, Harvey — and the desire to give her daughter a good social send-off. The conflict is resolved in the last act where the doctors are ready to give Elwood the "treatment" which will destroy his illusions and make him normal — and dull and humdrum. I suddenly realize that I don't want Elwood to change — I want him to stay as lovable and as happy as he is, Harvey or no Harvey. I begin to pound on the door, shouting, "Don't give it to him — I don't like people like that! I don't want my brother to be like that . . ."

'The scene brings all of Veta's scatterbrained comedy up sharply because it is straight drama. If it were not for that touch of pathos, the character of Veta Simmons would lose its impact. And that's my only theory of comedy — you have to find the drama underneath and let it come to the surface at the right moments.'

Because her last three parts — which have made her better known to the public than all the rest of her work in the theatre — have been ladies slightly mad, it is interesting to contrast them with Josephine Hull herself. It would be hard to find a more evenly balanced, integrated mind. She brought to the theatre a thorough grounding in the classics and in the history and tradition of the stage as art. Yet she says, 'I am just a worker in the theatre who tries to make acting real.' Thousands of playgoers and millions of film fans can testify to the degree in which she succeeds.

7 Laurette Taylor

Norris Houghton

December 1945

Laurette Taylor (1884–1946), petite, wide-eyed, ingenuous, was acting in a supporting role in *The Great John Garnton* when she met and married its author J. Hartley Manners. He devoted the rest of his career to building showcases for her distinct but limited talents. The most enduring of these was *Peg o' My Heart* (1912), the tale of a winsome Irish orphan grafted into a wealthy family. Taylor retired in 1928 but returned as Mrs Midgit, the charwoman with a problem son, in the 1938 revival of *Outward Bound*. Although she was something of a legend, producers avoided casting her because of erratic behaviour due to alcoholism, but she made a triumphant return as the fading Southern belle Amanda Wingfield in *The Glass Menagerie* (1945).

From an early age, Norris Houghton (1909–2001) was dedicated to bringing good plays to the stage. Designing scenery at Princeton University, he worked with Joshua Logan, and for the University Players of Provincetown, Mass., with Henry Fonda and Margaret Sullavan. On a Guggenheim grant (1934–5), he went to Moscow to observe great directors in action, which resulted in his book *Moscow Rehearsals*. In 1936, he assisted Guthrie McClintic and Katharine Cornell, and thereafter was an active force in the American theatre, particularly as a proponent of strong regional theatres. He co-founded the Phoenix Theatre Off-Broadway in 1953, but, a mediocre director at best, is remembered for staging a disastrous *Seagull* with Montgomery Clift in 1964.

'A VERY extraordinary woman, Laurette Taylor, a creature of curious beauty and charm and awkwardness — a dusty, tawny moth, miraculously fluttering . . . toward the light of an art in which personality is consumed by the fire of inspiration. Unmistakably she is in the company of the very few actresses of real genius that we have today.'

This notice might have been penned after the opening night of Tennessee Williams' *The Glass Menagerie* last March, but it was not. It was, in fact, written by the critic of the *New York Evening Globe.* (Kenneth Macgowan) about the leading lady of a play called *One Night in Rome* on December 3, 1919. More than a quarter of a century later it still seems completely pertinent, as accurate a description of that lady's quality, as correct an estimate of her worth as it did then.

It may seem ungracious to remind the world that an actress has been on the stage thirty-five years, since most actresses prefer their publics to believe that they have not been alive that long. But Laurette Taylor cannot dissemble, for she cannot escape the very public fact that as long ago as 1910, and in the succeeding years whenever she has appeared on Broadway, she has received such critical acclaim as has seldom been accorded any American actress.

Yet a generation of theatregoers and theatre workers has grown up in the years since Miss Taylor's last great starring vehicle, Fanny Hurst's *Humoresque* in 1923 — a generation to whom the name of Laurette Taylor struck no familiar chord. This generation, it is true, caught a glimpse of her magic in 1938 when she played Mrs. Midget in a revival of *Outward Bound*, but they were forced to wait another six years to see in its completeness what their fathers had meant when with glowing eye they recalled her in *Peg o' My Heart*.

The amazing thing to this new generation has been that the Taylor performance they saw in 1945 belonged to their own time. It not infrequently happens, when an actor of an earlier day 'returns to the stage' after an absence of some years, that the spectator is made acutely aware of the change in style that has otherwise imperceptibly affected our theatre. The older performer measures his playing by another yardstick, he speaks in a different key. Not so with Laurette Taylor. The new generation has 'discovered' her for themselves, and has found her to be, in a sense, one of themselves. I have heard such unanimous adulation of an older actor by the youngsters in the profession only among the neophytes in Moscow who worshipped at the feet of Stanislavski and Kachalov and Moskvin.

What is it that these younger artists, and all her public, as far as that is concerned, find so remarkable in the playing of Miss Taylor? Ah, that is the question — a question very nearly unanswerable. For when you talk to her most ardent admirers, when you question her fellow actors, when you study her yourself, when you ask her herself — no one seems to know. There is magic at work, everyone will agree (except perhaps Miss Taylor who keeps, one feels sure, many secrets to herself as the Irish are wont to do, and who only opens those great eyes with wonder and laughter and doesn't say).

The enigma of her playing has fascinated audiences from the beginning. In 1911 a critic remarked (and again his words might have been written of her current performance): 'Laurette Taylor plays the part [in *Seven Sisters*] in curious fashion, partly eccentric, partly pathetic, partly comic. She succeeds in holding the attention by mystifying the audience as to just what she is trying to do.'

Our purpose, however, is not so much to dwell on the mystery as to seek a key to unlock it. Perhaps the nearest thing to an answer lies in the one word — truth. The reason her playing remains today as fresh as it seemed to her critics thirty years ago is that it has nothing to do with fashions in stage convention, which are changeable, and everything to do with truth, which is lasting.

Now truth on the stage is very rare. It has really nothing to do with personality, a commodity that frequently passes in our theatre for acting. Miss Taylor, to be sure, has personality (to use the word in the advertising agency sense which is the sense in which the theatrical press agents use it too); five minutes in her dressing room are enough to prove it. And she has personality on the stage too (to use the word with a slightly different connotation): for the performance she gives as Amanda Wingfield is completely personalized, completely the creation of Laurette Taylor and of nobody else. But the thing that Miss Taylor contributes and that makes her seem different from so many other actors is the utter conviction of truth that comes from everything she says and does.

The student of acting sits before her performance and marvels at the series of constant surprises with which she rewards him: her phrasing and accent of a line is so often unexpected, her movement so unanticipated. But each surprise is confirmed and justified by its inevitability. If she throws away a syllable or the end of a line, it is right. If she gives double stress to a word as no other actor would have thought of doing, or draws it out to twice its normal length, it is right. It is right because it occurs not as a mannerism but as part of an inner rhythmic pattern that is organically of the truth. To traffic in the unexpected for its own sake is dangerous; when Miss Taylor offers the unexpected, you say, 'Of course. That is the only way it should have been done.' There is not a single cliché in her performance from beginning to end. That is why you sit so breathless to see what this woman will do next.

In the days immediately preceding the opening of *The Glass Menagerie*, those connected with the production were as nervous, as uncertain of success as people in such a situation always are. But a close observer reports that Miss Taylor alone was never uncertain. This was the more remarkable in that she had been known to throw over a play on the very eve of its presentation. Or was it so remarkable? Might it not have been that she knew in the other instances that she would not be good, just as this time she knew that she would be? When you are concerned with as fundamental and uncompromising a thing as truth, there can never be any doubt. Either you have it or you don't; and when you do, you know it and that's all there is to it.

Whence comes this knowledge of the truth? That is the next question we must face up to. Miss Taylor, of course, is the person to answer it and she would promptly reply: from the creative imagination. 'It isn't beauty or personality or magnetism that makes a really great actress,' she once said. 'It is imagination. . . . The imaginative actress builds a picture, using all her heart and soul and brain. She believes in it and she makes the people across the footlights believe in it. Unless she has done this she has failed.' But there is more to the imaginative process than that. 'She must stimulate the imagination of the audience as well. How often does an actress play a part so as to leave you with the feeling that you have so intimate a knowledge of the character that you could imagine its conduct in any position aside from the situation involved in the action of the play? Unless this happens . . . you have seen a limited portrayal.'

It is inevitable when talking about acting, and doubly so when talking about it in the way Miss Taylor has just been quoted, to hark back to Stanislavski, who could be more articulate on that subject than any other artist of the stage. It is idle speculation and completely unimportant to know whether Laurette Taylor ever read *My Life in Art* or *An Actor Prepares*, whether she ever heard of the 'Stanislavski System'. The interesting thing is that her acting approximates as closely as that of any other American the kind of art that the great Russian director was talking about. Stanislavski would undoubtedly have applauded her handling of the two telephone conversations in *The Glass Menagerie* which in Miss Taylor's hands are a revelation of conflicting psychological impulses, layer on layer, that take from the speeches that dullness and unbelievability that so often weigh down the stage telephone conversation.

In her insistence on the importance of the imagination she echoes the Russian's dictum that 'every movement you make on the stage, every word you speak, is the result of the right life of your imagination'. The connection between imagination and truth Stanislavski also recognized when he pointed out that what the actor uses on the stage is 'truth transformed into a poetical equivalent by creative imagination'. That transformation Miss Taylor is able to accomplish. Take the jonquil speech in *The Glass Menagerie* as an example of it. ('That was the spring I was obsessed by jonquils.') So alive is her imaginative conception that the spectator is made to visualize the whole youthful scene of the now faded matron.

In all this, technique plays its inevitable part. But in the case of Laurette Taylor there is such complete mastery of technique that its presence is unrealized by the spectator. For instance, when, after asking her son to bring home a 'gentleman caller' for her daughter, she goes to the door to call after him, again and again, 'Will you? Will you? Will you? Will you?' actually her voice rises scarcely at all with each iteration, but to the audience it seems, as she leans from the doorway, that her final cry must be heard three blocks away. Volume, rhythm, timing — over all these things Miss Taylor has complete control. Her magic is backed up by consummate technique.

As a rule, one does not go to actresses for definitions. Again Miss Taylor is an exception. Let me repeat what seems to me one of the most elucidating and all-embracing definitions of acting I have ever heard. To a newspaper reporter who came to interview her during the run of *Outward Bound*, Miss Taylor said, and I beg you to read this carefully: 'Acting is the physical representation of a mental picture and the projection of an emotional concept.'

Across the street on West Forty-eight Street in New York, opposite the Playhouse over whose marquee appears the lighted name of Laurette Taylor coupled with *The Glass Menagerie*, stands the Cort Theatre. This season its boards have advertised Fredric March in *A Bell for Adano*. Thirty-three years ago the Cort opened its doors for the first time. On that night in the early winter of 1912, when the first lights went on over the marquee, they spelled out the name of Laurette Taylor, coupled then with *Peg o' My Heart*.

She was already a star, you see, for in the three years since her first appearance on Broadway in *The Great John Ganton*, success had followed success: *Alias Jimmy Valentine; Girl in Waiting*, the first play in which she appeared written by J. Hartley Manners who, a few years later, not only was to provide her with her most famous role, Peg, but was to become her husband; *Seven Sisters; A Bird of Paradise*, in which she appeared as a South Sea island maiden, wore a black wig and danced the hula.

The Cort Theatre housed Laurette Taylor for almost two years while *Peg o' My Heart*, the sweet tale of an Irish-American waif accepted into the stiff aristocratic

English household of distant relations, ran up a near-record of 604 performances. The Cort was the scene of nightly ovations during those years, but probably the most memorable occasion was the day Laurette acted for Sarah Bernhardt. The 'divine Sarah' had heard a great deal about the young American actress, who sounded like the real thing to her; she expressed a desire to see for herself. But she was playing every night and matinees fell on the same day. What could be done? Laurette, honored as no other American actress had been honored, offered to give a performance for Bernhardt at eleven o'clock in the morning; so before an audience consisting only of the immortal Frenchwoman and her suite, she assembled her company and played *Peg o' My Heart*.

That Bernhardt joined the ranks of Taylor admirers is evidenced by the fact that when she returned to America in 1916 she again wanted to see Laurette play. This time Sarah was unable even to leave her theatre, so Laurette brought her whole company and production down to the Empire Theatre and there at three o'clock one afternoon she played *The Harp of Life*. I wish I might have been in that theatre filled with Miss Taylor's 'gentleman callers' (for this time there was an invited audience); to have seen the lights go out in the red damask and gold auditorium while Bernhardt was carried in and installed in the right stage box; to have stood, when the lights came up again, and cheered the *grande dame* with the rest of the audience; to have watched Miss Taylor play the mother of a son of nineteen, although she herself could not have been much more than thirty.

The Harp of Life was also written by Hartley Manners, and it was her first play after she returned from performing *Peg o' My Heart* for five hundred performances in London. If you ask Lynn Fontanne, she will tell you that Miss Taylor had seen her act during that season in London and had brought her to America to play with her, and that in this *The Harp of Life* the English-born actress played her first important role in New York, in support of Laurette. And that, incidentally, is another reason why I wish I had been at the Empire that afternoon in 1916.

During the years of World War I and in the season that followed the end of that war, Miss Taylor appeared in a series of plays written for her by her husband, Hartley Manners. In fact, for over ten years she never played in anything written by anyone else (if you except the rather disastrous special matinees of Shakespeare she essayed in 1918). There was *Out There* in 1917, in which she played a Red Cross nurse in Flanders to whom *The New York Times* reviewer referred as ' 'aunted Annie, a cockney Jeanne d'Arc'; there was *Happiness* in 1918, which told the story of Jenny, the little Brooklyn dressmaker's apprentice who turned fashionable shopkeeper; there was *One Night in Rome* the following season; *The National Anthem* in 1921, a jazz-age morality (the national anthem was, of course, jazz).

Before the not too successful production of Philip Barry's *In a Garden* in 1925 came *Humoresque*, from the pen of Fanny Hurst. It too was not a great success on the stage but Miss Taylor received thunderous personal acclaim for her performance of the Mother from the Ghetto. There is interest in the fact that the notices and descriptions of her performance of a mother in *Humoresque* echo in advance the notices of her performance of a mother in *The Glass Menagerie* more than twenty years later. Although the roles are dissimilar, there is a familiar strain in the

Hurst mother who fights for her child that Miss Taylor may have heard in her inner ear when she set to work on Amanda, who also fights a battle of a different kind for her child.

In 1928 Hartley Manners died. He had given Laurette Taylor a great deal more, she has always said, than a series of successful scripts. He had taught her much about acting and about life. 'He has given me', she once said while he was still alive, 'a sense of the fitness of things — and a sense of proportion.' But when he died, he took away from her for the time being that sense of proportion, as far as life was concerned. It was ten years before she was able to return to the stage in full power. Then she appeared as Mrs. Midget — again as a mother battling for her child, but a completely different character from the other mothers she had played and was to play. When *Outward Bound* closed, once more she disappeared. But this time it was not such a willing disappearance. She was ready to act again, but not unless the play were right, not unless the part were one in which she could believe, not unless her imagination were stirred. Truth being as rare as it is in our drama and on our stage, it is no wonder that she had to wait another six years before she found what she was seeking. But thank heaven she found it, and pray heaven she may find it again soon. For now that we have seen her once more and come to know her artistry, seasons will be bleak in the future that are not illuminated by the light that is her peculiar treasure.

8 Seven interviews in search of good acting

Aimee Scheff

March 1952

Because the United States has no national theatre, it has never had a conservatory or official school of acting. Independent teachers, often retired or failed actors, set up their own studios, without the need for official validation. Many of the fugitives from the Russian Revolution, unable to continue their own acting careers because of heavy accents, opened acting schools, claiming close acquaintance with Stanislavsky and the Moscow Art Theatre. The anomaly of these schools, unassociated with a working theatre, was that classwork often became the be-all and end-all, without relevance to performing before a paying audience.

Bown Adams, author of a play about John Milton (1943), ran, with his wife Virginia Daly, an acting studio in New York which advertised regularly in *Theatre Arts*. A pioneer collector and exhibitor of silent films, he left his collection to Phillips Exeter Academy.

Austrian-born Herbert Berghof (1909–90) had been educated by Max Reinhardt and Lee Strasberg. A member of the Actors Studio, he was first seen on Broadway in *Reunion in New York* (1940) and staged the first New York production of *Waiting for Godot*. A trusted teacher of acting, with his wife Uta Hagen he founded the HB Playwrights Foundation.

Stella Adler (1903–92) was the daughter of the distinguished Yiddish actor Jacob Adler and sister of Luther. A student at the American Laboratory Theatre, she joined the Group Theatre (1931–5) at the urging of Harold Clurman, whom she married. Her best part there was Bessie Berger in *Awake and Sing!*, but she left over disputes about how to interpret the teachings of Stanislavsky. She became a formidable acting teacher of her own version at a school she founded in 1949, with Marlon Brando among her students.

Sanford Meisner (1905–97) acted for the Theatre Guild before joining the Group Theatre where, with Clifford Odets, he co-directed *Waiting for Lefty* (1935). That same year he began teaching the Group's version of Stanislavsky at the Neighborhood Playhouse, whose "Acting Department" he led until 1959 and again from 1964.

Erwin Piscator (1893–1966) headed the left-wing Volksbühne in Weimar Berlin, where he experimented with constructivist settings, film clips, moving walkways and other technical innovations for propagandistic ends. During the Second World War, he lived in New York, directing at the New School for Social Research and a Dramatic Academy in the Capitol Theatre Building. He counted Marlon Brando, Judith Malina and Julian Beck among his students. When he returned to West Germany, he became the foremost director of documentary drama.

Galicia-born Lee Strasberg (Israel Strassberg, 1901–82) imbibed the ideas of Stanislavsky, Meyerhold and Copeau at the American Laboratory Theatre (1924–31), and then co-founded the Group Theatre in 1931. His successful productions there included *The House of Connelly* and *Men in White*. However, his dogged adherence to early Stanislavskian concepts of emotional memory led him to clash with Stella Adler, and they came to lead two armed camps. Strasberg left the Group in 1941, and ten years later became head of the Actors Studio, where he promoted the "Method", with intense exploitation of personal feelings. He strongly influenced three generations of actors, but lost the ability to direct a well-integrated production.

Vera Vasilievna Soloviova (1891–1986) was a Russian émigré, whose lovely voice had earned her admission to the Moscow Art Theatre 1st Studio (1908–24). Married to the actor Andrius Jilinsky, she went with him to the Lithuanian National Theatre (1929–35) and then to New York as a member of Michael Chekhov's Moscow Art Players (1935). She co-founded the School for Stage Art, and aided by her former student Christine Edwards, opened the Vera Soloviova Studio of Acting in 1951.

Aimee Scheff, sister of the critic Lionel Abel, was the regular reporter of Off-Broadway for *Theatre Arts* in the early 1950s. She later became a regional theatre director, and had a small role in the horror episode of Todd Haynes' film *Poison* (1991).

WHILE theatre critics and playwrights are constantly giving us their opinion on what constitutes good theatre, they tell us little about one of the most important elements, good acting. What makes good acting? For the answer we might look to those responsible for the training of actors. To this end we interviewed a cross section of teachers of acting in New York City.

1. What particular school of acting do you represent, and what are distinctive techniques?
2. What qualities are most essential for an actor? Just what is good acting?
3. How many years of training are necessary for thorough preparation?
4. Is experience in classic drama essential for the apprentice?
5. Are there new trends in acting corresponding to new trends in literature?
6. Is experience in stock companies and off-Broadway groups valuable?
7. Do you emphasize ensemble acting as opposed to the star system?
8. Is TV experience an asset?
9. Will the revival of the arena theatre overshadow the conventional stage and lead to more imaginative acting?
10. What is your opinion of Broadway?
11. Besides helping to solve the unemployment problem, would a subsidized theatre in the United States stimulate better acting?

Brown Adams

1. We represent the American school which inspires the creative outlet through individual coaching and maximum experience. Training emphasizes a good speaking voice, a relaxed mind and workshop productions.

2. Essential qualities in an actor are a mature mind, artistic warmth and sensitivity. Good acting is releasing in artistic form the spirit or truth of the part.

3. If the actor is mature, less than two years' training is necessary, otherwise five to ten years.

4. Experience in parts students can most easily play comes first; classics follow.

5. We are going away from externalities. More stress is placed on the actor's ability to sense the truth and moods of a play.

6. If the student has not developed bad habits, stock experience is helpful.

7. We emphasize ensemble acting, but train students to hold their own in the professional theatre.

8. TV does not add to the growth of the artist, but helps him face realities in the theatre.

9. The arena theatre has contributed to finding truth in the theatre. If the actor can create an illusion in arena style, he should be able to transfer it more effectively to conventional staging.

10. The Broadway theatre has made strides but has not reached its goal.

11. A subsidized theatre is a good thing, but at present impractical.

Herbert Berghof

1. I represent my own system of acting based on my experiences in the theatre, and what I learned from Lee Strasberg and Sanford Meisner. My methods include the study of human behaviour based on Aristotelian principles as outlined in the *Poetics*. My techniques involve exercises in improvisation, study of plot, character and motivation.

2. The actor must have sensitivity and imaginary power. Good acting is the marriage of a flawless technique with genius.

3. Two years of training, six hours a day, is necessary.

4. Experience in classic drama should be a part of training in the advanced stage.

5. We should have gone beyond the Stanislavski of the 1900s, which still seems to be a point of argument, and we should make use of new findings in psychiatry, psycho-analysis and semantics.

6. Experience in stock companies is helpful to actors who have defined their technique.

7. I emphasize ensemble acting.

8. TV only offers actors money to survive in the theatre.

9. The arena theatre is adventurous and therefore desirable.

10. Broadway is hopelessly in the clutches of merchants; nevertheless my students will enter its ranks.

11. In a country of boundless resources, a theatre aspiring to serve as a cultural force should be subsidized wherever it is.

Stella Adler

1. My methods evolve from my own experiences and influences. My earliest were my parents, Jacob and Sarah Adler of the Yiddish stage, and later, Madame Ouspenskaya and Stanislavski. My own technique involves breaking down separate elements of a system and putting them together again in terms of what the individual student requires.

2. The essential quality in an actor is the desire to act. There are two kinds of good acting — that which reaches the soul, and that which shows a sense of craftsmanship.

3. For the student, a minimum of two years' training is necessary; for the actor a lifetime.

4. An actor's range *must* include the ability to deal with classic roles.

5. If society, through any of its creators, produces a new form it must express itself eventually in the theatre.

6. If the actor is disciplined all experience is helpful, including stock companies.

7. No actor today is trained in the technique of the star system. The star is created by the theatrical street whether it be the Boulevard Theatre or Broadway.

8. TV can help the actor if he knows himself.

9. The arena theatre might stimulate the actor toward an independent way of work.

10. The theatre, to a certain degree, belongs to the actor. If he is strong he will turn it into something valuable, if only in self-preservation.

11. The American theatre can be helped by many things. Subsidy is one of them. This should be controlled by the most responsible and cultured elements in the theatre.

Sanford Meisner

1. I represent the school for Theatrical Realism, and employ methods and techniques as developed by Stanislavski and tempered by 20 years of practical creative experience. These methods are related to the individual actor and not on generalized intellectual theories or book exercises.

2. An actor must possess an arresting personality and the quality to bring his own truth of living to the use of the character. Good acting is humanly alive and theatrically vivid.

3. Two years' minimum training is essential, three years preferable; and a lifetime is needed for self-development.

4. Experience in classic drama is not a must but desirable after basic training.

5. The new technical awareness formulated by Stanislavski marked the most important departure from old patterns. We follow in the path of this modern development.

6. Stock company experience is helpful to actors if the companies are in the hands of talented directors.

7. The importance of every role's contribution toward the entire play is emphasized at all times.

8. TV, as such, makes no special contribution to acting.

9. Arena theatre will contribute more to art than conventional staging if it inspires plays written for this form.

10. In any season there is always the predominance of purely commercialized entertainment plus very few distinguished plays.

11. The only solution is subsidizing, under government cultural auspices, genuine theatres throughout the country.

Erwin Piscator

1. Method in the theatre is a means to an end, and that end, being art, involves the human being. Methods vary. One is not superior to another. The actor's method is *his* secret. Even when we open the fourth wall and the actor addresses the audience directly, the spectator does not think of method but accepts a new and adequate expression of modern man.

2. The actor must have the ability to create real characters. Good acting is convincing acting.

3. A basic three-year course is necessary, but there is no limit to learning theatre.

4. A classic background typified by European repertory theatre is a must.

5. Since theatre art encompasses all living art, new trends in acting presuppose new trends in writing.

6. If the actor is well-trained, stock experience will help perfect his skills.

7. Our emphasis is on ensemble acting rather than a star system; but the ensemble has produced great stars such as Olivier.

8. TV could offer an excellent opportunity for experience as it demands one's full knowledge of the stage.

9. The arena stage, handled with care, contributes much to theatre art. There can be no cardboard actors, no "best" profile. The actor must show himself in the whole.

10. Our students look forward to Broadway, not only because it provides for their material needs, but because they do not find in the avant-garde or experimental theatre the proper fulfillment.

11. The subsidized theatre is the ideal theatre. It permits experimentation as well as tradition and offers a greater opportunity for a livelihood.

Lee Strasberg

1. The actor functions as a real life instrument not as an imitator of life. Some of the basic processes used in training have been explored by Stanislavski and others of his school.

2. Good acting exists when an actor thinks and reacts as much to imaginary situations as to those in real life.

3. Two or three years of training is essential.

4. Great classic acting depends upon the same elements necessary for any kind of acting. However, if the actor approaches the classic drama without first having the ability to create real live characters, he is liable to wind up as an oratorical automaton.

5. Techniques remain the same regardless of trends; styles change constantly.

6. If the methods are good, there is value in an actor's constant work on stage.

7. Ensemble acting is emphasized. This is true of all modern acting.

8. TV is helpful. The actor gains authority.

9. Today we have a diversity of theatre styles for different types of plays. Emphasis on arena theatre or any one particular style may be detrimental to the growth of the theatre.

10. What Broadway suffers from today theatrically is a great waste of the greatest reservoir of theatrical talent.

11. The artistic problems will be the same, but it is advisable to have the security that a subsidized theatre offers.

Vera Soloviova

1. My method grew out of 21 years of working under Stanislavski in the Moscow Art Theatre and the First Studio. My training is highly individualized, stressing relaxation, group work in concentration, observation and improvisation.

2. The actor must possess a creative imagination, vitality and radiance. Good acting combines sensitivity, vitality, and technique.

3. Three years of training are necessary.

4. Acting experience in classic drama enables students to undertake any modern role.

5. Our techniques are elastic enough to encompass any new forms in acting that must result from new forms in literature.

6. Summer stock is a lot of fun but gives very little experience to student actors.

7. Only by accenting group playing can drama be faithfully presented. As my husband, Andrius Jilinsky said, "There are no small parts, only small actors."

8. TV under expert direction offers an opportunity for the Stanislavski technique in its demand for natural, sincere acting.

9. Arena theatre can be fascinating but cannot take the place of conventional staging.

10. Broadway the last few years has had better plays and better direction than previously. However, too often the accent is on the beautiful sets and costumes.

11. Subsidized theatre is very necessary if the theatre is to survive.

It is evident that the methods of all those interviewed are based on Stanislavski's theories, and the only variations among the schools result from the differences in the personalities of the teachers themselves. In their general opinion, individuality and imagination are the prime elements of good acting.

9 That wonderful, deep silence

Shelley Winters

June 1956

Shelley Winters (1920–2006) is remembered for her movie roles, ranging from blowsy temptresses to obese harridans over the course of her 50-year career. Before she came to Hollywood in 1943, however, she had gained experience performing before live audiences in Borsht Belt revue and on Broadway, serving as Julie Haydon's understudy in *The Time of Your Life* (1939–41) and playing the housemaid disguised as a countess in *Rosalinda*, Max Reinhardt's adaptation of *Die Fledermaus* (1942). Throughout the 1950s, she made sporadic stage appearances in New York (*A Hatful of Rain*, 1955, and *Girls of the Summer*, 1956), while taking classes at the Actors Studio.

BACK in 1948 I stepped out of the theatre and into movies, specifically out of the role of Ado Annie in *Oklahoma!* and into a seven-year contract at Universal-International Studios that started with a role opposite Ronald Colman in *A Double Life*. In those days such a move was like stepping from one separate theatrical world into another, because at that time there were two distinct kinds of actors—stage actors and movie actors. Today, so far as I can see, there are only actors, and they play both mediums, plus a third that no one thought about very much then—television.

When I left the stage, a player, in order to go into pictures, had to sign a seven-year contract that virtually kept him from going back to Broadway. Only a very rare movie star ever managed to obtain a contract with a clause permitting him to do an occasional play. The others, away from the stage too long (or perhaps never having been on it at all), were afraid of braving the New York critics and audiences. Today movie stars are not rarities on Broadway, and the tendency is for players to live in New York, travel to Hollywood for an occasional picture (the one that *interests* you, not the one you *have* to do) and squeeze in television appearances from time to time.

How does an actress feel, then, who returned to Broadway after seven years in which movies and stage stopped existing in separate worlds? For myself, I feel the stimulation, excitement and fulfillment that come with the freedom of being able to shuttle between the two mediums, with television always there to add a third dimension to my work. It is a healthy and challenging situation but, contrary to what theatre fans might think, it is not one that requires a great deal of adjustment for the player.

Granted, the mediums differ. Each poses its own problems. In movies there is plenty of time to learn lines but no chance to achieve continuity, to develop a characterization. In television there is continuity but not sufficient rehearsal time; you're always going on before you're really "free" from the lines. In the theatre there are both adequate rehearsal time and continuity, but there is also the risk of going stale. (I must say, though, that for me, one of the wonderful things about the theatre is the period *after* you've gone stale, when your role comes alive all over again and every audience presents a new challenge, a new opportunity to add shading to your characterization.)

There are also different techniques, tricks of each branch of the business. In pictures, for example, handling props is a very tricky thing because of the pure mechanics of the medium. If you move an ash tray from one table to another, you must be sure to pick it up on the same word and put it down on the same word in each "take," always with the same motion of your hand and arm; otherwise your movements will not match when the film is edited. For me this requires so much concentration that I try to avoid touching props wherever possible.

On the stage this is a simple matter. In *A Hatful of Rain* I perform a great deal of "business"—washing dishes, ironing clothes, doing ordinary household tasks. Yet I don't ever have to think about these things as I do them, because they are all part of the whole; they are natural to the character I am playing, and I find myself going about these tasks instinctively, just as though I were really keeping house on the stage of the Lyceum Theatre.

On the other hand, the problem of vocal projection, which is nonexistent in movies and television, is a real one in the theatre. Last year I opened a summer tour in *Wedding Breakfast* at the Salt Creek Theatre near Chicago. The critics there complained that they could not hear me, and they were right. By the time we got to Westport I had learned to project, and the notices were pretty good. Then, when we opened *A Hatful of Rain* in New Haven, I found that, where I had a particularly important line or where the situation was very dramatic, my voice would grow shrill. During the pre-Broadway tour I learned to project without shrillness, to be heard all over the house without actually raising my voice. It's a trick, and it takes a lot of work to master it.

Still, these things are technique, not art, and an actor who has only technique is not, in my opinion, an artist. To me acting is acting. whether it is in the theatre, in movies or in television. It consists essentially in seeing the truths and realities in the character you are playing and translating them into your own terms and experiences. Once this is done a truthful and honest performance will result, no matter the medium. The only difference will be that you are using, so to speak, another set of muscles.

Take Ado Annie, for example. The true humor of this character, as I see it, lies in the fact that she really can't say "No." For her this is a genuine dilemma. It constitutes the reality of the character. It is not enough for an actress to get a surface laugh by singing "I Can't Say No" with a toss of the head and a glib throwing off of lines. She must understand that for Ado Annie, who truly can't say "No," this is a real problem. Consequently, the real humor *of the character*, not merely *of the lines*, will come through.

For the actor the crux of the matter lies in learning to put a finger on that elusive thing that makes a character true and genuine. In this regard a good director is almost godlike. Yet again I am not at all convinced that directors, any more than actors, differ with the various mediums. They differ only in their sensitivities and in their recognition of the limitations of each medium. Right here I should like to say that I believe I have learned more about acting from Lee Strasberg than from any other person in the dramatic arts. But I have seen a good movie director accomplish as much as a good stage director.

George Stevens, with whom I worked in *A Place in the Sun*, is such a director. In this picture there was a scene in which, as a pregnant, unmarried mother, I visited a doctor in the hope that he would perform an abortion. When I originally played the scene I really felt every bit as distraught as I supposed the character would have felt. I began to cry, and I cried right through the "take." I was sure that I had played it right, yet afterward Stevens called me over and explained something I had not even considered:

As an actress I had wanted to *show* that the character was distraught, but the character herself would want to hide this, for fear that the doctor might not help her. When we did the final "take" I was trying so hard not to show anxiety that I had to take long pauses in the dialogue to keep from crying. It seemed to make the audience cry for me. That's what a good director can accomplish for an actress.

In the final analysis, though, it is the audience from whom a player really learns—and that is something you don't get in movies or in television. You can understand your character, you can profit from wonderful direction, you can master technique—but it remains for an audience to tell you whether or not you are coming alive. Every audience, as any actor will confirm, is a separate person, with a distinct character all its own. If you don't reach this person you have failed.

Wednesday matinée audiences are a case in point. They are mostly women. They want very much to see the show. They have probably gone to a great deal of effort to come. They will not tolerate talking among themselves. They will "shush" each other so that they can hear the actors. More important (and unlike Saturday matinée audiences who want more to laugh), they are very susceptible to getting involved in the drama.

Early in the run of *A Hatful of Rain* I began to notice that during the scene in which Ben Gazzara, as my husband, feels the movement of our unborn child, there would be a loud snapping noise. It would be particularly loud on Wednesday afternoons. I found it distracting and complained to the stage manager. He said, "When you *don't* hear that noise, worry." It seems that the noise was caused by the women in the audience snapping their handbags open to take out their handkerchiefs! Now at every performance I wait hopefully for that sound, and if we fail to get it. I really get upset.

Another sound for which I am always listening is the sound of the laugh that's hard to get. These are the laughs that come, not from the lines themselves, but from the actor's delivery. If a funny line doesn't get over, the actor is at fault. But if a valid laugh, growing out of the situation, can be gotten in precisely the same place every night when the line itself isn't funny, the actor has found that extra "something," and the sound of that hard-to-get laugh is a rich, personal reward.

In a sense it is those audience sounds that sum up the difference between acting in the theatre and acting in other mediums. It isn't the demands that are so different. It's the rewards. Every now and then, when you're on stage, you hear the best sound a player can hear. It's a sound you can't get in movies or in television. It is the sound of a wonderful, deep silence that means you've hit them where they live.

For myself, if I could get *that* every performance, they wouldn't have to pay me so much.

10 Shakespeare and the American actor

John Houseman

July 1956

The regular plaint of American dramatic critics was that there was no native way of playing Shakespeare. Despite a long train of illustrious actors in the major roles (Forrest, Davenport, Booth, Mansfield) and a somewhat more uneven record of directorial interpretations (Daly, Belasco, Hopkins, Orson Welles), no specifically American style had emerged. The founding of the Shakespeare Festival in Stratford, Ontario, in 1953 (albeit with a British director, Tyrone Guthrie and a British star, Alec Guinness) spurred the emulation of the U.S. theatrical community. In 1956 John Houseman became the artistic director of the new American Shakespeare Festival in Stratford, Connecticut, which aimed to provide a centre for an indigenous style to take shape.

Born in Bucharest as Jacques Haussman (1902–88), Houseman broke into the American theatre as director of Virgil Thomson's opera *Four Saints in Three Acts* (1934). With Orson Welles, whose excesses he tried to moderate, he organized the W.P.A.'s Negro Theater Project (the Voodoo *Macbeth* (1935), the Classical Theatre (*Dr Faustus; The Cradle Will Rock*, both 1936) and the Mercury Theatre (the modern dress *Julius Caesar*, 1937)). He became a successful film producer in Hollywood (1945–62), while continuing to direct on Broadway. Years after he left the Shakespeare Festival in 1959, he formed the Drama Division of the Juilliard School and its acting company (1968–76). Late in life, he won wider fame and fortune as the imperious law professor in the film and television series *The Paper Chase*.

"How do you feel about an all-American Shakespearean acting company?" is the question I have been asked most persistently since it was announced that I would direct the works of the American Shakespeare Festival Theatre in Stratford, Connecticut, this summer. My answer is a well-considered and most emphatic "fine!" The time is particularly propitious. For years American acting was a branch—a very honorable branch—of the English theatrical tradition. Then with the rise of a native American drama, there developed an unfortunate but ever-widening chasm between the classic and realistic schools of performance. For half a century they have seemed irreconcilable and mutually exclusive. Today the tendency seems to be reversing itself. It is to the great advantage of our theatre that this gap is rapidly closing.

The American actor of today is probably more conscious of the problems of his craft, and works harder at mastering them, than his fellow artist in any other country in the world. In the past two generations most of our best young actors have been preoccupied mainly with the inner mechanics of expressing human emotions—the much discussed "method" and its derivatives. The results have been stimulating and far-reaching. Of late, however, even among those actors who are most deeply committed to the subjective systems, there has been a growing preoccupation with a theatre possessing more style and eloquence. Returning to New York after an absence of several years, one is startled to see how far American acting has veered in this direction. The murmuring, introspective playing in vogue a generation ago is giving place to performances in which the communication between actor and audience has become more direct and more frankly theatrical. Julie Harris' Joan in *The Lark* exemplifies this, as does the acting and the staging of *Cat on a Hot Tin Roof*—to mention only two obvious examples.

It is not surprising, therefore, that American actors today should be casting eager eyes toward Shakespeare. The subjective actor, concerned with personal patterns of mood and feeling, has tended to regard the text as a vessel into which he can pour the emotions generated in him by the realistic situation in which the playwright has placed him. Much of the time we find him playing around and above and beneath the lines. In the sustained verbal stretches of poetic drama this cannot be done. The author's words *are* the emotion; and the actor's ability to illuminate and enrich them is the measure of his technical and emotional capacity to work in this no-less emotional but more formal theatrical medium.

How well are American actors prepared to meet this challenge? Very well indeed; for they can bring to it a keenness and a depth of interpretation sometimes missing in actors whose whole lives have been devoted exclusively to elocutionary theatre. On the simple level of speech, whenever the question of an American company comes up, I find an automatic and nervous raising of eyebrows. This is absurd. Purged of blatant provincialisms and phonetic vices, American speech is as good as any other kind of English. It is almost certainly closer to Shakespeare's tongue than the class-conscious and emasculated idiom known as "Oxford English." The truth is that we are far more conscious, in theatrical performance, of our "American" pronunciation than are the British. When the film *Julius Caesar* was reviewed in England, John Gielgud, as Cassius, and Marlon Brando, as Antony, were not placed in separate departments, but were hailed in joint headlines for their very different but very vital performances. (Indeed, from the start, Brando was accepted by English critics with a much freer, less reserved enthusiasm than was the case with our own movie reviewers, who were still worrying about Kowalski, while the British were listening to Shakespeare.)

What we will aim for at Stratford—what any American company must aim for—is not a mimicking of the British pronunciation but a constantly high standard of rich, vigorous speech. This we are confident of achieving. What is far more serious for the American actor is his lack of preparation, through training and practice, in facing the problems that go with the delivery of dramatic verse—an understanding and a capacity to handle, to maximum vocal and dramatic advantage, the beat, the stresses and the rhythms which make iambic pentameter, as used by Shakespeare, the greatest medium of dramatic communication known to the Western world. In this respect the new school of English classic actors is far ahead of us; in clarity, intelligibility and pace, they have achieved a perfection which we can only hope to emulate with time and work.

Generally speaking, however, in regard to enlightened and practical training for Shakespearean acting, the young people now in schools and colleges are better off than their predecessors. Not only are there today, all over the country, a number of excellent academic training grounds, but there have grown up several established and well-attended festivals to which the young classic actor can attach himself and develop his craft. Best known of these are the one at Antioch College in Yellow Springs, Ohio, and the Oregon Shakespeare Festival at Ashland, where B. Iden Payne, who has done so much work along these lines from Pennsylvania to Texas, is teaching and directing this summer. Already a national system is developing by which it is possible for a young actor to join a Shakespeare theatre, start by playing a modest role, then in subsequent seasons move on to bigger parts as his experience and capacity grow. In this development we hope to do our share. So much for the future.

But for anyone connected with the festival at Stratford, Connecticut, the problem has been the immediate and pressing one of assembling the best possible available acting company—here and now. Ideally the best American Shakespeare company consists of the best American actors playing Shakespeare. Many of them are with us this summer. Others still hesitate; they feel that they are unprepared and are unwilling to attempt the task. We have done all we could to persuade them; we must do more in the future. For here the festival can fulfill an invaluable function. It can provide the opportunity for these actors to undertake parts which they would be unwilling or unable to attempt on Broadway. In England, Laurence Olivier's forthcoming film *Macbeth* will mark his third or fourth major portrayal of the role—just as his Richard was an interpretation made up of elements accumulated through several previous performances. In America an actor of forty-five finds himself venturing into a major Shakespeare role for the first time in his professional life—and he usually has about three weeks of actual rehearsal to prepare it. At the festival the actor can play his part for the entire summer in repertory, and he can breathe and think while he is doing so without the attendant pressures of a transitory Broadway production. At the end of the summer his performance will be surer and richer than when he began. He will be that much closer to the interpretation of which he is ultimately capable.

In this very growth there is an element of excitement—and also a reason for caution. A great Shakespeare acting company cannot be developed in a single summer. Two, five, ten years from now the final fruits of our efforts will be harvested. In the meantime, what our audiences have the right to expect, and what we hope to give them this summer, is the excitement of a new organization performing great plays in an original and exciting fashion. For this reason we deliberately have chosen, as our first productions, two of the lesser known plays: *King John* and *Measure for Measure*. We want audiences to regard Stratford not as a museum for distinguished and familiar relics, with the added fillip of a competitive star performance, but as a home for living and exciting theatre. For this reason we believe that the choice of these unfamiliar plays is a good one. We hope that each of them will have some of that quality of revelation that is shared by actors and audience during the performance of a new work—in this case two new works by the world's leading playwright, one a comedy and one a tragedy.

The comedy *Measure for Measure*, which in Victorian times seldom was performed on the stage, and bowdlerized beyond recognition in book form, is enjoying a surprising renaissance on both sides of the Atlantic. It is a very controversial play and a very modern play. Highly contemporary are its twin problems of relative as against absolute morality—of informed tolerance against the rigid enforcement of an arbitrary law. Our world of today is much concerned with the liberal concept of civilized life as opposed to state-enforced codes of social and moral behavior. It is interesting to note that Shakespeare enthusiastically endorsed the former.

A play about power and human character under the pressure of power, *King John*, once very popular and now in temporary eclipse, also has much to say to the modern audience. On the one hand it is a play about loyalty and treachery in government and among nations; on the other it is the first of the series of historical plays (first in point of time of action) in which Shakespeare developed those basic and important themes about kingship which are recurrent in so many of his works. A key character, Faulconbridge, starts with a personal, opportunistic loyalty to King John, in the belief that this will benefit himself; we witness his disillusionment when he realizes the king's fallibility, and share his final realization that the crown and the state—comprising all its subjects in an organic and inseparable whole—are more important than the individual who wears the crown.

With these two plays, performed alternately in repertory, our season opens on June 26. A third play will be introduced into the repertory on August 5. On the physical level we are making certain fairly drastic changes in the stage of the Festival Theatre. There was talk last year of remoteness between the actors and the audience. To correct this we have extended the apron and widened it; we have raked the stage and restricted its depth so that the areas on the forestage, and upstage of the arch, are now just about equal in depth and width. In this new form we hope to make the stage a simple and potent dramatic instrument on which our American Shakespearean company may perform in the extraordinarily beautiful frame of the Stratford Festival Theatre.

Here again time—time, which was one of Shakespeare's favorite subjects—will be the final judge of our efforts. We know that we shall not achieve all our aims overnight. Certainly nothing would please us more than to achieve that consistent glow, compounded of local pride and artistic excitement, which has characterized the festival in Stratford, Ontario, since its inception. As of this writing we do not even know, exactly, what the source of our audiences will be. New England? The Eastern seaboard? The nation? Two or five or ten years from now we shall know the answer. For the present—having weighed with care our assets and liabilities, our ambitions and our inhibitions—we work in the earnest hope that we have found something like the proper formula for the American Shakespeare Festival of 1956.

11 Geraldine Page: The irony of a legend

Joseph Carroll

April 1953

Geraldine Page (1924–87) made her mark Off-Broadway as Alma in José Quintero's production of *Summer and Smoke* at the Circle in the Square (1951–2) and was confirmed on Broadway playing Lily in *Mid-Summer* (1953). She then went to Hollywood, returning, at the behest of Lee Strasberg, to play Olga in his turgid *Three Sisters* (1964). The stage career which seemed so promising in 1953 foundered for a while until she appeared in *Agnes of God* (1982), a sensation drama about a pregnant nun, which ran for 599 performances.

Joseph Carroll (1930–77) was on the staff of *Collier's Magazine* and an editor of *Theatre Arts* and, later, *Sports Illustrated*. He began publishing stories in the *Saturday Evening Post* in the 1950s. Although he had been born in Chicago, most of his writing dealt with Irish culture. His play *The Barroom Monks* enjoyed 300 Off-Broadway performances in 1962, and *Mr Bloom and the Cyclops*, an adaptation of the Cyclops chapter in Joyce's *Ulysses*, was produced by the Abbey Theatre in 1977.

GERALDINE PAGE, who became a star this season in her very first appearance on Broadway, is the newest version of the theatre's oldest legend: the overnight success. She is also a blunt refutation of the legend, being a young woman whose ironic habit of mind goes oddly with her fragile appearance and gentle manner. She herself simply does not believe in the legend, either in her own case or anyone else's. "In the theatre," she told an interviewer—not out of modesty but merely as a matter of fact—"there is no such thing as an overnight success. It only happens in Hollywood B pictures about the understudy who goes on for the star on opening night and wins an ovation from all the extras who have been hired to be the audience."

Miss Page's ovation at the opening night of Vina Delmar's *Mid-Summer* at the Vanderbilt theatre on January 21 was as close to tumultuous as reality ever is to Hollywood's fantasies. There were even members of the audience who yelled "Bravo!," too enthusiastic to care about any pedant who might remind them that the word should be "Brava" when addressed to a female performer.

When the reviews appeared the next day, the critics had already made Miss Page a star by acclamation, though she was technically co-featured with Mark Stevens, a movie actor also making his Broadway debut, and with veteran actress Vicki Cummings. Miss Page ran away with the notices, as the phrase goes, though Mr. Stevens and Miss Cummings were generally praised. The play got at best mild approval and at worst was written off as sentimental claptrap, creaking with its own contrivances. A few days after the opening, the producers of *Mid-Summer*, Paul Crabtree and Frank J. Hale, accepted the critics' and the public's view of the situation and elevated Miss Page to stardom. Her name was raised above that of the play on the theatre marquee. Mark Stevens' name was raised at the same time, so that technically she is now co-starred with Mr. Stevens, and his name appears before hers. This is related to some mystique of theatrical contracts, and no one concerned is willing to give any intelligible explanation of it. The best a Broadway outsider can do is to accept *Variety's* completely dead-pan analysis in its January 28 issue:

"Angle on Miss Page's elevation to stardom is that film actor Mark Stevens' . . . contract specifies that no one can be billed above him. So although he got only moderate reviews in the play, it was necessary to boost him to stardom in order to star her. Technically, Stevens could have refused to allow Miss Page to be starred, but he reportedly okayed it provided he retained top billing. Although the play itself received brush-off notices, Miss Page drew the most spectacular individual raves for any debut performance in memory."

So that is that, and had better be left to the contract lawyers. As far as the average playgoer is concerned, Miss Page is the star of *Mid-Summer* and is firmly established as an upper-case Theatre Personality and a Legend.

What are the realities of the legend, and how formidable is the personality? It is no discourtesy to Miss Page, who has the gravest skepticism about her present success, to say that the legend has no reality at all and that the lasting effectiveness of the personality remains to be seen.

She came to Broadway after a year's run as Alma Winemiller in Tennessee Williams' *Summer and Smoke* at the Circle-in-the-Square down in Greenwich Village. In that part she won better notices (so far as a casual examination of the archives can show) than any performer in a non-Broadway production since the epic days of the Washington Square Players, which had so spectacular a success down-town that it needed only the blessing of the drama critics to move it, almost part and parcel, uptown, where it still survives in the guise of the Theatre Guild. It is always a test of the innocent excellence of amateurism whether it can survive the hard-cash standards of the professional theatre. Even if the excellence remains or increases, the innocence is almost certain to be lost.

In any case, Miss Page was handsomely treated by the reviewers who managed to find their way below Fourteenth Street. Brooks Atkinson, Walter Kerr and almost every other critic emptied the lexicon of adjectives on her behalf. This magazine singled her out for "Theatre Arts Spotlights" [July, 1952] and applauded her "maturity of technique, charm of person and—the rarest quality in modern acting—intellect."

She was, if anything, even more handsomely treated in the reviews of *Mid-Summer*. The headline on John Chapman's review in the *Daily News* read: "Geraldine Page A Superb Actress." Richard Watts, Jr. in the *New York Post* gave his copyreader ample pretext to write: "The Arrival of Geraldine Page." Mr. Atkinson, who gave Miss Page her original accolade, did not retreat from his position, even though—in comparison with the perfervid notices of the others—he seemed to be almost lukewarm. "When the drama gives her something to work with," wrote Mr. Atkinson cagily, "Miss Page can break your heart, for she plays without artifice. But like the play, she does not seem quite certain whether the wife is a noble primitive or a moron. . . . It is hard to tell on short notice how much of the fault is hers or Miss Delmar's."

That was the chilliest notice Miss Page got, and many an actress would settle for a lot less. Even the weeklies, whose reviewers have a longer time to decide that their first-night ecstasies were inspired by drink or the fabrications of a press agent, gave Miss Page hearty notices. *Time*, which makes a point of never being really impressed, had this to say: "There is a rewarding extra element . . . the play has a brilliant and raved-over new actress and Broadway an almost certain new star." The almost equally laconic *Newsweek*, whose reviewer was tolerant of the play, called Miss Page "a talented and immensely appealing young actress . . . [She] contributes a nervous, self-effacing charm to the leading role that must be more than the author could have hoped for."

Miss Page also was given the highest marks within the command of Wolcott Gibbs, drama critic for the *New Yorker*, whose usual technique is to praise with faint damns and who is on record as being unmoved by the best that Shakespeare, Ibsen and Chekhov had to offer. Still unmoved, Mr. Gibbs wrote that Lily, the heroine of *Mid-Summer*, "may be the noblest woman put on the stage in my generation . . . who might be completely insufferable if the role were in any other hands than those of Geraldine Page, an actress of great charm and pathos and almost matchless technique."

Mr. Gibbs deals at all times in understatement, and these reckless remarks amount almost to drooling.

In the face of her press, Miss Page's aloof and critical attitude towards her career is record-breaking. Most actresses believe whatever their press agents write about them. Miss Page believes nothing—except that she enjoys acting, has always enjoyed it and will go on enjoying it as a highly paid star, just as she enjoyed it when she worked for beans in stock and in off-Broadway companies.

That is not to say that she pretends contempt about her success. She is having a hell of a fine time and makes no secret of it. Even the fact that it is no longer necessary for her to economize on cigarettes by saving the long butts is a constant delight. It doesn't stop her from economizing, but she thinks it's nice to know that she doesn't need to.

Now, as to the facts. She is not an overnight success, for she has been trying to survive as an actress for ten years. In fact, she *did* survive as an actress, earning her living from time to time and eking out a living whenever her theatre jobs didn't quite make it. She is not an amateur, in spite of the amateurish aspects of her pre-Broadway career. She never *wanted* to be anything but an actress, though—to stay alive—she took any job going, in the theatre or not.

The chronology of Miss Page's life reads much like that of any other actress—or, possibly, that of any other human being. She was born in Kirksville, Missouri, 1924, and insists that it is going to be her "gimmick" that she will abide by that date. When an interviewer suggested that it is not such a tough date to abide by, since it only leaves her approaching twenty-nine, she agreed that when she is fifteen years older she may feel different.

But even that is doubtful, for Miss Page's current acclaim is not related either to her youth or to her appearance. One reviewer, Mr. Watts of the *Post*, went so far as to say: "To those who have the fantastic suspicion that critics praise new actresses only when they are beautiful, I must add, perhaps impolitely, that Miss Page, like most distinguished feminine players, is not going to be given ecstatic notices for any such qualities."

Off-stage, Miss Page is so little like an actress that she causes alarm to her friends, who think that she is now entitled to swank about a little, and to her agent and her producers, who think she would make better "copy" if she put on some kind of act. Exactly what an actress is supposed to be like off-stage, no one is quite sure; but roughly, the idea is that she should radiate glamor or whatever it is that Tallulah Bankhead radiates. Miss Page radiates nothing of the sort and at first sight (until animation lights her face into genuine prettiness) is a rather plain girl whose clothes look like those of almost any other Greenwich Villager: dowdy and somewhat unpinned. She disdains hats, preferring those parti-colored kerchiefs which are almost an item of uniform in the purlieus of Washington Square. Her fair hair is worn in a long bob, rather tousled, and she gives the effect of a young incarnation of the White Queen in *Alice in Wonderland*, in a hurry but not at all sure what she is in a hurry about.

This causes some mild distress to her parents, Dr. and Mrs. Leon Page of Chicago, who are delighted with their daughter's success but believe that Geraldine ought somehow to start living up to it. Dr. Page, a sedate and pleasant-mannered physician of late middle age, feels that—apart from the usual parental consider-ations—he is entitled to have something to say about Miss Page's career because he really launched her on it. When she first began to act, in the drama group of the Englewood Methodist Church in Chicago in 1941, she was cast for the part of Jo in *Little Women*. It is a part that is supposed to call for certain tomboyishness (Katharine Cornell and Katharine Hepburn have played it in their time), and Dr. Page was convinced that Geraldine was badly miscast. He saw her as better fitted for the part of Beth, the Louisa May Alcott character who dies so prettily in *Little Women*. But Geraldine preferred to be Jo—as who wouldn't, since it is the most important part in the play? By this time, Miss Page had already decided that she wanted to study for the theatre, and her father agreed that if she came off well as Jo, he would send her to the Goodman School of the Theatre. She played the part to his satisfaction, though he still thought she was miscast, and after she was graduated from Englewood High School in 1942, she enrolled at the Goodman, with Dr. Page paying the bills.

The doctor and his wife—a comely and motherly person whose grooming is as careful as her daughter's is careless—seem to look on Geraldine's career with a kind of benevolent disapproval, especially the parts of it which involved working in non-theatrical jobs in order to continue acting. Like many another actress, Miss Page never found the theatre lucrative. By her own choice, she took employment at various times as a candy-counter attendant in a movie theatre, as a waitress, as a factory hand and as a hat-check girl at Lindy's. Miss Page is militantly proud of these economic makeshifts, whereas her mother and father are inclined to think they were never quite respectable and ought to be hushed up.

The disagreements are transparently friendly ones, though Dr. Page may be entitled to believe that his original estimate of his daughter's talents is being vindicated. She *does* suggest the wispy and pathetic Beth March, rather than the rowdy Jo. And it is the wispy aspect of her personality that is being exploited on Broadway.

The audiences who delight in her fluttering performance in *Mid-Summer* are given no opportunity to know that there is anything in Miss Page except what meets the eye: an actress with a reedy body, a bony face, a wheedling voice and omni-present hands. The hands, in fact, are so active that Miss Page has been likened to ZaSu Pitts, an actress who has no need for technique, for her personality is so immediate and compelling that a director would be wasting his time to tell her what to do.

Miss Page has also been compared to almost every other actress of the present and the near past remarkable for a set of distinctive mannerisms. Some see a resemblance to the late Pauline Lord, who—like Miss Page—spoke every line of a play as though it had just come into her head. Some are reminded of the late Laurette Taylor, with her wondering look and her heedlessness of the audience. Others see in Miss Page a re-creation of Helen Hayes, whose small voice always makes itself important and whose presence always contradicts the littleness of her physical person.

Whatever the comparison, Miss Page's mannerisms are also unmistakable. Her hand is forever finding its way to her hair or to the collar of the shirtwaist she wears in *Mid-Summer*. Her voice breaks at unaccountable times, trailing off into nothing or into nervous, apologetic laughter. She is never aware of the audience—or doesn't seem to be—but is always intensely aware of the other people in the play, as though her life depended on hearing what they are saying. This absorption is so intense that friends of Miss Page, watching from the audience, can never quite tell whether she is making a "fluff"—garbling her lines or speaking at the wrong time, or whether she is being true to the character she is playing and merely stumbling over her speech, as people so often do in real life.

That is where the guesswork comes in, both for Miss Page and for her admirers. She astutely chose the part of Lily in *Mid-Summer* for her Broadway debut because she had a ready-made set of mannerisms, developed in her year in *Summer and Smoke* when she played Tennessee Williams' favorite character: the appealing woman who is constantly apologizing for her own appeal.

As an actress in stock (mainly in the Middle West), Miss Page has played almost every part in the modern repertory. She played the gaudy whores, like Sadie Thompson in *Rain*. She played the able bitches, like Regina Giddens in Lillian Hellman's *The Little Foxes*, and simple ingénues, like Suzie in Sam and Bella Spewack's *Boy Meets Girl*.

She thinks of herself as a versatile actress, who can play anything at all. The parts she wants most to play are the strangely diverse ones of Hedda Gabler, Ibsen's most ruthless neurotic, and Roxane, the heroine of Rostand's *Cyrano de Bergerac*. Offhand, one would be inclined to think that Roxane would be more Miss Page's speed, being all sugar and cream and intolerable gentility. Miss Page insists that she isn't sugar and cream—that she is always played that way but is actually a woman of brains and character. Hedda, of course, is well stocked with brains; her character is, at the very least, positive. It is something for the drama critics to speculate on: whether Miss Page's air of refinement might not be exactly the touch of humanity that would make the grisly Hedda believable.

The question also arises, especially in the minds of her fellow actors, whether classic plays would be Miss Page's forte. She has a highly individualistic way of learning a part. She refuses to memorize lines and insists that she can only learn words by acting them out. That has worked well enough in Vina Delmar's play and Tennessee Williams'. But would it work in Ibsen, Rostand, or any other dramatist whose way of saying things is the very essence of the play?

It is one of many questions that only the future can answer.

Miss Page knows that she came to Broadway *typed* for a particular kind of part. She achieved stardom in that part. What next? Will Geraldine Page make her way as actress—or as Geraldine Page? Or both?

12 Jason Robards, Jr.

John Keating

April 1960

With the waning of the touring show, the 1950s saw the emergence of the so-called New York actor. This was a performer who, like his forerunners, may have served a long apprenticeship on Broadway or regional theatre, but was likelier to have studied at Actors Studio or other private classes and won critical attention in an Off-Broadway production. Many of the actors chosen for full-length interviews in *Theatre Arts* in the 1950s and 1960s fit this profile. Many of them, as well, had reputations as heavy drinkers, another theatrical tradition.

Although on Broadway from 1947, Jason Robards Jr. (1922–2000) soared to stardom as Hickey in the Circle in the Square production of *The Iceman Cometh* and Jamie Tyrone in the first American production of *Long Day's Journey into Night* (both 1956). They established him as the ideal O'Neill actor, leading to appearances in *Ah, Wilderness!, Moon for the Misbegotten* and *Hughie*. He also created the author's surrogate in Arthur Miller's *After the Fall* (1964). Later, in Hollywood, he enjoyed a position similar to the one Walter Huston had had before the war: as a type of the American character, whether as heroes or heavies.

JASON Robards, Jr. is a rare phenomenon on the contemporary American stage—a successful actor under forty who has never been a member of the Actors Studio, and who never intends to become one. Almost alone among his generation—the Canadian-born Christopher Plummer is one other who comes to mind—he has achieved stardom without ever having harked to the Stanislavskian exegesis of Lee Strasberg. But Robards is that even rarer being, an actor who is non-Method without being anti-Method.

"Just think of the people who have come out of the Studio," he said, and began ticking them off. "Eli [Wallach], Mo [Maureen Stapleton], Julie Harris, Kim Stanley, Brando, Ben Gazzara—all the others. You can't dismiss all that. The methods they use have obviously worked for them. It's just that I know they're not for me; I have to go about my work in a different way."

The actor, who burst out of obscurity four years ago in the Circle in the Square production of Eugene O'Neill's *The Iceman Cometh*, and established his right to star billing on Broadway several months later as the tragic Jamie Tyrone in the same author's *Long Day's Journey into Night*, was talking between assaults on a Lucullan breakfast consisting of a Bloody Mary, a platter of Oysters Rockefeller, lemon sherbet and black coffee at Locke-Ober, the Boston outpost of *la haute cuisine*. It was the night after the pre-Broadway opening of Lillian Hellman's *Toys in the Attic*, in which Robards had created the part of Julian Berniers, a thirty-four-year-old congenital failure who inadvertently sets tragic forces in motion when he returns to the genteel poverty of his New Orleans home, not as a bankrupt but spilling over with money, presents and an almost manic euphoria.

"I wasn't happy about last night's performance," he said, thoughtfully. (Neither were two of the three Boston morning-newspaper critics.) "I don't know about my own performance; that's something the audience has to judge. But in this play I'm off stage for long periods of time; I can see what is being done during some of the most important scenes in the play, and I know that what the audience saw last night was not the great play Miss Hellman wrote. But it's there, solid. This is not one of those makeshifts that is going to change from night to night, as the author listens to what this one and that one tell him he should do. Miss Hellman has told us that we are going to open with the play as written. You don't know what a comforting—and what an unusual—thing that is.

"*The Disenchanted* was never the same two nights running," he continued, "and I am sure it was hurt by the frantic revising. I think the play we did the night we opened in New Haven was a beautiful and moving one, much more than what we had when we got to Broadway. Characters kept being dropped out and put back in; scenes were switched; it became more of a vehicle for me, but less of a play. Lillian has promised that nothing like that will happen with *Toys in the Attic*. You know, I had almost made up my mind to take the role of the defense attorney in *The Andersonville Trial*—it was a much bigger and stronger part than it is now, as the play was trimmed and shaped for Broadway—and then I read this play and there was no doubt in my mind about which job I would take."

For Robards, a lean, volatile man nearing thirty-eight, with a furrowed brow, deep-set, fatigue-smudged eyes, and habitually hunched shoulders that make him seem less than his height (almost six feet), the enviable position of being able to choose his roles is a recent one. He had scuffled in the dismal tradition of the acting profession for more than ten years before his "overnight" success in *The Iceman Cometh*. "Nothing I had done before that seemed to matter," he said reflectively. "I had played in stock for years, doing everything from Noel Coward to Strindberg. I had been in and out of all kinds of terrible radio and television things. But nothing I did meant anything. I was nowhere, living in a cold-water flat on the outskirts of the Village, in the wholesale-meat district over towards the Hudson River. I had a wife and two kids and no visible means of support." Robards now has three children, Jason III, who is eleven; Sarah, eight, and David, three. And his second wife, Rachel, whom he married last year, is expecting an addition in a few months.

"I had played one of the leads in *American Gothic* [1953–54] for José Quintero at the Circle," he continued, "and when I heard he was going to do *The Iceman Cometh*, I made up my mind I'd get the Hickey role, come hell or high water. I had never wanted anything so much in my life. But José had me in mind for a different part, not a very important one, either. I had always been terrible at selling myself—and that is such an important part of being an actor that they should give a course in it at all drama schools—but I went into Louis' Tavern, next to the theatre, and got myself a couple of drinks, and went back in to see José and insisted that he let me read Hickey. And that was it."

Robards' electrifying performance of the guilt-ridden salesman who is the catalyst of O'Neill's drama was one of the outstanding events of the 1955–56 season, on or off Broadway. "I was a great success; every newspaper and magazine in town was sending interviewers and photographers to see me, but I was still starving." Robards said. "An off-Broadway actor's salary, you know, is less than any self-respecting soda jerk will accept. I was living on the money from whatever television jobs I could pick up—and on hope, just like the characters in the play."

Material success followed when the Circle in the Square producing triumvirate —Quintero, Theodore Mann and Leigh Connell—was tapped by Carlotta Monterey, O'Neill's widow, to put on the Broadway production of *Long Day's Journey into Night*, and Jason was cast in the role of Jamie, the tragic, drink-ruined older son of the actor James Tyrone, a thinly disguised portrait of O'Neill's own actor-father. Since then, his appearances as the F. Scott Fitzgeraldish novelist in *The Disenchanted*, as a wounded Hungarian revolt leader in the film *The Journey* (in which he starred with Yul Brynner and Deborah Kerr), and in a number of important television productions have banished the wolf from the door, and permitted him to leave the cold and depressing precincts of the meat district for the more stylish and comfortable East Sixties.

Rather surprisingly, Robards didn't enter the theatre until the comparatively advanced age of twenty-five, although he had been born, figuratively speaking, in a wardrobe trunk. The year was 1922 and the place Chicago, where his father Jason Robards, Sr., was appearing with Frank Bacon in *Lightnin'*. A few years later; Robards, Sr., who had become one of the stage's more successful matinée idols, was lured to Hollywood. For a time he lived the flashy, money-dripping life of a movie star of the 1920's. That lasted until Jason, Jr. was about twelve.

"Then they discarded Dad," he recalled. "It must have been a terrible, humiliating time for him—the terrific worry, the waiting for the phone that never rang, the phony talk, the need to keep up a cheerful false front. It undoubtedly had much to do with my lack of interest in acting. What I *was* interested in was sports; I wanted to be a baseball player or a sports announcer. I did take a course in dramatics at Hollywood High and I almost flunked out; I'm convinced the only reason they passed me was because I was the star miler on the track team."

Robards went from Hollywood High in 1939 into the Navy, and spent the next seven years as a sailor. He lived through the attack on Pearl Harbor. He took part in thirteen major engagements, and in one of them, the battle for Guadalcanal, the cruiser on which he was serving was sunk. (Some years later, when he answered a casting call for *Mister Roberts*, he was turned down, he says, by a casting director who told him he didn't look rugged enough to be a sailor.) During his Navy service, Robards' interest in the theatre was aroused, he has said, by reading a copy of O'Neill's *Strange Interlude* he found in a ship's library. When he was discharged, he enrolled in the American Academy of Dramatic Arts, which his father had attended thirty-odd years previously.

"After I left the Academy, I signed on with a stock company Tom Poston and his brother organized at Rehoboth Beach, Delaware," he said. "It was a great way to break in, but, when I got back to New York, the only job I could get was playing the hind end of a cow in a production of *Jack and the Beanstalk* for children. I made my Broadway 'debut' as a super, a spear carrier, with the D'Oyly Carte company when they came to New York in 1948. But until José Ferrer hired me for a bit in *The Chase* [1952], which didn't last long, most of the work I did was in radio, in soap opera. [The program for *The Chase* also lists Robards as the assistant stage manager.] Ferrer rescued me again by giving me a small part in *Stalag 17*, and I stayed with it as long as it ran. [The Broadway run of 473 performances ended in June, 1952, and Robards was also a member of the touring production that ran until May, 1953.] We were still living on what we had saved from that when *Iceman* happened."

Unlike most American actors in his age group, who are able to talk of their craft only in terms like "motivation" and "emotional coefficient," most of which seem borrowed from psychoanalysis, Robards is both articulate and enthusiastic about that old-fashioned concept, technique.

"As I said, I am not anti-Method, but on the stage I have to know what I am going to do every minute. For that you need technique; you can't improvise a performance every night. By the time a play is ready to open, I am so immersed in the character I am playing that I can be confident the lines will come, because they are the lines that character would speak in that situation. But the framework of the performance has to be set; it can't depend on the way the actor feels that night. Actors who become so absorbed in self-analysis that they disregard the other actors—or, worse yet, the play itself—are misusing the Method; they are using it as an argument to justify their own self-indulgence. That is inexcusable. The actor is there only to deliver the play the author has written. That is his only reason for being.

"When I take on a role, I place myself entirely in the hands of the author and the director," he continued. "The author knows what his play means, and the director knows. An actor has to believe that, and act on his belief. If the director tells me I must do something in a certain way, or that I am supposed to convey such-and-such an emotion or attitude in the reading of a line, I do not think it is my place to take that direction into the psyche and wrestle with it to decide whether it coincides with my own conception of what the author means. I don't mean that the actor should be a soulless, mindless puppet. I think I have contributed to the realization of any character I have played. But every actor must accept the idea that what he thinks is less important than what the playwright thinks. The actor's great achievement is to express what the author intends. The great sin is to twist the author's words so that they will exploit the actor rather than the play."

13 George C. Scott

Jack Balch

June 1960

George C[ampbell] Scott (1927–99) served a long apprenticeship in regional
theatres before making his Off-Broadway debuts as *Richard III* in the New York
Shakespeare Festival (1957) and as a stylish cardsharp in *Children of Darkness*
(1958). He later played Shylock and Mark Antony in the Festival, the latter opposite
his wife Colleen Dewhurst as Cleopatra. Scott's talent was matched by a demonic
and quarrelsome temperament, and after a breakout role in *The Andersonville Trial*
(1959) he decamped to the movies, making occasional sorties back to Broadway
(Ephraim Cabot in *Desire Under the Elms*, 1963; Willy Loman in *Death of a
Salesman*, 1975).

Jack S. Balch (1909–80) had been the assistant director of the Missouri Writers'
Project (1935–40) under the Federal Arts Project and wrote *Lamps at High Noon*, a
novel about its famous walkout in 1935. He was for a long time dramatic critic for the
St Louis Post-Dispatch.

THE house in which I interviewed George C. Scott is a throwback to the pre-
automobile era, when houses often consisted of two buildings: one, fronting
toward the street, for the "people," the other, in the rear, for the "horse-and-
groom team." Scott's two-room apartment, on the west side of New York's
Greenwich Village, near the Hudson River, is remodeled from the rear part of
one such old house. I rang the doorbell of the front building one rainy afternoon
recently; after a lengthy wait, during which I began to speculate on the possibility
that the actor had forgotten our appointment, the door was opened.

"I should have warned you of the wait," Scott said, after we had introduced
ourselves. "It's a long trip between the front and rear buildings." Casually,
as we began the trek, he remarked, "In a more refined age the trip wasn't made
at all." Then, as an afterthought, he added, "Protocol went kaputt in our
lifetime."

The actor—in appearance and conversation, as well—was as unexpected as the
apartment to which he led me, first through the corridor of the front building and
then through a rear yard with deep puddles. Oblivious to the stormy weather, he
wore a red-and-black striped dressing gown, blood-red slippers, dark glasses and
a long cigarette holder. In some men the obliviousness might have seemed affectation, even effeminacy. In Scott's case it seemed completely natural. He is a big,
slim, broad-shouldered, broken-nosed fellow who, as those who saw him on
Broadway this season as the judge advocate in *The Andersonville Trial* might agree,

would seem merely rough and tough if it were not for a certain intellectual and moral discipline that seems to control the physical side of him.

Inside the apartment, he asked, "Drink?" Then he waved me to a choice of seats: either of two armchairs or a sofa, none of which matched. It was a largish room that looked larger because it was neither perfectly square nor rectangular but an irregular thing of bays and crannies. Improbably but functionally located, several inches from one of the bays, was a red-brick fireplace with logs, cut to the proper length, stacked alongside. Books—the Bible, Will Durant's *Caesar and Christ*, a biography of Hitler—were scattered everywhere. So many of the books were open that I had the impression that Scott was in the midst of a crash program of reading.

"Ferdinand the Bull got his kicks smelling flowers," he said. "That's the way I am about books. Can't get enough of them. Funny, though; until about two years ago I did very little reading. One way of looking at it, I had lots of time to read. Another way, I had no time at all. You see, until about two years ago, I had never worked on the New York stage or in the big time anywhere. While I had lots of time, it was the wrong *kind* of lots of time—full of fuming, brooding, frustration and unhappiness. That's not the kind of time that's best for reading."

"But now?"

"Now every night and a couple of matinées a week, I go after poor Herbert Berghof [the defendant in *The Andersonville Trial*] and leave the stage all tuckered out from getting a conviction of the only Southerner ever tried and sentenced to death as a war criminal during the Civil War. And yet I feel wonderfully renewed each day. Saul Levitt [author of *The Andersonville Trial*] has written a wonderful play. It's not only full of questions for me to seek answers to in the character I play; it creates enthusiasm in me for questions and answers about everything." He waved his hand to indicate all the books. "Now, with no time at all, I've got time to read everything. I figure I've got about a million more books to go."

He saw me looking at a book about chess, which was opened and lying beside a half-completed chess game on a small table in front of the sofa. "I've got time for chess, too," Scott said. "I'm replaying both the black and white sides of a famous game between Morphy and Anderssen, about the time of the Civil War."

From upstairs, as we talked, had come a steady noise. The actor explained that it was being made by a carpenter fixing the paneling in the room above. "Once upon a time," he said with a straight face, "there was only one room here, with a very high ceiling. The ceiling's lower now, but I have two rooms."

Scott's tenancy of the apartment dates from an important time in his career: the period of his first role on the New York stage, as Richard III in a New York Shakespeare Festival production in the fall of 1957. Approximately seven years earlier he had earned his first pay in the theatre. As a student of journalism at the University of Missouri, he was also a member of the male resident company that appeared in plays with the students of Stephens College, a school for girls, in the same Missouri town, Columbia. From that he went into stock in much larger communities like Toledo and Detroit, where he had his own company in 1954.

Now, surveying his New York apartment, I said, "Now that you're an acknowledged star in your first Broadway hit"—

He anticipated the rest of the question, and broke in to deny that he is looking for larger quarters. "Not a chance. I like it here."

Two cats, walking in single file, had come down from the upstairs room, and perched on either side of him, just as he began to provide a résumé of his career. "I'd better tell you who these four-legged people are before I go any further," he said. "This one is Zorro, but I call him George Raft, because of the white handkerchief in his breast pocket." The other cat looked up at him and mewed. "*This* one," he said, stroking its head, "is named Tiger. In her case, that's ridiculous. She's a she. I hate to mix my genders, so I just call her Ladybird."

The résumé followed without further interruption. After *Richard III*, he did another show for Joseph Papp, producer of the New York Shakespeare Festival: *As You Like It.* Still another off-Broadway assignment followed. For José Quintero and Circle in the Square, Scott appeared in *Children of Darkness*. Then came a movie, *The Hanging Tree*, which starred Gary Cooper. Scott played a drunken faith healer. In November, 1958, he got his first Broadway role, that of a frightening psychopath in a drama called *Comes a Day*, which starred Judith Anderson. The play had only twenty-eight performances, but Scott received glowing praise, just as he had when he was appearing off Broadway (and winning a series of awards for acting). He returned to the Shakespeare festival as Antony in *Antony and Cleopatra* in January, 1959, then played Shylock in a University of Utah production of *The Merchant of Venice*. Continuing the westward trek, he played a lawyer in the film *Anatomy of a Murder*, for which he was nominated for an Academy award. Three television shows followed, and then came Broadway stardom in his second appearance there. *The Andersonville Trial* opened just before the arrival of 1960, and this time the actors (Scott, Albert Dekker and Herbert Berghof share top billing) *and* the play were received enthusiastically.

"You've been a pretty busy fellow these last two years," I said. "What was the record before then?"

"Failure," he said. "Nothing but failure. I'm thirty-two now. As a child, during the depression, I moved with my family from Virginia, where I was born, to Detroit. My father, who has done all right lately—he's an executive for a tool company now—found himself broke in 1935, permanently out of his job as a coal-mine surveyor. We arrived in Detroit, and my mother died the same year we got there. It was hell for a long time.

"My father believed in education, and knew why. I believed in it too, as I grew up, mainly because he told me I'd also eventually know why. I hung on to education until I graduated from high school. That was in 1945. I was seventeen. I wanted to see the world then, and my father didn't know how to keep me at home any longer. So I joined the Marine Corps, and they sent me to Washington, D. C. That's all the world I got to see. I was there four years, and it was the dullest four years I ever spent, though it was no fault of the Marines. I played a little baseball, did a little boxing, got on all right with the ladies, and made sergeant's stripes. But nothing much helped. I guess you might say I was suffering from a sort of life disappointment. Anyway, beginning with my arrival in Washington, a great liberty town, no matter what else you can say against it, I picked up a solid drinking habit that stayed with me from then on."

He saw me looking at the glass of water beside him.

"I've been a member of Alcoholics Anonymous for about six months now," he said. "I was a drunkard out of boredom and frustration for almost half my life, fifteen years."

"But why didn't you quit two years ago, when Papp gave you your break?" I asked. "Why only six months ago?"

"A man doesn't know how deeply enmeshed he is until he starts to cut his way out," Scott replied. "The expectation of failure is why I drank. It took a long time for me to replace that expectation with other expectations."

"How did you get your first break with Papp?"

"That's an interesting question," he said. He lit a cigarette and puffed a few times. "Up until that time I used to audition and then walk away. If they called me back, all right. If they didn't, the hell with it. I had my pride. But I was drinking more and more, even for me, and getting into some awful brawls that I couldn't even remember the next day. I suddenly knew it was now or never. And I decided to give up my pride. Either that or give up my sanity. I had auditioned for Papp and his director, Stuart Vaughan, and they had liked me enough to let me read a second time. But I knew my second reading was wrong. I picked up the telephone and called them back—and man, was that tough to do! I said, 'Please, don't judge me yet. Please let me read again. I know this sounds corny, like an actor talking, but Richard is my part. It was written for me.' And that did it. They let me read a third time. When I got my break, it did something more than start me on what I consider my proper life's work. It was the beginning for me of proof of my father's belief in education. I began to see failure for what it was: not as the ocean with me deep in it, but as one of the elements. Only one. I became aware of land, too."

"Do you mind my writing about your fifteen years of drinking?" I asked.

"I want you to," he said. His face broke into a grin, a rather rare expression for Scott. "Like all members of A.A., I'm a missionary," he said. "We're proud to use ourselves as the best argument for change."

"One last question: How did you become interested in the theatre?"

"Well, if I've seemed to blame the Marine Corps for my drinking, I'd like to give them credit for opening up this other thing for me. When I left the Corps, I took with me the best gift they could give me, the opportunity for a formal education under the G.I. Bill of Rights. I started going to college for one thing, and it wasn't panning out. I was bored all over again, or, should I say, *still*. And then, one day, I saw my first play, on the campus, and finally I knew what I wanted to do. I wanted to act. Funny thing. As in *The Andersonville Trial* and *Anatomy of a Murder*, the part was that of a lawyer. The play was *The Winslow Boy*."

14 Maureen Stapleton

Gilbert Millstein

July 1960

In the earlier part of the twentieth century, the roles created for actresses often demanded wide swathes of glamour to be cut across the stage. By the 1950s, although sex was still a major component in leading female roles, it was to be projected by neurotics, waifs and slatterns. In no way limited by her *zaftik* figure and plain face, Maureen Stapleton (1925–2006) played some of Tennessee Williams' steamiest heroines: Serafina in *The Rose Tattoo* (1951), Flora in *27 Wagons Full of Cotton* (1955) and Lady Torrance in *Orpheus Descending* (1957). A more matronly note was struck as Carrie in *Toys in the Attic* (1960) and Eva in *The Gingerbread Lady* (1970). Her performances were always workmanlike but rarely impassioned, and she was often a target for the critic John Simon's cruellest remarks.

Gilbert Millstein (1916–99) was a book reviewer and feature writer for the New York *Times* (1949–63) and *The Saturday Evening Post*. His greatest claim to fame is his glowing review of *On the Road* in 1957, which vaulted Jack Kerouac to celebrity.

———————

A PRINCIPAL quality of Maureen Stapleton, one of the stars of *Toys in the Attic*, an exercise by Lillian Hellman about a New Orleans family violently disabused of its fantasies, is an impressive capacity for audible rumination. This turns out to be at once comical, prickly, disarming and comfortable, rather than—as it might, with a slight jar—flat, presumptuous, tiring and uncomfortable. Miss Stapleton seems genuinely incredulous whenever apprised of the fact. She has an unwavering image of herself as an inarticulate groundling of Irish descent from Troy, New York. "Peasant stock, kid, sturdy peasant stock, or I'd've been dead by now," she started out recently, for example, with a broad declaratory swipe, and then racketed off into a long discursion that somehow held together.

"The folks broke up when I was eight," she said. "Years after, he sent Ma a birthday present. Nicely wrapped and so on. She put it on the table in the parlor—my brother and I were living with our grandmother—and didn't open it. It stayed there for years. That stubborn. I never did find out what was in it or what happened to it. I'm just telling you the funny thing's. Put it this way, when they were together they were pretty active and I was the youngest referee on the block. I spent my childhood figuring out how quickly I could get out of Troy. I remember at St. Mary's School a couple of us getting into a discussion with one of the nuns, a Sister of Charity. The talk got around to did any of us think we wanted to be a nun. I said, 'Maybe after I've done everything I want to in the whole wide world.'

'Do you think God would want you then?' the Sister asked. 'Sure, he would,' I told her. 'He knows the way I am.' "

Miss Stapleton, who was at home and wearing a black housecoat, rolled her eyes. She passed a plump, distracted hand through her hair, returned it to the table, fidgeted a cigarette out of a crumpled pack, lighted it, and glanced wildly around the room. "God," she said, "I feel so damn' disorganized. I like things *simple*. What the hell."

She went back to her reminiscences. She said she had decided to be an actress at just about the time she started going to the movies, which was at the age of six. "Nearly as I can judge," she said, wrinkling her forehead, "it seemed to me—on the outside, anyway—the actors all looked pretty, they seemed to be making a lot of money, and they looked as though they were loved. If you could be that, all of those things, my problems were solved. Well," she went on, directing a reproving aside at a wall, "we all know how true *that* is. But you can't knock that kind of dream."

By the time she was ten or so, Miss Stapleton was going to the movies seven days a week, from three in the afternoon, when school let out, until roughly eleven at night, when the picture houses let out. "I liked everything," she said. "I went to Proctor's, the Troy, the Lincoln, the American, the Rose. The Rose was the last stand. It was only five cents, a flea bag; the rest were a dime. I was always a little scared to go there, but I'd go. I used to try and get some of the other kids to stay right through with me. I'd think up anything to keep someone there with me, but finally nobody'd go with me any more. I didn't get off easy at home, either; I'd get whacked. It was a question whether they were going to stop me by hitting me, or were they going to give it up. They had to go through with the business of doing something about it, but they gave up. I kept a scrapbook on Robert Taylor when I was eleven. I was quite in love with him. I always assumed when I was sixteen— kismet!—Robert Taylor'd show up and we'd get married. He must have got on the wrong train. I fell in love with him because I couldn't get Clark Gable. That would have been like marrying the Pope.

"I guess I was a pretty nutty kid, hey kid? Actually, I think I was a very frightened child. I don't know what of. I've been going to a psychoanalyst for five years and I'm not at the sources yet, because now I'm a frightened woman and I still don't know what the phantoms are." She shook her head in some kind of private exasperation. "I was in one play in grammar school," she continued. "All I remember is I didn't know my lines too well. I got into two in high school, *Murder on a Ferris Wheel* and *Anne of Green Gables*. I played somebody's mother in both. I wasn't in the school dramatic society or anything. They just needed an ole fat girl, and I sure was. Nobody jumped up and down and said, 'You have got to be an actress,' but I had my mind made up. I started very early to lay siege to the family on that, so it wasn't much of a shock to them. Then it got to be a question of serving my time in high, saving my money when I went to work, and getting to New York."

Having served her time, Miss Stapleton was duly graduated from Catholic Central High School in June, 1942, and then worked, successively, as a junior state clerk in Albany, at an employment office in Schenectady, and in the arsenal at Watervliet, where she was what is called a "P. and I. man," or present-for-inspection clerk, which meant that every time a cannon got out of whack she had to take a sheaf of forms around to everybody concerned, and have them signed. By the fall of 1943, having accumulated $100, and considering that a nice round sum, she came to New York with another girl, took an apartment, got a job as a night billing clerk at the Hotel New Yorker, and set about the business of becoming an actress. By her own account, she was no beauty. Later, having slimmed down some, she worked as a weapons demonstrator at a window exhibit in the Chrysler Building.

She studied first at a school whose method consisted of dividing everything into three parts, "even your eyeballs," said Miss Stapleton. "In three or four months, it gradually penetrated—this wasn't for me." From there, she went on to Herbert Berghof, who was then teaching at the New School, and ultimately she became a member of the first class at the Actors' Studio with Montgomery Clift, Marlon Brando, Eli Wallach, David Wayne and Tom Ewell, among others. During the summer of 1945, she and twenty-one other Berghof students put up $150 each, formed a stock company that performed for eight weeks in Blauvelt, New York, and returned home exhausted.

In Berghof's classes, she was given one week the role of a prostitute, which required the wearing of a rather sketchy costume. For a fat girl who would never go swimming and who wore a light coat, even in the hottest weather, the experience was devastating. "I froze," she said, "but I lived through it." The next day, on the advice of a fellow student, she tried some homemade shock therapy. She went to the Arts Students' League and offered herself up—that was the sensation the act gave her—as a nude model. She stuck it out the first day, called in sick the second, gritted her teeth on the third, and finished out the week. Thereafter she modeled alternately for about a year and a half for Raphael Soyer and Reginald Marsh. She can now be seen as "Maureen" in a Soyer portrait, and as a burlesque queen in some of Marsh's wonderful genre paintings, and she now thinks of that period as one of the most pleasant of her life.

One small part succeeded another. (Her Broadway debut occurred in the 1946 revival of *The Playboy of the Western World*. The next year she was in the Katharine Cornell production of *Antony and Cleopatra*, and her other early roles were in *Detective Story* and Arthur Laurents' *The Bird Cage*.) Miss Stapleton was married to Max Allentuck, general manager for Kermit Bloomgarden, in 1949; a year later, she was the mother of a son. (Ultimately the couple had a daughter, too; she and Allentuck are now divorced.) In 1951 she got the part that made her a star, Serafina delle Rose in Tennessee Williams' *The Rose Tattoo*.

It was during the New York run of this play that whatever phantoms were frightening Miss Stapleton began to show themselves in the form of a particularly sinister symptom. "I began to think," she said, "someone in the audience had a gun and was going to kill me. It got so bad, Eli Wallach asked me what was wrong. I said, 'There's someone out there with a *camera* taking *pictures*.' I was trying to hide it. About the gun. The stage manager searched the house, but I couldn't stop that gun. I actually saw a gun, and it was always a man had it. I said it was everything, anything—short of a gun. Curtain calls were murder; I was an absolute target. Even on the street, I'd duck into doorways, so finally I had to let Eli know the truth, and I told Max and I went to a psychiatrist. The way I'd get through the night was I'd tell myself, 'Tomorrow, you'll be at the analyst's and it won't give me any trouble that night.' But, boy oh boy, you learn that doesn't help for long. This was just before the play went on tour. It didn't happen on the tour. That was all I wanted to cure, and I did, and I thought that was that, everything's rosy." By 1955, however, when she appeared in Williams' *27 Wagons Full of Cotton*, and had become a mother for the second time, Miss Stapleton realized her troubles had barely begun, that her marriage was breaking up, and she returned to psychoanalysis.

"One of my gifts is," Miss Stapleton continued, after a bit, "I can do nothing, nothing. I don't know whether it's morally good or bad, but I can literally do nothing and love it. I've acted a long time now. I've been married, in one play after another [more recently *The Crucible, Richard III, The Sea Gull, Orpheus Descending, The Cold Wind and the Warm*], two movies, television; I've had two children and been divorced, and I kind of need a rest. I need my batteries recharged and refreshed, and I want to have my children more. It's no big declaration. I'm glad to be working and all that, but things have happened too fast for me, and also, if you don't have time to do nothing, you find yourself doing a lot of things you didn't want to do in the first place." She grinned faintly and rubbed her chin. "It's terrible," she said, "if the sum total of what you can say of yourself after ten years is that you're tired."

Miss Stapleton stopped talking the length of another cigarette. She was then off in another direction. "I'm glad I act," she said earnestly. "It's all I know how to do, and I don't think it matters why. One thing—I like other actors. It's not like we're gypsies, it's like being related in some way we all know about. We're inside a land in which we all recognize each other and our relationship to each other. Only actors understand that; there's a silent bond, because we've all been through the same things. A company's like an organism, and you can't explain it to anybody outside. It's not tangible, but once there is a company, there is an instant family— protective of each other and caring of each other. I *know* that in this profession you're happy for other people's success. Maybe it's selfish, but that makes you a better human being.

"I'm proud to be an actor. Maybe I'm oversentimentalizing, but I'm thinking of when John Gielgud got a Tony—it wasn't only for *Ages of Man*—for me, it was the marvelousness of that man. Because I tell you, we know what people think of us—that we're irresponsible or childlike or egomaniacs. It's not so. Actors are extraordinarily nice, beautiful people. And that's part of what I mean by being proud of my profession."

15 "Dear Diary . . ."

Hume Cronyn
July 1961

By the early 1960s the Broadway theatre was, if only gingerly, beginning to deal with the theme of homosexuality. One of the first plays to test the waters was *Big Fish, Little Fish* by Hugh Wheeler (1912–87), who would later become known as Stephen Sondheim's librettist for the eminent musicals *A Little Night Music* and *Sweeney Todd*. The play, set in academe, had a veteran cast, headed by Hume Cronyn (1911–2003). Canadian-born Cronyn and his wife Jessica Tandy would come to be compared to the Lunts. He had studied with Max Reinhardt and had varied but undistinguished employment on the stage, when Alfred Hitchcock brought him to Hollywood (see headnote to Chapter 65, "Notes on film acting"). His best performances, in the Richard Burton *Hamlet* as Polonius (1964), Albee's *A Delicate Balance* (1966) and *The Gin Game* (1977), as well as several classic roles at the Minneapolis Repertory Theatre under Tyrone Guthrie, lay before him. Cronyn's comments on Method acting in a commercial enterprise are symptomatic of the climate of American acting at this period.

[*THE editors have long been intrigued by the idea of tracing the course of a production from the first day of rehearsal to opening night on Broadway—from the inside, so to speak. With that in mind, we asked Hume Cronyn, one of the stars of* Big Fish, Little Fish, *to keep a daily account of his activities and reactions during the production period of the Hugh Wheeler play, which began its stay in New York last March 15 and closed June 10, after 102 performances. Mr. Cronyn not only obliged; he also supplied a postscript whose interest quite transcends a single Broadway show—even one whose members won a series of distinguished awards. Mr. Cronyn himself received a medal, "for the most distinguished performance" of the season, from the Drama League of New York, together with the annual award of the Barter Theatre of Virginia. Antoinette Perry (Tony) awards went to John Gielgud, director of* Big Fish, Little Fish, *and to Martin Gabel for his acting in the comedy. The work of the entire cast was recognized by the Outer Circle's award for "best ensemble acting."*]

Cincinnati, Ohio
Saturday, February 4th, 1961

DEAR DIARY: (*Ugh!*)

Supposed to fly to New York for rehearsals starting 11 a.m. Monday. All flights canceled. New York snow-bound. Decided on train to Washington. About to leave hotel when college girl appeared, asking to see Miss Tandy. The unannounced visitor had attended the matinée of *Five Finger Exercise*. Long woolen socks, loafers, polo coat, and stars in her eyes. Intense fifteen minutes about THEATRE. Made me feel a hundred and eight! Anyway, let's go.

Sunday, February 5th

Arrived New York twenty hours later. "Where are the snows of yesteryear?" Right here, all of them! Walked fifteen blocks carrying three bags. Caught bus. Lew Allen [producer] called. Rehearsal postponed. Gielgud stuck in Montreal, Robards in Nassau, Grizzard lost. Cronyn pooped. Slept ten hours.

Monday, February 6th

Lew called. Rehearsals tomorrow—hopefully. Everybody converging. Nice note from Hugh Wheeler saying he thought I understood character of Jimmie Luton. Should be encouraged but shuffled around apartment in sweat of gloomy anticipation. Hate this feeling. It all becomes too important and too personal. Found myself remembering, "Once more unto the breach . . ." Also, "Charge once more, then, and be dumb!" Self-dramatization. Took some exercise, felt better. Opened script, looked at hen scratches. Closed it again. Tempted to learn some lines. Better not. Too soon and too rigid. Wouldn't remember them anyway.

> ". . . he never could recapture
> That first fine careless rapture."

Tuesday, February 7th

Arrived Ziegfeld roof ten-fifteen. Met Jason going up in elevator. Most of the company already on hand. Lots of nervous jokes and overplayed camaraderie. Started to read on the tick of ten-thirty. No formal statements from anyone—no welcomes, introductions, explanations, or psychological investigation. Just, "Shall we read it?" Rather a relief. We're off!

My voice sounds very loud, and the words meaningless. Must make myself *listen*. Ruth White reads beautifully. John Gielgud asks Hugh's permission to make a cut.

"Of course."

That's good. Hope it continues. Someone out front laughs. Who the hell is out there, anyway? The voices continue, some loud, some whispered, some quiet, some deliberate. All nervous. Halfway through the first act someone lets go with an unabashed and full-bodied fart. Everyone feels relieved. We begin, tentatively, to talk and to listen. Finish the first reading before the lunch break—start blocking afterward.

Wednesday, February 8th

Blocked, cut, rewrote and transposed all yesterday afternoon and today with only one official ten-minute break outside of lunch. Whew! Must wear other shoes and bring lunch with me. Finished long and complicated first scene of first act. Five more scenes to go, and only seventeen days before we face an audience. Well, don't think about that! Must remember to go slow and concentrate on relationships rather than business. Johnny G. seems to have sixteen new ideas a minute. Write in and erase, write in and erase. Script covered with lunatic markings.

Lost an actor today. Part written out. Homework little more than a mechanical review, and uninspired.

Thursday, February 9th

Long discussion today on the homosexual implications in the play and the exact nature of the relationships between various characters. Opinions differ widely. We begin to eliminate certain lines, and Hugh changes the color of one of the key situations to avoid a seeming stereotype. *The Best Man, Advise and Consent, The Devil's Advocate* and *A Taste of Honey* all involve homosexual incidents in one fashion or another.

These attempts to prejudge audience or critical reaction are always tricky. You may end up safe but regretful.

Friday, February 10th

Still blocking first act. Very complicated. Set table, serve meal, dress, undress, dress again. Set up cot, make bed, etc., etc., etc. This one is going to be a prop man's nightmare—and mine—at least until I get the book out of my hands. I have Marjorie [Winfield, secretary-assistant] cuing me at night now, but it doesn't exactly rush along.

Saturday, February 11th

Stumbled through first two scenes of first act. Hugh doing some revisions of later material, so we're repeating rather than forging ahead. Good thing as far as I'm concerned.

Hugh read new material to company at end of day. Very good, we think, and are all encouraged.

Got home and felt lousy. Skipped dinner and went to bed. What have I caught and how long will it last? Hell, hell, hell! Why do these bloody ailments always smack you in rehearsal?

Sunday, February 12th

No rehearsal today. Lucky thing, too. Felt as though I'd been worked over with a baseball bat. The doctor says it's food poisoning. Whatever, it gave me an acrobatic night and I'm limp this morning—oatmeal, dry toast, and back to bed. I *must* be able to work tonight!

Monday, February 13th

Props, props, props. This must be the proppiest play since the creation of time.

Tuesday, February 14th

Thank God—a moment of euphoria. Unreal, and probably quite unjustified, but at least a scene seemed to go! Books and all—*it seemed to go!* There was contact and a brief moment of happening. A genuine "illusion of the first time."

Wednesday, February 15th

Every new play in rehearsal is a new discovery of an old lesson. The audience only cares about what it *feels*, rarely about what it thinks, even less about what it sees, except as such elements contribute to the emotion of the moment. The actor may be loaded with "understanding," on time for rehearsal, word-perfect, responsive to direction, a paragon of actor's virtues and discipline, and terribly dull!

Thursday, February 16th

Lines, cues and business. Lines, cues and business! Here I am, having done more plays, or at least as many, as any member of the company, caught in the oldest of traps. Mechanical repetition! Why, why, why, do I never learn?

Friday, February 17th

One week from today we dress-rehearse in Philadelphia. Brr! Nine days of rehearsal behind us and eight ahead before facing an audience. I'm still carrying a script in the last act. Marjorie cues me until midnight when I stop making sense. For Valentine's Day she gave me a gold paper heart plastered with dexamyl spansules!

Saturday, February 18th

John ticked me off today. It was done gently and with considerable forbearance. I know I'm driving him up the wall.

"Perhaps you could concentrate a little less on the business."

Dear God! I see those technical rehearsals coming; no time, a thousand props, and a never-ending weave of movement. If I don't pantomime it now, what will happen then? Chaos. Still, he's right, and I know it and must do it.

Sunday, February 19th

Jessica called from Los Angeles.

"I hope you're enjoying rehearsals."

I managed only a civil grunt. And yet six weeks from now I'll say, "Oh yes, very much," and mean it—I think. It's a marvelous company. Perhaps the best I've ever been with. One of the depressing aspects of the crapgame theatre is the tendency to mutual disenchantment as rehearsals proceed and tensions mount. Here, of course, the director and principal players have an enormous responsibility. They set a tone, and you cannot do better than Gielgud, Robards, Gabel, Grizzard. They are not just talented, but thoroughly professional and generous as well, so the going is relaxed (my own tensions and anxieties being hopefully, if improbably, hidden). There is not an uncreative, let alone an incompetent player in the cast. And we are blessed in our author as well.

Hugh Wheeler, a successful novelist turned playwright, has extraordinary gifts. He is flexible, he is modest and very, very quick. Provided he approves a cut or transposition, it's done immediately. When a rewrite of consequence is required, he will look, listen, leave rehearsal, and return in a matter of hours—at the most, it's been a day and a half—with a really new and improved scene. Some of the best things in his play were written under great pressure. Many excellent playwrights find this impossible. I might add that collaboration with his director and actors is not beneath him. In my experience writers find this collaborative compromise (yes, it may mean compromise, just as it may mean significant improvement; compromise is not inevitably destructive) much more difficult than do their subsidiary creators. As for the obligations of the playwright to his first inspirations, I am aware of them—and their limitations.

Why then, with such a playwright, director and company, does the tenor of this diary seem so gloomy? Perhaps because of the accepted conditions under which we work. There is no continuity of work or practice. Even the actor in demand, provided he exercises any discretion—he better or he won't remain in demand for long—must wait months between engagements, and there is never room for him to fail. No wonder our courage is in question. Success, a hit, is all, and yet, after waiting, praying, and working for it, he must repeat himself, without seeming to do so, for hundreds of performances, a process almost guaranteed to stunt his development as an actor.

Are there no existing alternatives?

Yes: California, television, or off-Broadway theatre, provided he can afford the latter. None of these are satisfactory either in themselves or in combination, for the simple reason that the best the theatre has to offer in every department is neither required nor available in any one of them.

What then?

We must develop a new theatre, and we will, but only after considerable agonies of death and rebirth. As a matter of principle, I dislike having to agree with Mr. Tynan about anything, but when he suggests that, in a very short time, Broadway will find itself with not more than a dozen theatres and all of them given over to musicals, I have no other choice.

Monday, February 20th

At last I'm free of the script. Now all I have to do is act it.

Tuesday, February 21st

We're obviously overlength, but I'll worry about that tomorrow or the next day, or rather someone else will. We must get through this hiccough stage before an accurate timing can be assessed, or even before we know precisely where the cuts are indicated.

We have a new cast member: the cat. Martin barely tolerates "Pussikins." His affection for her in the play will be a triumph of illusion.

Wednesday, February 22nd

Washington's birthday, and I cannot tell a lie. I wish I'd never started this diary. There isn't time. They will expect penetrating insights or amusing anecdotes. I feel about as penetrating as a balloon, and the humor is graveyard. We are to run through for "a few guests" tonight, and catch a train to Philadelphia tomorrow morning.

Thursday, February 23rd

We were told we were to have our own parlor car, complete with two drawing rooms for conferences and those on-the-train rehearsals that rarely take place. I was lucky to get a seat in the diner. The Pennsylvania Railroad goofed, and "our" car was attached to another train. The company, mountains of baggage, a cat and a dog are spread through half a dozen cars. Pandemonium. It was almost worth it, as it's the first time I've ever seen the manager, Oscar Olesen, on the defensive—at least with actors.

Friday, February 24th

Stumbled through a technical of the first act last night. More of the same today. Dress parade and dress rehearsal tomorrow. Poor Mary Grant [the costume designer]—the wardrobe has gone astray. John Maxtone-Graham, our stage manager, looks more and more austere, and more and more like Prince Philip on parade. The cat scratched Martin, and she must be given a manicure.

Saturday, February 25th

Still no wardrobe. Dress-rehearsed in street clothes. John G. continues to restage the first scene of the play. Please God, let me remember what version we're to do on opening night. The prop men are in labor, and the squawk box over the switchboard competes with the dialogue as Ben Edwards sets his lights. Isn't this jolly!

Sunday, February 26th

Project! Project! The Locust Theatre in Philadelphia could house a musical, and is magnificently unsuitable for such an intimate play. We have an invitational preview tonight. Our first performance and our last to such an audience. It will *not* be a typical theatre audience, and the reactions can prove as misleading as helpful.

This is being scribbled while waiting for room service at the hotel. I must be back at the theatre in fifty minutes. In the interim, I shall try to drown a flock of enormous pale-green butterflies with a comforting slug of bourbon.

"Do you mean to say you drink before a performance?"

"Yes, ma'am, I sure do!"

The opening, February 27th

This is written the day after. I spent fifteen hours in the theatre yesterday. Not that there's anything very unusual about that, but it's trying! I had no lunch and a sandwich dinner in the dressing room. There were exactly seventeen changes to absorb, and I took them in very bad grace, becoming increasingly peevish as the day wore on. At one point Lew Allen gave me a friendly "How's it going?," and got a definitely surly "Don't talk to me" in reply.

I remember something Rex Harrison was quoted as saying in a magazine profile. He was seated in the house during rehearsals, and, pointing to the stage, he said to his interviewer, "You know it's very exposed up there."

Most of the changes were superficial, but they were changes and not calculated to increase one's sense of security. Half a dozen of them were serious, involving new or rearranged dialogue. John Long [dresser] was still cuing me at the half hour.

The reviews were one good and two indifferent, which is probably healthy. After all, this is another beginning rather than an end. To this point an essential element, the audience, has been missing. The next two weeks will be lived in a trancelike atmosphere of hotel bedrooms, rehearsals, performances, and round and round we go. Dear old Aunt Marcia who lives in Philadelphia will complain again that her favorite nephew failed to see her, and the room service, good or bad, will become intolerable.

In looking back over these entries I find I've said very little about either my fellow actors or the director. To have reported on the actors and the varying approaches to their work would not only seem presumptuous, it would require a greater objectivity than rehearsals allow. As for my own problems in finding and developing the character of Jimmie Luton, they've existed, but a discussion of an actor's kitchen work is inclined to result in so much argle-bargle, and to sound pretentious as well. One may do a little better with a director. You can see him, and feel his weight and influence almost as well as he can see and judge you.

I watched John Gielgud direct some of the *Five Finger Exercise* rehearsals last season, and have enjoyed the experience at first hand for the past three weeks. (Yes, that I did enjoy!) He has enormous vitality and enormous enthusiasm. While he may be dissatisfied, he is never defeated, and these are qualities the actor can lean on. He seems, at times, to be concerned only with externals, the mechanics of "staging," with form rather than content, but this is a matter of choice or individuality, and when the form reveals the content as vividly as in these two plays—he received brilliant notices in both cases—discussions of approach become academic. He expects his actors to do a great deal of work for themselves, which is perhaps a reflection of his own superb capabilities as an actor. At the same time he is better able to do those things for an actor that no actor can be expected to do for himself, and that lie purely within the realm of "direction," than any director I've ever worked for. This theatrical ability, a combination of taste, long experience and an unerring eye and ear, has become increasingly rare in our theatre. We are passing through and out of an era of director-analysts. To find John directing a group of our more self-conscious "method" actors (a quite inaccurate but recognizable label) would be hilarious. I don't know who would head for the couch first.

About nine and a half working days left before we open in New York. That excludes matinée days and one day of technical rehearsal at the ANTA—say, roughly fifty hours. With John, of course, it will be less than that. Much less. He has a positive aversion to rehearsals, which leaves me torn between anxiety and admiration. I am used to that numbing, frenetic grind out of town. Yet time and again I've seen this proceeding hurt a production, wringing all spontaneity out of the performance. No time for consideration and, in consequence, no time for brevity.

What will happen to us? How will we be received?

I haven't the faintest idea.

An answer that always mystifies the amateur and civilian. I do know that Hugh's characters are rich and honestly drawn, and that the actors are likely to fare well. Much that the playwright has done may be overlooked, yet reflect favorably on us. Perhaps there's a rough justice in this. The playwright *can* go back to his typewriter—he may not want to, but at least he has that choice. The actor? A year or two years if he's in a hit, and if he's not, another wait. Another season, another Philadelphia and another bout with time and the pale green butterflies.

Melancholy? No. Self-pitying? I hope not. On the other hand, no quotations from Dr. Coué either; no note of triumph in "There's no business like show business" or wry little jokes about "The Fabulous Invalid." The bed we've made on Broadway is bloody uncomfortable, and I for one would like to climb the hell out of it.

May 1st

Big Fish, Little Fish is now in its seventh week at the ANTA Theatre, New York. The play received "mixed" notices, but on balance they would be considered favorable if not "smash." There was particular praise for the direction and the perform- ances, and a variety of awards have been bestowed on individual members of the company. All very soothing to the ego.

"Was it worthwhile then?" That question seems to be on the minds of the editors, and is, I suppose, a logical springboard to an epilogue—a very brief one!

There are two answers. The working experience was emphatically worthwhile. More so in this case than in most, because it brought together a gifted new author, an exceptional director and a company of actors almost as sympathetic, and certainly as capable, as is to be found in most first-rate "Acting Companies."

Was it worthwhile as a commercial Broadway venture? (You have to stand judgment in the league in which you play.) I think *not*. And I believe the same answer must be given to the same question when applied to every other straight play produced in the 1960–61 season. There is one exception: Jean Kerr's *Mary, Mary*. Some of the current attractions may survive the summer and go on to recoup their investments next season, but it seems unlikely.

This atmosphere of continual commercial crisis is both depressing and restrict- ive. It inhibits all new production and particularly the type that might seem to justify the theatre's claim to an art form. In consequence, it must inevitably discourage the most creative elements in the theatre.

There are no easy panaceas, no single formula for stemming the tide of deterioration. The problems are too many and too complex. We will proceed, hopefully, to apply a series of economic Band-Aids because they will be forced upon us, but to this Cassandra only a basic and all-encompassing revolution of production procedures will restore the American professional and commercial theatre as a self-supporting institution. Let it come quickly.

16 Julie Harris

John Keating

January 1962

Julie Harris (b.1925) first caught the critics' eyes as the confused adolescent Frankie in Carson McCullers' *Member of the Wedding* (1950). Her red-haired, waif-like presence then incarnated Sally Bowles in *I Am a Camera* (1951) and Joan of Arc in *The Lark* (1955). For a while, it seemed that if any play or film had a neurotic or hypersensitive or excessively caring young woman in its cast, Julie Harris would get the part. Later in life, as she shed her dewy-eyed quality, she indefatigably toured one-woman shows about Emily Dickinson, Mary Todd Lincoln and Isak Dinesen.

ONE of the bitterest accusations against Hollywood made by champions of the theatre is that movie makers constantly raid Broadway to steal away the bulk of the most promising new talent uncovered by the theatre. It is a legitimate plaint—one thinks of Marlon Brando, Shirley MacLaine, Anthony Perkins and a dozen others who have shifted their interests either entirely or primarily to movie-making—but it is not a situation for which the theatre is entirely blameless. (As Gilbert Millstein pointed out in *The New York Times* Magazine a few months ago, not even a star of Julie Harris' stature can depend on Broadway for enough work to remain solvent, either artistically or financially.) Looking at it from another point of view, it is just possible that Hollywood, in spiriting away so many promising young players is merely reclaiming those who should rightfully have been its own all along and who, by some chance, strayed from the proper path. For the one inescapable conclusion to be drawn from interviews given by young actors and, even more, by young actresses, is that it was the movies which first attracted them to the actor's life. A generation or two ago it would probably have been the resident stock companies or touring shows. Today, even the most staunchly pro-theatre of Broadway's younger stars give full credit to Hollywood.

Tammy Grimes, for example, says: "I went to the movies all the time and I'd stay all day. I may be the only living person who has seen *The Foxes of Harrow* twelve times. I saw everything and I loved everything. I never analyzed the movies; I believed it all. When someone got shot, he really got shot, and I would cry for him. The movies were much more real than what was going on in my actual life."

Maureen Stapleton, whose background is in all other respects as different as night from day from the country-club-debutante existence Miss Grimes knew, says she started going to the movies when she was about six years old and decided to become an actress at almost precisely the same time. "It seemed to me the actors all looked pretty, they seemed to be making a lot of money, and they looked as though they were loved. If you could be that, all of those things, all my problems were solved," she told *Theatre Arts* (July, 1960). By the time she was ten, she was, like Miss Grimes, going to the movies "all the time, from three in the afternoon when school let out until eleven at night, when the picture houses closed. I liked everything."

Kim Stanley remembers seeing *Wuthering Heights* with Laurence Olivier and Merle Oberon "about twenty-five times," and Shelley Winters knew she wanted to become an actress "the first time I saw a talking movie: *The Jazz Singer*."

For Julie Harris, too, the movies were a girlhood obsession. With her, it was not enough just to see them, she had to recreate them on the rolling lawns or in the spacious rooms of her family's Grosse Pointe, Michigan, estate. She was, alternately, Vivien Leigh and Olivia de Havilland as those two ladies appeared in *Gone With the Wind*: family legend has it that she saw the Civil War epic thirteen times; at other times she became Ginger Rogers, Katharine Hepburn, Bette Davis, and whoever it was who was playing Tarzan in those days. One month, when she was seventeen, she saw fifty-two different films.

"The movies were like a wonderful dream," she recalled—dreamily—one recent afternoon, before trekking to the Bronx to work in a movie of her own, *Requiem for a Heavy-weight*, in which she is starred with Anthony Quinn and Jackie Gleason. "It was a kind of never-never land and the people were all like gods and goddesses. But it was all so beautiful and out of this world. I never thought for a moment I could really be one of them.

"When I saw my first plays in the theatre," she continued, "it was different. I could see these were people. Real people. It was all still marvelous. I remember that the first time I saw the Ballet Russe de Monte Carlo and saw Eglevsky make those miraculous leaps, I yipped out loud, my mother had to shush me; and I screamed in terror when the rat ran across the stage in *Native Son*—but on stage it was not only marvelous but real. I knew I had to become an actress."

Miss Harris, like most of her contemporaries in the theatre, has remained a movie fan (as a spectator, though not necessarily as a participant) and, after she had signed to play the part of Josefa Lantenay, the housemaid-heroine of her current Broadway success, *A Shot in the Dark*, she went on a foreign film binge, paying particular attention to Brigitte Bardot pictures.

"It wasn't that I thought Josefa should be like Bardot—or that I *could* be," she explained, "but she is the kind of French girl who would be most likely to use Bardot as a model for, oh, the way she would try to do her hair. She would be a fan of Brigitte Bardot, you know. Then I went to see the Italian picture, *Rocco and his Brothers*, and even though it was about a family in another country and they were all men and boys, I thought this is the kind of family that Josefa would have come from. She is a peasant like them and like them she wanted to get away from the farm and try her luck in the city; that required a certain kind of courage and a sort of intelligence that was different from the rest of the peasants she was brought up with."

A Shot in the Dark, an adaptation by Harry Kurnitz of a French comedy by

Marcel Aymé, will probably turn out to be the most successful play, at the box office, that Julie has appeared in since she achieved stardom in *I Am a Camera* ten years ago. It is one which she was most reluctant to accept. Harold Clurman, who had previously directed her in *The Young and the Fair*, *The Member of the Wedding* and *Mademoiselle Colombe*, attempted to forestall any objections about the part being "not right" by assuring her, with absolute certitude, "This is one time I won't have to direct you at all, except to say that you must gain five pounds."

"I knew she would say she couldn't play it," Clurman recounted. "And it *is* a far cry from Joan of Arc or the Irish nun she played in *Little Moon of Alban* or some of the other roles she has done so well. But when she said, as I knew she would, that it wasn't a part for her, I told her 'You can play anything—including Shylock.' "

It is Clurman's theory that an actor possessed of what he calls "mobility of temperament" is capable of playing any role in which he is not physically unbelievable. By mobility of temperament he means the ability to read quickly, easily and fully to each of the events of the play. These reactions must be not only fluent, readily tapped, they must also be of such quality that they have an exciting and memorable effect on the audience.

"Julie has that mobility," he explained one afternoon shortly after the play had opened to enthusiastic review with, as is customary with plays in which Miss Harris appears, particular excitement and enthusiasm for her performance. "And with it she has a special lightness of touch, great rhythm and absolute grace.

"She is an absolute joy for a director to work with," he said enthusiastically. "She will take in what you have to say, take the interpretation from the director, use her intuition and bring you a fresh and creative performance.

"I remember in *The Young and the Fair*," he continued "where Julie played a kleptomaniac in a girls' boarding school. Her big scene came when she was accused by one of the other girls of being the thief. At some point while we were discussing the character, I had told her that when a person is accused of some-thing of which he is guilty frequently the reaction is to feel sick. Several days later—I had forgotten all about the conversation—I happened to glance over at Julie and was shocked at the way she looked. Her face had gone gray and I could tell she was in some terrible distress. I stopped rehearsals, rushed up to her and asked if there was something wrong. I was really frightened. But no, there wasn't anything wrong with Harris: it was the girl in the play who was sick. She had held on to that idea I had mentioned in passing and had turned it into something frighteningly real and moving. She seemed literally to be on the verge of vomiting, and she was able to convey all this in the most graphic way imaginable without being at all disgusting. She stopped the show with that scene opening night."

Clurman recalled another time when Julie had taken to word he had dropped and built it into a memorable moment. During the first days of rehearsal for *The Member of the Wedding*, he pointed out that one of the characteristics of children was their penchant for imitation. They would "become" a dog by barking, or a train by hooting out an approximation—"choo-choo"—of a train whistle. Some time later, in a scene where Julie as the twelve-year-old tomboy of the play was ecstatically describing how she would go around the world in an airplane, he was surprised of and delighted to see her suddenly wheel around the stage with her arms extended, dipping and swerving like the wings of an airplane, and emitting "a wonderful child's imitation of the sound of an airplane's motors roaring away."

"In the present play," he added, "she does a wonderful thing with her elbows—lifting them, a kind of parody of a fighter's pose—on a line something about 'I'd belt him.' She gives it a wonderful quality of coarseness; you know this is the kind of a girl who starts street fights."

To the casual inspection of the audience, Josefa the maid and Julie Harris the actress might seem indistinguishable physically. Julie sees the two differently. Josefa's complexion is rougher and ruddier than Miss Harris' pale, freckled countenance; her eyebrows are heavier, her mouth wider and fuller. She is somewhat bustier and her hair is done up in a home-made Bardotesque mess.

"When I take off my make-up after the performance," she said, recently, with a rather puzzled frown, "I look in the mirror and I ask myself, 'Where did she go?' "

That is a question people have been asking about Julie Harris since she first came to public attention. No satisfactory answers have yet been recorded. The late John van Druten, who dramatized Christopher Isherwood's *Berlin Stories* into *I Am a Camera*, the play in which Miss Harris became a star officially, once told a reporter, "On stage, she is a flame, but as she leaves it she turns into a wisp of smoke." Van Druten, who obviously had given a bit of thought to the subject, on another occasion compared her to a crystal pitcher. "You pour in red wine," he said, "and the pitcher looks red; pour in crème de menthe and it's green. When she's by herself, Julie is almost transparent, almost nonexistent."

There is no question but that the life Miss Harris prefers to live when she is not acting is, even by non-theatrical standards, a quiet one, and that the personality she has developed is not likely to draw crowds any time she walks down a street. (She herself, as several writers have pointed out, would not be easy to pick out of a crowd without a great deal of conscious effort.) She and her second husband Manning Gurian might be living a thousand miles from the bright lights of Broadway rather than just across town and a few blocks north in a remodeled four-story house near Beekman Place which they share with their six-year-old son Peter. Gurian, a veteran stage manager who joined the producers' ranks with *The Warm Peninsula* in which Julie toured six months in the 1959–60 season, before bringing it to New York, is a notably protective guardian of his talented wife, and seems to care as little as she for the glamour and chi-chi without which *la vita* is not truly *dolce* for most celebrities.

Much has been written about the fact that Julie takes more busses than taxis (which is probably no longer true); that she doesn't go to night clubs or the city's more glamorous restaurants (which is); that she rarely takes a drink, even more rarely lets an unladylike expression escape her lips, is a dedicated and conscientious worker, a devoted mother . . . in short, a model of propriety and rectitude. It is an image seemingly composed equally of Alice Sit by the Fire and Goody Two Shoes.

This "image" is one which Miss Harris is undoubtedly sick to death of having presented to her, as it has been in just about every article ever written about her. While it may fit the observable facts, it cannot be the complete or accurate one. Neither Alice nor Goody nor any combination of that kind could provide the fire, passion and emotional comprehension that has shone forth in everything the actress has done, from the pre-teen tomboy of *The Member of the Wedding* through Sally Bowles, the Joan of Arc of *The Lark*, the Juliet she created for the Stratford, Ontario, Festival two years ago, and on to the lusty, uninhibited, strangely innocent bed-hopper she plays in her current vehicle.

The probable truth is that under the colorless façade lies a restless, vibrant, strongly individualistic personality, like the handsome and dashing thin hero who, Cyril Connolly once wrote, is hidden beneath the obese cloak of every fat man.

Elia Kazan, who auditioned her for The Actors' Studio in 1947, remembers being depressed by the description of Julie as he heard it from her sponsor. He girded himself for an interview with an ethereal, dundreary type. "I discovered that she is really quite the opposite," he recalled later. "She's violent, strong and wonderful."

She was still a student when she was hired for her first Broadway part, in a comedy called *It's a Gift*. Five days after rehearsals started, she was fired. The reason? Julie's preference for minding her own business and making herself unobtrusive.

"I had learned all my lines long before rehearsals started," she recalled the other afternoon, "so when the director would be working on scenes I wasn't in, I would go over to the side of the stage and read a book. I had no idea that this would irritate anybody, but it did. The director came over to me and said, 'How can you expect to feel the rhythm of the play if you don't pay attention to what's going on? There's more to a play than just the scenes you're in!' I was terribly embarrassed, of course, and for the rest of the time I was there, I kept my eyes glued to everything."

No one had to warn her to pay attention to rehearsals during her next job. This was with the touring Old Vic Company headed by Laurence Olivier and Ralph Richardson. She was a walk-on in the Old Vic productions of *Oedipus* and *Henry IV*, easily the most studious extra in the company. During the next few years, she played in a Guthrie McClintic production of *The Playboy of the Western World*; alternated with another young actress as the White Rabbit in an adaptation of *Alice in Wonderland*; was one of the three witches in the Flora Robson-Michael Redgrave production of *Macbeth*; had increasingly important roles in *We Love a Lassie*, *Sundown Beach*, *The Young and the Fair*, *Magnolia Alley* and *Monserrat*. By 1948, four years out of Miss Hewitt's classes, she had established herself as one of the busiest, most promising young actresses in New York. After her performance as Frankie in *The Member of the Wedding*, her future was assured.

Helen Hayes, who had been one of her childhood idols (after seeing Miss Hayes in a touring company of *Twelfth Night*, she had rushed to the hairdresser with a picture of the star clipped from a newspaper and had her long hair chopped off and styled to resemble the Hayes coiffure), came backstage one night and presented her with a small, delicate, lace-edged handkerchief which Miss Hayes had received from Julia Marlowe who, in turn, had been given the talisman by Sarah Bernhardt. Bernhardt's instructions to Miss Marlowe, which she had relayed to Miss Hayes, had been to pass it on to the young actress she deemed most likely to perpetuate the great tradition of acting. The following year, after fifty performances as Sally Bowles in *I Am a Camera*, she was officially pronounced a star and her name went up in lights above the title of the play on the marquee of the old Empire Theatre. It is a stardom she has enhanced with every subsequent performance: in *Mademoiselle Colombe*, *The Lark*, *The Country Wife*, *The Warm Peninsula*, *Little Moon of Alban*, *Romeo and Juliet*, and the current *A Shot in the Dark*.

She has also, occasionally, visited the land of the wonderful dream, first in the film version of *The Member of the Wedding*, again for *I Am a Camera*, *East of Eden* and two foreign-made films, *The Truth About Women* and *The New Gossoon*. She has enriched television on many occasions by her performances. This season she was seen in the television production of *The Power and the Glory* which starred Laurence Olivier, and in the role which Helen Hayes created on stage a generation ago, *Victoria Regina*, her most impressive video triumph to date.

The Harris career has been, from the very beginning, a markedly successful one. In addition to the Bernhardt-Marlowe-Hayes handkerchief, she has received just about every known award for acting excellence. Fellow professionals in the not-uncatty world of the theatre are unanimous and unstinting in their praise of her talent. The critics have lavished superlatives upon her, have indeed crowned her one of the authentic greats of the theatre.

Speaking with an acquaintance not long ago about her career, she was asked what had led her to embrace it in the first place.

"I think I was like one of those little dogs you see in the circus," she said. "They come out in their little costumes and they're so eager and anxious to do their act, to do their best. And when they've done it right, and their owner cuddles them and gives them a sweet or whatever they do, you can just see how happy they are. That is the way I felt. I thought: How wonderful it must be to feel all that warmth and affection rising up all around you from the audience!"

Have the warmth, affection and applause bestowed upon her in the past decade been satisfying? She considered her answer thoughtfully for a while before answering in a quiet, unaccountably Irish-tinged voice. The answer began equivocally but turned out forthright.

"Yes and no," she said. "The longer you live the more you realize how foolish it is to expect satisfaction from wanting to be loved. The real satisfaction comes from loving, from giving of yourself. In the theatre, the great satisfaction comes when you have worked with a play-wright and a director and have created something to give to an audience."

The difference between those two responses—the desire to be loved and the wish to give love—might be taken as a measure of maturity. It is, certainly, a maturity not many actors—or, for that matter, not many people in any walk of life—achieve.

Part II
The British legacy

17 A crux in English acting

Alistair Cooke

September 1932

Throughout the nineteenth century, English acting had been taken as a pattern for the American stage; many actors were themselves transplanted Britons (Junius Brutus Booth, Maurice Barrymore, George Arliss) or had English antecedents (the Wallacks, the Drews, the Jeffersons); other simply sported English accents. The quarrel between the genteel British tradition and the nativist approach had reached a murderous climax in the Macready/Forrest feud in 1849, but by the *fin de siècle* there was a regular two-way traffic between New York and London. Even though *Theatre Arts* admired the challenge offered to hidebound English traditions by Shaw and Granville-Barker, in the 1930s it began to carry a monthly review of West-End openings by Ashley Dukes.

Alastair Cooke (1908–2004), English essayist and commentator, first became acquainted with the U.S. when he attended Yale and Harvard as a graduate student on a Commonwealth Fund Fellowship. He served as a film critic for the BBC and the London correspondent for NBC, resolving this transatlantic schism when he became an American citizen in 1941, just before Pearl Harbor was attacked. His wartime broadcasts were high points of Anglo-American relations. Later he was the urbane host of the early television cultural show *Omnibus* and, less significantly, of Public Television's *Masterpiece Theatre*.

THE English actor is the best naturalistic actor in the world, according, we need to qualify, to English notions of how people behave naturally. We have no understanding of lyric acting, as it has been known in France and Italy. We have no knowledge of acting gymnastics, such as most German actors believe to be the basis, as well as the duty, of their work. And almost any competent visiting American player can demonstrate how poor is our sense of rhythm, especially in comedy. Yet these traits, quite apart from their being suspiciously labelled as evidences of national temperament, are likely to be cultivated by actors who regard acting as an art, as much in its own right as sculpture, poetry, or painting. A capacity that actors boast of but rarely possess. And one that is not popular in England. Consequently, our acting prefers to copy the detail of every-day conduct.

And since conduct in England is endlessly observed, discussed, and codified, we have evolved during the past eight hundred years a phenomenon more local than most Englishmen imagine: the idea of the gentleman, which—with afternoon tea—we may be said to have given to the world. We are duly sensitive about this preserve and most young actors would think twice of accepting small character parts before juvenile leads. A reputation for elegance is more coveted than one for accurate observation. We are interested to show how we ought to behave rather than how we do. And the result is that we have several hundred young men and women on the West-End stage who can give a minutely accomplished and humourless representation of a tea-party or an at-home, that our stage is ridden with type-actors, and that latterly play-writing has taken the enforced turn of a prescribed milieu and we have become the unquestionable and unquestioning masters of plays written to demonstrate the "fragrancy" of the suburbs.

There has so far been no enquiry into or analysis of post-war acting. The attitude of the actors may be fairly represented by Mr. William Farren, who is constantly writing to the papers to say that acting is not what it was. He is right but not as he wishes to be right. For the fact that there is an English idiom—"not what it was," meaning "vastly inferior to what it was," does not preclude the literal, truer statement, "is different from." Acting has lost its kind but not therefore its goodness. It has changed simply, not deteriorated; a conclusion not over-subtle, but more and more in English criticism the obvious badly needs saying. And yet between a histrionic tradition and a naturalistic one that is already at a dead-end there seems no choice, no reputable modern method. Except in the work of one actor, an analysis of whom may more directly illumine the present crux.

In staking this claim for Mr. Cedric Hardwicke the writer assumes that the reader is aware of more than one or two kinds of acting. Very few actors can imply, in a single performance, any other acting equipment than the one they are at the time employing. There is, on the contrary, a pleasing mystery about Mr. Hardwicke's control: he can probably act, we reflect, as suavely and naturally as Sir Gerald du Maurier and yet probably, too, knows all the Irving tricks. His interpretations are too consistent to allow us to discover whether any one performance is a sustained pose or a piece of unconscious behaviourism. But he has presented on the London stage a handful of creations that help us to decide what qualities are definitely not his. Some things we can with certainty deny him. He is surpassed in emotional resilience by Mr. Robert Loraine; in lyricism by Mr. Esme Percy, whose inheritance of French blood together with a French training may be the reason for a quality rare in English acting; in strangeness by Mr. Eric Portman, a handy example of an actor's making the most of a voice with abnormal intonation; and in individuality of method notably by Mr. Noel Coward, an actor who has intensified the ordinary naturalistic method by acting on his nerves. But in choosing to limit Mr. Hardwicke's talents we do not make a show, in the way that disciples of an artist often tend to win sympathy, of accepting limitations and then defending them. We are not concerned with virtues, absolutely considered, but with desirable, that is timely, qualities. And that Mr. Hardwicke's method is not obviously in any "grand" tradition and yet historically most timely and appropriate is what I hope to establish.

Every great actor, we must assume, has solved the difficulty of trimming his natural style to suit his material, of striking a balance between form and the content demanded by fashion, the supply of dramatists, or any other historical accident. And acting styles are not interchangeable across the centuries. To assume that what is called "the grand style" is always valid for certain plays is to betray a false understanding of the development of a tradition in acting, literature, and indeed in any of the arts. It is not fanciful to suppose, for example, that the bag of rodomontade that Betterton brought back from France and tumbled indiscriminately into classical and modern plays would be inappropriate to the presentation of, say, the Coward-Lonsdale milieu (though it might be very heartening as deliberate satire in Barrie) and, indeed, to the firm, unequivocal naturalism of post-war acting. Yet it must have invigorated much rhetorical writing at the time and given a unifying vivacity to a play like Dryden's *All For Love*. But that kind of vivacity would be embarrassing if it were applied to modern problems of conduct and is now better never practised.

The same may be said too for the technique of, for instance, Mr. Matheson Lang and Sir John Martin Harvey, what might be called the actor-manager technique, a kind of elaborate rhetoric possibly enlivening and stimulating at the end of the last century but no longer relevant to our dilemma because no longer surprising: it now seems glib, mechanical, unambiguous, and at so distant a remove from behaviour that it does not appear to be approaching the human problems it may be, indeed, interpreting. And being clearly under the control of an actor's whimsicality, and not of an outside producer, it is not likely to be mistaken for expressionism. Instead we become aware we are witnessing rhetoric in deflation. And the last war compelled us to a circumspection in conduct, and in pronouncements about it, that should prevent any sincere artist from acting rhetorically in a naturalistic play.

On the same score we may disregard the work of many less distinguished exponents of the same or closely related techniques. Mr. Hardwicke, on the other hand, more than any actor on our stage, seems to exist on the smallest store of working tricks, he acts by the negation of what is commonly called technique. His entrance in the first act of *The Barretts of Wimpole Street* was a pretty example. Each of the sick Elizabeth's brothers had entered her room to pay their respects and sympathies. They had grouped themselves submissively round her couch. The termagant sister suddenly announces that their tyrant father is leaving home. They form a jubilant circle and sing their thanksgiving, when down extreme stage-right the door slowly opens and discloses the father. This entrance was obviously written to assist the actor to a studied, rather crudely sensational impression. Mr. Hardwicke did not match his author, he just "came in" and one remarked only how beautifully he walks. It is this capacity for letting down one's expectations, for disclaiming what the critics call "theatre," for quietly seeming to refuse the great occasions, excusing himself from rhetoric on the grounds of a modern indisposition, and yet saving himself from the cigarette-smoking stigma by revealing in walk, voice, and general poise, that acting is a reputable profession, which endows him with the virtues of Mr. Matheson Lang and Sir Gerald du Maurier, of rhetoric and naturalism.

One might say it is the *honnête homme* returned in a lounge suit, and squeamishly press the point by reviving the conception of artiste as gentleman. Again, in *The Apple Cart* he broke up the long speech on democracy into three parts, consumed each at his ease, and the whole passed unnoticed as a plum. He has confessed that, whenever he received applause for this speech, or even on an exit, it was the result of tiredness. The scene of Barrett's praying for the redemption of his daughter illustrated another side of the same quality. He knelt down very slowly, very deliberately, without protestation or pretence of deep emotion. Then he prayed with a ruthless and shocking urbanity that reminded one of Raymond Asquith's parody of Tennyson,—"And I shall meet Him face to face, As gentleman to gentleman." This determination to preserve composure, to be aware of himself as an artist using himself as an instrument, is his best merit. And so constant a merit that his impulsive abandonment of it, the collapse of his composure, is terrible. As, after the single moment of the embrace with his niece in *The Barretts of Wimpole Street*, his fierce, suspecting reassumption of calmness offered one sufficing glimpse of the "tormenting abstinence" (of lust) he was later to mention, and revealed, as if by accident, the whole character, everything in fact that Mr. Hardwicke had so carefully excluded from his study. So that the character was pitiful not by the performance but by what the performance appeared to conceal. This is the method in all his work that is not openly comic creation. The only outward signs are a good presence, a graceful walk, and the ability to speak English, and not English, as Americans say, "with an English accent." In this way he has already superseded the "emotional" actor and the contrasting sort who stands wholly outside his part and directs it as policemen do the traffic. He is rapidly approaching a third remove, when the actor is neither losing himself in his part, nor acting like a good critic, but impartially dividing the actor's valid individuality with the critic's sense of form.

The doubts arise with his character acting. In the Stage Society's recent revival of *Widower's Houses* his performance was more notable than the play. It was more studied than either Magnus or Edward Moulton-Barrett. It suggested endearment in the composition, the slightest defection from its austere standards of martialling the material of his characters. Usually he appears to be playing for continuity rather than for "moments." Here one suspected his knowing it was a piece for the connoisseur. Mr. Hardwicke is too self-respecting an actor to be in danger of the actor-manager tradition, of lapsing into a moral and intellectual coma when the delighted contemplation by the actor of each of his gestures is all that is sought. But the smallest increase in the speed of his performance would have prevented our feeling that the others were assisting at an entertainment. This embarrassment apart, there was plenty to admire; he can use mannerism as if it belonged to the character and not to the actor's repertory. One is likely, ever afterwards, to associate Lickcheese with a sniff and a certain way of holding the bowler hat, and to think that Shaw could never have invented so personal a character. His timing, as has been suggested, betrayed his consciousness of the audience but was very varied and assured. And what began as a crisp piece of character-acting soon became an exciting impromptu, the words didn't seem to matter. There is, however, just this disturbing hint that his integrity and accomplishment may part company.

It may be that this analysis is actually a piece of transposed vanity, that our praising Mr. Hardwicke's fusion of rhetoric and naturalism is one way of keeping our heads over water. Dignity dies hard and we like to think that our behaviour in the drawing-room is still godlike even since we have resigned ourselves to cream horns. Whatever the cause, it is certain that Mr. Hardwicke's acting, much over-praised for the wrong things, implies a strong criticism of pre-war methods and offers a resistance to the contemporary substitution of photographic behaviour for acting.

An achievement one would like to think was representative.

18 Acting in my time

St. John Ervine

August 1935

The standard complaint about English acting was that it was too genteel. It was said to lack the natural ease of the Americans, the polish of the French, and the passion of the Italians and Russians. At the same time, no one questioned English authority when it came to acting Shakespeare. This essay weighs the value of youth in injecting fresh vigour into the English stage.

For a time the manager of the Abbey Theatre, St. John Greer Ervine (1883–1971) stirred up controversy with plays dealing with social conflict and religious intolerance: *Mixed Marriage* (1911), *John Ferguson* (1915) and *Jane Clegg* (1913). He was outspoken in his beliefs, but when he moved to England, switched to light comedy: *Anthony and Anna* (1926) and *The First Mrs Fraser* (1929). He also served as dramatic critic for a number of publications, including the London *Morning Post* and the *Observer*, and published a major biography of G. B. Shaw (1956).

I

MENDL, as did Darwin, asserted that evolutionary changes might be made in sudden spurts or leaps as well as in a slow accumulation of modified events, but neither of them went so far as to say that convulsive leaps ahead must result in 'progress', if by 'progress' we mean 'improvement' and not merely 'movement'. In my time, I have seen a great change in acting, but I doubt if the change is as much for the better, as some people, bemused with the notion that the latest thing must be the best thing because it is the latest, suppose. I ought to begin my reminiscences of 'acting in my time' by prefacing them with the remark that they are ampler than those of the majority of people, not because I am a venerable person, incredibly old, but because I began my play-going at an earlier age than any of my contemporaries in criticism.

I belonged to a family which liked, even loved, the theatre, although it had no other connexion with it than that of paying for admission, and in consequence of this fact, I was frequently taken to see plays at an age when other boys, if they went to the theatre at all, were taken only to a pantomime or a circus once or twice a year. I had seen a great variety of plays, ranging from Shakespeare's to George R. Sims', before I was sixteen, and I had seen Irving, Ellen Terry, Forbes Robertson, Wilson Barrett and (once) Sarah Bernhardt often enough to make those who are the same age as myself suspect that I must be much older than I am. I can scarcely recall a time when I was not a playgoer of some sort. If I could

not go to the Theatre Royal, I made my own theatre and gave my own performances in a shed in my grandmother's backyard. I must be one of the few critics of
my age, which is fifty-one, who really know what penny gaffs were like; for I have
sat entranced in a score of them. It is this fact, and not any venerability in me,
which enables me to write with some authority on my theme.

The War was the sudden spurt or leap which seemed to make a profound
change in human habits, but my recollection of the progress of events makes it
seem much less of a leap than it is commonly supposed to have been. All the
changes in beliefs that are now said to have been inspired by the break with
tradition made in 1914–'18 were, in fact, already inaugurated before the War
began. I listen without respect, and with scarcely any interest, to young men and
women who were mewling and puking in their nurses' arms in 1914, assuring
each other that *they* have altered the current of the world's opinions, for I know
that all this alteration was already begun before they were born. The sudden
spurts or leaps which might, Mendl and Darwin very tentatively thought, result
in progress, have, we had better know, resulted in less than Marxists imagine.
Mankind still moves on the slow accumulation of modifications.

The acting of Sarah Siddons subsided into that of Edith Evans or Kit Cornell
by such slow degrees that no one can point to a particular period and say, 'There,
that's the date on which the old acting gave place to the new!' And yet the change
between Sarah Siddons's acting and Kit Cornell's is obviously profound, although
no one can speak of it from his own experience. It is probable that we, could we be
transported with our twentieth-century minds to the last lustrum of the eighteenth century, would find Mrs. Siddons a tedious ranter. It is certain that if she
could be resurrected and taken to see a performance in one of our theatres,
she would not believe she was seeing any acting at all, assuming, of course, that
she could hear a word our 'natural' actors and actresses were saying. They would
seem to her, not so much mummers, as mumblers. But which of the two dispu-
tants on acting would be in the right, is a problem that no one can solve. The
methods are different. That is all we can confidently say about them. We shall
make fools of ourselves if we try to prove that one is superior to the other. Siddons
could appal her contemporaries to a greater extent than any modern actress can
appal hers. Miss Naomi Royde-Smith, in her book, *The Private Life of Mrs. Siddons*,
says that 'Mrs. Crawford had a shriek and a groan "that made rows of spectators
start from their seats". Mrs. Siddons went further; when she shrieked the house
shrieked with her; at her groan young ladies swooned in their boxes.'

Macready, in his reminiscences, says that Mrs. Siddons, in the last act of Rowe's
Tamerlane:

> worked herself up to such a pitch of agony, and gave such terrible reality to
> the few convulsive words she tried to utter, that the audience for a few
> moments remained in a hush of astonishment, as if awestruck: they then
> clamored for the curtain to be dropped, and, insisting on the manager's
> appearance, received from him, in answer to their vehement enquiries, the
> assurance that Mrs. Siddons was alive, and recovering from the temporary

indisposition that her exertions had caused. They were satisfied as regarded her, but would not suffer the performance to be resumed.

She threw an audience of Scotswomen into hysterics, and greatly upset Sir Walter Scott. When the elder Macready and another actor, called Holman, saw her in *Tamerlane*, Holman turned to Macready and said, 'Do I look as pale as you?' Our actors and actresses do not now move audiences as deeply as that, but their failure to do so may only mean that audiences are no longer capable of being moved in the way that Mrs. Siddons moved hers.

II

We shall waste our time, therefore, if we spend it in arguments on 'progress'. In such matters as these, and probably in most matters, there is no 'progress': there is only difference. Duse differed from Mrs. Siddons as much as Lynn Fontanne and Diana Wynyard differ from Duse, but who will dare to distribute prizes to them in order of merit? If, however, we cannot report progress, we can certainly report alteration. In searching my mind for recollections on which to base an account of the changes in acting in my time, I find myself obliged to take note first of all of the prominence now given to youth. We are all, even the old among us, a great deal younger than our fathers were at our age. His Majesty, King George V, was forty-five when he succeeded his father, Edward VII, that is to say, he was only four years older than the Prince of Wales is to-day; but he seemed much older then than the Prince seems now. It was not only that he was a bearded man and that all his children were born, but that an air of age, at all events middle-age, invested him. The Prince is forty-one, but the world still thinks of him as a young man.

This insistence on 'the blown feature of youth', as Ophelia calls it, is, I think, the most notable characteristic of our time, and its origin is undoubtedly the War, in which, it seemed, only the young went to their death. That, of course, is untrue. The old died, too, many of them in the trenches, but the temper of the time was set for admiration, amounting almost to idolatry, of youth, and the young were everywhere hailed as the saviours of civilisation and the only people whose opinions were worth consulting. The middle-aged and the old shamefacedly withdrew to the background, or ran to beauty specialists and youth-restorers and other quacks, and had themselves plastered and pummelled into some semblance of juvenility. It was the young man's, and even more the young woman's, day. Some of us look a little wryly on this youth-worship, especially when we see what lamentable results have followed on it in Italy, Germany and Russia. The governments of those countries, established and maintained by the young, do not encourage any sensible person to believe that we have only to turn our affairs over to those who are under thirty to have them well administered.

In the theatre, chiefly because of this absurd youth-worship, but partly as a result of the popularity of the moving-pictures, the young swiftly rose to the positions of stars, and girls, scarcely out of their 'teens, if they *were* out of them, became leading ladies. The world forgave their lack of accomplishment and technical skill in regarding their unlined, pretty faces. Hollywood had taught mankind to look for unblemished beauties. The heroine's features must not be marred by any defect. If there was a tooth out of alignment or a spot on her chin or a hair too many in her eyebrows, a manipulative surgeon must at once be brought to pluck it, like a rooted sorrow, out. Lines of thought were abolished from the film-star's brow. Thought is an ageing thing, and film-stars, therefore, must not think. The theatre, finding itself submerged in a vast horde of film-fans, most of whom were either illiterate or half-educated, attempted to pull itself up to the surface again by joining the Youth Movement. Nice-looking boys and girls supplanted actors and actresses. Our players no longer acted: they behaved.

III

But a craze of that sort could not last for long. It is not possible to go on for more than a year or two gazing ecstatically at mindless beauties and empty-headed youths. The world may not want to, but it has to, think. The thoughtless young are amusing for an hour or two, particularly on wet afternoons, but months in their society are unbearable. The father in Mr. Maugham's comedy, *The Breadwinner*, appalled his progeny by telling them that they bored him. They could scarcely believe their ears. They? Boring? Did not the wide world know that it was only people *over* the age of thirty-five who were boring? . . . The reaction, once begun, could not be stopped. The Bright Young Things became ridiculous and everywhere the subject of jeers. Film-stars, always a little absurd, became objects of derision, and it was regarded as a sign of silliness to take much interest in them. The expression 'film-fan' was recognised as a synonym for 'nit-wit' or mental defective, and even the highbrows who professed to admire the pictures were considered to be lacking in brains. They were, at all events, markedly inferior to other highbrows. People did not even trouble to be shocked by the revelations of awful goings-on at Hollywood that were occasionally made in the popular press. A film-actress's march from bed to bed did not upset a single mind. For these people were not thought to be real. How could anybody feel upset by the promiscuities of fakes? The marital misadventures of smoothed-out dolls are not marital misadventures as human beings understand them. There are no moral standards for puppets! . . .

A tendency to think appeared again in human society. The days of febrile emotion were ending, even in America, where the tendency to confuse emotion with thought is common and persistent. In 1929, the United States were full of boom-maddened men and women who seemed to think that the spurious prosperity they were enjoying would last for ever. The collapse came quickly, and recovery from it has still to be made. But the slump years gave the thoughtless something to think about, and America, which, in 1929, seemed able to dispense with intelligence, took to thinking hard in 1932, and has been thinking very hard ever since. Europe had already done a good deal of hard thinking, and the advent of America to the ranks of hard thinkers helped to discredit the Youth Movement. The effect on the theatre was instantaneous. The young still have authority on the stage, but it is given only to those young who have minds. The Nace Boy has been relegated to the chorus of the lesser revues. The Mindless Girl has been told that it is her legs that matter: her head is of no account; and legs are only useful for dangling purposes. There is no place for the Mindless Beauty except in the purlieus of Hollywood, where films for fatheads are still manufactured, and the front row of the 'additional ladies' in a musical comedy. A young man or woman who has omitted to have a mind has now little or no hope of obtaining any prominence on the stage.

IV

But this fact does not denote that Youth has lost its hold on the public affection. It means merely that the public, after a hectic attempt to fulfil the Mendelian law about sudden leaps in evolutionary processes, has returned to the sounder law that changes come about by the slow accumulation of small modifications. We have reverted to the tendency which was everywhere observable before the outbreak of the War, and are continuing it, with more modifications, some of which might better be called enlargements. Naturalism in acting had come perilously near to making the performance of a play seem like an intimate discussion among the players, a discussion which it was almost impertinent of the audience to hear. Acting, indeed, by turning into 'behaving', had begun to look like anybody's job, as it became during the Youth craze, and the amateur was everywhere treated with as much deference as the professional.

This was a tendency observable in other walks of life. The unskilled labourer expects to be paid as much as, even more than, the skilled: and tin-openers demand and receive the same pay as accomplished cooks. But the stupidest people, even if they are Russians, soon realise that an unskilled world is a perishing world, and Stalin is learning the lesson we all have to learn, that a world in which everybody is equally inefficient is one which cannot endure. He has introduced discrimination in pay and status between the skilled and the unskilled into the Soviet Republics.

The heresy which prevailed in the theatre immediately before 1914, in reaction from the star system, may be summarised in the term 'team-work'. The last remnants of this heresy are to be heard muttered in Russian film-studios by deluded directors in sloppy flannel trousers and dirty pull-overs. There were to be no more stars, no more prevailing personalities, but only a crowd of earnest mediocrities, all entitled to the same amount of limelight. The Hamlet of one evening was to be the noise outside in the third act on the next evening, and the possibility that one personality could be more attractive and interesting than another was to be denied. The result of this 'team-work' was a dull skilfulness which called for the applause one accords to a circular saw which neatly divides a plank, but does no more; but even in theatres where this 'team-work' was most strictly practised, a tendency for personality to assert itself became apparent, and one or two players soon rose above their fellows and were more applauded by the audience. It does not matter where the team-work theatre may be, in Dublin or in Moscow, sooner or later a player will pop his head above the shoulders of his colleagues and attract attention to himself. If he is dismissed from the company for receiving more than the allotted share of applause, the company promptly falls into dissolution, unless another personality appears; for a theatre cannot live on the talents of a crowd of undistinguishable mediocrities. It must have its genius.

This craze for teamwork was, naturally enough, synchronous with the craze for 'natural' acting. The players were to behave exactly as if they were in a parlour with no one to observe or listen to them. But the room on the stage is not, and never can be, a real parlour, and there are in the theatre a number of persons, perhaps a thousand, who have paid to observe and listen to the people who are playing on the stage. The effect of this insistence on 'natural' acting was to drive the audience out of the theatre. Why should people pay good money to hear no more than inarticulate mumbles and watch incomprehensible people lounging 'naturally' through meaningless movements? It was cheaper and more entertaining to take a penny ride in a tramcar and make up your own play about the total strangers you saw facing you. The characters on the stage were, of course, total strangers at curtain rise, but the purpose of the play was to make them less and less strangers, to make them so familiar that by the time of curtain-fall, they were intimates. The saddening paradox of 'natural' acting was that, attempting to achieve intimacy, it achieved only obscurity, and sent the audience away not only ignorant as it was when it arrived, but irritated and bewildered. The demented democrats of the 'team-work' theatre were destroying what they had set out to save.

V

In my time, therefore, I have seen a complete circle in the theatre. Robust acting dwindled to refined acting, and refined acting dwindled to 'refaned' acting. It could dwindle no lower, unless it dwindled out of existence, so it took a turn up and is in sight of robust acting again. The love mankind has for exuberant and distinguished personalities may be very sad, but it is a fact, and it is a potent fact in the theatre, more, perhaps, than it is anywhere else. We *will* have our stars, and will *not* be content with a general flare. God Who 'made two great lights: the greater light to rule the day, and the lesser light to rule the night: He made the stars also,' and we may be sure He knew what He was doing. Drab team-workers were, no doubt, desirable in the performance of drab drama, though even in its performance some distinction of drabness was observable, but the very fact that there was a drab existence outside the theatre made those who lived drably more eager to see plays and players full of colour and emphatic character.

The soldiers in France were utterly bored by khaki. Wherever they went they saw that dreary tinge, the colour of dung — the word *khaki* comes from Urdu and means *dung* — and they were not made content with it because those in authority told them that it was a safe colour and would prevent them from being seen. They were willing to take the risk of being seen by their enemies. It is only the timorous, shrinking animals and insects that are addicted to camouflage and must conceal themselves because they cannot defend themselves. The strong, fighting animals desire no disguise. 'Tiger, tiger, burning bright, In the forest of the night! . . .' Blake knew a *great* animal when he saw one, and had no wish to see those luminous stripes concealed.

Mankind, like the soldiers in France, desires colour and personality and distinction. If we cannot be distinguished ourselves, we long to see those who can: and if there is no distinction in our community, we will gladly pay for admission to the theatre to see men pretending to be distinguished. The team-workers, setting out to make us all alike, succeeded only in achieving one result, a result which denied its own intention: it made the small-part player attempt to obtain a distinction which he had not been encouraged to obtain in the past. The servant announcing on the stage that dinner is served seeks to make his announcement noticeably good, and speaks his lines as if he were saying, 'Sir, the universe has been created!' We have made the small-part players better than they were, and are ready again to give the geniuses their heads.

19 An artist's apprenticeship: Chapters from an autobiography

John Gielgud

June–July 1937

For those who complained that the English acted from the neck up, John Gielgud (1904–2000) was Exhibit A. He was also, by the mid-1930s, acknowledged to be the leading actor on the English stage. Beginning at the Old Vic, he had given outstanding performances in Shakespeare as Romeo, Mercutio, Richard II, and especially Hamlet, noteworthy for his vibrato delivery of verse. This psychologically febrile interpretation was a huge success when it came to New York in 1936. A member of the theatrical dynasty the Terrys, Gielgud was steeped in stage tradition and, aligned with the Noël Coward circle, popular in café society whenever he appeared on Broadway. *Theatre Arts* often turned to him for commentary and, when it learned he was preparing an autobiography, later published as *Early Stages* (1938), it offered to publish preliminary excerpts. Anecdotal in nature, Gielgud's memoirs cast light on how an actor managed to hone his art in an age when on-stage practice rather than classroom training was the norm.

1904–1914: 'Overture, Beginners' (as the English call boy shouts).

THERE were three of us upstairs in the nursery, my sister Eleanor, my brother Val and myself. We began our stage enterprises with our model theatre — an inspiring affair of cream and gold with a red velvet curtain. My brother Val wrote the plays for the toy theatre and I painted the scenery. I had no special desire to act. The architecture of the stage interested me most. This interest has not faded and I am still practical, and, I hope, inventive, in thinking of scenery for my plays. In those days, it was the scenery first and the play afterwards. We were also very mercenary in the management of our theatre. Val and I were partners in management, in the manner of our Uncle Fred Terry. My sister was 'Lady Jones', a fabulously rich patron of the drama, and we drew on her purse for our brave productions. As a family, the Terrys have not got a great sense of humor, Ellen always excepted, and we did all this with horrible seriousness. 'Lady Jones' financed us in a series of alarming plays, dealing with our grand Terry relatives. In one of these, we worked off our stored-up fears of Grandmother Kate Terry by putting her into the play, in the throes of sea-sickness, shouting for her deaf maid. Grandmother, by the time I knew her, was a gay but slightly alarming old lady, with a beautiful voice and a fine expressive face, and the Terry nose and mouth.

The nicest room in the South Kensington house — apart from our nurseries upstairs, of course — was the large white drawing-room on the ground floor which was only used for parties and celebrations. There was a grand piano — on which my father's playing sounded much finer than on the upright in our room — gold wallpaper and a large gold Chinese screen which hid the door from the people in the room and kept out some of the draught as well. On Christmas Day my famous Terry relatives used all to come to lunch or tea, and then my stage-struck heart would beat and I was in a state of unmitigated rapture. First Grandmother, stout and jolly, with a special armchair at table, and a special picking from the turkey (the Terry appetite is well known, and they are all gourmets), then Aunt Marion, with her gracious smile and beautiful sweeping carriage. After lunch, a great laugh and jingling of coins and Uncle Fred's big head and shoulders looming up over the screen, followed by Julia Neilson, his wife, in lovely clothes and laden with beautiful and expensive presents — finally a sudden hush over the room, and a little old lady is there.

She comes in quietly but she has the most vivid personality of them all. Everyone feels it in a second. It is Ellen Terry, bowed and already very blind, covered in hats and shawls and a big bag and two or three pairs of spectacles — like the most beautiful godmother in a fairy tale. She wore black or gray, very cleverly draped on her slim body, too long in front (as she always wore her stage dresses, too) and bunched up over one arm with inimitable grace. When she got rid of the hat and scarves there were coral combs in her short gray hair and coral beads, and the lovely turned-up nose and wide mouth, and then the wonderful husky voice — a 'veiled voice' somebody called it once — and the enchanting smile and laugh.

She adored children, and they her, and even though she was vague and you felt she was not quite sure where she was or who you were, her magic was incredible. 'Who is this? Who? Jack! Oh, of course, I remember. Well, do you read your Shakespeare? My Ted has written a wonderful book on the theatre — I'll send it to you.' So she did. I have it still (her own copy, scribbled all over with notes and comments).

'You know, I fell down this morning in Charing Cross Road, and when the policeman came to help me up I was laughing so much I could hardly move. Hullo, Old Kate — hullo, Polly. Who's this, Fred? Where's my bag? My other glasses are in it — Oh, I have to go on somewhere — I can't remember — oh, yes, Edy Gwynne's — I must be off — I have a nice new flat in St. Martin's Lane, near all the theatres, and do you know, the other day, who should come in but Jim (James Carew, her husband). Imagine, he's living in the same building. Wasn't it sweet of him to come in!'

And so with much bundling and kissing and chattering, she is gone.

1914–1922

I was a boy still, but I lived in time to see Bernhardt in a one-act play in which she was a wounded *poilu* of eighteen, dying on the battlefield. She seemed to be incredibly young and her voice melted my bones. I saw Adeline Genée dance and heard Albert Chevalier sing. I saw Marie Lloyd and Vesta Tilley and, one other day, I saw Duse in *Ghosts*. It was the last time she was to act in London, and I came away, rich with the memory of her voice, her wonderful hands, and of an audience bigger than the theatre would hold, crowding in the aisles, applauding and weeping at what seemed inevitably a last farewell.

I was lucky to be born in time to touch the fringe of the great century of the theatre. We were privileged, too, as Westminster boys, to see some great sights while I was at school there. I saw each opening of Parliament and was struck by the beautiful voice and perfect diction of Bonar Law in the House of Commons. I was in the Abbey at the wedding of the Princess Royal, and at the burial of the Unknown Soldier we boys, in our training corps uniforms, lined the path between the street and the Abbey. It was extraordinary to stand there, with arms reversed and faces lowered and know that the greatest men of our English world were passing close beside us, though we did not dare look up.

It was about this time that I made my first shy hints: that I wished to renounce an attempt at winning a scholarship at Oxford and try my fortune on the stage. I made this concession: if I did not succeed before I was twenty-five, I would follow my parents' plan obediently and become an architect.

Then fortune fell into my hands. I won a scholarship at Lady Benson's dramatic school, for my reciting of *Bredon Hill*. . . .

Between terms I walked on at the Old Vic. I have been told that I was simply dreadful. I was weedy and Lady Benson — a delightful and amusing woman, and splendid teacher — said that I walked 'like a cat with rickets'. Robert Atkins, the producer at the Vic, referred to me as 'that boy in the brown suit'. Of course, I thought I was frightfully good. In *King Lear* I had to hold the chair in the scene where Gloucester's eyes are put out, and the horror of the situation almost made me sick. Those were primitive days at the Vic, before Miss Baylis had enlarged her theatre. The dressing-rooms were inadequate. Many of the actors had to dress where they could, even in Miss Baylis' office. One would be cheered by the sight of Court Ladies scurrying into the bar at the back of the circle, where they dressed, re-appearing a few moments afterwards as nuns for Ophelia's funeral. We supers dressed in the top boxes, which were fitted with curtains through which we would peep at the stage. Once the curtain collapsed and we were revealed, half-naked, to the audience.

1922

MY COUSIN, Phyllis Neilson-Terry, gave me my first professional engagement on tour in a play called *The Wheel*, by J. B. Fagan. This important occasion in my life was made even more momentous when I received the following letter from my grandmother, Kate Terry:

> Dear old Jack,
>   I am delighted to hear of your intended real start in a profession you love and wish you every success. You must not anticipate a bed of roses

for on the stage as in every other profession there are 'Rubs and arrows' to contend with. 'Be kind and affable with all your co-mates, but if possible be intimate with none of them.' This is a quotation of my parents' advice to me and I pass it on as I have proved it to be very sound. Theatrical intimacy breeds jealousy of a petty kind which is very disturbing. I hope you may have many chances with your various studies and prove yourself worthy.

I am returning home on Monday and shall, I hope, have an opportunity to have a good old talk with you.

Meanwhile my love and congratulations.

Your affectionate grandmother,

KATE LEWIS

I worked hard when I was touring with Phyllis Neilson-Terry. I learned the routine of a stage manager, which is not often taught in the schools of acting, played three or four parts at understudy rehearsals, and held the book and rang the bells and hustled the actors at performance. I saw the properties and scenery out of the theatre and on to the train every Saturday night, and moved them in at our next 'date' on the following Monday. I would sometimes be on duty in the theatre for thirteen hours at a time. I felt that my duties were arduous, but old actors in the company assured me that I knew nothing of the real hardships of touring.

I was encouraged during these weeks on tour by letters from the family. Once, a parcel came from Aunt Nell herself, and inside was a copy of her memoirs. She wrote: 'Jack, my dear great-nephew, I am your most loving old great-aunt, Ellen Terry.' And her name, in her vaguely generous fashion, she had signed two or three times in different places in the book, and finally under the picture of herself as Imogen, the one she liked best of all. She died in 1928, and I am proud to think that, in the first six years I spent as a beginner on the stage, I was able to see her sometimes in the theatre and sometimes away from it, and to gather for myself something of the greatness of her personality at these times which has been precious to me ever since. . . .

One of the keenest memories I have is of an evening when she read Beatrice in Mrs. Cazalet's house in Grosvenor Square. I had never seen *Much Ado* on the stage, and here there were only gilt chairs in a semi-circle, a hushed and respectful audience, and a company of nervous amateurs in evening dress reading the play from little books. In the armchair in the middle sat Ellen Terry, also provided with a little book. Off she started, her spectacles on her nose, her eyes on the book, no showing off to frighten the others. Just a sweet old lady with a lovely voice – but not for long. The play seemed to catch her by the throat, she rose from her chair, and the years fell from her – she almost seemed to dance with high spirits. She no longer looked down at the book and, as her memory of the lines became more sure, she began to act the part as I can never hope to see it played again, her wit and pace and glorious gaiety making one forget the lack of lights, costumes and scenery. Then, in the Church scene, when she cried, after Hero swoons, 'Why, how now, cousin? Wherefore sink you down?' she rushed across to the girl who was reading Hero, knocking four slender chairs over on the way, and clasped her to her bosom, to that young woman's acute embarrassment.

I saw her act another time, in a theatre on the pier at Brighton. She played scenes from *The Merry Wives* (and what an entrance she used to make, dancing in to music) and the Trial Scene from *The Merchant of Venice*. Among those who were playing in her company and learning from her was Edith Evans. 'A girl after my own heart!' Aunt Nell wrote in a book she gave her, and Edith's own wonderful performance of Mistress Page some years later showed how apt a pupil she had been.

It was cold weather at Brighton when I saw the performance and Ellen Terry had to be wheeled to the stage door in a Bath chair, well wrapped up against the wind, down the long pier, past the penny-in-the-slot machines and the seats upon which girls and their mashers sat in the warm summer evenings. The Bath chair came to the stage door and the slight figure was helped into the theatre. But when she swept onto the stage in the Court Scene of *The Merchant of Venice* half an hour later and bowed to the Duke with the grace and spirit of a girl, the elderly lady of the Bath chair was forgotten in a moment and the illusion of loveliness was complete, though the hair was unashamedly white under the doctor's cap. Like Duse, she needed no artificial aids to express a spirit of youth on the stage, and it did not seem the least incongruous to see her still playing Portia. The Trial Scene was her favorite, and she never failed to remember her lines in it, though Edith Evans has a good story of a night at the Coliseum when they were playing it during the war in an air raid. Ellen, undismayed, had been watching the raid from the roof, despite the protests of the management, and was in high spirits at appearing before an audience at such an exciting time. However, her concentration, more than usually shaky, deserted her as she came to the line, 'This bond doth give thee here no jot of ——!' The company sitting round her on the stage began to whisper a prompt with one accord, when suddenly the voice of Edith Craig was heard shattering the silence from the prompt corner with — 'Blood, mother, Blood!'

It is no use pretending that I was a great success when I was touring, though I went on one night for an understudy and didn't do so badly. My self-confidence increased. But there was a danger here. I realize now that I must have been dreadfully raw and others thought so too, for one day a member of the company whispered in my ear that it would be good for me to go to the Royal Academy of Dramatic Art and master some more of the rudiments of my job. I went obediently. There I listened to a lecture by Bernard Shaw in which I remember his telling us never to accept less than thirty shillings a week, for, by doing so, we might keep the less fortunate in the gutter. Once Sybil Thorndike came and rehearsed us in Greek tragedy. What a rare example she is of a fine actress whose entire philosophy — but no, it is deeper than philosophy — is in unselfishness of mind and heart.

I was not to be merely a student for very long. During my first term, Nigel Playfair came to one of our student performances and engaged me for the part of Felix in *The Insect Play* at the new Regent Theatre. I studied during the day, and acted at night. But I was unfortunate in my part, which was that of a la-di-da poet, wearing a green sash and carrying a golden tennis racquet. I treated the part as seriously as if it had been Hamlet, and exploited its affectations in deadly earnest. I am glad now that I had no idea of the unfavorable impression I created. The play ran for six weeks, and was followed by Drinkwater's *Robert E. Lee*, in which I played a small part very badly and understudied Claude Rains. I went on for him one afternoon and acquitted myself fairly well, to the surprise of everyone. Is it easier, I wonder, to play a big part than a small one when one is a beginner? The play was not really a success, but it ran through the summer.

Soon after this run came to an end, I got a chance of going to Oxford, not as an undergraduate — though I was only eighteen and many of my school con-temporaries were studying in that capacity — but as an actor, with a new part every week to learn and play, and a handsome salary of seven pounds a week to live on. This was a wonderful piece of luck, and I don't know quite how it came about. Possibly Playfair may have suggested me to Fagan, who was producer and manager of the Oxford Playhouse which he was just trying to establish as a repertory theatre after he had had some years of brilliant but varying fortune in producing Shakespeare, Sheridan and others at the Court Theatre in London. It is sad to think that my first kind managers in the theatre are both already dead, for they were neither of them more than middle-aged. Both were men of great personal charm, besides being great gentlemen, and both gave of their very best to the theatre, risking their money cheerfully and spending again on the theatre anything they were lucky enough to make in it. Both were Oxford men, and very much at home working in the semi-professional atmosphere of Oxford, whether directing productions for the O.U.D.S., in the theatre or the open air, fathering repertory companies and giving chances to promising youngsters. Fagan had Edith Evans acting for him long before she was known in London, and Playfair gave her first distinguished success as Millamant in *The Way of the World* and afterwards in *The Merry Wives*.

In the company I was in at Oxford were Tyrone Guthrie, James Whale, Flora Robson, Veronica Turleigh and Richard Goolden — all of whom have had splen-did careers since that busy time. Fagan's wife, Mary Grey, was the leading lady, and we played in wonderfully varied programs of first-class plays: Shaw, Ibsen, Maeterlinck, Benavente and Sierra, Pirandello, Congreve's *Love for Love* (which shocked North Oxford and had to be kept on another week as a *succès de scandale*) and Chekhov's *The Cherry Orchard* which was so successful that Playfair transferred it to the Lyric, Hammersmith. At the dress-rehearsal everyone despaired of its chances, and a revival of *The Beggar's Opera* was hastily arranged to follow. Against all expectations, the first-night reception was tumultuous, the critics mostly enthusiastic. James Agate wrote a beautiful and illuminating notice, recommend-ing everyone to see the play and explaining why it was a masterpiece, and we moved to the Royalty Theatre and ran all through the summer.

Raymond Massey also came to play with us at Oxford. As we had a new play every week, learning our parts was sometimes beyond us and we resorted to the old trick of pinning the lines to tables and onto the backs of chairs. How little the audience dreamed of our duplicity as we bowed our heads apparently with emotion, but actually to read the next line off the top of a table. It was a minor disaster, therefore, when Raymond Massey spilled a bottle of ink over the script of a most important scene and the actors were left to struggle with their memories as best they could.

1923

I WENT to the Regent Theatre for an audition. There I stood on the empty stage, looking up to an imaginary balcony, while Mr. Ayliff, the producer, read Juliet's part from the wings and Sir Barry Jackson and his manager sat mute in the stalls. Two more auditions were to follow before I could convince them that I was fit to play the part. It was one of the most nerve-shaking ordeals of my life.

Gwen Ffrangcon-Davies was to be the Juliet. She was calm and efficient at rehearsals, but most divinely kind. How she worked over that production, both at her own performance and to help me with mine! Of course I was miserably self-conscious and inexperienced, though I did have some glimmerings of the difficulties of the part. . . . Nothing was ready at the dress rehearsal of this early *Romeo* at the Regent except Gwen's dresses, which suited her to perfection and most of which she had sewed herself. My costumes were not becoming — or it may be that I did not know how to wear them — and my efforts to look Italian were not assisted by an unfortunate coal-black wig, parted in the middle and long at the back, which made me look like a cross between Rameses of Egypt and a mid-Victorian matron.

To have played Romeo in London at the age of nineteen sounds, I suppose, a considerable achievement, but I enjoyed no fine flight of success, and remained on the dim edge of the limelight. My first Romeo got some bad notices and it deserved many more. One that I have always cherished said: 'Mr. Gielgud from the waist down means nothing at all. He has the most meaningless legs imaginable!' Ivor Brown thought me like Bunthorne. A. B. Walkley of the *Times* was very kind and encouraging, and Gwen had a wonderful personal success with both the press and public alike, but the production ran only six weeks, and I was out of the bill for a fortnight with pneumonia. Happily for my peace of mind, but dangerously for my future career, I lived at this time in a golden fog of delusion. I thought I was a marvel of virtuosity, and greedily lapped up the praise which my less discriminating friends served out to me. It was lucky for me that, though I had some fine chances at first, long runs and big salaries did not yet come my way to deceive me into thinking I was a genius. Something always seemed to happen to take the gilt off the gingerbread, and I had the sense to go back to Oxford again for another season when *Romeo* came to an end.

1926

I LEFT Oxford again to understudy Noel Coward in *The Vortex*, and played his part for a month at the end of the run. On top of this grand experience, in the most modern kind of play with a fine West End cast, I was given a chance of doing quite different work of an even more interesting kind: I became a highbrow. I had, while with J. B. Fagan at Oxford, already appeared once in spectacles and a bald wig as the perpetual student Trofimov in *The Cherry Orchard*. I had approached this part with some misgiving and was amazed afterwards when people told me I had made a success of it. I was even considered a bit of an intellectual. But I fear that this reputation was quite unmerited. I do not mind confessing that I had very little idea what these Russian plays were about, at first, though I had gone straight from *The Vortex* into Chekhov's *The Sea Gull*. The part of the young writer, Konstantin, was a very fine one, and I was thrilled to play it. Valerie Taylor made a big success as Nina and, though I had rather mixed notices, the production was much talked of and ran for some weeks. Chekhov was suddenly becoming fashionable. Komisarjevsky, the Russian producer, saw our performance and thought me promising, though he did not care for this production — small wonder, as he had worked in the original first production in Russia under Stanislavski and Chekhov himself, while his sister, Vera Komisarjevskaia, had created the part of Nina.

The manager who put on *The Sea Gull* now thought he might as well exploit this Russian boom to the full, and engaged Komisarjevsky to do the other Chekhov plays for him in a little theatre down at Barnes which he had taken and wished to run as a highbrow repertory theatre. I was engaged for the next play.

This production at Barnes of *The Three Sisters*, in which I played the Baron, was one of the most beautiful I ever saw — and certainly made one believe in the Russian atmosphere as no amount of boots and blouses and stygian gloom had done in the *Sea Gull* performance. I never enjoyed rehearsals more, and when we saw the scenery and lighting effects — to say nothing of all the other stage devices of which Komisarjevsky is such a master — the whole cast burst into applause. We had a great success on a tiny stage with minimum salaries and rigorous economy all round. I don't suppose the whole production cost much more than three hundred pounds — and smart people in cars thronged down to Barnes in evening dress for eight weeks to see it. Afterwards I played a man of forty — my first real character part except Trofimov — a weak but wildly jealous character, in *Katerina*, a play of Andreyev's, and Komisarjevsky again surpassed himself with ingenuity of settings on the tiny stage — and was fascinatingly helpful to work with. Ernest Milton and Jean Forbes-Robertson were also in the cast, and there was a wonderfully produced studio party in the last act. The first night was a nightmare, for the scenery was hardly finished — the stage-manager fainted and was borne below, while Komisarjevsky and a single stage-hand changed the flats themselves and held them up from behind during most of the play. The pianist exhausted her repertoire several times after every act, and the final curtain fell about midnight, most of the critics having crept away before the end.

The Barnes season is a time I shall always look back on with pleasure and gratitude. From Komisarjevsky I learned many things I had never suspected about the profession of the actor. I found out slowly that the most satisfying acting — for performer and audience alike — comes from within, that the contact with your fellow players is more important than your own selfish personal effect, that the audience can sometimes be forgotten altogether in certain kinds of plays provided the life on the stage is developed and made interesting to the utmost. My first ambitions — to appear more handsome, more sympathetic than in real life, to hold the stage alone, listen to my own voice, and take a solo call at the end of the play — these were gradually dawning on me as being cheap and easy and unworthy of the art which we call acting. Some of the difficulties of the craft began to penetrate my mind, and I started to experience for the first time the delights of playing with real sincerity in fine character parts and trying to contribute to the interpretation of the producer, the author and the other actors so that the play should live every night upon the stage, not merely as a vehicle for my own virtuosity, but as a complete and fascinating whole.

1928

I was never again to see Ellen Terry on the stage — though they told me she was in a box one day when I was playing in *The Constant Nymph*, and I heard her whispering 'What is happening?' when she couldn't see in a dark scene, and once again during the performance, at which, of course, I was dreadfully nervous at her presence, 'Now I know how he must have looked as Romeo!'

I have only one more remembrance of her and it is, in a way, the most vivid of all. From the beginning I had never been alone with her. Our meetings had always been in crowded rooms, at parties, or theatre boxes, or in public. But this time, which was the last time, there was nobody there to disturb my vision of her.

Her Elizabethan cottage was at Small Hythe and I was passing in a car on a sleepy day in June. Her house and garden, looking over the marsh, were very quiet, and it was very hot and beautiful. I couldn't resist stopping to knock at the front door, and they said yes, she was getting up, and would be down in a moment.

I went into the farm kitchen which had been made into a sitting-room. I remember that there was a picture of Irving as Becket and I thought: 'She must have so many memories and souvenirs of him, yet I have never spoken to her about them.' The house was simply, almost ascetically, furnished. The Terrys have always been great hoarders. Fred and Marion Terry's houses were full of the sentimental accumulations of years, and towards the end of their lives it was not easy to move in their crowded rooms. But Ellen Terry liked her little house to be unencumbered. She wanted more air and space.

A steep staircase led from the room in which I waited to the bedroom above. I could hear her moving about and speaking to her servant in a gruff voice, husky, but frank and distinct. Then I heard her say: 'Where is my bag?'

Her companion, Barney, whispered to me quickly: 'She will ask you to stay to lunch, but please don't as there is not enough.' Then she came down the staircase, and asked me who I was. She wore a gray dress, like a pilgrim's gown, with long, flowing sleeves, a high waist and something white at her neck. She carried the same enormous black bag with the padlock that I remembered from our Christmas parties, and the red coral combs which I had known as a child were still in her white hair.

She did not say very much to me. I had on a brightly colored shirt, and she liked that — and said how gay it looked, and laughed. As Barney had whispered, she asked me to stay to luncheon, but I said no. She seemed to remember who I was, and asked what I was acting in. One thing delighted her. 'They are driving me over to Bodiam one night soon to see the castle and the swans by moonlight once again,' she said. She always said she was moonstruck — and, they say, even as an old lady, she could still drive a pony at night without disaster. I did not stay long, for she seemed to be tired. But she came down the garden path with me, her gray draperies sweeping the early lavender at her side, and leaned on the gate when I had climbed into my car. She shaded her eyes then against the strong light with one hand, and lifted the other hand to wave goodbye. I turned when I had traveled almost a quarter of a mile along the road, but she had gone past the lavender bushes once more, back into the house.

1929

THE LATE J. T. Grein arranged two special performances of *Ghosts* in honor of the Ibsen Centenary. Mrs. Patrick Campbell had promised to play Mrs. Alving for him, and I was offered the part of Oswald, her son.

Rehearsals of *Ghosts* were great fun, although the producer didn't last very long, soon washing his hands of us. Mrs. Campbell was wonderfully patient with me and took great pains to help me with my part. Her instructions were couched in unusual but graphic terms.

'Use a Channel steamer voice,' she said when I came to a certain difficult line. I looked at her blankly. 'You know,' she went on, 'empty your voice of all meaning, as if you were going to be sick.' She has since told me that Pinero said this to her at a rehearsal and she thought it so good she never forgot it.

The notices for *Ghosts* were favorable. People seemed to think that I was good in the play. I certainly loved acting in it, though I do not greatly care for Ibsen as a rule, and I should never wish to see a performance of it from the front.

Ghosts seemed to set the seal on my reputation as an actor of neurotic or eccentric parts. Highly-strung poets, pianists, invalids and people of that sort, usually pale and, I hope, sometimes interesting, were the characters with which I became associated in the public mind. I have always enjoyed splendid health and I am much stronger than I appear. But, as Basil Dean once said to me, 'If you would strain less to show the audience how hard you are working, and relax and use your imagination more, you might be a better actor.' This is very true, and very difficult to accomplish.

I was anxious to make a success in less morbid roles, and I was delighted when I was offered a part in a farce. It was unfortunate that this play, in which I was 'starred' for the first time in my life, happened to be a somewhat poor specimen.

I should like to lay the blame for its failure on its inferior quality alone, but, if I am to speak the truth, I must admit that my performance was incompetent too. However, I felt I was a leading West End actor, earning a star's salary. I acquired some extravagant tastes, bought more new suits than I needed, and began to go to the Savoy for supper. But my swagger was premature. My first failure was followed by two others, in disconcertingly quick succession.

I felt empty and forlorn. My salary as a leading man had, it seemed, brought me nothing but disaster. I saw that people were beginning to be disappointed in me, and I had not the inner satisfaction of feeling that these experiences had taught me much about my work. It is a waste of time to attempt to play ineffective roles in unconvincing farces unless you are a genius at making bricks without straw, like Seymour Hicks or Leslie Henson. I hope, however, to be given the opportunity of appearing in a first-class play of this kind one of these days. The best thrillers and melodramas, written by men as different as Somerset Maugham and Edgar Wallace, afford magnificent chances to the straight actor. But it took me a long time to learn what a good actor you have to be to play them. . . .

One day Harcourt Williams, whom I hardly knew at that time, surprised me very much by begging me to join the company at the Old Vic, where he was to begin work as a producer. I was offered one or two leading parts, Romeo, Richard II, and there was even a whisper of Hamlet. But Miss Lilian Baylis, the beloved despot of the Vic, is too shrewd to make rash promises before she has seen how an actor shapes in her theatre.

The salary mentioned was exactly half of the money I was earning in the West End. This was an important consideration, for my short spurt of prosperity had infected me with extravagant tastes.

I put off making a decision for some days, as I usually do, and asked the advice of every person I met. It occurred to me one day between the matinee and evening performances of *The Lady With a Lamp* to place my dilemma before Edith Evans. Miss Evans is a conscientious worker, who always rests in her dressing-room between two daily performances. I felt guilty for disturbing her, and hesitated for a moment outside her door. Then my knock was answered by a musical 'Come in.' We sat in semi-darkness, and I timidly put my question. Miss Evans' beautiful, assured voice reached me from the depths of a vast sofa. She told me that it is best for each of us to make his own decisions. But, since she had been faced with exactly the same problem as mine, she could only say what she had done in similar circumstances. She had gladly interrupted a prosperous career in the West End to seek in the Waterloo Road a better fortune than money.

The next day I went to seek Miss Baylis in her office. I was in an exalted frame of mind and felt slightly condescending. I had, I told myself, made a considerable sacrifice, and I was determined to be very businesslike over my contract, and to demand a bigger salary than anybody else had ever been paid at the Vic. I was a little dashed when Miss Baylis, instead of greeting me with a grateful catch in her voice, said briskly: 'How kind of you to call. It would be nice to have you with us, but unfortunately we cannot afford stars.' She quickly convinced me that I was not wanted in her theatre at all. And I, who had entered the room prepared to offer my services graciously, found myself begging her to allow me to join her company. We both evaded financial topics until the last minute of the interview, and I am inclined to think that a little matter of fifty shillings, over which we obstinately failed to agree, was finally settled by letter.

Lilian Baylis sends distinctive letters. They are beautifully typewritten, but nearly all the typed words are crossed out, and the letter is re-drafted in her impulsive handwriting.

I think that a large number of the people who today support Shakespeare's plays in the West End first began to understand them through the productions at the Old Vic, which in recent years has given us the plays swiftly, simply and naturally, in versions which have not been cut and maltreated in order to afford an actor-manager the maximum of limelight. I did not feel, when I went to the Old Vic, that I was running into the danger of acquiring the peculiar booming voice and the exaggerated, meaningless gestures of the Shakespearean actor of the comic papers, with his astrakhan collar, spats and bibulous nose. I knew something of Harcourt Williams' fine reputation in the theatre, and I was conscious too that my equipment lacked breadth, sense of character and ability to handle big scenes effectively.

I was heartened, in moments of doubt, by a letter I received in the curious, decorative calligraphy of Gordon Craig. He wrote to say that he was delighted to hear of my new work, and in a postscript he added: 'Remember, stick utterly loyal inside to H. W. Then great things are possible.'

One golden September afternoon before the Vic season began, I made the first of my many journeys across Waterloo Bridge. Now I must confess to a small weakness. I have always loved to see my name on theatre bills. When I first saw it in lights in Shaftesbury Avenue I nearly dislocated my neck with my rapturous interest. Now perhaps you can guess why I chose to stroll to Lambeth on that fine day. But the journey was wasted; there were no names outside the theatre. It is the custom at the Old Vic. Rather disappointed, I walked home again. Then I realized that I had come in touch, for the first time, with the spirit of the Vic.

There can be no other theatre quite like the Old Vic in the world. It may seem odd to have to stress the fact, but it really *is* a theatre. In these days of concrete boxes, masquerading under the name, with their bleak and uninviting facades and cold, severe interiors, such a thing is becoming a rarity. The Old Vic is warm, alive; and it has a tattered magnificence about it. It smells and feels like a theatre, and it is able to transform a collection of human beings into that curious, vibrant instrument for the actor, an audience. At the Old Vic, the play, the actors and the audience are somehow welded into a single experience. And how I love the old theatre when it is empty (in the daytime only, of course) with all the dust sheets on and bits of light coming in through attic windows in the back of the gallery.

I was very happy during the two seasons that I spent at the Old Vic. The repertory system has always been my ideal of working conditions in the theatre, though for some reason many actors regard it as a penance and a bore. There is, of course, the hard work of constantly rehearsing new plays; but this form of labor is, for me at least, far less exhausting than repeating the same part for months on end.

Long runs are, of course, necessary, if an actor is to establish himself. I am grateful for *Musical Chairs* and *Richard of Bordeaux*, which gave me money and popularity as well as wonderful acting opportunities. I hope, therefore, that the public which responded so splendidly to those two plays will not think me churlish for confessing that, at the end of their prosperous careers, I was exhausted and tired of acting in them. I am not, unfortunately for my nerves and spirits, the type of actor for whom the playing of a part becomes, by constant repetition, a sort of mechanical feat. Perhaps I shall learn to make it so when I have become more experienced. At the present time I act from my emotions, which are liable to become falsely emphasized as the run of the play proceeds, and nothing is more disheartening than finding oneself elaborating and forcing one's effects through staleness, boredom and conscientiousness — when the ideal is surely to simplify and economize wherever possible.

We were very busy those two seasons at the Old Vic; we were often very tired. But we never had time to be bored. We had our failures; in fact, the first season opened in an atmosphere of gloom, amid the execrations of most of the critics; but we always had the next production to make us forget our disappointment. Our great strength and rallying-point was Harcourt Williams, the producer. He ruled us by affection, and by the trust he had in us. This trust was almost childish in its naïveté. Any little instance of selfishness, of disloyalty to the theatre or to the play, would merely throw him into a mood of amazement or disbelief. I am sure we all still remember his little notes of good wishes and thanks to the company and staff on first nights (why were there never notices of abuse and disgust occasionally to balance them?); his vegetarian lunches which we would regard with such anxious interest; the occasional cigarette which he would light with an air of recklessness in a moment of extreme crisis; and his frenzied attempts to concentrate on the last rehearsal of a play when the cast of the next one, to say nothing of the setting for the one after the next, must have been causing him sleepless nights of worry.

I know that Ellen Terry considered Harcourt Williams one of the most brilliant young actors of his generation. Her influence over his life shows itself in his straightforward manners, and in the fact that nothing which he accomplishes in the theatre is tainted by cheapness or vulgarity. I am sure that her sublime shrewdness and common sense and her artist's vision were with him to comfort him on the occasions during his four strenuous years (he stayed at the Vic for two more seasons after I did) when his acute sensibility was strained almost to breaking point.

I was aware of a sense of adventure every time I crossed Waterloo Bridge to attend our first rehearsals at the Old Vic. We used to rehearse in an enormous room at the top of the building. The roof was spanned by gaunt iron girders and the academic atmosphere was intensified by the presence of students, who sat watching us in rows, with enormous volumes of Shakespeare on their laps. I don't know which disconcerted me the most: those who apparently took no interest in the proceedings at all, or the painfully keen ones who balanced all the proceedings with a sort of pietistic fervour.

Harcourt Williams quickly won our affection and our loyalty and we were all tremendously keen for his sake that his plans should succeed. His ideas at that time seemed to be revolutionary; though now I feel certain that his Elizabethan productions, which preserved the continuity of the story by means of natural and speedy delivery of the verse and light and imaginative settings, allowing quick changes of scene, were very suitable for modern needs. Of course they influenced my own productions enormously when I came to do them. . . .

1930

I was very sorry when the Old Vic company disbanded for the summer, but it was nice to feel that I should be returning there the following autumn. I had asked for a rise in salary as a condition of a second season, and when it was given me without a murmur — at the Vic, where money really is a most earnest consideration — I felt I must really be something of a 'draw' at last. I had enjoyed rising early in the morning, the keen winter wind as I walked over Waterloo Bridge, and our rehearsals with their aspiring hopes and eager discussions. Then a quick lunch at the station buffet at Waterloo, during which we stopped arguing only when our mouths were too full of sandwiches and sausage rolls to speak, and back to the theatre to work until four o'clock. Afterwards I would go home and rest until the evening performance, play my gramophone, and perhaps have a drink with a few friends. On the evenings when the Opera Company held the stage at the Old Vic we were free, and I was able to go to the theatre. Now, when I am playing in a long run, one of the chief things I miss is theatregoing at night. I am an inveterate haunter of theatres at matinees, it is true, but that is hardly the same thing.

Our week-end dress rehearsals at the Old Vic were almost social occasions, though they were in a setting of earnest endeavor. The company were permitted to invite friends and relations. My mother, I believe, did not miss one of these functions. Besides friendly criticism, she brought sandwiches, juicy apples and an enormous thermos flask of hot, fragrant tea or coffee.

Before our first nights it was a sort of ritual with some of us to have dinner at Gow's in the Strand. We were too excited to eat very much. Old Vic first nights, although they occur with such frequent regularity, never seem to lose their novelty and excitement. Their fervour never becomes dulled. There is a feeling of excitement about a 'full house' at the Vic which I have never encountered any-where else. An audience makes the theatre come to life in a curious way. Some people think it a cold, unfriendly place when it is empty, as if it were sulking in the absence of the public. But on first nights it magnifies the sound of the chattering, expectant throng and assaults the eardrums and intoxicates the brain with a noise like the humming of a vast sea shell.

An actor must necessarily lose part of his identity at the Old Vic, for the spirit of the place is so much stronger than any of the separate personalities who serve it. One associates the feeling that fills the house with the short, dogmatic and very

English figure of Lilian Baylis. All eyes are turned on her when she enters her box. She glances at the huge audience for a moment. She has a right to feel proud, for it is her creation more than anybody else's. But there is no *hauteur* in her eye. She stands there for a moment, simple, homely and friendly, although an observant person could not fail to see traces of the martinet in her erect figure and in her eyes, restless and watchful behind the lenses of her authoritative pince-nez. Lilian Baylis left me alone while I was in her theatre. She did not tell me until I left her that she had appreciated my work. In the early stages, when it seemed that I might fail there, she refrained from criticism; and later, when success came, she never flattered me. But although she may have seemed outwardly indifferent, I was deeply aware of her ceaseless vigilance. It was astonishing how her influence permeated the theatre, although we hardly ever saw her in person. . . .

Harcourt Williams introduced Bernard Shaw to Old Vic audiences for the first time. We had already given *Androcles and the Lion* the season before. Now we attempted *Arms and the Man*. We were all very flattered and considerably awed when we learned that Mr. Bernard Shaw had consented to come and read his play to us. We waited for him in the theatre one winter morning. It was bitterly cold, and we sat muffled up in heavy overcoats and scarves.

Punctually at 10:30, the great author arrived — wearing the lightest of mackintoshes. There were grace and humour in his reading and his voice was clear and lively. He was in high spirits as he illustrated points in his play, and taught us the correct inflections for his lines. He compelled our attention, although we were shivering miserably. While we suffered we marvelled at the constitution of that wonderful man.

Later, he came to a dress rehearsal. We could not distinguish him in the darkness of the stalls, but we saw the light of his pocket lamp bobbing up and down, like some mischievous will-o'-the-wisp, as he made his notes. He assembled the company in the interval, produced his written comments, and reduced everybody to a state of disquiet. Then he departed, the spirit of the wintry wind rather than its victim, without bothering to wait to see me in my big scene.

20 The Gielgud *Macbeth*

Ashley Dukes

October 1942

Between 1937 and the outbreak of the Second World War in 1939, Gielgud consolidated his pre-eminent position by heading a repertory company at the Queen's Theatre, London, where he played Richard II, Shylock, Joseph Surface in *School for Scandal*, and Vershinin in Michel Saint-Denis' production of *Three Sisters*. He also re-appeared at Hamlet at the Lyceum and as Jack Worthing in his own production of *The Importance of Being Earnest*.

After stints with a wide variety of publications from *Vanity Fair* to *The Illustrated Sporting and Dramatic News*, Ashley Dukes (1885–1959) became the English editor of *Theatre Arts*, contributing a monthly letter from London. He was also a much-staged playwright, mainly of adaptations of French, German and Spanish drama. The best thought-of was *The Man with a Load of Mischief* (1924). In 1933 he founded in London the Mercury Theatre (not to be confused with Orson Welles's), which specialized in verse plays and, after the war, was adviser on entertainment to the British Military Government in Germany.

HERE is a production that arrives in London after months on the road, and must be taken as the considered work of the director (John Gielgud himself) and his cast. They have had time enough to correct minor faults, of which there must have been few from the start. The presentation has a smooth majesty within the simple frame that Michael Ayrton and John Hinton have devised. William Walton's music is composed for the occasion but played from recordings, and many of the cast double their parts as a wartime measure. All this detail has been well thought out and ingeniously woven into the pattern. Such a *Macbeth* could never fail for lack of pains.

Nor would any members of the company pay much heed to the old tradition that this is an unlucky play — the old actor's way of saying that it has been the grave of many reputations. Gielgud is far from being an old actor in years or anything else, and he has broken fresh ground enough in our time to smile at the ancient mutterings of Drury Lane and its insalubrious alleys. His authority springs from years of the Old Vic and his place is down West in Shaftesbury Avenue. After his Hamlet and Lear, his Macbeth was any way inevitable. In a true career there are certain stiff fences every actor must face, and this is the biggest of them.

Take the physical nature of Macbeth to begin with — the man and not simply the monster. His entire presence is implicit in the spectator's conception of him;

there is next to nothing of the explicit humanity that makes Othello, for instance, easier to understand and to play. (Think of Iago's suspicions of Othello and Emilia, and all that they do to complete the character of the Moor.) Nor is there much of the self-analysis or self-pity that brings Hamlet continually close to the listener as if they were talking man to man. There is not the pathos of Lear or the passion of Romeo. The private life of the Macbeths, up to the beginning of their joint career of murder, arouses no speculations whatsoever; it was presumably as dull as a Scottish Sabbath. We are asked to believe of them that they are suddenly consumed by an awful lust for power; and we believe it, but only by a convention like that of the Greek drama.

Faced with this unusual introduction of Attic concepts of guilt into the framework of Scottish historical tragedy — unusual because Shakespeare is a man of the Renaissance and has very little to do with such notions in general — we find it convenient to apply our own *kothornos* to the Macbeths and to raise their physical stature in our own imagination as the Greek player raised his stature on the stage. Such a proceeding is in the highest degree illogical, but it has a kind of dramatic necessity. It is true that Zoffany paints one of his greatest theatrical pictures of Garrick and Mrs. Pritchard in *Macbeth*, and shows the actress towering a full head and shoulders over the tragedian with his very modest inches. But we do not know just how good a performance that of Garrick and Pritchard was, though it was much praised by their contemporaries. Nor do we know how much better it could have been if both had towered physically instead of only one of them. Other things being equal, we are right to prefer the Macbeths to be figures rather larger than life-size. It is also a help if we can see in our imaginative background that gloomy Cawdor bedchamber with the four-poster bed in which they beget their progeny of crimes; for Lady Macbeth, 'Unsex me here' has no dread significance unless she first be well-sexed.

Gielgud's Macbeth is not only nobly but tremendously spoken; it would be hard to name another living actor in any country with a finer, swifter understanding of what he has to say. I think he takes most of the passages from the apparition of Banquo to the death of his lady too fast, and the speech of 'all our yesterdays' too slowly; but there is thought in all he does and no doubt in this as well. Everything that authority can do to give flesh and grandeur to Macbeth is done; yet the ultimate vitality is not there. This is a figure who would pass better in the mask and the high shoe of Attic tragedy than on our modern proscenium stage. He would pass better, perhaps, on the Elizabethan stage with its simple hangings and its apron for the player's rhetorical appeal. It seems to me certain that the visual background and the 'atmosphere' of the tragedy, well realized as they are, only augment the unreality of this Macbeth's relation to them. He lives in the dramatic poetry well enough, but scarcely on the heath or in the castle courtyard or at the banquet. The more substantial these facts, the less substantial is the incorporation of the Thane.

And nothing, surely, but some understanding of this could have prompted him to choose Gwen Ffrangcon-Davies for his Lady Macbeth. The choice looks like a deliberate piece of protective coloring or compensation or what you will by way of distraction and contrast. This actress can both move and speak with grace, and nobody will blame her for being slightly shorter than David Garrick himself. But she, far more than her Macbeth, lacks the vitality of the character. She is beautifully dressed and moves beautifully with the exception of some abrupt gestures ending in outstretched and insignificant fingers; but grace is never the thing that is needed. She carries not the most elementary conviction, but flutters through the tragedy with the best of will and intelligence, as far as these things will serve.

It was not even necessary to cast an Edith Evans for Lady Macbeth; a dozen young and more or less unknown actresses could have made an effective showing opposite Gielgud and could have helped his own performance immeasurably. In the matter of physical lightness for the task, one and one do not cancel out but simply double themselves, much more than doubling the toil and trouble of the spectator. Nor is it necessary for either reviewers or actresses to go about saying, on the score of such a production, that Lady Macbeth is unplayable. She is not at all unplayable, save that Shakespeare has set the player a hard problem in bringing this tragedy so much nearer the neo-classic than any other of his work. It is hard to succeed in the part — and even harder to fail.

Gielgud as director shares credit for the grand Macduff (Francis Lister) and most likeable Banquo (Leon Quartermaine) who between them sustain the tragedy at full height. Young players like Alan Badel come into the picture too, promising a future Romeo or Hamlet. Ernest Thesiger leads the Weird Sisters, and what might have seemed an affectation becomes a satisfying achievement. The Porter is an affectation that does not succeed; it is easy to catch the spectator's fancy with the caperings of such a figure, and hard to repair the damage he does to a grim scene. Nobody yet knows if this *Macbeth* will run three months or twelve; but it deserves full record as an accomplishment of our stage in the third war year. And the Old Vic company, which is just coming into town with *Othello* and *The Merchant of Venice*, should take up the challenge and establish somewhere its London home of Shakespeare again.

21 John Gielgud: Actor

Alan Dent

February 1947

Gielgud had been busy during the Second World War touring for ENSA and staging a repertory season in London, playing Oberon in *Dream*, the Duke in *The Duchess of Malfi*, Valentine in *Love for Love* and Arnold in *The Circle*. A tour to Burma was followed by his Raskolnikoff in Rodney Ackland's adaptation of *Crime and Punishment* (1946), which he would revive in New York the following year. By this time, his pre-eminence was being challenged by Laurence Olivier and Ralph Richardson, and his thralldom to the powerful theatrical management of "Binkie" Beaumount meant that his talent was soon to be squandered on trivial projects.

Alan Dent (1905–78) had been encouraged to go into dramatic criticism by James Agate. Although he rose to be London critic for the *Manchester Guardian* (1935–43) and the *News Chronicle* (1945–60), he was deeply disappointed not to be named critic of the *Sunday Times* at Agate's demise in 1947. His critical credo was "to be just and nothing but just". A good friend of the Oliviers, he served as "screenwriter" (that is, script editor) on Olivier's films of *Henry V, Hamlet* and *Richard III*; but he detested *A Streetcar Named Desire* and deplored Vivien Leigh's participation in it.

LIKE THE rest of the handful of first-raters since Roscius was an actor in Rome, John Gielgud is liberally endowed with faults. Kemble was cold, and Macready was pompous, and Irving dragged one foot and croaked like a bull-frog — so they tell us. We can see for ourselves, now and without having to be told, that Gielgud's physique seriously limits his range and choice among the great acting parts. He cannot, for example, walk across the stage without suggesting that his knees are tied together with a silken scarf. This is a crying fault, of course, but it cannot be mended now. Kemble could not warm himself up. Macready could not condescend. Gielgud cannot walk. There it is.

He also has to contend — and usually, it must be said, contends successfully — with a natural hauteur of being. This has wittily but not unjustly been likened to William Hazlitt's description of Kemble — the abstracted air of a man just about to sneeze. It expresses itself in a certain aloof poise of the head, a certain diffidence in the glance from the half-closed eyes and in the general bearing a certain fastidium (if one may coin a word to denote something not quite fastidiousness), something between the hoity-toity and a plain distaste for things common, mean or blatant.

Vocally, too, it must be said that he always could on occasion, and still can on occasion, lose control and lapse in excited passages into hysterical whining or petulant shrieks. But this happens less and less often as his career goes on, and it should be said at once that this is the rare defect of his most valuable quality. That attribute, his speaking voice, is supreme in our time for lyrical flexibility. It has made him, and it keeps him, incomparable as a lyrical actor. It is an inheritance. Gielgud's maternal grandmother was Kate Terry who retired young but whose Juliet I have heard praised — by very old playgoers with very long memories — above any of her younger sister Ellen's performances. The Terry voice is something unique in timbre — warm, tender, glowing, expressive.

Gielgud has a higher share of this peculiar vocal beauty than any of the family since Ellen's prime. Over the past twenty years I have been won to and moved by his various performances through the sheer exquisiteness of his verbal delivery. Thus I said of his Mercutio: 'With this actor's delivery of the Queen Mab lines they become a scherzo, the words fluttering from Mercutio's brain as lightly as the elfin vision that they drew. Even the death-scene, following hard upon, and made the more poignant by the vitality with which this Mercutio had been sketched, was hardly more moving than the famous speech.' Dealing with his Romeo I see that I pounce on another of his shortcomings in those days (he has much improved since, in this respect) — his inability to pay court, to make stage-love: 'This new Romeo is more the worn young philosopher wondering about himself than the sultry young lover wondering about his Juliet. He seems, in fact, not particularly in love with that young lady; but he is particularly in love with love itself and with the poet's unexampled expression of it.'

Dealing, on the other hand, with his Richard II — one of the minor-key roles in Shakespeare in which he continues to be matchlessly fine — I said: 'Mr. Gielgud's face, growing more and more haggard with his eager woe, his voice ranging from a moving whisper to the keenest pitch of the King's unavailing imperiousness, and most of all his hands, modeling the lines as they were delivered and in themselves poetical, suave, regal — these attributes make the character a shining monument to human sorrow. The actor rightly luxuriated in Richard's griefs, and obliged us to luxuriate along with him.'

It is in these introspectives — with Hamlet at the head of them — that this actor has always been at his best. Of his 1939 Hamlet I said: 'Mr. Gielgud's interpretation of the Dane has now passed from faulty exquisiteness to something nearly perfect in its way. There is now a logic in his anger and a wildness in his calm. There used to be in this Hamlet something lackadaisical and weak here and there. Now, from the beginning to the late end, we can sit back and heed the fine artist over and over again excelling in his own delivery, in his own *phrasing* in the musician's sense of the term. Or we sit forward to observe the new excitements he has added — the unhesitant handling of this uncut Hamlet's morbidity, for example.'

In two Old Vic revivals of *The Tempest* he gave Prospero a towering eloquence which made that obstreperous old bore wholly tolerable for once — I mean, for twice! In *Macbeth* he put up a performance of the most taut and tingling sensibility — a performance marred only by the fault that we just could not believe that this Thane was the murderer of that King Duncan. The great virtue of his Raskolnikoff in Dostoievsky's *Crime and Punishment* — another introspective who commits murder — is that he plays cogently and piercingly and expressively enough to make us believe that he really has committed his crime this time, and committed it unfalteringly, with an axe. This is a hauntingly poetical performance delivered in the plainest of prose. He may be saying something as bald as 'Don't thank me, Sonia — we are the same, you and I!' to the poor girl next door who has been driven by poverty to prostitution. But he delivers every nuance of this prose part with the vocal beauty and with the imaginative intensity that he usually keeps for Shakespeare. He does so because he has the intelligence to realize that the great Russian is near-Shakespearean in his soarings and plumbings into the metaphysics of humanity.

Gielgud's last presentation of King Lear, in a production directed by Granville-Barker himself, had several marvelous moments which have not been obliterated from memory even by Laurence Olivier's triumphant exposition of that supreme part the other day. Must any decision be come to as to which is the better of our two best tragedians? Is comparison necessary, and not merely what Dogberry would call 'odorous'? Does one ask a traveler in Italy whether he prefers Florence to Venice? Both have their glories — that is all.

One thing must be said if any comparison must be instituted. It is that Olivier is obviously and by nature better suited to the heroic parts, the extroverts, than is Gielgud, who very rightly and shrewdly leaves the King Hals and the Richard Crookbacks well alone. Outside Shakespeare the ways of these two major actors lie far apart. Possessing remarkable style and elegance in costume, Gielgud has several times excelled himself in the English comedy of manners between Congreve and Wilde. Of his Joseph Surface in *The School for Scandal* I wrote: 'It is to his credit in the part that he does not at all remind us of his suffering Shakespearean kings and princes. He is specious and not at all villainous, having mastered the vitally necessary *plausibility* of the role. He clothes the character in a grey-and-white silken hypocrisy, and with each sentiment he is far more in and of the period than any other character in the production!'

Wilde in his best and lightest comedy is in the direct line of descent from Congreve and Sheridan, and *The Importance of Being Earnest* would certainly be included in almost any critic's list of the six best artificial comedies in the English language. Gielgud's Jack Worthing, the last time I saw it, had attained a cool and easy perfection. Building up this role in several revivals he has gradually succeeded in making a comic virtue of that natural hauteur which I began by instancing as one of his handicaps. His icy gravity as Jack, mocking but never consciously mocking, proud but without the petulance into which this actor can too easily fall, witty but with no self-approbatory knowledge of the fact, is now as dead-perfect as his late-Victorian man-about-town deportment.

And finally, going back to Congreve and his *Love for Love* — a Restoration play in quite the highest tradition of old English comedy — we have Valentine, the comic-romantic lover who feigns madness to achieve his purpose. It is said to have been the great tragedian Betterton's first part in comedy. Gielgud has to be seen to be believed in it. The famous mad scene in this play oddly evokes memories of all the best things he has done in the far-removed world of Shakespearean tragedy. Among its many astonishing suggestions is an astonishing suggestion of Romeo defying the stars in his half-insane pet against circumstance in general. This immensely witty and engaging performance is indeed a compound of all the crackbrains, set out with the most delicate sense of burlesque. Here, repeatedly, is Hamlet mad as the wind, but with none of the Dane's slight but admitted bias towards the west; Valentine is mad due north, and hawks and handsaws or heron-shaws are all one to him. Here is a hint of Macbeth's frenzy at Banquo's unexpected return from his gory ditch, and here is even a suggestion of King Lear storming at the storm. Here, too, are all the lunatics of Renaissance tragedy rolled together and dished up for sheer fun.

It is a startling performance — one to startle those who only know their Congreve on paper. Valentine in the study seems only a rather puzzling and inconsequent part. But given a delivery so varied, so choicely phrased, so con-summately elegant in mood, speech and gesture, and so deliciously fantasticated in the mad scene, the part is revealed as a superb one — certainly one of Gielgud's best. Let those who imagine any over-stating partisanship here go and view this production of this rich, bawdy, heavenly comedy. And then let them note particularly the crown of this Valentine's performance, the lovely, low-toned sin-cerity of one of the last of his speeches to the melting Angelica: 'I have been disappointed of my only hope; and he that loses hope may part with anything. I never valued fortune, but as it was subservient to my pleasure; and my only pleasure was to please this lady: I have made many vain attempts, and find at last that nothing but my ruin can effect it; which for that reason, I will sign — Give me the paper.'

This doubtless reads quite frigidly. Spoken as it is spoken by John Gielgud it becomes the testament — warm, tender, glowing, expressive (like the Terry voice) — of a heart filled with the purest and most disinterested kind of human devo-tion. But perhaps I grow laudatory! Why not, after all? Can one, quite seriously, withhold paeans of praise from an actor who throughout a career of the greatest distinction — and he is still only in his earliest forties — has displayed the purest and most disinterested kind of devotion to the highest order of stage plays, stage direction and stage playing? We think of his early Old Vic seasons, from 1929 to 1931, when he made his name in classical tragedy and comedy. Of his bringing Shakespeare to the West End of London and reinstating him there apparently for good. Of his encouragement of new playwrights — Gordon Daviot, Ronald Mackenzie, Rodney Ackland, John Perry, Eric Linklater. Of the exquisite and unforgettable revivals of Chekhov plays he appeared in and associated himself with — *The Seagull* (directed by Komisarjevsky) and *The Three Sisters* (by Michel Saint-Denis). Of his exciting evolution as an actor, of his high integrity as director and manager, of his unquestioned taste and artistry — even in some few blunders which were honorable blunders. All in all, is it possible to mention any man alive who has done more to raise and sustain the artistic standard of the English theatre? As a final well-merited paean we may repeat of Gielgud what Andrew Marvell said in his Horatian Ode: 'He nothing common did or mean upon that memorable scene.'

22 The actor as biographer: Wilfrid Lawson

Rosamond Gilder

December 1937

Wilfrid Lawson (1900–66) had had an extensive but checkered career on the English stage before he rose to stardom in J. B. Priestley's *I Have Been Here Before* (1937). He had been hailed for his John Brown in Ronald Gow's *Gallows Glorious* (1933) but damned for his Mark Antony in an Old Vic Production of *Antony and Cleopatra* (1934). He continued as a highly respected character actor to the end of his life, despite his legendary drinking bouts and his unmistakable gravelly voice.

Rosamond Gilder (1891–1986), daughter of the crusading journalist Richard Watson Gilder, began writing for *Theatre Arts* in the 1920s and became its editor from 1945 to 1948. Her first article had been a survey of dramatic theory from Aristotle to the nineteenth century. She ran the Federal Theatre's Bureau of Research and Publication (1935) and by this time had published her pioneering books *Enter the Actress* (1931) and *John Gielgud's Hamlet: A Record of Performance* (1937).

———————

When the Broadway show-shop and its companion on Shaftesbury Avenue turn International Portrait Gallery, as they have during the last few seasons, the actor is presented with a new facet of his many-sided problem. Wagner and Napoleon, Benedict Arnold and Keats, Richard II and Crown Prince Rudolph, Queen Victoria and Franz Joseph, appeared on Broadway last year in their habits as they lived. To these, Shaftesbury Avenue has this year already added King James I, and promises more historical portraits.

What happens when the actor is not at liberty to create out of the playwright's script a new and un-patterned being? Is it easier or more difficult to give authentic life to a character about which so much is known or imagined as Napoleon, Lincoln, Disraeli, Chatterton, than it is to built from the playwright's words the complete physical embodiment of a new personality? Does the creation of an historical character come from within by a process of assimilation, or from without by a process of imitation? How does the actor adapt his own known characteristics, his gesture, movement, voice, to a model already known to the audience? What approach is necessary when the actor must permit a personage already existing both in outward form and inward life to take possession of him; when, in other words, the part may be supposed to attack the actor, rather than the actor the part?

No one could answer these questions better than an actor who created so subtle and exact a portrait of Wagner that many people objected to its too revealing truthfulness; and who recently presented in London a James I 'with such terrific gusto,' one critic said, 'that you cannot resist the sheer impact of his acting.' Another said, 'Mr. Lawson fills the portrait with so much and such odious vitality, such fullness of voice and such rich theatrical bravura that it gives the play an enormous lift whenever he takes the stage;' and a third, 'everything is there — the sly intelligence, the timidity, the degrading pleasures, the underlying force of character and touch of majesty.' By one of those quick changes in fortune which come in the theatre, Lawson is now playing a very different part, 'a hag-ridden, whisky-sodden, suicidal business man', in J. B. Priestley's play that has stirred London, *I Have Been Here Before*, a performance which makes Ivor Brown call him 'the most exciting actor on the stage today; his performance in this piece jumps sheer up from the stage and gets you by the throat.' And even Mr. James Agate grows lyric enough to ask, 'Is this a great actor? Let me shelve the difficulty by boldly stating that he is a grand one, whose present performance is something to dream about.'

Wilfrid Lawson's long registry of roles includes many historical portraits. He knows whereof he speaks, when, with a malicious glint in his eye, he insists, of a true portrait in the theatre, that 'it's chiefly accident'.

'I hate the word technique,' he says — and, he might have added, all high-sounding, vague terms. 'The actor is not a creator anyway. He just uses a little of this and a little of that — things he sees around him. Like the lawyer in *Libel!* I never put my hands in my pocket myself but I saw a friend of mine, a barrister, do it, so Foxley does it. It seems natural for him to do it. With Wagner it's the same thing. After you've spent two hours day by day making up — it takes about two hours — looking at yourself, as you add each detail seeing yourself becoming more and more like Wagner, the part overwhelms you. I would begin to shrink in on myself as I worked — I lost about thirty pounds on that part — my neck, shoulders, elbows, knees, as well as my face, acquired Wagner's shape. By the time that had happened and I was ready to go on, it would have been hard *not* to feel like him. I am the character while I'm on the stage and I let him do the acting. It's much easier not to think of every movement to make, but simply to let them come. There's nothing to it!'

Nothing, Mr. Lawson calls it! Only weeks, months, of intensive study of every-thing written about Wagner, James the First, John Brown and the rest. A search for every detail of outward appearance — pictures, busts, masks, descriptions, inferences, parallels — a thorough immersion in the history, psychology, personal-ity of the character as the record of his life shows him. Sometimes the records which he has to go on are rich, sometimes they are inadequate.

'One great difficulty in a biographical play', Mr. Lawson adds, thoughtfully, 'is that both the author and the actor are apt to imagine that the audience knows as much about the character as they do themselves after they have spent months of hard work finding out about him.'

Fortified with long study, the actor emerges triumphantly with as exact a physical and mental portrait of, let us say, Wagner at the age of forty-five as he can achieve, but alas, that is not the noble, grey lion of the later portraits, nor the abstraction of genius which the name alone evokes. The actor of a biographical role is faced with a *fait accompli*. No matter in what period of life, in what circumstances, in what psychological or practical predicament the character of the play may be, on the broader stage of life his role is already fixed as hero or heroic villain. His reality is lost in his legend. The actor who evokes that lost reality from oblivion will be accused of inaccurate portraiture. 'We get an idea that it is important to present the truth about a character. I probably made this mistake with Wagner. I thought that since he was that kind of man — since he had those imperfections, meannesses — I should play him that way, and not as a straight hero. But it won't do.

'It seems to me that the actor is always wrong if he doesn't put over a part. If you don't convince, overwhelm your audience — carry them with you in your interpretation and presentation of an historical character — then *you* are wrong, not they, no matter how correct, photographically, psychologically, historically, you may be.' Biographical acting, far more than biography, must have in it both reality and the illusion of reality, both truth and its appearance.

The actor-biographer, Mr. Lawson could have added, has not only the historical and the legendary models for his portrait, but also the playwright's creation. And often the playwright's character differs from the other two. What you do, in that case, especially if the created man does not ring true is a problem that Mr. Lawson dismisses with a grin. 'You don't do the play at all if you think the playwright is wrong in his presentation of the character. What's the use in bothering?'

Obviously there are many plays that are worth bothering about, for four hundred roles in the last twenty years is the record of Mr. Lawson's devotion to a career that is more than perfunctory, and of an achievement more than accidental. It is difficult to find a role he hasn't played, including most of Shaw's leading men — Alfred Doolittle in *Pygmalion*, Mr. Gilbey in *Fanny's First Play*, Mangan in *Heartbreak House*, the Premier in *The Apple Cart*. Shaw, he avers, is fatal to actors — ruinous. 'He writes so well for the actor that no one can fail in those parts. Take Doolittle, for example. I did it pretty well myself, brought down the house both times I made an exit. I might have thought I was pretty good if I hadn't known that any amateur could do it. I directed the play myself that year for an amateur group and the fellow who did the part got just the same reception I did.'

Shaw's plays also include historical characters, as do Shakespeare's (if Mr. Shaw will permit us to bracket the Bard with him). Each of them has his peculiar angle for the biographical actor. Shaw tempts toward caricature; his two Premiers, for example, can, with the addition of a faint accent or a slightly exaggerated curl to a mustache, become a mocking commentary on a Ramsay MacDonald or a Lloyd George. 'It's a terrible temptation,' says Mr. Lawson. 'I often give way to it. One shouldn't do it on the stage, but it's such fun and the audience loves it.' Shaw's Joan and her companions, his Caesar and Cleopatra, are in varying degrees types of historical characters in which the author's reading of history can be interpreted by the actor directly from the text with little reference to historical originals.

In a sense, Shakespeare's historic figures are also more Shakespeare than history to us, and they have the added complication of theatre tradition, which drapes them in layers of garments acquired from the wardrobes of countless generations of actors. When a player returns cold-bloodedly to the text, reads it in relation to historical fact, and portrays, for instance, Mark Antony in *Antony and Cleopatra* as an aging libertine, paunchy with good living and beset with an instinct for theatrical effects (as the text and Antony's age at the time justify him in doing), then again the image of a 'hero' existing in the collective audience mind is cracked. 'It was a dismal failure,' so Mr. Lawson cheerfully records, 'but a good idea, nevertheless.'

Portraiture of Mr. Lawson's sort, scrupulously accurate in detail of make-up, costume, movement, pace and gesture, prohibits the exploitation of personality. If you are truly Caesar you cease to be Mr. Jones. 'Actors should never be known at all. You should forget the actor altogether and never know he is an actor. It should be Mark Antony through the medium of Lawson, not Lawson as Mark Antony. Of course you should have your own idea of the part but I don't think the actor should shine through. In fact, it might be better [perish the revolutionary thought!] not to have the actors' names on the playbills at all.' Names or no names, the giants of the old days tended to imprint their personality on every part they performed. Irving was always Irving; Bernhardt was Bernhardt, whether she played Frou-frou or the Unknown Soldier. Certainly these great ones served what Mr. Lawson insists is the theatre's only major function — to enthrall. 'Sometimes we forget that our mummers' business is to entertain.' And — although he did not say so — to be entertained.

There are a number of things, including acting in the movies, which Mr. Lawson finds not sufficiently diverting and therefore not worth bothering with. Since the director, more or less futile in the theatre ('You shouldn't have to direct an actor. Directors are a modern invention. Perhaps that's what's wrong in the theatre!'), is all-powerful — and often more inane — in the movies, Mr. Lawson gave up the whole idea after two attempts. He played something called *Ladies in Love* in a make-up which he achieved after much battling with the official make-up man. The success of his monocle and pointed beard and generally continental and sophisticated interpretation was so marked that when he was cast for his next picture, involving a totally different type of man — a munitions manufacturer and a hunter of big game in Africa — his director had but one idea for make-up, as the following note pinned to the wall of the dressing room indicates: 'INTER-OFFICE COMMUNICATION. Dear Ern: As per telephone conversation, Mr. Zanuck wants to play Wilfrid Lawson in exactly the same make-up he used in *Ladies in Love*, also using the monocle.'

Mr. Lawson pocketed this document and went into the jungle, monocle and all, but it was too much for his actor's integrity. In spite of the glittering rewards of such foolishness and a contract in hand, Mr. Lawson would have none of it.

The theatre and the actor's business in it makes a little more sense and from looking over Mr. Lawson's record and watching him in the theatre, one might be inclined to believe, over his protest, that technique — or, out of deference to an expressed prejudice, craftsmanship — as well as natural endowments, has something to do with success.

23 Gertrude Lawrence

Theodore Strauss

May 1942

Gertrude Lawrence (1898–1952) enjoyed a reputation as one of the great comic talents of the Anglo-American stage, a true "nymph errant". She had toured England from childhood as a singer and dancer, and first appeared in an André Charlot revue as understudy to Beatrice Lillie. She came to New York in *Charlot's Revue of 1924*, which featured her singing "Limehouse Blues." This was followed by the lead role in the musical *Oh, Kay!* (1926). Lawrence was best partnered in brittle repartee with Noël Coward in *Private Lives* (the role of Amanda was written for her) and *Tonight at 8:30* (1935). New York also saw her in *Susan and God* (1937). Her musical-comedy skills took on a darker tinge in Kurt Weill's *Lady in the Dark* (1941). Despite a less than sterling singing voice, her last role was as the Welsh governess Anna Leonowens in *The King and I* (1951), which she toured widely; the strain may have contributed to her early death.

In the early 1940s Theodore Strauss wrote film reviews for the New York *Times* and celebrity profiles for *Collier's*, before he established himself with the novel *Moonrise* (1946). After it was made into a film in 1948, he turned to screenwriting and narrating documentaries whose subjects ranged from the Nazis to Jacques Cousteau to Marilyn Monroe.

IT HAS been reported in occasionally reliable quarters that drama critics, like Ulysses on the fateful passage, have asked to be lashed to their aisle seats at the opening of a Gertrude Lawrence play. Like a man downing a double hooker of brandy to steel his nerves, they are apt to repeat slowly several times: '. . . after all, you couldn't say she's beautiful. Her features aren't at all classic, and Venus de Milo or Ginger Rogers has a more nearly perfect figure' — and so on. Alas, their mumbo jumbo preparation comes to nothing. The curtain rises and when it finally comes down, their critical credos have gone, leaf by leaf, with the wind, their resistance quietly and surely sapped. Afterward they reach not for the thesaurus but for Palgrave's *Golden Treasury* to find suitable refrains. Years ago, after Miss Lawrence's American debut in the first Charlot revue, the late Percy Hammond wrote that her 'conquest of last night's audience was the most definite thing of its kind I have ever seen. . . . Every man in town is, or will be, in love with her.' Just last season, in no less of a dream, Brooks Atkinson murmured: 'She's a goddess, that's all.'

In the clear cold light of day, no doubt these gentlemen have felt a trifle foolish, their memory a little fuzzy as to exactly what happened. But there, in irremediable print, is their paean of praise, and, gently closing their eyes, they may go back to the previous evening, trying to reconstruct the circumstances of their fall. Is it the completely infectious frivolity of movement, or the changeling and unpredictable moods that make each moment a surprise, or is it the voice, musical, varied and full, clinging to words like Salome clinging to the last of the seven veils? What makes Jenny's naughty personal history so delightful but the vixenish coyness of a lady withholding secrets and then, in a sudden fling, revealing all? Are these the compound of Miss Lawrence's sophisticated stage magic — or is it something more, hidden behind a brilliant and knowing technique? Whatever the secret of her sorcery, it is well-nigh unique. Among the women of the theatre she is perhaps the most volatile, the most versatile. And in Moss Hart's *Lady in the Dark*, as the heroine bothered by tantrums she can't explain, Miss Lawrence these evenings is giving a performance that probably she alone could give.

The legend of glamour follows her away from the footlights; if this were antebellum Vienna, Miss Lawrence no doubt would arrive at the stage door in a carriage drawn by panting youths. Her comings and goings are chronicled in sundry collections of social chaff. When once she went back to England minus stockings, the editors of *Vogue* and *Harper's Bazaar* suffered a sharp intake of breath, but quickly inferred that after all anything Miss Lawrence did was *ipso facto* fashionable. Broadway's backstage has fed the legend with stories, sometimes edged with malice, of Miss Lawrence's coloratura temperament. Out of it all has emerged a portrait of a lady enveloped in folderol and clothes by Molyneux or Carnegie; of a lady born to be served indulgently; of a lady impossibly fascinating but nonetheless a little feckless, a little irresponsible.

No doubt, Miss Lawrence is aware of it. She knows that she is an actress and that for an actress 'the curtain is always up'. But she has proved that glamour can also serve; she has been shrewd enough to use it as a means of luring the spotlight of the press to a hundred causes. Today, with or without the spotlight, she is engaged to the last free minute in soldiers' benefits and war aid. During her summers on Cape Cod, her zeal and hard work have stirred the inhabitants into providing several canteens and thousands of knitted garments for the fighting fronts; even now she is industriously studying advanced first aid so that she in turn will be able to teach it.

In New York, in addition to the exhausting requirements of her role in *Lady in the Dark*, she is one of the most aggressive leaders of the American Theatre Wing, she prepares regular recorded programs for rebroadcast to armed forces all over the world, and appears in an endless series of benefits. Although she rises early 'out of sheer curiosity, I suppose', there are other reasons. On one recent matinee day Miss Lawrence attended a Theatre Wing council meeting, sold defense stamps in the box-office, was photographed for a newspaper rotogravure section, chatted with convalescent soldiers after a performance and worked for three hours after midnight at NBC studios recording her *Broadway Calling* program for distribution in the war zones. It is Miss Lawrence's response to war-time demands; it is also her answer to the portrait of the giddy prima donna.

'I believe I have always been a very responsible person,' Miss Lawrence said rather passionately in her dressing room after an evening performance. 'I was trained to it. I came of modest little showfolk where each one had to pull his weight in the boat. I can cook, sew and scrub — things you learn of necessity and never forget. After all, you have to remember that most actresses had to work very hard for a living before they became successful.'

It was hard to remember as Miss Lawrence, wearing a wine-red dressing gown, curled up in an easy chair. She spoke with the quick excitement of a woman who has just returned to the stage for half-a-dozen curtain calls. She had come off singing and now the exhilaration of the performance was still there in the luminous eyes, made to seem much larger by the high arching brows. Her chuckle was rich and spontaneous, warming as a fine cordial. Though she seemed relaxed in the chair, the eyes, the restless inflection of her voice, the animated hands were a contradiction. Miss Lawrence's energies are highly inflammable. The sorceress onstage is still the sorceress.

But even sorcery, it seems, must be partly learned. The World's Inamorata was once, temporarily, a barmaid; the lady who now hums Kurt Weill's haunting tunes once warbled 'A little bit of ribbon, a little bit of lace, a little bit of silk that clings . . .' in an English provincial music hall; the consummate actress of *Lady in the Dark* or the earlier series of one-act Noel Coward plays presented in *Tonight at 8:30* today admits that 'I was once the comedienne of comediennes. I had discovered that I could get a laugh by a shrug of my shoulders, a roll of the eyes, or a play of the voice. Then someone said, "What are you doing up there? The audience is laughing at you, not with you." ' The Gertrude Lawrence, whose name on a marquee today is usually sufficient to turn even a poor play into a hit, once had to take any job she could find.

Her education was Hogarthian. Her father was a traveling song-and-dance minstrel possessed of a basso profundo that miraculously increased in richness and depth after a few beers; her mother played Britannia in the tableaux. At two, little Gertie was toddling up and down the aisles of English music halls crying 'croprams! croprams!' — by which of course she meant programs and of which she sold a great many. Not long thereafter she had already paid for the printing of a large number of personal cards which bore the simple legend: 'Little Gertie Lawrence. Child Actress and Danseuse.' She handed these about to agents and managers and hoped for the best. Meanwhile, she managed to see all the shows in the towns through which they passed by the simple device of taking calling cards from her mother's purse and scrawling upon them: 'Please give my daughter two seats for this afternoon's performance.'

Of formal schooling she had very little; born in a family of strolling players, she learned arithmetic and geography in fits and starts. To the deep envy of her classmates, she never appeared in the schoolroom on matinee days. But meanwhile she was learning other things — long before she was out of her childhood she had done blackface, clog and tap dancing, ballet and singing. At ten she played in her first Christmas pantomime, *Babes in the Wood*, as one of the urchin sparrows that blanketed the lost babes with forest leaves. A little later she appeared briefly in the Max Reinhardt-Morris Gest production of *The Miracle* at the Olympia and after that she went to Italia Conti's studio to learn posture and elocution. Here she first met the gangling Noel Coward who later recorded that Miss Lawrence 'told me a few mildly dirty stories and gave me an apple and I have loved her very dearly ever after'. Though Miss Lawrence's memory is not quite so exact, she does remember that she did not see him again until years later, after each had won separate successes, when they tightly clutched hands in the wings and listened to the deafening applause for their co-starring performance in Coward's *London Calling*.

At fourteen, she struck out for herself. For seven long years she toured the provinces in vaudeville or dire little 'fit-up' shows such as *Miss Lamb of Canterbury* or *Miss Plaster of Paris*, most of which were rather tattered hand-me-down copies of London musicals. Her chores were various. She would sing, or act, or dance. In the earliest show she can remember, she sang a naughty little ditty, 'Whom were you with last night?' and, after the first stanza, produced a mirror to reflect the beam of the spotlight on embarrassed countrymen in the auditorium. Once, when an erratic manager had absconded with the box-office take, leaving his company stranded, Miss Lawrence drew ale behind the bar and swept the sawdust-covered floor of the Red Lion Inn at Shrewsbury until another traveling company stopped in the town and required some local talent. Informed of a 'little nifty at the Red Lion who used to act a bit', the company manager immediately brought Miss Lawrence onstage in a nun's habit to sing 'The Rosary' between the acts. After her stint, she returned to the Red Lion and thus gained an early and considerable local reputation for versatility. 'It was awfully good for trade,' Miss Lawrence recalls with a chuckle.

Ultimately, Miss Lawrence was seen in *The Little Michus* by Lee White and Clay Smith, a pair of agents for Charlot, and not long thereafter she was called to London for audition. Charlot at once hired her as the featured dancer in *Some* and subsequently gave her the leading role when the show went on tour. In 1917 she understudied, and sooner or later appeared in, all the leading roles in *Cheep*, and a year later she sprang into the starring role of *Tabs* when Bea Lillie was thrown by a horse and suffered serious injuries. From that time onward, Gertrude Lawrence had an assured place in the firmament of musical comedy and revue stars in England. As furiously energetic then as now, she appeared in night clubs after performances in a West End musical and if a season lagged, she set out with the first touring show that came along.

Miss Lawrence first discovered America and vice versa when with Bea Lillie and Jack Buchanan she arrived in New York in 1924 with the first of the Charlot revues. Though all three were then immensely popular in England, they were not at all certain what their welcome would be in this land of politicians and Indians. Out of sheer home-sickness and misery Miss Lawrence and Miss Lillie sat on their assembled luggage at the pier and wept. But a few nights later the revue began its run of a year and after that Miss Lawrence stopped being sad. Although Bea Lillie won most of the adjectives in that show, Miss Lawrence's way with 'Limehouse Blues' was never quite forgotten by any who heard it.

Thereafter, she moved rather briskly to and fro across the Atlantic, first in Charlot's next revue and subsequently in *Oh, Kay*. In 1928 she made her first attempt at a straight dramatic role in *Icebound* for a London Sunday-night society. Then came *Treasure Girl*, *Candle-light*, another drama, and *The International Revue*. In 1930 she frolicked through Coward's *Private Lives* to prove once and for all that her talents weren't confined to the musical stage, and with the wide gamut of the one-acters of *Tonight at 8:30* she showed that she had high talents as a serious actress as well. Next Miss Lawrence swept gaily through *Susan and God* and *Skylark*; and now in the fabulous *Lady in the Dark* she has finally made use of all that she knows, moving from the pathos of Liza's retreat to her childhood to the lowdown shenanigans of Jenny's saga — all with unerring authority.

She knows quite a great deal, partly instinctive, partly conscious. Today, after an experience that has overlooked hardly a nook or cranny of show business and the theatre, Miss Lawrence says 'I can sense the temper of an audience just as Raffles at a safe is guided by his fingertips. Even before the curtain goes up, I know the mood of the people out front by the noise of the programs and the talk and bustle they make.' That is an intangible knowledge, not at all like multiplying 2 by 2. But there are tricks to be used knowingly when need be. The wag at a recent comedy who watched Miss Lawrence's restless performance and later asked, 'Who did your choreography?', was unconsciously criticizing the play rather than the star. Miss Lawrence is no tyro. She has the craft to conceal the shortcomings of a poor play under the sequin-like glitter of her own personality.

'Being a person in the theatre after many years', said Miss Lawrence, 'is like slowly building up a terrific sort of general store in which you know your wares from top to bottom. For a thin play you pull out all the tricks you can use. But a good play you cheapen and insult by using devices. The secret lies in not allowing yourself to fall in love with your own tricks and in knowing when the time has come to put them back on the shelves. Even audiences aren't always trustworthy. If they are too easy or too hard, they may trap you after you have responded by exaggeration or overplaying. Every play has a line and it is your job to follow it; like a melody, you may vary the tempo or the nuance slightly from moment to moment but never essentially. Otherwise it is simply Gertrude Lawrence or Minnie Smith on the stage — not the play.'

Outside the dressing room the house was silent. The curtain had gone down long ago and bit by bit Miss Lawrence's response to the stimulus of the perform-ance had subsided. With it the actress had slowly vanished and there remained only a relaxed and totally unaffected woman talking quite simply of her work. For a moment she drew a hand across her eyes in obvious fatigue, then added, as if summing up: 'If you have patience and intelligence to criticize yourself, you grow. When I was a young girl, I wanted to be a star some day but I didn't have much time for daydreaming. I had to earn a living. Managers would try me in roles, and some I kept and some I lost. But I myself was never in a position to refuse what was offered. And after a while I found that I was getting along bit by bit. Whatever I have learned in the theatre I have learned out of necessity — and a good thing it was, too.'

The interview was over. Miss Lawrence changed into a tailored suit and walked across the darkened stage, her high heels echoing sharply among the ghostly shapes of Harry Horner's settings. Outside, Sam, the chauffeur, was waiting to drive her home through the fogbound streets in which the lamps hung like expanded phosphorescent halos. 'It's much like London tonight,' Miss Lawrence began and fell silent. It was not difficult to guess what she was thinking. For when the blitz fell on London, Miss Lawrence set out to do her share. It was pleasant afterward to think of what a great deal she had done and to fit it into some sort of a pattern. Behind the artistry lay the long apprenticeship; beneath the giddy antic for publicity's sake was a spirit genuine; beneath the glamour the World's Inamorata had a heart.

24 The Oliviers

Sewell Stokes

December 1945

Americans first knew Laurence Olivier (1907–89) as a good-looking juvenile in comedies by Noël Coward (*Private Lives*, 1931) and S. N. Behrman (*No Time for Comedy*, 1939). By then he already had varied stage and film experience, first gaining notice as Captain Stanhope in *Journey's End* (1928), and winning plaudits as a promising, if not definitive, Romeo, Mercutio, Hamlet, Henry V, Macbeth and Iago. More athletic and dynamic than the usual English leading man, he was presented to the filmgoing public as a matinee idol in costume pictures, and his own film of *Henry V* was a stirring contribution to the war effort. After four years in the British airforce, he rejoined the Old Vic in 1944 and, with Ralph Richardson, ran a repertory, astounding spectators with his versatility, playing Oedipus Rex and Mr. Puff in *The Critic* on the same night (1945). He pulled off a similar feat with his Hotspur and Shallow in the *Henry IV* plays, shown to New York in 1946.

The first association of Olivier and Vivien Leigh (Vivien Mary Hartley, 1913–67) was in 1937 when she played Ophelia to his Hamlet at Elsinore Castle. Three years later, while Juliet to his Romeo in New York, she married him. She continued on the London stage, making a powerful impression as Blanche du Bois in *A Streetcar Named Desire* (1949), directed by Olivier (re-directed by Elia Kazan, the performance is recorded on film). They were seen as the ideal stage couple, but even at that time, her mind was coming unbalanced and the marriage grew increasingly fragile.

Sewell Stokes (1902–79) was a successful English playwright and screenwriter. Most of his plays were written with his brother Leslie, among them *Oscar Wilde* (1936, New York 1938), which launched the career of Robert Morley. From 1941 to 1945 he served as a probation officer at Bow Street Magistrates' court. A close friend of Isadora Duncan, late in life he co-wrote the film script for Ken Russell's BBC film of her life (1966), and also worked as script adviser on *Loneliness of the Long Distance Runner* (1962) and *Tom Jones* (1963).

IF PROOF were needed that solid fame has now come to Laurence Olivier and his wife Vivien Leigh, it is to be found in the surprisingly large number of people one comes across in the profession who constantly refer to them as Larry and Vivien: the same people who, actuated by a desire for reflected glory, refer always to John and Noel in the fond hope that by this familiar form of address they will lead you to imagine them on intimate terms with Gielgud and Coward. 'Larry was telling me only the other day . . .' 'What Vivien wants to do next . . .' Such phrases are heard all over London, because all over London these two stars and their work are at present being discussed.

For some years now the Oliviers have certainly been celebrities. He was considered an excellent actor who might have improved his position in the theatre had he not sold himself to the movies. She was adored by the film fans, and politely told by the critics when she appeared on the stage that she was lovely to look at. But after he had played *Richard III* in the Old Vic's repertory season last year, and early this year she (under her husband's direction) had given English audiences her version of Sabina in *The Skin of Our Teeth*, the general attitude toward them changed. Thereafter, Olivier was reckoned a very fine actor indeed; and of Miss Leigh it was said that now she not only looked lovely, but acted too.

For the record, Laurence Olivier rushed into the world — he could only have rushed, one feels — on May 22, 1907, just six years before Miss Leigh first saw the light of day in Darjeeling, India. He first appeared on the stage, after a course of training at Elsie Fogarty's dramatic school, at the Shakespeare Festival Theatre, Stratford-on-Avon, where in a special boys' performance he somewhat surprisingly played Katherine in *The Taming of the Shrew*. Shortly afterwards he was engaged by Sybil Thorndike to more or less walk on in her and Lewis Casson's production of *Henry VIII*, about the last play to be staged on an elaborate scale. However, Gielgud's production won the day, Olivier agreeing to go into it. Of the two performances, Gielgud wrote:

'Larry had a great advantage over me in his commanding vitality, striking looks, brilliant humor and passionate directness. In addition he was a fine fencer, and his breathtaking fight with Tybalt was a superb prelude to his death scene as Mercutio. As Romeo, his love scenes were instantly real and tender, and his tragic gift profoundly touching. . . . I had an advantage over him in my familiarity with the verse, and in the fact that the production was of my own devising, so that all the scenes were arranged just as I had imagined I could play them best.'

But to leave an American student of the English contemporary stage with the impression that most critics think as I do regarding the rivalry between Gielgud and Olivier, would not be honest; for while I am not alone in my belief that comparisons ought to be avoided, there are not a few others — staunch supporters of Gielgud until now — who declare him to have lost ground, if only temporarily. Among these is my brother, Leslie, who has written as follows:

'If we may believe the remembered early judgments of one of our more aged critics, there had been no great English actor since Irving. It is the early judgment which is in doubt, for we may check his current estimates of contemporary actors by a visit to the theatre, but we shall never know for certain whether some of the beauty of those performances witnessed so long ago did not lie in the young eyes of the beholder. The greatness of an actor cannot be measured exactly, like the speed of an athlete, but only by comparison with his rivals, as the skill of a boxer is measured against that of his opponent. We can, however, award the championship.

'The present champion of the English theatre is Laurence Olivier, who wrested the title from John Gielgud with his performance in *Richard III*, during the last Old

Vic season. Gielgud had held his position against all comers for about fifteen years, and it was his own skill which enabled him to do that, not merely the lack of it in his rivals, for he was challenged many times by Olivier himself. Gielgud had played Hamlet, Macbeth, Lear, Shylock, Richard II, Romeo, Mercutio, Joseph Surface, Vershinin, Trigorin and John Worthing.

'The skill by which Gielgud held the title for so long, and the faults and deficiencies which prevented Olivier's gaining it, may yet result in a great come-back for the Old Champ. Perhaps he was only a little out of training, or a little stale; perhaps Olivier was on his top form for that one bout only. It remains to be seen.

'What were those faults and deficiencies which prevented Olivier's gaining the title for so long? There was one all-important deficiency: he lacked poetry. And there was one basic fault: a kind of vulgarity which showed itself in over-emphasis. He was too loud, too agile, and too obvious where he was most original. We remember how he played Iago with one eye on the gallery and almost winked at the audience to underline his points.

'The deficiency has to a large extent been made up. The fault is still there — even in *Richard III*. We could say of his performance that "it should have a little more solidity, depth, sustained and impassioned feeling, with somewhat less brilliancy, with fewer glancing lights, pointed transitions and pantomimic evolutions." But those are the words which Hazlitt used to describe Edmund Kean's performance in the same play. And we could also say of Olivier, as Hazlitt said of Kean, that "he gives an animation, vigour and relief to the part, which we have never seen surpassed".'

In the future, the question may be asked countless times by those yet unborn — What of Olivier's *Hamlet*? And a reference to the opinion expressed by Mr Agate on January 5, 1937, after seeing the performance at the Old Vic, will reveal the following:

'. . . I detect in Mr. Olivier none of the vulgarity which Lewes (G. H. Lewes, the critic) found in Lemaitre. But I do observe a modern jaunty off-handedness which is presumably a legacy from parts of the Beau Geste order. I do not refer here to the one quality in which Mr. Olivier's Hamlet excels any Hamlet of recent years — its pulsating vitality and excitement. After Claudius has left at the end of the play scene this Hamlet acts literally all over the stage, his "why, let the stricken deer go weep" being accompanied by a tremendous leap from the perched-up throne on to the mimic stage below, and thence down to the footlights in an access of high hysteria. That is matter for the most compelling admiration. The jauntiness complained of occurs in the philosophical passages, which too often take on a note approaching pertness. This is due to, I will not say a fault, but a characteristic of Mr. Olivier's playing which prevents him from being Hamlet. . . . To sum up, this is obviously a performance carefully thought out, consonant with itself, and taken at admirable speed. On the other hand, it is not Hamlet, but a brilliant performance of the part such as Stanhope in *Journey's End* might have put up in some rest interval behind the lines.'

To return to Miss Leigh, whose first appearance on the stage was made in a now forgotten play at a tryout theatre on the fringe of London, during the same year in which her husband-to-be joined forces with Gielgud. *The Green Sash* was the title of the play. It never reached the West End; but Miss Leigh did, only three months later, when she made what at the time was called 'a sensational success' as Henriette Duquesnoy in *The Mask of Virtue*, a period comedy translated by Ashley Dukes from the original of Carl Sternheim. 'London's latest dramatic discovery' was a phrase used to describe Miss Leigh at this time; though the more discerning critics were in agreement that it was her youthful beauty, rather than any exceptional ability as an actress, that caused her to shine so brightly in the public's favour. Her stage career after this initial success was not astonishing, though she steadily gained in popularity as a film actress, and finally so much impressed David O. Selznick, that he decided she was an improvement on his choice of Paulette Goddard for the part of Scarlett in *Gone with the Wind*, and gave it her. Whether a film star need be an actress too, is a question outside the scope of this article; but it was undoubtedly the public's eagerness to see their film idol in the flesh that kept *The Doctor's Dilemma* running for a year in London, when Miss Leigh appeared in it on her return from Hollywood during the early days of the war. Which brings us to her recent performance as Sabina in Olivier's production of *The Skin of Our Teeth*. After this the majority of the critics were undivided in their belief that when Miss Leigh stepped on to the stage, she knew very well what she was about. She did, too.

Even to suggest what the Oliviers' future in the theatre might be is pointless unless one knows how frequently they intend to make films. Film and stage audiences are so entirely different, that what time and energy an actor devotes to one must of necessity be a loss to the other. Which is why, since screen stars with no dramatic talent whatever manage to persuade patrons that they have plenty, it is such a great pity that actors who have the real thing have not also a sufficiently strong love of the stage to enable them to turn their backs on the studios forever.

25 Sir Laurence and Larry

Alan Pryce-Jones

February 1961

Between 1945 and 1961 Olivier's reputation as the foremost actor on the English-speaking stage had been consolidated. With Vivien Leigh he had gone on tour as Mark Antony and Shaw's Caesar, and opened up a whole new vein of tragedy in Peter Brook's production of *Titus Andronicus* (1955). Scenting the change in the direction of British drama, he seized upon Archie Rice in Osborne's *The Entertainer* (1958) as his introduction to a younger generation. After a stint playing Becket and then Henry II (which he realized was the better part) in Anouilh's *Becket* in New York (1960–1), he was appointed first director of the Chichester Festival Theatre. Two years later he would fill the same function at the newly founded National Theatre.

Alan Pryce-Jones (1908–2000) was a distinguished man of letters, as novelist, travel writer, critic and, especially, editor. He became editor of the *Times Literary Supplement* in 1948 and remained there for 11 years, increasing its international scope. After he stepped down in 1959, he was theatre critic of *The Observer* for a year, while its regular man Kenneth Tynan was on leave, and then signed on as adviser to the Ford Foundation in New York. He settled in America permanently, with a regular column in *Theatre Arts* for a while, and, as a BBC radio commentator, interpreted American life for the British, as Alastair Cooke had done before him.

MOST of those who work in the theatre—whether as actors, producers, or directors—are very much of one piece. That is, each tries to develop a consistent personality, so that his hallmark is visibly present on anything he may do. Not so Olivier. He has divided himself, to begin with, into two pieces sharply contrasted—one being labeled Sir Laurence, and the other Larry. And within that framework he has encouraged a rare proliferation of talents to spread in whatever direction may serve his purpose of the moment.

Sir Laurence is the son of an Anglican clergyman. He is the young man of twenty-nine who James Agate, in 1936, prophesied would be "our next great actor." He is that actor knighted before middle age, a representative talent who followed close on the heels of John Gielgud as obvious leader of the British stage. Larry, on the other hand, is a different man altogether. He dines out; he delights his friends with salty and wide-ranging conversation; he runs a substantial country estate. Larry may even collide head on with Sir Laurence by half-suggesting that actors are too big for their boots. The play's the thing; the director must know how to use his resources so as to impose a pattern on actors who are unlikely to be clever enough to understand it for themselves. The whole matter of stagecraft, Larry might conclude, is to avoid the high seriousness of Sir Laurence. After all, gentlemen have to ride their profession on a light rein.

This double vision accounts for both the successes and the failures of a remarkable career, extending from Katherina in *The Taming of the Shrew* (he was in his teens at the time) to Becket. When all goes well, his merits are wonderfully balanced; to bring that about, a classic play is usually required. He is more likely to be remembered for his Oedipus of 1946 than for *The Sleeping Prince* of nearly a decade later, for his Coriolanus at Stratford-on-Avon in 1959 than for the splendidly handsome account he has given of Shakespearean heroes in the films that spread his popularity all over the world. Likewise, when things go wrong, it is on account of a passing astigmatism. There are certain complexities of the human spirit into which he cannot enter. His Hamlet, like his Macbeth, remained much the same on stage or screen over nearly twenty years, simply because Sir Laurence failed to look Larry in the eye—perhaps in fear of the small but unreassuring wink he was likely to find.

It is refreshing to watch an actor of such eminence so unwilling to sink into a rut. If the great classical roles come to him most easily, he is willing to expose himself to severe tests in such pieces as John Osborne's *The Entertainer*, or Ionesco's *Rhinoceros* in London last year. His performances in those plays alone give the lie to a remark he is on record as having made a year ago: "Personally, I loathe all abstract discussions about the theatre. They bore me." We may doubt if even Larry is really bored by anything that touches the theatre, and Sir Laurence must agree that, although the craft of the theatre is essentially concrete, some element of theory has to support logical practice.

Olivier is above all a realist. This is not, I think, because he rejects the possible sterility of too intellectual an approach to the stage, but because Larry maintains an obstinate sympathy for the human race even when Sir Laurence feels no more than businesslike about depicting it. He is an extremely subtle actor, therefore. Writing in 1946 of *Uncle Vanya*, Eric Bentley recorded that he would "never forget Astrov, as played by Olivier, buttoning his coat." And the memorable events in Olivier's career—as actor still more than as producer—have all been accumulated round tiny touches of this kind. In *Rhinoceros*, for instance, he varied the scale of his playing with extraordinary virtuosity. The climax to which it led came at the very end of the play, and it amounted to a final assertion of human dignity. In order to drive the last ten minutes home, Olivier had modulated the entire evening from an almost inconspicuous start toward a dominating crescendo. A play in which the characters turn successively into rhinoceroses cannot be said strictly to be realistic; but the force of Olivier's acting came from the contrast that he imposed between the fantasy of Ionesco's theme and the realism of its central character.

No doubt instinct rather than theory tells him how to achieve the effect he aims at. He is certainly not the kind of theatre man who would spend midnight oil evaluating the concepts of Stanislavsky or Brecht—Larry would never allow Sir Laurence so much latitude—but the evidence of nearly thirty years suggests that

Olivier leaves nothing to chance. Whatever is done by him is controlled down to the least detail.

There can be very few great actors who are personally so unfamiliar to the public. In an age when personality is ruthlessly exploited by anyone who can get his name into the press, and when publicity and success go hand in hand, Olivier keeps his own counsel. Even a divorce does not bring him into the limelight, despite the fact that for twenty years his marriage to Vivien Leigh had been accepted as one of the most stable institutions in the modern theatre. They made a remarkable pair, from the days of an unsuccessful *Romeo and Juliet*, at the beginning of the war, to a high point in the Stratford-on-Avon *Macbeth* of 1955. Olivier was a generous husband; he took immense pains to assemble and burnish the latent talents of a wife who might by herself have been content simply to be ravishingly pretty, and in *Macbeth* the combination of the two was irresistible. The critics, I recall, were more enthusiastic about Olivier. But there was an icy, serpentine quality about Vivien Leigh that has stamped a far deeper imprint on my own memory. It made her the most dangerous Lady Macbeth in my experience; and if that is so, the credit must go as much to Olivier's perception as to her own skill.

To the public, however, he has been, by choice, little more than an exceptionally handsome man who is also an outstanding actor. That is partly because he has always set his face against giving newspaper interviews. Apparently some journalist once attached to him the oddly inappropriate epithet "elfin"—it was a long time ago—and the risk has not again been undertaken willingly. The reluctance has brought its own revenges. Of late years the press has not been particularly kind to Olivier. Journalists lose few chances to point out that even the brightest stars wane in the end. Critics, on the other hand, who pause to take a backward look, must notice that Olivier has greatly extended his range, and his technical equipment as well, over the years. Some twelve years ago, for example, Stark Young was writing of him that "his voice is fairly light, has small warmth or continuity of tone; his delivery of verse is based often on a kind of jerky energy." With that in mind, listen to him speaking the part of Becket. Not that the text has any distinction, or any hint of poetry. Simply by using his vocal resources so as to convey the possibility of poetry, Olivier persuades an audience that it has been listening to something rather splendid. There is no jerkiness, no absence of warmth in that voice nowadays, and he has overcome an old tendency to heighten emotion by a sudden rise of pitch.

What is most interesting about him, however, is that he is clearly still looking for new conquests. I doubt very much if even ten years ago he would have cared to tackle *Rhinoceros*. For nearly thirty years he has either been giving the classics, from Shakespeare to Sheridan, Chekhov to Shaw, or else trying his hand at the kind of play for which natural charm and responsive sympathy were enough—from *The Green Bay Tree* to *No Time for Comedy*. It is a pattern that cannot be repeated endlessly, and in spite of his success in films, he is known to prefer the living stage; therefore he is unlikely to enlarge his experience in the cinema. I find it significant that he should now be turning to Ionesco and John Osborne. The theatre is stirring, if patchily, into fresh life, and it is a symptom of Olivier's vitality that he should be moving with it. This may well mean that in future Larry will take over more and more from Sir Laurence. Olivier now has the technical means to do whatever he chooses, and he may well reverse the procedure of the late Sir Johnston Forbes-Robertson. Quite lately, in London, a film was unearthed some forty-six years after it was made. The film was Forbes-Robertson's *Hamlet*, and at a single semi-private showing it confirmed that at sixty he was still probably the best Hamlet of this century. It will be fascinating if Olivier, instead of perfecting his Shakespeare over the next ten years, turns toward modern experimentation. The trouble with experiments is that by their nature some are bound to fail; it needs an exceptionally clear head to foresee which are worth the undertaking and which are not. It is in helping the growth of the contemporary theatre from a noncommercial standpoint—and Olivier has never been especially interested in money—that Sir Laurence and Larry may finally come together and reach their full stature as a single whole.

26 Shaw and the actor

*Interviews with Rex Harrison and Siobhán McKenna
(author unknown)*

March 1957

Rex Harrison (Reginald, 1908–90) headed the list of English actors skilled at projecting sophistication and elegance in light comedy. He had won that title in Rattigan's *French Without Tears* (1936) and Coward's *Design for Living* (1939). Perhaps it pigeon-holed him unfairly, since he was equally good in Shaw, Pirandello and Chekhov. After a stint in the R.A.F., he varied the farcical fare with Henry VIII in Maxwell Anderson's *Anne of the Thousand Days* (1948) and the Uninvited Guest in T. S. Eliot's *The Cocktail Party* (1950). However, it was his reputation for easy badinage that won him the role of Professor Henry Higgins in *My Fair Lady* (1956). With no singing voice, he talked through his numbers, conveying a petulant charm.

Siobhán McKenna (Siobhán Giollamhuire Nic Cionnaith, 1923–86) began her career acting in Gaelic, before she joined the Abbey Theatre in 1944. She made her own the role of Pegeen Mike in *Playboy of the Western World*, but even that was overshadowed by Shaw's *Saint Joan* which she first played in her own Gaelic translation in Galway in 1952. She then acted it in English at Dublin's Gate Theatre (1953), in London (1954–5) and New York (1956–7), and on a European tour. Critics admired its peasant directness and spirituality, while pointing out that it ran counter to Shaw's own concept. Her West End and Broadway debuts were as Miss Madrigal in Enid Bagnol's *The Chalk Garden* (1947, 1955) and she was then seen in *The Rope Dancers* (1958). As this article appeared, she was booked to play Viola in *Twelfth Night* at the Stratford Ontario Festival.

Rex Harrison on Henry Higgins

Q. What scene, line or sequence of lines by Shaw do you feel best sums up the character of Higgins?

A. I think the last scene with Eliza in which Higgins, by his violence of independence, shows to the audience, but not to himself, that he is not as independent as he thinks. This is a key to the character, in a way. Higgins says: "I can do without anybody. I have my own soul: my own spark of divine fire." From the start of the play I believe that Higgins "protests too much" for Shaw to have meant the things he says on misogyny to be taken with anything but a grain of salt. The two subjects occupying Higgins' mind are misogyny and phonetics—the passion for the latter is quite another matter; it is much more serious, like Shaw's own interest in the subject.

Q. It has been said that Shaw's heroes in many ways are not dramatic characters but merely mouthpieces for the author's opinions. Do you believe this applies to your current role? What are the Shavian opinions you enjoy expressing as Higgins?

A. I think the statement applies in general, but I do not believe it wholly applies to Higgins. I think the writing of *Pygmalion* was involved to a large extent with Shaw's infatuation with Mrs. Patrick Campbell, as he wrote the part of Eliza for her, and that either consciously, or more likely, unconsciously, he wrote *himself* as Higgins. If I have followed a model in my movement, it is based on my memory of Shaw, and the way he used to move and stand.

The Shavian opinions which I find most amusing to express are largely the ones on misogyny, because they are so witty: ". . . the moment I let a woman make friends with me, she becomes jealous, exacting, suspicious, and a damned nuisance . . . the moment I let myself make friends with a woman, I become selfish and tyrannical." Or, in answer to Pickering's question, "Are you a man of good character where women are concerned?" Higgins replies, "Have you ever met a man of good character where women are concerned?"

Q. How much do you think Shaw's *Pygmalion* contributes to the astounding success of *My Fair Lady*?

A. I think that one could not do without the other, for *Pygmalion* might not have been a successful musical had it not been for the great talents of Alan Jay Lerner and Frederick Loewe; and on the other side of the coin, Lerner's and Loewe's talents would not have been so fully realized had it not been for Shaw's play. Many persons have commented that it is difficult to know, when you are watching *My Fair Lady*, where Shaw leaves off and Lerner's additional dialogue and lyrics begin—and I think that's the great secret of the production's success.

Q. Why do you feel that *Pygmalion*, which had its London première in 1914, has such an appeal for audiences today?

A. The Cinderella story has always been successful, and this is a wonderful Cinderella story.

Q. Having played not only in prose works but also in verse drama by Maxwell Anderson, Eliot and Fry, would you consider Shaw a poetic dramatist?

A. I do not consider Shaw a poetic writer any more than, I think, he would have considered himself one. Commenting on verse dramatists at the time he was a critic, Shaw wrote: "Since his [Shakespeare's] time, every poor wretch with an excitable imagination, a command of literary bombast and metric facility enough to march in step, has found himself able to turn any sort of thematic material, however woodenly prosaic, into rhetorical blank verse; where-upon foolishly conceiving himself to be another Shakespeare, he has so oppressed the stage with yards upon yards and hours upon hours of barren imagery, that at last the announcement of a new historical play in verse . . . produces an involuntary start of terror among the critics . . ." (from *Our Theatres in the Nineties*)

What Shaw writes is good prose—great prose. An actor realizes this because you can't interchange the smallest preposition, let alone a word of three syllables, and get a better one. It is true that Shaw's lines have a definite rhythm, and if you drop an "and" or a "but," the rhythm goes. My approach to playing Shaw is not so different from my approach to Fry, Eliot and Anderson, in which I would try to break down the verse form partially, to allow the audiences to understand the meaning of the words.

Q. What are some of the qualities you would say are important for an actor to have, in order to play Shaw?

A. If you try to speak Shaw with reverence as though he is a classic, you will go wrong. Shaw is a modern writer. Most of his heroes should be played with a little more warmth, vitality and heart than they would appear to need in the script. They have to be "off-cast" a bit. An actor like Charles Laughton, by his talents and personality, can infuse a great deal of richness into a part such as that of Undershaft in *Major Barbara*.

To the aspiring actor who wants to play Shaw I would say: Forget this was written fifty years ago; pretend it was written yesterday and play it like that. I think this applies to all his plays—they are all satirical comments which are just as valid today as when they were written.

Siobhán McKenna on Saint Joan

Q. Referring to particular scenes and lines, can you discuss your interpretation of Shaw's Saint Joan?

A. The performance moves in a cycle—that's why I start off in a red peasant dress and finish in the same dress. Joan traditionally appears in shining armor, but I feel that everything stems from her country upbringing, which Shaw greatly emphasizes. He stresses this in his preface, and even makes the point that her military leadership comes from that particular type of common sense which country people have.

I also feel that the spiritual quality of Joan is not an ascetic one, removed from life, but one of sheer goodness and a natural communication with God. I don't feel she is a mystic, but I do feel she is a visionary. While she lives with her saints, she never neglects to love human beings as well. Scene I. is important, for here one gets the very innocent girl. Some have said there is a slight element of the clown in my first scene, which I think is correct, for Joan does not realize here the importance of her mission; she is just being obedient to her friends, who happen to be her voices.

What I love about Joan is her common sense; the voices are always backed up by practical things. Consider her answer when she is asked why she wears men's clothes: "If I were to dress as a woman they would think of me as a woman; and then what would become of me?" She is a practical saint. She is like Al Capp's Bald Iggle, which insists that other people tell the truth. It was Joan's absolute, burning honesty and truthfulness, her refusal to compromise by flattering any-body, that was her downfall. She just couldn't pretend. Country people don't. If I buy a hat and wear it to Mass in the country, and someone else doesn't like the hat, that person will tell me it's awful—tell me the truth just as an act of charity.

When I played Saint Joan in London I was asked why I thought God would tell Joan to get rid of the English, but Joan answers this very well herself when she says that we are not subject to feudal lords, but "We are all subject to the King of Heaven; and He gave us our countries and our languages, and meant us to keep to them." A wonderful thing that Shaw portrays, and that Joan accomplished, was the breaking of the feudal system, which was very bad for the church because the bishops were inclined to be feudal lords. Joan's love for the common people is very evident not only in her historic life but in the play. The thing I find interesting is that the common people all accepted her—it was only in the hierarchy that she was rejected, out of fear of diminishing their own power.

One of the most important things I feel about Joan is that she is not a rounded saint until the epilogue—she has the makings of a saint, but at the trial she is not a saint because she commits one of the greatest sins, that of despair. So you can't play her as a complete saint. She is absolutely in communication with God, and is being used as an instrument of God, but all her military achievements are, to my mind, not hers but God's, and she is the instrument used to obtain these victories.

Her great achievement occurred when her voices left her. This puzzled me for many years until I came across an explanation: In the final analysis, no matter how blessed or chosen by God one has been, the greatest gift God gives to man is free will. The voices left Joan to stand on her own two feet. This, to me, is her greatness—that, having been blessed with this extraordinary communication with God, when she is in prison, weak and alone, and it comes to a choice, she makes the choice of faith, of her own free will—without God's help, but with his grace. This is what made her a saint.

Shaw points out that we pay lip worship to truth and saintliness, that we really don't want them with us if they are going to interfere. Joan asks in the epilogue, "Shall I rise from the dead, and come back to you?" The offer is rejected. The last speech of the play is the greatest of all. Joan asks, "O God that madest this beautiful earth, when will it be ready to receive Thy saints? How long, O Lord, how long?"

Scene V. is true for everyone, not only for Joan. In the final analysis every single one of us is alone—we have great communication with people, but in the end there is no one human being to whom one can go about the essentials; you have to go to yourself and to God.

Q. Does the charge—that Shaw's characters in many ways are only mouthpieces for the author's own opinions—apply to Joan?

A. Joan is never a mouthpiece. Shaw himself says that it was as if the Saint stood at his shoulder and wrote the part herself, that he could not write the words as quickly as they flowed. And why shouldn't an author have an opinion? He gives both sides of the argument in this play. Joan speaks for herself rather than Shaw; the others around her may express Shaw's opinions, but they are still dramatically correct.

Q. Why do you think that *Saint Joan*, after three decades, still has such wide appeal for audiences?

A. Saint Joan, the most remarkable woman who ever existed, stands for the spirit of freedom. When the Hungarians revolted I thought, "How great is the human spirit; when it has no chance to survive, it will still flame out." The human spirit is Godlike to me. Even though the world gets more and more materialistic, the spirit of the world is not that way. It is a stronger force.

Q. You have appeared in many plays by Irish dramatists, including Yeats, O'Casey and Synge. What qualities do you feel Shaw shares with them?

A. They all have a tremendous command of words. I think Shaw shares with the others the quality of poetry which many people deny him. Many musicians and composers have said Shaw's work is like an orchestral composition. And in order to have poetry, you don't need to have rhyme. In the "alone" speech (Scene V.) you have assonance, interior rhyme, rhythm and flow. That is why Shaw and Synge and O'Casey have said that the actor must always obey their punctuation. If they have a comma, you put it in. In O'Casey you get a laugh by that tiny pause he has indicated. Another quality Shaw shares with the other Irish dramatists is his comedy. Shaw has been accused of being dried up. One critic, commenting on a recording I did of *A Village Wooing*, said that when I play Shaw, I give him heart. This is not true—his heart is there, big as anything. The two speeches he has [in *A Village Wooing*] on the relation of man and woman are intensely poetic and moving.

Q. What in your own background, either your training for the stage or your past life, has been especially helpful to you in the role of Joan?

A. I have lived many months of every year on a farm, and my grandmother had a farm. Though I was born in Belfast and love it dearly, I left at five. My mother was definitely "country," and I base my interpretation of Joan on my mother. She had the same extraordinarily unshakable faith. Once when my father was going for the chair of physics, for which he had been beaten twice before, she predicted that he would get it by thirteen votes because she had said thirteen Masses that morning, and asked one vote for each. She would talk directly to a picture of the Sacred Heart she had on the wall, and on this occasion she said, "I've never asked for anything in my life, and I'm asking this one request." When we heard a knock at the door that afternoon and received a message of congratulations announcing that my father had won the chair, my mother rose like a queen. She was not at all surprised that he had won by thirteen votes.

Q. What do you consider the most important qualifications for an actress who wants to play Shaw? What advice would you give her?

A. You need style as well as heart. You need to realize that there is a particular style necessary for Shaw, and it is not a wooden style, nor disembodied. I would play Shaw more realistically than many have done, who are inclined to superimpose didacticism upon him. Never break up the passages; they must flow on with passion until they come to a particular point. I feel passion is very important in Shaw. When some say I bring something that was not there before, it is not true. I have discovered this something in the part—I know it is there.

Some Irish people have said that Shaw didn't love Ireland, but a dustbin man named O'Reilly showed me a copy of a letter Shaw had written him. O'Reilly had sent him a silver shamrock, and Shaw wrote to say, "I have hung your shamrock on my watch chain, and there it remains until I myself drop off it." When O'Reilly sent him some handkerchiefs, Shaw replied, "Don't waste your money on me—all I want from my Irish friends are their prayers, which are invaluable."

Shaw was a very religious man and a very human one; he loved humanity, and one can't do this without an understanding of it. He had a wonderful feeling for the common people and a great love for Joan. There are two things at his home on the grounds at Ayot St. Lawrence which symbolize this. One is a little sculptured figure of a lamb, and the other a statue of Joan, not in armor but in a red peasant dress.

27 An actor stakes his claim

Cedric Hardwicke

February 1958

One of Bernard Shaw's favourite actors, appreciated for his keen intelligence and clipped diction, Cedric Hardwicke (1893–1964) had played Caesar in *Caesar and Cleopatra* (1925), and created King Magnus in *The Apple Cart* (1929) and the Burglar in *Too True to Be Good* (1932). These performances built on a long period in Frank Benson's company, the Old Vic and the Birmingham Rep. Hardwicke arrived in New York in 1936 as *The Amazing Dr Clitterhouse* and Canon Skerritt in Paul Vincent Carroll's *Shadow and Substance* (1938). Richard Boleslavsky had earlier brought him to Hollywood to play the saintly Bishop in *Les Misérables* (1935), but Hardwicke's dry, sepulchral voice and gaunt features led movie producers to cast him as villains (Death opposite Lionel Barrymore and the lustful Claude Frollo to Charles Laughton's Quasimodo). He was one of the few actors to contribute regularly to *Theatre Arts*.

WHEN I was a young man in the theatre, it was an actor's theatre. It was dedicated almost entirely to the enjoyment of the art of acting. Then Bernard Shaw came along, attacked it and created the theatre of ideas: in other words, the playwright's theatre. The actor naturally receded in importance. Now we have a director's theatre—and actors have become even smaller cogs in the machine. The directors influence the actors—and the playwrights.

Actors have tended to become puppets. Ironically enough, the better the playwright, the more is done for the actor. Now, with the greater importance of the director, still more of the actor's work is done for him. It has always amused me to hear playwrights say that a good play should be actor-proof. I have never heard of a composer saying that his work is pianist-proof. If our playwrights feel that the actor is an unfortunate handicap in the creation of a work of art, a kind of necessary evil, I can't help thinking that they would be better off writing novels. The novel *is* actor-proof. If playwrights write parts that are actor-proof, what is the point of training actors—or even having them?

I claim for the actor the same privileges afforded the great musical interpreters, men such as Heifetz and Menuhin. If everything is written out for the actor, there is nothing for him to do, and no room for great interpretations. An actor is a good actor only when he is a creative actor, when he is different from any other actor. As a related example, let us consider a situation in another art. A horse may be painted or drawn by six different individuals. It is not the representation that is most like a horse that is best, but the one that tells us something about a horse that no other artist has told.

Creativity in acting has almost entirely disappeared. There is a craze for stark realism. The world is composed of fairly ordinary people, for the most part. The more intimately people can identify themselves with the little man, the more they can get from the characterization. To watch someone bigger than life disturbs the audience. When acting glorifies the weakness and mediocrity of man, as it often does, this tends to pull the theatre down to the level of the least interesting people.

No generation has a monopoly of great talent. There is as much today as ever, but it is not used. In order to become a great surgeon, a doctor must perform a great operation. There must be a great challenge. It is only when we see an actor in a great part that we can tell whether he is great. Classical training is almost a handicap for an actor in the theatre today. In speaking to students, I have often asked them why they don't learn to talk and to walk properly. They reply, "We can't earn a living if we do that; nobody wants us." Why, indeed, train for a classical play if they are going to perform only the mediocre characters of the modern play? The real craft of acting is not only valueless; it is definitely a handicap. Film directors say, "Stop acting!" If you stop acting, what is the point? You are then just talking and behaving. All that film directors require is that you lose any self-consciousness before the camera. I was fascinated to read not long ago that Marilyn Monroe had decided to give up films in order to "learn to act." She was at the top of her profession—but she was giving it up to "learn to act"!

I do not say that the theatre that I remember with so much pleasure was better, but it was different. The older actors were spellbinders. They were true to something bigger than life—too good to be true in the literal sense. The difference between them and today's actors is the difference between a portrait by a great painter and a photograph or snapshot. Irving, Booth and Barrymore wouldn't belong in the theatre today. There is no place for such actors. Where could Booth get a part? The theatre today makes no demands on the actor's talents and craft. It has become too much of a business, too commercial. If, when I began in the theatre, there had been an opportunity to earn ten times the amount of money one could then earn—and by doing less work, after one had made a little success—I would have succumbed to the temptation. Young actors today have the impatience that Americans have for immediate success. Ours is an impatient age.

The actor has a better opportunity to learn his craft in England than in America. Every small town in England has a repertory theatre. Its actors receive thorough training and grow up to understand all sides of the theatre. In this country there are no repertory theatres. When an actor does one or two plays a year, how can he learn anything about acting? In England we have Stratford-on-Avon and the Old Vic. Geographically, too, there is a difference. London is the center of the British theatre, just as New York is in this country. But unlike New York, London is also the center of the film and television industries. In the United States, if an actor is a success, he is rushed across the country to Hollywood to live comfortably among palm trees and smog, and is no longer in touch with life. Hollywood is not so much a place as a state of mind. There is certainly a very good place in the world for this sort of fairyland, but it doesn't tend to make good actors. In England there is no such thing as a film actor. There actors work in all three mediums, and within and near London.

I also believe that there is a distinction to be made about the theatregoing publics of England and the United States. In America there is really no instinctive love of theatre among the people. They love hits, but there is no compulsion to go to the theatre. In England people must go to the theatre. It is a part of their lives. And I think one reason is that in London and in other cities there are at least ten plays produced for children at Christmastime—works such as *Peter Pan* and the pantomimes. At an early age children acquire a love of the theatre, of its color, excitement and imagination. In this country virtually no one goes to the theatre until he has approached adulthood. By that time it is too late; a deep love of theatre will never develop.

I have never found the so-called Method articulate in any sense. Persons with special interests form circles in which there is interminable shoptalk. I cannot believe that any method can be applied to developing so individual an art as acting. What one method could produce a Rex Harrison, a Laurence Olivier and a Sam Levene? All are masters and necessary in the world of the theatre. I don't care for anything that tends to standardize acting in any way. I cannot believe there is any method that will make a good actor if God didn't make him one.

Any art that must do without its masterpieces is in trouble. Take the classic operas from the opera, ballets from the ballet, old masters from museums, symphonies from orchestras, and what is left? It is a disaster that the younger generation may never see many of the great plays of the past. Revivals are not news. The production of a new play is news – a story of a hit or a flop. Newspapers are not interested in revivals. There is nothing much or new that the critics can say about a revival, in so far as the play is concerned. At one time in the history of the theatre, when the theatre depended on revivals, critics had to know about acting or they had nothing to write about. Today critics have difficulty in distinguishing between a good part and a good performance. We must see different actors in the same part in order to judge acting.

"Playwright" means the maker of a play, just as "wheelwright" means the maker of a wheel. A person aspiring to write for the theatre must have working knowledge of the theatre. Most good dramatists have been actors or speakers, not merely writers. The average play is never committed to sound until it goes into rehearsal. Shaw was a wonderful speaker and actor. Pinero, too, was an actor. The only plays that have lasted are the actable plays, plays that present actors with great opportunities. We go to the theatre to enjoy the acting, not to enjoy literature; if the emphasis is on the latter, then the play becomes long-winded and dull. Shaw and Shakespeare were conscious of the actors, knowing that the play had to come to life through a group of human beings. Shaw once told me that his stage directions were not put in for the actor, but for the reader. The reader must have some indication of what the actor is doing. Good actors should never read those directions!

When you go to the concert hall, you go to hear and enjoy the musician who is performing. When you go to the theatre, you should go to enjoy the acting. The theatre is the actor's art. It is not the writer's art. The memorable plays achieve that quality because of the actors. Good actors are good because of the things they can tell us without talking. When they are talking, they are the servants of the dramatist. It is what they can show the audience when they are not talking that reveals the fine actor.

I suppose what I miss most in the theatre today is a sense of gaiety. As I said in *Shadow and Substance*: "There is great safety in laughter." There is no gaiety—even in the musicals. *Oklahoma!* and *Carousel* had a few very ugly moments. And this season's *West Side Story* has a full share of them. Everybody is taking himself too seriously. There are too many fears. If it isn't the Asian flu, then it is mental health or the H-bomb. This seems to imply a lack of faith in the human race, and the lack is very obvious in the theatre. What we see is not the entertainment of a relaxed people, but that of a tense, taut people. At times audiences must ache to see some nice people who like each other. I like a little fun and good manners in my theatre. It is surprising that the two biggest hits in the theatre and the movies are *My Fair Lady* and *Around the World in 80 Days*—both about nice people. Bernard Shaw once said to me that you can make people cry by hitting them in the stomach, but making them laugh is much harder. Shaw dealt with social and economic problems. But he treated the most serious matters with a kind of intellectual gaiety.

28 Albert Finney

Audrey Williamson

October 1963

By the time he made his New York debut in 1963 as John Osborne's *Luther*, a role he had created two years earlier, Albert Finney (1936–) was hailed as a typical exponent of the Angry Young Man school of acting. Stocky and plebeian in appearance, he seemed perfect as Willis Hall and Keith Waterhouse's working-class fantasist *Billy Liar* (1960) and, later, the leads in John Arden's *Armstrong's Last Good Night* and Peter Nichols' *A Day in the Life of Joe Egg* (1967). In fact, he had had a strong classical background, having worked at the Birmingham Rep and the Shakespeare Memorial Theatre (Edgar to Laughton's Lear), and was soon to show he was as strong a character actor as a leading man.

Audrey Williamson (1913–86) was one of the most prolific theatre journalists of her time. Her innumerable books include not only periodic surveys of the West End scene, but also monographs on the London and Bristol Old Vics, Gilbert and Sullivan, Wagner, ballet, the Pre-Raphaelites, biographies of Shaw and Paul Rogers, a study of the Princes in the Tower, and detective novels.

JOHN Osborne's play *Luther* is giving American audiences a close look at Albert Finney, the young British actor who has been seen up to now in this country only in the film *Saturday Night and Sunday Morning*. Finney's giant step from Arthur Seaton, the factory hand rebel in *Saturday Night*, to the great Protestant dissenter, Martin Luther, is not quite as astonishing as it may at first seem, for although Osborne's *Look Back in Anger*, which revolutionized English stages, was produced before Finney's own rise to fame, it was the progenitor and symbol of the style of Angry Young Man who has swept all before him in literature, plays and films in England today, and it was on the crest of this wave of the "anti-hero" that Finney surged to success.

Luther, in one aspect, was a rebel against society no less, and Osborne in dealing with him is moving more, as a playwright, out of period than out of character. But the society and mentality are, of course, very different in outward forms, and if Osborne's talents must adapt to them in the literary sense, Finney's no less must throw off contemporary gracelessness and disgust and delve into the manners and ideologies of a more formal, spiritually expansive age. But for Finney this is nothing new, for he was reared in English repertory and on classics of the theatre, even though his major success has come from the Tony Richardson-Royal Court Theatre group, from which *Look Back in Anger* and the "kitchen-sink" theatre formula emerged.

Finney may be said to have established himself as international leader of the young English actors whose names have been associated with naturalism, the working-class background and dissent against the Establishment. He is himself a Salford lad, sturdy product of that district near Manchester which also spawned Shelagh Delaney and her play, *A Taste of Honey*, in a sudden surprising rainburst (in Manchester rain is the natural meteorological order) of precocious local talent. Young Finney, only son of respectable middle-class parents unconnected with the theatre, went to Salford Grammar School; he had no interest in the stage whatsoever, and to this day is flummoxed as to the exact reason why his head master singled him out as a possible candidate for an acting career. (He suspects it was a last desperate resource to find something for which he might show the slightest talent.) Anyway, his head master called him into his office one day to discuss a possible future career, and countered his pupil's total lack of ideas on the subject with the mysterious-sounding sentence: "You ought to go to RADA." (The Royal Academy of Dramatic Art in England is invariably referred to as RADA, pronounced as in Rajah.) Young Albert, who had never heard of RADA, immediately demanded, "What's Rada?," and was sufficiently impressed by the answer to go home to his parents with the important-sounding observation: "The head master thinks I ought to go to RADA." Whereupon he was able to feel satisfyingly grand and knowledgeable when the family instantly echoed his own earlier query: "What's Rada?"

Finney's manner of telling this story is a guide to his not always realized gift for humorous self-deflation, and also to his cajoling charm. It was perhaps the charm, something innate and easy about his manner that transfers without technical difficulty to the stage, that impressed his schoolmaster; perhaps, too, an element of cheek that is without offense but something, some inner indestructible sinew against adversity, that is for the actor a necessary bulwark for survival. An actor has to have both nerves and nerve—not at all the same thing, but producing together a conflict of tensions with out which no player is likely to reach the top rank.

Finney therefore learned his piece of Shakespeare, and went up to London to audition for RADA. He was stopped after a few lines and accepted without difficulty; but still it was all to him a kind of game, and it remained so, he says, for at least two terms. He even had serious doubts about wanting to be an actor at all. Then suddenly, in his third term, he was given a part to study and play, and for the first time something "clicked." The lens had snapped, the picture was irrevocably taken; and from then on he was seized by a burning interest in the whole process and business of acting, and knew he could be nothing else but an actor.

Even before he left RADA, he had attracted attention in end-of-term productions; and he naturally gravitated to the Birmingham Repertory Theatre, which had nurtured the young Edith Evans, Laurence Olivier, Ralph Richardson, Cedric Hardwicke, Paul Scofield and many others, and has come to be looked on as the repertory "plum" for actors straight from dramatic school. Here for two years, with a three-weekly change of play, he was to play an enormous number of parts and at twenty-two make his first London-echoing success, as King Henry V in a production by Douglas Seale (who was this year's director of the same play at Stratford, Connecticut). The London critics, as frequently happens with prominent English repertories (few are more than 100 to 200 miles from the capital), had been invited to Birmingham to review this production, and that Finney was a future "winner" none doubted at the time.

I myself (who did not then know Finney personally, though he later married a gifted young actress, Jane Wenham, who was one of my close friends) covered the performance for the London *Times*, and it might be of interest now to resurrect this first impression of a talent in embryo, only six short years ago:

"The lasting emphasis of this production proves to be informality, its center a humanized King Henry who at the conference table, not on the throne, carefully, and without casuistry, weighs his decision to invade France. Rhetoric throughout is played down – the Harfleur speech flung by a crouching King in hoarse whispers at his cowering army. . . . It is, in fact, a production without loftiness, and Mr. Albert Finney as the King, too, as yet cannot command the pulse and flow of the verse. Always intelligent, moving after Agincourt, he takes the stage with an engaging charm of youth. Sturdy rather than royal, in the Burton tradition rather than the Olivier, he is a king who tends the wounded and is himself wounded, a king close to his subjects if not yet with the mental maturity which in the speech on ceremony can grasp at disillusion without bitterness, but with the resigned wryness of political experience."

It should be added this was an infinitely more cautious appraisal than most of those Finney received, which frankly proclaimed a full-fledged Henry and an unmistakable "star." And though it is tempting to wish one had let the spirit of prophecy carry one away more unquestioningly, I still feel (and believe Finney does too) the estimate was just of one of that age in a part in which Olivier and Scofield (twenty-three to Finney's twenty-two) had both been memorable when young (Scofield, his face already traced, like a saddened Rembrandt, with fine ascetic lines, certainly got more out of the speech on ceremony). Henry is not the hardest of parts for a young man to succeed in; romanticism and *panache* will go a long way with the audience. Finney did more than that, certainly, but in some ways I was more impressed by his potentialities a few months later when I saw him play a purely character role, that of a hard-headed young modern business go-getter, in a play called *Be Good, Sweet Maid* at the same theatre. Here, in fact, was a hint of his future as Arthur Seaton, an incisive piece of work in which the charm was used deliberately as a veneer for a cool and egoistic calculation.

When he was twenty-three, Birmingham took a greater plunge and put him on as Macbeth. To expect him to be ready for such a part would, of course, be stupid. He likes to joke about it now and say that Charles Laughton, who saw him in it, told him he was "bloody awful." This, like Mark Twain's death, is an exaggeration; Laughton of course (he had himself, at a maturer age, been a controversial Macbeth at the Old Vic a quarter of a century before) knew what was inevitably lacking, but was impressed enough by the quality to insist that Finney be given the part second to his own in a modern play, *The Party*, he was about to present in London. Finney's Macbeth was by no means lacking in weight; his robust build helped him here, and though the full macabre poetry and imagination were lacking it was a characterization well thought out, intellectually and technically an advancement in his powers. By now I knew him well enough to discuss it with him offstage, and was surprised at the grasp he showed of the problems raised by the character, and the methods he had taken to solve them onstage. He was too young to have seen other great actors in the part; he had to build from his own instincts and his own reasoning, without at that time even much experience of life to help him. Both the instincts and the reasoning were those of a born actor.

He admits that at Birmingham he owed a great deal to Seale; the work had been hard and all-absorbing, and the experience of a six-month run in a West End play, without heavy daytime rehearsal of a new part and with all the social distraction West End success entails, was a new one for him. It may be for the first time he was able to relax, to discover his own ego and his own capacity for enjoyment. Certainly it was after this that a new Albert Finney began to emerge—a more feverish, unconventional individual, aping his idol Laughton in clothes (like Laughton, he began to sport the English working-class man's cloth cap), less fettered domestically in spite of the fact that a baby son, Simon (very much a laughing red-blond Albert in miniature), had by now arrived.

From the West End he went to Stratford, to the Shakespeare Festival. Stardom at Birmingham is one thing, and possible to a youngster of talent; Stratford is another matter, with its players of greater achievement (this year Edith Evans and Laurence Olivier led the team), and although Finney was far too intelligent to expect the kind of parts he had had at Birmingham, it is nevertheless not easy for a young ambitious actor, recently playing principal roles and being acclaimed in them, to readjust himself to the line of romantic "juveniles" that tends to be the lot of the rising young actor supporting established leading players in Shakespeare. He also went through that period almost inevitable in the changeable world of the theatre, when critics who have lavishly praised a young newcomer tend to "think again" when seeing him in less over-powering parts.

This was, in fact, though it happened to a small degree, unfair to Finney, for he played even a romantic idiot like Lysander with an engaging "bounce" of virile youthful vitality, and got more character into parts like Cassio in *Othello* and Edgar in *King Lear* (Laughton was the Lear) than sometimes happens. But he was not happy at Stratford, either in his work or private life (no fault of his charming, slightly older, understanding wife, and perhaps not entirely of his own, depressed by new difficulties in his work and the stirring of new, hitherto unanalyzed, psychological factors which had never had time to reveal themselves or develop in the work-absorbed days in repertory). When his marriage broke up, he said quite frankly in interviews that he had married too young, his character unformed and with no sense of the responsibilities involved, and these weighed on him. He was, in fact, a deeply troubled boy; soon, however, he found a new center among the Royal Court Theatre group, with the Laughton cap replaced by casual clothes which in New York would tend to be labeled "Greenwich Village."

Although decidedly virile, he was still not quite mature either as actor or person—unlike Peter O'Toole, the traditional "Wild Irish" actor who simultaneously at the Bristol Old Vic, at the same age, was engrossing the critics with authoritative Popes and Molière fantastics and Hamlet. The boyish ring in Finney's makeup, now troubled by adult "growing pains," made him a successful Coriolanus and gave him a last brief blaze of triumph when Olivier, who had been playing it, left Stratford. For Coriolanus, as Olivier has always brilliantly realized, is a hero in war and a schoolboy in his emotions, and it was this quality of an adolescent rebel, with an adolescent charm, that irradiated Finney's Arthur Seaton in the *Saturday Night* film and worked that histrionic miracle that often happens when great interpretative skill is allied to a temperament emotionally in tune with a part. Finney's troubled stirrings of conscience in this film were a token of a natural warmth that might flower in less dissonant circumstances, and in a society less intolerant of breaches in bourgeois reasoning and established order. And Luther gives those stirrings more room for development, in a rebellion based less on youthful egoism than on integrity of vision—the vision of something larger than man, outside himself.

In the meantime Finney had a brilliant success as another contemporary youth, trying to burst the bonds of his environment, in the long-running West End play, *Billy Liar* (when he left the cast to make the film *Saturday Night and Sunday Morning* the part was taken by Tom Courtenay, himself now well-known as star of the film *The Loneliness of the Long Distance Runner*). In *Luther* London critics found in Finney again all those qualities that originally dazzled and lifted him above the rut, now richened with time into a more profound penetration of character, a new authority. He has also made a new film as Fielding's *Tom Jones*, an incursion into past romanticism he found difficult to readjust to, though it is a part well suited to his springs of sincerity and charm. Beneath the skin, he is searching for some hidden truth—about himself, about modern man, about the art of the actor. His full achievement may not come until he has found it; but the quest is an exciting one, throwing up glancing lights of a formidable actor in the making. Providing he maintains his grip, and continues to mature, the prospects for Albert Finney can only brighten with time.

Part III

Foreign modes of performance

29 How Reinhardt works with his actors

Gertrud Eysoldt

October 1921

The notion of a "stage director" was a novel one for the ordinary playgoer at the beginning of the twentieth century. Plays were staged, somewhat mechanically if efficiently, by their author, or a stage manager or a functionary referred to as the "producer". Max Reinhardt (Goldmann, 1873–1943) personified the new concept. Dominating the German-speaking theatre, he managed a number of playhouses in Berlin and Salzburg and had become internationally known for his large and disciplined choruses in *Oedipus Rex* (1910), his orientalist pantomime *Sumurûn* and his musical pageant *The Miracle* (1911). His skilful deployment of crowds, his canny use of lighting, stage revolves, orchestrated voices to create a mood, his managerial proficiency in delegating tasks to assistants wound up characterizing what a director is supposed to do. Here one of his favourite actresses, the elfin Gertrud Eysolt (1870–1955), who played Puck and Wedekind's Lulu for him, provides an impressionistic account of Reinhardt in rehearsal.

––––––––––––

Morning. The rehearsal about to begin. Daylight in the dusty morning-grey of the theatre. A grouping through the dark rows of the parquet, hands feeling their way along the backs of the seats. The eyes blind with darkness. The stage ahead a light cutout in a hazy blue glow. A faded daylight falls in streaks from above through the flies. The stage is empty—two scene walls, fastened together, are leaning against one side. This emptiness of the stage. Its purity. So touching to the actor. Like a stretched but untouched canvas for the painter!

   The actors come one after another. Slow, ill-humored, drowsy. Reserve in every feature. The attitude of saving up for something. Complete inertia. Reinhardt's face and figure reveal themselves through the dark in front of the first row of parquet seats. The actors blink down at him with sidewise glances. Something stirs within them, although they seem indifferent. There is a blending of the fighting spirit and unrest. Reinhardt has his book in his hand. His features are apathetic. Morning pushes all of these night-folk wearily ahead of her. Phantasy is settled all about, absolutely motionless. And we know we must set her free. We are afraid. Great energy is needed for that. What you win in the prosiness of a morning rehearsal lives doubly in the inspiration of the night. The artificial light that now illuminates the stage insufficiently for the rehearsal does not awaken the evening mood—the streaks of daylight cut through it. And yet this hostility of the daylight that breaks in everywhere upon the brain and seeks to tear your inner life to pieces, at last fires you by contrast. Suddenly you understand how the deepest sorrows flit like shadows over white plaster at sunny noontide through the indifferent, hurrying crowd.

Reinhardt calls us out of our first lethargy. We begin hesitatingly. Ashamed. Listening within ourselves. Our voices are strange to us. Suddenly a ring, a well-known tone in our voice rouses us! The melody moves shyly. Reinhardt's look answers with a flash of interest. He puts an emphasis into the speech, quietly, as you call to one who is just awakening. His glances are more firmly fixed on his players—we bestir ourselves. Again that inward hesitation. Reinhardt takes his book, we listen—divided between an eagerness to understand and a resistance, half-assumed. Our own damming up of the inner stream appears as modesty. We are off the track. Nothing convinces us. We suffer. Reinhardt pretends not to be especially attentive in order to give us a chance to free ourselves of our confusion. He indulges us. Then if he catches a soaring tone from us he holds it pitilessly fast and will not let it go; no falling back is granted us. He tortures us, he drives us, he resolves every doubt. He repeats. Once again we hold the reins, we pull them taut, we slacken them, until we know the pace. Once warmed up, all the repressions melt away. A rhythm of intensity and exhaustion swings us in a circle. Reinhardt takes hold of it and bends it. We give ourselves up to the play. We feel this part-ner—his face, his glance, his hands, his figure, his aspiration and his opposition, his hope and his conflict. Reinhardt binds voices together, pulls distances to pieces. He draws us up to rapture, drags us back to syncope. On his exit from the scene a player drops down worn out upon a stool or a part of the set, to quiet the tumult within him and not to give it up to the meaningless horde back of the scenes outside of the play. Things are set to rights. A self-mastery conquers the player, holding him until he sets foot on the stage again—setting himself free or listening, from time to time, to the quiet progress of the play. Reinhardt has his book. We have our parts. Each of us has brought his own, worked out or learned, and carries it in momentous hands. And book and parts and ideas are remolded here by the stream of new minds they meet, are given new lines written in blood. What was letter and thought grows to feeling, that which was feeling grows to an inner picture. The "magic sap" drowns us too in the ocean of madness. Beautiful and vivid are these dreams on the blank canvas of the stage. Out of the morphia of inspiration grow new measures of infinity for us. We try to be a part of them, to drag reality closer. With uncertain footsteps we feel for solid ground. Now tables and chairs and walls and stairs are thrust upon us, color surrounds us. Our strength must live in them. We give warmth to lifeless things. The balustrades of the stairs offer us the one and only gesture that clarifies our pain or our pride. The bench calls to our trembling knees, the window laughs love to our lips. The wind and the trees call. Restlessly creation stirs in us, flows into us and forms us. Nothing that is not stirred into life by us, the players, on the stage has a right to be there.

The property-man goes on tiptoe to the footlights and says to Reinhardt: "The red carpet is going to act, too, isn't it?" And in those words he uncovers the spirit of the theatre.

30 The Month of Duse

Kenneth Macgowan

January 1924

At the time of her death, the Italian actress Eleonora Duse (1858–1924) was, along with Sarah Bernhardt, one of the two legendary divas of the world stage. Her fame derived in part from their rivalry, which was grist for critics' mills, Shaw and Chekhov much preferring her understated style. Journalists loved to report her refusal to wear make-up and her expressive hands. She was as good in Goldoni's comic *Mistress of the Inn* as she was in Dumas' pathetic *Lady of the Camelias*, which exercised a serious influence on Eva Le Gallienne. Duse's indefatigable touring in an eclectic repertoire of Sardou, Ibsen, Sudermann, D'Annunzio (her sometime lover) and others spread her celebrity as well. She died while on tour in Pittsburgh on 21 April 1924, a few months after this article appeared.

Kenneth Macgowan (1888–1963) was on the staff of *Theatre Arts* from 1919 to 1925, at the same time assisting the Provincetown Players and the Greenwich Village theatre as a producer and director. An ardent apostle of the New Stagecraft, he promoted its ideas in The *Theatre of Tomorrow* (1921) and *Continental Stagecraft* (with Robert Edmond Jones, 1922). In 1934, he moved to Hollywood where he worked as a successful producer to 1947 (the first all-Technicolor feature *Becky Sharp*, 1935; Hitchcock's *Lifeboat*, 1944). After his retirement from the movies, he became chairman of the Department of Theatre Arts at the University of California at Los Angeles. His *The Living Stage: A History of the World Theater* (1955) was a standard textbook for many years.

BEFORE the fifty-two weeks of 1923 are passed New York will have seen the art of the three most powerful figures of the European stage—Stanislavsky, Duse, and Reinhardt. Two other men and one more woman share with them the crown of the modern theatre; Chaliapin and Isadora Duncan have been frequent visitors to the United States, while no stage has seen more of the Achillesian Craig than the American. Six great artists of the theatre leaving their impress upon our stage, and, of them all, none so impressive as the frail lady with the dun cheeks and the corded neck who makes us live with beauty.

Arthur Symons once spoke of Duse as "a chalice for the wine of imagination." I doubt if that perfect phrase ever fitted more perfectly than it did in the sixty-fourth year of her life when she came out, a very remote figure, upon the yawning stage of the Metropolitan. Then she was doubly the chalice. To the mystery and exaltation of her art was added a strange element of aloofness which made her, not the hybrid of actress and dramatic character to which this curious art of the theatre accustoms us, but a great person in the cast of another drama, which we call Life. Our imagination rose to the art of voice and hands and body, but it rose, too, to an art of living which brought this extraordinary woman before us. It rose higher, I think, to the woman Duse than to the actress; for not only an alien tongue, but the vast gulf of the Metropolitan intervened between our emotions and Ibsen's Lady from the Sea. Duse's art is more than realism, but it is founded, nevertheless, upon the intimacy of the realistic theatre, and neither at the Metropolitan nor at the Century, where she played the remainder of her brief engagement, can the living word of the playwright and the living presence of the player fuse with the soul of the spectator. In both houses Duse was not so much an actress ministering to emotion as an extraordinary person, a legendary heroine, perhaps a goddess, come before us. And it was not quite as though she were a great woman appearing in our midst as Wilson appeared in Paris. Behind the footlights, and across the gulf of these abominable theatres, Duse became a kind of story. She seemed to be a legend of herself.

All of which is a very murky effort to say how strangely the figure of Duse moved many of us on this epochal occasion, and how oddly the art of Duse left our playgoing emotions cold. Concede this anaesthesia, admit that we did not suffer with the women of *Ghosts* and *The Lady from the Sea*; then let us look more closely at the art which, under happier circumstances, might have left us wrung with the emotion of Ibsen.

Duse has reached an age at which actors retain none too much of their vigor, and actresses are so sapped that only the greatest—Bernhardt and this Italian— can keep a grip upon their art. Duse has lived more truly and more fully than Bernhardt, and given more of herself to life. Duse is weak; she can play only twice a week, and two hours on the stage leave their mark upon her as she takes her final curtain. Duse has never tolerated make-up or any artifice of wig or clothing to imitate vanishing youth. So today her Ellida Wangel would be aged, and her fascination for the young sailor a disgusting absurdity, if it were not for the soul and the art that still animate her so fully. The voice is endlessly musical and shadowed with infinite expression; it runs light as a bird's for the most part, singing note after note of beauty colored by hope, doubt, fear, love, exaltation; it plunges suddenly into deeper tones that carry suffering upon their dark, slow wings. Occasionally the voice breaks or goes dull, but these weakenings are very few. Duse's body, Duse's hands above all—for D'Annunzio was the true-seeing poet when he called her Duse of the Beautiful Hands—play a symphony of movement. There seems nothing studied in her actions, nothing deliberate; sometimes her hands flash nervously across her face when we are most anxious to see her expression. Her movements are not an artifice but an inevitable outcome of emotion felt in the very soul and irresistibly commanding a body fashioned consummately to obey. It is here in the soul of Duse and in the mystery of the body made one with it that we sense the ultimate of her art. And we cannot tag and label it.

We can be downright and documentary, however, on one aspect of Duse. It is the relation of her acting to current modes. We have had, roughly, three kinds of playing in this first generation of the twentieth century. We have had the exploit-ation of personality colored by artifice, a thing that begins with any one of our agreeable women stars and rises to the brittle pinnacles of Bernhardt. We have had the exploitation of personality fitted to type parts, a cast of characters by mail-order, a kind of stock-room realism. And we have had—most notably in the Moscow Art Theatre—true impersonation, made up of the surface art of wig and grease paint, and of the deeps of emotional identification. Duse gives us a fourth art, an art unique in its combination of qualities. She is unforgettably a person; she is Duse. She is skilful with voice and body, but by inner emotion, not by artifice. The bare, clean skin of her cheeks speaks both sincerity and a kind of realism that stands against the theatrical even at its best. She turns her back on all the deliberate maskings of face and body which make so much of the art of the Russians, and which they make so much of. Duse dresses her hair differently for the Lady from the Sea and the mother in *Ghosts*, and she wears appropriately different garments; yet it is essentially by the movement of hands, face, and voice that she defines the gulf between the two characters. Through the hands, the face and the voice, Duse remains Duse. It is only that an inner spirit has changed, and emanations appear before us in wrist or smile or intonation. Duse understands more completely than any actress I have ever seen the mysteries by which the inner spirit is kindled and the emanations arise. [. . .]

31 Eleonora Duse: The last phase

F. Bruno Averardi

September 1931

Franco-Bruno Averardi was an Italian scholar and diplomat, who made an Italian translation of John Ford's Jacobean tragedy *The Broken Heart*, and co-authored the screenplay for the documentary *More about Nostradamus* (1941).

WHEN she seemed to have reached the highest summit of her art, Eleonora Duse left the stage. Her long silence, twelve years, was considered by the world not as a pause, but as the end. But it was not the end. At the age of sixty-two she suddenly returned. She felt that she had a last word to say, especially to that younger Italian generation which had suffered in the Great War. She could not have ended her life without revealing and offering to others what had ripened in her during that silence. She felt that if this last word was really to be what she meant it to be, she must throw away every artifice, and come to the stage with her white hair and her old face, with no embellishing, deceiving veil between her public and herself. She decided to appear in Turin, the city of her first triumphs, as Ibsen's *Lady from the Sea*. She selected this play because the figure of Ellida was the one which responded more deeply than any other to what she felt herself to be and to what she had to say: The lady wedded to the sea, the symbol of the infinite.

There are a few great scenes in the play, but, on the whole, it is not one of Ibsen's strongest works and the ending is conventional. The character of Ellida, however, as it passed through the last spiritual vision of Eleonora Duse became something greater than it had been: a feminine Hamlet, one could say, who loses the sense of life's laws and realities in the inward ocean of timeless, endless contemplation. Eleonora deepened, developed and perfected the finest of the drama: Ellida's inward abandonment to the over-powering attraction of the sea. She left in the shadow the less significant motif of the woman's right to freedom of decision.

Eleonora had known all the profound happiness of life, if by happiness we mean exaltation, "the intensified feeling of the worth of man's being and becoming, and not a mere smirky contentment with one's lot", as Eugene O'Neill says. She had known all the torments which a human being so great and so essentially lonely can know. And from this exaltation and this suffering she had emerged greater and more beautiful, with an inward beauty which shone through her face and made it perhaps more fascinating than it had ever been. Already, in the second phase of her career, when she had played some of the tragedies of D'Annunzio, a critic had said: "The infinite shines through her art," and this spiritual transparency had increased more and more.

So Ellida, the woman whose soul has become restless and strange, obscure to herself since she first heard the call of the sea, of the infinite, appeared to Eleonora Duse as the incarnation through which she could best express herself now that she felt her life's end approaching, now that she stood almost on the threshold of the infinite.

One of the most inspiring portraits of Eleonora is that in which she appears as La Cieca of *Citta Morta*. She leans against a pillar facing the sea and we feel, we almost see her soul wandering away from her eyes. She appears there as the true daughter of the sea, of St. Mark, as D'Annunzio calls her. The sea with its endless movement always attracted her restless soul as the visible expression of that continuous movement and progress towards an unknown goal which was the predominant sentiment in her. Once somebody asked her which among the countries she had seen was the dearest to her; she answered: "*La traversata!* (the crossing)." Her great friend Matilde Serao called her "the passionate pilgrim." When her friends accompanied her to the station they found her quite different from the day before; the feeling of leaving behind her a particular place and of going away in search of the unknown inebriated her.

She was, therefore, profoundly sincere when she selected the Lady from the Sea as her first role after her long silence. Before her first performance she spent an entire day at Genoa, alone in the room of her hotel, contemplating the sea from her window. She longed to make the breath, the perfume, the soul of the sea, her own, to be really the lady from the sea. Once more, or rather, more than ever, her acting was no fiction to her, but superior life. She did not want to see, in the days preceding the performance, the actor playing the part of the man from the sea, because she felt that, if she had seen him, his face would have become too familiar to her and would have lost, at his sudden appearance in the third act, that strange, distant, dream-like quality which made Ellida start back and hide herself from him.

The evening in which she appeared in that little theatre at Turin before an assembly of the best known personalities of Italy, is one of the unforgettable evenings of my life. All through the first scenes of the play nothing could be heard of what the other actors said, because everybody in the theatre was restless, whispering, or expressing somehow his growing impatience to see Eleonora. And on a sudden a voice ringing with inexpressible music, as clear as silver and as soft as velvet, called from behind the scenes:

"Are you there, Wrangel?"

A profound vibration, followed by a passionate exclamation, ran through the audience. It was still the voice of Eleonora. A moment later, when Eleonora herself appeared on the stage, everybody felt that Eleonora was really there, entirely there, undiminished, more profoundly she than ever. And all the crowd rose and burst out in a great outcry: "*Viva la nostra Duse! Viva l'Italia.*" They all felt in that moment that during her long silence the echo of her art had become more and more intense, that Italy had realized more and more what she thought to have lost with Eleonora. They saw that she was not lost, that she had come back, and they greeted her with that passion of tenderness which we would feel and express if a beloved dead one suddenly returned.

A friend of mine told me that a few hours before the performance he had visited Duse and had been terrified by her aspect. She was leaning back in a chair, weak, exhausted, like the shadow of herself. Now she appeared on the stage erect, walking with light, sure steps toward Zacconi. I shall never forget that in the dim light of the stage I thought I saw on her head a wreath of white roses; then I realized that it was the blending of her white and black hair or rather, of her white and gray hair, which had created this illusion. In one scene of the first act she was sitting, talking to somebody about herself, but with increasing hesitation and long pauses, as if she could not or would not find the words expressing what she had in mind. While she spoke, an umbrella in one of her unforgettable hands was slowly tracing designs in the sand and everybody in the audience followed the movements of that umbrella, as if she were tracing secret words about herself which her lips would not speak. All her performance was a sequence of such unique nuance and details. When we see some other actress, we leave the theatre with a general impression of excellent acting, but with Duse we took into our hearts each of those nuances, to remember it always. It was as if each of those details had been a touch of color from the hand of a painter. One touch followed the other, and when the curtain fell, when everything was over, it was *less over* than ever, and we saw spiritually the final painting, the total vision of beauty and truth which all those unforgettable little touches had composed.

The greatest miracle of the evening was perhaps that scene of the second act in which Ellida tried to explain to her husband why she could not forget that other man. He asked her: "Of what did he speak to you?" She answered: "Of the sea." But she pronounced these two words: "*Del mare*," quickly, with a reluctant and shy inflection in her voice, as if the sea had been a secret which she feared to profane—with the accent which another woman would have had in pronouncing the dearest of all names. Then she overcame her reluctance and began to speak about the sea in all its moods: when it is still, silvery and fragrant in the morning; when it seems to dissolve itself in the golden dream of sunset, when it darkens and threatens in a sudden storm . . . in her voice all the sea was chanting with its thousand musics. That voice could have, within the same sentence, the profound, dark echoes of a cello and the delicate, airy lightness of a flute.

When the lady from the sea crossed the sea to visit America she knew that she would never come back. This is not merely an impression I had; she told me so herself with one word.

I shall never forget an afternoon which was one of the most inspiring and at the same time one of the most irritating afternoons in my life. It was then that I met Eleonora, in the house of one of those ladies who possess the fatal secret of loading the atmosphere with banality and of spoiling a conversation as soon as it has begun to be really interesting. When I entered the room Eleonora was alone with her hostess. She looked annoyed and when she heard my steps she seemed to feel still more annoyed, judging by the expression of her face when she turned around to look at me. Eleonora was tremendously expressive—just as much in life as on the stage. But she seemed to realize that I was not merely somebody else anxious to contemplate that strange and famous creature called Duse—that I was dumb with emotion, and there was a sudden change in her expression. After a moment of silence she slowly opened her hands in an inexpressibly melancholy gesture, while a kind, sad smile passed over her face, and she said: "*Ecco*"—that little Italian word of which "Here I am" is only a diluted and weakened version. I had the feeling that this one word expressed so many things. It said: You desire to see me, here I am. And it said also: Look at me, here I am, old, ill and tired. She could not have said anything containing more kindness and more sadness. Two profound, tragic furrows cut her marvelous face, which age had exempted from its usual net of tiny wrinkles. The conversation which followed was painful because of the frequent unfortunate interruptions of the hostess with remarks such as "How fatiguing it must be to play for evenings and evenings, Signora Duse! I think I could never do it," etc. . . .

But the afternoon was followed by another in which I could abandon myself to the happiness of listening to Eleonora and of speaking to her without being checked by exhausting dissonances. She spoke to me about Shakespeare: "He is too great for our age. Our theatre cannot contain him."

"But how is it with the other Elizabethan dramatists?" I asked. "Is it impossible to give life to some of their great visions on our stage? Would it not be worth while to make a great effort?"

I told her how deeply fascinated I was by the Elizabethan drama, by such masterpieces as Webster's *The White Devil* and *The Duchess of Malfi*, and even by some minor but delightful works such as Heywood's *A Women Killed with Kindness*. I spoke to her about that scene of this last play in which Nan, having lost her children, her home, through her unfaithfulness, receives from her husband several things which belong to her and which he sends to her as if to express more definitely their separation. Among these things she sees the lute which use to cheer her loneliness. She takes it and tries to play on it, but it does not respond as it used to, and she murmurs: "We both are out of tune." I had always seen the face and heard the voice of Eleonora while reading this scene, and now, while I was speaking, she said again and again to herself: "Beautiful, beautiful!"

To my great surprise I found that although she did not speak English, she knew perfectly well and loved passionately Ford's great tragedy of Giovanni and Annabella, *'Tis Pity She's a Whore*. "Oh, that scene in which Giovanni appears before his sister's husband, with her heart on his sword!" And she stretched out her hand, while her face changed entirely, became young and fierce and seemed to be on fire with triumphant revenge. Her eyes looked straight before her, as if hypnotized by the vision of Annabella's heart on the point of the sword.

I told her that I intended to translate John Ford's other great tragedy, *The Broken Heart*, and I described that scene in which Calantha, while she is dancing, receives the news of her father's and then of her lover's death, and continues her dance without revealing the terrible emotion which will break her heart. In that reckless, heroic dance, Eleonora perhaps perceived what I perceived: a vision which had a secret affinity with her life.

"I am too old to be Calantha myself," she said. "But I would like so much to direct a performance of *The Broken Heart* in Italy. When will your translation be completed?"

"It will not be completed before you leave for America, but when you come back it will be ready for you."

It was then that Eleonora suddenly looked at me with a strange, sad astonishment in her eyes and repeated: "Come back?"

Her accent was that we have when we repeat something absurd or at least very improbable which has been said to us. Her voice and her eyes asked: "Do you believe what you say?"

I did not attach much importance, then, to this particular moment of our conversation. But when, approximately a year later, walking in a crowded street in Naples, I suddenly was struck by a crude, monotonous voice crying: "Eleonora Duse dies in Pittsburgh," the first thing which flashed through my mind was her incredulous, dreamy "Come back?".

Two weeks later something strange occurred. I was sitting on the balcony of my little home overlooking the Bay of Naples, making some corrections in my translation of the final scene of *The Broken Heart*, in which Calantha dies. Suddenly a man working in the garden below, called up to me:

"Did you hear that sound?"

I had not heard anything. I looked up and saw a ship towering against the horizon in front of me.

"That ship brings Duse back to us," the man said.

Nothing could have been more beautiful in that moment than the words and the accent of that simple Neapolitan. Whenever I think of Eleonora I hear that man's voice, I see the resplendent bay, I perceive that ship approaching and approaching, bringing back the Lady from the Sea to her beloved Italy.

32 Giovanni Grasso

Stark Young

January 1922

Scion of a dynasty of Sicilian puppeteers which had its own house, Teatro Machiavelli in Catania, Giovanni Grasso (1873–1930) went on stage as a child and took over the family business at the age of 15. The great tragedian Ernesto Rossi persuaded him to move to the live stage, and his Sicilian-dialect touring troupe soon became famous, playing at the Teatro Argentino in Rome in 1902. From 1908 he took his company to Berlin, London, Paris, St. Petersburg and, later, New York (1921, 1928), collecting such illustrious admirers as Hauptmann, D'Annunzio and Meyerhold. Grasso was considered an interpreter *par excellence* of Pirandello, especially in *La figlia di Jorio*, and carried on the tradition of Salvini as a frantically emotional Othello.

THERE is something ironical in the fact that in the place in New York where least scenery and equipment has been this season there has been the finest acting. Grasso at the Royal Theatre on the Bowery has packed the house with Italians night after night for weeks. His presence there and the power that carries his art along serve very well to remind us that after all the actor has something to do on the stage as well as the lights and costumes and scenery and dramatic problems about which we talk so much.

Grasso belongs to the naturalistic school of Sicily. This art of his gets its life through improvisation. It comes from a land where there is an abundance of animation, vitality, fire and spirit and flexibility. It is free; it invents, glows, strikes, is shattered; it is life itself, naked, simple, inevitable, though never very psychological or complex. It exercises us not by refining on our reflections and adding nuances to our inner experience; but by putting into play those more open and universal faculties of the heart and mind that make us a part of all human experience everywhere. Such art has not the subtlety of mists and shadows and visionary depths; but for all that it may have a subtlety of its own, the subtle and infinite simplicities of light on a wall or of the sky at noon. Grasso's effects come straight to us. Within an elemental range and definite limitation they are perfect. From the minute he comes on the stage his absorption and his complete possession by the part give to him a magnetism and a kind of violent unity that are more alive in their way than life itself. For any student of acting Grasso is a veritable school; in his art the foundation of all acting can be studied, however different the method or school may be that will ultimately be followed.

33 Mei Lan-Fang

Stark Young

April 1930

Whatever impression Americans had of Chinese theatre before the arrival of Mei Lan-Fang (1894–1961) came from trips to Chinatown, where ignorance of the meaning of music, words and costumes led to descriptions of such performances as outlandish and discordant. *The Yellow Jacket*, a pseudo-Chinese play by George Hazelton and Ben-Rimo, made some of the conventions familiar to adventurous audiences. However, the real revelations came with Mei Lan-Fang's world tours. He inspired Bertolt Brecht and Vsevolod Meyerhold, who saw him in 1932, to experiment with a more conventionalized style of acting. Mei was the member of an acting dynasty and, under the protection of powerful warlords, distinguished himself as a *dan* or player of women's roles. By combining two previously separate types and amalgamating martial arts to delicate behaviour, he created his own repertoire and became internationally famous. Despite his acceptance by Charlie Chaplin and Douglas Fairbanks, audiences in the United States were bemused by a man playing a woman, critics comparing him with the vaudeville female impersonator Julian Eltinge. Stark Young's response to Mei is a more thoughtful analysis of the qualities which make a great actor and their contribution to a definition of classical art.

THE conventions of the Chinese theatre are more or less known to many foreigners, and if not, can be easily read about. One way or another, such conventions as stooping, to show that you pass through a door, the property men who are to move things about and to be regarded meanwhile as themselves invisible, the whip to represent a horse, are fairly common knowledge. There are numberless others, from such simple representations as the duster of horsehair that denotes divine or eminent persons, or walking on the knees to denote trembling with fear, to the more elaborate conventions in the dancing, the music and musical instruments, the usage of the sleeves, the diverse modes for entrances and exits, the costumes, the masks of the faces, painted—by formulas, for the most part ancient—with a predominant red to signify the heroic, with blue for cruelty, and so on. These conventions are sometimes distant and elusive; in their simpler forms they are innocently smiled at among foreigners, in much the same way as the tilt of the head and arrangement of the limbs in Byzantine painting or in Botticelli or the archaic smile and eyes of early Greek sculpture, are smiled at; and are naively taken to imply that the artist did not know how things actually look and had stumbled but blindly toward the light. It is of course easier to dwell thus on any departure from reality than it is to learn the alphabet of an art and to read its language. But to dwell very much on these conventions in Mei Lan-fang's art is a mistake.

An account of Mei Lan-fang's life and work is as readily found as an account of the Chinese theatre. He was a musician at seven, a successful player of female roles at twelve; he is the greatest Chinese actor, is "Foremost of the Pear Orchard" and head of the Ching-Chung Monastery, the highest titles in his art. He has a repertory of four hundred plays. He has made profound studies into the arts of China, has revived many old forms in plays, music and dancing, and through his tact and genius combined these with his country's modern theatrical art; for example, the old classical dances of China, which he has set to the music of today. He has combined styles hitherto strictly separate in Chinese tradition—the operatic and histrionic female roles, for example—and from either of them has drawn at will, in order from such a fusion to enrich and increase the flexibility of his portrayal. He has created a school or tradition that involves every element in the theatre, costume, music, realism, stylization, spoken and sung speeches, and so on. As a medium for the art of acting we may record that, however foreign his music may be, his voice is plainly one of great flexibility, brightness and dramatic timbre; his muscular control, based on dancing and acrobatics, is remarkable; his mask mobile, accurate and trained to that passive and exact restraint that we see in good Chinese sculpture; his eyes somewhat larger than those of most Chinese and highly expressive; his famous hands slender and trained to the utmost in the conventional and complex uses of his art. He is medium height; the face oval; the waist, from which so much of his gesture and movement pivot, is supple, well-knit and thoroughly disciplined. The nervous co-ordination is so manifestly responsive to the action around him on the stage, and so almost supernaturally sensitive to the audience, that it becomes one of the chief sources of his magnetism, and might indeed become, if he should play too long for foreign audiences, a source of danger to the purity and wholeness of his art.

This Chinese theatre brought to us by Mei Lan-fang is not necessarily the greatest kind of theatre art; we should only waste time getting into that discussion. What counts for us just now, and makes the event of so much point, is that, far beyond anything in the Western theatre, it is a theatre that is pure and that is complete. Saying that it is pure art does not mean that, like music or architecture, it exists solely within its own terms, entirely without reference to any thing outside itself, for no theatre could be without some degree of verisimilitude. This Chinese theatre, like any other, is constantly based on resemblance, on a truth to the life we see among men and to the world that we look upon or dream of. Even its conventions are largely stylizations of actual conditions of place or action. This is the point and is a matter that must be put carefully: the purity of this Chinese theatre art consists in the fact that everything employed in it—action, facial expression, voice, movement, speech, the story, the place and so on—is so subordinated to the artistic intention that the resulting work is in itself an entity wholly ideal, a work of art, at no point to be mistaken for actuality. To say that this Chinese art is not necessarily inclusive of all human experience but is as theatre art complete, means that it draws on every medium of this particular art, acting, speech, singing, music, dancing in the wide meaning of the term, visual décor and, finally, the audience, for the players include the audience in their technique as definitely and frankly as any other element. Furthermore, this is a theatre with an exact and passionately felt tradition behind it, a severe discipline and apprenticeship and an exacting public, so that whatever, good or bad, is done, can be taken as settled and intentional and ready to be judged. And it is based on great sophistication, for the audience, with the story and characters already known, and all merely incidental realism dispensed with, is concerned with the performance itself, its quality and progress. Mei Lan-fang's theatre, then, is a veritable school of principles for us to consider.

We watch *The Death of the Tiger General*. It is a play from the Ming Dynasty, a sixteenth century piece. I take it because it is the most complete and admirable number on Mei Lan-fang's present program, less flexible, free or intimate than the play about the slipper; and more austere, fixed and in the grand style. The walls, a permanent set, painted to represent open brick work or lacquer, with two doors, left and right, at the back, are hung with embroidered tapestries. Fei Chen-o, a court lady, has taken the place of the imperial princess, who has promised to wed the Tiger General in order more securely to kill him and avenge her family, whose ruin he has worked. She enters, sings an aria in which she sets forth her intention, and in this and her soliloquy and dance, expresses her varying states of mind, the vengeance, shame, horror, resolution, seduction and murder. The Tiger General enters, somewhat overcome by the wine with which his fellow officers have toasted him in honor of his betrothal. Fei Chen-o beguiles him into drinking more wine, the nuptial couch is brought in by the property men, the General takes off his helmet and coat and falls asleep. Fei Chen-o calls her maids to make her ready. They remove her head-dress, her belt studded with jade, and her magnificent coat. She sends the attendants away, looks behind the curtain to see if the Tiger General is asleep, plunges her dagger into his breast. A struggle follows in which an old wound is struck, he falls, she kills him with his own sword, which she snatches from where it hangs above the couch. Then follows a song of her dread of the soldiers, of shame, of death; she cuts her throat with the sword and falls lifeless.

I am shaken with an excitement that is curiously stronger than I am likely to get from any mere photographic portrayal of death and horror and is yet at the same time vaguer and more exalted; and then gradually the points that are important to me, and greatly so to our Western theatre, begin to range themselves in my mind.

I hear the music of the orchestra, the ti-tzu, or flute, once used in the older aristocratic theatre and reinstated in Chinese favour through Mei Lan-fang's influence, the cymbal, flutes and other instruments. The scale is foreign to our ears but much of the music becomes easily distinguishable and dramatic in effect. I see that this Chinese theatre art is based on music, or at least musically seen, it is felt as moving continuously within the realm of music. I note the fine accentuation of the gesture by music, the tapping of a drum, or, in this classic drama especially, the noble line of the flute, without the quarter notes, without the trills that some of the musical modes allow, but grave, austere, leading on the tragic emotion. Sometimes the emotional content of the scene opens more fully and follows the musical idea given to it by the orchestra. I realize more than ever that the final quality, pure and ideal, of a work of theatre art is measured by the degree of its motion toward music, the sense, whether the music be heard or only felt continuously, of resting on musical life.

I note the rising into song whenever the pitch of the emotion seems to demand it, which is biologically true—since with an access of vitality it is natural for us to burst into song—and which seems to me a natural and necessary condition in the highest development of the theatre art. The Greeks practiced it; the Church has always known how to preserve, in the drama of the mass, this alternation of spoken and sung levels of feeling; and Shakespeare and Marlowe, in the absence of such a technical possibility, did what they could to make up for the lack by an extreme heightening of the style, straining their poetic medium to its last mad divinity.

I note in this Chinese theatre that of the mediums involved that of the actor is quite frankly the chief; which is sound doctrine since he, of all these mediums, has most connection with the audience, who are human beings like himself.

I notice at once that Mei Lan-fang's make-up is the most beautiful I have ever seen, those various carmines that shade his eyes and give them the contours of the eyes in classic Chinese sculpture, that black of the eyebrows underlaid with red, and blended into the surrounding white, like painted porcelains, that sharp outline of the hair arranged about the face in order to define the type desired. The face of the Tiger General is painted into a complete mask, black, white, red, in flat patterns.

I notice in Mei Lan-fang's acting that the rhythms of the body are complete throughout. If a gesture is made with the right hand, it not only proceeds from the right shoulder (in much of the acting we see hereabouts not even that occurs) but affects the left shoulder as well; so that the entire torso falls into the justly related rhythms. The head is constantly moving, subtly alive on the neck, a motion that may often be unnoticed, as we may overlook the vibration of line and plane in fine sculpture. The use of the sleeves, from which hang the long white cuffs far down below the hands, is, in Mei Lan-fang, regarded by his Chinese public as the height of all his accomplishments. The variety of these usages and conventions a foreigner could only observe after a long familiarity with his art, but the beauty and drama of the dance that he creates from them is evident. At one moment in the play, after Fei Chen-o has put off her head-dress and coat, and stands dressed in her blue jacket with its white linings and white sleeves and the long dress of white, she flees in terror from the maddened Tiger General, and you see the sleeves go up, wildly fluttered, like a white dove, you even hear the flutter of wings in quick flight; a thing so subtly done and perfect that you can hardly believe it happened, and yet it was done with great certainty and design, even to its exact position on the stage.

I note the acrobatic display in this Chinese acting, softened or stiffened according to the character. Of this fact we may say that, for one thing it is based on a fundamental muscular impulse within our bodies; and, for another, that this acrobatic technique serves to relate the actor, through the medium of his body, more fluently and more accurately, to the musical basis on which his art relies.

Of the many conventions and symbols, I note how, even those that are as symbolic as a word—which, of course, means nothing until you learn what it represents—have tended, because of their significance and association, to acquire a degree of perfection in themselves – the stooping to enter a door, for example, the hiding of the face during emotion at certain times, the symbolic objects themselves, those decorative whips, dusters, parts of the costume. I note the precision where precision is desired for the whole effect—a movement of blowing out the light is as exact as the most realistic actor of great talent could make it.

My mind experiencing all this is filled with the various imports. The first of these concerns realism in art. This is, after all, the greatest question in art, and parallels what is the greatest question in our life: the relation of the actual around us to ourselves, of our own bodies to our minds and souls, of what is permanent in time to what is passing, the extent to which the world is related to us and restated within us for our own uses, the necessity we feel for signing the world of our experience with the name of our dreams. This Chinese theatre is spoken of as completely unrealistic art, entirely ideal in character. But while this is in a larger sense true, we must be careful not to be misled. This theatre art of Mei Lan-fang is not completely without realism, not in the sense that a cubistic painting would be, an abstract Arabic decoration, a geometric dance design. Its exact parallel is Chinese painting and sculpture. In these the impression that remains in the memory is of the abstract and decorative, but we are constantly surprised at the exactitude with which nature, a leaf, a bough, a bird, a hand, a mantle, has been observed, and are amazed at the dazzling notation of characteristic details and at the manner in which they are made to supercede and concentrate their own actuality. This exact notation is marvellously set into the whole work of art, which taken in its completeness, is ideal and dreamlike. To judge even by their common paintings and statuettes, the delight felt by the Chinese in this dexterous realism combined with tradition, convention and abstract pattern, must be very strong. We are to remember this when we hear it said that Mei Lan-fang's art is wholly unrealistic. We must also remember that one of the things to learn from this Chinese theatre art is not the need for unrealism or its contrary, but rather the exactness of the degree to which, in every part of it, realism is employed. The gestures, the narration, the acting, even the much discussed falsetto voice employed for the female roles, the movement, and so on, all are the same distance from the actual; which is another way of saying that the whole achieves a total unity of style.

But there is a reverse observation about this art that is also misleading. With the matter of the commonly heard phrase, the female impersonator, we need not concern ourselves. The Chinese themselves have often warned us, and we have only to use our senses, to see that Mei Lan-fang does not attempt to represent a woman. He seeks to discover and recreate certain essential qualities in movement, emotional rhythm, grace, force of will, seduction, vivacity or tenderness; and from these to present a figure, secure in its feminine attributes and persuasion, created into the pattern of a dance, poetic in essence. But in the matter of those impersonations of emotion and states of mind of which we hear so much—of fear, hate, love et cetera—we must get the point straight. There is no intention of acting out an emotion or of portraying the actual expression that would accompany such an emotion in life. The intention, again, is that which we see in good Chinese statues and paintings. The motion is stilled into something less immediate than the actual emotion in life; it contrives to give us the shock of truth without the incidental intrusion of imitation or photography; we have the sense of action in repose, of finalities within a flux of forms, of something beautiful and elusive. Words can scarcely express this point, but, from the realm of our own culture, we have, in order to realize it, only to look at some work of Mino da Fiesole, Desiderio da Settignano, Rosellino, for example, or Duccio, noting the flow of the essential lines, the concentration toward some ideal harmony, the sense of some beautiful transcription of reality and that elusive flight from it to the permanent.

This idealistic flexibility, with regard to the use of the actual, leads the Chinese theatre art into the freedom of our profoundest human truth, into purities of rendering essential quality, and into confirmations of the human mind, not as dependent for its proofs on things outside itself, but as a reality among other realities. In that last scene of the play where Fei Chen-o grovels with her despair, draws the sword across her throat, and falls, crumpled and motionless, down on the floor—that stillness, which is like the stillness and sudden darkness that must come suddenly thus into that anguished soul—is more exact that any blood or final convulsions could be. The mingling freely of supernatural beings and mortal men, which we see constantly in these plays as a mere matter of course, is a simple rendering of one of our commonest feelings; I mean the gods, memory, the great dead, dreams, the ghosts of love, these presences that are so often within us, even beside us they seem, so real are they. There are some inner realities of which all outward evidence is only a weak obstruction to their full intensity; there is no outer reality in action or expression that would not obstruct the full effect; and here if necessary, this Chinese method permits of no reality whatever; the face, for instance, at some terrible moment is hidden with the sleeves, leaving the grief suddenly hidden from us, as, even in life, another's grief at its greatest depths must be, no matter what outward signs of it occur. Such instances as these are only a few among the many advantages of such flexibility as the Chinese theatre enjoys. As a matter of fact, to come to the point, Mei Lan-fang is freer from the bonds of these conventional traditions in his art than our theatre is from its realism; for, wishing to work a certain shock and check, whenever he likes he can successfully insert a certain amount of realistic detail, whereas one of our actors, no matter what removal and style he may long for in some passage dear to him, is tied to such gestures, manners and actual possibilities as are conceivable in life.

I have seen various survivals from other epochs—at the Théâtre Français, for instance, but never before this Chinese theatre of Mei Lan-fang's have I seen a high, contemporaneous instance of the classical minded in the theatre arts. By classical in this sense I do not mean any reference to Greece and Rome necessarily but to a state of mind, an attitude in art, that on the whole accepts certain forms, certain type ideas, characters, working patterns, and takes for granted that it is within these that the artist is to express himself. In this sense Beethoven, using the strict musical forms and altering, refuting and enriching them with his own romantic soul, was not classical; nor was Michelangelo, whose magnificent and sometimes perverse treatments, in the Campidoglio, for instance, are so full of a secret and personal violence. Racine, the ancient Noh plays of Japan, the sculpture of Phidias, the mass ritual of the Catholic Church are classical minded. With regard to Mei Lan-fang's theatre it is just at this point, that one of the gravest misconceptions has arisen. We are told that in it there is a fixed way to do everything, unalterable conventions and rules, and that the secret of its beautiful persuasion lies in the fact that it is not original, not disturbed with egotism and individualism, but is all set, established, approved of by tradition, perfected by the centuries. As a matter of fact, though this is not an uncommon way of speaking of the classical, to say so is only to describe an art that is dead. When such an imprisonment within form exists, there is no art but mostly only husks, dry husks unable to contain the living content that waits to be expressed. No, the essence of the classical mind is that within this form and typicality you do not evade or nullify yourself but express yourself. Fixed though a pattern may tend to be, the creative impulse, working on it, finds itself; as many diverse men may find themselves or may express themselves, looking on the sea, which remains in its character nevertheless, or at the wide sky, in which each one creates an image. There are people who understand, and those who do not, that a prayer repeated through a thousand years by millions of lips may still contain the essence of fresh needs, just as the human body, always the same, always different, still carries the inexhaustible variety of countless souls. This classical mindedness in art, however, is not, of course, the only kind of mind, and not necessarily the most admirable. With time and movement the largest patterns and forms are due to change. The point merely is that in the Chinese theatre so far, for reasons deep within the soul and history of the race, this change has not been convulsive or obliterative; the classical mind remains.

As a matter of fact, however, Mei Lan-fang's art is by no means so fixed as all this might imply. He has not only forced traditional forms to express his own poetry and energy and wonder, but has originated many treatments, revived and illuminated many lost features of the Chinese theatre, presenting them singly or in a creative fusion with contemporary forms. His performances are alive with their individual immediacy, never dry or academic. Like everything that is art instead of being merely mechanical, they press constantly against the pattern, at the same time staying within it, and by that very pressure and conformity they keep themselves alive; an exact parallel of what happens elsewhere: in life a man's individual self struggles against the human type in which he exists, remaining at the same time, unless he be a freak, within the type; in art a pattern made by hand differs from one made by machinery by this same living combination of assertion and restriction. On the whole, nevertheless, this Chinese theatre is classical; the forms remain like great aspects of the natural world, which a man accepts, and the image of which within himself he bends to his own uses.

Not only upon this quality of the classical, which may occur in any country, but also on the Greek, Mei Lan-fang's theatre is a luminous comment. The Elizabethan parallels with the Chinese theatre are obvious and more or less external. There is the fixed scene, with certain properties and conventions, naive or not naive, according as you may happen to see it; there is a bush for a forest at the Globe, a whip for a horse at the Pekin theatre, there are the four men to stand for an army, certain arbitrary positions on the stage to indicate various places, and so on. There is the prologue. There are couplets said at the Chinese actor's entrance and others said at his exit, very much as the end of the scene was often indicated in Shakespeare by a couplet:

> The time is out of joint: O cursed spite,
> That ever I was born to set it right!

There are the men playing female roles. There is the possibility of shifting back and forth between prose and verse, and of writing the play in any number of scenes.

But the comment of Mei Lan-fang's theatre on the Greek is the most profound that I have ever seen. I have seen German and English revivals of Greek dramas, done often with ingenuity, spaciousness and, at certain intervals, even with power. But the Greek element in these was only in retrospect, too self-conscious, often too theoretical, though now and then out of its own secure universality quite compelling and convincing, whether there was an authentic slant or not to the interpretation afforded us. I have seen Italian productions of Euripides and of *Oedipus Rex*, careless but not without vitality and eloquence, superbly aired beneath the sky and amidst the ruins of classic Rome; given too with some feeling of the hail and farewell that time has only increased in these tragic poems. But in none of these was the Greek element inherent and not the result of studious interest, however much we felt its poetry and beauty. I have seen numerous pieces from the classic French period, *Polyeucte*, for example, *Andromache*, with their classicistic set, and courtly version of the Greek spirit; and I saw once Mounet Sully do his Oedipus. This last, by virtue of three hundred years of tradition in the French classic theatre, had an inherent spirit, very elegant and august and often magnificently moving. And, through this authentic French tradition, plus the force of Sophocles' genius and the Greek character of the powerful story, a considerable degree of Greek quality seemed genuinely implicit in it, though a very late Greek quality, long after Athens was a mere eclectic centre of art. But this Chinese theatre is a profound comment because the qualities reminiscent of Greece represent for China a natural way of thought, a spirit deeply inherent. There are not only the patent resemblances like the men in female roles, the Chinese faces often painted into masks, with traditional styles and conventional meanings, scarcely to be distinguished from the actual masking in Attic theatres, the limitation in settings; there are also resemblances in qualities that proceed from the inmost characteristics of mind and spirit. There are the fixed patterns for exits and entrances and stage movement, there is the use of the dancing medium, in the fullest sense of the term, the basis of musical accompaniment, musical accentuation, the rising into music where the emotion demands the very fullest expression, there is the fusion of words, speech, singing, music, dancing and décor into one art. There are the standard scenes, built on familiar patterns, set scenes as it were, which, as with many of our musical forms, are to be enjoyed and admired for the treatment afforded them—Recognition Scenes, Parting Scenes, Scenes Based on Irony, Dialectic Scenes and so on. There is the search for pattern, and the subordination of personal emotion to some passionate abstraction and secure outline. There is the unceasing stylization throughout. There is the intention of beauty, grace or exaltation.

It must be said, however, that there was a boldness or shock in the Greek sometimes that would be excessive for the Chinese. In *Oedipus Rex*, for example, the king, after digging out his eyes, enters with his bleeding face and his speech that begins with the pain and the physical detail of his voice seeming so far away, and moves on to the thought of that horror awaiting him in the world of the dead. In this scene the physical detail is used to clinch the impression on the audience' mind, to send the moment into their bloods and make them believe it; and the poetic details are used to create the ideal significance that lies in the moment, and to give it wings. There is nothing like that in Chinese, not in its authentic theatre. The reluctance on its part to present such physical extremes, has no doubt something to do with the racial soul, in which death and horror have their due place but are seen in a long avenue of centuries and patient thought. When Fei Chen-o approaches the Tiger General's couch, she has drawn a strand of her hair across her mouth, on which her teeth are clenched—even the abysm of hate must be covered like that or in some way prevented from ugliness, it must ultimately be beautiful.

This brings us to a final point on which there is much misconception and mistaken writing with regard to Mei Lan-fang's theatre. It is often said that the sole end of this Chinese art is to achieve grace and beauty. This is entirely confusing, though, it must be confessed, to such persons and races as may have a smaller sense of beauty and grace, it is something of an easy way out.

To say that we seek grace and beauty in themselves is as foolish as to speak of seeking freedom for its own sake: we seek freedom only in order to be the better able to achieve something that we desire and aim at. We must go farther back now and start again. Then we shall say that what this Chinese art seeks primarily is the lack of what we may call effortism. That means that you have not achieved your end when you have merely arrived at an execution of what there was to do, however excellently and skillfully your effort came off. What you strive for is something that follows on this expert and complete accomplishment; I mean that when all else is accomplished, there remains the direction to be finally taken; that when all else is done, there remains to be achieved the flower, the fragrance, the soul, the last grace of it. Hence the attempt to present to us that quality of the beauty, discovery and permanence of patterns. These patterns denote and contain the soul of us. Watching Mei Lan-fang through one of his tragic scenes, I am absorbed with the thought of how this persistent weaving of life among its own beautiful forms binds and delights us. But even this grace or soul or beauty— whatever name we want to call it by—does not remain left to itself like that. It constitutes a sort of continuum, a something by which is provided the continuity that runs through one action to another, through phrase to phrase, idea to idea, and so on through all the successive parts of the play, establishing thus for it a kind of music or free essence in which it moves. We may say, moreover, looking at the drama as a social element, that it may be this final quality of grace and beauty that has given the whole Chinese theatre a freedom from which derives, more than from anything else, its continuity and endurance within the race, as if it were not only an art but a quality of soul.

34 Between curtains: The acting of the Abbey Theatre

Andrew J. Stewart

March 1933

The Irish National Dramatic Society was founded in 1902 by E. F. Horniman as a theatrical outlet for the Celtic Revival, and two years later moved into a permanent position as the Abbey Theatre, Dublin. Those who wanted it to be a political mouthpiece defected, and it became known for the poetic vagaries of W. B. Yeats and the earthy comedies of Lady Gregory, until it discovered J. M. Synge, who worked in both modes. More than the repertoire, it was the subdued and low-key nature of the acting that attracted the critics. The riots around Synge's *The Playboy of the Western World* (1907) won the Abbey a notoriety that was repeated during its tours of the U.S. in 1914 (the cast was imprisoned in Philadelphia). With subsidies from the new Free State Government in 1925 it became *de facto* the Irish national theatre and enjoyed a resurgence with such actors as Maire O'Neill, Barry Fitzgerald and Sara Allgood. The plays of O'Casey were met with the same kind of negative reaction as *Playboy* had been, however, and by the early 1930s, frequently on tour, the Abbey was in an artistic doldrums.

For three years I have been in close contact with the Abbey Theatre and with the theatre's audience. What has especially interested me is the general criticism of Abbey acting.

As if reciting from the multiplication table, people say that an actor from the Abbey Theatre in Dublin is noted for sincerity, naturalness, and simplicity. I owe thanks to the German chess partner who forced me to look carefully into these qualities. He wanted to know why naturalness didn't imply simplicity, why naturalness and simplicity weren't ingredients of sincerity, and why, if this were so, the term sincerity couldn't be omitted. "I'll try to explain on paper," I told him.

The Abbey actor is sincere, as any conscientious actor is sincere, in his love of acting and in his effort to present life as he sees it.

He is natural in his interpretation of character. He speaks and moves like a human being. He does not overstress his words and emphasize his gestures. His pauses are no longer than those heard in daily conversation. By playing in many parts he learns to run the gamut of human emotions, but he is not true to Abbey standards if he girds up his loins for a dramatic killing. He has at his command a choice of voice and accent, of tone quality and volume. His naturalness does not necessarily come naturally: it is a matter of conscious technique.

The Abbey actor of today speaks of Abbey tones and delivery. Lennox Robinson writes that it takes a long time to train a player in the Abbey method. As far back as 1903 Lady Gregory told a youthful actor that all he had to do when he walked across the stage was to walk across the stage. "No, not like an English actor. No facial expression required. Let your legs do the work." For ten years before this a group that subsequently became the Abbey Company had been instructed to avoid bombast in speech and action by Frank Fay, an admirer of Antoine, and Willie Fay, who, through acting part of the time in England, was in touch with the exaggerated acting displayed there. As the Fays worked with untrained amateurs (most of them were profoundly unaware of the artificial conventions of English acting) they were able to devote themselves to the training of voices and to laying the foundation of honest character portrayal. The Fays, not being in favor of over-emphasis on the stage, insisted that the actors should forget the footlights and act just as the people would whom they were presenting. This aim was facilitated by rehearsals and appearances in private houses and upon small stages. This early insistence upon natural acting has become, in the course of years, a tradition in the Abbey Theatre, and new actors have to learn it from older actors and often from a producer who also has had the technique of naturalness handed on to him.

The naturalness of the present company is just as consciously an acting convention as the subtle simulation of human action on the English and American stages or the declamatory method of the French actor of tragedy. The French tragedian moves like a dancer, poses like a sculptor's subject, and with an ear for applause trumpets a purple passage. A tragic role is a chance for him to display his virtuosity. An English or an American actor says to himself, "I do not have to be natural. I only have to appear natural." In his performance he allows for the toning down of his work to approximate naturalness as it penetrates forward from the stage through space and light to the eyes of watchers in the audience. If he practised his stage deportment in a living room he would be considered affected.

The Irish actor is the one actor who becomes more lifelike the closer we get to the stage. He should be seen only in an intimate theatre. From the rear of the balcony of a large theatre, or worse yet, from its gallery, his performance seems flat, particularly if it is the first time you have seen him and are not aware of the Abbey convention. When the Irish actor leaves his dressing room he leaves himself behind. When we see him he is Captain Boyle basking in squalor, or Christy Mahon boasting in the shebeen, or John Ferguson weighed down by anguish. These men have no interest in footlights and tier on tier of eyes. They have their own affairs to attend to. The Irish actor on the stage has a major preoccupation: being Captain Boyle exactly as he is in life, or Christy Mahon exactly as he is in life, or John Ferguson exactly as he is in life. And as conscientiously as he strives not to overdo the part, in the same degree he strives not to underdo it. While on the stage he is, to the best of his ability, the character.

The Irish actor's simplicity cannot possibly imply that he lacks acting technique. It can only mean that he gets his effects in an unobtrusive fashion. For the Irish actor to be natural he must be simple. Although he occasionally plays a poetic role, he is occupied most of the time with the study of characters in realistic plays. These characters are usually drawn from the lower walks of life. They are the poor, the humble, the unheeded, the unknown and unsung who make up most of the population in all parts of Ireland, the country, the small town, the city. Such people, as a rule, do not build around themselves a shell of standardized behavior. They have a tendency to speak less guardedly and to act more spontaneously than the upper class, trained to conformity in conduct. W. B. Yeats urged young dramatists to study the Irish folk because of their straightforwardness. Despite their emotional complexities, which might be as involved as Phedre's or Nina Leeds's, their visible deeds and spoken words are stamped with a directness uninfluenced by the moving picture, the stage, literature, and the machinery of sustained education.

But naturalness, let it be remembered, does not always walk hand in hand with simplicity. The complicated characters that we see on the stage so frequently today—those frustrated by life, those philosophical to the point of neutrality, those neurotically introspective; the nervous wreck, the sextossed, the diseased—such characters, too, are natural in the sense that they are actual products of nature. Compared with these, the characters seen upon the Abbey stage are simple. The Abbey actor, in portraying them just as they are, has to be simple, too.

The American and English theatre-goer does not always have in mind a simple presentation of simple people when he says that the Irish actor's performance has an air of simplicity. He more than likely means it is different from what he is used to seeing, and as he is accustomed to watching a simulation of life on the stage, a form of representation more heightened than life itself, the Abbey actor's manner, by contrast, is simple.

As much has been written and said about the Irish actor's voice as about his sincerity, naturalness, and simplicity. It takes years for news to get around, and many people who today comment on the exquisite voices of the present Abbey company are unconsciously re-echoing reactions to the earlier Abbey group that came over in 1911, 1912, 1914, and 1927, and in which there were many splendid voices. Although strong and pleasing enough, there is not a voice of exceptional quality in the Abbey company now in this country other than Eileen Crowe's, which is far richer than the average professional's.

This past summer I saw Sara Allgood of the original company at the Rotunda in Dublin, in *The Cherry Orchard*. Her voice is deep, rich, flexible, and astonishingly beautiful. As she had studied under Frank Fay, the first voice teacher at the Abbey, I asked her after the play what he stressed when teaching voice production. "Frank Fay emphasized clearness of speech, strength without loudness, and particularly the greatest possible tone variety." U. Wright, who has been with the Abbey company since 1902, gave me additional information about Fay's methods. "He would make us sing A's and O's for hours, raising and lowering the key. He insisted on distinct final D's and T's. The ends of our sentences had to be well out. Sharp! He saw to it that we took breathing exercises." This thorough voice training, given and followed without benefit of contract or fat pay check, developed sound voices and made the Abbey players famous for their beautiful speech. The present company has no voice teacher within the theatre, and has no formal drill in voice production. But both the old and new groups have in common three attributes: lovely pronunciation, variety of inflection, and the gift of phrasing.

There has always been a decided difference of opinion over the Abbey manner of acting. One English professor I know went away disgruntled after traveling from Richmond to Philadelphia to see the Abbey Theatre Irish Players. Another English professor itemizes their merits for me once a week. The New York dramatic critics sing their praises like publicity agents. One afternoon last summer I visited in Dublin an eminent poet, painter, mystic, and economist. "If I want to be bored I go down to see some quiet Abbey acting," he said. That same evening I went to see an actress once a member of the original Abbey group. "The success of both companies," she told me, "is due to quiet acting."

The next night I walked out of the Abbey behind two Americans. Said the wife: "I didn't see a bit of acting all evening." Said the husband: "That was acting. Our players are too cocained up."

35 The actor and the revolution

Pavel Markov

September 1936

The first years following the October Revolution in Russia had been a time of great ferment in the theatre. Despite the privations of civil war, avant-garde experimentation by Meyerhold, Eisenstein, Tairov and Tretyakov had been the norm, an attempt to find an artistic equivalent of the social upheavals. Constructivism, cubo-futurism, eccentricism, circusization were talismanic concepts. By the mid-1930s, however, Stalin had made everything in the Soviet Union subservient to the Five Year Plans and his own hold on power. "Formalist" experiments fell into disrepute and Socialist Realism was prescribed as the national style in literature and art.

Under these circumstances, Pavel Aleksandrovich Markov (1897–1980) had the ticklish task of explaining theatrical current events to an American reader. He had published his first book on modern theatrical trends in 1924 and was instrumental in creating the Satire Studio in 1920 with Vladimir Mayakovsky. Invited to work at the Moscow Art Theatre in 1925, he ran its literary department from 1948. Whatever the changes in artistic policy dictated from above, he found ways of working with them without compromising his own principles. In this survey of the Soviet theatre, there is, of course, an undercurrent of Marxist thinking, but Markov manages to be more even-handed and less tendentious than many of his colleagues.

———————————

I

IN THE early days of the revolution, and in the bitter Civil War that followed, with hunger and blockade threatening the young Union, Moscow, Petrograd and every centre of theatrical activity became conscious of the growth and spread of a new theatre movement. Schools and studios sprouted on every side, forming a chain that eventually became the main strength of the theatre.

These schools and studios were intent on formulating the principles of the art of the theatre and discovering new techniques of acting. Many succumbed after completing this task; others, finding themselves unable to exert any essential influence, passed quietly away. The few remaining, in spite of deprivation and a lack of the most fundamental necessities, developed into large and important theatres.

The 'studio', as a conception, born on the eve of the revolution and reaching its culmination soon afterwards, played an extraordinarily significant role. One of its primary statements was a new basis for group acting—not groups based on immediate box-office returns but formed along lines of a common artistic program.

Any attempts to form a 'new' theatre before the revolution, besides the handicap of lack of precedent and feeble social grounds, had to meet the problem of considering first the existing acting forces. The young Kamerny Theatre, for example, at the time of its organization in 1914, was obliged to mix unskilled apprentice actors with actors already marked with the distinctive style of an established theatre. To avoid this, several theatres decided to form school groups, or studios, within their own systems, to train young actors in a single method. As early as 1906–1907, the First Art Theatre drew its actors, with few exceptions, from its own school, with the assurance that these actors had not been subject to any other influence.

When the revolution exposed the inner decay of the existing theatre, it became clear that a renaissance (the dream of the finest artists) could never become a fact with the old actors alone, even though, among them, there were many who eagerly and sincerely tried to understand the new demands of modern life: the revival of the theatre had to be grounded in the cultivation of a new generation, growing up under modern conditions and ready to serve as flexible and sensitive material for creative experiments. The education of the actor was understood not merely as technical development but as a sharpening of his social viewpoint. This new approach affected not only the individual but the group.

Students, after having worked together and having spoken a common language for four years, were reluctant to break away from the group. Instead of actors trained for any chance occupation, entire groups with a single method and a common purpose came out of these schools. (Most of the important Soviet theatres of today had such a beginning.) This differentiates our actor from the actor of Western Europe. In Germany, for example, the most distinguished actors would, within one season, play in various theatres differing radically in style — say those of Reinhardt, Jessner, Piscator — even dropping from time to time into other genres, such as operetta (Kathe Dorsch and Pallenberg). In the Soviet theatre there are very few actors who work in more than one style or genre, and even these have only one style in which they feel at home.

A production meant, for the studio, not the sum of more or less successful rehearsals, but a means of discovering new ideas and new forms. It is easy to imagine groups spending months or even years realizing new principles of composition or the best methods of demonstrating acting or production schemes. They all burned with belief in themselves and in freedom; they were ardent patriots of their fatherland — the theatre. Even studios long dead and forgotten were regarded by their students and founders as first chapters in as many glorious histories.

But some of the studios did live on, actually making history. Starting their activities in one of the tiniest halls of Moscow, presenting at first only single episodes and acts, the students of Vakhtangov carried their collective to the present fame of the Vakhtangov Theatre. The young Meyerhold students, clustered around the banner of the Theatrical October in 1920, laid the foundation for the Meyerhold Theatre. The young students of the Maly Theatre, instead of scattering, formed the collective now known as the State New Theatre. The First Art Theatre, actually the initiator of this type of school studio, gathered into its own ranks all the members of its Second Studio. Its First Studio, working directly under Stanislavsky since before the World War, developed into the Second Art Theatre. The musical workshops of Stanislavsky and Nemirovich-Dantchenko are now known as the Stanislavsky Opera and the Nemirovich-Dantchenko Musical Theatre. The Kamerny, no longer drawing its actors from miscellaneous sources, has built up a school of its own. More recent studios go on blossoming out into public life — the Simonov Studio-Theatre, the Zavadsky Theatre and Dikki's new Studio.

Not all studios, however, grew up painlessly and easily. Very often growth was a grim process, and more than one studio gave way under it. Two of the main difficulties were the conception of the studio as an end in itself, and a separation from the actuality outside the walls. Many a studio acquired the character of a monastery, with its own morals and customs, satisfied with a limited audience of an unchanging group of friends, preventing any possible new stimulation. The very qualities their founders had rebelled against were again cultivated in this atmosphere. Their artistic revolt no longer grew out of the social revolution around them. Within a few years, once promising organisms rotted away. This is the story of Foregger's studio, killed by its blind dependence on vaudeville forms. Thus Ferdinandov's studio died unnoticed, after going into its shell of obstinate experiments in rhythm and metrics.

But, during these years, many studios grasped the significance and opportunity offered them by the renewed life outside. A new kind of actor took shape. Exposed as they had been to all literature, painting and music during their studio years, they began to feel it natural for an actor to have a wide culture. Artistry and craftsmanship were no longer separated from culture and social consciousness. That is why, when speaking about the actor of a revolutionary era, one must think not of the few striking individuals of the epoch but of the sweeping change in the standards of the entire acting level.

The problems of acting technique are inseparably related to the problems of contemporary culture. The evolution of the actor's attitude towards the theatre, which has remodelled his life and his consciousness, has not yet come to an end. Stanislavsky's principle—'not the theatre for the actor, but the actor for the theatre'—is being more profoundly interpreted than ever before. Yet the actor today exists not *only* for the theatre, but also for the social ideas and artistic aims that the theatre expresses. The actor no longer performs a series of attractive, successful roles; success now means the ripe expression of a definite artistic program and a world viewpoint. The actor is the artist who, by means of theatrical expression, embodies the theme of the play and the ideas of its characters; he is no longer the merchant-craftsman, selecting, from the established clichés, a role and an interpretation that seems suited to his abilities.

The process of change concerned older theatre groups as well as young ones. The perfect craftsmanship of the old theatres acquired new incentives and new materials. The artists who had preserved the traditions were given the opportunity to participate in renewing them. Naturally, the most passionate participators in this process were the young people who had entered the theatre in the first years of the revolution. For them, the theatre meant not only a theatre education but an experience of life. (The majority of theatrical students of that time came from the middle-class intelligentsia; the working class has taken the opportunity to send its artist sons and daughters only within recent years.) So eagerly and passionately did they throw themselves into the struggle that it was only to be expected that theatrical life, rooted in the studios, should become a stormy scrimmage of different tendencies.

Meyerhold, Tairov and other regisseurs were searching for new methods of acting. However, behind all methods, one thing was clear to the majority of students: the old theatre, the box-office theatre, with its hastily digested concoctions and its concentration on entertainment, was dead forever.

As time went on, the civil war generation began to enter the studios. This new blood again forced a new regard upon the art of acting, scorning the characteristic sentimentality of the old theatre and the decadence of the formal theatre. The young actors wanted to pour into the images that they played the new store of experience they had accumulated, a bright new light on values, new emotions, thoughts and sensations. For all this they demanded new forms; it was impossible to be abstractly beautiful and aimlessly rhythmical after the actor had seen the severity of class justice and the power of partisan struggles. This is how the inner experience of the actor caused a change of outer forms.

This is how the social character of the actor changed.

II

One of the new acting systems, of considerable significance in the first years of the revolution, was the eccentric. Brought from the West, it was closely related to bohemian and anarchistic tendencies, in opposition to all academic art. This was a world-outlook as well as a theatrical form. The eccentric openly fought all truths, raising up the essential artificiality of acting as a banner to lead the attacks on the realistic or naturalistic theatre.

The exponents of the eccentric claimed that the modern audience, unlike Shakespeare's, was unable to endure five acts and hours of orated tragedy. They claimed that the quickening tempo of modern life demanded a corresponding change in theatre forms. They drew the laws for these new forms from the music-hall and circus, with acting technique taken directly from those of clowns and side-show performers. Ideas were not to be developed in psychological detail—the eccentric proposed relative and opposed associations. The eccentric actor was to select the most prominent features, exaggerate them to (sometimes beyond) the maximum, and, after exhausting one situation, to move on to the next, different but equally sharply presented.

One cliché was removed only to make way for another. The standardized expression of love, passion, rage, which Stanislavsky often ridiculed, was replaced by another over-simplification in which clowning was the means, and which stressed absence or balance and incongruity. Instead of a live face, the eccentric actor would show a mask, choosing two or three dominating features, accenting them and discarding the rest. He proudly announced that he represented the non-existent.

Could the laws of vaudeville, however, be interpreted as theatre laws? The music-hall program, where the eccentric technique originated, is a series of items, musical or acrobatic or comic, each expressing its point in the shortest possible time. Was the audience, for whose sake presumably the form was invented, able to watch hours of a brilliant, concentrated eccentric ensemble, undiluted by alternating numbers as in its parent form? Was such a performance preferable in any way to the normal, mature theatre? Did not the eccentric kill its own raison d'être, stab itself with its own sharp weapons?

A single eccentric actor, playing in the midst of other styles, gave one the impression of a visiting star; Martinson, for instance, developed this discord as a strength, letting his partners act as foils to his wild ingenuity and tricky transitions. I am doubtful whether a production performed by dozens of Martinsons could be accepted, even granting that it could be created, which in itself is highly doubtful.

Pure eccentricity is rarely to be seen on our stage. It was bound to acquire a psychological and social interpretation. A group of Martinson roles (often found as a group within one role—witness Meyerhold's *Revizor*) is a sort of social masque. In the hands of an actress of such significant and original talent as Glizer, eccentric methods rise to a new plane.

Judith Glizer's most important contribution is her attempt to combine eccentric methods with her rich observation of life. Much less formal than Martinson, like him she builds her character on principles of association. The structure of the character of Mme. Skoblo in Glebov's *Power* is a perfect model of the maximum effect of such an approach. Here, as in several other roles, are episodes in which every second is saturated with rich psychological content. Glizer's appearance, her make-up, carriage, costume, is invariably extraordinary. But there is always a conflict between her bare method and her rich content.

One of her best roles, Inga, was constructed out of a fund of human observation with monumental results. In each new act, Glebov shows an advanced step in the growth of the character, without the intermediate stages. Glizer regarded each act as a new play, presenting in each a sharp, fully shaded characterization, different but always typical. The series of characters remains close to life, and Glizer interprets them as clearly and unforgettably as though through a microscope. However, when confronted with the role of the Englishwoman in Zarkhi's *Joy Street*, her eccentric method of interpretation ran counter to the entire production. I am not sure whether it was the fault of Glizer or of the production, but it was clear that Glizer was a hindrance to the author, and the author a hindrance to Glizer. The clash between a poster style and non-poster material showed Glizer the need for a deeper development and adaptation of her method.

In Glizer's development we can trace the course taken by the eccentric through the Soviet stage. The dominating position it occupied during the first years of the revolution now appears not to have been justified. It has left behind it some acting forms, but no production forms. With the development of social depth in Soviet playwriting, the sphere of eccentricity grows narrower. It helped to break up the clichés of the naturalistic theatre, and in so doing brought several new images into the theatre. But, in its purest form, it long ago arrived at a point where the only step it could take was a step backward to the special type of theatre that gave it birth.

III

The struggle against the naturalistic theatre was being fought on other fronts at the same time. In the so-called 'aesthetic' theatre, the actor put primary emphasis on making the theatre aesthetically attractive, and his control of rhythm, movement and voice was determined by this. Movement and gesture were minutely composed. Speech became a peculiar song. It seemed that the actor sang and danced his role, a method that helped him learn rhythm and composition but could not give him a firm psychological foundation.

These contradictions were particularly obvious at the early Kamerny Theatre, the pillar of these principles. One needed to possess Koonen's talent and Tairov's critical objectivity to develop compact contemporary images out of their early formalistic gropings. With considerable pain and many mistakes, the Kamerny actors learned that rhythm, music, and so forth, were not an aim in themselves, but only a part of the countless means of expressing content.

It became obvious that Tairov would have to revise his principles. Curiously enough, it was through the American playwright, O'Neill, that Tairov found the needed incentive for socio-psychological investigations — in *The Hairy Ape, Desire Under the Elms* and *All God's Chillun Got Wings*. For example, when the young actor Alexandrov created the leading role in *All God's Chillun*, Tairov gave him a typical rather than a detailed conception of the role, although he guarded against narrow naturalism.

All experiments in the aesthetic and formalistic education of the actor ended in disaster; none passed limits at which Tairov himself deserted.

Meyerhold, in his theory of bio-mechanics, found a different way of freeing the actor from naturalistic clichés. The revolutionary significance of bio-mechanics consisted in its fight against detailed naturalism, on the one hand, and against decorative aestheticism on the other. Meyerhold sought liberation for the actor's creation in the teachings of the reflexes and in production processes. He found the methods of outer expression in the folk-theatres, in Shakespeare's and Molière's theatres, and finally in the Kabuki. Lately, the classical Chinese theatre has added its influence.

The Magnanimous Cuckold in 1922 confirmed the craftsmanship of the actor in its purest form. In it, Meyerhold freed the actor from the ballast of exquisite costumes and make-up; he dressed the whole cast in overalls (with little variation) and gave them flexible faces free of make-up. He regarded movement not for its abstract prettiness but as the clearest expression of inner content. Of all the actors, Ilyinsky employed this method most brilliantly, without allowing the structure and continuity of his role to escape him.

Meyerhold is forever seeking a way *through his actors* to the most vivid expression of a given theme.

In this respect it may be useful to parallel the varied but equally successful accomplishments of Ilyinsky and Bogoliubov. Ilyinsky likes to play queer simpletons, social outcasts and the like, while Bogoliubov is personified strength and courage, performed in laconic, compact and heroic outlines (in *The Final Conflict, The List of Benefits*). Neither Bogoliubov nor Ilyinsky play with pretty plasticity, nor with the encumbering inheritance of Duncan and Dalcroze; nevertheless they are eloquent in movement — one might say exquisite except that the word would insult them, so perfect and precise is their movement based on counter-movement. Here dialogue is not only words, it is carried on in gestures as well, in an unbroken chain of steadily fused movement and counter-movement.

Babanova, beginning her career with Meyerhold, uses to this day this same method in the Theatre of Revolution where she now works. She composes the basic lines of a character (whether it is Masha in *After the Ball* or Shakespeare's Juliet) with the same purity, the same exactness of accent and the same scorn of petty lifelikeness, for the sake of more profound truths. Meyerhold denies calm objectivity in acting; he insists that the actor give subjective evaluations on the basis of a revolutionary world-outlook.

One cannot refrain, at this point, from a comparison of the Meyerhold and Vakhtangov methods.

Vakhtangov's contribution is that, on the basis of the whole psychological theatre and Stanislavsky's great culture, he was able to break through to new forms. Being a consistent pupil and master of the methods and principles of the Art Theatre, Vakhtangov subordinated the problems of form to the exposition of the image. The more passionately, deeply, the actor looked into life, the more natural and clear seemed the exposition. This was his guard against an actor's photographic and indifferent approach.

Vakhtangov's concept of a production as a typical general event, built up with chosen specific features, was best demonstrated in his *Miracle of Saint Anthony*, in his studio, and his production of *The Dybbuk* at the Habima Theatre. The educational system he left behind him has led to splendid results in social penetration of theatrical material. (*Princess Turandot* was only a scenic exercise, and not to be taken seriously. His earlier creations are more permanently significant.)

Shchukin, a characteristic Vakhtangov actor, adds rich reservoirs of observation to clean outer forms. It is extremely satisfying to see how Shchukin understands how to be simple. Artistic economy, in him, throws aside all exalted moments, retaining only the substance of the role. He walks along the narrow edge between naturalism and exaggeration, but so far has escaped the former as well as the latter, fusing, in his acting, the inner theme with a depth and understanding of life.

An example of the second direction of the Vakhtangov Theatre is Simonov, with excellent exterior characterizations, boldly drawn and colored. At the same time he relishes more the inner contradictions of the type than Shchukin does. He is interested, not in the heroism of men, but in their contradictions, thus inclining, in his selection of roles, towards negative types. His performance is invariably of an inner-sceptical character. In the playing of his men, he neither sympathizes with them nor believes in them, keeping a sharp eye on everything that is queer and negative in man. The history of his heroes is the history of horrible or comical downfalls.

Nevertheless, the *Turandot* line is taken by the present Vakhtangov Theatre not as study material but as the genuine Vakhtangov principle — much to our regret. Too often, depth and inner sureness are displaced by technical skill and shallow tricks, much the way a professional jockey rides a horse.

The latest productions at the Vakhtangov Theatre illustrate vividly the presence of this inner struggle in their understanding of the actor. Their *Hamlet* need not be further abused here, but the fact remains that the production did not show a single performance of power. But they can well be proud of their *Yegor Bulichov*, with its ensemble of acting strengths — notably those of Shchukin and Mansurova.

IV

At the present stage in the growth of the Soviet theatre, the most responsible task facing the Soviet actor is that of depicting the contemporary man. No matter how successfully the playwright draws the image of civil war and socialist construction, the actor is obliged himself to become acquainted with the people. Often the author has hastily sketched a figure in outline that the actor must fill in the round. Behind the play, behind the warring scenic battalions, behind the studios, a vital new method of portraying actuality has had to emerge. The actor has lost his right to skim over the surface of his types. It is easy to gather certain characteristic features and arrange out of them a superficial naturalistic image. It is much more difficult, but much more important and honest, to show the inner sense of social events. This is, perhaps, why the methods of the First Art Theatre have begun again to attract attention.

As a worker in the First Art Theatre, I believe that its methods, correctly applied, give fine and true results. And this is what has happened during the past few years. It is a fallacy to consider the degree of psychological exposition as equal to the degree of naturalism in the drawing. On the contrary; Vakhtangov was right when he strove to reveal simultaneously a deep insight and an expressive exterior. The best performances in the last period of the Art Theatre have been interested not in a narrow, purely psychological approach but in a class-psychological interpretation of a role — its growth, its development through complex inner channels. When Dobroliubov created the character of the bolshevik Mikhailov in *Bread* he steered away from cluttered naturalistic detail as well as from false exaltations, keeping the image clear of pretensions. Kudriavtsev made the Young Communist Nikolka (in *Blockade*) emotionally moving without sentimentality. Livanov brought to his role of Kambayev (in *Fear*) sharp and typical theatrical features. A full psychological penetration was given the student by Yanshin and the white-guard officer by Khmelev in *The Days of the Turbins*. And Batalov brought convincing partisan pathos to his bit in *The Armored Train*.

The new qualities that the revolution has introduced into the technique of the First Art Theatre actors has found its clearest expression in the ensemble of

Gorky's *Enemies*. Nemirovich-Dantchenko, who directed, brought a new meaning out of the phrase 'acting of attitude', once interpreted to mean the deliberately personal attitude of the actor towards his image. Now the attitude is at once personal, group, and social. Kachalov plays the liberal manufacturer Zakhar Bardin. He gives a splendid image, which never for a second swerves from a determined inner core, from which all the outer features have developed. He chooses only typical details, peeling off everything and anything not directly related to the core of his image. Together with the entire ensemble, he gives a performance that, perhaps more than any other production of the Art Theatre, well illustrates the tendencies of the theatre towards simplicity, concentration and depth.

The goal is in sight. Out of the most varied methods, a Soviet acting style is being synthesized.

36 Child of silence

Jean-Louis Barrault; translated by Eric Bentley

October 1949

Jean-Louis Barrault (1910–94) was the all-purpose *homme du théâtre* of the twentieth century. He acknowledged his debt to two creative fathers: the actor Charles Dullin at the Atélier in Paris, and the exponent of pure mime Étienne Decroux. The wiry, vital Barrault was a paradoxical actor, highly cerebral in his concepts yet flexibly physical in his technique. Drawn by his love for the classical actress Madeleine Renaud, he joined the Comédie Française, breathing fresh life into its heroic roles and introducing it to Claudel. In 1946 the couple founded the Renaud-Barrault company at the Théâtre Marigny, which became one of the leading repertories of the world. With government support, it widely toured its productions of Shakespeare, Marivaux, Kafka, Claudel, Anouilh, Offenbach and Feydeau to 1956. The company's fame was aided by the audience's familiarity with Barrault through film, especially his Baptiste in *Children of Paradise* (1945), an avatar of the great nineteenth-century mime Jean-Gaspard Deburau. Ahead lay his work at the Odéon with Beckett, Genet and Ionesco, his unceremonious ouster after the "events" of 1968 and his total-theatre adaptations of Rabelais and Jarry.

WE ALL receive a weird education. We are taught how to write. We are taught, to a lesser degree, how to speak. But we are rarely if ever taught how to move. We know writing, therefore, and can recognize its fine points, can recognize poetry; we have an idea of the word and can usually appreciate eloquence; but, having little notion of the significance of gesture, only with the utmost difficulty can we appreciate any art that proceeds from it.

If we appreciate dance, it is because dance is to gesture what song is to diction. The word and the gesture are the resources of self, the means of expression. Nothing could be more foolish than to neglect one of these dual means, yet it has been happening—and for a long time. The word has been kept going thanks to writing, its subtle and passionate derivative; thanks to an idea of genius, that of fixing what the mouth spits out in bubbles with signs executed by the tip of the hand. Writing, a miraculous artifice, partly preserves the word; *nothing helps to preserve gesture*. Dance and sport may help incidentally, but not consciously. To prove this point, it is enough to take a walk in the street. All the people coming and going around you are people who can write, who talk (more or less), who know their native tongue. Watch them move. Follow them a second or two. Observe the way they step off the sidewalk, the way they pass other pedestrians or walk side by side with them. Watch them shift from one foot to the other when they talk with someone they meet. And then ask why these persons, who know their own tongue, don't know their own feet.

We have lost our instinct for gesture. This is very clear when, during the training of a theatrical company, any given series of gestures must be enacted: the result is chaos. Most people refuse even to give their attention to gesture. They at best deem it a language for the dumb, the *primitive* form of action. In our age writing has drawn everything to itself; we live in an age of talkers.

We must re-examine gesture. For the sake of our education, of our "cultivation", we must clear this terrain so long abandoned. Just as the theatre has for its mission the preservation of the so-called spoken language (as against the so-called written language), we must invest this same theatre with another mission: that of preserving gesture. Tragedy and comedy keep language going. Pantomime will preserve gesture.

Pantomime is not simply a child's diversion or an artist's mania; it is the Art of Gesture in the broadest sense of the word. It is not the feeble art of trying to ape the word by a conventional system of gestural language; it is the re-creation of life by gesture. It is a region of artistic creation that has been so long unexplored that it seems to have regained its virginity: a region across which in the past twenty years, one or two pioneers have advanced, guided solely by the echo of an instinct more or less lost, their sole resource an intellectual intuition. The task is a double one: that of restoring the notion of gesture to those who are going to be mimes and to perform publicly; and to rehabituate the eyes of the public, restoring to them a taste for gesture, covertly guiding them towards the rediscovery of a lost sense.

A certain taste for pantomime already seems to be returning. In a few years this art will probably have won back its proper place. It will no longer be considered an inferior form of theatre, good only for fair-grounds and half-literate audiences. It will be recognized as a legitimate department of theatre art. When a man has acquired a taste for the right gesture, he will presumably make his own gestures "right"; and if he moves rightly he will have a better chance of living rightly, and might even end by reasoning rightly.

PROUST once wrote about Sarah Bernhardt in "Phèdre": "The gesture of these artists said to their arms, and to their tunics, 'Be majestic'; but their unsubmissive limbs allowed a biceps that knew nothing of the role to strut between shoulder and elbow." Let us take "Phèdre" as an example of gesture in spoken theatre.

The verbal form of "Phèdre" is the Alexandrine. The Alexandrine is founded on Number. The way in which the Alexandrine is spoken does not correspond to the ordinary way of speaking: it is a diction whose rhythm is dictated by Number. Nor is the way in which the actions of the play succeed one another the ordinary way. They have been filtered and strained off from a narrative which was already abridged. Their form is circular; they come one upon the other in perfect symmetry. The total action of "Phèdre" is a pure geometric figure. In composing "Phèdre", Racine obeyed the exigencies of Number and pure geometry. The language is elliptical, the action is crystallized. In order that this purity may be safeguarded throughout, the actor should also *move* in a way that is not ordinary. His gestures, like the Alexandrines he speaks and actions he performs, should be regulated, chosen.

If this is not observed, it becomes impossible to pass from a gesture to a sound. The required synthesis of the seen and the heard cannot take place. If, in the theatre, one thinks oneself in the presence of ordinary life, one asks why the characters talk and act in so unnatural a way. But if one regards the stage as a magic circle, a mysterious box of illusions, one is disappointed to see such ordinary characters on it. Sensing this weakness, this lack of cohesion, many spectators consider theatre an impure art, vulgar or second-rate. An audience that is used to naturalism in the plastic realm is, in general, bored by tragedy. When they ought to be protesting against the false notes struck by actors ignorant of gesture, as they would against an orchestra playing cacophonies, the Alexandrine rhythm lulls them to sleep.

To acquire the science of gesture, to learn to create a language of gesture, which is regulated, chosen, and rhythmic, and which can be concerted with the vocal language of the author, the actor must submit himself to a training which will educate him and make him supple. Let us not hesitate to say it: *there should be, deep in every actor, an element of the robot.* The function of art is to lead this robot towards the natural; to proceed by artificial means towards the imitation of nature. It is because the violin is a hollow box, like a dead body, that it is so satisfying to furnish it with a soul. To re-create life is to defy death; creation must start from death. Exactly like the breath and the voice, gesture has its language. Exactly as the heart beats in iambs (systole-diastole), exactly as breath respires in iambs (inhalation-exhalation), gesture too has an iambic rhythm (contraction-relaxation). We walk iambs. Exactly like the spoken language, the language of gesture has its syntax and its metrics.

Every gesture, indeed, is a phrase. The "attitude" one takes up, the "movement" one makes, and the "pointing out" of something into which the movement is decomposed, do these three phases not recall to our minds "subject", "verb", and "object"? It is, moreover, by the respiratory apparatus that gesture is related to breath. Are not our respiratory movements visible? The thoracic area is the headquarters where "news" converges, and whence orders for the smallest actions depart. *Why regulate the word and not the gesture?* Without analyzing our gestures further, let us say that there exists a tonic-sol-fa of gesture, an alchemy which every actor should know. And the "transposed" gesture is just as far from the ordinary gesture as it is from dance, even as the Alexandrine is just as far from prose as it is from song. There should be an absolute similarity between gesture, regulated, chosen and given rhythm by the actor; and the vocal form, regulated, chosen and given rhythm by the author.

The plastic behavior-pattern of the characters does not duplicate the behavior-patterns revealed by the words: it completes them. Very often we express in words only what we wish to show, while our smallest gestures reveal what we would like to hide. For the psychoanalyst, careful observation of someone's gestures is a valuable way of finding out what that person is concealing. In rehearsing

"Phèdre", a whole plastic language has therefore to be constructed bit by bit. This plastic language constitutes in some sort the secret, subterranean and sub-conscious revelation of the action. Conjointly and simultaneously with the spoken language, one can thus observe a visual language completing it, matching it or contradicting it. Buried secrets, bad faith, dissimulation, involuntary compulsions, weaknesses, escapes and so forth, will find themselves a place *beneath* the official behavior-patterns. Sometimes a character behaves in relation to what he has already experienced; sometimes, in relation to what he is preparing to experience, something he fears; sometimes, in direct relation to the present. Thus gesture, to a greater or lesser degree, departs from the text in one direction or another, just as in certain pictures at Epinal the color does not stay wholly within the contours of the design.

It is night. The theatre is deserted, haunted. The audience has gone home with a rich deposit of "present moments" bespangling its head, the innumerable "present moments" of a three-hour performance. The auditorium has almost stopped vibrating with the monstrous beat of the collective heart, and approaches the total silence that reigns on the stage, now emptied of all illusion. The auditorium is a heap of bones, the stage an enormous black cube where silence coagulates and freezes. Time has stopped. All movement is blocked. The air sleeps like dust. *But now, look!* There rises from the orchestra pit, like those gyrating insects whose bodies hang down like long tails, a kind of sonorous comet that is just starting to whirl. It cuts the frozen block of the stage, rending it from one end to the other. It warms the atmosphere. It rotates faster and faster. The ice melts. The silence softens, and liquefies into music. Music, in fact, has invaded the stage. It is music that now stirs up the theatre. This magic spot has now become an immense whirlwind.

And now in the sonorous cyclone, as from the dust that is flying in all direc-tions, a little whirling heap of something starts to rise off the ground. The little heap grows, grows, and rises, accelerated by the music, which has the devil in it. It takes form like earth on a potter's wheel. It no longer touches the floor except at a single point, vertical and arched, which is the point of a slipper, no less; above it, a contracted calf, then the tense ham, then the delicate strong thigh; then, spreading out like a cup, the outline of a gyrating tutu. End this delicate column with the upright bust, the tensed neck, the face drunk with movement, and the dancer is there, turning like an enchanted spinning-top under the impulse of music.

Then the music recedes, its revolutions slow down, the dancer loses her shape. The living sheaf of wheat dwindles as the music withdraws into the orchestra pit, the dancer is again a little heap, then stops revolving altogether. The music has gone to rest in the bowels of the stage. The dust falls again to the ground. Silence reasserts its right, and the air freezes once more. *We have looked on at the birth of the dance. It is music which creates it. It is sound. It is an interruption of the silence. The dance is brought to birth by noise.* And now that silence reigns once more, there is little hope of seeing our ballerina again.

BUT what is it we see there, at the back of the stage? This being with the convex chest that slowly advances like an explorer's ship forcing a passage through the ice? With his chest protruding like the breastbone of a bird, he lifts the coagulate air before him. At each side of him floats a V-shaped wave. In his wake follows a small whirling cone. Who is this man who undertakes to make the silence melt by movement alone? Here he is, accelerating his walk, starting to pace the stage, tracing and retracing his steps, running across, jumping, leaping, fighting, debating, recoiling, pulling himself together, attacking: a victim of the delirium of action. It is he, this time, who cuts the silence to pieces like an angry samurai, who devours it piece by piece, who makes it bite the dust—or rather who makes the dust bite it, for the dust awakes once more; once more impelled by man, it hovers in space and turns, dragged in his wake.

Man has provoked the silence, has defied it. He maltreats the dust, dragging it along. Now he makes the air vibrate; and music, by means of rhythm, reappears, but this time as an accompaniment. This man is the mime. Let him stop, and every musical echo will cease. The dust will fall again; and, like the explorer's ship, man, the mime, will be taken back into the ice of silence. *The dance is the child of music. Pantomime is the child of silence. That is the difference between them.* But, though they come from opposite poles, the dancer and the mime are running to meet each other.

I REMEMBER from my schooldays that our art teacher explained to us one day that the art of painting (that art of nuance and complication) reduced itself in the end to the play of three fundamental colors, and to combinations of the related component colors. He drew a diagram for us. Later I added to this enormous simplification of painting the influence of white and black, in order to better understand the infinity of "broken" tones, "cold" tones, "warm" tones. Later still, in our walks through sleeping Paris, my great friend Antonin Artaud had, I might almost say, "initiated" me into the "ternary" system of the Kabbala. Always *three* elements: the masculine, the feminine, the neuter. In my mind I found this triangle in painting. I believed in all this and did not believe. I was frequently confused.

One day a certain man of letters instilled in me, despite myself, a certain suspicion. He claimed that the theatre was not an art but ersatz-literature, a sort of annex. He felt no need of theatrical performance. He would ten times rather read Racine by his fireside. No company, no performance, could give him what his imagination gave him on reading such a work as "Bérénice". I was struck, but not for long. I discovered that the theatre was certainly an autonomous, pure and independent art, distinguished from other arts by the fact that it, alone among them, was appointed to *re-create the present*, and to do that by the simultaneity of the seen and heard. I rediscovered my Nietzschean Dionysos and Apollo. I was confirmed in the idea that the theatre, far from being a satellite of literature, could only live at a "present" moment, in "presence" of crowd, and thanks to the "presence" of certain people; and my love for this collective communion was redoubled.

What could be the ideal instrument of this independent art, an instrument that could retranslate into the present the simultaneity of the seen and the heard? Only *the human being* answered these purposes. I was more and more convinced that the human being (and not the writing of a man of letters . . . seated) was the essential instrument of theatre art. The seen and the heard, the body and the voice; and, as a third element of the ternary system, the heart: these, respectively, are the seat of movement, exchange, and rhythm.

There remained to find the equivalent of black and white. I noted that the theatre did not make use of the human being alone, any more than painting made use of color alone; but that theatre art consisted of a presentation of the human in space, just as painting consisted of a presentation of color on canvas. Hence: just as blacks and whites influence opposite colors, so space or the human being entered in to influence actions set in motion on the stage. Sometimes it was space that imposed its movement on the human being; sometimes the human being asserted his will. The same gesture or the same cry could be expressed either in an *imposed* fashion or in a *voluntary* fashion. *Example*: Fear seizes me, makes me breathe in despite myself. On the other hand, the illness that empties me of life makes me want to breathe in, to suck life back again with all the will-power I possess. In both cases I breathe in; but under contrary influences.

I didn't need much more encouragement to find for myself my respiratory or vocal ternary (source of the voice, the word, and diction); and my plastic ternary (source of corporal expression and mime in general); along with the two influences, black and white, of the imposed and the voluntary. And I have all the broken tones of my audible actions, corresponding to this fundamental ternary of action: receiving, giving, keeping. In other words, feminine, masculine, and neuter, plus components and complements—and always the two influences, the imposed and the voluntary. Such was the starting point of my method. It may seem complex, but in the development and application of pantomime I have found it most useful.

37 Louis Jouvet: The triumph of deceit

Monroe Stearns

January 1953

A member of the Cartel des Quatre, a consortium of directors which stood opposed to French boulevard theatre in the 1920s and 1930s, Louis Jouvet (1887–1951) had studied with Jacques Copeau as a young comedian and designer. At his Comédie des Champs-Élysées, he staged primarily modern comedies, especially his great standby, Jules Romains' metaphor of hypochondria as a cause of fascism, *Knock, or The Triumph of Medicine* (1923). Jouvet discovered and promoted the plays of Jean Giraudoux at the larger Théâtre de l'Athénée, and was named director of the Comédie Française in 1940; that ended with the German occupation and Jouvet spent much of the war touring his company around South America. He was the first to stage Jean Genet, with *The Maids* in 1947, although he refused to follow the author's directives and cast men in the roles. Jouvet was considered a leading authority on Molière, his own performances as Scapin, Arnolphe, Dom Juan and Tartuffe ground-breaking re-interpretations. His posthumous writing on theatre had just been published when this article appeared.

Monroe Stearns was an art historian and professional translator of French novels.

FOR THIRTY years before his death in 1951, Louis Jouvet kept notebooks on his career as an actor. These were recently published in two collections in France under the titles *Écoute, Mon Ami (Listen, My Friend)* and *Témoignages sur le Théâtre (Testimony on the Theatre)*. The notes were jotted down as they occurred to him after a performance, a rehearsal or a class in acting. The two books create an intimate portrait of a great actor. Into them went his studies of the roles he played, his observations of students and playwrights and his comments on the vagaries of the playgoing public.

"Listen, my friend," Jouvet wrote, in the phrase that gave the title to one of the books, "listen, brother comedian: the most important thing in our profession is to forget self in order to advance ourselves."

"Comedian" is the term Jouvet chose to describe his art. He preferred that word, although his famous roles were in that high form of comedy which sophisticated critics find hard to distinguish from tragedy. The term has its irony, but it should certainly not be interpreted to mean a mere "funnyman" of the kind that abounds on radio and television.

Jouvet used the word in its classic sense. To him, a comedian was a member of humanity and interpreter of the *comédie humaine*, the vast and intricate passing show of life itself. It meant that he tried to see human beings as they are, creatures of feeling, not always true to their intelligence and yet somehow wonderful: wonderful because of their flaws rather than in spite of them.

The tragic hero, essentially an idealized creation because he is greater than the common man, seemed to interest Jouvet less than the comic figure. Perhaps this preference was due to the fact that the tragic actor must think, and so the character he portrays emerges more as an extension of himself than as an independent being. The effect of thinking in the game of the stage is that of a puppeteer suddenly thrusting his head and arms upon his tiny scene, annihilating the dream that surrounds his diminutive players and their world.

A tragedian, Jouvet maintained, builds everything on himself; a comedian, on the character he is playing. The two stand at opposite poles of dramatic talent: presumptuousness and humility. But because both these qualities exist in his own personality, the performer must find a point of balance between them. Only this equilibrium can give breadth to acting. The talent of the comedian is that he does not know how to think. Thinking is contrary to the nature and exercise of his profession. His function is to assimilate through sensation and thus to reconstruct.

These are the principles by which Jouvet found a key to the enigma of the theatre, than which nothing is more false, nothing more true. He believed that it is the only beneficial enigma in human life—but an enigma it always remained to him. It is the business of drama, he said, to ask questions, not to answer them. Life must necessarily appear enigmatic to any human being, anyone with humor. Let the philosophers find fixed laws; the theatre, like the life it clarifies, is always changing. Aristotle's dogmas, for instance, only make drama sterile, for they are the result of analysis, not of synthesis.

All that is stable in the theatre is the Tradition, the Convention. Its basis is a twin illusion—the actor's and the spectator's, both of which spring from the same source and cause. Even so, this Convention changes from era to era. The public, the playwright, the comedian must agree on their search for a common illusion for their own time. Being a state of mind, the Convention of the theatre is imperishable.

To JOUVET, a play was a kaleidoscope of endless questions which no one can answer. The greatest danger for the actor lies in his finding his own personal answer, for the question itself has more value than a so-called Truth. The audience must answer the question; each person must find his own Truth. The problem for the actor is to interpret the question satisfactorily for his own time so that his audience may do likewise. Given this aim, he can approach perfect timing, which is the essence of comedy and, Jouvet thought, of success in life as well.

The problem is solved by intuition, not by logic. In the first place, a good actor chooses his vehicle by intuition alone. Only by that means can he make universal an attitude which exists in the loneliness of the abstract exclusively within the play or in a single character. For a brief time, the actor causes the spectator to share a human solitude which is necessary to the audience's spiritual survival.

The art of the man of the theatre is fundamentally no more than remaining human himself.

In this living by intuition, in being truly human, the actor is alone. The comedian becomes the true tragic hero whose tragedy is his aloneness. The comedian is a sacrificial offering on the altar of obedience to the laws of the theatre and the dramatist. In shrugging off his identifying personality, he becomes an ironic sort of wanderer, an empty body searching and waiting for a tenant. "For us comedians," Jouvet insisted, "everything is suspect except the body."

"I NEED NO moral laws," Jouvet wrote of himself as a comedian. "Alone, I am a law unto myself, simple in my complexity, honest though I live in a false world. I am an impartial judge, law-abiding though lawless. I quest for no ideal. What right have you to judge me?—our codes are utterly different. I have nothing in common with your desires, your whims, your behavior. Reader, spectator, comedian—whatever you are—you can approach me only in the isolation in which I live. Yet the same desolation unites us. Since I myself have neither vices nor virtues, it is your aspirations and feelings that mold me."

This sensitivity to his audience is one of the actor's greatest responsibilities, morally as well as professionally. If he has sufficiently forgotten himself, then his audience will forget what they knew about him and what they have been conditioned to look for in his performance. In every play, the comedian must be fresh and different. Stripped of substance, living in unreality, he waits to be incarnated by the imagination of the spectators. It is his duty to enter into a mutual communication with them. The audience then dissolve their own personalities to evoke the phantom which the actor is. He is never more than they make him seem to be.

"To be unknown," Jouvet wrote an aspiring actress, "is the ideal state for establishing complete communication with people. That anonymous solitude justifies our profession, which—never forget—is first of all a betrayal of self. It is the triumph of deceit."

Sincerity Jouvet regarded merely as a gratification of the ego, a desire to win the approval of others. True sincerity in an actor is the search for deception, for the mystery of the possession-and-loss of self. This is the essence of theatre.

ACTORS ARE prone to speak of their vocation as if they were priests, monks or nuns and as if it were an impulse from the metaphysical world. But an actor's calling is not the cause of his choosing his profession. It is only after many years of exercising it that there comes to the actor the decision to continue his career. This decision might be termed a call. The same choice made over and over again is all a "vocation" amounts to.

"I couldn't truly tell you," Jouvet's advice continued, "how I happened to go into the theatre. In my childhood I hadn't a sign of inclination that way. Certainly I was not predestined to do it. Then one day there I was in a theatre, in a rehearsal room, on the stage. I am still surprised, but the astonishment does not embarrass me; rather it pleases and satisfies me. The most fortunate thing in life is the capacity to be surprised. It is the knowledge of what one has wished for, or done, swimming into the light from the depths of one's personality. That is life. One need only yield to one's feelings, take the consequences of them, be faithful to them. Freedom lies in accepting the fate you have chosen and in obediently fulfilling the demands of the profession."

There is no clear definition of the profession, Jouvet added, for the comedian lives between being and seeming, between releasing and governing his self. It was easier for Jouvet to trace the phases through which an actor must pass. Even this, he said, does not give a portrait of a comedian, only an idealized and arbitrarily systematized description.

IN THE first phase, the actor is totally ignorant about himself. This is the period of his "sincerity." To be something other than himself disturbs him violently. In order to acquire a new identity he naïvely believes that Orestes or Hamlet is waiting for him to bring them to life by lending them his own soul. Everything in the theatre begins in him and exists because of him.

Then from the first phase the second develops normally and logically. The comedian cannot long endure the frenzy of his egoism. Tired, disillusioned, unsatisfied, he begins to see that his taking possession of a character like an evil spirit has deceived no one but himself. His undisciplined attacks yield not to a knowledge of himself but to an awareness of himself. His mind becomes a labyrinth in which he strays until he encounters the wall which is himself. After he has met himself, found out what he really is, he becomes conscious of what he is doing.

At the same time, he discovers the Convention of the theatre and the restrictions of his profession. He sees his position as both instrument and instrumentalist. He perceives that his existence on the stage is composed of the audience, his fellow actors, the character he must play.

Thus, he learns the art of pretending, the lie in which he is and must remain embedded. He acknowledges now his own "insincerity," understands that he has a double nature, that he must live in a limbo of half being and half seeming. What he used to call his art, he recognizes as a craft, a trade.

Most difficult to reach and hardest to explain is the third phase of the actor's evolution, in which the performer finally masters his feelings. What he experienced in the second stage of his development here becomes sublimated to a lofty, vibrant sensitivity which may be called intuition. With a strange independence the actor arrives at the true intention of the drama. He has found the meaning of his profession; now he can give meaning to his life.

The great moment for a true actor is not the final curtain when a cheering house rises to its feet to reward him with applause, but his realization that he has managed to plunge into the sea of feelings in which the audience has been submerged. He has found a new and straighter path to their hearts, discovered unexpected reactions and unsuspected thoughts. What seemed to him hopelessly complex, he has been able to reduce to a single value. This is the actor's moment of divinity.

Living as he has been in the innermost core of the play, the actor has become one with the private and inexpressible intention of the author. He understands and can explain to himself all the different interpretations of the part, the different critical opinions and appraisals. These finally appear to him merely as various ways of saying the same thing, for true interpretation to an actor is only the expansion of his own receptivity.

The man who accustoms himself to living on the surface of his personality becomes the vessel, the body, in which the intention of the drama is formed and is born. He is the link between the author and the public, the vital organ of the reality and unreality—one and the same—which is the phenomenon of theatre.

This metaphysical process can never be accomplished by thought but only by a state of sensitivity and sympathy through which the character in the play is freed by a kind of magic incantation from the printed page and becomes a living soul possessing the actor. While he is on the stage, the actor is a sleepwalker.

All life to Jouvet, regardless of the objections of philosophers, was a duality whose highest achievement was this somnambulistic power to keep control at a time when willful control is suspended. That power he called the justification of the actor's double self and the dynamic conflict in which he lives.

Jouvet was too rational, however, to believe that the penetration of the actor into the heart of a play and his assimilation with the author's spirit, could be achieved by hocus-pocus. Few actors or directors have studied their authors and their texts more thoroughly. Of the three dramatists Jouvet most admired—Molière, Romains, Giraudoux—he had the advantage of working with the latter two. In the case of Molière, he had to resort of painstaking research to discover the dramatist's intention. The principle of interpretation which guided him was that only by knowing the total environment of an author at the time of composition can one arrive at the true and complete meaning of a play.

Jouvet, for his productions of Molière's *Tartuffe* and *Don Juan*, has left copious records of his researches as well as penetrating analyses of the plays themselves. This work led to so perfect an understanding of the dramas that Jouvet's productions were masterpieces approaching the genius of the playwright.

Yet Jouvet, forever the true artist, doubted his accuracy, suspected his understanding of the original spirit. Always there hovered the specter of the ego between the inspiration and the realization. "A classic," he wrote, "is a piece of gold that has never been wholly minted into coin."

No one can be sure of what a dead author meant. "Your Tartuffe," said Jouvet, "is not mine, that's all that can be said. Beyond that there is no possible judgement, for what standard of judgement exists? Tartuffe resembles no one in particular, yet everyone in general. Doubtless that is why Molière wrote the play; that is why I mounted it."

Toward the end of his own life, Jouvet recalled an anecdote about another great actor after his farewell performance. " 'I looked,' said the retiring performer, 'at the costumes scattered about my dressing room, and I got the feeling that the characters whom I would nevermore bring to life, were dead. Later I dreamed that those characters suddenly invaded my bedroom, glistening, animated by a collective life—that of all the actors who had played my parts before me. Then one of the characters said: "How dull you are! It's not we who are dead, but you who are going to die. You never created us, you only dressed us. Now we shall just go to some other costumer." And,' said the actor, 'I awoke very humble.' "

"That," remarked Jouvet, "shows what a character in a play really is."

38 Lotte Lenya

David Beams

June 1962

Wife of the composer Kurt Weill and member of the original cast of *Die Dreigro-schenoper* (1928), Lotte Lenya (Karoline Blaumauer, 1900–81) was regarded as a living relic of Weimar Berlin. Her hoarse renditions of Brecht's songs were considered definitive, as rendered in Marc Blitzstein's versions in the Off-Broadway recension *The Threepenny Opera* (1954) and the revue *Brecht on Brecht* (1961), as well as on long-playing records. Her status as symbol continued when she was cast in the musical *Cabaret* (1966).

David Beams was a contributor to *Films in Review* and a specialist in German literature.

It is 1954, but for a few pennies Off Broadway we are inspecting Edwardian Soho, a brothel etched in fog. The shock of recognition will come; at the moment there is only the shock of Bert Brecht's jeering vision, dressing everyone equally in fine irony. And what are we to make of Kurt Weill's stale, nifty dance tunes, their peaked sweetness defying us to be fine even in irony, their acrid harmonies forbidding even nostalgia?

Yet there *is* something familiar about Gin Mill Jenny at the bordello. Topped by a mess of carrot-root hair, her face is long and bold, high-boned with tilting eyebrows and a red slash of mouth. Black-striped purple binds the pale, sagging chest, and there is a jet ribbon around her neck and a heart with purple stones. Incurable rhythms lurk in the lean body slung indolently into view, one arm sinuous along the raven skirt. With a draftsmanship as thrifty and merciless as his own, Lotte Lenya has re-created a Toulouse-Lautrec, the satirical, foot-lighted canvases of Montmartre clowns, tarts and tired divas. It is not only an unerring clue to the impudent new world of Brecht but a kind of last collaboration with him, by which Lautrec joins Gay, Villon, Kipling, Piscator and cabaret in the Brechtian hash. No painter was more of the theatre, and Bert Brecht would be the first to authorize the blowzy poster Jenny, in the tradition of his own placards, unfolding his new Moulin Rouge.

In the current Off Broadway hit *Brecht on Brecht*, Lenya does Jenny's songs, the pulsating tramp of Mutter Courage and a visionary speech of St. Joan of the Stockyards in a simple jumper and shirt, neutral and distancing. The analogy to Lautrec is no longer needed, only the stark eyes misting for the ship with eight sails—"und fünfzig Kanonen." For this Brechtians have Lenya mainly to thank. The current show, with the six actors seated on high stools, sometimes resembles a tea party at which the Mad Hatter, Brecht, is catered to but not allowed to get out of hand. But Lotte Lenya, pursuing her task of a decade now, in Robert Brustein's words "cold, metallic, seemingly detached from the proceedings, conveys the steel and ice that were in Brecht."

When Kurt Weill died in 1950, Lenya's task was before her. Broadway had cherished the balding, chunky little man with thick glasses over intent saucer eyes, the musician with a shy, lovable personality. But one half of Weill's life seemed forgotten, the years when he and Bert Brecht had articulated the brutalization of Germany with the fierceness of embittered yearning. There had been a record of it all in the original recordings, proper Brechtian tools to estrange the listener from "empathy" and permit reflection, but they were forfeited to the oppressors.

Probably Lenya's most gallant song was "Surabaya Johnny," the aching reproach of a girl plundered by a good-for-nothing Burma sailor: "Surabaya Johnny, why are you so cruel? Surabaya Johnny, my God, and I love you so." Not only did Lenya no longer have the record of her voice; she had lost the memory of ever joining Theo Mackeben and his jazz orchestra to engrave it. "If you have to leave your country overnight, you're not going to take some records with you if the Nazis are on your heels. I knew nothing about it."

Lotte Lenya belonged to the Twenties with the far-away swing of Mackeben's band, but in early 1951 Lotte Lenya-Weill was half-caroling, half-croaking old omens in *Dreigroschenoper* at Town Hall. "I don't remember even being alive at that time. I did it because I had to do it, so this was the beginning." The next year Leonard Bernstein introduced *The Threepenny Opera*, Marc Blitzstein's English adaptation of Brecht. Finally Lenya launched the same on a six-year Off Broadway run because she deemed it a "masterpiece," necessarily softening the German but loyal both to Brecht and to Weill's trenchant scoring. For others Blitzstein's colloquialisms dampened Brecht's poetry; and the production, apart from a rich-throated, bluesy Mrs. Peachum, was a little *too* beggarly of Brechtian craft, failing the easy fraud of the original style. However, Lenya's first purpose was soon achieved in the eighteen hit records of "Mack the Knife," a bleak, compulsive ballad memorializing infamous crimes in the vein of old street-fair singers.

With an audience widened by Louis Armstrong, Tito Puente and Constance Bennett, the next problem was to consolidate the style and point of Brecht-Weill, to restore nasality and expose Mackie Messer, the swaggering bully and ravisher whose shark colors became a uniform. Encouraged by Goddard Lieberson of Columbia Records and by her second husband, the editor George Davis, Lenya began her series of new recordings: the Brecht-Weill document of lawless Berlin in its plunge through grime, cosmetics and the dregs of glasses to its fate.

In certain respects the new enterprise was blessedly remote from the original *Threepenny* recordings, where Carola Neher had appropriated Peachum's "Useless Song" and Lenya herself sang Jenny, Lucy, Frau Peachum and the Streetsinger. In those days, "except for Ponto and Gerron, the original stars were too big, they didn't think so much of *Threepenny* and didn't show up to make the records." Now, however, Lenya exercised a firm supervisory hand. She located a conductor with eighteenth century affinities like Kurt Weill's; she summoned Willy

Trenk-Trebitsch of the old crew for an unctuous, implacable Peachum and the Munich cabaret star Trude Hesterberg, of the disconcertingly rock-bottom voice, for a shrewd, bawdy Frau Peachum. On the other hand, the portly Hesterberg was not invited to re-create her 1931 Begbick in *Rise and Fall of the City of Mahagonny*. "I wanted to get away from the half-spoken cabaret style. Kurt Weill wrote *Mahagonny* with sustaining melodies he wanted to have *sung*." Lenya secured artists of the Hamburg Staatsoper to sing them, including a famous Florestan for Brecht's parody of the liberated Florestan, Jimmy Mahoney "aus Alaska."

Although she made restitution of all songs to their rightful owners, Lenya's chief donation to the project was her own art, especially in *Mahagonny*—Brecht's nightmare in which the Florida Goldküste decomposes in a ravening capitalist typhoon amid the honky-tonk stridencies and rah-rah songs of "anti-opera" (which Kurt Weill keeps traducing into baroque magnificence). Here again was the prostitute Jenny's artlessly alluring introduction of herself, "Jenny Smith aus Havanna," and the sublime doubt and reproach in her question at her worth, "Dreissig Dollar?" Lenya's original "Havanna Lied" had been one of her fondest tracings of a vocal line, but here was the same tender pliancy and solemn didacticism, the same limpid diction and almost the same honeyed tone, a miracle of incongruity in sum. Here in the "Berlin Theatre Songs" was a sturdy belting-out of the Sailor Tango from *Happy End*, along with the sassy saloon nostalgia of "alter Bilbao Mond" in the "Bilbao Song." Above all, here was the new "Surabaya Johnny" with its recriminations, its loss of control, its final erotic loftiness.

Undoubtedly the years had defrauded Lenya the singer of a point here and there. She no longer commanded of quite the silveriness of the old "Alabama Song," quite the glistening soprano in the mysterious refrains of "Pirate Jenny." Gone was the numbing impact of Jenny's original guilelessness where even the martially accented "Und es werden kommen hundert gen Mittag an Land" was virginal in tone. A more conscious violence replaced it. But as compensation "you put in all the wisdom you have accumulated as a human being. It's a maturer Jenny or 'Surabaya Johnny' than in 1930, although the emotion, the meaning are unchangeable."

Equally unchangeable are the amusing moments where she merely brandishes her voice at the notes, the rhythmic precision, the Brechtian pungency. Yet the whole remains elusive. Lenya is enchanted by analogies to Fritzi Massary, royalest of Berlin operetta stars; but for all her exemplary diction, she happily lacks Massary's archness. And there is none of the drowsy narcissism of Dietrich's Lola-Lola either. The reason Lenya remains indefinable, says Goddard Lieberson, is "that she has an individuality that grows out of her own giving of herself to Brecht and Weill. Her individuality comes out of them, like a person assuming his full potential by falling in love with someone else."

From 1955, making the records in Berlin and Hamburg, Lenya conferred on Brecht-Weill productions throughout Germany. Sometimes she was gratified, as by German response to Weill's "Schubertian" *Down in the Valley*. Although "Broadway has a smelly taste in Europe," *Street Scene* remained in the Düsseldorf repertory three seasons, with Caspar Neher sets. But the 1957 West Berlin revival of *Die Burgschaft*, Weill's 1932 *vale* to Trust in a police state, was a jolting travesty by the librettist Neher and the original producer Carl Ebert. To spare Berliners' feelings, blithe scarlet uniforms transported the original fascist roughs to never-never land, and because of East Berlin, potent Brechtian symbolism of economic inequalities was scrapped. The nihilistic ending, disputed by Weill's music, was sentimentalized with quantities of the score cut. Lenya also had to contend with a Darmstadt *Mahagonny* staged in "Mexican Hayride" style. "If you come just for the dress rehearsal and the opening is the next day, all you can do is hope you can keep your mouth shut. Whenever they let me sit in, I tell them what I know about it, but whether they take it or not, that's another thing." In Frankfurt and elsewhere they rejoiced to take Lenya herself in concerts and *The Seven Deadly Sins.*

Lenya's real headache was the American theatre. "Is there ever any revival in this country? That doesn't exist. The whole theatre is not geared for revival or repertory. So whenever they do revive anything on Broadway, it's rarely successful. The one exception was *Pal Joey*. They're not trained for seeing a thing twice or three times, different casts and conceptions. In Europe they're subsidized so they have their companies. The Berlin Ensemble is solid. It is sad."

Nevertheless, the late Fifties witnessed City Center revivals of Weill operas and Lenya singing to 9500 at Lewisohn Stadium. Antony Tudor's ferociously sardonic ballet *Judgment of Paris*, with the *Threepenny* music, had been resurrected. There was also the indicative American vogue of Carl Orff, the racy primitivist who helped himself to Brecht-Weill although burying the moon over Soho in a Grimm forest. The culmination was the New York premiere of *The Seven Deadly Sins* in 1958. Mirthless in a patchy sweater, short skirt and high heels, belligerent with revolver, Lenya was the "practical" Anna who convinces her instinctual sister that to dance modestly is Pride, to eat instead of starving for the strip-tease is Gluttony, and to love a poor pimp when she has a generous protector is Lust. Under the original choreographer George Balanchine, Lenya lacked only the sultry vampirism of her 1933 Anna, which Brecht had cloaked with Tillie Losch to make sleek, exotic twin lilies on a single stem. Weill's score humidified Louisiana with a taut, sickly melodiousness and percussive humdrum, ceasing to ironize in the final march. And Brecht's stinging wit abided in W. H. Auden's translation, "as close as you can get to Brecht in English" in Lenya's judgement.

On opposite walls of Lenya's sunny East Side apartment are a silhouette of her 1928 bustled Jenny and a record jacket of the Toulouse-Lautrec Jenny. The small woman seated at the telephone table between them is neither. "Lenya" is a stage name, and this is Karoline Weill-Davis, an astute but amiable businesswoman with the latest telegrams about Prague and Lucerne *Mahagonny* grasped in her long fingers. Her hair is red, but as Milton Caniff has told her, it somehow tolerates red sweaters, and she wears them, often turtle-neck. With her bangs and the large, musing eyes in a slender, eager face, she looks to be a Carson McCullers waif grown up. Her enthusiasm is infectious as she plucks from a shelf of Balzac a new photo of Brecht's widow Helene Weigel, inscribed in quaint Brechtian English "from the oldest sexbomb." Her gestures are succinct, her voice patient and a touch husky as she deliberates new projects.

Lenya's accountability to Brecht and Weill forced her to withdraw from "the shambles" Edinburgh made of *The Seven Deadly Sins*, although she permitted the work to be heard. But she is optimistic about Hamburg's forthcoming *Mahagonny*, which was delayed by uneasiness over Brecht's side of the Berlin wall. A reliable performer of Berg's Lulu is to be Jenny, but maybe the Negro soprano Mattiwilda Dobbs would be even better. "Jenny sings 'Ich bin aus Havanna, meine Mutter war eine Weisse'—so that shows her father was a Negro. So that would be my choice, a very Brechtish and Weillish idea." Although it is the poorest selling of Lenya's albums, *Mahagonny* may also descend upon Lincoln Center, if Kurt Weill's orchestral battery can be managed. Meanwhile, there is a recording of the energetic *Happy End*, with its Johnny songs and more Mandalay, still to be issued here, and Lenya has recently recorded the *Brecht on Brecht* material. Hanns Eisler's mournful "Song of a German Mother" (who gave her son the brown shirt that became a winding sheet) was brought to her attention by Eric Bentley after Bentley's sure vocalizing of Brecht on the radio impelled her to write a fan letter. Queerly, the two foremost Brechtians in the United States have never met although Lenya is reported contemplating Bentley's new *Threepenny* translation for the bilingual edition of Brecht.

Lenya is devoted to Brecht but not especially devout, an imperfect Brechtian as it were. For one thing, the theories of epic theatre, of socialist actors narrating or reporting or demonstrating in an estrangement from the audience and the role, have never been her portion. Perhaps she encouraged audiences to reason rather than to identify, but "whatever I did, it seemed to be right without his theory. I went to Brecht's house, I worked with him as you work with a director. He sang a little bit, phrases, snatches. Try it this way, try it that way. And don't forget, there was always Kurt Weill at the piano." Directing *Threepenny* and *Mahagonny* in 1928 and 1931, Brecht "never once talked to me about *Verfremdung* and all those things. Either it was right or wrong and no more and no theory *ever*."

That it was right in retrospect is proven by the notes on the *Threepenny* "Process" and *Mahagonny* which Brecht published immediately afterward. "There is a kind of speaking-against-the-music which can have strong effects," he wrote, "the result of a stubborn, incorruptible sobriety which is independent of music and rhythm" and which intensifies the dialectic already present in text and music. Lenya allows that Jenny is aware of her outburst in "Pirate Jenny," that it is not overflowingly emotional but calculated, yet "I can't describe it, I can only *do* it."

The fact is, however, she could do it if "somebody would take me right in the middle, say, and ask me a question. I would stop and answer the question and go right on because I don't need any mood to create. I don't have to get into a trance to do what I'm doing." The last word on what she is doing is probably Brecht's after all. Shortly before his death she visited him and told him about her proposed record of Berlin theatre songs. "Brecht, I'd like to make this record, but we have to discuss it because in the meantime you have that theory about epic theatre and all that." The answer was, "Lenya, whatever you do, it's epic theatre enough for me."

As for Jenny's place in the Brechtian menagerie (to use Eric Bentley's term), she is a figure of love in her pining tango with Macheath, but she betrays. The keynote of "Pirate Jenny" is revenge: "the eternal underdog, she dreams of the day when she can pay it back, all those rats." And Lenya does not suffer merrily talk of parodistic effects in this song, its reference to kitchen maid's fiction on the one hand or "Senta's Ballad" on the other. "It is as earnest and sincere as can be." Yet if "Pirate Jenny" seems helpful, Lenya reminds us that it was originally Polly Peachum's song recited as entertainment at the stable wedding, and only later switched by Brecht to Jenny, who has since defended the favor.

The only solution to Jenny is the *other* Jenny in *Mahagonny*, who will wear undergarments or not as her lover pleases. She is the same character, Lenya affirms. In the anarchy of the pit, Jenny Smith too prefers to kick rather than be kicked and will not reclaim the woodcutter from the electric chair decreed by his whiskey debt. But as she perches on her little suitcase in the long black stockings of a frail, bangs over her forehead, straw hat tipped cockily, and elegizes her lost innocence to the Moon of Alabama, or as she joins Jimmy in the fragile, dreamy duet of the cranes, she defies us to doubt her values. And she is herself many times more valuable than her price in the golden city of nets. In the paradox of Brecht's makebelieve, the moon is a paper disk, hot floodlight over the stage because "we are workers, friends, not wizards." Jenny is both in that she transcends the brassy clang of horror in which Brecht's helpless workers are indistinguishable in license from their exploiters, thus becoming a humane reference point where one is fervently desired.

In general, Lenya is inclined to stress Brecht the romantic and humanitarian "liberal," like Clifford Odets in this country. "Brecht was very romantic, which is almost sacrilegious to say now because they know him only from his cynical side, which is very misleading." Random and domestic in her apartment, Lenya becomes theatrical only now, palm raised to explain Brecht's thinking. "That's the only thing, you can *hope*. This is what Brecht says a thousand times. He hopes for a better future, but you who are born where man to man is helper at last, think of us in the past with some understanding, that we who wished to plant the seed to kindness could not ourselves be kind. You who are born with the advantage that you don't have to go through a war of classes and to change your country more often than shoes—he *says* it. This is Brecht, and it is not a Communist talking. It is a great humanist talking. This is what I can tell over and over again."

It is what she is afforded a prime opportunity to tell in Jenny's "Solomon Song," a docile litany of great souls whose virtues shine like naughty deeds in a society which makes them remarkable. But there is always the peril of confusing Brecht with wise old Solomon. Lenya has been known to deny there was anything Marxist in her 1931 film of *Dreigroschenoper*, where the pretty and well-trained Polly Peachum becomes a banker with portfolio and the beggars march like the proletariat in Eisenstein. In the early Fifties, when she piloted a recording of the Brecht-Weill *Der Jasager*—a utilitarian "school opera" teaching Communist sacrifice to participants and audience—Brecht's politics were a curious mystery in the sleeve notes. And Lenya's choice of Brecht poems for her recorded anthology of German verse omits any of his more searing visions.

Inevitably Lenya's expectations of America were colored by the perverse Brechtian romance with this country. However, though "coming home" to sky-lines out of von Sternberg movies, she and Kurt Weill did not find the Here-You-May-Do-Anything Inn at New City, New York. For that matter, they did not find Negroes in Hoboken, as *Lied von Hoboken*, a mistranslated Berlin play in which Lenya was a mulatto, had assured them they would. "You're in the wrong department. Try Harlem."

Brecht had been in the wrong department, too, but Lenya recalls that not everyone thought so. When Lenya did *Mahagonny* in Vienna in 1932, one of her fans was Ernest Krenek, composer of the world-gladdening if rather naïve and slight jazz opera about a Negro band leader and white women, *Jonny spielt auf*, which eventually suffocated at the Metropolitan. Krenek had introduced locomotives to opera but his verdict on *Mahagonny* was: "I'm sorry, Lenya, I loved you but I hate that work. It's raw and vicious." By 1937, however, visiting the Weills, Krenek had changed his mind. "After living in this country for two years, now I understand *Mahagonny*." Lenya considers this movingly honest, but still, she insists, "only the locality of America is taken. *Mahagonny* is a play about Germany, about capitalism, about anywhere." Brecht himself was grateful to America during his time here and "had a very healthy feeling," but saw no future because he could never learn to write the language.

Kurt Weill, on the other hand, visiting radio studios, *Porgy and Bess* and Harlem, learned the musical language so nicely that Todd Duncan would find his role in *Lost in the Stars* more challenging than Porgy. The question is whether Weill didn't also waive some of his old refractoriness. In the German years he had impeached the puffy apparatus of late Romanticism because it induced sleep instead of recognitions. Resolved to communicate intelligibly in vital theater, to be the "poor man's Verdi," he likewise abandoned atonality and declined the frigid academi-cism of his friend Hindemith. Essentially conservative but aware of experiments by Stravinsky and Milhaud, he effected a kind of counter-reformation in German romanticism during the Brecht period, fusing Mahlerian harmonies, classicist ideals and ragtime into a highly accessible-theatre idiom. With its flat melodies and jaded syncopations, so-called "vulgar" music was simple and incisive, in Brecht's mind ideal for expressing social attitudes as against useless individual psychology. (As for why music at all: it is a kind of presentable garb for Brecht's derelicts although the whole point remains, for Brecht as for Peachum, that they are pretty threadbare.)

Yet in the U. S. the revolutionary Weill was doing, not the importunate Marc Blitzstein subjects or even a *Guys and Dolls* but *One Touch of Venus*. And how did Brecht's old comrade in the brutal recoil of the "Kanonensong" join up with Maxwell Anderson, who thought his heroes must "take arms against what enemies assail them and come out of the battle with their morale intact," of all things? Anderson probed the psychology of exceptional protagonists representing the forces of good; were his "Ballad of Magna Carta," the fatuous *Knickerbocker Holiday* and the racial drama *Lost in the Stars*, incorrigibly healthy-minded, material for the satirist Weill? Didn't Weill's magisterial African choruses—even the anguished "Cry the Beloved Country"—tend to mawkishness where the old fox trots were electrifying in their banality? Was Weill an original genius only when the text was so invincible as to require him to say something for himself?

"People say Kurt Weill got soft in this country; he succumbed to Broadway. But I think that an opera like *Street Scene* could very well have been written by Brecht. It attacks the poverty of those people in the brownstone tenement. Remember, when Brecht went back he still had some things to attack as before, but here in this country there was less to attack." For Lenya, Weill's story is the clear and natural development of a "romantic, a great romanticist" committed above all to his music. Lenya's first allegiance is to that music, American as well as German—but not without paradox so far as her own career is concerned.

Exiling all but the most selfless sense pleasure from the tidings in their ballad opera, *Lehrstück* and *Zeitoper*, Brecht and Weill set a premium on the untrained voices of singing actors. The voice of Lenya, the actress Weill had married in 1926, was as "popular" and merely approximate as any other, not apt to entertain so imperiously as Maria Jeritza's. It was sufficiently wrong to be reasonably right from a boxing ring beneath ghoulish Caspar Neher projections at the 1927 Baden-Baden "little" *Mahagonny*. The sound was a plaintive moan in Brecht's Tin Pan Alley "Is here no telephone?," yet it was chastely melodic for the rest of the "Benares-Song," heightening the ironic wistfulness for another sin city. The words were clear even as Jenny champed an apple, and this new kind of singer was eligible for whistling back, in Brecht's uproarious design, at a yowling apoplectic audience. In all, Lenya belonged where music, as Brecht felt, was in counterpoint to the text, taking issue with it, songs providing opportunity for medicating rather than an intensity of purgation. Music and speech were on separate levels; the former could be no more voluptuous than the latter, and with Lenya it wasn't.

But by the sixth collaboration of Brecht and Weill, the big *Mahagonny* of 1930, Kurt Weill's musicianship was straining at the leash, unsettling Brecht with continuous music, an orchestra of forty-strong (cheek-by-jowl with accordion and zither were the dreaded violins), fugue developments and drum-punctuated ensembles of Verdian power. Had there been any pretense of rationality it would have been handily "washed away," from Brecht's point of view, by the music. There *was* that pretense in *Die Burgschaft*, Weill's 1932 grand opera in which the Commissars of the New Order are beckoned by the totalitarianism of force and money within everyman. Humanizing Casper Neher's nearly unbearable book, Weill's music was lyrically elaborate in arias, giant orchestral ritornellos and enormous choruses. Although the Nazis were dismayed, Brecht was only less so, finding in the Handelian polyphony the mandragora of "culinary theatre" lulling the mind and the will. Brecht pronounced it "bourgeois." And there was no role for Lenya.

Kurt Weill was to assert his ideal at the time of the neo-Puccinian "dramatic musical" *Street Scene*. Reserving his jazz rhythms mainly for children among garbage pails, he sought an illusional "blending of drama and music in which the singing continues naturally where the speaking stops." This is the exact reverse of

Brecht's prescription, "but who makes Brecht the great expert on music, I want to know?" Lenya asks. "Kurt Weill was a full-blooded musician and not just what Brecht, I must say, reduced his composers to—to a level where the music serves his needs as a dramatist and no more. I am convinced that opera is an art in itself and will exist as long as Mr. Brecht's theories."

Except that circumstance wouldn't have it so, Weill would have created operas in Germany, a few musical plays in between, and no songs for the labor movement. This view of Lenya is admissible since Weill ended by fashioning Broadway opera, sophisticating the musical with adroit orchestration, a relatively superior gift of melody and a measure of the old concern with mores—paving the rather luxurious way to Bernstein's *West Side*. "I think surely Leonard Bernstein know every note of Kurt Weill, and he is the closest to Kurt Weill, taking up where he left off at his death." Of course, Bernstein's Manhattan is not only polyrhythmic but shark-infested where the onetime Moritat-singer was looking to *Green Mansions, Gone With the Wind* and Herman Wouk for subjects. But Weill's *Huckleberry Finn* with Maxwell Anderson might have been major folk opera by a man whose assimilation of American history, culture and idiom was gracefully complete. At Weill told Lenya in the hospital: "Darling, I will float it in beautiful music." And *Moby Dick*, according to Weill's notes, might have followed.

The fact remains that Lenya's career as exponent of her husband's music halted with the leave-taking of Brecht and Weill. To be sure, since her comeback she has recorded Weill's American theatre songs with glamorous, supple mastery. The warmth and inflection of her "Speak Low" (the song at which Dietrich balked when proffered *One Touch of Venus*), the suave, expansive "September Song," the caressingly spun "It Never Was You"—all reveal tonal bloom, poised phrasing and the utmost imagination in dynamics. She is buoyant in the tripping "Green-Up Time" and insistent in the outcry of the torch song "Trouble Man." Best of all, she transforms herself as lustily as did the svelte Gertrude Lawrence for the swinging "Saga of Jenny," third of Kurt Weill's "four Jennys in one generation." ("Look," says Lenya, "for me Gertie Lawrence was tops in *Lady in the Dark*, so you can't tell me I'm doing just as well. Oh God, I loved her.")

Still, Lenya appeared in only one of the Broadway musicals, *The Firebrand of Florence* in 1945, and this was Weill's one flop. Lenya as a roguish Duchess on the make was up to the really opulent music; there was twinkling insinuation in her "Sing Me Not a Ballad" with an almost silken beauty in the refrain. But when her co-star. Walter Slezak withdrew at the last minute, she was left on a limb: "My style would never ever jell with Melville Cooper's." And John Murray Anderson's overproduction, the heavy Florentine costumes, "moved like goo." Thereupon, although she might have known better than to make up her mind, Lenya decided to sing no more.

Through most of the Forties she embraced the new role of audience. Her husband's songs infallibly came to his inner ear "in Lenya's voice," but Lenya sat in the house while they sounded in the trained voices of the "fabulous" Mary Martin or even the celestial Polyna Stoska. "Kurt Weill trusted my judgment very much when it came, for instance, to the first orchestra rehearsal. He wanted me there because with my untrained ear, which he called such a highly musical ear, I was already audience. And he never allowed me to learn to read music. He said no, it would spoil you. Leave it alone." Lenya was still dead center in the theatre with Weill and his lyricists Ira Gershwin, Ogden Nash and Alan Jay Lerner, with Anderson, Moss Hart, Elmer Rice, directors Elia Kazan and Rouben Mamoulian, conductors Maurice Devine and Maurice Abravanel. But her own occupation was ironing shirts on South Mountain Road in Rockland County, in the home elegant as a Swiss chalet, replete with a decoy duck. She collaborated with Alfred Lunt's valet in a Victory garden of colossal watermelons and belonged to the woods and tranquil brook and Kurt Weill's sheepdogs with the shaggy bangs.

She would sing again, but mainly as custodian of the Brecht-Weill tradition. Her habit of discriminating between herself and "real singers" is implanted from a time when she carried the trains of *Sängerkrieg* contestants into the Hall of Song. The truth is "I don't like to sing. I like to *act*." Currently her feline, pictorial Contessa in the film *The Roman Spring of Mrs. Stone* has fastened on the public consciousness like the movie work of Magnani and Paxinou, though in a radically different tradition. With it Lenya has resumed a career no prima donna would fathom.

If self-possession in the midst of tensions is a Lenya trait, it can be traced to her days on the tight-rope. Born in a Vienna tenement surrounded by rubber factories, she could look down from the kitchen window to a small permanent circus in the field below—bleachers, stage, three-man orchestra and no tent. When the summers were not too rainy, neighborhood urchins were recruited to fill in the program. Lenya was taught to walk on a small wire between poles, moving just above the ground but nobly encumbered with an umbrella between tiny fists. "A little kid with an umbrella—that's what they mean when they say 'she started in a circus'!"

From this she proceeded to ballet, studying in Zurich where she lived with an aunt during the War, also acting boy's parts in fervent operettas like *Polish Blood* and singing wherever necessary in her natural voice. Excelling as a Wagnerian extra, she stood for hours in *Parsifal* but also danced in the Venusburg bacchanale. In *Rheingold* she was a dwarf carrying the Rheingold on her back. Although hers was short of being a vocal contribution, her intimacy with Wagner would be a lasting delight to Kurt Weill. "I sang whole stretches of the bass because I happened to stand behind the chorus who sang bass. 'My God, what are you singing now?' Kurt Weill would ask. Well, I learned it this way."

Tending more and more to serious acting in Zurich, Lenya moved to Berlin in 1923, where the recompense during inflation was mainly practice—as Juliet, Rosalind and Maria with an "idealistic" company which toured the suburbs. Recalling that time Lenya, with typical diffidence and perspective, savors the memory of other actors. Paramount among them was Bergner doing, for instance, Shaw's *St. Joan* for Max Reinhardt and his dramaturge, one Bertolt Brecht. It is probable that Lenya shared some of Bergner's slim, juvenile unworldliness in

Shakespeare, the boyishness which recaptured the Elizabethan stage. (Oddly in view of her own orientation, Lenya mentions first among German actors the inveterately histrionic Eugen Klöpfer and Lucie Höflich.)

Then, spending a country summer with the Georg Kaisers, Lenya agreed one day to row across the lake to fetch a week-end guest. The guest was Kurt Weill, ex-conductor in the provinces, student of the arch-nationalist Humperdinck and the austere Busoni, quiet rebel. He and Kaiser set to work on a one-act opera about traveling actors with a title suggesting Lenya's own future role, *Der Protagonist*. Shortly after it was finished, Lenya and Weill were married. Much later Weill mustered some of his noblest music for another Kaiser text, *The Silver Lake*, a winter's tale from which Lenya was to sing the proclamatory telling of Hitler, "Cäsars Tod." In the meantime, however, Weill had been drawn to Brecht's urgent poems and productions and drew his wife with him.

Lenya auditioned the new "Alabama Song" for Brecht and his remark—"Not quite so Egyptian"—was the key note for the relaxed style she was to evolve as an actress. She found this relaxation prevailed only on stage. However unshaven, lank and idle looking with his leather cap and cigar, Brecht was ensnarled in endless propositions of his disciples, and Weill lost time with forlorn pupils in his dingy apartment. Yet somehow the confederacy succeeded in being a very "inter-woven" one with exchange of ideas from the start, Weill scrupulously attentive to Brecht although not always mindful of his guitar and Brecht long-suffering with the actors. Conceivably Lenya's presence in the sanctum was relaxing; with her piquant face and chic bangs she was the only member of the Brecht retinue safely untempted to resemble Brecht. And she was well aware of the sight and sound of "working women in the backyards of tenements on Sunday afternoons," Brecht's ideal according to Hanns Eisler.

The premiere of *Dreigroschenoper* was as precarious as the tight-rope. Producer Ernst Aufricht was afraid of Kurt Weill, an "avant-garde" composer, and contemplated using the original *Beggar's Opera* airs until Lenya's singing of the Tango bedeviled him into conviction. Brecht, for his part, was undone by Aufricht's deadline and fled with Helene Weigel and the Weills to the Riviera to complete the play. During rehearsals the idea of it all had to be pounded into Harald Paulsen, the handsome tenor doing Mackie Messer, and, besides, Paulsen wanted an entrance aria. The cabaret *chanteuse* Rosa Valetti, on the other hand, herself a model for Brecht, pulled up short at Mrs. Peachum's idea that by nightfall men are "lying again on top" and refused to sing her "filthy" song. (Says Lenya: "Brecht is never vulgar, and the advice he gives two people in the 'Procurer's Ballade,' for example, is almost, for me, a *Lehrstück*. He just tells you what to do when a woman is pregnant and not to disturb that pregnancy. If you have a dirty mind, you can say it's dirty. For me it's pure.")

Although she lost her "Solomon Song" in the bawling mayhem of the last rehearsal, Lenya was saluted for the Danubian lilt in her voice, and Lenya the actress entered permanently the lore of Berlin. Dancing Macheath into the arms of the police, she delivered a saucy wave of farewell which became a symbol in the great era of betrayal. Gesture as Brechtian *Gestus*, it persisted on the streets of

Germany long after Lenya's records were labeled "degenerate" and dissolved in acid. *Gestus* or embodied attitude, again, was the adoption of Lenya's songs as codes in concentration camps.

Dreigroschenoper ran indefinitely in Berlin, besides spreading everywhere else, but Lenya surrendered Jenny for other roles, some of remote pertinence to Brecht. Defiant in brimmed hat and trench coat, dragging a cigarette, she was the free-living Ilse in Wedekind's sex calamity *The Awakening of Spring*, with Peter Lorre. Max Reinhardt sent his pupils to see this Volksbühne production of 1930, and Lenya also joined Lorre in *Pioneer in Ingolstadt*. A sovereign experience was *Danton's Death* where, although sensuality palled, sullied mistresses and wives so unhinged as to doubt the revolution knew, with Danton at the guillotine, that "you cannot keep our heads from kissing at the bottom of the basket." At the Staatstheater Lenya had also acted Sophocles, Moliere and Schiller.

Returning to *Dreigroschenoper* she played Lucy instead of Jenny because of Brecht's boyishly informal and impartial relation with Macheath's ladies. But Lenya was reappointed to Jenny in the celebrated Pabst film with Carola Neher, Ernst Busch and Theo Mackeben conducting. The cameraman Fritz Arno Wagner apparently imagined himself back with Murnau's eldritch *Nosferatu*, for his traveling shots kept the brothel uncannily gliding, at it were, like Dracula's coach and spectral ship. But in the midst of over-enriched or melting realities, Lenya restored some of Brecht's mordancy with her drawn face, her slumping posture and neck choked in long black ribbon. Pabst's film was sober at times, but not the quintessential Pabst, still less the quintessential Brecht as Brecht apprized the public in a lawsuit and sixty pages of derisive, righteous commentary. But despite a mellowing in the part itself, Lenya remained the demoralizing image of Jenny.

It is the Brechtian fraternity of actors which Lenya remembers best. Peter Lorre played with Weigel in the 1931 *Mann ist Mann*, Brecht's first consciously "epic" production (with music by Weill, now lost). Rational and explanatory in the Brechtian method, he was unforgettable, "such an extraordinary actor." For Lenya his trip to Hollywood, thence to China or wherever as Mr. Moto, was peculiarly unfortunate. Even more unfortunate was the slightly Carola Neher, whose frail, ingenuous voice introduced "Surabaya Johnny" in the Brecht-Weill *Happy End*, where she was Lilian Holiday, the girlish salvationist turned moll to subvert gangsters, with Lorre, Weigel and Oscar Homolka. The irony there was intransigent enough, the Salvation Army finally affiliating with the gang in respectable commercialism. Reality was worse when the fetching woman for whom Brecht wrote Polly Peachum and St. Joan of a Chicago insurgent, and to whom he dedicated poems, emigrated to Soviet Russia and disappeared in Stalin's liquidations. On the other hand, the massive Therese Giehse, alumna of the Munich *Dreigroschenoper*, was to become the first Mutter Courage with Brecht in Zurich.

And there was Weigel, of course, whose crippled Madam in *Threepenny*, legless on a wheeled platform, was critically overcome by appendicitis. She would be Lenya's counterpart as the keen superintendent of the Berliner Ensemble, the obedient, lucid, weather-beaten actress and dry-voiced singer of the later Brecht. Today Lenya and Weigel are on "the best of terms," although these are of the nature of peace terms since their firing of peremptory telegrams over a Berlin *Threepenny* production (and a certain amount of Lucy-Polly discord over rights in general).

Part IV

Stanislavsky and his followers

39 Stanislavsky to his players

Konstantin Stanislavsky; translation from the Russian
(arranged by Lucie R. Sayler)

January 1923

Founded in 1898 by the amateur actor and industrialist Konstantin Alekseevich Stanislavsky (Alekseev, 1863–1938) and the playwright Vladimir Ivanovich Nemirovich-Danchenko (1858–1943), the Moscow Art Theatre was a high-minded enterprise directed at the middle-class intelligentsia whose attitudes it reflected. Its greatest early successes were with Chekhov, Gorky and Hauptmann, for its innovations came chiefly in the realm of controlled directing, team acting and naturalistic stage effects. However, by 1905 Stanislavsky felt that it was in a rut, and began to experiment with symbolist drama and the classics. Hence his interest in Maurice Maeterlinck, the most popular symbolist playwright of the time. His production of *The Blue Bird* (1908) turned out to be a great success: it was copied in Paris and London and was kept in the repertoire throughout the Soviet period, a must-see for every Muscovite child.

Theatre Arts was instrumental in making the Moscow Art Theatre known in the U.S. Earlier, the occasional article in a specialist journal might refer to "The Seagull Theatre", associating it with Chekhov's play. In 1917, Oliver M. Sayler, dramatic critic of the *Indianapolis News* and reporter for the *Boston Evening Transcript*, headed for Moscow to record its achievements "before it was too late". He arrived on the eve of Revolution and his front-line reportage appeared in *Theatre Arts*. In 1923–4, the Art Theatre toured the U.S. and proved to be immensely influential on many theatre activists, among them Eva Le Gallienne and the Group Theatre. Ironically, the repertoire it toured was made up mostly of its early naturalistic hits and contained none of its more extreme experiments.

I AM happy that you received *The Blue Bird* so enthusiastically when you read it today. In a few days we will begin to study the play in preparation for rehearsal, and will produce it at the beginning of next season, that is in October or November. Not only Moscow will watch us but our beloved and gifted author, Mr. Maeterlinck, may perhaps honor us by attending the first performance. We must justify the confidence which he has placed in us. Could anyone think of greater encouragement for the work before us? We know how great and responsible a work this is.

There are three main difficulties to be overcome. First of all, we must express on the stage the inexpressible; Maeterlinck's thoughts and feelings are so elusive and subtle that they can be transmitted across the footlights only if we, artists, regisseurs, painters, musicians, decorators, machinists, electricians, penetrate as deeply as possible into the author's mysticism, and create on the stage a suitable atmosphere irresistible to the public. Second, the sensibilities of the public are not ready to receive and comprehend abstract thoughts and feelings. Third, we have to personify sleep, a dream, a presentiment, a fairy tale. This is lace work, woven of fine threads like a cobweb, while the scenic means of modern stage technique are coarse and clumsy.

I shall let my imagination play with the impression made by this poetic creation, and with its different themes: what the author himself means, with what impressions the public will leave the theatre, and how to get those impressions.

To begin with the main theme, the author's idea. Man is surrounded by the mysterious, the awful, the beautiful, the unintelligible. These mysterious intangible things fall upon something young and vital and frail and quivering, or cover with snow the hopelessly blind, or astonish and dazzle us with their beauty. We are drawn toward the mysterious, we have forebodings, but we do not comprehend. At times, in exalted moments, our eyes perceive barely visible contours beyond the clouds of reality.

Man by his animal nature is coarse, cruel, and conceited. He kills his own kind, he devours animals, he destroys nature, and believes that everything was created for his caprice. He reigns on the earth and hence thinks he understands the mystery of the universe. In reality he knows very little. The most important things are hidden from man. Thus he lives absorbed in material blessings, getting farther and farther from spiritual, contemplative life.

Spiritual happiness is given to only a few of the elect. They strain to hear the rustling of the blade of grass in its growth and to see the phantom-like outlines of worlds invisible to us. Having caught a glimpse and a sound of the world mysteries, they are greeted with the wide open eyes and distrustful smile with which men look upon geniuses. Thus centuries go by and the rumbling of cities deadens the sound of the growing blade. The smoke of the factories hides the beauty of the world from us; manufactured luxury blinds us; plastered ceilings separate us from the sky and the stars. We are stifled and look for happiness in the stench and smoke of the life we have created for ourselves. Sometimes we attain real happiness, out in the open fields in the sunshine. But this happiness, like the blue bird, becomes black as soon as we enter the shadow of the ill-smelling town.

Children are nearer to nature, from which they came not so long ago. They love contemplation. They are able to love toys and cry on parting with them. They enter into the life of an ant, a birch tree, a little dog, or a kitten. They are capable of great joys and pure dreams. That is why Maeterlinck, in *The Blue Bird*, has surrounded himself with children to undertake the journey through mysterious worlds. He succeeded perfectly in this world of children's fantasies, horrors and dreams. Let us, too, attempt to turn back to youth.

The production of *The Blue Bird* must be made with the purity of fantasy of a ten-year-old child. It must be naive, simple, light, full of the joy of life, cheerful and imaginative like the sleep of a child; as beautiful as a child's dream and at the same time majestic as the ideal of a poetic genius and thinker.

Let *The Blue Bird* in our theatre thrill the grandchildren and arouse serious thoughts and deep feelings in their grandparents. Let the grandchildren on coming home from the theatre feel the joy of existence with which Tyltyl and Mytyl are possessed in the last act of the play. At the same time let their grandparents once more before their impending death become inspired with the natural desire of man: to enjoy God's world and be glad that it is beautiful. Let the old people scrape off from their souls the scum that has befogged them, and look attentively into a dog's eyes and caress it as a sign of gratitude for its dog-fidelity to man. Over there in the quiet of the sleeping town, perhaps, they will feel in their souls the distant land of memory in which they will soon be slumbering.

If man were always able to love, to understand, to delight in nature! If he contemplated more often, it he reflected on the mysteries of the world, and took thought of the eternal! Then perhaps the blue bird would be flying freely among us.

I believe the author will be gratified if we convey a hundredth part of this impression to our audience, but how can we do this with a thousand-fold public? The Moscow theatre public is usually late for the performance, enters the hall noisily, looks for a seat for some time and settles itself gradually amid a rustling of clothes and programs. Such a crowd will frighten away the mood of Maeterlinck's phantoms, deaden the fluttering spirit of the mysterious, and disturb the dream of the beautiful child's sleep. People will not be carried away at once and quiet down. First of all they will have to shake off the daily worries which they bring with them to the theatre in their minds and their tired nerves. Thus will the first act pass.

Yet not a single word of Maeterlinck's play must be lost. It is necessary to get the attention of the public at once without waiting for the development of the play to draw them away from their cares.

Formerly this was attained by simple means. In the days of our grandfathers they did not quiet the audience, they produced an artificial cheerfulness with an orchestra which played a deafening march or a polka with castanets. Then the play and the actors were different, and the decorations and costumes bright and loud. Everything acted sharply on the sight, the hearing, and the primitive imagination of the spectator. Now both the purpose and the manner of seizing hold of the spectator have changed, and the old theatrical manner no longer satisfies. The theatre does not wish to amuse the public under the guise of diversion, it has more important aims. The author and the artist use the theatre as a means of conveying noble pictures and thoughts. Through it the poet Maeterlinck sings his liturgy and Ibsen the thinker preaches the freedom of the human spirit.

Everything abstract is less intelligible to the middle class public and therefore our task is more complicated, but happily we have new means of expression more effective than the old methods. The theatre has become strong through the cooperation of representatives of all the arts and crafts of the stage, and their creation is irresistible. We do not need striking decorations or costumes; exquisite paintings and materials in subdued tones take their place. Old, strait–laced actors with wheezing voices are replaced by modest people of culture and quiet manner. They do not need to go to the extreme of what they feel, for it is only to the stupid that you have to explain everything in words. The regisseurs have learned to bring into common harmony all the creative elements of the performance, and in this harmony lies the strength of the theatre. Therefore we shall attempt to win the audience at the rise of the curtain.

The leading role in the ensemble belongs to you artists. In order to make the public listen to the fine shades of your feelings you have to experience them intensely yourself. To live through definite intelligible feelings is easier than to live through the subtle soul vibrations of a poetic nature. To reach them it is necessary to dig deep into the material which is handed to you for creation. To the study of the play we shall devote jointly a great deal of work and attention and love. But that is little. In addition you have to prepare yourselves independently.

I speak of your personal life, observation which will broaden your imagination and sensitiveness. Make friends of children. Enter into their world. Watch nature and her manifestations surrounding us. Make friends of dogs and cats and look oftener into their eyes to see their souls. You will be doing the same as Maeterlinck did before writing the play, and you will come closer to the author.

Just now I cannot stop longer on this most important point, the work of the artists, to which we shall devote many sittings and rehearsals. I must hurry on to that part of the production the realization of which does not permit of delay. I mean the decorative, the musical, the electro-technical and other phases of the work for which the craftsmen of the theatre are waiting.

40 Perspective in character building

Konstantin Stanislavsky

July 1949

As early as 1902 Stanislavsky wanted to put down his ideas on acting and by 1922 he had compiled a number of notebooks with his fugitive observations. None of this constituted a "system", although he planned a book on the "history of a production". Stanislavsky's teachings cannot be congealed into a frozen set of exercises, for his thinking was always in flux. He aimed at liberating the actor from his tension, teaching him to concentrate, to develop his imagination within the author's "given circumstances", to refine his sensory and emotional capabilities, notably by seeking out personal inner images (affective memory). Inner and outer techniques were to be combined to achieve a creative state of mind resulting in the human truth of the character. As émigrés, his students, who had encountered an early period of his researches, spread their own interpretations throughout the world, disseminating a vocabulary of "re-experiencing", "through action", "the task", "the super-objective", "the magic if". At the American Laboratory Theatre in New York, Boleslavsky and Ouspenskaya trained Lee Strasberg who, in turn, stressed personal psychology at the Actors Studio.

Late in life, Stanislavsky tried to formulate his principles in *An Actor's Work on Himself*, of which only the first part was completed by his death. In its fictional guise, a young actor follows the instruction of a teacher who is the author's spokesman. The American versions by Elizabeth Reynolds Hapgood – *An Actor Prepares* (1936), *Building a Character* (1950) and *Creating a Role* (1961) – were much abridged and rearranged versions of the originals. Still, this excerpt from the second book tries to move beyond "affective memory" to create characters who are distinct from the actor.

IT WAS exactly 9 o'clock when Paul and I reached Tortsov's home.

I explained to him how crushed I had been to find that inspiration had been replaced by theatrical calculation.

"Yes ... by that too," admitted Tortsov. "One half of an actor's soul is absorbed by his super-objective, by the through line of action, the subtext, his inner images, the elements which go to make up his inner creative state. But the other half of it continues to operate on a psycho-technique more or less in the way I demonstrated it to you.

"An actor is split into two parts when he is acting. You recall how Tommaso Salvini put it: 'An actor lives, weeps, laughs on the stage, but as he weeps and laughs he observes his own tears and mirth. It is this double existence, this balance between life and acting that makes for art.'

"As you see, this division does no harm to inspiration. On the contrary the one encourages the other. Moreover we lead a double existence in our actual lives. But this does not prevent our living and having strong emotions.

"Do you remember what I told you back in the beginning, when we were working on objectives and the through line of action, about the two parallel lines of perspective?

"The one is the perspective of the role.

"The other is the perspective of the actor, his life on the stage, his psycho-technique while he is acting.

"The stream of psycho-technique which I illustrated for you in the 'Othello' speech is the line of the *perspective of the actor*. It is close to the *perspective of the role* because it runs parallel with it, the way a foot path may stretch along beside a highway. But at certain moments they may move farther apart when, for one reason or another, an actor is drawn away from the main course of his part by something extraneous and irrelevant to it. Then he loses the perspective of his role. Fortunately our psycho-technique exists for the very purpose of giving ways constantly to attract us back to the true path, just as the foot path always leads the pedestrian to the highway.

"I went to the theatre recently to see a five act play," he said. "After the first act I was delighted with the production as well as the acting. The actors gave vivid characterizations, showed much fire and temperament, acted in a special manner which interested me very much. I was curious to see how the play and the acting would develop.

"But after the second act I found they had shown the same thing as in the first. Because of this fact the interest of the audience, as well as my own, suffered a definite decline. After the third act the same thing was repeated to an even more marked degree because the actors plumbed no new depths, their characters were transfixed, there was still the same fiery spirit to which the public was by now accustomed. The same manner of acting by this time had become so routine that it was boring, dull, and at times annoying. By the middle of the fifth act I was unable to take in any more. My eyes were no longer on the stage, my ears were deaf to the lines, my mind was preoccupied with the thought: How can I get out of here unnoticed?

"What is the explanation of this descending scale of impressions gathered from a good play, well acted and produced?"

"Monotony," I ventured.

"A week ago I went to a concert," Tortsov went on. "The same 'monotony' was evident in the music. A good orchestra performed a good symphony. They ended it as they began it, they scarcely altered the tempo or the volume of the sound, there was no shading.

"Why did they have no success, this well acted play and this good symphony performed by a good orchestra? Was it not because in both cases they were playing without perspective?

"Let us agree that the word 'perspective' means: the calculated, harmonious inter-relationship and distribution of the parts in a whole play or role.

"This means further that there can be no acting, no movement, no gestures, thoughts, speech, no word, feeling, etc., etc., without its appropriate perspective. The simplest entrance or exit on the stage, any action taken to carry out a scene, to pronounce a phrase, words, soliloquy and so on, must have a perspective and an ultimate purpose (the super-objective). Without those an actor may not so much as say 'yes' or 'no.' Even a tiny phrase taken by itself, has its own brief perspective. A whole thought expressed in a number of clauses is even less able to do without it. A single speech, a scene, an act, a play all need perspective.

"It is customary, in referring to speech, to have in mind the so-called logical perspective. But our practice in the theatre leads us to a broader descriptive terminology:

1   The perspective of the thought conveyed. This is that same logical perspective.
2   The perspective in conveying complex feelings.
3   Artistic perspective, used to add color, vivid illustration to a story or a speech.

"In the first, the perspective used in conveying a thought, logic and coherence play an important part in the unfolding of the thought and the establishing of the relation of the various parts to the whole expression.

"This perspective is achieved with the aid of a long series of key words and their accents which give sense to the phrase.

"Just as we underline this or that syllable of a word, this or that word in a phrase, we have to throw into relief the most important phrase carrying a whole thought, and do the same in a long story, a dialogue, a soliloquy. We follow the same principle of choosing the significant component parts in one large scene, a whole act and so on, the important episodes. Out of it all we evolve a chain of outstanding points which vary among themselves as to their volume and fullness.

"The lines of perspective which are used to convey complex feelings move on the subtextual, inner plane of a role. These are the lines of inner objectives, desires, ambitions, efforts, actions which are grouped, inserted, separated, combined, accented, toned down. Some represent important fundamental objectives and appear in the foreground. Others of medium or minimum value are grouped on a secondary plane, or sink quite into the background, according to the peculiar factors causing the development of the emotions throughout the play.

"These objectives, which go to make up the lines of an inner perspective, are to a large and important degree expressed in words.

"When we come to the laying on of color along the lines of artistic perspectives we again are obliged to adhere to qualities of consecutiveness, tone and harmony. As in paintings, artistic coloring does a very great deal to make it possible to distinguish planes of speech.

"The important parts, which must be filled out most, are most highly colored, whereas those relegated to the background are less vivid in tonal shades.

"It is only when we study a play as a whole and can appreciate its overall perspective that we are able to fit the various planes correctly together, make a beautiful arrangement of the component parts, mold them into harmonious and well rounded forms in terms of words.

"ONLY after an actor has thought through, analyzed and felt himself to be a living person inside his whole part there opens up to him the long, beautiful, beckoning perspective. His speech becomes, as it were, far-sighted, no longer the myopic vision it was at the start. Against this depth of background he can play out whole actions, speak whole thoughts, rather than be held to limited objectives, separate phrases and words.

"When we read an unfamiliar book aloud for the first time we lack perspective. Moment by moment we have only the immediate action, words, phrases in mind. Can such a reading be artistic and true? Of course not.

"Broad physical actions, the conveying of great thoughts, the experience of wide emotions and passions are made up of a multiplicity of component parts, and in the end a scene, an act, a play cannot escape the necessity of a perspective and an ultimate aim.

"Actors who play a role they have not studied well and thoroughly analyzed are like readers of a complicated, unfamiliar text.

"Such actors have only a dim perspective of the play. They do not understand where they must lead the characters they portray. Often when they play a scene they are familiar with they either do not distinguish or they do not know what lies still unrevealed in the obscure depths of the rest of the play. This obliges them to keep their minds constantly fixed on only the nearest action, the immediate thought expressed, utterly without regard for the whole perspective of the play.

"Take as an illustration of this fact that some actors who do the part of Luka in Gorki's 'The Lower Depths' do not even read the last act because they do not appear on it. As a result they cannot possibly have a true perspective and are unable to play their role correctly. The end hinges on the beginning. The last act is the outcome of the old man's preaching. Therefore one must have one's eyes always trained on the climax and lead all the characters whom Luka affects towards that end.

"In a different way the tragedian who plays the title role of 'Othello' knowing the end but without a careful study of the whole play begins to roll his eyes and gnash his teeth in the first act, gloating over the prospect of the murder.

"But Tommaso Salvini was much more calculating than that in preparing the plan for his roles. Take 'Othello' again. He was always aware of the whole perspective of the play from the moment of his fiery outburst of young passionate love in his first entrance to his supreme hatred as a jealous killer at the end of the tragedy. With mathematical precision and unrelenting consistency, from point to point, he plotted out the evolution of the emotions as they matured in his soul.

"Let us suppose you are playing 'Hamlet,' the most complex role of all in its spiritual coloring. It contains a son's bewilderment over his mother's suddenly transferred love—'or ere those shoes were old' she had already forgotten her beloved husband. In it, too, is the mystic experience of a man who has been afforded a brief glimpse into the world beyond where his father languishes. After Hamlet learns the secret of that other life this one loses its former meaning for him. The role embraces the agonizing recognition of a man's existence and the realization of a mission above his strength, on which depends the liberation of his father from his sufferings beyond the grave. For the part you must have the feelings resultant from filial devotion to your mother, love for a young girl, renunciation of that love, her death, the emotions of revenge, horror over your mother's death, of murder, and the expectation of your death after you have fulfilled your duty. Try jumbling up all these emotions on one dish and you can imagine what a hash will result.

"But if you apportion all these experiences along the perspective of the part in logical, systematic and consecutive order, as required by the psychology of such a complex character, and the life of his spirit which unfolds and develops throughout the whole course of the play, you will have a well built structure, a harmonious line, in which the inter-relation of its component elements is an important factor in the gradually growing and deepening tragedy of a great soul.

"Can one project any single part of such a role without bearing in mind the perspective of the whole? If, for example, you do not convey in the beginning of the play Hamlet's deep pain and consternation caused by his mother's frivolity, the famous scene with her later will not be properly prepared.

"If you do not feel the whole impact of the shock Hamlet receives from what the ghost tells him of life beyond the grave, there will be no understanding his doubts, his painful efforts to uncover the meaning of life, his break with his beloved, and all the strange conduct which makes him appear abnormal in the eyes of others.

"Does all this not suggest to you that it is the more incumbent on the actor who plays Hamlet to take care how he plays his first scenes, because so much will be required of him in expanded passion as his part unrolls?

"The result of that kind of preparation is what we call 'acting with perspective.'

"As a part moves along we have, as you might say, two perspectives in mind. The one is related to the character portrayed, the other to the actor. Actually Hamlet, as a figure in a play, has no idea of perspective, he knows nothing of what the future has in store for him, whereas the actor who plays the part must bear this constantly in mind—he is obliged to keep in perspective."

"How is it possible to forget about what is coming when you play a part for the hundredth time?" I asked.

"You cannot and need not do it," explained Tortsov. "Although the character being played should not know what lies ahead, still perspective is necessary for the part so that he can appreciate more fully each present moment and more fully give himself up to it.

"The future in a part is its super-objective. Let the character keep moving towards it. It will do no harm if the actor meanwhile remembers for a second the whole line of his role. This will only reinforce the meaning of each segment as he lives it and it will pull his attention with increased power.

"Let us suppose that you and Paul are playing a scene between Othello and Iago. Is it not important that you should remember that you, the Moor, only yesterday arrived in Cyprus, were forever united with Desdemona, that you are experiencing the best days of your life—your honeymoon?

"Where else would you get the joyousness necessary to the opening of the scene? It is all the more important because there are so few gay colors in the play. Moreover is it any less important for you to recall for a brief moment that from this scene forward the lucky star of your life will begin to set and that this decline must only gradually become apparent and distinct? There must be a powerful contrast between the present and the future. The brighter the first the darker the second.

"You need that rapid glance into the past and the future in order to make a proper estimate of the present action, and the better you sense its relationship to the whole play the easier it will be for you to focus the full extent of your attention on it.

"Now you have the necessary basis for the perspective of a part," concluded Tortsov.

But I was not satisfied and pressed him further with the question:

"Why does the actor himself have to have that other perspective?"

"His own perspective, as the person playing the role, is necessary to him so that every given moment while he is on the stage he will be in a position to assess his inner creative powers and ability to express them in external terms, to apportion them and make reasonable use of the material he has amassed for his part. Take that same scene between Othello and Iago. Doubt steals into the former's jealous soul and gradually grows. The actor who plays Othello must remember that he will have to play many more scenes of mounting passion between that point and the end of the play. It would be dangerous for him to break loose in this first scene, to show all his temperament without holding it in reserve for the gradual reinforcement of his unfolding jealousy. To squander his inner powers here would throw the whole role out of proportion. He must be prudent, calculating and always have his eyes on the final, culminating point of the play. 'Artistic emotion is weighed not in pounds but in ounces.'

"We must not forget one extremely important quality inherent in perspective. It lends a breadth, a sweep, a momentum to our inner experiences and external actions, all of which is of extreme value to our creative achievement.

"Imagine yourself running a race for a prize, but instead of pressing on over a long distance you stopped every twenty paces. If you did this you would never get into your stride or acquire any momentum, and that is enormously important in a race.

"We actors face the same problem. If we stop short at the end of every bit in a role and then start over again with the next we never get up momentum in our efforts, our desires, our actions. Yet we must have it because it prods, stirs, inflames our feelings, our will, thoughts, imagination and so on. You should never spend yourself on a short sprint. You must have the depth, the perspective, the faraway beckoning goal in mind.

"WHAT I have said here is equally applicable to the sound of the voice, to speech, gestures, movements, actions, facial expression, temperament and tempo-rhythm. In all these fields it is dangerous to break loose, to squander your all. You must be economical and make a just estimate of your physical powers and means of transposing the character you play into terms of flesh and blood.

"To regulate them you will need not only your inner powers but also the perspective of a dramatic artist.

"Now that you have made the acquaintance of perspective in a play and in a part, think it over and tell me if it does not bear a close resemblance to your old friend the through line of action?

"Of course they are not identical, but there is a kinship between them. The one is the other's closest aid. Perspective is the path through the entire extent of a play, along which the through line of action constantly progresses.

"*Everything happens for the sake of these two elements, perspective and the through line of action. They contain the principal significance of creativeness, of art, of our approach to acting.*"

41 Fundamentals of acting

Richard Boleslavsky

February 1927

Polish-born Bolesław Ryszard Srzednicki (1887–1937) changed his name to Richard Valentinovich Boleslavsky when he entered the Moscow Art Theatre in 1908 and acted and directed in its first studio. He served with the Polish Lancers in the First World War, and left Russia when his fellow cadets were executed. He came to New York from Paris as the *conférencier* of the *Revue Russe* (1922). In the summer of 1923, Boleslavsky learned English through 18 hours a day of constant instruction in order to get a job directing Melchior Lengyel's *Sancho Panza*. With Maria Ouspenskaya he founded the American Laboratory Theatre (1923–30), where they taught a full curriculum. His approach to acting stressed units of action ("beats"), the "spine" of the play and emotional-memory exercises; his student Lee Strasberg would later convey these teachings to the Group Theatre (although Boleslavsky believed that Strasberg was wrong to emphasize affective memory over dramatic action). Boleslavsky's Princess Theatre lectures and articles in *Theatre Arts* (1923–32) introduced Americans to the Stanislavskian concept of "concentration" in acting and were the basis of *Acting: The First Six Lessons* (1933), which is still in print. From 1930 to his death, he was a busy Hollywood film director.

To DEFINE the art of acting is a difficult problem. The mere size of the subject is bewildering. Acting, in the first place, has the widest range of any art excepting perhaps architecture. It extends all the way from the highest level of human development down through the animal world, where a kitten, for example, will act out a mouse-hunt, knowing perfectly well all the time that the supposed mouse is merely a scrap of paper tied to a string. The fact that this art is not confined to the limits of the theatre complicates the subject still further. Acting is inextricably interwoven into our everyday life. Let anyone follow closely his actions as he goes about his daily tasks and try to separate those moments when he is acting a part from the times when he is really himself. He will soon realize that in the matter alone of those formal smiles of salutation, with which he greets many people, he does not actually feel in the least like meeting with a smile, there is a very considerable amount of histrionic material. It almost seems as if the art of acting were born with us.

Even our good manners—which are pure theatre—do not, in the last analysis, come from governesses, tutors, books of etiquette or dancing masters. They come rather from that logical sense of perfection which resides in every normal human being and this longing for perfection may be said to be the true source of that acting power and theatricality which pervades our life. Sometimes this desire to idealize and to avoid things as they really are leads us to absurd lengths, as, for example, when we put ornaments on coffins and feathers and draperies on the hearses going to the cemetery.

While it is true that the theatre is only a part of what might be termed the huge acting industry of the world, it is, at the same time, the field where the art of acting can best be analyzed. If the "acting" of everyday life is the attempt to perfect reality, within the theatre you get the further attempt to perfect this first perfection. There the art of acting is set before you in its essence and for that reason offers a better opportunity of analysis.

There are many definitions of the art of acting, already thoroughly familiar. At the risk of being repetitious, I will quote a few of them. First there is the opinion of Fanny Kemble written in 1882. She declared that:

> The art of acting has neither fixed rules, specific principles, indispensable rudiments nor fundamental laws; it has no basis in positive science, as music, painting, sculpture and architecture have; and differs from them all in that the mere appearance of spontaneity, which is an acknowledged assumption, is its chief merit.

Coquelin, on the other hand, following Diderot's paradox, says:

> I am convinced that one can only be a great actor on condition of complete self-mastery and ability to express feelings which are not experienced, which may never be experienced, which from the very nature of things never can be experienced. And this is the reason that our trade is an art, and this is the cause of our ability to create.

Talma has his own opinion:

> Acting, like every other art, has a mechanism. No painter, however great his imaginative power, can succeed in pure ignorance of the technicalities of his art; and no actor can make much progress till he has mastered a certain mechanism which is within the scope of patient intelligence. Beyond that is the sphere in which a magnetic personality exercises a power of sympathy which is irresistible and indefinable. That is great acting; but though it is inborn, and cannot be taught, it can be brought forth only when the actor is master of the methods of his craft. He must remember, first, that every sentence expresses a new thought and therefore frequently demands a change of intonation; secondly, that the thought precedes the word. (The actor should have the art of thinking before he speaks.) Of course there are passages in which thought and language are borne along by the stream of emotion, and completely intermingled. But more often it will be found that the most natural, the most seemingly accidental effects are

obtained when the working of the mind is visible before the tongue supplies the words.

And finally I would take you back nearly two thousand years to Quintilian, who somewhere between the years 35 and 95 A.D. wrote:

> The great secret . . . for moving the passions is to be moved ourselves; for the imitation of grief, anger, indignation, will often be ridiculous if our words and countenance alone conform to the emotion, not our heart. . . . Wherefore, when we wish to attain verisimilitude in emotion, let us put ourselves in the place of those who really suffer; and let our speech proceed from the very state of mind which we wish to induce in the judge. Will he grieve, who hears me declaim unmoved? Will he weep, who sees me dry-eyed? But how shall we be affected, our emotions not being at our command? This too I shall try to explain. What the Greeks call *paviaolas* we call *visiones*; whereby the images of things absent are so represented to the mind that we seem to see them with our eyes, and to have them present before us. Whoever shall have conceived these thoroughly will have complete power over his emotions. I have often seen histrions and actors, on laying aside their masks after some mournful scene, continue to shed tears. If, then, the mere pronouncing of another's words can thus beget unreal emotions, what should not we effect, who ought to think our own words, and to be moved on behalf of our clients. . . . I have often been moved, not only to tears, but to pallor and every symptom of grief.

One is tempted to add parenthetically, at this point, Shakespeare's definition of acting, in his characterization of one of his fools, who after all were actors too. The definition is short and not without humour—"A Corruptor of Words"—that is all. What a marvel this Shakespeare was, to foresee a condition hundreds of years ahead and give such an excellent definition of 90 per cent of the average acting today!

I have chosen these contrasting opinions on the art of acting to bring out the four different schools which they represent. Miss Kemble represents the opinion that acting is nothing but inspiration, nothing but flashes of the mere appearance of spontaneity. I might term this the School of Inspiration. To Coquelin's followers, acting is the "ability to express that which never did happen"—in other words the ability to falsify. This might be called the School of Counterfeiters. To Talma, acting is a mental process, the result of brain work, an exhibition of intelligence and mentality—a very honorable, but none too happy opinion, belonging to the School of the Scholars. Finally we come to the definition of Quintilian, which begins "for moving the passions, is to be moved ourselves." This we may call, with William Archer, the School of the Emotionalists.

This last definition precipitates us at once into a controversy that has raged intermittently from before the days of Quintilian up to the present time. I do not intend to bore you with a dreary catalogue of the arguments and quarrels brought about by the discussion of the questions "Should you feel what you act or should you not?" "Is it easier to move the audience when you actually feel on the stage or when you only pretend or perform the feeling?" But having laid all the various points of view before you, it may be profitable to consider them a little more at length—particularly the classic debate between the Emotionalists and the Anti-Emotionalists.

The followers of both sides can bring you, to support their contentions, a mass of evidence, all of which is witty enough and true enough to leave the decision in the air. Take, for instance, the old story about the French actor Quinault Dufresne, who was required in a highly emotional scene, where his cheeks were bedewed with tears, to utter an aside in a low tone. It is related that on one occasion, some one in the pit called out to him at this moment "Plus haut" (Louder) and that without a second's hesitation the actor shot back "Et vous, Messieurs, plus bas" (Softer). Your Anti-Emotionalist will maintain that it would be impossible for a man who was really feeling to the point of shedding tears to answer an interruption of this kind as promptly and so to the point. He must, they say, have been merely pretending to feel, while his mind was actually free and untrammeled by emotions. It is, however, quite as easy to argue for the other side that only because the actor was in a state of genuine and significant emotion that had been rudely interrupted could he summon the requisite courage and strength so boldly and unhesitatingly to defend himself. There is another story which concerns Lekain. Of him it is told that once in the midst of an exceedingly tragic scene, where, as the son of a murdered mother, he entered her tomb with a raving monologue, he noticed a valuable diamond, dropped by the leading actress, lying on the floor before him. Without interrupting his lamentations, he quietly pushed the diamond toward the wings with his foot. Anti-Emotionalists insist that a man capable of such presence of mind could not be truly feeling his tragic emotions. To be genuinely absorbed in grief and quietly to save a diamond at the same time is to them altogether incomprehensible. The Emotionalists counter with the assertion that if such a situation were duplicated in real life, it might be quite instinctive for a distraught son to bend down and slip the diamond into his pocket.

Personally I admire Joseph Jefferson's statement. "For my part, I like to have the heart warm and the head cool," which seems to come rather close to the crux of the problem. One might term the followers of this point of view the School of Emotion Makers or creators. It is only comparatively recently, however, that the new psychology and psycho-analysis have made such a thought practical.

It is obvious that no actor, no matter how endowed, can enter absolutely into the character of, let us say, Lady Macbeth, Othello, or Hamlet. If such a thing could be done, the unfortunate actor would be able to play the part but once and then would be a candidate for the mad-house. As a matter of fact, I have actually known a case similar to this. There was once a very talented member of the Moscow Art Theatre, who dreamed all his life of playing the part of one of the Brothers Karamazov. When he finally had the opportunity to do this, he played for a few weeks and then was taken to the insane asylum. He recovered two years later, but had completely lost the power to appear on the stage and perform. Some of us who were youngsters at the time took him to our hearts and helped him to start again from the very beginning. We arranged performances where he, like the veriest novice, trembling and perspiring with nervousness, played small parts before an audience of one, two, three and four, gradually working up to a full house. I am proud to say that our group of young actors actually cured him and brought him back to the stage. When the Moscow Art Theatre visited the United States two years ago, this actor was with them and played several parts. For me, however, his experience is adequate proof of the impossibility of 100 per cent pure emotionalism on the stage.

I must admit that I find it more difficult to present any evidence other than my own feelings, based largely on my experience and observation of theatre audiences, to prove as conclusively that the School of Anti-Emotionalism is without meaning. A counterfeit sincerity no matter how cleverly contrived never moves an audience. Pathos which is not genuine never stirs the emotions. I am sure that the main explanation of why the plays of Shakespeare are not especially popular nowadays in certain countries of the world, while they are exceedingly popular in others, lies in this fact. I think you will find that in those countries where Shakespeare is not popular, the actors approach his plays with the most complete reverence for literary tradition, but with an equally complete lack of genuine feeling for Shakespeare and his people. On the other hand, in those places where Shakespearean performances are successful, the actors tend to run away from tradition and try to feel Shakespeare and play Shakespeare as if he were someone who lived in the same street.

With the exception of a few French actors like Coquelin, Sarah Bernhardt, Guitry and one or two others, I must admit that I have never seen any very good representatives of the Anti-Emotional School. I am sure that a really fine Anti-Emotional actor must always be a genius in the most exalted meaning of that word. The School of Emotionalism is difficult enough. It demands an actor's very life. It requires that his entire being should be sunk in his work. It leaves him after a performance robbed of his very soul. But I can understand that it must give him a very considerable amount of creative pleasure and probably a profound sense of satisfaction in his moments of inspiration. The School of Anti-Emotionalism, on the other hand, requires him to be cold, analytical, watchful, to walk, so to speak, along the edge of a precipice and at the same time to control all the resources of his body—physical, mental and emotional. That must be positive torture. It takes a man of the genius of Coquelin so to coordinate his bodily resources that every single move even to a minor muscle of the face is remembered and employed with the accuracy of a scientific instrument to produce a desired effect. When playing the part of Tartuffe, in the scene, for instance, where the hypocrisy of Tartuffe is discovered it is with a single move of a muscle above the eye-brow that Coquelin reveals the man who knows he is lost, but who has not yet surrendered. It was a supremely clever detail in the artificial performance of a complicated state of feeling. It aroused my intense admiration for the work it represented, but not the least tingle of emotion. Every part that Coquelin undertook was deliberately prepared down to the smallest detail and was built up of countless little moves purposefully fitted together like a huge mosaic with its thousands of small, differently colored stones. I should say that while the craft of the Anti-Emotionalist may be very great, his art is more open to question.

I have often wondered how the Anti-Emotionalist School of acting ever came into being and having appeared how it could continue to exist and find followers. I think that the best answer to this question is furnished by our old friend Talma, when he says:

> Moliere and Shakespeare had given excellent reasons to their brethren, the one in his *Impromptu de Versailles* and the other in *Hamlet*. How comes it then that in spite of the advice of these two great masters, and no doubt of that of many of their contemporaries, the false system of pompous declamation had been established in almost all the theatres of Europe and proclaimed as the sole type of theatrical imitation? Is it because truth in all art is what is most difficult to find and seize?

Yes, truth is the most difficult thing in the world to find, but at the same time it is the only thing worth looking for. Truth on the stage is the same as truth in any other art. Like the other arts, the stage is not concerned with what might be called life-truths, but with artistic truth, which is something quite different. Truth in life is positive and materialistic. Life defines truth naturalistically. Truth is simply that which we know to be so. Art, on the other hand, has its own laws. Murder in real life is not what would be termed a truth, but murder on the stage may be a truth—even a wonderful truth. To prove my contention, which may seem to you a little paradoxical, I might mention a certain scene in *Broadway*, now playing in New York. In it a girl kills the villain, as an act of justice to herself and her slain lover. When I first saw this play, I surprised in myself a distinctly pleasurable feeling that this man was getting his just deserts. When I went to the play a second time, I watched the faces of the audience at that particular point and as far as I could see there was not a face that did not express pleasure and satisfaction at the sight of this stage murder. A stage truth had overridden a conventional truth. It can only do this, of course, when it is entrusted to the hands of a master, who knows how to interpret it. This master is the talented actor. The actor's art can not be taught. He must be born with ability but the technique, through which his talent can find expression—that can and must be taught. An appreciation of this fact is of the utmost importance not only to students of acting but to every actor who is interested in the perfection of his art. For, after all, technique is something which is perfectly realistic and quite possible to make one's own.

What is generally referred to as the technique of acting, limited as it usually is to a certain development of the actor's physical resources, is not really technique in the strict sense of the term. I would call it rather a tuning up of the instrument, just as one might tune up a violin, before starting to play. But even the most perfectly tuned violin will not play by itself, without the musician to make it sing. The equipment of the ideal actor, even although he is perfectly tuned up is not complete unless he has what I have already called, for want of a better name, the technique of an "emotion-maker" or creator; unless he can follow the advice of

Joseph Jefferson to "Keep your heart warm and the head cool." Can it be done? Most certainly! It is merely necessary to try and think of life as an unbroken sequence of two different kinds of steps, which I would call Problem steps and Action steps. For instance, if I were meeting you face to face instead of through the more indirect medium of print, I would attack the task of making you understand my argument quite in the manner of an actor, playing a part on the stage. Your willingness to follow me and consequent understanding of my point of view would be materially affected by many details, which I, as an actor standing before you, could bring to bear on my discourse—as, for instance, a clear voice, slow speech, a firm delivery and, not least, my ability to make you feel that I myself understood what I was talking about. You will see that the first step is for the actor to understand what the problem is that confronts him. Then the spark of the will pushes him towards dynamic action. A play has the same structure as life itself, although it may be more condensed, differently expressed and very often abstract. When an actor realizes that the solution of a certain part may consist merely in being able first, to stand on the stage for perhaps no more than one-five-hundredth of a second, cool-headed and firm of purpose, aware of the problem before him; and then in the next one-five-hundredth of a second or it may be, five or ten seconds, to precipitate himself intensely into the action which the situation requires, he will have achieved the perfect technique of acting. With such fluidity of resource he will never be in the position of being handicapped by the emotion itself or of becoming a nerotic from a too constant and too strenuous expenditure of his emotional forces. At the same time he will not have constantly to cheat himself and his audience, working hard at building castles in the air and trying to define what is by its very nature essentially indefinite—thus limiting his art to the production of a series of elaborate tricks.

Such a technique of acting, if completely mastered and diligently practiced, is not so tremendously difficult, because its secret lies so close to nature. It is based on the very essence of that form of acting which we use in our daily life. It is the same realization of a problem with its appropriate sequence in action that is seen in our individual daily dramatic efforts. This idea is exceedingly difficult for the average experienced actor to grasp. He generally is altogether convinced that should he pause while acting a part to consider his next move, although it might be only for an unnoticeable part of a second, he would come out of the character and so destroy the illusion. As if he did not do the same thing a thousand times in his daily life without coming out of his own character! The younger generation, on the other hand, are very easy to convince on this point and exceedingly sensitive as to this simple method of connecting problem and action. In my experience with American actors, particularly those of Anglo-Saxon origin, I have found this the only effective way of arousing the emotions and of making their nervous emotion on the stage count for something real and sincere.

42 An actor prepares: A comment on Stanislavsky's method

John Gielgud

January 1937

The appearance of Stanislavsky's first book on the actor's education was the result of a long and tortuous process. The original manuscript, Part One of what was intended to be a much longer work, had been translated by Elizabeth Reynolds Hapgood, wife of the editor and dramatic critic Norman Hapgood, who had managed to obtain the world rights to Stanislavsky's writing (and who is responsible for the French spelling Stanislavski). In the process, she invented a new vocabulary, translating Stanislavsky's "task" and "super task" into "objective" and "superobjective". When Yale University Press turned down the unwieldy text, Hapgood asked Edith Isaacs to help her prune it into something commercially viable. The truncated and lexically garbled book that resulted, *An Actor Prepares* (1936), became accepted as the authoritative English-language enunciation of Stanislavsky's ideas. *Theatre Arts*, its publisher, ran a series of commentaries on this watershed publication, beginning with John Gielgud, a somewhat unlikely choice, given the wholly pragmatic nature of his own training.

> It was Lee Simonson who suggested to the editors that there was something more important to do with Stanislavski's 'grammar of acting', *An Actor Prepares*, than to review it as a work of literature. The important thing was to discuss, or invite leaders in the theatre to discuss, the value of Stanislavski's method of actor-training to actors and directors outside Russia and for plays of all kinds. Mr. Gielgud's is the first contribution to this symposium. Mr. Simonson's, with others, will follow. — Editors' Note

It is a marvelous thing for the theatre of the whole world that Stanislavski should have taken the time to write what he calls his working text book. Over and over, as I read *An Actor Prepares*, I came to passages which expressed exactly the things that every actor must have felt but been unable to express, must have known subconsciously but never quite realized.

What he says, for example, about knowing, or learning, how to relax, how to control the body, is marvelous. There is no doubt, too, that his actual teaching of the approach to a part, of the preparation and the inner realization of a role, his theory of imagination, of the give and take between actors, the study of the audience, how to hold them, whether to play with the fourth wall down or up, are all of inestimable value. Good actors who have not been trained in this school would have to — and, no doubt, would — find out these things for themselves, but training of this sort would shorten their apprenticeship and help them over the hard spots.

I am not sure whether *An Actor Prepares* is really an actor's book. I think it is, perhaps, of principal value to directors and to students. Above all, a great lesson for directors. But I do know that it should prove fascinating reading for any person in the theatre. Personally, I was entrapped by it. I could not put it down.

There are those who will say that Stanislavski's method is not practical for the commercial theatre. In a way, I agree with them. And for this reason. It could not be applied to the poor play. It would be no use for a Boulevard company, for popular plays. One can hardly imagine Stanislavski's being bothered to produce romantic or comic melodramas, or even plays as good as *The Barretts*, *Dear Brutus*, *The Royal Family*, or any other plays in themselves essentially theatrical — plays written by sophisticated, commercial minds for sophisticated, commercial audiences. There would be no sense in attempting to direct these plays in Stanislavski's way.

But for the classical play, the really serious play, and modern poetic dramas like *Murder in the Cathedral* and Maxwell Anderson's works (actors, I can tell you, welcome plays like these), the approach would be admirable. One can apply the Moscow Art theory, of living every moment of the part, to Shakespeare and it means something. But apply it to *Hay Fever* and it becomes ridiculous. I don't say that the actor trained in this school might not carry a tray in a farce comedy *better* than any actor trained in the normal Anglo-Saxon manner, and, I suppose, that's something. On the other hand, while a Russian production of *Hay Fever* might be quite different from Noel Coward's — entirely removed from his intention or conception — it might still be able to amuse a Russian audience hugely and intrigue an English audience. The Habima Theatre production of *Twelfth Night*, for example, was altogether different in spirit from Shakespeare's intention. Yet it could hardly have failed to delight Shakespeare's as much as it did London audiences because the acting and the direction were so extraordinarily inventive.

A school working with Stanislavski's theory ought to be of great value to the student of acting, though, of course, it is a question whether anyone but Stanislavski would have the ability to direct it, without his genius to guide him. Craig has always demanded a school but never achieved one. And there are all too few schools run by men of real discrimination in the theatre. In England now there is the London Theatre School, created by Michel St. Denis, a nephew of Jacques Copeau, and leading actor and director of the famous Compagnie des Quinze, which works on much the same theory as Stanislavski's. And at Dartington Hall is the newly organized Chekhov Theatre Studio. The Compagnie des Quinze, which created André Obey's *Noë*, *Viol de Lucrèce* and *Bataille de la Marne*, is, alas, broken up.

I don't see any reason why Stanislavski's system should apply only to Russia. All schemes of training rest on the fact that you must get people when they are young and are prepared to go through a training course. The only danger is that unless these studios are able, out of their own groups or with another commercial management, to develop a working group of players — who can act plays before paying audiences — they are apt not to go far. This is the intention of St. Denis, and I believe he will achieve it. Every young actor must wish, when he is very young, to be told the things that Stanislavski tells of in his book. And for the director, and the actor, too, Stanislavski's ability to distinguish between a cheap effect on the audience and the real effect of the artist must be immensely valuable. Another value of a studio like Stanislavski's is that it may lead young people into designing, directing and other branches of the theatre, even if they have no talent for acting, but a real talent for other service to the theatre, as very often happens.

In Russia and on the Continent the theatre is taken seriously as an art. In Anglo-Saxon countries, it is, if you generalize, a business. The actor's looks, his sex appeal, his personality, count for far more in our theatre than in Stanislavski's. People fall into the acting profession for a dozen reasons besides real ability. There is not, at present, the same opportunity to build up a serious repertory theatre. There is no theatre for the classics — and it is deeply needed for the good of the theatre itself, both for actors and for audiences — and without it an actor has very little chance to play the great parts. The actor, in these days, almost has to make up his mind whether to be popular or to be a good actor. And often it is hard to gauge the difference between popularity and real talent. Alas, the modern commercial theatre is bound to be a bitter disappointment to those trained in Stanislavski's theories. But it is our theatre which is wrong and not the training.

I am not sure that a great personality, a really great actor, would not be liable to disrupt Stanislavski's type of theatre. I should like to ask Stanislavski how he can reconcile the supreme art of the great players of the past with the bad companies and the bad plays they appeared in. These actors — Bernhardt, Duse, Salvini, even Henry Irving — had a curious unevenness and a passion for the limelight which conflict strongly with Stanislavski's ideas. I have a feeling that one must have a classical impersonality to work well in Stanislavski's theatre. A Schnabel can attain that magical quality. Playing Beethoven, he almost *is* Beethoven. But whether an actor can, I am not sure. Are the Russian and the Continental theatres the only ones that produce great actors with true genius for direction also? The great ones I spoke of just now were all directors, and very good ones too. But this direction was focussed around themselves and they could not, or would not, have directed or acted in great productions of *The Cherry Orchard* or *The Government Inspector*, plays which were not written for a single star.

I would give anything, myself, to know how to produce a play in our commercial theatre with a star part in it where every part is perfectly cast. I doubt if this has ever been done — except, possibly, in Stanislavski's own theatre. Meanwhile, in our theatre, actors and producers must labor to produce really fine plays, to build up repertory companies. There is no better training than working over and over again with the same actors, especially in a theatre of short rehearsal periods and long runs.

If only Stanislavski could now take the time to travel, to see foreign productions, to lecture and criticize, to bring his own companies to Europe and America!

43 An actor prepares: Comments on Stanislavsky's method

Robert Sherwood, Harold Clurman and Norris Houghton
February 1937

Robert Emmett Sherwood (1896–1955) had started out as a humorist and critic for *Vanity Fair* and the old comic magazine *Life*, and was a sporadic member of the Algonquin Round Table. At this juncture, however, he was known as the successful playwright of *The Road to Rome* (1927), *Reunion in Vienna* (1931), *The Petrified Forest* (1935) and *Idiot's Delight* (1936). He was about to launch *Abe Lincoln in Illinois* and co-found the Playwrights Company (both 1938). He won three Pulitzer prizes and during the Second World War became an adviser to F.D.R.'s White House.

Harold Clurman (1901–80), a native New Yorker, had found his calling in Paris and served as playreader for the Theatre Guild (1929–31). He had co-founded the Group Theatre in 1931, where he nurtured Clifford Odets and modulated Russian acting techniques into a distinctly American style. He directed several of their best productions including *Awake and Sing!* (1935) and *Golden Boy* (1937). He later was a much-sought-after Broadway director, effective with Arthur Miller, Eugene O'Neill and Carson McCullers; an inveterate Francophile, he also embraced Giraudoux and Anouilh. His pointed and perceptive theatre criticism appeared in *The New Republic* (1949–52), *The Nation* (1953–80) and *The Observer* (1955–63).

For Norris Houghton, see the headnote to Chapter 7, "Laurette Taylor".

---

by Robert Sherwood

ALL I KNOW is that acting *is* an art, requiring the same general sort of psychological abnormality in its practitioners as poetry, sculpture, music or any other art. An inexperienced actor, given that psychological abnormality to begin with, will find, in my opinion, that Stanislavski's method is the ideal one for developing his talent. Of course, that method is useful in our theatre — in every theatre.

by Harold Clurman

TO ASK if acting can be taught is only a little less paradoxical than to ask if music or painting can be taught. Obviously no teacher can make a Kreisler, but no one will deny that a normally endowed person may be taught to play the violin with respectable musicianship. The Kreislers are not 'made' through training any more than the Salvinis, but rare indeed are great virtuosos or great actors who have not worked hard and, very often, systematically at some form of training in their respective crafts. The fact that many of the old actors did not attend a formal school does not invalidate the truth that acting not only can be taught but has been taught to most of the major talents in the history of the theatre. Those people who scoff at the idea of actors' training will generally point to recent stars of screen and stage, mistaking momentary success or the vogue of a type person-ality for the real achievements of mature craftsmanship. The Bernhardts, Duses, Irvings, Chaliapins, Michael Chekhovs may all be set down as trained actors, though some derived their training in stock companies, others in conservatories and still others through the instruction of older masters. 'Talent without work is nothing more than raw, unfinished material.'

One of the things that bring discredit to the idea of a formal training for actors is the dilettantism, not to say charlatanism, of so many dramatic schools and teachers. Personally I know of only one complete modern acting technique which seems wholly sound as a method for actors' training and actors' work, and that is the so-called Stanislavski method, of which Stanislavski's *An Actor Prepares* gives the best summary. That it is sound does not strike me as a matter for debate since almost the entire Russian theatre of today — and almost all Russian acting — is based on it. Even Meyerhold, whose directorial style and general aesthetic is far removed from that of Stanislavski, recommends the Stanislavski method as fun-damental to all actors. The Vakhtangov Theatre in Moscow, though diverging in some respects from Stanislavski's approach, likewise regards 'the method' as basic. And, it must be noted, this is not a method for students only, but for seasoned actors in their work on production.

The Stanislavski method is not a theory; it is an actual way of work which has been practised now for over twenty-five years by some of the finest actors and directors in the world. Nor, it may be added, is Stanislavski's method an 'inven-tion'; it is a formulation of the creative process as it manifests itself in actors, a formulation intended as a technique for a genuine interpretation of parts and plays. There is nothing esoteric in the Stanislavski method; he came upon it by observing great actors, by reflecting on his own problems as an actor (he is a brilliant actor), by studying nature and art generally, and by working as a director with actors. And, for all his authority and experience, he is quite humble about his method. I heard him say to an actress quite recently, 'If the "method" disturbs you, throw it away. The "method" is intended to help the actor. If it fails to do so or if the actor is really good without it, let him forget all about it.'

Many people who admire the Moscow Art Theatre and who are quite willing to agree upon the value of the Stanislavski method feel at the same time that it is probably suited exclusively to a foreign or Russian temperament. This is nonsense, based on a vague theoretic knowledge of the method. As a matter of history, the actors of the Moscow Art Theatre, when Stanislavski first presented his new ideas to them, were just as averse to this 'intellectualization' of their art as any non-Russian actor might be. There is nothing 'national' in the method, and the resistance that the method might encounter anywhere is based on the old fear of 'consciousness' that is believed by many of the 'inspirational' school to rob the actor of his 'spontaneity' and so forth. Furthermore, the Stanislavski method is not a method exclusively for tragedy or for realism as some suppose. The method, in short, does not by itself guarantee a specific kind of result. Thus the Group Theatre, whose work has been influenced by the Stanislavski system, has done productions like *The House of Connelly, Men in White* and those of the Odets plays, which have been generally admired, while other productions by the same theatre that were less admired appeared to some critics to prove the unsuitability of this method for the American actor. Actually this method (like any other) depends on the actor who uses it and the director who applies it. . . . A young actor like Franchot Tone was trained almost exclusively in the Stanislavski method.

The only thing which makes the use of the method difficult in the American theatre is the lack of unified permanent companies, for it is hard to practise a definite technique with partners or directors who are practising another technique — or none at all.

by Norris Houghton

I CAN speak of the Stanislavski method only from observation of the results in the American theatre and in the Moscow Art Theatre and from more or less careful examination of Stanislavski's theories both as practised in his rehearsal rooms in Moscow and as he has codified them in *An Actor Prepares*.

From such observation, however, I conclude that acting can, up to a certain point, be taught. That limiting point is the same one that Stanislavski faces in his last chapter: the threshold of the unconscious. The inspiration which is the mystical quality, as it were, of creativeness, the thing that Arthur Hopkins calls 'unconscious projection' comes or does not come to each artist alone; inspiration cannot be taught. But these moments of inspiration, this ultimate kind of creativeness, can, as Stanislavski makes indisputably clear, be fostered and encouraged, the way can be paved for their appearance, the personality of the artist can be strengthened to receive them — if one knows how. And when such inspiration fails, knowledge can go far to fill in the gap.

If music or painting or architecture can be taught, why does it seem strange to talk of teaching acting? Certainly a Beethoven sonata is as intangible as *Hamlet*. An inspired performance of the one is as little concerned with technique as the other. But any kind of performance, inspired or pedestrian, of either is, at the same time and quite obviously, completely concerned with technique (to which something may or may not be added). This technique — acting, if you please, in this case — can and must be acquired, a process that involves learning and being taught. 'For how without technique', as Stark Young says, 'shall the actor know a way to discover out of many possible devices and symbols those suited to his own physical case and at the same time intelligible to men in general?'

How anyone who has worked in or even seen performance of the Moscow Art Theatre and has witnessed the results of such a method of acting could question the soundness of this method is inconceivable. During but four months of daily intercourse with the artists of the Art Theatre, watching the evolution of a play into a living organism, I became convinced of the truthfulness, the rightness and the beauty of their work–work based on these same principles which Stanislavski enunciates in *An Actor Prepares*. The book comes as but a refreshment of that conviction.

The Art Theatre's method can be challenged, it is true, by those who demand some abstract 'style' in the theatre, who want a heightening or a sharpening of artistic form, who sense that on the stage there should be a quality of 'theatricality'. This tends to be lost, as one can imagine, in the work of the Art Theatre, which abhors stylizations. Such people, however, have been more pertinently answered by Stanislavski himself than by anything I might say: 'This type of art is less profound than beautiful, it is more immediately effective than truly powerful; in it the form is more interesting than its content. . . . You can receive great impressions through this art. But they will neither warm your soul nor penetrate deeply into it.'

When I consider the question of the usefulness of this method to the American theatre, I pause. If I believe that acting can be taught and that this is a sound method, why do I hesitate at championing its practice here? If it could be universally taught, if all our theatre workers could base their attitude toward creation in the theatre on these Stanislavski ideas, as do all the theatres of Moscow (whether they carry his theories to their conclusion or not), then I would be convinced not merely of its 'usefulness' but of its power to give our theatre a new truthfulness and a greater beauty. But it is quite apparent from *An Actor Prepares* that this method, although completely personal, is at the same time a cooperative adventure.

It would be of little use to our theatre if an actor here and there were trained in and practised these methods. It would be of little use (although of more use, I admit) to the actor himself if the 'partner with whom he played had no knowledge of these methods, if his director knew nothing of such ideas. To be completely useful to the artists of our theatre, these methods should be understood and practised not only by all our actors but by the directors under whom they work; for a director, working at the high speed and tension of Broadway, could readily undo all the good such a method was accomplishing for an actor.

Such widespread unanimity of attack on play production is, however, unthinkable in our present theatre world, organized as it is on individualistic and temporary bases. Although the individual actor can and should find much that is useful from the Stanislavski method and will find much that is already familiar, our theatre must wait for the day — perhaps not too far distant — when actors working together as permanent groups under permanent directorates can practise this system collectively as Stanislavski would have it done.

44　The Group Theatre: In its tenth year – a critical estimate

John Gassner

October 1940

Co-founded by Harold Clurman, Lee Strasberg and Cheryl Crawford in 1931, the Group was conceived as a collective inspired by the Moscow Art Theatre and Stanislavsky's approach to acting. Precisely what the latter consisted of was open to debate, which led to a schism in 1934 between Strasberg (who preferred emotional memory and private moments) and Stella Adler (who insisted upon physical action and characterization). Meanwhile the Group had fostered such playwrights as John Howard Lawson and Clifford Odets and such actors as John Garfield, Morris Carnovsky, Elia Kazan and Sanford Meisner. Unlike the original Art Theatre, it was politically engaged and far to left. The tension between its activist goals and its artistic platform eventually led to its dissolution, and by 1940 many of its leading performers had moved to Hollywood.

John Gassner (1903–67), indefatigable anthologist, had just published his massive history *Masters of the Drama* (1950). This would win him a teaching post at Yale as Sterling Professor of Playwriting and Dramatic Literature (1955–67) and form the cornerstone of his reputation as doyen of American dramatic critics.

CELEBRATIONS are inappropriate in the desperate world in which we are living, and there will probably be no extraordinary festivities in November when the Group Theatre begins its tenth year. But this fact should not disturb that valiant organization, since the meetings that launched it on its notable career took place in another dreary and desperate year, twelve months after the historic stock market disaster. After a difficult, financially unstable decade, it is nonetheless generally recognized that the Group Theatre's history constitutes one of the brightest chapters in our theatre.

The Group has not been particularly successful in finding a critical understanding of its approach and its problems; it has been subjected to uncritical rhapsodies, on the one hand, and deprecatory, vague skepticism, on the other. Actually, however, the truth is simple and clear: namely, that the Group's work was grounded in the principle of collectivism in art and life, with due respect, at the same time, for individual self-realization and democratic procedure.

In the middle-'twenties, a number of young people who appeared in various Theatre Guild productions discovered that they had common interests. The 'new art' in the theatre propounded variously by Gordon Craig and Stanislavski, which had by now spread to this country, had one aim in common — namely, that all the arts of the theatre must be completely integrated in a production. Artists worth their salt subscribed to this principle, and many extended it in practice by striving for community theatres and permanent acting companies. It was not extraordinary then that Harold Clurman, fresh from Paris, should have been fired by Jacques Copeau's community theories of acting, and that Lee Strasberg should have immersed himself in the Stanislavski 'system'. In the winter of 1928 these progressive young artists and their associates began a seventeen-week rehearsal period on two strongly stylized, uncommercial plays, and a number of the actors were actually included in a short-lived experimental Theatre Guild studio which aroused interest with its production of the Soviet play *Red Rust*. By then, however, collectivism in the theatre reached a clearer definition, probably under the stimulus of the social idealism of the period, and the upshot of a series of meetings that began in the fall of 1930 was a resolve to establish a true 'group theatre' which would embrace a great deal more than the idea of simply acting together.

In April 1931 Harold Clurman drew up a provocative program for submission to the Theatre Guild's Board of Directors, in the hope that the Guild would give his company the permanent status of a First Studio. This was not to be, and the Group became an independent organization. Clurman's 'Plans for a First Studio', however, remains a classic statement of first principles. The theatre, if it is to be an art, must have 'singleness of meaning and direction'. It 'must create from the chaos which is the common experience of its members an expression that will have . . . an identity and a significance with which people, sharing the common experience, may sense their kinship and to which they can attach themselves'. Its artists must be 'confident all the time that the thing that binds them together must be a reflection of a sentiment that animates many people in the world about them'. This 'thing', it was evident from both Clurman's statement and the Group's later history, was to be the collective way of life and of art: 'The generations before us seemed to have been strenuously individualistic without believing very steadily in any particular good for their individuals. . . . We believe that the individual can achieve his fullest stature only through the identification of his own good with the good of his group, a group which he himself must help to create.' It would be difficult to find a more comprehensive definition of the Group's subsequent policy as exemplified by its close unity, its partiality for plays that had reference to social realities, and its persistent discovery or underscoring of such meanings in every script selected for production.

Clurman's program, moreover, recognized the importance of the individual in the collective enterprise. The actor was expected to develop himself continually, instead of contenting himself with superficial success. The actors spent their summers together, engaged in mutual criticism, and participated in special productions not intended for Broadway or in experimentation with scenes from plays. In order to make such an enterprise possible the Group kept its actors on an annual salary basis for six years, even adjusting the scale in accordance with the needs of its individuals. Nor did actors have to prove their adequacy at their first reading of a part, as is customary on Broadway; instead, they were enabled to grow into their roles under sympathetic guidance, and for the early education of the group, Lee Strasberg, in particular, proved himself an accomplished teacher. It is not surprising then that the Group developed many young actors of sterling quality, as well as directors like Harold Clurman, Robert Lewis and Elia Kazan, and that its ensemble received unstinted acclaim; it was not unusual for critics to refer to the Group as the best acting company in America. Incidentally, too, the same painstaking 'group' approach was contemplated for the playwright in the 1931 program, which held that the organization 'should not confine itself to doctoring his plays but criticize them, not simply criticize them but come to grips with him on fundamentals — in other words, actually collaborate with him'. It was precisely such collaboration that Odets received.

The Group has been chary of calling its methods the 'Stanislavski system'. Nevertheless, no other theatre has adhered so closely to Stanislavski's approach to acting. The Group actor realizes, among other things, that he must recreate a given situation in terms of his personal associations, and that he must perfect sense memory, as when that superb actor Morris Carnovsky acquired his gait in *Golden Boy*, in which he played the old Italian father, by striving to realize what would happen to a body shoving a fruit wagon for years. The actor must develop to the highest degree his ability to find inner justification for his conduct, to believe what he is saying or doing; he must master the kernel or spine of his role until it assumes a distinctness that is the acme of individuality or personality. He is expected to place himself in a 'circle' which keeps him real to himself, at the same time making sure that he is responding to the other characters on the stage instead of merely addressing their ears. Characteristic of this approach are Clurman's recorded injunctions during rehearsals of *Rocket to the Moon*: 'The spine of the character should be found by the actor himself. What's the simplest thing an actor can do today? He knows immediately he's talking about his [own] life.' To encourage a maximum realization of each role in terms of the actor's personal experience, Clurman exhorted them to express themselves freely: 'If you feel the impulse to do something, to do more than is called for, do it. If you are doing too much, I'll stop you.'

It is necessary only to add one cardinal element to the Group's production procedure — namely, the realization of the social significance of the play and of its parts. No one must regard the play or the role as an isolated experience, but virtually as a social one. Thus the larger content of the dentist's love story in *Rocket to the Moon* was for its director, Mr. Clurman, the thesis 'that the free exercise of the passion of love is impossible in middle-class life today'. Clurman's introductions to Odets' published plays teem with such references to the purport of the playwright's fable. *Golden Boy*, according to its director, was 'the picture of a great fight — a fight in which we are all involved, whatever our profession or craft. What the golden boy of this allegory is fighting for is a place in the world as an individual; what he wants is to free his ego from the scorn that attaches to "nobodies" in a society in which every activity is viewed in the light of a competition.'

Any evaluation of the Group Theatre is impossible without at least this fractional analysis of its approach, which has made it not only a redoubtable producing organization and a repository of impressive acting talent but also the only social theatre of our day that has refused to content itself, in the main, with presenting elementary, one-dimensional conflicts. Clurman, for example, criticized the Theatre Union because it thought that 'one aspect of the whole thing which is the art of the theatre is enough'. Whatever the future of the Group may prove to be at a time when we can only regard the future of all civilization with a shudder, its past has been honorable and fruitful. Confirmation of this fact, regardless of any esoteric contribution that the Group or its friends may claim, is abundantly present. It developed the most important new playwright of the 'thirties, Odets; it introduced Saroyan to the theatre; it produced notable experimental plays like *The Case of Clyde Griffiths*, *Johnny Johnson* and *My Heart's in the Highlands*; and it was largely, if not wholly, responsible for the rise of such outstanding actors as Franchot Tone, Morris Carnovsky, John Garfield, Elia Kazan and Luther Adler. However, every enterprise suffers from the limitations or problems imposed upon it by its approach, and a survey of the Group's noble record must take account of some understandable shortcomings.

Although comedy is one of the potent forms of social drama, this theatre has thus far found few occasions to exploit its actors' impressive comic talent. Perhaps, too, the Group would have been in a sounder financial condition if it had successfully tapped the resources of comedy. Its commendable immersion in social significances also left that organization vulnerable when the social picture no longer held out any direct hope of social change for the better, and even before then. Almost unavoidably, in presenting social plays devoid of simple and direct militancy — that is, allegories, so to speak, or oblique social commentaries — the Group Theatre often favored weighty but foggy dramas. This was conspicuously the case in such items as *Gentlewoman*, *Gold Eagle Guy*, *Weep for the Virgins*, *Casey Jones*, *Thunder Rock* and *Night Music*. At the same time, the Group's insistence on discovering social significances in everything it touched led to occasional straining of effect without actually achieving the desired clarification. A supposedly significant but fugitive detail, like a minor character's longing for window curtains in *Night Music*, may too often elude attention; it may not be safely expected to exemplify the central meaning of a play. Symbolism or allegory often possesses an esoteric character, and to communicate it to an audience it is not sufficient to assume an air of profundity. When the actors perform certain movements or scenes slowly and with high seriousness, they do not actually convey any meanings that the playwright has failed to precipitate completely in his script. Moreover, such emphases may labor the point unnecessarily, retarding its tempo and giving it a lumbering pretentiousness such as prevailed in a frequently beautiful play and production like *Night Music*. Lightness of touch, in fact, has not been one of the Group's virtues.

High tragedy has not been conspicuous in its repertory, which has favored little people and their problems, consequently keeping Group audiences on the plains and in the depths instead of lifting them to the heights, as the theatre must do at least now and then. Nor has this organization given sufficient scope to the imagination. That the company is abundantly endowed with this faculty was apparent in *My Heart's in the Highlands* and *Johnny Johnson*. But the realism that has dominated the Group's approach to acting appears to have inhibited inventiveness or freedom of treatment. A certain heaviness was apparent in the staging of *Johnny Johnson*, and despite the fine fantastication of Lee Strasberg's production idea many of the performances lagged or seemed pedestrian. Although the productions of *Thunder Rock* and *Night Music* were effective whenever some actor evoked that veracity of characterization which is the Group's crowning glory, they somehow lacked the free flow of imaginative beauty. The treatment tended to be solemn rather than inspired.

The staging of *Casey Jones* should have evoked folk poetry and theatrical opulence, instead of contenting itself with a flatly realistic presentation of a drab plot. In all such instances the scenic designer, Mordecai Gorelik, was sufficiently creative, but other elements of the production fell short of his achievement, due perhaps to the company's realistic orientation rather than to any flaw in the director. It may also be noted that enthusiasm for the 'little man' has encouraged a certain sentimentalization of the weak and foolish in Group productions; this was evident in the casting and direction of the heroines in *Rocket to the Moon* and *Gentle People*, as well as in the text of the plays. These characters were far less appealing and 'significant' than its directors seem to have believed; it was only too easy to dismiss them as trite and silly girls.

Regrettable, too, has been the Group Theatre's avoidance of revivals to which many of its actors and so brilliant a director as Clurman could have brought new values. Nor has the acting company been efficacious in enacting other than proletarian or lower middle-class types, most of them markedly and specially metropolitan. A notable example was the otherwise sensitive production of *Paradise Lost*, which nevertheless failed to convey the representative qualities of the American middle-class beyond certain, seemingly exotic, areas of New York City. Its predecessor *Awake and Sing*, on the other hand, was plainly a realistic play about the Bronx, apart from its larger significance, and Clurman's staging came as close to perfection as anything in the American theatre. It may be no accident that the Group Theatre has rarely invaded the road successfully, and its influence, too, might have been greater if its productions could have been less local in color and tone. It is not impossible to maintain, as some people do, that the Lunt acting company has achieved greater effectiveness within a much shorter time, and without the seemingly herculean labors of the Group. No doubt the redoubtable Alfred Lunt and Lynn Fontanne deserve much of the credit, but their company's greater elasticity and its unprovincial character have furthered its success immeasurably. Against this claim the Group may well argue that no collection of actors has such a consistent record of deeply realized characterizations. But this does not remove the limitations of a too localized appeal.

In its tenth year, this gallant company is at the crossroads; it is contemplating some reorganization, and it is considering a broader program, possibly based on a more popular price scale. It intends to interest itself in anything that is simply good theatre. More than ever, too, it disclaims being a cult or 'mystery', pointing to the fact that even arrivals from Hollywood like Frances Farmer and Jane Wyatt found no difficulty in working in harmony with the regular members. Owing to its admirable combination of social awareness and respect for individuality, it is capable of becoming even more distinctly a theatre for varied, broadly acceptable and nationally pervasive dramatic experience. It has gone far; now it may be expected, if external circumstances permit any growth, to go further.

45 The Actor's Lab

Dwight Thomas and Mary Guion Griepenkerl

February 1947

The Actor's Laboratory was founded in Hollywood in 1941 by Group Theatre members Roman Bohnen, Morris Carnovsky, Phoebe Brand and J. Edward Bromberg to fill the gap left by the dissolution of the Group. It concentrated on teaching film acting along the Stanislavskian lines introduced at the American Laboratory Theatre by Boleslavsky and Ouspenskaya. Centered on the use of "given circumstances", this was the interpretation approved by Stella Adler. Students included Sanford Meisner and Judy Holliday. It also established a non-profit professional theatre. The Lab was harassed from the start by the FBI, which claimed it was inculcating Communist ideology and, as its members were blacklisted or called before the House Committee on Un-American Activities, it weakened and folded in 1952. Its disappearance allowed the newly founded Actors Studio to impose its reading of Stanislavsky with minimal competition.

Dwight Thomas, co-author of a documentary life of Edgar Allan Poe, and Mary Griepenkerl were occasional contributors to *Theatre Arts*, always in tandem.

ONE DAY in June, 1946, a modest sign was placed in front of a small theatre in the heart of Hollywood. In contrast to the protracted electrics which blazed around the corner on Hollywood Boulevard movie palaces, the printed words merely stated that The Actors' Lab, Inc. presents *Awake and Sing* by Clifford Odets, with a cast including John Garfield, Morris Carnovsky, Art Smith, Phoebe Brand, Alfred Ryder, J. Edward Bromberg and Roman Bohnen, and setting by Boris Aronson.

This simple marquee was enough to cause the theatregoer with a long memory some astonishment. These same names, not then so famous, had appeared on a similar sign in front of the Belasco Theatre in New York in February, 1935, when *Awake and Sing* was given its premier performance by the Group Theatre Acting Company. Was this a revival of the Group, supposedly defunct since 1941? Or had these few members of the old Group, chancing to meet in Hollywood, decided to take a holiday from the films and revive one of the pleasanter mementos of 'the fervent years' as a tour de force?

The performance invalidated this theory. Here was a painstaking production, played with as great earnestness and enthusiasm as the original, but with the players showing the greater artistic maturity which comes after eleven years of continuous work on stage and screen. This revival captured the fresh spirit of the first production in New York, even though the actors contributed their services, working together again because they loved the theatre.

The Actors' Lab was organized by professional theatre people for the purpose of cultivating, through a program of work and education, a permanent non-profit theatre organization which they hope will grow to be a vital cultural force in the community. There is a definite link with the old Group Theatre; besides those already mentioned, Mordecai Gorelik, Ruth Nelson, Robert Lewis, Larry Parks, Lee Cobb, Will Lee, Richard Conte, James O'Rear, Michael Gordon, Henry Morgan, Phil Brown are Lab Workers with former Group affiliations. This, however, is not the whole story. Sam Levene, Hume Cronyn, Aline MacMahon, Hugo Haas, Rose Hobart, Jessica Tandy, Vincent Price, Marc Lawrence, Mary Tarcai, Danny Mann, Anthony Quinn and Lloyd Bridges are among many artists of theatre and motion pictures who share in the work of the Lab. Michael Chekhov spent several months with the group directing *The Inspector General*.

The original impetus came from three of the old Group, Bohnen, Bromberg and Mary Virginia Farmer, who, along with Jules Dassin, were invited to supply the leadership for a small circle of actors who had been meeting in a Hollywood loft to work out problems of their profession. As other former Group members gravitated to Hollywood it was only natural that they should join up. Non-Group people began to join the circle, and from these humble beginnings emerged the plan to build a fine theatre. Now, nearly six years later, the members still regard the project as far from maturity but full of the potentials of an exciting child. Their purpose seems to be identical with that of the old Group as expressed by Harold Clurman in *The Fervent Years*: 'to combine a study of theatre craft with a creative content which that craft was to express.'

For the study of theatre craft the group which had met in a loft acquired a small theatre on Laurel Avenue in Hollywood and became the Laboratory Workshop. Many of them worked with younger actors and taught them from the wealth of their background and experience. Plays were produced, not for the public but as classroom exercises — *Liliom*, *The Green Cockatoo*, *The Showing-Up of Blanco Posnet*.

War changed the plans of the Laboratory Workshop. The members offered their services to the USO as a unit and prepared a number of typical light-entertainment shows, *Brother Rat*, *Three Men on a Horse* and the like — thirteen in all — which played Army camps both here and overseas. At the close of the war there still remained a duty to the servicemen: to give the returning actor a chance to work and reestablish himself in his profession. Thus, a GI Workshop was set up to present all-veteran plays, this time in public performance. The first production was *A Bell for Adano*, sponsored by John Garfield and given at the Laurel Avenue Workshop theatre. This was so successful that it was soon followed by *A Sound of Hunting* and *Home of the Brave*.

A number of the GI players from these shows have accepted offers from the films or elsewhere, so that the purpose of the program has been realized. For further training of veterans the Workshop School, under the direction of Mary Tarcai and Danny Mann, offered a course approved under the GI Bill of Rights, and many of the one-hundred students now enrolled at the school are former servicemen.

Even during the war, however, enthusiasm for the permanent theatre and workshop continued. Funds were needed, and playing before an audience was the logical means of raising them. In August of 1944, in the fourth year of the Lab's existence, the tiny theatre was opened to the public for the first time with a bill of one-act plays: Irwin Shaw's *The Shy and Lonely*, Anton Chekhov's *The Bear* and *On the Evils of Tobacco* and O'Casey's *Pound on Demand*. The following May the Lab gave *Volpone*, directed by Morris Carnovsky and acted by J. Edward Bromberg, Phoebe Brand, Norman Lloyd, Hugo Haas, Rhys Williams and Housely Stevenson. The success of these public performances made the Executive Board of the Actors' Lab decide to present a definite program of plays in a regular theatre, with all proceeds to go into a fund for the ultimate erection of their own theatre and workshop facilities.

By the spring of 1946 a theatre was leased, the Las Palmas, less than a block away from Hollywood Boulevard, and the program was under way with a revival of *Volpone*. Though it played to standee audiences for five weeks, it was closed to make way for a run of *Awake and Sing* during June and July. In August the Workshop production of *Home of the Brave*, which had not been intended for presentation in the 'big theatre,' found its way there and later played a successful week in San Francisco.

The fall and winter season opened in October with Gogol's *The Inspector General*, directed by Michael Chekhov. Then an original script was produced, a first play by Anthony Palma, a twenty-four-year-old student from the University of California at Los Angeles. Entitled *To the Living*, the play recounted his experiences in a German concentration camp. Although the Actors' Lab has presented thirty-five plays during the past five years, *To the Living* is its first new script.

Every production at the Las Palmas Theatre has been a success but each was closed at the end of four or five weeks because 'long runs stultify everything but the cash register.' Eventually the plan is to tour with an occasional play and to keep the best few in repertory. A first try at this was made in January when *To the Living*, classified as a 'heavy' play, ran on a split-week schedule, alternating with a bill of one-acts, three by Tennessee Williams and one by O'Casey, all on the 'light' side. Another experiment was inaugurated for the Christmas holidays: *The Wizard of Oz* was played for two Sunday matinee performances, especially for children.

The Lab is a cooperative concern. All students at the Workshop, and everyone received into membership in the organization, must demonstrate a serious interest in the theatre and in the Lab. It is duly incorporated, with a lengthy constitution in which the point is reiterated that every member must be willing to perform all assigned duties for the good of the Lab as a whole. It is a permanent organization, with a goal not unlike the Moscow Art Theatre but with the important distinction, according to Roman Bohnen, chairman of the Executive Board, that 'the leadership is composite and elected,' meaning the Board members, who apparently function harmoniously.

This is because they feel that no one director should dictate the policy of the organization; 'any few of us can drop dead without causing the collapse of the Lab.' In the words of Mr. Bohnen: '*The Lab is bursty* at the seams with health, growth, talented people, money in the bank, plus a new brand of planned insolvency ahead — a payroll in excess of $80,000 annually for teachers, secretaries, plant maintenance, a few technicians. For five years the artists have contributed their talents; soon they must be paid. The plan, however, is to operate theatre, workshop, school and apprentice body at a deliberate deficit of about $200,000 annually. Until there is a cabinet minister of fine arts to foot such bills, we will simply be obliged to make a motion picture annually in order to "squander" its profits on basic subsidy for the entire operation.'

46 Past performances

Lee Strasberg

May 1950

For Strasberg, see headnote to Chapter 8, "Seven interviews in search of good acting".

———————

THE idea that performances of the past are completely lost and cannot be completely recreated is obviously and unfortunately true. But much more can be accomplished than is commonly supposed. While the actual performance is forever gone, the style, the character, the interpretation, the *soul* of the performance can be arrived at. And this can be clothed in an *ideal* performance, one that while lacking the actor's actual presence also misses his individual imperfections, so that we *see* the performance as it might ideally have taken place.

Look at the picture of Edmund Kean in "Shylock." A famous actor in one of his outstanding roles—the one he chose to stake his reputation and career on, when he made his debut in London on January 26, 1814. At first glance there is nothing unusual. There is nothing pictorially exciting or intriguing about the picture. But examine it a little more closely; compare it with illustrations of other well known actors in the same part—Rudolph Schildkraut, Albert Basserman, perhaps Werner Krauss, Edwin Booth, or Henry Irving—and we may perhaps share to some slight extent the experience of Coleridge when he spoke of seeing Kean as reading Shakespeare by flashes of lightning. Where is the outcast in the midst of a foreign society—dressed usually either in demeaning clothes to hide his wealth, or else orientally ostentatious, with the typical hair accouterments of the Ghetto Jew? Shylock here is young; Shylock is Italian! Notice that though he wears the clothes demanded by law of all his coreligionists his neckwear is peculiarly decorative; his attitude bold, aristocratic, an intelligent Italian of Jewish faith—fiery, young. His wife died young and he has only one young daughter. That is exactly the way Kean played him. "There was a lightness and vigor in his tread, a buoyancy and electricity of spirit, a fire and animation" which the great dramatic critic Hazlitt, though enthusiastic about the performance, found unsuitable to the "morose, sullen, inveterate, inflexible malignity of Shylock"; only to admit two years later that he had been in error, that he had "formed an overstrained idea of the gloomy character of Shylock, probably more from seeing other players perform it than from the text of Shakespeare. Mr. Kean's manner is much nearer the mark." Is it far-fetched to imagine that in observing this picture we have almost a glimpse of Kean in the part? And that a complete performance of Shylock might be built out of the suggestions derived from this observation?

Recently, by playing before some young actors records of a few speeches of Hamlet delivered by Sir Johnston Forbes-Robertson, we were able to glimpse a kind of Hamlet that none of us had ever seen or visualized—though we had read the stimulating remarks of Shaw on this performance. We are on the verge of a new, revitalized and dynamic conception of the performances in the ancient Greek theatre by means of a study of the dramatic aspects of extant vase paintings. The behavior, gesture, business of the commedia dell'arte actors will ultimately be reconstructed. That was already partly accomplished by directors Meyerhold, Evreinoff, and others working with a number of theatrical students on the eve of the Russian revolution. And one of the experimental projects of the Group Theatre was a reconstruction of a commedia dell'arte performance based on the available evidence. Most of this material that now exists can be found only in numerous doctoral theses, specialized philological or other research, and much is still to be accomplished before this becomes readily and widely available.

But material of a different kind, as difficult of access but more easily understandable, has just been made available in an excellent anthology "Actors on Acting" edited by Toby Cole and Helen Krich Chinoy. This comprehensive collection contains a selection of actors' thoughts and writings about their own art, in their own words. It is a comment on the existing cultural level in the theatre that we have had to wait for it till now, and that it is almost the only book of its kind in any language. There is a Russian collection which attempts the same task, but the present achievement is much more comprehensive. There are very few books which contain such factual and germane information on the theatre. It is a book to be enjoyed, perused, or studied. It can be opened at random and one is sure to find something stimulating. The juxtaposition of this material becomes an exciting experience as the confrontation of differing and opposing viewpoints takes on the aspect of dramatic conflict. It should at the least serve to introduce the young actor to the names of many previous practitioners of his art he will want to know more about. For the general reader it may serve to arouse a modicum of respect for the acting profession. This is truly one of the few indispensable books on the theatre. For it is obvious from the material that the actor, interested in amusing and entertaining his audience, is like other artists or craftsmen at least equally concerned with the correctness and truthfulness of the means he uses to accomplish that task. Interested in gaining the applause of his audience, he still insists on using the means he considers to be true and valid, and will not permit the success of another actor to sway him from the use of those he considers to be right.

The publication of a work of this sort is a great accomplishment, but poses a big responsibility for the editors. The material must be found, selected, sometimes translated and excerpted and must also be properly introduced and presented. The editors have done a capable job of annotating the book by supplying simple, pertinent, factual, biographical or chronological notes. But the basic value of a book of this sort resides not simply in the pleasure and stimulus one derives in reading it, but that it extends the knowledge of the craft the artists are concerned with. The editors must therefore supply not only the kind of historical material mentioned above, but the necessary theatrical knowledge in the light of which the extracts can be properly understood and evaluated. Otherwise the reader will receive entirely erroneous impressions. For instance, the editors use Edwin Booth's comments on Kean's Shylock, lumping it with that of Macklin and Cooke. Booth explains Kean's use of a black wig instead of the traditional red one on the assumption that Kean "was very poor and probably had a limited stock of props—he doubtless had no other old man's wig"—an assumption completely unwarranted. In fact Kean used the wig deliberately as part of a consciously original interpretation, and against the advice of his fellow players who, on his first appearance, warned him against doing so. Booth is unaware of the whole character of Kean's interpretation, and shows equal failure to differentiate it from that of Macklin's. Yet unless one is aware of these facts he will be unable to evaluate correctly Mr. Booth's understanding of Shylock, and thus will gain a wrong impression of Kean.

To take a more significant example. David Garrick is one of the outstanding actors of all time. His influence in the eighteenth century spread over the entire continent of Europe and affected not only the theatre but other arts as well. What he did and what he thought is obviously of the greatest importance. The editors manage to give the mistaken impression that Garrick agreed with Diderot's ideas on acting. They quote words ascribed to Garrick . . . "that a man was incapable of becoming an actor who was not absolutely independent of circumstances calculated to excite emotion, adding that for his own part, he could speak to a poet with the same feelings and expressions as to the loveliest Juliet under heaven." And they add that "anecdotes confirm the fact that he was not completely immersed in his role." The statement of Garrick is completely true, but the deductions drawn from it are entirely wrong. The statement has nothing whatsoever to do with the problem of emotional identification. No actor of any school would maintain that an actor can act only under the real circumstance demanded by the play. In fact the exact opposite is true. Vakhtangov, Stanislavski's outstanding pupil, points out that it isn't acting at all if you cry when someone really hits you. Acting arises only when you are not really hit at all and yet you cry just as if you had been. There seems also to be a completely wrong idea of what it means to be immersed in one's role. The fact that Garrick could joke in the wings after his exit does not in any way indicate that he was unidentified with his role. It simply means that he was not strained or forced, that he possessed the muscular relaxation Stanislavski considers so necessary for acting, that his concentration was excellent when it had to be. He could stop and start easily and at will. There are other actors who do not make the transition so easily. This indicates nothing about the style or character of their acting, but has to do with the ability to concentrate at will. Garrick himself is quite clear about this point, and in a letter said about Diderot's favorite actress, Clairon, that "the heart has none of those instantaneous feelings, that life-blood, that keen sensibility that bursts at once from Genius . . . Madame Clairon is so conscious and certain of what she can do, that she never, I believe, had the feelings of the instant come upon her unexpectedly; but I pronounce that the greatest strokes of genius have been unknown to the actor himself, till circumstances, and the warmth of the scene, has sprung the mine as it were, as much to his own surprise as that of the audience." This is in flagrant disagreement with Diderot's admiration for Clairon. That Diderot appreciated Garrick should cause no surprise, but it should not be construed to indicate Garrick's agreement with his ideas.

The basic controversy in the art of acting is that between reality and imitation. Does the actor really experience the emotion of the character he is portraying, or does he only imitate the form by which these emotions are expressed while he himself feels nothing. The problem is usually simplified ad absurdum or totally misconstrued. Many actors of the "emotional" school have resented the imputation that their results were achieved accidentally. Kean complained that "because my style is easy and natural they think I don't study, and talk about the 'sudden impulse of genius.' There is no such thing as impulsive acting; all is premeditated and studied beforehand. A man may act better or worse on a particular night, from particular circumstances; but although the execution may be not so brilliant, the conception is the same."

The emotion that the actor experiences is also not an exact parallel to that of the character. It is not necessary for the actor to have been a murderer in order to play Othello, to have died in order to play a death scene, to be a drunkard in order to play a drunk scene, to be in love in order to play Romeo. This is a simplification which is nonsensical. All good actors of whatever school have gone back to nature for their models. The extent to which they should do so, the degree to which one must actually experience at the moment of creation, and the nature and training of the actor's creative process are the field of disagreement. The words which actors speak or write express not abstract ideas, but relate to the methods which they use and the results they achieve. In reading about the art of acting, it is important to keep constantly in mind the reality to which the words of the actor or critic refer, if one is not to become confused and wind up with a hopeless "plague on both your houses" feeling, or an attitude of forced neutrality.

One of the outstanding documents in the discussion of acting is Diderot's famous "Paradox of Acting." The philosophic reputation of the author, his eminent and assured position in the history of culture has served to single his essay out from amongst the rest. The fact that he was a naturalist and materialist, that he advocated that "classical tragedy be replaced by a serious drama of everyday bourgeois life" has given his essay an appeal to the intelligent lay audience which few theatre writings have ever attained.

Diderot had previously held and expressed somewhat different opinions on the importance of sentiment in acting. "An actor," Diderot once wrote in a letter to Mlle. Jodin, a young aspiring actress, "who has only reason and judgment is cold; one who has fire and sensibility is crazy. A certain proportion of good sense and of warmth makes the sublime man; and on the stage and in life, he who shows more than he feels makes one laugh instead of affecting you." What made Diderot change his ideas? I must admit that when I first posed this question to myself I was unprepared for the answer. Nothing I had read about Diderot or his life had prepared me for the answer. For the essay is filled with a shocking, vitriolic, bitter, and insulting attitude not towards acting but towards the person and character of the actor! Listen to this diatribe and consider what it signifies. "In society, unless they are buffoons, I find them polished, caustic, and cold; proud, light of behavior, spendthrifts, self-interested; struck rather by our absurdities than touched by our misfortunes; masters of themselves at the spectacle of an untoward incident or the recital of a pathetic story; isolated, vagabonds, at the command of the great; little conduct, no friends, scarce any of those holy and tender ties which associate us in the pain and pleasures of another, who in turn shares our own. I have often seen an actor laugh off the stage; I do not remember to have ever seen one weep. What do they do then, with this sensibility that they arrogate and that people grant them? Do they leave it on the stage at their exit, to take it up again at their next entrance.

"What makes them slip on the sock or the buskin? Want of education, poverty, a libertine spirit. The stage is a resource, never a choice. Never did actor become so from love of virtue, from desire to be useful in the world, or to serve his country or family; never from any of the honorable motives which might include a right mind, a feeling heart, a sensitive soul, to so fine a profession."

What had the actors done to him personally to arouse this attitude and to create a change from his previous opinion? Is it perhaps permissible to imagine that they are the reflections of an embittered and unsuccessful playwright? Imagine what it must have meant to a man like Diderot to have an actor exclaim "My Lord, I cannot laugh today." The basic implication of the essay is not its concern with the problem of the actor's sensibility, but rather that a great actor should be "a most ingenious puppet, and his strings [should be] held by the poet, who at each line indicates the true form he must take" (shades of Gordon Craig's Uber-Marionette). Diderot after all recognized that actors did possess sensibility, that those who did at times were "strong," "fiery," and "sublime." But what confirmed him in his view was "the unequal acting of players who play from the heart. Their playing is often alternately strong and feeble, fiery and cold, dull and sublime. Tomorrow they will miss the point they have excelled in today." Had Diderot really been interested in actors and their problems he might perhaps have asked as Stanislavski many years later was to ask—how was one to make this condition no longer a matter of mere accident, or "are there no technical means for the creation of the creative mood?" But had he asked this question he would not necessarily have been able to answer it. He was neither an actor nor did he possess the requisite theatrical knowledge to compensate for that. His great contribution to the history of culture should not hide the defects of an unsound, basically bigoted and insulting diatribe.

One could go through "Actors on Acting" and comment on each of the selections and also on the notes of the editors. But that would mean writing a history of the theory and techniques of acting. Perhaps this will some day be done. The present publication will serve as a valuable reference text for such a work.

One of the most affecting statements by an actor I have ever read is the article by Walter Huston written after the failure of his "Othello." What touched me particularly was that Mr. Huston seemed willing to acknowledge that he might be wrong but he wanted to know why. And except for the fact that the critics hadn't liked it he could reach no constructive answer. As Max Beerbohm once remarked about dramatic critics, "Our mimes can derive no benefit save such pride as there is for them in knowing they are 'admirable,' or have 'never done anything better' or have 'seldom been seen to greater advantage'; and such shame as there may be in the consciousness that they are 'somewhat disappointing' or 'evidently suffering from the proverbial nervousness incidental to a first-night performance.' " Perhaps the volume we have discussed and others like it may help to train and stimulate not only good actors, but good critics without whom no significant theatre can today exist.

47 An actor must have three selves

Michael Chekhov

December 1952

Nephew of the playwright, Michael Chekhov (1891–1955) was a favourite student of Stanislavsky. At the Moscow Art Theatre and its first studio he astounded the public with his mythomaniac Khlestakov in *The Government Inspector*, Caleb Plummer in *Cricket on the Hearth*, 1914; Frazer in *The Deluge*, 1915; Malvolio in *Twelfth Night*, 1917, Strindberg's Erik XIV, 1921. From 1924 to 1927 he was the artistic director of the 2nd Art Theatre, where he played a despondent Hamlet. Passionate about Vladimir Solovyov's mystical theories and Rudolph Steiner's anthroposophy, Chekhov devoted himself to the problem of the actor's psycho-technique, and evolved a theory of imitation, in which the actor incarnates an image imbedded in his imagination, using the "psychological gesture" which radiates beyond one's own body. In 1928 he left Russia, going first to Berlin to work with Max Reinhardt. At the invitation of impresario Sol Hurok, he came to New York in 1935 with a troupe of émigrés. The Group Theatre invited him to discuss a collaboration, but his lectures on the creative process divided its members. Instead, he was asked by the actress Beatrice Straight to found the Chekhov Theatre Studio in 1936 at Dartington Hall in Devonshire. On the eve of war, it relocated to Ridgefield, Conn.

Freed of political and commercial restraints, Chekhov proved to be an inspiring teacher. The last phase of his life took place in Hollywood (1942–55), where he appeared in 11 films, usually cast as benign codgers. His passion was channelled into his teaching, his pupils including Yul Brynner, Joan Caulfield and Gregory Peck.

IF YOU were to ask two equally talented artists to paint the same landscape with the utmost exactitude, the result would be two markedly different pictures. The reason is obvious: each will inevitably paint his individual impression of that landscape. One of them might prefer to convey the landscape's atmosphere, its beauty of line or its form; the other would probably stress the contrasts, the play of light and shadows, or some other aspect peculiar to his own taste and mode of expression. The same landscape will serve for both to display their *creative individualities*.

Rudolf Steiner defines the creative individuality of Schiller as characterized by the poet's moral tendency: Good fights Evil. Maeterlinck seeks subtle mystical nuances behind outer events. Goethe sees archetypes unifying the multitudinous phenomena. Stanislavsky states that in *The Brothers Karamazov* Dostoievsky expresses his search for God; which, incidentally, is true of all his major novels. The individuality of Tolstoy is manifest in the tendency toward self-perfection, and Chekhov quarrels with the triviality of bourgeois life. In short, the creative individuality of every artist always expresses itself in a dominant idea which, like a leit-motif, pervades all his creations.

It has been reiterated that Shakespeare created only one Hamlet. But who will say with equal certainty what kind of Hamlet existed in Shakespeare's imagination?

In everyday life we identify ourselves as "I"; we are the protagonists of "I wish, I feel, I think." This *I* we associate with our body, habits, mode of life, family, social standing and everything else that comprises normal existence. But in moments of inspiration the *I* of an artist undergoes a kind of metamorphosis. Try to remember yourself in such moments. What happened to your everyday *I*? Did it not retreat, give place to another *I*, and did you not experience it as the true artist in you?

If you have ever known such moments, you will recall that, with the appearance of this new *I*, you felt first of all an influx of power never experienced in your routine life. This power permeated your whole being, radiated from you into your surroundings, filling the stage and flowing over the footlights into the audience. It united you with the spectator and conveyed to him all your creative intentions, thoughts, images and feelings. Thanks to this power, you are able to feel to a high degree your real presence on the stage.

Considerable changes which you cannot help experiencing take place in your consciousness under the influence of this powerful other *I*. It is a higher-level *I*; it enriches and expands the consciousness. You begin to distinguish *three different beings*, as it were, within yourself. Each has a definite character, fulfills a special task and is comparatively independent. Let us pause and examine these beings and their particular functions.

While incorporating your character on the stage you use your emotions, voice and your mobile body. These constitute the "building material" from which the higher self, the real artist in you, creates a character for the stage. The higher self simply takes possession of that building material. As soon as this happens, you begin to feel that you are standing apart from or rather above, the material and, consequently, above your everyday self. That is because you now identify yourself with that creative, higher *I* which has become active. You are now aware of both your expanded self and your usual, everyday *I* existing within you simultaneously, side by side. While creating you are two selves, and you are able to distinguish clearly between the different functions they fulfill.

Once the higher self has that building material well in hand, it begins to mold it from within; it moves your body, making it flexible, sensitive and receptive to all creative impulses; it speaks with your voice, stirs your imagination and increases your inner activity. Moreover, it grants you genuine feelings, makes you original and inventive, awakens and maintains your ability to improvise. In short, it puts you in a *creative* state. You begin to act under its inspiration. Everything you do on the stage now surprises you as well as your audience; all seems entirely new and unexpected. Your impression is that it is happening spontaneously and that you do nothing but serve as its medium of expression.

And yet, although your higher self is strong enough to take command over the entire creative process, it has its tendon of Achilles: it is inclined to break the boundaries, overstep the necessary limits set during rehearsals. It is too eager to express itself and its dominant idea; it is too free, too powerful, too ingenious, and therefore too near the precipice of chaos. The power of inspiration is always more intense than the means of expression, said Dostoievsky. It needs restricting.

That is where the task of your other, everyday consciousness begins. What does it do during those inspired moments? It monitors the canvas upon which the creative individuality draws its designs. It fulfills the mission of a common-sense regulator for your higher self in order that the business should be carried through correctly, the established *mise-en-scène* kept unchanged and communication with stage partners unbroken. Even the psychological pattern for the whole character, as discovered during rehearsals, must be followed faithfully. Upon the common sense of your everyday self devolves the protection of the forms that have been found and fixed for the performance. Thus, by the cooperation of both the lower and higher consciousnesses, the performance is made possible.

But where is that *third* consciousness previously referred to, and to whom does it belong? The bearer of the third consciousness is the Character as created by yourself. Although it is an illusory being, it also, nonetheless, has its own independent life and its own "I." Your creative individuality lovingly sculptures it during the performance.

The terms "genuine," "artistic" and "true" are frequently used to describe an actor's feelings on the stage. A closer inspection, however, will reveal that human feelings fall into two categories: those known to everybody and those known only to artists in moments of creative inspiration. The actor must learn to recognize the important distinctions between them.

The usual, everyday feelings are adulterated, permeated with egotism, narrowed to personal needs, inhibited, insignificant and often even unaesthetic and spoiled by untruths. They should not be used in art. Creative individuality rejects them. It has at its disposal another kind of feelings—those completely impersonal, purified, freed from egotism and therefore aesthetic, significant and artistically true. These your higher self grants you while inspiring your acting.

All you experience in the course of your life, all you observe and think, all that makes you happy or unhappy, all your regrets or satisfactions, all your love or hate, all you long for or avoid, all your achievements and failures, all you brought with you into this life at birth—your temperament, abilities, inclinations, whether they remain unfulfilled, underdeveloped or overdeveloped—all are part of the region of your so-called subconscious depth. There, being forgotten by you, or never known to you, they undergo the process of being purified of all egotism. They become feelings *per se*. Thus purged and transformed, they become part of the material from which your individuality creates the psychology, the illusory "soul" of the character.

But who purifies and transforms these vast riches of our psychology? The same higher self, the individuality that makes artists of some of us. Therefore, it is quite evident that this individuality does not cease to exist between creative moments, though it is only when being creative that we become aware of it. On the contrary, it has a continuous life of its own, unknown to our everyday consciousness; it goes on evolving its own, higher kind of experiences, those it lavishly offers up as inspiration for our creative activity.

It is the degree of inner activity of the higher self, producing those purified feelings, that is the final determinant of quality in the creations of all artists.

Further, all the feelings derived by the character from your individuality are not only purified and impersonal, but have two other attributes. No matter how profound and persuasive, these feelings are still as "unreal" as the "soul" of the character itself. They come and go with the inspiration. Otherwise they would become forever yours, indelibly impressed upon you after the performance is over. They would enter your everyday life, would be poisoned by egotism and would become an inseparable part of your inartistic, uncreative existence. You would no longer be able to draw the line of demarcation between the illusory life of your character and that of your own. In no time you would be driven mad. If creative feelings were not "unreal" you would not be able to enjoy playing villains or other undesirable characters.

The other attribute of creative feelings is that they are compassionate. Your higher self endows the character with creative feelings; and because it is able at the same time to observe its creation, it has compassion for its characters and their destinies. Thus the true artist in you is able to suffer for Hamlet, cry with Juliet, laugh about the mischief-making of Falstaff.

Compassion may be called the fundamental of all good art because it alone can tell you what other beings feel and experience. Only compassion severs the bonds of your personal limitations and gives you deep access into the inner life of the character you study, without which you cannot properly prepare it for the stage.

There is yet another function of the actor's awakened individuality which should be dealt with here, and that is its ubiquity.

Being comparatively free from the lower self and the illusory existence of the character, and possessing an immensely extended consciousness, individuality appears to be capable of straddling both sides of the footlights. It is not only a creator of the character but also its spectator. From the other side of the footlights it follows the spectators' experiences, shares their enthusiasm, excitement and disappointments. More than that, it has the ability to foretell audience reaction an instant before it takes place. It knows what will satisfy the spectator, what will inflame him and what will leave him cold. Thus, for the actor with an awakened awareness of his higher *I*, the audience is a living link which connects him as an artist with the desires of his contemporaries.

Through this ability of the creative individuality the actor learns to distinguish between the real needs of contemporary society and the bad tastes of the rabble. Listening to the "voice" speaking to him from the audience during the performance, he slowly begins to relate himself to the world and his brothers. He acquires a new "organ" which connects him with life outside the theatre and awakens his contemporary responsibilities. He begins to extend his professional interest beyond the footlights, he begins to ask questions: "What is my audience experiencing tonight, what is its mood? Why is this play needed in our time, how will this mixture of people benefit from it? What thoughts will this play and this kind of portrayal arouse in my contemporaries? Will this kind of play and this kind of performance make the spectators more sensitive and receptive to the events of our life? Will it awaken in them any moral feelings, or will it give them only pleasure? Will play or performance perhaps arouse the audience's baser instincts? If the performance has humor, what kind of humor does it evoke?" The questions are always there, but only Creative Individuality enables the actor to answer them.

To test this, the actor need only make the following experiment: He can imagine the house as filled with a specific type of audience, such as only scientists, teachers, students, children, farmers, doctors, politicians, diplomats, simple or sophisticated people, people of different nationalities, or even actors. Then, by asking himself the foregoing or similar questions, he should try to sense intuitively what the reaction of each audience might be.

Such an experiment will gradually develop in the actor a new kind of audience sense, through which he will become receptive to the meaning of the theatre in present-day society and be able to respond to it consciously and correctly.

48 A study of the Actors Studio

Maurice Zolotow

August and September 1956

The Actors Studio was founded in New York in 1947 by Elia Kazan, Cheryl Crawford and Robert Lewis as a natural successor to the Group Theatre. Originally, it was intended not as a school, but as a workshop for professional actors. However, under Lee Strasberg, who was its artistic director from 1951 to 1982, it became part classroom, part therapy ward, dedicated to promulgating his idiosyncratic view of Stanislavsky's teaching. "The Method" stressed stripping bare the emotions and a psychological striptease, breeding actors who were best at projecting tormented personalities on screen. Only occasionally did the Actors Studio stage full-scale productions of plays, and Strasberg was very disappointed not to be named the artistic director of the new Lincoln Center Theatre.

Maurice Zolotow (1917–91) was an all-purpose entertainment reporter, who began writing for *Billboard* and by the end of his life had had his byline on articles in magazines from *Life* to *Reader's Digest*. He was best known for celebrity profiles which he would occasionally work up into full-scale biographies, as with the Lunts (*Stagestruck*).

THERE is a very neat symbolism in the location of the Actors Studio, one of the most powerful forces vitalizing the American theatre today. The studio is located in a three-story building at 432 West 44th Street, New York City. The building, set back from the sidewalk, is freshly painted in gray and white. It has a strange triangular roof and odd flat pillars set into the front. It is an old building and was formerly a Greek Orthodox Church. It is quite fitting that actresses and actors should come to perform the often painful and terrifying rites of their profession in an abandoned church.

The importance of the Actors Studio to the acting profession is one thing—and I shall go into that in great detail later. But for the theatre as a whole the importance of the Actors Studio is precisely that it is a temple, a church, a shrine, a place where a hundred human beings have come together to dedicate themselves—often to give themselves up as sacrificial lambs in a dramatic experiment—to an ideal: the ideal that dramatic perfection is a pure and noble goal, an aim that is good to labor for and agonize over. Just as the example of a man, who is anxious enough about his own salvation to be willing to withdraw into a Trappist monastery and give himself up to contemplation and prayer for the rest of his life, tends to irradiate the lives of innumerable persons who are either unable to, or lack the utter desperation to make such an extravagant commitment, so the

Actors Studio, by setting an example of artistic dedication, has set up rippling waves of stimulation all over. Wherever men and women care about the theatre, either as spectators or participants, the Actors Studio has, in subtle, indirect ways, been an inspiration. It never intended to do this. It still does not consciously strive to do this. But it has managed to set up another criterion for theatrical success—in addition to money, fame, good critical notices, long runs and public adulation.

Although we are probably one of the most romantic and unselfish countries in history, we are self-conscious about our tender impulses and cloak them in the mucker pose of hard-boiled, carefree, cynical vulgarity. Since the cultural atmosphere in which we breathe has a compelling effect on our choices, the very fact that there is a solid group of actors and directors, who are not ashamed to say that dramatic beauty is a good thing to shoot for, provides an example beneficial to every actor—even those actors who may think Stanislavsky is the name of a new brand of vodka.

A good example of what I mean is the case of Bert Lahr and *Waiting for Godot*. Lahr is one of the most perfect low-comedy actors who ever capered on a stage. For some thirty years his artistry has been stifled by a succession of revues and book musicals in which he has rolled his eyes, stretched his mouth, and moaned "un-gah, un-gah, un-gah." In 1955 he decides to go into a play, a fairly serious play. For any actor to leave the security of his tried-and-true tricks, that have always brought him laughs and applause, is an act of courage. But Lahr does not merely decide to play a dramatic role. He decides to play a lyrical role in an unusual play, one of the most unusual and unconventional plays of our time, the sort of play that ordinarily might have been performed in one of those reconverted cafés of the off-Broadway theatre. He knows that *Waiting for Godot* is a controversial, perhaps an obscure work. Nor is he an intimate of Lee Strasberg or Elia Kazan. He does not spend his evenings chatting about Meyerhold and Vakhtangov with *avant-garde* intellectuals in the San Remo Café in Greenwich Village. If you brought up the *Partisan Review* in a chat with him, he might say, "Who wrote the sketches for it?"

Mr. Lahr, however, happens to be as ardently dedicated to his art as Eli Wallach or Maureen Stapleton—to name two of the most conscientious devotees of the Actors Studio—but for him to play Gogo required an even more violent act of faith than for Wallach to undertake the role of Kilroy in *Camino Real*. He could do it in 1956. I do not think he would have been able to do it in 1946. Lahr may not know why, himself, but I believe it is largely because the Actors Studio has impregnated the atmosphere with this quality of dedication. He was given a shield with which to defend himself from the ribbing he would get from his cronies around Blair House and Toots Shor. Well, finally *Waiting for Godot* was opened by producer Michael Myerberg at the Coconut Grove Playhouse in Miami last winter. Since Florida and California always have been intensely competitive, Miami was anxious to prove that not even Los Angeles could exceed it in vulgarity. On opening night the audience became restless and its members started walking out in large numbers. Tom Ewell, who played Didi, was replaced by E. G. Marshall for the New York engagement. Lahr would have a perfectly justifiable excuse for ceasing to wait for Myerberg. But he doesn't. He remains with the play—throughout more weeks of rehearsal, and he opens on Broadway. He opens to more controversy and wisecracks and, fortunately, appreciation. Walter Winchell, an old friend and admirer of Lahr, suddenly develops an acute personal resentment against *Waiting for Godot* and carries on an almost daily vendetta against the play in his column. You would think *Waiting for Godot* had been written by Ed Sullivan instead of Samuel Beckett. But Lahr remains indefatigable. And he is right. He is not going to get rich because of *Waiting for Godot*. Metro-Goldwyn-Mayer will not adore him. The Columbia Broadcasting System will not give him $25,000 a week to star in a situation comedy on television. But he is ahead of the game. He has enriched himself as an artist and as a human being, by meeting a real dramatic challenge and triumphing. He may have achieved the high point of his life as an actor. He has felt the joy that comes of performing at the top of one's potentiality.

Whether the Actors Studio has discovered an alchemic formula by which it magically transforms stones into stars is really not the chief concern of Cheryl Crawford, Elia Kazan and Lee Strasberg—the three directors of the studio. Nor is the principal accomplishment the fact that actors like Marlon Brando and Eva Marie Saint and Jimmy Dean and Kim Stanley were helped to perfect themselves by working in the studio. Nor is it the fact that both Marilyn Monroe and Shelley Winters, at crucial turning points in their lives, were able to turn to the studio for artistic and emotional support. A theatre does not live by hit plays and a handful of glorious stars. A theatre of any vitality, depth and extension can flourish only in a healthy atmosphere. And this the Actors Studio has helped to bring about—not by words but by actions, by dedication.

The idea of dedication makes some people squirm. But everyone, or at least everyone who makes a success of anything, has to be dedicated, whether it's a mother dedicating herself to children, or a fisherman dedicating himself to fly-rod casting, or those who dedicate themselves to power or money. There isn't anything inherently evil about dedicating yourself to money. The desire to acquire large sums of money certainly does less mischief to the human race than the desire to reform other people, for instance. I know people who have happily dedicated themselves to sex or alcohol. Unfortunately what happens to many actors who stop dedicating themselves to dramatic art is that they come to dedicate themselves to sex and alcohol and road racing. There doesn't seem—at least for an artist—to be any middle-of-the-road policy. He either dedicates himself to self-fulfillment or self-destruction. What has made the Actors Studio a moral force is that it has said in a loud voice to any actor who cared to listen: You do not have to be ashamed of dedicating yourself to self-knowledge as a person and self-fulfillment as an artist.

One further point: There seems to be a general impression that the Actors Studio, suddenly and in splendid isolation, has rediscovered the principles of acting enunciated by Stanislavsky, and that it is earnestly manufacturing a new and potent miracle drug known as The Method. In the first place, as Lee Strasberg, the artistic director of the studio, pointed out to me, Stanislavsky himself did not discover or invent anything new. He organized and schematized in a usable form certain psychological principles and habits of stage behavior which had been used by every good actor that ever lived.

Secondly, the Stanislavsky techniques for applying these universal principles in any dramatic situation have been known and used by American directors and actors for over thirty years! To be more exact, since 1923, when the Moscow Art Theatre played a season of Chekhov, Gorky and Dostoevski in New York. The ensemble acting of the Moscow Art Theatre took the city by storm in 1923, just as the ensemble acting of the Old Vic company did when Laurence Olivier played Oedipus Rex. When the Moscow Art Theatre returned to the workers' paradise, two persons, oblivious to the blessings of Communism, remained behind: Maria Ouspenskaya and Richard Boleslavsky. They opened a school and gave lessons in acting. Madame Ouspenskaya herself acted in films and plays. Boleslavsky taught and directed. When, in a conversation with Strasberg, I cited Ina Claire as an example of an artist with a highly polished technique of high comedy which, it seemed to me, the Actors Studio was not able to develop in its students, he said, "Didn't you know she studied with Boleslavsky? It was in 1928 or 1929, maybe later. I think she studied with him for a whole year. She was going into a play by Behrman and she felt there were certain things she wanted to master and that Boleslavsky could help her, and she went to him."

In 1929 a group of actors and production personnel who had been working for the Theatre Guild received permission from Guild executive directors Theresa Helburn and Lawrence Langner to rehearse experimental plays in their spare time. At first this offspring was called the Theatre Guild Studio. Later it changed its name to the Group Theatre. With Cheryl Crawford, Lee Strasberg, who had been a professional actor since 1925, directed his first play—and the Group's first achievement—in 1931: Paul Green's *The House of Connelly*. The Group Theatre was in existence until 1941. Probably its most important long-range contribution was to give a platform to Clifford Odets. Odets' ability to make dramatic emotions out of the lives of poor people in terms of a highly tinged vernacular influenced not only Tennessee Williams and Arthur Miller, but every one of the television realists like Paddy Chayefsky and Robert Alan Aurthur. People, I think, would be a little less impressed by Chayefsky's originality if they would bother to read *Awake and Sing!*

The Group Theatre also started the careers of Sidney Kingsley and William Saroyan. Out of it came several important acting talents, including John Garfield and Lee Cobb. The Group Theatre was run by Strasberg, Cheryl Crawford and Harold Clurman. Many of its plays were being done in the muted, naturalistic style when Marlon Brando was a little boy in Nebraska. In the company of *Golden Boy* (première at the Belasco Theatre, November 4, 1937) were Robert Lewis, Elia Kazan, Martin Ritt. All were to become directors ultimately. All have been using "method" notions for years and years. And Karl Malden, who frequently is described as a product of the Actors Studio, also was in the cast of *Golden Boy*. *Golden Boy* was directed by Harold Clurman, a true-blue Stanislavskyite if ever there was one. Even Joshua Logan, whom nobody thinks of as a "method" director, studied with Stanislavsky in Moscow and has employed many of the "method's" methods in his work. Strasberg took pains to point out to me that the Actors Studio does not claim to have a monopoly of the "method"; one or another of its many elements is used by drama coaches and drama teachers throughout the country.

The Actors Studio was born in 1947.

49 A point of view and a place to practice it

Robert Lewis

April 1960

Robert Lewis (1909–97), a member of the Group Theatre from 1931 to 1941, had a spotty career as a film actor, usually cast as perfidious Asians (the Japanese general in *Dragonseed*). After the Second World War, he was much in demand as a Broadway director, with such hits as *Brigadoon* (1947) and *Teahouse of the August Moon* (1953). One of the co-founders of the Actors Studio in 1947, he soon found himself at odds with the dogmatic methods of Lee Strasberg. His book *Method – or Madness?* (1958) tries to disentangle some of the basic principles of Stanislavsky-ism from its later distortions.

"Is it just a coincidence that so many people, like yourself, who came out of the Group Theatre are still doing major theatre work today, almost thirty years later?"

It is a question that I hear often, and the frequency with which it is asked is perfectly understandable. Consider the Group alumni who are acting, directing, producing, teaching, writing, and otherwise carrying on the ideas and ideals of their work of 1931–41, the period of the Group, in the 1950's—and who soon will be continuing the process in a new decade. A partial list includes Harold Clurman, Lee Strasberg, Cheryl Crawford, Elia Kazan, Kermit Bloomgarden, Franchot Tone, Morris Carnovsky, Sanford Meisner, Stella Adler and Clifford Odets.

Of course, no one can say with complete assurance that the Group was responsible for shaping their subsequent careers. Some of them might be pursuing their present activities even if there never had been a Group Theatre. But I don't think it can be denied that a ten-year period of concentrated work with a specific point of view has left a strong imprint on all of them; or that that imprint has influenced the American theatre, and is continuing to do so.

The Group had significance—but why? Was it because these people were inherently special? There is no doubt that the members were all chosen fairly carefully in the early 1930's. Some of them, it is true, were already successful when the Group was formed: Tone and Carnovsky had played good parts on Broadway; Strasberg, Clurman and Crawford were stage manager, playreader and casting director, respectively, for the Theatre Guild. Others, like myself, had had only a little previous acting experience. But I'm sure the truly important factor was that, for ten years, we all had a *place*. A place to work, a place to study and learn, a place to develop, a place to fail. Yes, a place to fail, too. The privilege of failure, by which I mean an opportunity to "try things," is essential to a growing artist. That opportunity could not have been ours if we had been involved in the usual rat race of doing one show after another, and faced with two possibilities: succeeding virtually every time or going under. I was always experimenting, in class work, on problems of style. That activity eventually led to my first Broadway directing stint (in 1939): staging William Saroyan's *My Heart's in the Highlands*. The production introduced Saroyan as a playwright, too. To this day, people speak kindly of it to me. But by show-business standards, its run of six weeks could only be counted a flop.

As a matter of fact, the whole measure of success and failure is different in a theatre such as the Group was. Broadway has a different yardstick. In the Group we were proud of good work done, whether or not we were always fortunate enough to hit the commercial jack pot, too. I remember the first time I had a big "money" success on Broadway, as director of the musical *Brigadoon* (1947). When I would pass some of my former Group colleagues on the street, they eyed me as though somehow I had betrayed them. Now, if I do a show that doesn't meet with all-out financial success, the hat-check girls in the Broadway restaurants scowl at me as if I had offended them personally.

What I am saying is a prelude to a point that bears constant repetition. In addition to the obviously desirable and necessary entertainment industry, there ought to be permanent theatres devoted to specific artistic points of view. Great Britain has its Old Vic along with its West End. France has the Comédie Française, the Barrault and Vilar companies, and others. Additional examples on the Continent are the Josefstadt and the Moscow Art. Those organizations nourish and influence their theatrical worlds, which, let us not forget, also contain all other forms of show business. Here in America we have continuing attempts to create such theatres, but, so far, the results do not measure up to the resources. Why? Well, I suppose the old answer of "prohibitive costs" will have to stand as one reason. At the risk of triteness, I must point out that it is a shame that some form of subsidy is not forthcoming to meet the necessary deficits of such operations. Would the Group Theatre have survived longer than ten years and twenty-five productions (at that, something of a record for a permanent acting company performing on Broadway) if it had had a subsidy? No doubt it would. But since this is a continuing problem and a highly complex one, it is important to glance back and see if there were reasons, other than economic, that led to the Group's dissolution in 1941. Its avowed purpose for ten years was to train a company of actors to present new plays by American authors, and consequently to relate, theatrically, to the life around it. Sometimes I wonder whether that purpose couldn't have been served additionally through fresh productions of classics. They would have broadened the base of the theatre and expanded the style of its actors and playwrights. They might have enabled it to tide over the arid stretches—the periods when we were waiting for that third act to be finished by the always-too-few available working playwrights. Such additional productions might have saved the Group's life.

Actually, it was not too bad a bet to be a Group Theatre actor, in a financial sense, though some players of the thirties sniffed at our comparatively modest salaries ($200 a week, top). When you consider that we often played throughout all or most of the season, while some others were averaging many fewer weeks on the hit-or-flop basis, you can see the advantage. There is another, perhaps even more far-reaching point. Any actor can tell you that there is a solid feeling that comes from *belonging*, from knowing that one's theatrical life goes on regardless of the fate of the current production. In my days with the Group, I used to parody Stanislavsky's "There are no small parts, only small salaries" (I was often a lower-bracket Japanese butler), but the all-round training that I got in those ten years can only be described as a lifetime annuity.

Recently, in Paris, I saw Jean-Louis Barrault bring down the house in his five-minute appearance as a lively Brazilian in his company's production of Offenbach's *La Vie Parisienne*. I don't remember feeling that he had "come down" from the success of his performance of Hamlet. I don't suppose he felt that, either. The show, by the way, was an enormous financial success.

50 Wanted: More stars, less "method"

Sherman Ewing

January 1961

As the Method came to dominate the New York school of acting, *Theatre Arts* opened its columns to articles by its exponents, without endorsing its principles. The performances of Marlon Brando had familiarized the public with a distorted notion of what the Method was supposed to be. Although caricatured as a matter of torn T-shirts and mumbled lines, it was congenial to the American taste for realism and the fad for psychoanalysis. Those who objected to its inadequacy in playing the classics or poetic drama had a hard time making themselves heard.

Sherman Ewing (1902–75), veteran producer, director and choreographer, offered a reasoned argument for an alternative.

NOT so long ago, through the columns of the New York *Times*, Laurence Olivier poked fun at the modern American approach to directing, and the American actors' approach to their parts. What he wanted of an actor was the ability to take orders, to do what he was told to do. He would have none of the psychological approach to acting. Clearly he belonged to the "Get On With It" school, and had no use for the "Method."

Now, as almost everyone knows, the "Method" is the holiest cult of the modern American theatre. Since the Moscow Art Theatre came here in the 1920s, and Stanislavsky's books were published in English, no serious student of the craft has dared to be without at least a superficial knowledge of the "Method." It is the basic course in the majority of the schools of acting in this country, and there are hundreds of them. It was the inspiration of the Group Theatre, it is the creed of the Actors' Studio. Lee Strasberg, Stella Adler, Robert Lewis and Elia Kazan are its High Priests.

The "Method" by which an actor prepares his part begins with reading and study of the play. Then he concentrates on the character he is to portray; he absorbs every facet of it as it appears in the script; beyond that, through research he fills in the gaps that the author has left. For example, if an actress is asked to play an Irish biddy, she should know something of the poverty-stricken slum district of Cork from which the biddy has fled, and of the mores as regards drink and wenching that might typically be ascribed to her father, who is not mentioned in the script. If the biddy is a liar, it is necessary for the actor to consult Freud for motivation of that trait of character. Not that a profound knowledge of psychology is required, as Kazan explained at one of last year's ANTA Assembly panel meetings, at which Sir Laurence's controversial article was a lively topic of conversation; only the ordinary knowledge of psychology that in this enlightened age we all have. Kazan himself, in preparing to direct, goes further than that, he said; he studies the author, mixes with him socially, plays tennis with him, sees how he ticks in various situations, until he has a complete psychological picture not only of the characters in the play, and the meaning of the play, but also of the creative personality of the author. An actor, of course, rarely has the opportunity of studying the author, and must confine himself to the reconstruction of the psychic biography of the character he is to portray.

After the preliminary groundwork, there enters the magic "If," which is, I believe, Stanislavsky's greatest contribution. It is the key for unlocking the flood-gates of creative energy, and like many great ideas, it is simple. Our actress, in preparing to play the Irish biddy, must not say to herself, "I am an Irish biddy, and therefore I will act like this." Such an approach is obviously untrue and unreal, and has the effect of choking off the essential emotional response. On the con-trary, the actress must say to herself, "*If* I were an Irish biddy named so-and-so, who left Cork in 1958 to escape the poverty and drunkenness, etc., then I would act in the given situation as follows—"

Such an approach is, beyond question, a useful spring-board for creative writ-ing. Whether it is also useful for an actor is another matter. Stanislavsky thought that it was useful, and he created a great theatre. But is the approach appropriate for our modern needs? Do we want acting that is psychologically motivated, or do we prefer something else?

A few days after publication of the Olivier article, the *Times* reported on a speech by Willi Schmidt of Berlin, a distinguished German director. He was quoted, in part, as follows: "The American actor is afraid to be *unnatural*. He has a way of mistrusting himself, and belittles his own talent. . . . Actually he does not play at all any more. He talks to himself in a kind of monologue, and he is constantly and forever tracing his own feelings, which very often do not get across the footlights." Professor Schmidt thought that the reason for the difficulty was perhaps that the American actor is shy and uncertain.

Is there a historical basis for such a surmise? Let us examine some recent history. The coming of the depression was coincident with the sharp reduction in the extent of the legitimate theatre, both in New York and on the road; it was also coincident with the rise of motion pictures. The opportunity for "on the job" training for stage actors also declined sharply. Fewer and fewer jobs were available on Broadway, and if an actor did make a name for himself, he fled to Hollywood where the big money was. But the movies and television are not a training ground for the actor in stage roles; consequently there has been no considerable group of actors able to develop techniques for the stage.

I recall an excellent illustrative case from the successful revue *Angel in the Wings*, which Marjorie Ewing and I produced in 1947. Elaine Stritch had her first con-siderable part in the musical, and she received excellent notices. For several weeks she stopped the show in her big scene (who can forget the bongo-bongo girl of "Civilization"?); she was fresh, beautiful, enthusiastic and altogether alluring. And yet, basically, she was an amateur. After a month or two, her performance lost something indefinable. The director could not help her, or even detect what was wrong. All that could be said was that the applause had become perfunctory. The harder she tried to recover her enthusiasm, the less it paid off. She was in despair. Then, because she had character and real talent, she began to rebuild her performance, slowly, night by night. It took months, but fortunately the revue had a good run. Eventually she was back in stride—but no longer an amateur. She was a professional actress who knew how to dominate an audience, and bring out the desired responses. She is now, of course, one of our established stars.

It is that sort of experience which few of our present-day actors have had; yet it was the basic training of all of the great performers of the theatre of old, and is still a common experience in England and Europe.

Since our own young actors, by and large, have had no such training, they are in great need of something to take its place—something to provide a feeling of security as they face a live audience. And that is where the "Method" enters the picture. Instead of relying on body and voice control, on stage-craft and stage manners—in short, on the technique of the stage, which they don't possess— they find emotional and spiritual values in the creative approach to their parts. Doubtless such values are of enormous satisfaction to the actor. But does the audience give a rap for them?

Let us consider another example, the case of a schoolteacher in a Welsh mining town. The play is *The Corn Is Green*. I have forgotten the name of the teacher, but I shall never forget the name of the actress who played the part: Ethel Barrymore.

In preparing the part, did she study the background of a schoolteacher in a Welsh village? Did she go down into the coal mines? Did she join a choral society and steep herself in the lovely music of the district? Did she brush up on the subjects that she presumably had been teaching, or worry about the moral or intellectual level of her Welsh associates? I refuse to answer my questions. But the result of *her* method was not realism—not a psychological and painstakingly accurate sketch of a little Welsh schoolteacher. The result was an Ethel Barrymore performance—sheer theatrical bravura. That's what the customers came in droves to see and applaud.

Ethel Barrymore was a star, the sort of performer that a large audience will pay money to see. We have some stars left in our theatre, but most of them are old, or English. There are few stars among our young American actors who fit my definition. I am not thinking of the multitude of film stars who are little more than pin-up girls. As for television, it has its great personalities, men like Arthur Godfrey, Jack Paar, George Gobel, Ed Sullivan. But the stars made by television are not even actors within the scope of my definition, much less stars.

For a great many theatre people, the star is one of those Gilbertian characters who "never would be missed." The mine-run actor obviously won't miss him. The author without a star can write as he pleases, and such dubious freedom may even rid him of the thought of creating a theatrically effective role. The director? Well, the director without a star has himself become a star.

Some of those I have mentioned may argue that the demise of the star has been a boon to acting. They will suggest that stars are not essentially actors at all, but performers. Such a suggestion is an example of the Catty Cliché, something worth contempt, if indeed worthy of a reaction at all. By my definition the star is always an actor, albeit a special one—something very like the virtuoso performer of the concert stage.

Now we come to the choice. On the one hand there is the "Method," developing a group of actors able to approach various roles along the psychological avenue, to the great satisfaction of theatre folk in general; on the other hand, technical training in stagecraft, developing a group of actors able to obey the behests of their directors with faultless technique, and developing also from among the group a few personalities of outstanding talent. Which should we choose?

That we have a choice is due to a new element that has sprung up in the last few years. I refer to the off-Broadway theatre, and to the huge development of little theatre and community theatre, which is largely amateur but coming more and more under the influence of professional directors and guest artists. Since we now have a training ground that is showing great vitality and increasing scope, we should ask whether we are going to continue to train in the school of the "Method," or whether the "Method" has served its purpose and should be relegated to limbo.

Michel Saint-Denis, who is one of the most distinguished trainers of actors, recently made a survey of American schools of acting. I had the privilege of hearing him speak of his findings at the annual meeting of the New York chapter of ANTA. He speaks English fluently, and he has a direct, hard-hitting style of reporting, which is tempered by a delightfully diplomatic French accent. Although I am unable to quote him blow by blow, I gathered that, in his survey of our schools, he did not like what he saw. The ideal school of acting, in his view, would stress voice and body control, and those elements of stagecraft that can be taught; then, through practice in acting, he would help the actor to develop an individual style, or stress personality.

If we put our choice—"Method" actor or star performer?—to a vote, I suggest that a major part in the choosing be given to one who, although seldom mentioned in such symposiums, is the most important person in the theatre. I refer to the man out front: the audience.

I believe that the audience would vote unhesitatingly for "performers" rather than "actors," for personalities rather than psychologists. Let no one protest that the audience should be educated to like good acting, even though it may prefer something else. Some folks say that the theatre does the audience a great favor, and that the mere mention of audience preferences is out of order. Nothing could be further from the truth, which is simply that the audience does far more for the theatre than the theatre can ever repay. The audience is essential; if its members do not find what they want, they will not be found when they are wanted.

What they want, I contend, is personalities. Let the reader think a minute before he denies that, and he will not then deny it. Perhaps he will say that nothing can be done about such a preference, since a personality (or, if you prefer the more literal definition, "magnetic personal quality") cannot be created by teaching, any more than talent can be imparted by teaching. I recall that Lillian Hellman opened her address to Hatcher Hughes's playwriting class at Columbia University with the statement that playwriting cannot be taught. Very true, though rather tough on Hatcher, who was trying to teach it. Greatness is innate, but even the great must be trained in the basic techniques. And that preliminary to greatness assuredly *can* be taught. I have in mind all the things, largely physical—control of voice and body, stage manners, relaxation and concentration, pantomime—that are fundamental, but all too often relegated to second place by the devotees of the "Method" (though not, of course, by Stanislavsky himself).

I was directing, some years ago, at the Barter Theatre. Most of the kids had copies of *An Actor Prepares* tucked in their pockets. But it was easy to spot the real devotees. Their two distinguishing marks were that they refused to make any meaningful movements of hands or bodies on stage (that was considered "ham"), and they could not be heard. One girl, cast as the ingénue in *Night Must Fall*, had talent and a pleasing personality, but she was the clumsiest actress I ever set eyes on. A class in calisthenics and ballet was available in the mornings. I begged, implored, cajoled and commanded, but my ingénue had other ideas. She had come to act, not to dance; she spent her mornings in the subconscious, emotionally creative approach to her part.

As for voice control—well, it made a singer out of Rex Harrison!

So let us forget the "Method," and concentrate on perfecting the physical techniques of stagecraft. From such training come the Gielguds, the Oliviers, the Fontannes, the Audrey Hepburns. Let's have more of them. Let's go to school with Marcel Marceau, not with Sigmund Freud. The analyst's couch is as out of date in the theatre as the casting couch. Let's send them both to the dump!

Part V

The actor and his role

51 The actor attacks his part: Lynn Fontanne and Alfred Lunt

Morton Eustis

November 1936

The careers of American Alfred Lunt (1892–1977) and British Lynn Fontanne (1887–1983) took off when they married in 1922. Lunt had a wide range, from naïveté to brutality, and Fontanne was a past mistress of cool sophistication. Formidable talents individually, as a team they were incomparable, capitalizing on their physical intimacy, conversational delivery, and long hours of rehearsal together. They were stalwarts of the Theatre Guild, rising to stardom in scintillating high comedy, such as Molnár's *The Guardsman* (1924), Sherwood's *Reunion in Vienna* (1931) and Coward's *Design for Living* (1933).

As ANYONE on Broadway — with the possible exception of Alfred Lunt and Lynn Fontanne — will tell you, The Lunts approach the problem of acting in a manner all their own. From years of working together, they have developed a technique in which each actor complements the other to an extraordinary degree. The play selected, The Lunts do not waste much time analyzing it from a literary viewpoint nor ponder long upon nuances of character and interpretation. They visualize a drama instantly as theatre — a stage, settings, props, costumes, musicians in the pit. When they study the script, they do so with the *aperçu* of the actor, director, designer and producer rolled into one. Only *after* they have already begun to act out their parts do they concentrate on subtleties of impersonation, on definitions of character.

Mr. Lunt, perhaps because of his early training in stock and vaudeville, may have a more immediately intuitive, spontaneous reaction than Miss Fontanne. Reading *The Taming of the Shrew* he may be the first to feel: 'Really, this is a *shameful* play! It has *something*, but we've got to build it, hoke it, play it like a three-ring circus. . . . We must have midgets, acrobats, two men to make a horse!' Miss Fontanne, reared in the more gentle school of English pantomime and acting lessons with Ellen Terry, may reason a little more sharply, more analytically — though this reaction may stem as much from temperament as from training. She may inquire: 'Will midgets be *right*? Will they be the *best* people we can use?' But, between them, they reach the same conclusion. Miss Fontanne rides from her wedding on a bouncing steed, midgets and acrobats caper all over the stage. And Shakespeare is removed from the library into an actor's theatre.

The Lunts rarely plan out a scene in advance. Their first move is to learn the lines mechanically, by rote, to get them out of the way. Then, in the privacy of their home, where they do most of their work, they improvise their scenes together and 'see what happens'. They throw themselves into the extra-curricular rehearsals with even more gusto than they exhibit in their playing. Acting the same scene over and over, they discard what is bad, keep what is good, then 'polish, polish, polish'. There is nothing objective about their method. At the same time it is not a casual, undisciplined charade. No actors could have compassed parts by Shaw, O'Neill, Maxwell Anderson, S. N. Behrman, Noel Coward, Robert E. Sherwood, Sidney Howard, Shakespeare, without an essentially serious under-standing of, and respect for, their craft. They enjoy themselves enormously in their improvisations. But they are always careful, to the point of exactitude, to work within the script. And always they are guided by the reactions of an imaginary audience, composed of stern, uncompromising critics, most exacting among them Mr. Lunt and Miss Fontanne — a group which has grown in stature and severity ever since Miss Fontanne first captivated London and New York audiences as Dulcy in 1921 and Mr. Lunt romped gaily to stardom in *Clarence* in 1919.

Stock in the Castle Square Theatre in Boston ('every different kind of play'); an eighteen-months' tour with Margaret Anglin in a repertory of *As You Like It, Medea, Iphigenia* and other plays; then, reversing the usual order but not the happy results, knockabout training in vaudeville, with Lillie Langtry — this was Mr. Lunt's previous apprenticeship. A first stage appearance with Ellen Terry in a tour of *Alice Sit by the Fire*; pantomime in London — a reputed first entrance on a tightrope; touring in the English provinces; spasmodic appearances in London and New York, culminating in an engagement in 1916 with Laurette Taylor's company, had started Miss Fontanne on the road to fame. But not until marriage in 1922 and electric lights in Molnar's *The Guardsman* in 1924 joined their names together and a second apprenticeship began under their own observant tutelage, and that of the Theatre Guild, did Lunt and Fontanne, as Broadway affectionately knows them, begin to develop the technique which is now second nature with them.

Appearances together in *Arms and the Man, The Goat Song, At Mrs. Beam's*. . . . then a theatrical separation: Mr. Lunt the racketeering Babe Callahan in *Ned McCobb's Daughter*, the first high-pressure salesman in O'Neill's *Marco Millions*, Mosca in *Volpone*; Miss Fontanne as Eliza Doolittle in Shaw's *Pygmalion*, Nina Leeds in five hours of neurosis known as *Strange Interlude*. Then reunion, not yet in Vienna, but in a Viennese setting for *Caprice*, in New York and London; the sky tops of Manhattan in *Meteor*; sword play and fustian in *Elizabeth the Queen*; high comedy and gusto in *Reunion in Vienna*; high comedy and nerves in *Design for Living*. Melodrama and more neurosis in *Point Valaine*; high jinks in *The Taming of the Shrew*; song and dance, sin and sadness, amid the threatening war-clouds of *Idiot's Delight* — these and other plays, other performances, cemented a union at once mystical and practical, real and theatrical. From a dramatic instinct, sharpened, heightened, tempered and chastened by years of acting experience, emerged order and discipline.

When The Lunts enter the stage door for official rehearsals, they adapt what they have already created to the playing, to the personalities, of the rest of the cast, to new ideas they are constantly developing — even during the run of the play. Working tirelessly, they seem to infect everyone in the company with their enthusiasm for acting. Rehearsals, with them, are stimulating and delightful occasions.

The Lunts find it very difficult to analyze their method of attack. Mr. Lunt dismisses all the preliminaries with: 'Miss Fontanne and I do a lot of work at home together. But I can't just describe what it is. We've done it so long, it's become almost instinctive.' Miss Fontanne, almost as inarticulate, calls it: 'Something that's grown so with the years that I wouldn't know what it was. Our playing together, and our rehearsing, is like a note of music that we then enlarge into a chord.' Both are extremely loath to talk about technique, personally or impersonally. If talk they must, however, they are adamant on one point. They must take the stage individually. 'Mr. Lunt's opinions about technique, his reactions to the theatre, are often quite different from mine,' says Miss Fontanne. 'Just because we work together is no reason we should be classed as a team.' 'What Miss Fontanne does on the stage,' choruses Mr. Lunt in the adjacent dressing room, 'what she thinks about acting, is a personal equation. I wouldn't dream of intruding on that side of her life. You must talk to each of us alone.'

Bowing, accordingly, to their mutual wish, we raise the curtain to present Mr. Lunt and Miss Fontanne as individual actors, trusting that they will pardon the liberty taken in introducing them into the Actor's Forum on Acting Technique as a 'team' — a course which they themselves, by the very nature of the 'technique' they claim to despise, have made almost obligatory.

Lynn Fontanne

THE first essential of acting technique, Lynn Fontanne believes, is voice control — 'knowing how to pitch and throw your voice so as to fill a theatre'. This is the one histrionic facility which Miss Fontanne is willing to admit may be classed as 'technique, pure and simple' — one requiring long and arduous training. All the rest are amalgams of many qualities.

Timing, for instance, so vital a factor in acting, especially in the projection of dialogue by Shaw, Behrman or Coward, is 'purely a matter of ear — something instinctive, which the actor either has or has not got'. A good *raconteur* at the dinner table or in the drawing room 'has just as much sense of timing as the actor'. The actor's timing must be adjusted to other actors and to an audience. 'Perhaps that may be technique, though even it is largely ear training.' But the moment timing becomes methodical, deliberate and overstudied — simply an exercise in technique — the actor becomes like a clock ticking. 'And precision is bad. *It is far better for the actor to be a little off beat, to jangle!*'

Set movements and gestures, symbolizing the tragic or the comic, are absolutely meaningless, in Miss Fontanne's judgment. The actor supplies the movement, the gesture, the carriage, out of his sense of character, his natural instinct of rhythm and mobility. For a long time, Miss Fontanne was convinced that she never used her hands on stage, except for obvious movements called for by the action.

Alexander Woollcott, to whom — 'rashly' — she confided this belief, laughed her out of that fond assurance. But, to this day, she insists, she is rarely conscious of what she is doing with her hands. Instinctively, she will raise her arm or move her body as she speaks a line — 'just as you do in real life' — but she never, in *preparing* her part, maps out a mechanical line of movement.

Technique, likewise, cannot teach an actor how to know, before he has finished speaking a line, that the expected laugh, the gasp of horror, the ripple of merriment, will not be forthcoming on a particular evening. 'That is a telepathic quality, born with the actor — an essential sixth sense that every fine actor must possess.' The actor, perhaps, may learn by technical device how to carry on the next line, or piece of stage business, without a pause, so that the audience is unaware of its delinquency that evening. 'But that, too, is something more than technique . . . Call it *acting*!'

Miss Fontanne used to read a play primarily with an eye to her own role. Her first reaction was: 'There's *a part* I should like to play.' Lately, she has shifted her point of attack. The play itself now engages her first attention: consideration of her own role is a secondary step. When she first read *Idiot's Delight*, her own part was only 'blocked in very sketchily'. She signed the contract, however, because she had faith in the play. 'It is the most incredible feeling,' she says, 'to read a play on paper and suddenly to realize that, four weeks hence, you must *be* on the stage a personage as remote from yourself as Queen Elizabeth, Katherine the Shrew, Lady Castlemaine of *Old Drury*, or the vixen innkeeper in *Point Valaine*.' The instant Miss Fontanne reads a play a visual picture of the person springs to her mind. She does not attempt, however, to probe her character until she has worked on the part as an actress — a diametrically different attack from that used by Helen Hayes. Acting out the part with Mr. Lunt, improvising details of character — walk, gesture, carriage, tone of voice — she begins, 'slowly, to get into the character of the person'. And without analytical reason — 'I try not to use my intellect at this stage at all' — a conception gradually, 'mysteriously', emerges.

'Suddenly, on the stage or in the dressing room, walking in the park or motoring to the theatre, you discover something about the character you never knew even existed. In a flash, you derive a new slant on an action, a motive. Bit by bit, you sink deeper and deeper into the person. You see that you are wrong in one scene; the woman could never use that tone of voice. No sooner is that place rectified than another horrible gap appears. This refining process continues all during the run of the play. The impersonation is *never* complete, though it is truer on the last night of the run — if you are a real actor — than at any other time.'

It is impossible on the face of it, for an actor to disassociate himself completely from his own self. 'You remain the same size and you have the same vocal chords. But, if you are a good actor, you should not be bound by your physical presence.' Creating the part as Miss Fontanne does — working inward from without — the problem of adapting her own self to the role is 'something that seems to do itself'. Playing too many one-color parts, an actor is apt to imagine that he cannot play any other type of role. After acting a string of comedy parts, Miss Fontanne began to feel that way herself. Then she realized that 'acting is a bastard art, if it is an art at all. The author creates the character. The actor's only job is to *go ahead and play the part*. With a well-trained voice and the proper use of make-up, an actor should be able to compass any role. And the less he *reasons* about the complexities of impersonation, the better.'

Although Miss Fontanne does not rationalize movement when she is building a part, she follows the same general routine at each public performance. Lighting cues, if nothing else, would force an actor to adhere to a more or less rigid pattern. Too many unexpected movements, also, would throw the other actors into confusion and destroy the play's flow of action. 'Too much movement, at any time, by the way, is bad. The eye is so much quicker than the ear that movement tends to destroy words.' None the less, she says, 'you do change the part very much during a play's run. Little things, here and there, are added or left out. If a certain scene doesn't jell — and there always is a scene that doesn't — you try to go to the bottom of what you've got and find out what is wrong. In other words, you don't fritter a part away, playing it mechanically.'

This is where the 'dangerous subject' of emotion enters the scene — how much, how little, emotion the actor actually feels. Although — 'emphatically' — Miss Fontanne does not live the part or lose herself in the role, she plays emotional scenes — such as the famous 'my three men' speech in *Strange Interlude*, or the abandoned comedy love scene in *Reunion in Vienna* — with a much surer touch if she, herself, is 'highly emotional' while playing them. 'When my senses — or perhaps it's just my nerves — are keyed to a high pitch, I find I have a sharper ear, a much quicker response, to anything going on in the audience. I have, too, an uncanny awareness of the rightness or wrongness of my performance.' This quality of emotion is 'probably a form of self-hypnosis'. She does not actually feel the emotion, but she hypnotizes herself into thinking that she does — 'always being perfectly aware of what is going on, of how I am playing the part'. This hypnosis, however, cannot always be turned on and off at will, 'which is probably why my performances vary so distressingly. Sometimes, you know, they are so bad I should like to advance to the footlights and urge the audience to get their money back. At other times, well, I feel they have not paid enough.'

People often ask Miss Fontanne: 'Why is acting in a play so tiring? You work only a few hours eight times a week.' The usual answer to this question is that acting is a nervous job, and physically tiring from the strain of using tremendous breath control. Miss Fontanne believes there is still another reason why a big role is so exhausting. 'Being the focus of thousands of eyes produces an hypnotic magnetism which makes the actor physically stronger than he is himself, so that when the eyes are withdrawn and the current is switched off he feels like a pricked balloon.'

The hardest role Miss Fontanne ever played — 'by hardest, I mean the most wearing' — was the Shrew. 'She is not written angrily enough to convince a modern audience, or oneself. The role has to be played at what seems like almost a silly pitch to make it come across at all.' As she was physically injured in almost every performance of the *Shrew*, the role in *Idiot's Delight* 'was like going from something which is driving you to a nervous breakdown to lying in a feather bed'.

Consequently, *Idiot's Delight*, at the moment, takes first place as the pleasantest role ever essayed.

One of the pleasantest features of this role, too, was the way in which the part developed. Perhaps owing to the way in which the part was written, or played, the character was never quite projected at the beginning. Audiences were always a little puzzled as to what the woman's background was — whether she was a complete fake or not. Working on the part, during the summer holiday of the show, Miss Fontanne added some cockney speeches, a few bars of a song in an early scene, to indicate that the woman had a cockney rather than a Russian background and immediately — to the intense excitement of both Miss Fontanne and the cast — the whole characterization took on a new meaning, became rounded where formerly it had been flat. 'And so it goes.'

'The bad parts are the most difficult. The best you can hope to do with a bad part is to make it human, to fill in gaps.' Once Miss Fontanne had a very bad part to play — a costume role. She did not know how to play it. 'I went to the Metropolitan and saw all the Peter Lelys. I copied one person exactly, down to the jewelry. My make-up and my appearance were so startling that the part made quite an impression. But that was only trickery. In some respects, however, the parts that do one the most good as an actor are the bad parts. If a good actor plays a lot of bad parts he can become endlessly resourceful so that when, at last, he plays a good one, *something happens*! And then he never wants to play *another bad part*!'

Alfred Lunt

I*f* Alfred Lunt has any *idée fixe* about the actor's place in the theatre's sun, it is this: 'The actor is not a creative, but an interpretive artist. His one and *only* job is to work *within the play*, to translate the ideas of the author. The play itself is what counts.' Mr. Lunt entertains quite violent opinions about the actor — star or bit player — who tries to 'hog centre stage', who puts himself on a loftier plane than his fellow-actors and the author's script — 'not that I know any such actors today'. The important thing is for everyone in the show to make good.

He is convinced that the reason *Idiot's Delight* is a hit is that it is a good play, well cast. 'People don't just come to see Lunt and Fontanne. That's absurd. If a play is bad, all the stars in the world can't save it. Look at *Point Valaine*. The reason *Ghosts* was a success last year was not simply because Nazimova was starred in the play, but because Nazimova, a great actress, did not sacrifice play to performance. She acted faultlessly herself, but she also stepped aside and gave the play to the other actors. With the result that *Ghosts* was projected as a play rather than as a vehicle for a star actress.'

It is not surprising to discover that Mr. Lunt, holding these views, always reads a play first to see whether it is a good play, only secondly to determine whether or not it is a good play for him and Miss Fontanne — or him alone — to act in. The wide range in which Mr. Lunt's parts have fallen — youth without illusion as Prior in *Outward Bound* to maturity without scruple as Rudolph of Hapsburg, Clarence to the Emperor Maximilian, Shaw's meek Chocolate Soldier to the bestial Stefan in *Point Valaine*, Dmitri Karamazov to the blustering Petruchio — indicates great variety and flexibility of interpretation in the actor. Mr. Lunt professes to be ignorant of the actual method by which he creates a part, differentiates one characterization from another. Like Miss Fontanne, he believes that is something that does itself. He is sure, however, that he always attempts to make each role something new and non-characteristic of himself. He has little respect for the actor who simply projects his own personality, charming or otherwise.

'I never play myself in a part — at least, I never mean to,' he says. 'Take Harry Van in *Idiot's Delight*. I pieced him together — accent, personality and appearance — from three people I used to know in vaudeville . . . By the way, I don't know Harry Richman, and I've never seen him perform . . . I took something from each one of them and added a general impression based on my own experiences. Vaudevillians, I have found, may be pretty terrible when they're giving "their all" in a number. But most of them, fundamentally, are pretty nice, simple fellows. I tried to put that quality in Harry Van. Externally, I envisaged him with a pasty-faced expression — the look you see on men around Times Square who don't get out enough into the air — and black, shiny hair, slicked back around graying edges. I spend about an hour before each performance covering my hair and face with grease to get just the effect I want. Perhaps it's foolish. I could go out with hardly any make-up and get away with it. But it wouldn't be the same thing. Harry's accent came direct from vaudeville acquaintances — I think accents and dialects are terribly important — from standing listening to the chatter at Times Square corners.'

Rehearsals to Mr. Lunt are even more fascinating than actual performances. He never tires of standing on a bare, ill-lighted stage, watching others perform, acting himself. His improvisations with Miss Fontanne are elixir to his actor's soul. He never relies on the director to shape his concept of a part. 'If you know your job and work for the play and not for yourself, you don't need a director to develop the part for you.' The director must work to perfect every detail in the show, to pull together all the loose strings. For that matter, so must each member of the cast. *Idiot's Delight*, he says, was really an actor's show, directed by the actors. Bretaigne Windust actually staged the play, but everyone contributed something — 'which was what made it so exciting'.

How Mr. Lunt achieves his effects is a question he cannot — or will not — elucidate. Technique, he admits, is part of an actor's equipment. 'But no actor can define what his own technique is, or tell how he uses it.' He is extremely scornful of theories and rules. 'No good actor is bound by any rules. It's absurd to say there are any set formulae for acting comedy or tragedy — one set of gestures the actor pulls out of the hat when he is a clown, another when he is a tragic figure. *What* you do and *how* you do it depends entirely on the play and the part you portray. Harry Van is one type of person, the Earl of Essex another. You *play* serious and comic scenes differently. Of course. The timing is quite different, the whole inter-pretation — just as it is in life. But that depends on character more than on technique. Often you do the best you can and then something happens you hadn't expected at all. You plan one piece of business to get a laugh. It falls absolutely flat. Something you hadn't thought out at all brings down the house. *You can't be sure of anything.*'

Mr. Lunt's description of his playing, once rehearsals are done, is this: 'I try to relax into the part and play it as nearly the same way as I can each night. But when I say relax, I *don't* mean get slovenly. Every performance, whether in New York or Squedunk, is as important as the opening night.' One evening last spring, the whole company of *Idiot's Delight* slumped. The pace went wrong. The show was very ragged. '*That was a terribly serious thing.* We had a big shake-up. Rehearsals. You *can't* let things like that happen, ever. You've got to be on your toes all the time.' Stage business, as a rule, is set in rehearsal and the actor goes through the same routine every night.

In certain types of comedy, however, business may vary considerably with each performance, especially when the play is *Design for Living* and the three leading actors know one another as well as The Lunts and Noel Coward. One night, Mr. Lunt admits, in the hilarious drinking bout he and Mr. Coward staged each night, Mr. Coward — 'by accident, or dire intention' — took Mr. Lunt's line. Not to be outdone, Mr. Lunt promptly took Mr. Coward's next line. They played out the entire scene — 'a full half hour' — with each one speaking the other's lines. 'The scene was just as funny as ever,' Mr. Lunt declares, 'but obviously ad libbing or changing business would be *outrageous* in anything but a very special type of comedy, and then one in which you happened to be playing with the author. Still, in every play, you are consciously studying your part, adding new shades of meaning, building it all the time. *And you know what you are doing every second you are on stage.*'

Rin Tin Tin, in Mr. Lunt's opinion, was 'a great emotional actor, *simply marvelous!*' But, he points out, he could never have acted on the stage. When he barked, he barked for as long as it suited his canine pleasure. The only way he could be controlled was by cutting the film and piecing it together. 'But you cannot cut on the stage. That's why an actor can never let himself be overcome by emotion. If he started to cry during a scene, there wouldn't be any play.' Emotion can play a big part in acting. 'Sometimes a role can tear you to pieces. But it must always be *controlled emotion*, which is what makes it all the worse.'

Mr. Lunt refuses to place on the record the names of his favorite roles, the easiest, the hardest, or most rewarding. (He dislikes putting anything at all on the record about his acting.) All his roles were hard. They all taught him something. He liked them all. In general, the comedy roles were the 'toughest' assignments. 'Anyone who says comedy isn't harder to act than tragedy doesn't know what he's talking about. Timing in comedy is so much more difficult. Waiting for the laughs. Not waiting for them when they don't come, which is even more important. And no emotional undercurrent to sustain the interest.' The chief reason Mr. Lunt hates to expound on his technique is that, despite all his experience, he is 'never overburdened with confidence at any time'.

He acts 'because it's fun — more fun than anything else I know'. He loves to dress up, just as a child does. If rehearsals are his greatest joy, long runs are never tiresome to him. He is always learning new things about the part, playing to new audiences. He is never bored in the theatre. He never has been bored. The only time languor may creep over him in the dressing room is when he finds himself trapped by a fool reporter who wants him to describe the technique of his performance . . . Enough — too much — of theory! Ring up the curtain! Let the play begin!

52 A play in the making: The Lunts rehearse *Amphitryon 38*

Morton Eustis

December 1937

The Lunts had just come off a slapstick *Taming of the Shrew* (1935) when they asked one of their favourite playwrights, S. N. Behrman, to prepare for them an English version of Jean Giraudoux's *Amphitryon 38* (the title refers to the alleged number of the times the theme had been treated in drama before). The Greek legend of Zeus wooing a mortal lady by taking the shape of her husband was an unlikely subject for a Broadway hit, but it fit the Lunts' reputation for elegant sex farce.

———————

'ALL RIGHT. Let's get going!' It is Alfred Lunt speaking. The scene is the stage of the Shubert Theatre one afternoon early in October. The occasion, the first rehearsal of the 'Alfred Lunt and Lynn Fontanne production' of Jean Giraudoux's *Amphitryon 38* after the West-Coast try-out three months earlier.

A cold, white light from the first border strip overhead illumines a semi-circle of straight-backed chairs facing the auditorium. In front of the footlights, centre stage, are a table strewn with papers, two or three more chairs. Right and left, at each corner of the proscenium, is a single chair, its back to the empty theatre which fades into a black void beyond the first rows of orchestra seats. The scenery for *Babes in Arms*, playing in the theatre, is stacked against the grey brick walls of the stage house. Stage left, their faces standing out in pale relief in the light of a single bulb above the entrance, a group of people are gathered, exchanging the usual badinage of friends reunited after a summer.

At Lunt's informal command, the group disperses; individuals assume their identities as actors or technicians, and the human machine that is in ten days' time to resume its collective role as *Amphitryon 38* begins to 'get going'. Lynn Fontanne, who is wearing a black silk dress, a hat with a wide brim, walks across the stage with Lunt, reading to him a few lines from her 'sides'. 'It's better, don't you think?' The actors take their places in the semi-circle of chairs. Bretaigne Windust, who is staging the play, sits at the table with two assistants. The prompter and the stage manager, each with a script, occupy the chairs at either side of the stage. Lunt and Richard Whorf, who play the first scene together as Jupiter and Mercury, pull forward two chairs centre stage, turn them round and sit straddling them, facing the non-existent audience. Miss Fontanne puts on a pair of blue-rimmed spectacles and watches from one side. Lunt nudges Whorf, makes a jest that has no connection with his role. The whole company laughs. Then Jupiter and Mercury, their chins resting on the backs of their chairs, look down from their celestial abode to the earth — 'The only star that smells like an animal' — They discourse, in witty and Rabelaisian tenor, on the art of love as humans practise it, and connive for Jupiter, in the guise of the mortal Amphitryon, to descend to Thebes and make love to Amphitryon's wife, Alkmena.

The 'run-through' of *Amphitryon*, now being staged, is obviously quite different from an ordinary first rehearsal. The actors have already acted the play before audiences in San Francisco and Los Angeles. They are meeting to reassemble and restage a pattern of production that is, in the main, already set. Changes will be made of course; scenes and lines that didn't go over will be reshaped. But the most arduous business of rehearsal, the long and infinitely complicated process of creating a play out of a dramatist's script, is already a thing of the past.

The play, when it opened, was much too long. S. N. Behrman, in translating and adapting the French original, had already compressed the text considerably. (Translations from the French, if they are to approximate the French meaning, always have to be pared down, a word made to do the work of a phrase, French speech is so much faster, more musical than English.) But it needed more than an hour's further pruning. The principal object of today's run-through, then, is to let the actors listen to the new arrangement, to let everyone concerned decide in the light of past experience and present observation what parts still need elision or revision. The main emphasis is on the scenes and lines that did not, or do not, jell; on the play's weakness rather than its strength.

Lunt and Whorf speak their lines hurriedly at first, in low tones and without any dramatic emphasis. 'It always takes time,' Miss Fontanne explains, 'for actors to get back into the theatre after a holiday. One of the greatest thrills of a first rehearsal, in fact, is the exhilaration that comes from suddenly hearing your voice expand to twice its normal volume, the words springing from a source completely untapped in everyday conversation.' But gradually they work into the scene. Jupiter orders 'a special cloud' to conceal them as they speed towards the earth, and the scene ends in laughter as Lunt makes an impromptu gesture which almost dislodges Whorf's chin from the back of his chair. (In the play, the actors appear to be suspended in the middle of a cloud and only their heads and arms are visible; hence their positions.)

Sydney Greenstreet (the trumpeter), George Meader (Sosie, Amphitryon's servant) and Alan Hewitt (the Warrior) go into Scene Two. Greenstreet is blowing his trumpet (a cane) to celebrate peace on earth, when Hewitt, very martial in the armor of a grey flannel suit, and brandishing a broom for a spear, stalks on to announce that Thebes is at war. He runs off, calling the Thebans to arms. . . . 'You've got to hold that spear close to your side when you make that turn,' Windust admonishes him. 'Otherwise you'll brain Sydney or the scenery.' 'I don't know which would be worse,' Lunt adds.

Miss Fontanne rises, strolls back stage and makes her entrance. Perhaps because she thinks the rehearsal has been a little casual so far, Miss Fontanne plays the scene in which she bids her husband farewell with an actor's full equipment. The effect on the other players is electric. They stop whispering, reading their lines, pacing up and down, and watch in silence. The lights seem to dim, the scenery to rise into place. Amphitryon is no longer in a brown suit. As Alkmena embraces him, you can almost see and feel, as she does, the armor that encases him. (Miss Fontanne, in stroking him, keeps her hands a fraction of an inch from his body and follows, in pantomime, the curve of his armor.) The scene drops, with an audible thud, as Jupiter — 'forgetting the law of gravity' and his lines — strides on. Lunt repeats his entrance, and, catching the tempo Miss Fontanne has injected into the performance, plays with great gusto the scene in which Mercury transforms him into a mortal. Miss Fontanne walks up and down back stage. Lunt hesitates. 'I think that line's too long. Why not just cut it all out?' 'Not all of it, Alfred, just the first half' — Miss Fontanne never even looks up. 'O. K.'; he tries it again. A few speeches further on he again mixes up his lines. 'What version *are* we playing!' Despite the interpolations, the scene has pace and humor. And when Lunt stands outside Alkmena's bedroom window (a row of chairs) and pleads to be admitted, it is not difficult to forget that he is wearing a double-breasted blue suit and that Miss Fontanne is, unromantically, chewing gum.

Refused admittance as a man, and accepting Mercury's sage advice, Jupiter tries again, this time as Alkmena's husband. Miss Fontanne interrupts the action: 'Can't you change all that to just "Very well"? That's really all it amounts to in French.' Lunt does not agree: 'Behrman had a very good reason for emphasizing the speech.' 'O.K.' Jupiter and Alkmena take the solemn oath of marital fealty — Jupiter with his fingers crossed — and he gains admittance to her chamber.

The curtain, metaphorically, descends on Act One. Lunt strolls up to the footlights: 'Isn't this an amazing play? It's like no play I've ever acted in before. It's as much of a farce as *Room Service*. Yet it's got a quality, something like a Gauguin picture that you see for the first time. No, not that. You can't quite put your finger on it. I don't know if it will go over. How can you tell? It's poetic, profound. You can't *ever* set the laughs.'

Mercury recites the soliloquy that opens Act Two. (Never before has the master of the gods tarried so long in the arms of a mortal woman.) The cast wanders round. Whorf slips up several times in his lines. 'It's so impossible,' Miss Fontanne points out, 'with nine different versions of the play floating in our minds to remember what lines we are supposed to speak. Try it as Berrie (Behrman) wrote it for the Los Angeles opening, Dicky. No, that didn't go, did it? . . . I know. The third night in San Francisco. That was much better.'

Now it is the Lunts' 'big scene'. The company strolls down into the orchestra to watch. Miss Fontanne sits on a chair, her feet up on a bench. Jupiter crosses in front of her and she gives him a smart tap with her hand. Laughter from the cast greets this bit of business, which is new. Lunt sits facing her during the dialogue which follows; then he gets up, goes over left stage, crosses back. 'No, I crossed too soon.' He repeats the manoeuvre. . . . 'Change the order of that speech, Alfred, so that you'll cross before you speak instead of after, the way we tried it last night at home.' The scene runs on. The Lunts are playing faultlessly; they obviously relish both the scene and the laughter it evokes. As Miss Fontanne is darning a hole in

Jupiter's sock (she does it so expertly, in pantomime, that the needle and thread seem to materialize out of thin air) she breaks the scene: 'That's wrong, that speech. I must say something much simpler, something direct like "Do let's", only that's too modern.' 'What about: "Swing it"?' Lunt suggests. A tentative compromise, until Behrman is consulted, is reached in the word 'Proceed' and a delightful high comedy scene closes on appreciative comment as Alkmena exits to do her marketing.

Mercury enters and chides Jupiter: 'Jupiter, you have the naivete of a superman.' 'Cut that line,' Miss Fontanne calls sharply from the wings. 'Thank God!' Whorf says, 'I've always hated it.' Soon comes the part that has never jelled since the play opened, the Leda scene. Behrman has revised it. 'But there's still something wrong. It's all there, but it's got to be pulled together, rearranged,' Miss Fontanne declares. 'Anyway, let's run through it.'

Edith King, in a blue silk dress, with a brown fur round her neck, makes her entrance as Queen Leda. 'Wait a minute,' Lunt says. 'We've got to get Berrie to write in a line before Edith comes on so that the audience will know, *positively*, that she was the girl whom Jupiter loved as a swan.' 'Everybody'll know that anyway,' someone calls out. 'Audiences don't know *anything* that a playwright doesn't tell them,' Lunt responds. . . . 'I knew a woman who was named Leda and had never heard the legend of the swan,' Miss Fontanne volunteers.

Although the situation has obvious dramatic possibilities and some of the lines are amusing, the scene, unquestionably, does not jell yet. Miss Fontanne and Miss King analyze it at some length. Lunt makes suggestions about the staging. He reads Leda's line, crosses on a new beat. Then where Leda describes her affair with Jupiter: 'Up to a certain point, he was like a cloudburst, a gust of swans,' etc., the accent is wrong. 'The first part should be stressed, not the last. "Up to a certain *point*" — gesture — then, on a descending scale, as memory is obliterated by the tempestuousness of the god's appeal, "He was like a cloudburst," etc. Oh, let's leave this scene now. It's very bad. It's got to be completely rearranged.'

They go into the last act, where Jupiter confronts the husband and wife and Amphitryon defies him. (The intermediate scene is being re-written, and is not ready yet.) 'This scene is too complicated,' Lunt says. 'Let's try ad lib-ing it, Lynn, and see what happens. Windy, take this down.' Lunt and Fontanne make up their lines as they go along. Although the result is rough, 'It's the right idea, anyway,' as Windust puts it. 'We'll give it to Behrman this way and let him work it out.'

At this moment, Behrman arrives with the new scene. There are only two scripts. All the cast clusters around Greenstreet and Meader as they read their parts. 'That's *much* better, Berrie,' Lunt says. 'Much more philosophical, much more style.'

For Behrman's benefit, they run through the scene they have just fabricated, to show him how they think the lines might be filled in — 'It was all in the French, anyway' — and then, hurriedly, they rehearse the last scene to show him where they have made cuts and changes, where further work still needs to be done. Lunt comes to a phrase: ' "I know your strategies" . . . I hate that word, strategies, Berrie. I can never remember it.' 'That's not the word's fault, Alfred,' Miss Fontanne says. . . . 'Oh well, it will come.'

The run-through is over. 'Tomorrow, eleven o'clock, and tonight, at the Guild, for the Leda scene and the Third Act.'

It is noon, three days later. The Lunts have finished rehearsing a scene. It seems to have gone badly, for both of them look tired, discouraged. They sit silently on a bench. The cast wanders about in the wings. Every one seems tense and on edge. 'It's been a perfectly terrible rehearsal,' Whorf says. 'Everything's gone wrong. I don't know how we'll ever get it fixed in time to open in Baltimore in five days.'

'Let's try it again,' says Lunt, standing, the picture of dejection. They go through it listlessly. 'It's smoother, but there's something gone out of it.' 'Where's Behrman?' Miss Fontanne asks. Behrman cannot be found. He was expected at the theatre that morning. No one knows where he is. Lunt sits down again, eying the script grimly. There is silence for several moments. Then Lunt stands: 'Let's go home. I'm so tired I can't think any more.' He sits down again, picks up the script. Another long silence. Miss Fontanne looks up: 'It's *very* simple,' she says, in low but diabolically clear tones, 'we simply won't open if we can't get the scene fixed. *We won't open!*' She and Lunt look at each other, with comprehension. They know they will open, on schedule, that the scene will be fixed if they and Behrman have to sit up four nights working on it, but it's soothing to pretend.

'Let's run through the whole play again,' says Lunt, by this time quite a tragic figure. 'Something's gone out of it, but still —' He and Whorf straddle their chairs. Windust sits in the orchestra. The play starts, almost inaudibly, as Lunt is saving his voice, and his temper, but it does start.

Suddenly the house lights go on and a loud hammering commences in the rear of the theatre. Lunt never even looks up, but a wild gleam comes into his eye. Windust runs back, returns dejectedly. 'It's some construction work that has to be finished before the evening performance of *Babes in Arms*. They'll make as little noise as possible.'

The actors go on with their lines. The hammering stops; now there is a loud scraping sound, uneven, rasping. Miss Fontanne and Barry Thomson play their love scene. Miss Fontanne forgets her lines, once, twice. 'I'm sorry, Barry, but I just can't keep my mind on the play with all —' She tries again. *Scrape. Scrape. Hammer. Hammer.* The 'big scene' in the second act arrives painfully. Four days earlier, it was hilarious, full of pace, innuendo and abandon. Now it is flat and weary. Lunt is so tired he does not even attempt to act. Fontanne makes an attempt, but it's difficult to act alone. *Bang. Bang. Scrape. Scrape.* 'Don't let's finish this scene,' Lunt implores. 'It can't be as bad as it sounds now.' They go on playing. The Leda scene has been revamped. But it can't hold its own against the barrage of sound which seems to pierce right into the brain cells. It may be better, or worse.

They go into the Third Act. Behrman arrives. He had been unavoidably detained. The Lunts play out the questionable scene in a kind of forlorn desperation. Their gaiety is that of a tragic mask. *Scrape. Scrape.* The scene ends. Behrman thinks that 'something has gone out of it'. *Hammer. Hammer. Hammer. Hammer.* 'Let's not tear it apart now,' says Lunt; 'that will take hours.' They go into the last scene. Mercury and Jupiter prepare to disappear in a cloud for the finale. *Scrape. Scrape.*

'Oh God,' somebody calls from the wings, 'why go on?' Why, indeed. The play's going to be a flop. *Crunch. Crunch.* It can never be pulled into shape. They might as well start rehearsing the new play now. *That's* a lovely play. *Hammer. Hammer.* Gloom. Gloom.

'Come on, Berrie,' say the Lunts in unison. 'Let's get out of here.'

'We'll have something to eat, then we'll all tackle the scene at home. We'll get it right if it takes all night.' *Hammer. Hammer. Scrape. Scrape.* 'God, what a rehearsal!'

'George Jean Nathan,' Whorf announces, 'has written that we've ruined the play by cutting out the scene with the nurse.' 'That settles it,' says Lunt, 'we now have a chance.'

It is the next afternoon. If any gloom still hangs over the rehearsal, it is dispelled by the news that Nathan thinks the show is going to be bad. The actors, immensely cheered, go to work with spontaneity.

Lunt opens proceedings by directing the scene between the trumpeter and Sosie that Behrman finished the day of the first run-through. It is not a big or an important scene — the two merely discuss Jupiter's projected arrival that evening — but to watch Lunt, Greenstreet and Meader working on it, you would think that the failure or success of the whole show hinged on it. First they run it through without interruption, while Lunt paces up and down in the wings, apparently not paying any attention to them. Then he takes hold. The intonation was wrong here, the gesture there. This speech must be cut, that transposed. That cross is bad. In high good humor, he plays both roles himself, exaggerating each effect he wants the actors to achieve, giving a vastly entertaining if somewhat burlesqued performance. Then the actors try it while Lunt, watching, unconsciously moves his lips and hands with them. Again he interrupts. Meader has to cross the stage to sit down on a certain line. There is no line to cover it, yet cross he must. 'I've been thinking,' says Lunt, as he becomes Amphitryon's servant for the moment, 'how about using superstition to get you across, like this?' Greenstreet gives the cue. Lunt, in pantomime, expresses his fear of the gods. He puts his hands up, backs across in front of Greenstreet, playing to him. Greenstreet inserts a new bit of business. 'Perfect!' Windust exclaims.

'Now play the rest of the scene that way,' Lunt exhorts them. 'Remember that the gods hear everything. But you hope they don't if you talk low.' Catching Lunt's idea, the actors deliberately overplay, score their innuendoes. Both of them know they are overplaying, but do so deliberately. Then they act it again, in a lower key, and, miraculously, a scene that was an hour ago dull and inconsequential becomes gay and spontaneous — an entirely new scene, in fact.

'That's what comes of playing together,' says Lunt with enthusiasm. 'Actors that hadn't played together like we have for three years couldn't possibly create a scene like that out of the blue' (really, Lunt's imagination). 'It'll probably be cut and changed entirely before the opening, but still, it's exciting now.'

The First Act scene in which the Warrior calls the Thebans to war is next on the schedule. Seated on a high stool, at one side, Lunt watches as Alan Hewitt declaims his speech loudly. 'Stop,' he says. 'You can't go on, Alan. You've got no place to go. You started on such a high key, you haven't anything left for "War! War! This is war!" Start much lower. *Pull out your words.* You don't have to yell to create excitement. It's a question of tempo, not of volume.'

Hewitt starts lower, but again Lunt interrupts. 'The *sound* is wrong — the tempo. Look, speak it in the tempo of a militant Winchell. Don't think of the *meaning* of the words — not in this kind of speech. It doesn't matter what you're saying. Try it just repeating: "You *son* of a *bitch*! you *son* of a *bitch*!" ' He bangs the beat on the table. 'Get up! To arms! You son of a bitch! Get up! To arms! You son of a bitch!'

He breaks into a laugh, and continues pounding. Hewitt goes into the speech. He pulls out his words, speaks in the clipped tempo of the pounding beat. His voice is keyed much lower but he is making twice the effect. The scene immediately becomes exciting, electric. 'That's fine,' Lunt exclaims. 'But don't go on. You strained your voice before. You were speaking from your throat instead of your diaphragm. Go home now and rest.'

Lunt plunges into the scene in which he arrives at Amphitryon's home. Just as if she knew exactly what second her cue would come, Miss Fontanne arrives at the theatre and runs into her lines almost before the actors know she is there. Signaling to the prompter to take her gloves and purse, she goes on without a break. Her interpretation is quite different from what it was before. It is shrewder, more penetrating, and much sharper. Lunt plays up to her, changing his own interpretation. 'Terribly exciting,' says Windust. 'Entirely new.'

Lunt, it seems, spent most of the night revamping the Leda scene. He took speeches from all the numberless versions, transposed and rearranged them. 'At first it was awful,' says Miss Fontanne. 'Then suddenly it crystallized. Edith and I have been rehearsing it all morning.' They play it out, and Miss Fontanne's judgment is substantiated. The scene has more variety; the points are clearer. 'But it still needs more work.'

After lunch, they go through it over and over. 'Listen,' Lunt steps forward. 'How about this? Play the whole scene as if you were two girls letting your hair down together. She makes you realize, Leda, that you have been *very* badly treated by Jupiter. He abandoned you. He never gave you any presents, "not even a little colored egg" — I love that line. You know it's true, but you're not going to let another woman see that you know it.'

Miss Fontanne and Miss King try it in this way. 'It's coming, isn't it?' says Fontanne. And it is. They do it again. 'Not quite right, Edith,' says Lunt. He sits on the bench next to Miss Fontanne. 'Your dignity is wounded, but you're not petulant.' He casts his eyes down, speaks the Leda lines, with occasional winks at the actors. Everyone is convulsed. Miss Fontanne overacts her part (but in the right key). They both laugh, half in character, half out. 'That's marvelous,' Miss King exclaims, and tries it herself. Behrman arrives at this moment and they play the scene for him, acting it to the hilt. He is as delighted as everyone else. 'We didn't do much,' Lunt tells him. 'All the lines are either yours or Giraudoux's. We just transposed — Last scene, everybody!'

Mercury walks to one side as Alkmena enters. 'I'm supposed to be invisible now,' Whorf says. 'What do I do to indicate that?' 'Make a gesture of invisibility, of course,' Lunt says, as he twirls his hand in a curlicue gesture and laughs.

Now they have reached the last lines, Jupiter's farewell speech, translated literally from the French. Lunt reads it slowly, improvising a little. 'It's there, if we can get it out.' They dissect the speech. Lunt loves a line which ends, 'affecting complete indifference'. Miss Fontanne can't bear it, neither can Behrman. It is cut. Lunt acts the scene this time. . . . 'Berrie, may I use "except" instead of "save"? It's a two-syllable word. It will sound better.' . . . His hand raised, he intones: 'We disappear then, all of us, *except* these two.' A few more lines and then, his eyes raised, hand outstretched: 'Curtain fall!' . . . 'No,' Fontanne exclaims. 'That will get a laugh. It's not right. The audience will look up to see if the curtain is falling. It will spoil your last line.' 'How about this?' says Behrman. ' "Curtain of the night, descend." ' It's better, they all agree.

Dominant, majestic, tragic and titanic — very much a god — Lunt stands backstage, his hat tilted backward on his head. He speaks his lines slowly, with force and dignity. Raising the hand that can cause the sun to rise, the waters to cover the earth, he commands: 'Curtain of the night, descend!' A few more lines, then he and Mercury disappear — in a cloud — and the stage manager bangs a crescendo of thunder on the table, as Alkmena waves farewell to the gods.

Seated in the darkness of the auditorium, you expect the curtain to fall slowly in a climactic burst of sound, a flash of Olympian light. Instinctively, your hands meet to applaud. Then, rather sheepishly, you get up as Windust calls out: 'Back at eight, everybody.'

Amphitryon 38 is still only a rehearsal.

53 The actor attacks his part: Nazimova

Morton Eustis

January 1937

Alla Nazimova was in fact Adelaida Yakovlevna Leventon (1879–1945), an Odessa-born actress who briefly appeared as an extra at the Moscow Art Theatre. By 1904 she was the leading lady of a Russian touring company which came to New York, where "Nazimoff" was persuaded by the producer Henry Miller to learn English, which she did in five months. Her popularity was so great that in 1910 the Nazimova Theatre (later the 39th St. Theatre) opened with her as Rita Allmers in *Little Eyolf*. By 1918 she was reduced to playing an anti-German propaganda sketch *War Brides* in vaudeville. A film of *War Brides* (1916) brought her to Hollywood, and for some years she triumphed as a star in her own films, most memorably *Camille* (1921, with Rudolph Valentino as Armand), and *Salome* (1923, with designs based on Aubrey Beardsley). After 1928 she appeared with two prestigious acting companies: Eva Le Gallienne's Civic Repertory (Ranevskaya in *The Cherry Orchard*, 1929) and the Theatre Guild (Nataliya Petrovna in *A Month in the Country*, 1930; Christine Mannon, in *Mourning Becomes Electra*, 1931; O-Lan in *The Good Earth*, 1932). In 1935, she directed and starred in her own version of Ibsen's *Ghosts*, which toured across the U.S.

IF *The Chosen People* is remembered at all today by Broadway statisticians, it is only as the play in which Nazimova, speaking in Russian, directing and acting with an obscure St. Petersburg repertory company, made her American debut many years ago. The drama was not a theatrical 'event' in its time — as the Moscow Art Theatre's American premiere was years later. It received but scant attention in the press. It was ignored by the rank and file of theatregoers. And it was practically forgotten before many moons had crossed the Great White Way. Yet among the small audience who, by good fortune or necessity, attended the opening at the old Herald Square Theatre, there are a few people who still look back to the event as a theatrical landmark, not only because it introduced to America a great artist and a vivid personality but because it was the first production to point the way to a style of acting and direction, altogether foreign to the American stage, which has exerted a major influence on our theatre.

Gone was the cloak-and-sword school of acting, so popular at the time; in its place was realism and restraint, feeling and emotion expressed in psychological instead of physical terms. Moreover, stranger still, no star held centre stage while the supporting company hovered discreetly upper left and right fearful of encroaching upon the hallowed domain. Emphasis in both acting and production values was apportioned according to the demands of the play. Although a young actress named Alla Nazimova radiated qualities of ability and presence far superior to those of the other members of the company, no spotlight shone on her. Each member of the cast was as important as his role; the entire company, playing in harmony, shared the emphasis and applause. A revolutionary innovation, to say the least!

Although a few ardent enthusiasts at once grasped the significance of the lesson that the production of *The Chosen People* had to teach the Broadway theatre and spread the word that both the play and Mme. Nazimova must be seen, it was hardly to be expected that an unknown Russian troupe, presenting an unknown play in an unknown tongue, should 'panic' the town. Broadway remained unmoved. Lack of patronage forced the group to move to a hall on Third Street, where a repertory of Ibsen plays was presented in Russian to the accompaniment of the music from a dance hall on the floor above and the clatter of a bowling alley in the rear. The small band of the faithful, their numbers gradually reinforced by others drawn by 'word of mouth' praise, crowded into the hall night after night, seemingly unperturbed by the fact that 'the pauses for dramatic effect were made hideous by foreign and irrelevant sounds,' as the *Theatre Magazine* phrased it.

Although the hall was not large enough for an audience that would make the enterprise pay, the enthusiasm and applause may perhaps have helped to persuade Mme. Nazimova to accept the contract tendered by an astute Broadway producer. At any rate, she remained in this country when the company sailed for home. Six months later, having learned in that short time to speak the language, she made her English-speaking debut in *Hedda Gabler*, the same play she is reviving this season. And adding the roles of Nora in *A Doll's House* and Hilda Wangel in *The Master Builder* to a quickly acclaimed characterization, she went on tour, bringing her style of acting and her personal glamor to the rapt attention of audiences all over the country.

The visit of the Moscow Art Theatre and the Moscow Musical Studio, the influence of producers like Komisarjevsky in England and Boleslavsky in America, have taught modern audiences to accept — and to regard highly — the style of acting which we call psychological, or 'spiritual realism', a style of playing that Mme. Nazimova was perhaps the first to introduce effectively into this country. Today we are familiar with the results, both for the individual player and for the ensemble, in the work of many of our own best actors and directors. But the method and especially the long training which produced the results still remain foreign to our Anglo-Saxon stage.

Almost all our experienced actors have been trained in the hit-and-miss school of long runs, in a theatre whose only permanence rests on the talent and perseverance of a few of its finest actors, producers and playwrights. Almost all Russian playing, on the other hand, implies a preparation for permanence, for association with a company remaining together for many years in one theatre under one director; and for the study of many and varied parts for performance in continuous repertory.

An artist like Mme. Nazimova is obviously not the result solely of training. Emotion, intellect and heritage all had their part in her make-up. As a child she studied the violin at Odessa. Four years in dramatic school, and studying direction at the Moscow Art Theatre, followed swiftly, but not casually — four years of improvisation, rigorous training in body control, voice culture, facial mobility, to achieve an ability first to understand and then to project. The logical aftermath of this training was repertory, first with provincial companies, later in leading roles in St. Petersburg and touring the Continent. Add to that background of Russian birth and repertory the creation of a long list of Ibsen heroines, an instinctive insight into character and the special gift and presence that is hers, and you have the actress who has earned the right to be known, quite simply, as Nazimova.

Nazimova's fundamental attack, one which expresses well her basic approach to acting, is best told in her own words: 'The actor should not play a part,' she says. 'Like the Aeolian harps that were hung in the trees to be played only by the breeze, the actor should be an instrument *played upon* by the character he depicts. All the impulse which sets him free as a technician, or artist, should stem from the creature of the dramatist's imagining. The actor himself should be of clay, of putty, capable of being molded into another form, another shape. The wind had but to ripple through the trees and the harp would play without conscious effort. The actor's assignment is more difficult. The breeze which stirs the player must sift, from the character, through the player's brain, his imagination and his body. And then, by conscious *technical* effort, the player must create the sound or fury, sense or sensibility, which the characterization demands.'

No automatic process can teach the actor how to fulfill his task. Much depends on the individual and his equipment, much on the part. The hardest role, always, is that which is not true — 'the silly role, in which there is nothing to probe; where suddenly the actor is called upon to be charming, beautiful, amusing, out of thin air. But every part is hard. Every part requires infinite study and patience.'

Perhaps the pleasantest role Nazimova ever played was O-Lan in the Theatre Guild's *The Good Earth*. She loved that part because it was the antithesis of any she had played before — 'something square, with no kinks, all white, clear and simple; no psychoses'. By far the most rewarding, however, have been the Ibsen roles — of which she has played all the most famous. 'If any playwright can teach an actor how to play, Ibsen has taught me,' Nazimova says. 'The reason is that he is true. There is not one line, one word, whose origin of thought you cannot trace. The same is true of Chekhov. But it is a very rare quality in a playwright.'

Nazimova creates a part 'something as follows': The first time she reads a play, she is 'simply an audience'. She judges the drama as if it were a novel, an essay or a biography. The one essential is that it shall interest her. If she falls asleep in the second act, she reads no further. On the second reading, she concentrates on her own role. 'But I never see myself at all. An actor must never see himself in character. I study the woman. I look at her under a magnifying glass and say to myself: "Is she right? Is she logical? Is she true to herself?" ' Not until the third reading, after she has analyzed the character as an individual remote from canvas and grease-paint, does she ask herself: 'Can *I* act that woman? Can I make *myself* over into *her*?'

The farther away a character is from herself as a type, the more interesting is the role to her. She approaches the part feeling: 'I am nothing. I am nobody. I have to reconstruct my whole self into this woman I am to portray — speak with her voice, laugh with her laughter, move with her motion.' If the part were written for her, this detachment would be hard to attain. Self-analysis would always intrude into the picture. 'But if you can see the person as a living creature, quite removed from yourself, you can work objectively to adapt yourself to the part. Personally, I am no more like Hedda Tesman, Madame Ranevsky in *The Cherry Orchard*, or the brooding Christine in *Mourning Becomes Electra* than I am like the earth-bound O-Lan. But if I can project the character so completely that the audience believes I *am* that character, then I have done my job well.'

The first thing Nazimova seeks to determine about a character is 'what she is thinking, what her inner response is, her feeling, when some other character is holding the stage. Once you know what she *is*, what she *does* becomes easy to interpret. . . . You see that she could not possibly wear red, could not tie a pink bow in her hair, that she must wear gray, that she must be a blonde, that she must move in a given way, speak with a certain inflection. Sometimes, even, you may conceive a character as a blonde and play her as a blonde, though you do not wear a blonde wig. Nora in *A Doll's House* will always be a blonde to me, though I have always acted her with brown hair.'

Unlike The Lunts or Katharine Cornell, who try to get the lines out of the way at the earliest possible moment — before rehearsals, if they can — almost the last thing Nazimova does is to memorize the words. Sometimes she does not even know them at the dress rehearsal. She is so immersed in the study, and delineation, of character that the sides, as such, are of secondary importance. Moreover, she feels that if a part is written correctly, the dialogue will spring so naturally from the characterization that it will almost learn itself. 'Once the actor knows everything there is to know about a character's thoughts — far more, even, than the author — he should grasp the vocabulary almost instinctively.'

In the early readings, Nazimova always reads the play aloud to herself. At one such session, she lets herself go, forgets about technique and allows the emotion of the play to carry her where it will. Studying her reactions closely, as a critic, after the 'performance' is concluded, she makes careful note of the passages where the emotions flowed freely and naturally. These points remain as touchstones. Then she analyzes the '*minutest cause* behind the emotion' which she felt instinctively and thereafter 'tunes down the emotion — or, rather, the actor's expression of that emotion — to the key in which it will be projected across the footlights.'

Nazimova has such a clear picture of the character in her mind by the first rehearsal that, except for the lines, she is able to give almost a finished performance. Stage business is 'instinctive'. The director never shapes her conception or steers her through the mechanics of playing. Only very few directors, she has found, know much about acting. 'Still, a good director can be of far more help to an inexperienced actor than training in stock, which, on account of rushed and inadequate rehearsal, is apt to make a player shoddy. The director, however, should tell the actor only what *not* to do. If he attempts to read lines, to show the actor the gesture he should use, he is a murderer — or he realizes that, unfortunately, he has to deal with an actor devoid of brain and imagination, and therefore must *drill* him as he would a parrot!

'Directing is like conducting a symphony. There are musical sentences — light motives one can trace through the play. They grow and fade. Each act, like a piece of music, is divided into sections and each section has its own inner rhythm.' When Nazimova directed *Hedda Gabler* this year (she also directed *Ghosts* last season), she divided the play into scenes. She made notes on the margin of the script: 'Scene begins here, ends here.' This did not mean that the curtain fell but merely that a new motive was born, that one thought-sequence had built to a climax and that a new attack was needed. Nazimova has always played the Ibsen dramas on the piano, improvising music for each character, each scene, 'to find the musical, the symphonic beat of the play — a rhythm not only of sound and movement, but of pause and thought, *especially thought*'. When Iturbi said of *Ghosts*, 'The play, the production, is like music,' Nazimova felt that he had heard, had seen and had felt the rhythm she had conceived in terms of music. Tempo, she believes, is a delicate two-edged sword hanging over the heads of the actors. The slightest slowing-up or speeding-up at the wrong time destroys the rhythm of a scene. Variety in tempo is one of the vital elements in the direction of a play.

In one of the first interviews she ever granted in this country, Nazimova was quoted in the *Theatre Magazine* as saying: 'Sincerity and the correct use of voice is the greatest thing in the art of acting. . . . If I were to advise any American actors, I would say: "Make gramophone records. One false note or inflection may ruin an entire performance." ' Although the actress has long since forgotten these words, time has not altered her opinion. In a recent production she begged an actor in the company to have a record made of a long speech so that he could hear, for himself, how monotonous, how flat, his rendition was. She believes that work in the movies can be of immense help to an actor for the same reason, provided he has first been well-grounded in stage technique. '*Seeing* himself, he can say: "That was bad. That was good. That is a mannerism. That expressed nothing." He can feel the rhythm of his performance, can learn to recognize the value not only of speech and action but of a pause. He can learn what *not* to do, which is just as important as learning what to do. *Hearing* himself talk, he can feel the quality of his voice, the scope of its projection, can determine its ability to express in tones the thought and feeling of words. And he can realize what good diction really means.'

Once the pattern of a role is established, Nazimova follows that pattern absolutely in performance. Often, however, it is four or five weeks after the opening before she can say to herself with confidence: 'Now I have my pattern.' Until then, 'I am constantly experimenting, playing a scene softer, louder, more harshly; digging into the role, dissecting it until I am sure it is right.' She does not change her style of acting because of audience reactions. 'A good actor', she asserts, 'should be able to *make* an audience, any audience, feel what he wants it to feel. This is his assignment.' The one thing that may cause her to alter her playing slightly on a given night is a variation in the playing of another actor. 'If one actor is a little slow, you have to come in faster. If a scene lags, you have to pick it up. But no losing yourself in the part! No being transported into other worlds by the emotion of the play!'

The time is long since past, Nazimova believes, 'when an actor can rant all over the stage and call it acting'. Inspiration plays a part, sometimes a large part, in acting. 'But one is never carried away *during* a performance. One watches oneself always. And the inspiration, the emotion, that the actor may feel — and often does feel — depend not so much on himself or on the character as on the interpretation, on the realization that he is projecting the desired illusion.'

'First, last and always', Nazimova adds, 'an actor must have imagination. Without imagination, he might as well be a shoe-black as an actor. Imagination kindles the feelings, steers the actor through the character into emotion, enables him to reproduce feelings he himself has never experienced.' Nazimova never attempts to relate the emotion of a scene to personal experience. 'If I thought for one second about *my* emotion while acting, I would be completely side-tracked.' Her entire concern is with the character she personifies, '*her* feelings and thoughts, *her* actions and reactions'. While Nazimova, the actress, is on stage, Nazimova, the woman, exists only as a captious critic appraising the performance from a seat on a mythical aisle.

54 The actor attacks his part: Katharine Cornell

Morton Eustis

February 1937

Known far and wide as "The First Lady of the American Theatre", Katharine Cornell (1893–1974) was one of the last stars to tour cross-country on a regular basis. She won large popular audiences as Shaw's Candida (1924), Elizabeth Barrett (*The Barretts of Wimpole Street*, 1931) and Juliet (1934) under her own management in productions staged by her husband Guthrie McClintic. (The seamy side of her tours has been described hilariously in Fitzroy Davis' 1942 novel *Quicksilver*.) Cornell's heavy-lidded eyes and husky voice lent an exotic tinge to her interpretations. A carry-over from the nineteenth century, she needed the proscenium arch to frame her large-scale romantic acting and never made a movie.

―――――――――――

THE YEAR was 1919. The place, London. The scene, the stalls of a playhouse during the matinee of a current hit . . . Katharine Cornell, a young American actress who had come to London to achieve her first success as Jo in *Little Women*, was seated in the darkened auditorium watching a tense drama unfold on the stage before her. At the climax of a highly emotional scene, tears welled up in the eyes of the leading lady; they fell slowly, drop by drop, down her fair cheeks. Instantly, a woman sitting in front of Miss Cornell in the audience nudged her companion: 'Look,' she whispered admiringly, 'real tears.' Through the entire house ran the same electric consciousness. '*Real tears!* The actress is so overcome by emotion that she is crying. She is *actually* crying!' The curtain, like the tears, fell slowly. It rose again. The star, still in the throes of emotion, took her bow. Her face was streaked with mascara where the tears had coursed. She wiped her eyes. A salvo of applause ran through the auditorium.

Miss Cornell was not among those to applaud. A season of trouping, the year before, in a small part in the tear-jerker, *The Man Who Came Back*, had made her realize that tears, real or glycerine, could easily be induced into an actor's eyes. How the actress in this play made herself cry, even the fact that she did cry, did not concern Miss Cornell as she walked out of the theatre. What did affect her was this: the moment the actress dramatized her own tears, held them on show, as it were, for all observers to see, *the character lost her audience*. Every person in the theatre thought only of the fact that the actress, herself, was crying. At the one time, of all others, when the audience should have been hypnotized into forgetting it was in a theatre watching a play, its thoughts had been diverted from the character to the actor, from illusion to reality.

Then and there, Miss Cornell made up her mind that when she had a 'big scene' to play, she would use her authority as an actress to melt the eyes of her audience rather than her own. How much better, she thought — looking into the future, perhaps, to parts like Candida, Juliet, Joan of Arc — for the spectators to believe that a character on the stage is moved to laughter or tears and, believing it, to laugh or cry themselves, and for the actor, conscious every moment of what he is doing, always a step ahead of his part, to use his powers to create, sustain and heighten that illusion! 'Acting is only the creation of an illusion of reality,' Miss Cornell insists. '*The essential thing is to make the audience believe all the time.*'

Although any form of personal exhibitionism on the part of the player at once destroys illusion, every actor is, on the other hand, faced with the necessity of building each role within the framework of his own personal presence. His body, his voice, and his ego are the scaffolding around the edifice of character which he creates. For Katharine Cornell this problem was made more than usually difficult by the very distinction of her presence. When a young assistant stage manager, named Guthrie McClintic, saw her act with the Washington Square Players during her first season on the stage, he scribbled on his program the words: 'Interesting, monotonous, worth watching.' Yet his comment at that time was kinder than that of other critics and friends. Miss Cornell was told, variously, that she was too tall; she looked awkward, gawky; her features were striking but far from beautiful; her voice musical but uninteresting; her whole presence was *wrong* for the theatre — too marked, perhaps; she should never consider a stage career. Two seasons of minor roles with the Washington Square Players, an arduous year with the Jessie Bonstelle Stock Company in Buffalo (playing parts of maids, scrub ladies and the like) and the road season with the *Man Who Came Back* company endowed Miss Cornell with the technical facility and poise to confound her former critics with a gracious and charming performance in *Little Women*. But the actress had not yet solved the problem of relating her own uncommon presence to a theatre's stage. The special radiance and grandeur that was to add lustre to many insignificant plays and enrich fine plays — qualities that must have been hers even then — still shone but fitfully in the actress' performance.

The task of 'making audiences believe' is made doubly hard for the young actor by the fact that he is compelled, through inexperience and lack of opportunity, to play many unimportant roles in mediocre plays. He has to make the audience accept not only a playwright's character but often a story essentially false. Miss Cornell's career, in this respect, was no exception to the general rule. Despite her success in London, she could not get a part in New York. After a brief tour in *The Man Outside*, she rejoined Miss Bonstelle's stock company, then in Detroit, playing the leading roles in works no better or worse than the usual stock fare. Her early critic, McClintic, happened to be a stage director for the company and he not only displayed a personal interest in Miss Cornell — they were married the following year — but he coached the actress in her roles — a new one each week. 'Don't play down your height, your peculiarities of presence,' he must have told her. 'Use them. . . . Attack each part as if it were new and vital. Learn to project character *through* your own personality. Use your God-given gift of glamour to make audiences believe even the silly parts. When the good parts come along, half your work will be done for you, and through them you will mature.'

The role of Sydney Fairfield in *A Bill of Divorcement*, the next year, offered Miss Cornell her first chance to enact a believable characterization on Broadway. (She was engaged for this part, against the judgment of the producer, on the insistence of the British actor in the lead who had seen her play Jo in London.) The play and the characterization were an instantaneous hit. And, even today, people who have entirely forgotten the drama still remember the feeling of sympathy evoked for the young girl who remained faithful to her father, shell-shocked and mentally injured in the War. A lovely character-portrait of Mary Fitton the next year (she impersonated Juliet for one scene) in the Winthrop Ames production of *Will Shakespeare* proved that Miss Cornell was not simply a one-part or a 'modern-play' actress. Years of less fruitful appearances were to follow in melodramas like *Tiger Cats, The Green Hat, The Letter* and *Dishonored Lady* — *Candida* alone, in 1924, breaking the spell of tawdry parts, giving true scope to the actress' powers and receiving, in grateful return, a glowing impersonation. Yet such was Miss Cornell's determination to make the audience care that she made Iris March, and the other murderesses and adulteresses she depicted, seem vibrant people and she built, for the moment, some universal truth out of the unreal stories these plays told. Not entirely incidental, too, was the fact that she made enough money out of these portrayals to enable her to set herself up under her own management.

Her own best development as an actress grew — as McClintic had told her years earlier that it would — out of the good parts in good plays that she then selected for production. The changing elements of character in the roles provided by *The Barretts*, *Lucrece* (the first classic role), *Romeo and Juliet*, *Saint Joan* and, this year, *The Wingless Victory* gave the actress the chance to create something more than excitement. And the presence and technique — in speech, timing and projection — used to such good effect in the trashy roles, found their ultimate expression in genuine characterization.

How Miss Cornell attacks a part — more specifically, how she adapts her own presence to contrasting characterizations — is, she says, 'very hard to describe'. Where Nazimova, with the Russian background of training, approaches a role with a complete sense of detachment — feeling that she, herself, is 'nothing, nobody' — Miss Cornell quite consciously attempts to relate a part to herself. 'Every character', she feels, 'is both near and far from an actor's own personality. The player must understand the person, have a cerebral as well as an emotional sympathy with the role, to act it. Then he has to present it through his own qualities of mind and physique.

'There may be actors who completely disguise themselves. But if the process is absolute, I doubt if the desired effect is produced. Every part must mirror something of the actor, himself, just as every book, every painting, every piece of music, reflects something of its creator. If an actor lost his personality, the public would lose interest in him, just as it would in a Rembrandt or Whistler painting that bore no trace of the style or personality of the artist. A good actor can play diverse roles, be a distinctly different character in each one of them, and yet retain his own personality all the time. I believe, for instance, that my Elizabeth Barrett, my Juliet and my Joan were three different people. You could not imagine Elizabeth, as I acted her, behaving as I did as Juliet or as Joan — at least, I hope you couldn't. . . . The three characters, even with contrasting make-up, all looked like Katharine Cornell. But each was — perhaps I should say, was *intended* to be — a person with distinct individual reality.'

Acting technique, Miss Cornell believes, can never be reduced to formula. In every art, there is 'much that is instinctive, much that is subconscious'. In acting, these qualities are observed especially in the relation of the character, and the actor, to the other characters, the other actors in a cast. 'To understand one's own character thoroughly one must see it in relation not only to itself but to the other characters in the play.' For this reason, Miss Cornell always tries to hold her impressions of a play 'in a state of fluidity' until rehearsals commence. Reading a play for the first time, she concentrates principally on her own role, to determine whether the part is suitable for her, one to which she can — 'perhaps' — do justice. Once she has decided that she likes the part, she studies the play as a whole, examines the relation of all the roles, the reactions of one character on another, the influences and emotional disturbances of the play. Then she re-studies her own part in relation to the play and to the other roles. *The Barretts of Wimpole Street*, her first production as an actress-manager, was one of the few plays she visualized at once, not in terms of the central part but as an entity. This, she confesses, may have been because it never occurred to her then that she could portray the frail poetess. (Perhaps the Iris March influence was still too fresh.) It was only later, through the suggestion of Guthrie McClintic (who had, and has subsequently, directed all her plays since *The Green Hat*), that she undertook to essay the role.

Although certain moments in every play immediately stand out in imagination as scenes played by actors, Miss Cornell spends a long time studying the character as a character before she attempts to project herself as an actress into the role. The actual development of the part is 'a slow, cumulative process'. Certain details — of gesture, speech, costume and manner — communicate themselves the moment the actor reads the play. Working out the part, in terms of a stage and of herself, Miss Cornell 'develops, refines and heightens these automatic suggestions'.

As soon as the 'sides' are delivered to her (her part typed out in full, with only the first and last lines of the other speeches included), she begins to 'break' the part. She reads the lines aloud, over and over, without any expression, without giving any thought to their meaning, in order to have them tabled in the back of her mind by the time rehearsals start. She deliberately leaves them 'suspended' for the first week of rehearsals and reads her part with the other players in order that her reading should not become set and conflict or jar with other voices or person-alities. Listening to the other actors, concentrating on their interpretations more than on her own, she is apt to read very poorly herself for the first few days. In the first day's rehearsal of *Saint Joan*, in fact, she gave such 'a stumbling, frightened reading' that Maurice Evans, the Dauphin, confided to a friend that Miss Cornell could never play the part. At the end of the first week, she will try out the role without sides to help her, and this time will draw on her reservoir of memory. With the lines 'out of the way' she can devote her whole attention to character development.

The finest hair line, in Miss Cornell's opinion, separates the good actor from the so-called 'ham'. The difference, nine times out of ten, lies in 'the power of selection, *the ability to seize upon essentials* and throw away the alluring temptations that clutter up a performance. Almost every imaginative person has a certain instinct for acting. But few have the power to execute, to put into practice, *to make real to an audience*, what they see or feel. . . . Lines, situations, character, all suggest an infinite number of things to "do". The artist is the one who has the ability to select, and select accurately, the right and significant things. . . . I have seen promising actors go wrong because they could not choose. They could not resist the impulse to "do, do, do".'

Rehearsals are the period during which the actor must edit his performance. After the opening night, except for minor readjustments, it is too late. Miss Cornell as a rule works out the details of stage business by herself and then lets the director 'add and subtract'. The director, Miss Cornell feels — and by 'director' she means Guthrie McClintic — 'is the editor, the critic, the eye of a production. He is like a conductor who, with a fine, or poor, instrument to play upon, is able to lead his men so that he obtains the best out of them. He does not set the part or impose the conception. He draws the reins or hastens the outflow, guides the actor in the direction he is taking. When the goal is false, when the actor is getting away from the play, he sets him on the right path.'

Although Miss Cornell plays the dual role of actress and manager, she is probably less concerned with the physical routine of production than most managers. Having worked for so many years with Mr. McClintic and his associates, she is able to 'throw off' all the production details onto their shoulders, convinced, through long experience, that they will be handled with sagacity. Her faith in Mr. McClintic is so implicit that she will let him, even, engage a Romeo and a Mercutio in London whom she has never seen. Her main concern, as a manager, lies in seeing that the play receives the best possible production, in engaging the best available actors for all the roles. Her chief responsibility as an actress is to give the best rendition she can of her own role *in relation to the play and the other players*. 'And, obviously, one acts best when one is surrounded by the best actors, for the give and take brings life not only to the play but to the players.'

All the productions under Miss Cornell's management have reflected — in the quality of presentation, the 'give and take' between the actors, the lack of emphasis upon the star — her conviction that 'the play's the thing!' The increasing excellence of the Cornell productions, however, has been due not alone to Miss Cornell's ambition and Mr. McClintic's flair for presentation but to the fact that Miss Cornell, working toward an ultimate repertory company, has gradually set up the nucleus of such a troupe — a permanent director and technical staff, and actors who have played together in many of her productions, both on Broadway and on the road. She has in that way been able to start work on each production well ahead of other Broadway 'hit or miss' producing units; to take short cuts and spend her energy on fine points instead of on routine work.

Once the performance is 'set' in rehearsals, Miss Cornell changes her acting little. The receptiveness, apathy or antagonism of an individual audience have their effect. But, in the main, she follows the one pattern, though striving, always, to improve the part. 'The actor', she says, 'is always conscious of whether he is making his points or not. He may give a good account of himself in character and yet realize that he is not making the audience understand, or feel, all that he finds in the part. Certain scenes will always worry and vex him. Instinctively, he will feel that they have not come across as well as they should. This may be due to faulty writing, bad casting, the wrong tempo, lighting or scenery, as well as the playing. Whatever the reason, the actor always struggles with such a scene. He will try different readings, gestures and movements on different nights, but only after he has thoroughly considered, and practiced, each in turn. Often it takes long playing to make a characterization satisfying to an actor. It took many months to break through the shell of Juliet. And if I played the part until I was ninety — which I shan't — I am convinced I would still find things to do, or, more likely, *not to do*.'

When a playgoer says to an actor, 'You *lived* the part!', he thinks he has paid the player the highest possible compliment. But the good actor, Miss Cornell declares, 'does not live the part; he *cannot* live the part. All the actor does is to *recognize* the emotion of the character and endeavor to transmit the illusion of that emotion across the footlights.' Emotion in acting, Miss Cornell believes, is a subject which should only be debated in private among players. Nevertheless, she is willing to state — 'flatly' — that she never loses herself in a role. Nor does she believe it is necessary for an actor to have experienced an emotion, or its equivalent, in real life to be able to portray it effectively on the stage. 'The truth of that is shown clearly in the other arts.' She agrees wholeheartedly with George Arliss, who once said: 'If the actor really feels an emotion, there is no sensible reason why he should continue his performance on a confined stage. He should rush into the public square and play out the scene there!'

'Spontaneous or inspired acting — meaning that something which drops from the sky at the moment when the player, Heaven help him, is on the grill in front of an audience — is equally unreliable. By a miracle it might save an actor once. But it would be unfair to tempt fate twice. Inspiration can be of real and lasting value to an actor when he is *studying* a role. But, even then, the actor must be careful to see that it has its roots in his work and is not a misleading flash. . . . *The actor should know, at all times, what he intends to do* and he should practice each bit most carefully before he puts himself in front of spectators. If the actor does live the role at all, it is only in the sense of concentrating on it, and it alone, from the moment he reads a script until the last night of a play's run.'

Audiences often wonder how an actor can play the same role, night after night, without going stale, without losing interest in the part. One reason he can is because 'each performance is a challenge. No two audiences are alike and each audience has to be convinced. Audiences, moreover, teach a player a great deal. Their reaction is the thermometer. They cannot show an actor how to act, but they can — and do — register whether the actor is ringing true.' Miss Cornell loves trouping not only because she believes that the salvation of the theatre lies in building up a theatre-minded audience outside of New York, but because the road audiences can often teach the actor more than the sophisticated New York public. 'Their reaction is less consciously analytical, more spontaneous.' The longer an actor plays a part, too, the better he is bound to be. 'I know that after over seven hundred performances of Elizabeth Barrett, I more nearly approached Mr. Besier's characterization that I did the first one hundred times, and Juliet at my last performance was nearer to Shakespeare than at any time before. The value of repertory is great, for alternating roles gives variety and freshness. But I know that I need a continuous spell at a part to get well into it, perhaps because of my training. The important thing, as William Gillette once said, is to give on the one-hundredth or the one-thousandth night the same illusion of freshness as at the premiere. . . . Oh, it's very difficult to make it all clear!'

The hardest role Miss Cornell ever played was in *Tiger Cats*, not because the role itself was unusually difficult, but because she was expected by the leading man to play it in the same style that Edith Evans had used in London. The most difficult role in another sense, was Leslie Crosby in *The Letter* because, as an avowed murderess, she had to fight every minute against the antagonism of the audience. Joan — 'without any question' — was the most rewarding part, 'for I feel that the audience got a tremendous lift out of Shaw's play and this exaltation reacted on the actors'. The most valuable training a young actor can get is — 'banally enough' — the chance to act. '*We need stock companies and touring companies. Young people must learn their craft with seasoned actors, not novices like themselves.*'

'All this', Miss Cornell says, 'is a groping and very personal viewpoint, subject to change. Opinions alter and methods grow. We all know actors who are perfect technicians but who can never interest the public. We know people on the stage who, truly, are not expert and yet enchant hosts of admirers. . . . The final answer — if there is any final answer — rests with the gallery gods.'

55 The actor attacks his part: Burgess Meredith

Morton Eustis

March 1937

In the series "The actor attacks his part", Burgess Meredith (1907–97) was, although nearly 30, featured as the representative of the younger generation. Short in stature, with craggy features and a husky voice, he ran counter to the traditional image of the leading man. Meredith had started in Eva Le Gallienne's Civic Repertory playing three small, masked roles in *Alice in Wonderland* and then attracted critical attention as dynamic youths on Broadway. He consolidated his success in three poetic plays by Maxwell Anderson: as the anarchist's son Mio, a role written for him, in *Winterset* (1935), the idealist Van Van Dorn in *High Tor* (1937) and the escapist inventor Stephen Minch in *The Star Wagon* (1937). More intellectual than many young actors and conveying a sense of wry skepticism, Meredith was valued by Orson Welles who cast him as Prince Hal in his short-lived Shakespearean cycle *Five Kings*. Nowadays, he is known primarily as the grizzled trainer in the *Rocky* movies.

THERE are as many theories rampant concerning methods of technical training for the young actor as there are styles of acting itself. Every school of the drama has its own doctrine; every artist or man of commerce in the theatre, his own conviction; and there is something to be said for almost all of them. No oracle can speak with final assurance and say: 'This theory is omnipotent.' No opinion is incontestable. It is not through any inherent, absolute rightness in them that the conclusions reached from an actor's personal experience are illuminating, but as reflections of the actor's accomplishments, the quality of his artistry, the craftsmanship of the theatre where he works.

When Burgess Meredith hazards the opinion that 'the actor's best opportunity to learn his craft lies in the chance to work under a good director', he lays no claim to originality or to infallibility. The twenty-nine-year-old actor, who was 'starred' last year in *Winterset* and who prefers to be 'featured' this year in *High Tor*, says, quite simply: 'I am sure that I never would have had any success if I had not been lucky enough to play under excellent direction, both in New York and in summer stock. Directors, I don't mind saying, made me. Without their aid and inspiration, I should still be sitting in casting offices. A really good director, I think, can teach the novice, *in one production*, more about himself, more about acting, than years of misguided playing in stock or repertory.'

So far as Meredith is concerned, these remarks are prompted by no false modesty. In his experience, so far, the director has been 'all-important' — that much is a matter of fact. At the moment he sincerely believes he would 'flounder helplessly' without astute direction. Yet his point of view — as he himself admits — reflects his youth and limited experience. As he grows in maturity, he may not rely so implicitly on 'stern guidance'. There are implications, however, in what he says about the importance of the director which can (without straining for effect) be read into both his experience and the opinion he bases upon it — implications that seem to presage a change of focus in the theatre of the rising generation.

Few mature players who have received their training in the Anglo-Saxon theatre would stress the importance of the directors under whom they played in their youth as a major force in molding their talents. The theatre in which Helen Hayes, the Lunts, Katharine Cornell and Ina Claire served their apprenticeship was, essentially, an actors' theatre, in which plays were built around stars and star parts. Meredith's theatre seems to be headed towards a different goal — a theatre in which, to quote Meredith again, 'the director's control is absolute'. And his experience is an indication, at least, of the fact that a new approach to acting, which centres to the playing group as a unit and not to a single player, is already well over the threshold of our stage.

Meredith does not understate the case when he declares that he was fortunate in his directors. His tutelage began under the shrewd and observant eye of Eva Le Gallienne, first in her apprentice school and then in her Civic Repertory Theatre. He played no big parts there but a large variety of small roles. In the summer seasons, to vary the routine, he stormed the barn theatres as Marchbanks in various revivals of *Candida*. The first role that brought him sharply to the attention of Broadway was that of Red Barry in *Little Ol' Boy*, the Albert Bein play of reform-school life, which was staged by Joe Losey in the spring of 1933. Brooks Atkinson said then of him: 'Burgess Meredith puts into the role all the implications and shades given it by Mr. Bein' — high praise for a first major assignment.

When *Little Ol' Boy* failed, Meredith returned to Fourteenth Street and threw himself, almost at one and the same time, into impersonations of The Duck, The Dormouse and Tweedledee in *Alice in Wonderland*. November of '33 found him again on Broadway, cavorting upstairs and down as the tap-dancing Princeton student in the riotous *She Loves Me Not*, this time under the precise, vigorous and meticulously-paced direction of Howard Lindsay. In that play, as in *Battleship Gertie* under Arthur Sircom's baton a year later (the play ran for only two nights), Meredith gave evidence of having a robust comic quality which responded well to direction. But he hardly led the critics to believe that he could compass a part like that of Mio in *Winterset* in less than a year's time.

To Guthrie McClintic must go the full credit for drawing out of Meredith the qualities which have since led him to be dubbed 'the Hamlet of 1940'. McClintic, however, would be the first to insist that what he did was not to impose his stamp on Meredith but to set free in the young actor the talents for which he could not, himself, find release. McClintic directed him first in a small role in Miss Cornell's revival of *The Barretts*; then, again with Miss Cornell, in the part of the half-mad youth in *Flowers of the Forest*, when, to quote John Mason Brown, he 'came near to walking away with the production'; last year in the savage, poetic intensity of

Winterset, and, this winter, in *High Tor.* It might not be amiss to note here, as an aside, that what Meredith calls his 'luck' has held not only with directors but with dramas. Few actors have been granted the opportunity, so early in their careers, to essay a part like that of Mio, and to learn from it the deeper truths of acting which only fine parts can teach. Perhaps that is one of the major virtues of a director's theatre — when a director has not only the vision to recognize undeveloped talent but faith enough in his own judgment to risk a fine part on his ability to make the actor compass it.

The director's primary job, Meredith holds, is to 'designate a form for a part'. The form need not be a fixed, rigorous mold in which the actor has no chance to expand ideas of his own. Like Helen Hayes, Meredith responds much better to direction which suggests the impulse but does not denote its expression. Staging which aims to shape an actor's whole conception, which illustrates each gesture and supplies each intonation, makes him feel 'stifled, self-conscious'. He prefers to work with a director, like McClintic, who 'lets the actor feel his way around, ascertains where he is going and then guides him along the path. But whether the director', Meredith continues, 'indicates the form at the beginning or the end of rehearsals, whether the form is more, or less, stringent, is unimportant as long as he says "yes" and "no" with definitiveness at some point during rehearsals.' Absent treatment direction is not Meredith's ideal.

'Form', as Meredith views it, 'is the theatrical relation of the actor's own conception of a part to the play and to the other actors.' It is expressed in the stage business, the tempo of speech and performance, and, most important of all, in the rhythm of an entire production, when the individual is subordinated to the play as a whole. The majority of actors like to create their own stage business. Meredith, however, prefers to have the director suggest the business. 'I would never have the imagination', he says, 'to think up the stage business. Unless the director told me to move, I would probably stand still' — a passive state of mind which his acting certainly does not suggest and which, he admits, may spring from lack of experience rather than an innate inability to move on his own volition. If the director makes a suggestion which Meredith feels, instinctively, is not in character, he will tell him 'after trying it out two or three times' that 'it doesn't work on this particular machine'. Then the two of them will either fight it out or compromise. 'The main thing is for the actor to be plastic — though not putty — in the director's hands.'

It is after the first complete run-through of the play that the director assumes his 'all-important' function. 'Having viewed the drama in its entirety for the first time, he tells you from the copious notes he has made: "That line was strident. That one was soft. That speech didn't mean anything; it conveyed no feeling. . . . The act lacked humor, poise or assurance. It was self-pitying, or too strong." Then it is that the director teaches the actor how to see the play as a whole; to realize where his performance is in, and out of, key with the other interpretations.'

The less creative the actor is, or thinks he is, the better, in Meredith's judgment.

'If the actor is an artist at all, he is strictly an interpretive artist. The more translucent he is, the easier it is for him to adapt himself — or to let the director adapt him — to various types of roles.' Meredith is somewhat sceptical of the 'value or the sense' of any analysis an actor may make of his own technique. 'The important thing for the actor is to achieve effects. Let the critics worry about *how* he succeeds or fails.' For this reason, he will only 'sketch briefly, inadequately and somewhat fearfully' a few salient characteristics of his approach to a performance.

Meredith has one 'peculiarity' which makes itself apparent at the very outset. He cannot, he has discovered, form 'a definite feeling about a play as a whole' except when it is read to him. If he reads a script to himself, he reads mechanically until he reaches his own lines and thus loses the essential impression of the drama. All the best plays he has acted in were read to him first by the author or by the director. And, in each case, he 'signed up' before he ever read the manuscript himself.

Once the part is delivered to him, his immediate reaction is in the first person singular: 'What am I going to do? How am I going to deliver this line?' And, most important of all, 'What *am* I?' He reads his sides aloud 'to obtain certain instinctive reactions about the character and the playing'. His next move is to determine: 'What characteristics of this person do I know from my own feelings?' No part was ever written, he believes, which does not have in its main conception some relationship to the actor's own personality — unless the actor is a complete moron. The character may be weak, strong, arrogant, supercilious, snobbish, headstrong. The actor, himself, may not be any one of these things *in toto*, or even in part. But, certainly, he will have had moments in his life when he experienced the emotions these qualities produce. 'He may not have killed anyone, but there are times when he would have liked to.'

Meredith next tries to recall the reaction the emotion produced in him at the time he felt it. With that as a base, he then 'dresses the character' in his mind, and endeavors to make it conform to his ideas. If the character is a conceited prig, automatically he reads the part, feels the part, as if he were a conceited prig. If the person is shy and defensive, he approaches the characterization shyly, defensively. 'From that point of view technique is simple. The only thing that really counts is: *Does it get across? Does it project?*'

The moment rehearsals start, the whole conception of how to read and play a part — '*not* the conception of the part itself' — is apt to change. In the privacy of his home, the actor may strike 'some perfectly grand inflection for a big line'. The instant another actor gives him the cue, however, he may realize that 'the inflection is all wrong'; the tone of voice of the other actor, his tempo or movement, has killed it. The reading is out of key with the style of the play. The same type of realization is apt to occur after the first audience reaction. Then the conception may have to be altered 'to fit what goes over and what doesn't'. It is extremely difficult to be sure, especially in comedy, that a line or scene will affect the audience according to advance expectations. '*Battleship Gertie*, for instance, was so funny in rehearsals that the technicians watching the dress rehearsal were literally rolling in the aisles. It needed an audience to prove how terrible it really was.'

Learning lines is a 'turmoil and headsweat' to Meredith. He cannot memorize a part, as most actors do, simply by reading it over and over. He must see the lines photographically. Reading the part, he conceives the lines in terms of the emotions behind them, gets 'the general idea of hate, bitterness, love or humor'. Then he writes them out — 'filling hundreds of pages of scrap paper' — until they are indelibly printed on his brain. Once they are learned — 'usually quite late in rehearsals' — they are put aside and he concentrates thereafter on the fine points of the characterization — a concentration which does not cease when the opening-night trial is over and the play settles down to a run. 'That is only the beginning. You work on the part each night you play it. You try, always, to think of it as something alive and fresh. You refine the interpretation each time you play it. Meredith purposely alters the pattern of a role slightly each time he goes on the stage, 'in order to avoid getting into a rut'. The main outlines remain the same, but he will 'graduate an emotion, vary the shades of intensity. And, suddenly, one night, you will hear yourself giving a line twice the meaning. *That's* a great thrill.'

Every moment that he is on the stage, the actor must be able to 'hear himself'; in other words, he must be conscious of what he is doing. Of itself, this fact makes it impossible for an actor to lose himself in a role. Such emotion as Meredith may feel during a performance is 'probably a form of non-alcoholic intoxication. You tap your reservoir of emotions while you are *creating* the part. *Playing* it, you merely carry this feeling objectively in the back of your mind. You are conscious of the effect this emotion should produce, but you don't let it affect you. For instance, in a scene in which I have to be very angry, I carry in the back of my mind the sense of "I'd like to sock you in the eye!" which would probably be my own personal reaction. The words I pronounce may be altogether different, but I dive under them with a sock-you-in-the-eye feeling to find the right reaction. I don't attempt to feel angry, or even to think of what it feels like to be angry. I couldn't possibly recreate a conscious emotion every night. I knew an actor who told me that always, when he played one scene in which he had to commit suicide, he tried to think of his emotions just before he stepped into a cold shower; that was his key to the scene. When he was able to visualize the emotion he played the scene beautifully. The trouble was that nine times out of ten he couldn't get near the cold shower in his mind and then was unable to project anything. If I have to play a suicide scene, I always strive to keep a physical picture in my mind, to imagine how it will feel when the bullet enters my head — the shock of steel tearing through my brain. In *Winterset*, when I was shot, I always thought of something striking me forcibly in the pit of the stomach; then I doubled up in pain. I have never been shot, but I have been hurt at sports and, knowing the feeling, I tried to simulate the *effect* it had on me at the time. But I didn't *feel* the emotion it produced.'

Like every actor, Meredith finds it 'very difficult, if not impossible', to illustrate the part emotion plays in acting. The attempt to dissect his method of playing — 'if there is any method' — rather frightens him also. He is, like all actors, quite unsure of ways and means. The one thing he is completely certain of is this: 'The role Mio in *Winterset* was one of the hardest, the pleasantest and the most rewarding role I ever played. Difficult, because the diction was so exacting and I had, besides, to overcome the immense technical hazard of presenting a great and poetic line spoken by a lowly person.' He had to find the emotion of the lowly person and 'let it speak with the tongues of angels, without sounding silly or losing the sense of character.' Pleasant, because the role 'gave lasting pleasure. The play lifted people up. It exalted them. You felt that all the time you were on the stage.' Rewarding, because each performance, each line, was a challenge. 'Sometimes, you felt you had really realized the part.'

56 The actor-dancer attacks his part: Fred Astaire

Morton Eustis

June 1937

From the beginning, *Theatre Arts* embraced the dance as a significant contributor to the New Stagecraft. It devoted articles to Isadora Duncan, Ruth St. Denis and Jaques-Dalcroze, as well as to Asian rituals and vaudeville chorus lines. The magazine also began, tentatively, in the 1930s to include the occasional article on film. So it was not out of keeping for Morton Eustis to include Fred Astaire in his series "The actor attacks his part". Astaire (1899–1987) is best known now for his appearances in a series of great film musicals, paired with Ginger Rogers from 1933. However, he had had a lively stage career from 1917, usually appearing with his sister Adele as stars in the Gershwin musicals *Lady, Be Good!* (1924) and *Funny Face* (1927), as well as in *The Band Wagon* (1932). Astaire had perfected his elegant yet seemingly casual persona long before leaving for Hollywood and regarded himself as a dancing actor rather than a dancer *tout pur.*

———————————

To DESCRIBE Fred Astaire as an 'Actor and Dancer' — in the manner of that reliable and informative volume, *Who's Who in the Theatre* — is to state a simple and obvious truth. But the delineation, though accurate, is inadequate. Like the monograph on Astaire, prepared by the movie press department, which reads: 'Fred Astaire was born in Omaha, Neb. Height: five feet, nine inches. Slender. Dark brown eyes and hair. Once owned racing stable in England. Likes tennis, golf and prize-fights. Birthday, Nov. 26,' it errs on the side of understatement and tells only part of the truth. If histrionic talent and the ability to dance with grace and precision were Astaire's only attributes, he would never have been able to create a form of entertainment as popular with tennis, golf, fight and racing fans as with students of drama, dance and film — a blend of song and dance, sense and nonsense, beauty and agility with an almost universal appeal.

Leaving out of consideration the intangible elements of personality, presence or genius — which, in the final analysis, determine the true validity of any artistic accomplishment — a large measure of Astaire's success as an actor-dancer must be ascribed to the fact that he is an expert choreographer, who designs, and has, since childhood, designed his own routines. Out of an innate sense of form, of balance and of rhythm, complemented by a natural gift of showmanship, Astaire has created a diversified group of dance patterns, on stage and screen, which are almost perfectly adapted to his own special capabilities as a dancer. Another achievement to which the actor-dancer must plead guilty is that of being what might be called a 'choreographer in terms of camera angles'. As the critics have noted, Astaire seems to be the one actor-dancer who is equally good on screen and stage. Credit for this has been imputed (naturally and rightly) to his excellence as a dancer and a comedian. But little or no stress has been laid on the equally important fact that Astaire himself (perhaps without realizing it) has evolved a method of photographing the dance which sets free its qualities as a medium where formerly they had been stifled. To add another item to the tally of attributes, it should be noted that Astaire, without any voice, in the operatic sense, has found a way to inject a dancing rhythm into song which makes his singing, if not a joy forever, at least a most immediate pleasure — as gay and buoyant as the tapping of feet. And, as a postscript, it might be observed that lately he has even popularized the dance in the most talkative but least articulate of all mediums — the radio.

Being imbued with a passionate dislike of anything which is even faintly spurious or 'arty', Astaire will probably resent being characterized as a choreographer of the dance, or of the dance in relation to the camera angle: for one reason, because of the slightly highbrow ring of the word 'choreographer'; for another, because he does not like to believe that he applies that kind of technical approach to his work. He will admit freely that he plans all his own dance routines, thinks them through first in the mind, sometimes even charts them on paper or on the blackboard, and then works them out with his 'own two feet'. He will acknowledge that he has definite theories about the way a dance should be 'shot' in the movies and that he plans all his own camera angles. But try to make him concede that in this 'planning' there is any deliberate application of a studied technique and he will shy away from the suggestion. Like so many people who have thought most about the problems of the actor or the dancer (those who really know the most about technique because they know how to apply it) Astaire is inclined to scorn the thought that technique is anything more than 'a sort of instinctive knowledge derived from years of experience'. He dislikes shackling his technique with words as much as he objects to talking about himself — qualities which make him both the bane of the RKO publicity department and an extremely agreeable subject for an interview. For when you examine his rather hesitant and reluctant replies to inquiries about his work, you discover that it is not difficult to read into his remarks certain conclusions about how the singing actor-dancer, who is his own choreographer, and a resourceful technician, applies the very technique he would like to disavow.

One reason why an artist finds it difficult to analyze his technique is that, by the time he has reached the point in his career where anyone is interested in the analysis, the technique is already second nature. It has saturated his being for so long that its application is a mystery to him. A brief résumé of Astaire's career should illustrate, better than any argument, the fundamental reason why his technique is to him (as to the Lunts) a practically subconscious asset.

Astaire started dancing in public performance at the age of five and he has been dancing ever since. At his birth, the proverbial gold spoon was strongly in evidence, not in worldly assets, but in the presence in the household of his sister, Adele, who was to become a perfect foil for him, both as comedian and dancer, in a twenty-five-year partnership. The two kids danced whenever and wherever they could, and a professional New York debut in vaudeville was the reward, when Fred Astaire was only twelve. There they ran into the child-labor laws and were forced to bow out of the act. For four more years (discouraging years to the dancers who were already professionals in all but name), they had to seek engagements elsewhere. But, in 1916, they were judged sufficiently mature to tour the United States and Canada, again in vaudeville, and the next year — Astaire was then seventeen — they appeared as full-fledged professionals in New York, to be acclaimed as the most talented youngsters who had yet graced the vaudeville stage. The following season, they danced their way into the hearts of the audience in that patriotic medley, *Over the Top*, and then for two seasons whirled through the mazes of *The Passing Show* (runway and all) at the Winter Garden. There followed a long succession of musical comedies and revues — in New York, on the road, in London and the English provinces: *Apple Blossoms*, *For Goodness' Sake*, *The Bunch and Judy*, *Lady Be Good*, *Funny Face*, *The Band Wagon*.

Then the brother and sister act was dissolved (by marriage), and Astaire had to look for a new partner. Although the ardent admirers of the Astaires believed that he could never find an associate who suited and graced his style of dancing as well as Adele Astaire — especially in the delightful, rough-and-tumble 'run-arounds' they used to do in almost every show — Astaire found in Claire Luce a partner who, under his astute guidance, danced gracefully and pleasingly through *Gay Divorcée* for a season in New York and another in London. Then came the 'Hollywood offer', and the rest (except insofar as his own comments are illuminating) is too well-known to bear repeating.

Astaire, according to his own estimate, was 'probably the most surprised person in the world' to find that he 'clicked' as a dancer in the movies. It never occurred to him that any dancing he might do on the silver screen would be more than incidental to a picture. It was strictly as an actor, or comedian, that he hoped to romp through the golden gates of movieland, retaining enough compensation on the way out to guarantee more security than the stage could afford when he became too old to dance eight times a week. Most of the dancing he had seen in motion pictures had not seemed to have any great authority as art or entertainment. Perhaps the flat surface of the screen robbed the dance of any three-dimensional quality. Perhaps the lack of personal contact with an audience destroyed an emotional vigor essential in dancing. It was with some reluctance that he essayed his first dance in the new medium (with Joan Crawford in *Dancing Lady*) and it was not until he saw the previews of the 'Carioca' (his first big dance number with Ginger Rogers in *Flying Down to Rio*) that he was willing to admit to himself that dancing might project as well on the screen as on the stage. Oddly enough, he reached this decision not because he liked the 'Carioca' as a dance. He did not like it; but the fact that it undoubtedly 'went over', that the audience enjoyed a routine which was, in his opinion, only fair, stimulated him to say to himself, 'If they think that's good, surely I can do something better than that.' Dancing could, after all, be made to project as effectively in black and white shadows as in the flesh.

Three years of dancing on the screen — *Gay Divorcée, Roberta, Top Hat, Follow the Fleet, Swing Time* and, now, *Shall We Dance* — have forced Astaire to the somewhat reluctant conclusion that his dances are even more persuasive on the screen than on the stage. 'From my own observation, I know that some of the same steps that people never even noticed on the stage are phenomenal on the screen, and any number of people tell me that they get twice as much kick out of my dancing in the movies as they ever did in the theatre.'

Astaire, at one moment, professes ignorance of the cause of this phenomenon. In the next, he tries to find an explanation for it — and out of his explanation emerges (perhaps unwittingly) the clue to his success in the motion picture medium — the very simple method, in short, which he evolved to make the dance register photographically.

'In the old days', he says, 'they used to cut up all the dances on the screen. In the middle of a sequence, they would show you a close-up of the actor's face, or of his feet, insert trick angles taken from the floor, the ceiling, through lattice work or a maze of fancy shadows. The result was that the dance had no continuity. The audience was far more conscious of the camera than of the dance. And no matter how effective the trick angles and cock-eyed shots might have been in themselves, they destroyed the flow of the dance — a factor which is just as important on the screen as on the stage.

'I have always tried to run a dance straight in the movies, keeping the full figure of the dancer, or dancers, in view and retaining the flow of the movement intact. In every kind of dancing, even tap, the movement of the upper part of the body is as important as that of the legs. Keeping the whole body always in action before the camera, there are certain obvious advantages that the screen has over the stage. You can concentrate your action on the dancer; the audience can follow intricate steps that were all but lost behind the footlights, and each person in the audience sees the dance from the same perspective. In consequence, I think that the audience can get a bigger reaction watching a dance on the screen than behind a fixed proscenium arch — probably because they get a larger, clearer and better-focused view, and so derive a larger emotional response.'

Chorus numbers, Astaire believes, should be used sparingly. Shots which show a thousand girls pirouetting, or in military formation, are meaningless because there is no individual audience reaction to that type of dance. 'Chorus numbers should be used only when you have a definite idea of something for the chorus to do which will heighten the whole dance number. On the stage, you can bring them close to the audience and get a visible emotional reaction. In the movies, the chorus should be used largely as background, because you cannot recreate that same kind of reaction. By the time you line up thirty girls in the forefront of a screen, they are so small that their individuality is lost.' Even in the more enlightened movie studios there still exists the feeling that the fans demand one flashy number, with lots of girls, in every first-class musical film. Astaire disagrees with this theory.

In planning out the angles from which to 'shoot' the dance, Astaire is always guided by the principle that the audience should never be aware of the camera.

He places it at approximately eye-level and lets it shoot the dance as 'straight on' as possible. Usually, he shoots a sequence with three cameras, working simultaneously. The 'A' camera is allotted the position he thinks will be best, the 'B' and 'C' cameras are placed at either side of it. Each 'take' is thus recorded, in entirety, on three rolls of film. When the 'rushes' are viewed the best shot is selected for use in the finished film.

'The "B" rush, taken a little from one side', says Astaire, 'sometimes has a more interesting composition than the direct shot. One shot may be more alive than the next. It is almost impossible to be sure which recording will be the most satisfactory; the eye of the camera is so entirely different from the human eye. It can look at you from different angles, follow you without altering the perspective. If possible, one "take" will be used for the whole dance. If, however, the "B" take is much better in one sequence while the "A" is better in another, the best sequences are pieced together, but the sequence of the dance itself is never broken. The audience may be conscious of a change of angle, but it will never be conscious that the flow of the dance has been interrupted.'

Astaire plans his dances for the screen in the same manner he used for the stage. 'On the stage you are bound by the limits of a 40-foot proscenium arch, whereas in the pictures you have a little more scope, though not much more, as the dance should not wander all over the lot. What the first approach is, is almost impossible to tell. Often the story, the character or a piece of music will be the inspiration for a dance routine. Sometimes the conception will come right out of the blue. You get an idea that it would be swell to do a dance on roller skates, or to your own shadow. When this happens, you have to fit your idea into the book, or, perhaps, even build the book around the idea. For instance, I had the idea for the *Top Hat* dance long before the picture was even planned. The picture, even its title, grew out of that idea.' Generally speaking, however, the book is planned first, and the dances are then built around or fitted into the framework.

This 'fitting' process may vary with each dance, but usually the next step — 'an all-important one' — is to have the music written. 'I find that I have to have music that will give my idea some inspiration before I start working out the actual steps. If the music is bad, I am completely stumped. I can't do anything.' Once the music is written, Astaire begins to devise the pattern of the dance. He experiments a great deal with the steps, always remembering that each dance has to be *something new*, as well as something good.

'Working out the actual steps', Astaire says, 'is a very complicated process — something like writing music. You have to think of some step that flows into the next one, and the whole dance must have an integrated pattern. If the dance is right, there shouldn't be a single superfluous movement. It should build to a climax and stop!' As already noted, Astaire works out his own steps and those of his partner. In pictures, he usually leaves the chorus routines to the supervision of the dance director, unless the dancing of the chorus has an important bearing on his own work, in which case he will outline routines for the girls and tell the dance director what he wants. Also, the floor space available for the dance is such a vital part of the routine that Astaire tells the director ahead of time exactly how much space he will need for each dance.

Astaire will often work for weeks on a routine to get it perfected before he even tries it out in rehearsal. He will rehearse it as long as necessary — the length of time depends on the dance — and, once he starts to shoot, he will keep on shooting until it is right. The average dance is recorded on film from six to ten times — each time in its entirety. But if there is something very difficult — physically or technically — about the routine, they may shoot the sequence as many as twenty times before a 'take' is selected. The roller-skating sequence in *Shall We Dance*, for example, was shot almost thirty times.

'Planning the pattern is not all there is to a number by any means. Once it is planned in the rough, you have to know how to start and end it. This may appear to be a simple affair. Go into your sequence when the orchestra strikes up and stop when it finishes. But it is not as simple as that. It is extremely important for a dance cue to flow naturally in and out of the story. I think the audience always slumps — even more in the movies than on the stage — when they hear an obvious dance cue, and both the picture *and the dance* seem to lose some of their continuity. Each dance ought to spring somehow out of character or situation, otherwise it is simply a vaudeville act. Also, you have to be able to sense the moment when the audience reaches its peak of exhilaration and feels like applauding. Then it's over.'

Astaire does not believe that any straight dance routine should run for more than three minutes. 'I doubt if it could hold an audience longer than that.' How to decide, without an audience, when you have reached the 'natural ending' is unquestionably difficult. It is a matter of 'training, talent, ear — whatever you want to call it'.

Astaire tries, as far as possible, to record the sound right on the set, while the dance, or song, is being 'shot'. This might appear to be the only logical procedure, but it is different from that employed by most singers, or dancers. Usually the song is recorded first in the recording room, and is then played back on the set on a gramophone record, the singers matching the movement of their lips to the already-recorded song. With Astaire, the orchestration is recorded first (to avoid the expense of engaging a high-priced orchestra to wait for hours on the lot), and the singing or dance is done to a play-back, which later, on a separate sound track, is made a part of the film. The sound of the dancing — if there is any sound — is usually recorded on the set, too. But, occasionally, especially for an intricate tap, he will do the dance on the set without any sound recording and then dub in the steps in another room with a good floor, matching the sound exactly to the picture.

If you ask Astaire whether he prefers the movies to the theatre, whether he plans ever to return to the legitimate stage, he will parry your questions by saying that he likes working in pictures for several reasons: 'Even though it is hard work and the hours are very long, it is, in some respects, less of a grind than the theatre. You have your evenings free. The holidays are longer. And the salaries, unquestionably, are much higher than anything the stage could ever afford.'

If it seems a fairly safe assumption that he will not return to the theatre, it is equally safe to say that he would not continue to dance for the motion pictures — no matter how great the largess was — if he did not feel that he was doing good work in that medium. For you have only to watch Astaire at work to realize how great his artistic integrity is. He refuses to do bad work, of any kind, before the public. He is never satisfied that he has done his best before the cameras. Always he is convinced that 'just one more shot' would be better than the last one. He is a prodigious worker and he cannot tolerate sloppiness. A scene — straight or dance — can never be just good enough. It must be exactly right. In one of his recent radio broadcasts, he slipped up in a tap-dance routine. He 'covered' the slip instantly, so that no one who either saw or heard the program realized the error. But he was miserable for days and could talk of nothing else at the studio. So many young dancers all over the country, he said, were listening. It was awful to disappoint them with a shoddy performance.

Emphatically, he does not subscribe to the belief — held by some theatre people — that it is unnecessary to act to be successful in the movies. 'You might get by in one picture on personality plus, but not more than one.' The technique of movie acting is different from stage technique. The camera can detect the ham and magnify it much more quickly than the naked eye. Most stage actors find that they have to 'tone down' their performances in front of the camera as it tends to exaggerate expression and gesture. Astaire, however, has always been inclined to work 'somewhat on the under-playing side'. As a result he did not have to alter his technique very much.

'It's a different kind of acting. You don't have to sustain a scene or carry a performance for two hours, as you do in the theatre no matter how you feel, but it's very difficult to shoot out of sequence and to match the long and close-up shots. It may be a more mechanical technique, but you have to act. Don't fool yourself about that.'

The audience, in the theatre, had been so 'absolutely vital' to Astaire — rehearsals, when he played to 'thin air', were a nightmare to him — that he expected to miss it tremendously in the studios. Much to his surprise, he found that the lack of an audience 'didn't mean anything' to him. 'In the theatre, when you expect a laugh, or applause, and it fails to materialize, you almost die. In the studios, when you don't expect it, you don't miss it. You don't need an audience to show you how to time your speeches' (not after years of stage training, perhaps). 'And on the comedy lines, we get the laughs in rehearsals — from the director, technicians and others — which helps us to see what will go and what won't. When we play the scene, we never consciously wait for laughs, as you have to on the stage. If you wait for a laugh and it doesn't come when the picture is shown, it is awful. Whereas if the laughs do overlap and you lose some of the lines in consequence, that is a good thing. The same general thing is true about the dances. I would much rather have the audience feel that they had missed something than that they had had too much. And it's good box-office. They will come back again to see what they may have missed.'

Astaire feels that movie technique, so called, is a help, rather than a hindrance, to a dancer's future stage career. 'A good actor can cover a line he has missed on the stage. The dancer can cover a slip in the routine. But in the movies, the relentless eye of the camera catches any slip-up. On the other hand, you can take a scene over and over again in the movies until you have the supposedly perfect shot, so perhaps the two things balance.'

Stock questions — like: What is your favorite dance? What type of dancing do you prefer? What is the future of the dance? — put Astaire on the defensive. 'I have no favorite dance routines,' he says. 'I find that I usually like my most recent numbers the best.' He has a great attachment for many of the dances he did with Adele Astaire on the stage — especially the 'Run Around' and the 'Whoops' number in *The Band Wagon* — but, generally speaking, 'there is no one type of dancing that projects better than another, on stage or screen. It all depends on the dance and the dancer. Not every dancer's type lends itself to the screen. I am not sure what type does click, but I know that certain types don't — no matter how excellent they may be.'

On one general topic alone will Astaire expand with any degree of fluency: the most valuable training for a young dancer. 'The novice in dancing', he feels, 'should get the fundamental points first — he must know what to do with his hands, which are just as important as feet in dancing. Ballet training is very useful but should not be allowed to penetrate your style, unless you plan to restrict yourself solely to ballet dancing. The dancer should use what ballet can give for its value as a smoother-cut process, but it should not dominate his work. First and foremost, any young dancer should realize that it is as an *individual* that he will make his success. You cannot teach dancing, as you can teach singing or music. You can teach only the abc's; the dancer himself has to do the rest. And if he doesn't, no matter how technically proficient he may be, he will have no character as a dancer. If the greatest dancer in the world has no stage personality, I defy him to get across! For the movies, a dancer should be able to act as well as dance. Otherwise, his field is strictly limited. And, even on the stage, the dancer who cannot act has little opportunity except in specialty numbers — which narrows his opportunities enormously.'

From the thousands of fan-mail letters Astaire receives, those that worry him most are those asking for advice, couched, often, in the general phraseology: 'You got all the breaks. Now tell me how to do it.' He would willingly disclose the secrets of success if he could. He would like, above everything else, to be able to give good advice to young dancers. 'But what can I tell them? My own training was this: I went through ballet school when I was a very little kid — then I taught myself the rest, by doing exercises and by dancing and acting anywhere and any time I could get a chance. It was only by going through dismal disappointments for twenty-odd years, by working in vaudeville, night clubs, anywhere I could, and by learning to dance, that I ever got ahead. I don't know *how* you do it. But I do know that unless the young dancer is willing to take an awful lot of set-backs, he's never going to get any recognition.'

57 The singing actress attacks her part: Lotte Lehmann

Morton Eustis

April 1937

Richard Strauss's favourite soprano, Lotte Lehmann (1888–1976), created the Composer in the revised *Ariadne auf Naxos* (1916), the Dyer's Wife in *Die Frau ohne Schatten* (1919), and Christine in *Intermezzo* (1924) and *Arabella* (1933). In *Der Rosenkavalier* she began as Octavian and matured into a wise and witty Marschallin. With age, she also took on Wagnerian roles such as Sieglinde and Eva, and was esteemed the ideal Fidelio of her generation. As skilled an actress as she was a singer, she lent warmth and charm to every role she inhabited.

She fled the Nazis to the U.S., where she sang in concerts and gave master classes.

THE APPROACH to a new part in opera is a highly individual problem for each singer. The obvious approach is, of course, through the music, and most singers focus their attention first upon the music as the only real clue to the dramatic action.

This is in direct contrast to the method of approaching a song, however. In studying a song I never begin with the music, but first consider the text, to which the accompaniment is, in the beginning, of secondary importance. I build up my songs from their actual foundations — the words — my interpretations flowing always from a deep sense of the poetry in the music. It is this poetry which inspires the composer to build up the wondrous interweaving of speech and melody that is a song; it is this poetry which inspires him to interpret the verse in his music and to create a harmonious entity. To many singers the poetry will necessarily seem secondary until it is recreated through union with the music, and thus expressed more clearly and more meaningfully to all the senses. But to me the actual sound of the words is all-important; I feel always that the words complete the music and must never be swallowed up in it. The music is the shining path over which the poet travels to bring his song to the world.

For an operatic part, on the other hand, I always start with the score as a foundation for the interpretation. Only from a study of the score can there come a true emotional understanding of the dramatic action of the opera, and it is only after I am thoroughly familiar with the music that I immerse myself in the libretto, to study my role from its purely dramatic aspect in order to judge whether I am suited to it.

The singing actress must always find the clue to a character in opera for herself. A stage director can help her, to be sure, but the greatest stage director, the one whom one follows as a final authority, is the music. The singer who approaches his part, looking on the music as of secondary importance, as though he were approaching a play instead of a music-drama, is not only a bad musician but a bad operatic artist. In the true artist there is an inherent inner capacity to sense musical and dramatic values simultaneously, and without this sixth sense the opera singer will never be able to give a convincing portrayal, no matter how much study is put into a role.

The singer who is creating an operatic part is naturally less free than the dramatic actor. He is, to some extent, the slave of the music, and must follow it and adapt all his actions to it. I have sometimes envied the freedom of the stage actor, who has the opportunity of unrestrained surrender to the character he is portraying. But when I once confessed this to a great actress whom I admired, she answered: 'Good Gracious! — and I envy you, who have the mighty stream of music to carry you on, to release the underlying emotion, so that an inappropriate gesture or a falsity of mood is almost impossible.' On closer thought I realized how true this was. To the opera singer the music is the basis of all stage behavior, a fine restraining force, at the same time as it is the root of all character interpretation.

My own acting always stems from personal experience and a mental conception of what is true and beautiful in life. But when I am on the stage I forget self and audience, everything but the role I am playing and the music I am singing. For only when heart and mind fuse into perfect union can one produce a characterization of poetic vitality and basic truth.

The most rewarding parts I have played in opera have been those in which I could express a really vital, human quality, while still retaining a correct singing style. A pure singing role, however, whose ultimate success lies only in a correct vocal and technical approach and not in the living character, has never interested me. The parts I have enjoyed the most have been the Marschallin in *Rosenkavalier*, Leonora in *Fidelio*, Elisabeth in *Tannhäuser* and Sieglinde in *Die Walküre*, roles of varied type; I should be sorry indeed to be limited to Wagnerian parts.

The Wagnerian singer must, of course, suit her mood and action to the nobility and flow of the music, which dictates this action. In a Strauss role, however, the singing actress must act her part freely and with seeming inattention to the restrictions of the music. That is, perhaps, why Christine in Strauss' *Intermezzo* was, for me, the most difficult role to prepare and sing. I did the premiere in Dresden, where Strauss himself was present at all the rehearsals and made very clear to me the manner in which he wanted the role to be treated. He wanted a new vocal style, half speaking and half singing, and emphasized that, although he had written exact notes for the part, he wished me rather to build up my own interpretation than to adhere too meticulously to these notes. As Christine I played the part of a shrew (incidentally a caricature of a composer's wife); in her scolding and tempestuous moods I was required to be fully cognizant of the music and yet to subordinate it entirely to the action and speech. I found it very difficult to acquire this technique, but Strauss was pleased with the results. Probably the reason this role has never become popular in Europe is because its new singing style is completely foreign to the usual opera technique.

To sing the Marschallin in *Rosenkavalier* on one night, striving for a mellow, understanding characterization, and on the next night to sing the youthful, passionate Leonora in *Fidelio* is to exercise one's full range of emotions. It is continual exercise of this sort from which the singing actress and her audience benefit, the actress acquiring new means of expressing music and drama, and affording new satisfaction to the audience.

In every detail of performance a singing actress is dependent on the singers who play opposite her. I have never understood the star who enjoys playing with a mediocre cast in order to shine out the more brilliantly himself, for the essence of any fine dramatic or operatic production is harmonious integration of all performances. Alfred Jerger, with whom I sang in Strauss's *Intermezzo* and *Arabella*, and the unforgettable Richard Mayr, furnished perfect complements to my acting efforts, I found. I will never forget our *Rosenkavalier* rehearsals in which Mayr, playing the part of Baron Ochs, struck the keynote of the whole performance for me in his vivid characterization. Stage association with other inspiring actors is a stimulation for one's own performance that cannot be measured. The final integration of the work of one actor with another comes, of course, through the stage director.

We have come to realize the close integration between all aspects of opera, to know that neither music nor action, nor staging, is sufficient unto itself, or unto an operatic production as a whole. A practical and effective stage director will not attempt to force his ideas on an actress, nor will a sensitive interpreter persist in a portrayal which does not jibe with the rest of the production. There must always be give and take between stage director and singing actor or actress, to bring two dissimilar interpretations into a satisfactory dramatic balance. Most conductors concern themselves solely with the music, but there are exceptions. Toscanini and Bruno Walter, for example, have an eye for the stage as well as the music, and with such men as these one hardly needs a regisseur.

I shall always remember with gratitude the man to whom I owe the original decision to attempt *Fidelio*. It was on the occasion of the Beethoven Centenary in 1926 that Franz Schalk inspired me to try this. I trusted his friendly advice and can never forget his interpretation of this noblest of all operas, his humble, wholly forgetful musicianship, and — I may rightly be proud to say it — his joy in my Leonora. I have since sung the role under various conductors, but I shall always remember most fondly Franz Schalk to whom I owe Leonora, Bruno Walter who led me to a deeper conception of the part, and Arturo Toscanini who raised me above myself with his strong, suggestive will. Schalk, if he liked a voice very much, was apt to forget in his enthusiasm that there are limits to a singer's powers. Walter, on the contrary, was careful always to eliminate the element of strain. His deep understanding and great sympathy for the singer are perhaps not to be equaled. The artist is continually protected by his consideration, and technical difficulties of singing and nervous inhibitions alike are easily overcome under such a conductor. When first I sang opera under the inexorable Toscanini I was a little apprehensive. One hears everywhere of Toscanini's inspiring rehearsals, but also a good deal about his lack of consideration. I had even heard that he required ten hours a day of singing with full voice. (My hair stood on end at this thought.) Actually Toscanini was full of consideration, always advising us to save our voices when, under the spell of his magic, we spent ourselves too lavishly. One thing, to be sure, he demanded: concentration — unconditional devotion to the task in hand and complete, perfect understanding of its scope. But no true artist could possibly remain passive in the presence of this passionate, almost fanatic will. Toscanini knows no concessions, he despises all incompetence, and where Walter overcame difficulties with understanding and sympathy, it was Toscanini's glowing will that wrought perfection. It is an overpowering force that would impel one to follow him even if the Maestro's own selfless devotion to his work did not immediately rule out anything but uninterrupted concentration on the part of the musicians under him.

It may be of interest to the reader to know something of the rehearsal procedure for a new opera. After thoroughly studying the libretto and music by himself the singer has several rehearsals with the co-repetitor. It is the co-repetitor who assists the conductor at all rehearsals and often conducts the singers from the prompt-box at a performance, so that the conductor can give more attention to the orchestra. When he has thoroughly mastered the part, the singer goes over it with the conductor at the piano for several rehearsals. Then follow more rehearsals with the other singers, but without chorus. These rehearsals take place on the stage with the co-repetitor at the piano and under the direction of the regisseur. During stage rehearsals the regisseur makes constant suggestions, since he sees the stage as a whole, which of course the singer is not able to do. The regisseur is, as it were, the mirror in which the unified production is reflected. Next come rehearsals with chorus, and, finally, with the orchestra. It is important to note that there is never a rehearsal without music, and that the action is never disassociated from the musical background.

The physical means of projecting a characterization in opera — the gesture and movement — are, of course, affected not only by the scale of the music but (just as a dramatic performance would be) by the scenic production and the size of the stage and auditorium.

Where there may be three or twenty-three theatres in a large city, there is rarely more than one opera house. The opera auditorium must, therefore, be large enough to accommodate a goodly audience at one time. Then, too, where the theatre stage may be intimately proportioned for drawing-room comedy with a small cast of characters, operatic stages must be large enough to accommodate huge choruses.

Wagner was the first composer to take the size of the opera house into consideration and to write operas of broad universal theme which the sweeping and elemental gesture (which the size of the open house demands) is far more suited than is the minute and intimate gesture of the small stage. Perhaps the reason that the public recognizes a tradition of convincing operatic acting in the Wagner operas because of their very adaptability to the large operatic stage. The old Italian and French operas, on the other hand, with their small scale action, have had to be over-acted on the big opera stages, in order to be projected across the footlights at all; and so an audience, accustomed to fine nuances of acting on the legitimate stage, is often apt to think of the opera singer as over-playing his role.

Dr. Herbert Graf's Philadelphia production of *Der Rosenkavalier* two years ago, in which the stage was cut down to proportions suitable to the action of the boudoir and tavern scenes, which are on small comedy scale, enabled the opera actors to play the opera with a new respect for its subtle comedy values. The reverse problem presented itself to Dr. Graf at Salzburg this past summer, however. There it was found necessary to enlarge a very small opera stage. Dr. Graf did an extraordinary job with the tiny Salzburg Festival stage in putting on the mob scene and the final festival scene in *Die Meistersinger*. In each case he had two-hundred-and-twenty-five people on a tiny stage, and, since he could not fit them gracefully on one level, he built up various levels, accommodating three times as many people as would have been possible otherwise.

Whatever questions of technique and problems of production may precede the operatic performance, it has been my own experience that in the instant of the actual singing of an opera role we are apt to forget all technicalities. When I am giving myself over completely to any part, I do not have time to analyze my approach or attack. I am afraid I play the part only as I know in my heart that it *must* be done unconsciously echoing Mephisto's advice to Faust in Goethe's illuminating lines:

> Grau, teuerer Freund, ist alle Theorie —
> Und grün des Lebens gold'ner Baum.

> (All theory, dear friend, is drab —
> And fresh the golden tree of life.)

58 Great roles reborn: Bette Davis tells Ramon Romero how Regina, the Old Maid and Miss Moffat came to the screen

Ramon Romero

March 1947

Typically, when Hollywood studios purchased a Broadway hit as a "property", they seldom used the stage stars who had made it a hit. They preferred a tested box office certainty. Thus, Bette Davis was cast in roles originally created by Tallulah Bankhead, Helen Menken and Ethel Barrymore. The New England virgin Ruth Elizabeth Davis (1908–69) had had scant stage experience when she was contracted by Universal Studios in 1929. It was at Warner Brothers that she began to forge a real career, often by accepting or seeking out unsympathetic roles distasteful to glamorous stars. The venal waitress Mildred in *Of Human Bondage* (1934) and the spoiled Southern belle in *Jezebel* (1939) established her as a powerful actress. She then moved to sympathetic parts in romantic tear-jerkers such as *Dark Victory* (1939), *All This and Heaven Too* (1940) and *Now, Voyager* (1942). Her popularity was also enhanced when she founded the Hollywood Canteen, a nightclub for service men in 1942. However, at the time this article was written, her films were getting poor reviews and losing money; and in 1949 she was to break out as a freelance, revitalizing her career with *All About Eve* (1950).

Ramon Romero (1904–81) had begun as a screenwriter in the silent era, and continued to publish short stories. One of them, *Swan Song*, was dramatized by Ben Hecht and Charles MacArthur and appeared on Broadway in 1946. In 1953 he wrote the screenplay for *City Beneath the Sea*.

WHAT HAPPENS to a famous theatre role when it is reinterpreted by an actor for the screen has long been the subject of debate. Knowing that Bette Davis has recreated more famous Broadway characterizations for the camera than any other member of her craft (*Dark Victory, The Old Maid, The Man Who Came to Dinner, Watch on the Rhine, The Corn Is Green, The Little Foxes, Deception*) I went to her for the answer.

'The stage actor whose talent is expected to carry a performance straight through two and a half hours of a play to its climax is like the conductor of a musical trio. He must convey the composer's emotions and thoughts to a limited audience,' said Miss Davis. 'The motion-picture star portraying the same role for the screen becomes the conductor of a vast orchestra whose music is for the millions. Just as the arrangement for the trio, because of its fewer tones and less complicated blending of melody, may be truer to the composer's original concept so the stage actor's portrayal, confined to a narrower compass of sustained interest, usually adheres more closely to the playwright's intention and construction. The screen actor, on the other hand, sometimes finds it necessary to enlarge upon the mood and the coloring of the role.'

Seldom does a musical composition or a play progress verbatim from the originator's brain to public exhibition. Unless he be a ventriloquist's dummy, the interpreter as an artist in his own right must express his talents too in an individual style.

Inseparable from the magic of making make-believe believable, whether on stage or screen, is the ever-present problem of adjusting the mechanics of acting to the mechanism of the medium itself. Miss Davis has no illusions about the fact that in these days of scientific marvels the actor's life is bound up with steel and iron, aluminum and tin, bolts and screws. Whatever honors there are must be shared with inanimate partners like a theatre curtain, a lighting switch-board, a camera more merciless than the severest critic and a microphone that makes no compromise with an off-key voice.

Since Bette Davis has scored top honors in the films and on the radio networks and garnered a backlog of experience that includes a brief career in summer stock and on Broadway, it is reasonable to assume that this two-time winner of Hollywood's coveted Academy Award knows whereof she speaks.

'In which medium do you find it easiest to express yourself as an actress?' was a natural question.

'The medium in which I happen to be working at the time,' she answered. 'If I am repeating a role on the air which I have already played on the screen I don't attempt to give merely a carbon-copy performance. I start from scratch. I make it my business to find out how I can get the best results technically with the machinery which carries my radio playing into the ether and on into homes. Once I have solved this and know how to use the tools I can throw myself into the part wholeheartedly. After I've accepted the stark fact that my listeners, sitting impatiently with their fingers on the dials, must visualize what I look like, how I am dressed, my minutest facial expression, all in their imagination, it becomes logical that what was all right for the camera won't do for the radio microphone. Like a magician who brings a rabbit from nowhere out of his hat, I must hold the attention with my voice alone, and a sixth sense of timing. That is radio, at least until television supplants it.

'When I did *Jezebel* for one of the big networks,' she continued, 'I got only lukewarm results with the same part which had won me an Academy Oscar. It obviously was not the ideal radio role. It failed to surmount the test of being transplanted into another form of dramatization, just exactly as some plants will not grow in alien soil. Dialogue and sound were not enough to give reality and scope to a story that cried for visual action and emotion.'

The reverse, she pointed out, could be true in the adaptation of a successful radio drama to the screen. What had been tense, exciting and ear-satisfying on the air-waves could become dull and static on film, like certain Broadway hit plays that have been transferred from footlights to celluloid. 'Very often a conscientious producer feels morally obligated to the public who have made a book or a play a success. He feels he must produce the Hollywood version with absolute fidelity to the original as insurance against resentment from millions of potential movie-goers and also to appease those critics who still accuse the movie studios of wrecking every fine book or play which falls into their hands.

'There is no law about this,' she insisted. 'Personally, I'm for as few changes as possible, but in the final analysis it depends on the elasticity and adaptability of the material. This is especially true in what I call one-dimensional plays. There are many plays which can be told without effort or strain in one setting but there are also a good many which have obviously been cramped into a single set because of economic pressure. These are the plays which best lend themselves to the expansive range of the camera. Retold in the language of motion pictures they seem to grow up and acquire a new dimension, so that very often a play which has been damned in New York will emerge from Hollywood a sensational success.'

This recalled *Dark Victory*, for which Miss Davis won her first Academy Award, and in which Tallulah Bankhead had starred on Broadway. As a play it had got a bad press and a brief run, yet the Hollywood play doctors, taking only the basic theme and plot outline, had managed to carve from it a distinguished and moving portrait of a doomed woman.

Another Bankhead role which Miss Davis played on the screen was Lillian Hellman's *The Little Foxes*. 'Lillian Hellman is a great writer,' Miss Davis declared. 'No matter for which medium she is writing, her material is successful because her characters have meat and bite and a reason for being. It is when studios attempt to change and distort plays like hers that my blood pressure goes up, and I battle for the original lines and situations.

'I thought *The Little Foxes* as a play was far better than the picture,' Miss Davis went on. 'It remained always true to Miss Hellman's conception and Miss Bankhead's characterization of Regina Giddens is unequalled. It made no concessions to sympathy, Legions of Decency or accounting departments. It was a flesh-and-blood realization of what Miss Hellman had written.'

The Davis enthusiasm for the Hellman mind was further shown in her acceptance of the comparatively minor role of the wife in *Watch on the Rhine*. 'I played Sara Muller because I believed *Watch on the Rhine* had something important to say at a time when it could do the most good.'

In the course of her career Bette Davis has recreated roles on the screen first performed on the stage by such gilt-edged Broadway names as Katharine Cornell, Lynn Fontanne, Jane Cowl, Tallulah Bankhead, Ethel Barrymore, Helen Menken and Mady Christians.

'Aren't you stirred each time by the challenge,' I asked, 'to make your picture equal to if not better than their plays?'

'It would be stupid egotism for me or anyone else to challenge the individual creation of any great artist,' she retorted in the brittle Davis manner, 'particularly when, as my predecessors in the same roles, these actresses established inimitable standards of their own.'

Only in rare instances, she remarked, has she ever seen an original production in which she was later to star on the screen. Occasionally she has caught a road production with the original company and star but she prefers to see the play after the picture has been finished.

'I'm convinced I can do a better job if I study the play itself rather than the work of the actress. I don't like to get preconceived ideas on how a part should be played until I've made a thorough breakdown of the final shooting script. What Miss Cornell or Miss Barrymore might make effective with their backs turned to an audience, I might have to do in pantomime, in a closeup, with my face full in the camera. There is always the camera to consider. That is the deciding factor.'

She remembered how, when she was a stage struck youngster in Boston, she had gone wide-eyed and worshipful to see Katharine Cornell in *The Letter*. Then her great dream had been to conquer Broadway. She wanted to get up on a stage and play that part just as Cornell was playing it. But when, years later, she was ready to portray Leslie Crosby in the second film version of *The Letter* she could barely remember the details of what Cornell had done with the part. Her Leslie Crosby was as much Somerset Maugham's as Cornell's had been; but Davis, like the conductor of a symphony, had played her own arrangement.

Miss Davis frankly admits that she enjoys working with stage actors, and whenever possible likes to have members of the original cast in her pictures. She is grateful for the opportunity of having worked with the late George Arliss; with the beloved Leslie Howard in *The Petrified Forest* and *Of Human Bondage*; with Paul Muni in *Juarez*, playing the Clare Eames role of Carlotta; and twice with Miriam Hopkins in *The Old Maid* and *Old Acquaintance*. Now she appears with Claude Rains in her latest release, *Deception*, from the play, *Jealousy*.

Of late she has had a hankering to get back to Broadway. Not since she played the ingenue in *Broken Dishes* and was shipped off to Hollywood on a Universal contract has she set foot on a stage. That has been almost seventeen years. She admits that she has not regretted a minute of the time she has been locked up in the film box. She also admits that the prospect of facing audiences and critics across the footlights frightens her. But when the time is ripe to do a play she knows she would be a coward if she didn't seize it.

If she goes to Broadway, however, it is certain she will not be the great Hollywood star lending her glamorous name to a stage production, but an actress in a play, giving her best to her part. She has said that no one is so big he cannot be replaced. Perhaps it is this attitude that gives her such zest, enthusiasm and desire to attack each new role as though it were her first big opportunity. Perhaps this is what has earned her, in more ways than one, the right to be called Hollywood's most 'legitimate' actress.

Part VI
Technical matters

59 The voice in the theatre

Stark Young

October 1921

In the pre-microphone age, an actor's voice was a vital tool of his profession
and Young had a keen ear for the spoken word. While a graduate student at Yale
(1901–2), under the theatre critic Brander Mathews, he had regularly attended
theatre in New York and New Haven. He had the opportunity to see the American
stars the Barrymores, Maude Adams, John Drew, Otis Skinner, E. H. Sothern and
Julia Marlowe, as well as such foreign visitors as Eleonora Duse and Mrs Patrick
Campbell. These experiences seasoned him as a spectator and gave him a wide
variety of examples to draw on.

IF the psychology of our day has stressed anything it is the fact that the life of the
mind rests on historically ancient processes, on the constituted matter of the
universe. That is to say we are grown out of and into Nature; we are a part of
its texture, of its tissue even; and what we call ourselves is only the little conscious
point at which we connect with the whole; and through which we enter on a
conception of the whole. The life of the mind has the same relation to Nature as
the fragrance of a flower has to the earth; our consciousness is the light fragrance
of a flower, but this fragrance is the odor of reality. It is only through all this
accumulated history that is in us, the remembering organisms, the unforgetting
cells and growths, that we share in the life of the world. And only through the
exploitation and use of this sharing can we express for the rest of the whole the
living part of it that we are.

That is to say that art depends first of all on the life of the body, that body
which is at the same time the ancient storehouse of the forms and pulses and
directions of a whole; and yet is its feeling organ, its every moment's intimate
perceiving. In the art of the theatre, then, to throw away such an avenue as is the
sense of sound is shortsighted and suicidal. It is a way of limiting the expression of
life, of forgetting the necessary earth, of telling lies. And in our theatre it is a fact
that sound is almost a forgotten thing. The voice is used in our theatre almost
entirely as an articulate medium. But a part of every truth is its inarticulateness;
all the half-conscious elements, delicate implications, the radiant and shadowy
emanations, that make up every human truth and that words can never express.
And sound itself has significance. The articulate meaning of the word *pain* is a
symbolistic accident; the sound of it goes vaguely but farther in. Regardless of
word-concepts the mere voice is another medium to express the ancient and
imminent life that lives itself in us.

Everyone knows the part a dramatist's sound takes in his complete effect. Shakespeare obviously is always recognized first of all by the ear. Very much of Galsworthy's failure to convince me, I think, lies in the abandoned drought of his music. And I believe that one of the obstacles in Ibsen's progress with us, something that makes his work seem dry and dutiful and Euclidian, is the sterile sound of the acting translation; a humble ear would take Mrs. Alving for Madam President calling the ladies to order and stating her case for their consideration. And every actor has his own sound, his voice. And every country's theatre has its own quality of voice.

The horrors of the American voice spread to our stage, naturally. I listen in the New York theatre for a beautiful voice, for a fine voice, an expressive voice. I do not often find it, not often, sometimes, yes. I listen for a sense of style in the use of the voice. I find that even less often. A sense of style in the voice would mean a constant variation of the quality to suit the kind of play it carries or the mood. In a comedy of manners like *The School for Scandal* the voice would be clear, finished, the lips expert, the tongue striking well on the teeth; the tone would go up and down but always be sure of its place in the throat, be crisp, shining, in hand, like the satin and gold of the furniture and costumes, the rapier at the wrist, the lace over it, the worldliness and the wit. In Chekhov it would have the last naturalness, every closeness to feeling and impulse that the moment reveals. In Shakespeare a range of elaborate music, suited to the style, a clearness, with a warmth of poetic emotion. In D'Annunzio's drama the voice would have to be rich and sensuous, metallic, shading infinitely, the voice of a degenerate god. And so on through the styles and moods of all drama.

Every language has its voice. Though it must be remembered that the voice is inextricably tied up with its language. We complain of the Italian singer's voice as "white"; but Italian is a "white" language. They complain of the German tone as "dark"; but German, and English too, are "dark" languages. Mimi Aguglia's voice, amazing in Italian, animal, pathetic, inexhaustible, becomes light and uninteresting when she speaks English. Ben-Ami is one of the few foreigners I have heard who can place exactly and naturally in English the tone they have always used. And Doris Keane is the only actor I have ever seen who could reproduce the Italian tone precisely in English. In a way the voice of a country's theatre, like the English or French or Italian, gets to be as definite perhaps as any actor's.

The characteristic of the American stage voice is, apart from bad enunciation, a tone driven through the nose, an inflexible upper lip, a very insecure placement in the throat, and a tendency to monotony. It has the distinction of being the worst voice on any stage in the world; and has very likely contributed no little to the success of the silent drama of the screen. And so we are always admiring the English voice. Often enough, as everybody knows, the quality is pleasanter in the English voice than in the American; that goes without saying. But I think that very much of its supposed excellence on the stage is really a matter of superior enunciation; it is pleasant to hear the English after too much of the Broadway language. The chief characteristic of the English male voice on the stage, however, is a kind of dry, balanced quality, the balance of a country house and the dry poise of the town club. It suits the comedy of manners admirably, and character parts. It has whimsicality, it has urbanity, the light touch. For tragedy on the elevated or very poignant scale it is a very poor voice indeed, despite the British claims. It has not enough bottom, its range is not wide and fluent enough; its resonance in the head is limited; it lacks mettle. It can be simple and quiet if it does not get too much of the breath in it and become prosaic. Most of all it lacks fine, virile roundness and volume. And all too often this voice betrays self-consciousness; an English tragic actor sometimes has a way of seeming infatuated with merely hearing himself speak. The women on the English stage have very often charming voices, suited to comedy, to romantic plays, or sentimental, and to noble or delicate tragedy; but not for great, passionate tragic moments. They have the English tendency toward affectation too often, especially in sounding the *s*, where an overhissing occurs, and not rarely in the silly Georgian lisp. And a sort of bellowing tone comes in also and is admired very frequently in these actresses, a tone that is large but a little hoarse, deep but not round, and used too much for its own sake. Moreover the English throat, in general, is not always free, and frequently gives a sort of choking effect. Too often the breath is heard rather than the tone, and the vowels are lost; or the sound is thrown against the roof of the mouth when it should vibrate the bones of the head. As in most other English things compared to the French or Italian, there is little sense of style in the English voice. Britons never will be slaves, and least of all in technical standards; and however pleasing, however fine, well-bred and even noble an English actor's voice may be, it is apt to be arbitrary, individual, and unfinished.

The French voice has style and training. Like most French things it has been made adequate for its own uses, as far as those uses go. In a burlesque it has all the musical resources of the jungle. In a drawing-room comedy it has every kind of variety and breeding. In witty farce the French voice is like the mind itself, leaping about over the furniture; it is clear, high, deep, brittle, inane, persuasive. But in one of their own tragedies like those of Racine the voice of an actor like Mounet Sully is complete as a noble orchestra; it has timbre, volume, melancholy flat tones, and a prolonged and even resonance never heard on English-speaking stages. Like Bernhardt's it is an artificial quality, very much finished, trained, electrified, charged with magnificent nervous power. In one respect only does the French voice fall far beneath what I have heard in Italian theatres: that is in the last accent of naturalistic tragedy.

The Italian voice is the most tragic of all, in the tragedy of the earth, the heart, the supreme rendering of a surface of life that reveals at the same time the inner content. There was something in Duse's voice that reminded you of Dante at his best; a trembling inevitability of effect, a passion of transparency above the life it expressed. There is no voice with a quality so immediate, so forlorn and irrevoc- able as the Italian. Not any voice so easily placed in the throat. The tone is open, it comes straight out, with no impediment or forcing down the throat or up against the nose. I remember when *The Bacchanals* was given in the Roman Theatre at Fiesole the voice of Agave, and when she said, "Addio, padre!" The uplifted hands of the chorus below her, the shadows of the columns on the stone, the fluttering of the leaves nearby, seemed all to serve that voice and to be summed up and expressed in it. It was the voice of the earth itself, over which she was to wander forever. It was a white voice, clear, exact, fatalistic, the voice of the animal and the soul. Only in styles that are more elaborate or artificial, whether in farce or comedy or tragedy, does the French voice surpass the Italian. But then only in elaboration and artifice. The Italian remains always more natural, more profound, more robust and subtle, more abundantly endowed, more easily resourceful.

It is, of course, a platitude in aesthetics of say that music is the most ideal of the arts. That music can be the thing itself where words can only be the concept of it or painting one selected phenomenon. In the light of this you may say that the tone an actor uses can move us more than any other thing about him; the word he speaks gives the concept, the gesture he makes exhibits a single phenomenon; but the voice may be anger itself or longing and go straight as music does to the same emotion in us. So that there is something strange and ironical in the realization of how much more our theatres—and our education for that matter—have cultivated the eye rather than the ear. We have all sorts of instructions about stage production, about light and its uses and diversities, about the effect of colors and their combinations. In Gordon Craig's design for *Electra* we have the idea of that door, high and fateful and unrevealing, the domination of visual proportion over our sense. Through a fine gift like Robert Edmond Jones' we have sometimes had light and color and line made as ideal almost and as abstract as music. But, after all, that is the realm of the visual, it is eye learning.

So that we may well recall what education the Greeks thought wise for the uses of their sons. Philosophy, rhetoric, oratory and recitation, and music, were the main branches of their endeavor. Sculpture and painting and architecture, those arts whose life is in the eye, they learned to know by seeing them and by the images arising from the perfecting of their bodies in the daily palestra. But often enough the philosophy that they learned, the history and poetry and logic, came through discourses and argument and reading aloud, and much of what they knew well they may never have seen in writing; they had received it in sound images instead of visual. The Greek ear was trained to hear the value of syllables and rhythm and cadence in speech, the modes of music and the quality of the voice in reading and singing. Through years of discipline and practice a Greek arrived at this perfection of exercise and perception.

In the Theatre of Dionysos the lighting was that of the sun; the scene was but slightly varied either through shifts or through light. The gestures were simple and restrained, as we may infer from the spirit and the style of the plays, and may be sure of from the difficulties that the costume, the onkos, the padding, and the high-soled cothurnus would have put in the way of animated motions. The expression of the mask remained unchanged, but it was made so as to serve as a resonator for the actor's voice. So that the larger part of the effect in the Greek theatre was due to the voices, trained as we train for the opera and exerted for a trained public taste. However beautiful the lines of those garments may have been, their grave and exquisite rhythms and their subtlety of color in the bright air, the blowing on them of the wind from the Bay of Salamis, it was the voices of the actors that achieved much of that effect of tragic beauty. The words of the dramatist were conveyed through the voice, animated by the beauty and variety of its music; and sometimes heightened further still by the music of pipes and strings that followed the voice, dilating further the poetic meaning, making it yet more poignant and unerring.

"Cynthius aurem vellit, et admonuit," Virgil wrote, when the god of poetry came to him; and Milton, translating, "Phoebus replied, and touched my trembling ears."

To all that antique world the ear was the seat of memory. And memory is half our life, and more than half of all beauty.

60 Illusion in acting

Stark Young

February 1924

Young's objection to working as a reviewer at the New York *Times* had been the daily grind, the need to come up with an immediate response to a show just seen, devote much of his column to plot summary and provide puff pieces. His preferred method, indulged at *Theatre Arts* and the *New Republic*, was to select a performance for review, see it several times if necessary, and mull over his impressions, before composing a well-considered essay. Not only could he convey the sense of the performance to a reader who had not attended it, but also he could illuminate those who had shared the experience, and perhaps the actors as well.

THE accident of the medium employed happens in the art of acting to be the cause of many confusions in the theories of the art; and of these the worst concerns illusion.

In the art of music nobody but the simplest creature expects the sound to deceive us by making us think it a storm, or pasture bells, a waterfall or anything whatever but music. Even if a piece of music is called The Storm most people know too much to demand that the stormy sounds be heard in it always or even from time to time. Almost anyone knows that a great composer might write a piece of music about Niagara Falls that would never in the least portray the falls; which in philosophic terms might be, as well as not, represented by the general theme of the individual's relation to the universe, or of time to eternity; and so have nothing whatever to do with water or slashing or roaring. In architecture everybody knows enough not to demand that a façade look like a forest or an ocean or a turtle or a hat or anything else in the visible world; everybody understands that music and architecture, and some few at least that painting and poetry, are purely themselves and complete in themselves.

But in the art of acting it happens that the medium employed is very close to the result achieved. The actor who plays Hamlet is a man with a body, a voice, a mind; and so is Hamlet. The man loves, hates, fears, dies, and so does Hamlet. The resemblance in this case between the medium and the art makes a perception of the nature of the art itself more difficult. And what this does for the average man is to lead him to assume that the business of acting is to duplicate something that he has seen. He sets himself up as judge, then, in what he takes to be a matter of imitation, reproduction, verisimilitude.

This whole point of view and assumption falls over its own feet at many turns. In the first place it assumes that there is some fixed aspect of things, that there is always some is-ness for everyone to see, if he can only see it; and this is by no means certain. It assumes, also, that the average man will know the perfect reproduction, the resemblance, the verisimilitude, when it arrives. But that does not hold either; for the average man does not know the color of his uncle's eyes, the tone of red roses in the moonlight, or even whether a cow's ears, though he has seen a thousand cows, are above or below the horns or where. And lastly it assumes reproduction as the final measure of approval and the final perfection in acting; and establishes for it the test of identity; the actor should not act the character, the actor should be the character. But obviously art is art, not life. The pleasure we get in art is not that it is the same thing as its subject but that it is different. We go to see the stars floating on the waves not because they are but because they are not the stars in the sky. The charm of art is not duplication but presence and absence, likeness and unlikeness. The truth of art lies not in reproduction but in idea.

The famous demand for illusion in acting, then, in the first place, makes no sense. It is refuted indeed by the mere mention of it, though it is mentioned or implied almost always when acting is discussed or a piece of it debated. When people coming away from the Moscow Art Theatre say that they can't believe that the actors are not the real characters there on the stage, Ivanoff, old Luka and Fyodor, they are either amiable in temper or confused in the head. If these players were the people they play we should not mention our belief at all.

This theory of acting, however, which demands illusion, is not in itself so bad, since art is art, not æsthetics. If people receive the experience to be conveyed by a work of art, if they respond to it, in sum, it is not so important what æsthetic or moral explanation they get up after the experience. If a man is in love it does not so much matter immediately what are the explanations and comments that he gets up about it. But in the end this explanation and theory does matter after all, because it affects the progress of his love and its movement toward perfection; it affects also the relation of this particular experience, this love, to the rest of his life and all life. And so the disaster about this business of illusion's being the end to be desired in acting arises from the fact that such a theory is harmful in two respects. It does not allow the artist to judge the distance from reality that he will choose to make when he sets about creation. And it leads the audience to judge a work of art by its subject-matter.

It ought to be obvious that an artist must be free to choose—always at his own peril—the degree of actuality that he wishes to preserve in his art. He can be as photographic or as conventional or abstract as he likes, always at his own risk. He may paint a tree as Gainsborough paints it, pushing natural masses toward the character of tapestry, or as Corot paints a tree, drowsy with vague mists and a dream of light, or as El Greco paints a tree, taking from it only those forms that may go up as lines and shadows in that ascending flame of his composition, or as Hokusai or some more ancient painter in China might do, seeking from the tree only a line, a pattern of nuance. It is not the distance from actuality that the tree painting must stand or fall by, but by itself, by the idea expressed in it. All of which means only that a work of art is complete in itself. You judge it first by its intention, its idea, and finally by the value or significance of this idea to you. And a work of art is art only in so far as it can be experienced as complete in itself; and—though it may gain in every way by its subject—the element of art in it exists only in so far as it is essentially free of its subject.

The illusion theory of acting blinds its followers to the very first thing necessary to know of it, which is that acting, in so far as it is an art at all, and not mere human material that remains human material and nothing else, is a language we must learn to read. In this respect it is precisely like music, painting or any other art. Not knowing this, people conclude, merely because of the closeness of the material to the result, that they can be at home with acting; and that they need for it only what they need in life generally, sharp eyes, feelings, memory and interest. To perceive acting they need to know men, places and events, of course, as a painter needs to know a tree when he sees one, or a dancer to know his legs from his arms. But what they are going by has little more relation to knowing acting as an art than knowing bricks from paper boxes has to architecture.

And so people will say, meaning to bestow a great compliment, that an actor playing a hobo is a hobo. If this were true, it would clearly be as good to see the hobo and never go to see the actor at all. People will say that when an actor in Hamlet dies you feel that he is dead. Clearly, it might be better to take these people and things as we find them in life, and to go to the theatre only to see events and people that we can see nowhere else, as we go to an aquarium to see the fish we cannot see in the pantry. But in that case we could not talk at all of illusion in the theatre; because, not being able otherwise to see these events and things, we could judge them only by what we see of them there on the stage. Obviously—too obviously—then, an actor is not the character he acts. And the lowest form of acting—not necessarily the worst performance of course—is mere impersonation, in so far as it tries exactly to copy the original person, which of course no good impersonator does. It is the same with the incident portrayed. What the actor does need not fool us by making us think that the thing is actually happening to him. And as for emotional illusion the point remains the same. In order to convey to us the emotion in its essential quality the actor must no doubt, if you insist, give us the effect of feeling it, otherwise the emotion is interfered with by a defect in the medium that expresses it. But this does not imply that we must be certain that the actor at the time feels the emotion, though it should not occur to our minds at the moment that he does not; all we need is that he give us the emotion free and pure in itself; the rest is his affair. All we can ask of the actor is that he has discovered what the emotion is and the means to convey it to us. The significant actor, like any artist in any art, uses as much actual, photographic reality and reproduction as he requires. He uses the illusion of being the character, duplicating externals, feeling the emotions, undergoing the incident, exactly as a painter uses natural objects or men. The art of acting owing to the nature of its material may use this duplication or reproduction more often than the other arts, but the principle of its use is the same.

What the actor gives us is a reality and no illusion. It is truth, not lies. He creates, embodies, isolates his idea; but he depends ultimately on no deception.

He gives us an essential, the idea, the characteristic, the personage, the point, as related to itself and to life outside itself. He can simulate and counterfeit externals, but only in order to give us his truth; which does not stand or fall by the extent to which we are fooled into believing it. When an actor does a torture scene we are harrowed and sickened not because we think him tortured, but because we receive from him at that moment an idea of torture so compelling that it moves us and moves us more powerfully perhaps than the sight of the same blood and wounds in life might have done. He does not blur any truth but that of mere accidental externality. He does not, in so far as he is good, blur truth at all, but isolates and intensifies it to fuller power.

The test of acting as an art consists in the extent to which its effect depends on some illusion that you undergo. Say, for instance, an actress plays a scene in which a woman is beaten and killed by her son. You can test the art of such a scene by how much it loses its effect upon you when you are reminded that it was only a play after all, that it was not the real woman who was killed after all, but only the actress, who was not dead now but having a cup of tea. If the pressure of the scene can be relieved for you by such a reminder, the acting was of no importance.

The test of your approach to acting as an art consists—exactly as it does in painting—in the extent to which you depend on illusion for your ultimate satisfaction.

For what has come off from that scene, if it was greatly acted, in no matter what style or school, is only a greater truth; the actor gives you the eternity of love, grief and death; you are moved as by a great building, or poem or great music. The art of acting in that scene is ultimately to be judged by the completeness and significance of its idea. Every work of art endures at last not by its body's likeness to things outside itself, but by the depth and freedom of its soul.

61 The lazy actor

John Shand

February 1928

John Shand was a regular reviewer of books, theatre and films for the *New Statesman* from 1925 to 1939. His animadversions on the indolence of actors in some ways prefigure Peter Brook's definition of the Deadly Theatre in *The Empty Space*.

> "Know, then, there is a certain set or society of men frequently to be met in parties about this Kingdom, who by a peculiar kind of magic, will meta-morphose an old barn, stable, or warehouse, in such a wonderful manner that [these] shall appear, according as it suits [their] purpose, at one time a prince's palace, at another a peasant's cottage. . . . Nay, so vast is their art that, by pronouncing audibly certain sentences, they transport the said barn, stable, or outhouse, thus metamorphosed, over sea or land. What is still more wonderful, they carry all their spectators with them, without witchery of broomsticks. These necromancers, although whenever they please they become princes, kings, and heroes, yet no sooner do their sorceries cease, though but the moment before they were banqueting with Jupiter himself, it is a safe wager of a pound to a penny that half of them go supperless to bed. A set of poor but pleasant rogues, miserable, but merry wags, that weep without sorrow, stab without anger, and die without dread. . . ."

THIS charming description of "the profession" is quoted from the *Autobiography* of Thomas Holcroft, the eighteenth century actor and dramatist. The actor's life today is the less "romantic" as it is the more "respectable," but there are traces still of those centuries during which the player was a rogue, who at one moment was robed in royal dress and at the next was going "supperless to bed." The most noticeable characteristic of the majority of players is their careless, vagabond attitude towards life in general and their own future in particular. "Today we drink, tomorrow we die" is the invisible motto over every dressing-room door. This gay nonchalance seems to be generated by the stage; it seems to be a special atmosphere which, scented with greasepaint and powder, fills every theatre and which every player carries about with him, as a snail its shell. Even those players who are naturally of a sober constitution, while in the company of their fellows will assume the vagabond's virtue even if they have it not.

A less attractive attribute of many actors, which may or not be an inheritance from those days of outlawry, is their careless attitude towards their art. I would not dare to agree entirely with Stanislavsky when he says, in that very fine book, *My Life in Art*, that "The majority of actors are interested, not in their art, but in rôles. To them it is important not to create, but simply to find out how to play certain parts. All their calculations are based on the continual presence of that inspiration which is given only to a few. Denying laws and fundamentals, they are proud of the *accidental* quality of their art, and think that this negation is a symptom of true talent." I would not dare, I repeat, to agree whole-heartedly in this statement, but I suggest that too large a number of players seem to be unaware that the *art* of acting is based on anything more than the acquisition of tricks and dodges. These actors are content to learn the surface technique which anyone can acquire with a little practice: how to walk, to speak, to make-up; and then they "sit down," as it were, and play variations on these accomplishments for the rest of their lives. This is surely to turn the art of acting, as the hack-writer turns the art of literature, into a trade.

Mention of the hack-writer will remind you that I do not suggest that this trading in the surface tricks of an art is confined to actors. There are, of course, hack-writers of music, and hack-painters of pictures. But there is this important difference between those who make acting a trade and those who make a trade of the other arts. The hack-writer of moderate talents in the world of music or literature has to work hard most of the time in order to live. But the hack-actor, whether he tours or whether he squats in the metropolis, has a very large allowance of spare time. Even during most of the time in those few hours in which, technically, he is at work, he may be chatting and smoking in his dressing-room. And even during that short space of time when he is actually working, that is to say, standing, sitting, moving, or talking on the stage, his job is so easy, when once the first night is over, that he can almost do it in his sleep, and very often seems to do so. Time for time, money for money, the actor who is only a competent hack has the best paid and easiest hack-work in the world. He takes the prize for salaried leisure. So long as he has a number of facial tricks at his fingers' ends, and a tolerable memory, he may settle down to an existence which may, indeed, be hazardous in these days of overcrowding but which will require a very small expenditure of effort and knowledge on the work obtained.

For the Tired Time of art, the theatre, as Mr. Frank Vernon remarked in *Modern Stage Production*, is the "Palace of Insolence." The profession of acting is, then, evidently one that will also attract born idlers in search of a "soft" job, and the failures of the world. The casualness with which it may be entered, the facility with which the surface tricks of the trade can be acquired, has always been a drawback to the art. You remember how Nicholas Nickleby, whilst he was wondering how to earn a living, encountered Mr. Vincent Crummles and the Infant Phenomenon; how he was immediately engaged to play leading parts, and how, in a short time, he became quite a box-office draw? This may still stand as a type case of the ease with which the average person can take up acting. It is one of the thousand illustrations of Diderot's contention that the stage is often a refuge for those who have nothing better to do, or cannot do anything better. But, if the stage-door has ever been too widely open to the knock of incompetent or worthless people, the hours of leisure which should be such a valuable gratuity to the actor's salary, are quite a modern development. Until quite recent times, "theatricals" were very hardworking people. In the provinces, people of a stock company, or of a "fit-up," were constantly rehearsing new plays or reviving old ones; and in London also, since the length of a play's run was generally quite short, metropolitan mimes had little more leisure than their provincial brethren. But nowadays the provincial actor tours in one play only, and has most of his weekdays entirely at his disposal; in the same way, the London actor learns his part, then settles down to a run of fifty or one hundred, even five hundred or a thousand consecutive performances.

The grinding work of the old days at least taught the players their job. But the system had many bad points, and no one wants to revive it. It very definitely encouraged the cultivation of stereotyped tricks, what Stanislavsky calls "stencil or rubber-stamp acting," and much of the so-called versatility of the old stock actors merely meant that they could do a lot of things very badly. There is much to be said for the present leisurely existence of the constantly employed player, but there is everything to be said against the use so many of them make of it. Actors have now more time than most members of the other arts to improve themselves, to cultivate their powers and increase their range; but most of them waste it, talking, sleeping, playing games, or grumbling about these long runs, or long tours in one part, and how they prevent all chance of a full experience in every kind of acting. The dancer and the acrobat practice every day merely to keep themselves on the same level of ability; the violinist and the pianist play their scales as if they were still pupils. Only the actor gets up late and wonders how he shall spend the day, as if he had nothing more to learn, and no art to grow rusty by want of exercise.

62 Type-casting: The eighth deadly sin

Edith J. R. Isaacs

February 1933

Type-casting had long been a tradition in the theatre, at least from the time of the *commedia dell'arte* with its assigned masks. By the time stock companies were a norm in the nineteenth century, most actors were expected to have an *emploi* or line of business, from which they seldom varied. At the same time, from Garrick on, actors were praised for their versatility. From their inception, the movies tended to prefer the *emploi* system (the vamp, the heavy, the pure girl) and, barring such exceptions as Paul Muni and other character actors, performers tended to be locked into types.

Edith Isaacs (1878–1956), a seasoned journalist, was drama critic for *Ainslie's Magazine* before joining *Theatre Arts'* editorial board in 1918. Eventually she became editor (1922–46) and majority stock-holder, expanding it from a quarterly to a monthly. By this time, she had published *The American Theatre in Social and Educational Life: A Survey of Its Needs and Opportunities* (1932). Later, her belief in a national theatre would lead her to be involved in the Federal Theatre Project.

"AND furthermore"—as a delightful old professor used to begin, when he wanted to imply that the subject was not, altogether, a new one—and furthermore, there never was a fine theatre that did not respect actors and the art of acting. The need for the Actors' Equity Association, and the actors' overwhelming response to the organization, is proof enough that the trade theatre did not really respect the actor in spite of all the money spent for names in electric lights that should outshine the rest of Broadway. For actors, like other artists, are notoriously individualists and not organizers except under great stress and oppression.

The trade theatre respected a featured player's ability to bring money into its coffers, and responded to it generously, and that was right enough. Every theatre needs money and the actor who can earn a great deal of money for his theatre is entitled to a fair share of what he earns. But it is a far cry from making large salaries available for star performers, during the few years in which they are a big business asset, to maintaining a theatre in which all actors can develop their talents and share, with the theatre, the burdens and the rewards of that development; from gambling on the gifts that nature brings to hand, to fostering the theatre's resources through opportunities essential to the permanence of the theatre.

What real actors want most, and need most, is the chance to act. They need steady work, at once liberating and restraining, under stimulating direction, plenty of rehearsals, constantly renewed association with other actors more experienced, and with a more developed technique, than themselves. They need little parts and big parts; easy parts, hard parts; old parts to refresh, new parts to bring to life; realism and stylization; prose and poetry; in short, the chance to create—not just to appear "in person" on a stage.

There were a great many good plausible reasons why the trade theatre that neglected the art of playwriting, scorned the art of acting. Most of the reasons were inherent in the trade system. When you pick up a new cast for each new play, when the theatre in which you rehearse carries an exorbitant rent because it is so expensively built on such expensive land (all roads come back to this fundamental evil), you must, to live, save money where you can. And time is obviously money. To anyone who does not know what acting is and does, or who will not trust what it can do, it seems like saving time in the preparation of a play to pick, for a given part, a man or a woman whose appearance is already close to the surface of the character he must set out to create. So type-casting on a large scale was a trade theatre invention, almost a trade theatre necessity. The dramatist, their theory said, writes his character clearly into his script. If a clever director can find the dramatist's man already made instead of bothering to create him, so much the better, so much the faster, so much the cheaper. The theatre of the speed age, they said, could not wait for actors. And they were almost right.

A really vital director can whip a group of type-cast players into shape on short notice, on condition that they are the kind that take orders easily and clearly. In other words, on condition that there are not too many artists among them, with ideas of their own. Artists have a way of getting out of hand in a type-cast play. But even without them there is often another trouble. A director can whip these players into shape but he cannot keep them whipped, or perhaps it would be more accurate to say that he will have so completely whipped whatever creative qualities they possess that, as soon as he stops giving orders and setting the pace, they cannot play. After a few days (their acting having acquired none of the inner automatic controls that are the outcome of fine training, technique, and experience) their performance slips away and begins to show exactly those qualities most annoying to the watchers of the average non-professional show.

Type-casting is, in fact, the sublimation of the unprofessional in acting. It is, moreover, one of the theatre's deadly sins. Fortunately, or unfortunately, it carries within itself its own withering revenge as anyone may know who has seen the futile trek to Hollywood, or who has seen what the trade theatre's so-called "Royal Family" has done to it—deserting one by one. And why? Not only because the theatre has nothing more to give them, but because they have nothing more to give the theatre; nothing added by years of experience to the rare tradition and real gifts with which they began; nothing left within themselves from which to help the theatre renew its life.

Some years ago I had a call to come at once to a certain producer's office, one of the most delightful, successful, responsive of the whole Broadway group. He wanted to show me an example, he said, of what he called "good directing". It was just before noon so it was obviously not a play in performance—probably a rehearsal in progress. And since rehearsals, good ones, have so much dramatic excitement in them that is often lost before an audience, the opportunity to share it seemed worth a trip uptown. The theatre, however, was dark. The director was in his office overhead. What he called an example of good directing lay inanimate on the desk before him. It was a photograph, or rather two photographs mounted as one. Two identical photographs they seemed at first, but they turned out to be a portrait of a New York company (still playing to crowded houses in a highly diverting comedy) and a portrait of a new company just setting out for Chicago in the same play. Height for height, color for color, pound for pound, this director had doubled these actors. Casting offices had scoured the town to make this perfect match. Each one of those actors had, moreover, the producer assured me, watched his original over and over again in performance until he had copied squarely every gesture, every bit of business, every facial expression. "And that," said the dear man, "I call good directing. They say we don't give Chicago as good as we got. There isn't one of them can tell the difference."

Yet somehow they did. Chicago didn't like that company. It was strange—they were so like New York's favored ones. They looked alike, they played alike. All, that is, except one. The leading man in the original company happened to be a really creative comedian. He played like a flash. He pulled the other players up to his speed; he gave strength to the weaker ones playing with him and added point to the keenest of his fellows. His style set the style for the show and kept it steady week by week. You could mimic him easily enough but you could not copy him unless you had his talent and his technique. Such an actor is always a hitch in duplicating casts. You can't buy his double either by the inch or by the pound.

But copying another man, either from life or from a play, is the very least of the complications that come into the theatre with type-casting. Copying yourself is a much harder and more destructive job; playing, over and over again, in a dozen different plays, year in and year out, the single role of beautiful young woman or good-looking young man in which nature has cast you. If you give an able actor enough to do to fill his time and talent and imagination, the real world is far less real to him than the world he plays in. He hardly knows how long or how hard he works or whether he has money in his pockets. His rewards are his own; you cannot understand them. He does not need too great material recompense. But certainly the opportunity for personal exhibition cannot pay any actor for the labor and the human deprivations and the uncertainties of life in the theatre. He might as well be a manikin in a show window. He must have plenty of money and electric light to make up for what he loses by that deal.

In the old repertory companies, every actor played many parts. And only an actor who has worked for many years within such a tradition of training and experience, or a member of the audience that has watched such players, knows what a different thing that training makes of acting, what it gives you for yourself in security and variety and creative quality as the foundation of your own part, and what it leaves you of understanding and response to spare for the actors who play with you. The Russians use the word "connection" to express that essential element in ensemble playing by means of which each individual actor can rise to his full height and yet add to the stature of the others around him, so that the scale of the group is larger than the scale of the individual players. It is utterly impossible to achieve that quality in a theatre where actors are cast to type. You must lose yourself to find it.

It is a commonplace in defence of type-casting to say that most famous actors are always themselves no matter what they play—Sarah Bernhardt, Henry Irving, and so forth. Such a statement has, of course, its basis in truth. An actor can never altogether escape his form and his features. They are the medium of his art. But the able actor uses them simply as a springboard. He does not act himself—ever; he acts from his own presence upward and outward, which is quite another thing. It is perhaps easiest to see this in the case of a successful comedian, who creates, for his constant use, a stage character quite unlike himself, from which all his roles emerge. Charlie Chaplin has worked this stage presence out so completely that the created type is more real to most of his audience than the original. So when we say Charlie Chaplin is "always himself" what we mean is that he gives us always, and by intention, the work of actor's art which is his creation, and of which we never tire. Great comedy has, traditionally, been based on these created types; from the days of the Commedia dell' Arte, every actor assigned to the part of mezzetin, or harlequin or pantaloon, designed a figure for his own use to the scale that suited him best, created a voice and gesture and movement and stock of tricks that pleased and satisfied him and used the character made up of these elements in a hundred ways—the created character, not his own.

What actors like Bernhardt do is much the same thing except that instead of one part in endless variation, they play many parts of great range all based on a stage presence that they establish for themselves. Phaedre and her fellows, in Bernhardt's acting, are not Mme. Damala (called Sarah Bernhardt on the stage) but Bernhardt-Phaedre, Bernhardt-Lecouvreur, Bernhardt-L'Aiglon.

One of the most astute of New York's casting directors has her own rationalization of the type-casting process. "The New York theatre is so systematically organized," she says (or something like this) "that it is today practically one large repertory theatre. In it there are hundreds of players, instead of a score, at the constant service of twenty directors, instead of one. They are all essentially a single large company from which a director may make his choice for a play. And obviously he must ease himself where he can in his difficult task, as for example, by removing the burden of creating an outward resemblance. This is so much the day of the director that an actor rarely creates anyhow. The director finds the spine of the play and the spine of the parts and molds the actors to his idea of what they should be." Which is, of course, completely specious. What the theatre modernist means, when he says this is the director's day, is something very different. He means, to begin with, that instead of tearing up the theatre into its elements—play-writing, acting, design, dance, etc.—and giving each element a day of glory and a day of punishment as history has done, there is a new desire, expressing itself in a new leadership, to harmonize all of these elements and establish them permanently in their due place and proportion. But this new leader, this new director, is no actors' bully. His work is to find out what they can do, to help them to do it better than they think they can do, and to unify their playing.

Whatever Max Reinhardt's faults—and his great days being just over, this seems to be the hour when his faults loom large—his appreciation of fine acting was his most creative virtue. There are two stories that Vladimir Sokoloff told of him that illustrate this well. Sokoloff himself, coming to Germany from Russia, suffered so from stage fright in his early rehearsals that he found himself practically tongue-tied. Try as he would he could not speak the first lines assigned to him in the voice, at the speed, or with the intonation he wanted. Over and over again he faltered, purred, stumbled. Reinhardt sat quietly and encouragingly opposite him. Suddenly Sokoloff heard those first three sentences said in exactly the right voice, tone and rhythm. Yet he knew that he had said nothing. He looked at Reinhardt, questioning. "That is good" said Reinhardt quietly, giving no indication that it was he and not Sokoloff who had spoken. "Now go ahead." And Sokoloff went on, realizing only gradually, as his power and self-confidence returned, that Reinhardt had caught and expressed for him, better than he could himself at that moment, exactly what he wanted—not the thing that Reinhardt wanted, but rather what Reinhardt expected Sokoloff to do and Sokoloff wanted to do, but couldn't. And that, if you please, is good direction, finding for the actor, and from within the actor, powers that he cannot master alone, and passing them over to him securely for his use.

The other story tells of a late rehearsal at which a leading lady, new to the company's ways, was prancing up and down, waiting to go on, while Reinhardt made Hans Moser, the delightful comedian, go over and over a little scene.

"Poor Moser," said the leading lady, "why does the Herr Director torment him? He is doing it well enough." Well enough, indeed! Moser was doing the scene so well that Reinhardt could not resist the sheer pleasure of having him repeat it over and over again. That is how he learned from actors. That is why actors learned from him; why a whole theatre world of them joined on Reinhardt's twenty-fifth anniversary at the Deutsches Theater to praise his direction. You cannot look at the extraordinary sets of actors' portraits in character in Reinhardt's anniversary book, you cannot look at the portraits in the Moscow Art Theatre or in the Vieux Colombier or, for that matter, at the old Empire Theatre Company or Daly's, or at the Abbey Players with us now, without knowing that here in control were directors who respected acting.

63 The moribund craft of acting

Cedric Hardwicke

February 1939

For Hardwicke, see headnote to Chapter 27, "An actor stakes his claim".

IN A season so distinguished as the present, with performances like Robert Morley's Wilde, Maurice Evans' Hamlet, Raymond Massey's Lincoln and Walter Huston's Stuyvesant, it is perhaps a little far-fetched to suggest that acting as an art seems to be dying. But I think of the younger actors when I say this.

Nor is it more than passing strange that in the midst of all this superb performing one should complain of slow strangulation: great art, great acting, always come at the end of an epoch, not at its beginning.

It may be possible that the younger actor will be able to meet the many new obstacles in his way and emerge as equal to the artists of any generation. But the way is difficult, more difficult perhaps than he realizes. Fashions have changed; points of view have shifted. It would not be amiss at this time to set forth what is in the way of good acting and what seems to be strangling it.

Today the mode is to say that the actor is merely one cog in the machine, like the designer, the director, the author and the ticket-taker. Recently when the Moscow Art Theatre celebrated an anniversary the hat-check girls were applauded equally with the directors and the actors. No one denies the cooperative nature of any theatrical enterprise; still less does he wish to make the function of the actor more important than it need be. But we seem to forget that it is the actor and only the actor who can make a play breathe. Until he speaks and moves, the play is a closet-drama, interesting perhaps but utterly lifeless.

It is therefore with some slight amusement that I have heard playwrights say that a good play should be actor-proof. I have never heard a composer declare his concerto pianist-proof, but it has always made me think that, if our playwrights feel that the actor is an unfortunate handicap in the creation of a work of art, a kind of necessary evil, they would be better off writing novels. The novel *is* actor-proof.

The novel, too, has many advantages which the theatre cannot offer. It is more free; it gives the writer greater scope. The novel is a better form in which to handle ideas or propaganda. The theatre, being the most explicit of the arts, demands ideas and truths in their most abstract form: poetic truths.

Since Ibsen, however, playwrights have been more pleased to enlighten us than to stir us. We have received sermons on divorce, youthful sinning, getting married and a variety of topics. The theatre for its own sake seems just a little shameful and not quite worth the attention of an intelligent individual. Of course, a propaganda play can be great theatre; Ibsen and Shaw are master dramatists. But the same cannot always be said of those who have been influenced by them.

In its search for realism the modern theatre has discarded many old techniques. The term *theatric*, for example, has come to be one of derision. Today all motivations tend to be clear, and all characterizations sharply etched. Shakespeare knew better. Lear is one of my favorite parts, but I cannot for the life of me understand why the old man should be so foolish as to ask his daughters which of them loves him most. It is the actor's task, however, to make this preposterous situation credible; nor is it surprising that a good actor does just that which we, in the quiet of our study, cannot do. And as for *theatric*, what could be more unrestrained, more turbulent than the picture of Lear at the end of the play? What contemporary modes of underwriting and underplaying could convey the old man broken by tragedy, wild with grief?

Shakespeare always allowed scope to the actor's art, always left hidden, secret meanings for the actor to bring to light. Hamlet, of course, is the classic example: the pundits are still learnedly mulling over his motivations and his character.

I have been playing Canon Skerritt in *Shadow and Substance* for more than a year now and I confess that outside the theatre there are many things the Canon does and says that I cannot fathom the meaning of. Brigid will have left him one moment quite charmed by her and the next the Canon sees of her he will be sharp and cross to her. That is, however, as it should be. Before the footlights there exists another world, not the 'real' world, and it has its own laws and meanings, its own spatial and temporal limitations. Mr. Paul Vincent Carroll has been willing to trust his effects to the actors; many of his contemporaries, I daresay, would not be so eager.

Nor are the playwrights alone in their distrust of the actor. In England I have directed plays, and when I chide the director I can take part of the blame. To the man who stages a play the actor is a kind of mimic who parrots back his every inflection and gesture. There was a time, I suppose, when actors champed under this kind of treatment but it is not evident today. I once directed a play in which the actors were given their sides some days before the first rehearsal. They came to that first reading, each one knowing every word of his part perfectly but without one bit of sense to it. They studied words mechanically; the rest they left to the director.

Can I hear the voice of the playwright say, 'That is just the reason why a part must be actor-proof. That is why we cannot trust our effects to the actor, why we must be sharp and precise. Leave it to the actor and you will have nothing more than a senseless repetition of words.'

But, I contend, the reason one encounters actors like these is that one has playwrights and directors like those who flourish today. The actor must bring to his part no intelligence, no understanding and a minimum of sympathy. He must look right, speak right and be able to follow directions. From long, sad experience the fledgling star knows it is wiser to study nothing more than words.

In our day we have witnessed a hundred theories about training actors, most of which have been advanced by directors, regisseurs. There is much in these theories that is valuable. What is true in them is not particularly novel nor does it often consist of more than a technical restatement of verities our common sense tells us are true. One or two of them, like that of Stanislavski, have added to the body of knowledge about the craft of acting. But what I distrust in all of them is their tendency toward cultism, toward forming special little groups, which, though they give lip-service to 'studying life', do nothing more than function as circles where one may talk shop interminably. For after an actor has mastered the few principles of his trade, the place for him to study is in the world, people, if you please. A portraitist, after he has learned to put brush to canvas, is better off studying people than other portraitists. You would never have had Goya's mordant studies of Spanish royalty, Greco's pictures of the aristocrats, had they done all their studying inside their studios. How can a man whose every friend is an actor, who lives in an hotel or apartment with other actors, eats where they eat, wears what they wear, reads only the theatrical pages, play anything but an actor?

The modern theatre puts yet another obstacle in the way of the young actor. That is the stage designer. Now there are stage designers and there are men to whom a play is an excuse to erect some kind of circus, preferably on a revolving stage, which they must necessarily suffer actors to punctuate with speeches before the scene can change to permit another round of applause. What is wrong with some of these magnificent designs we have all admired? They are impressive, they are expensive, they are ingenious. Their only flaw is that they so reduce the actor in stature as to change the focus of the whole play. Impressed by the technical dexterity of the designer we do not hear the actor or the author. That is why, incidentally, a mediocre play must have the best and most impressive settings money can buy.

The very nature of the modern stage, even when the case is not so extreme as I have made it, relieves the actor of his old function of scenewright. When we can build a magnificent castle for our audience to see, why should our playwrights trouble to describe it as beautifully as Shakespeare does in *Macbeth*? Shakespeare had no modern lighting board, nor could he call upon the genius of the scene-builder; so to create a magic island he had to create magic poetry for the actor who plays Prospero. In a sense, therefore, the technical progress the modern theatre has made is the actor's irreparable loss. Necessarily, he is called upon to do less and less.

Though I am not an antiquarian and though I do not suggest to modern playwrights that they employ the old devices when they have newer techniques at hand, it is interesting to point out that one of the most beautiful plays of our day, Thornton Wilder's *Our Town*, used a stage much like the Elizabethan and achieved much of its eloquence because the author asked of the theatre that it give him nothing more than four walls and a few lights: for the rest he depended on his own genius.

As well as being sinned against, the modern actor sins against himself. Since the theatre began striving for realism, the actor, always an humble fellow, began striving for lifelike effects, too. His voice fell from the declamatory to the sweet, sugary tones of a crooner. Instead of gesturing and posturing, he now limits himself elegantly to flicking the ash from a cigarette or adjusting his shirt-cuffs under his jacket. It is of course perfectly true that there is no longer any necessity for the excessive gesturing of yesterday when stages were poorly lit and acoustics bad. But here is another instance where progress has hurt the craft. The result is that today an audience must comprehend a play entirely with its ear and, since it has given up adequate gesture as being too theatric, acting has tended to become more and more inarticulate. The cult of the inarticulate reaches its height in Chekhov and it is not surprising that the modern actor is always little less than perfect in the Russian's plays.

Behind all this lies the contemporary trend toward realism in the theatre. No one wants to go back to the days when every room was the size of a room in Buckingham Palace. And it is quite natural that in a democratic era our theatre should concern itself with life as everybody knows it and lives it. But we have gone further. We have *excluded* the colorful, the dramatic, the excessive because it is too theatric. The fallacy behind the realistic theatre, I think, is that there is no reason to go to the theatre if it must consist only of the drab and commonplace, of events that could occur to any individual in a multitude. The world outside is too exciting, too full of conflict, of drama, of struggle, for us to care very much about the prosy problems of some *petit-bourgeois* merely because they transpire on a stage. Today the world is a theatre: we see men in politics as personalities engaging in a great drama in which we are at once spectators and participants. Politicians rant, they cry, they storm the very Heavens, they threaten, they perform before vast multitudes. Only the realistic theatre is still anxious about the problems of the little man.

This is not to say that our theatre is all realism. Everywhere one sees evidence of growing poetic awareness on the part of dramatists, a growth of vision, a working with newer, more heroic materials. Maxwell Anderson comes to mind for his historical plays and Robert E. Sherwood for his beautiful evocation of Lincoln, the hero.

But these hopeful signs are not the rule. Otherwise, the realistic theatre is another evidence of the moribund craft of acting. In this country these problems take on a very special significance. I have outlined the new problems all younger actors must face today; in America they are especially acute. You have so much here that is matchless, such an audience, such technical perfection, such a body of vastly talented young people, that you will forgive an Englishman for inquiring where — with some very honorable exceptions — are the American actors? Your actresses are the best in the world. But what of the men?

Alfred Lunt is always a joy to watch; Walter Huston is a grand actor and there are many others that one could list easily and confidently. But one October day I glance at the theatrical page and I see that Messrs. Massey, Evans, King, Lawson, Keith, Bruce, Digges, Morley and Bateman are engaged in leading roles. We await Messrs. Merivale, Kortner, Sokoloff, Homolka, Lukas, Waram, Oscar and Daniell. There is not an American actor in the list. What is it that makes the New York managers seek outlanders?

I think Americans must soon begin to ask themselves whether the very structure of their theatre is not unnecessarily adding to the burdens under which acting is laboring. Does the American theatre hinder the development of the craft in so far as it offers no training for the very young actor?

In England we have touring companies. It is possible for a young actor to master his craft in many years of touring and playing a multiplicity of roles. We have repertory theatres all over the country. An actor can gain poise, technical assurance and authority by actually working before audiences. The young American actor Orson Welles began his career by taking advantage of the opportunities our theatre offers younger actors. An actor will never gain the experience he needs by interviewing managers, playing before cameras or lunching in the right restaurants.

What, then, do you offer the younger actor here? Your tributary theatres, as you call them, can offer him some employment; but it is exceptional, not usual. Unselfish, theatre-wise people like Katharine Cornell and the Lunts are developing what amount to repertory companies and offer untold opportunities for the younger actors in their companies. The Mercury Theatre offers similar opportunities; the Group Theatre has developed a number of actors. There are in the hinterland, I am told, a few stock companies which employ professionals.

But all this is still not nearly enough. You have to develop hundreds and hundreds to get one great artist. The system must by its very nature be superabundantly generous. It requires more than individual effort. Today the only way a young American actor can gain experience is to be the perfect 'type' for a play and, luckily, find the play a hit.

In a country where the psychology of the frontier still exists, most people, I daresay, expect success early and lavishly and dread the day-to-day work it demands. Thus I have often heard young American actors tell me they have turned down jobs with stock companies in, say, Louisville or New Orleans because they 'would just be wasting a year'. It makes me wonder if I wasted a year playing in churches, hotel dining rooms and lecture halls in South Africa in 1913?

Now you can say that all these things I have been pointing out are true enough but that it has been ever thus with supreme genius — yet somehow it will emerge, whatever the conditions. I will not deny it. There is something mystic, unknowable about genius: the spark is there and it fires us. An inexperienced child can make technically competent people seem cold and lifeless. But in truth I have not presumed to speak of supreme genius: that does not bear speaking about except perhaps by geniuses, of which I know I am not one. I have really been speaking of competent, fine craftsmen. *They* must be developed. And we can tell how well the system functions by examining the performances in the lesser parts.

Our theatre can learn much from yours, but in almost every English play you will find the small parts played to perfection. The dramatist Somerset Maugham, when he came to writing his artistic testament, *The Summing Up*, singled out only one actor for special mention, not a star, sometimes not even featured, an actor who has played small roles in Mr. Maugham's plays and played them perfectly: Mr. C. V. France. When a dramatist does that, he does more than pay polite respects to a few stars: he pays tribute to an institution. And the reason you will find these small parts played so beautifully is that the English theatre, for all its faults, gave the actor just the training and experience he needed to do his job well.

Where — lacking a system of touring companies, stock companies, repertory theatres — is America to recruit its leading actors ten or fifteen years from today?

People are afraid of a 'shortage' of good playwrights. It is a justifiable concern. But how much more acute not to have actors — trained, capable actors! Mr. John Golden and the Dramatists' Guild are giving some thirty fellowships to young playwrights. Americans must now ask themselves if they are doing enough for their younger actors. Are they being given every opportunity to master the tools of their craft? The very nature of the modern theatre, as I have shown, militates against the growth of the art of acting: it now stands still and indeed loses much of its old function. But the structure of the theatre, which is man-made, should not as well be permitted to hamper the development of a body of fine actors.

64 Speak the speech, I pray you

John Gielgud

April 1951

By 1951, Gielgud had returned to poetic drama, his latest success being the roisterer Thomas Mendip in Christopher Fry's verse comedy *The Lady's Not for Burning* (1949, New York 1951). Then, for the very first time, he starred at Stratford's Shakespeare Memorial Theatre, playing Angelo in *Measure for Measure*, directed by a very young Peter Brook (1950) and Leontes in *The Winter's Tale* (1951), performances which have been preserved on LPs. Brook was about to direct him opposite Paul Scofield in a stunning revival of *Venice Preserved* at the Lyric Hammersmith (1952).

THE popularity of Shakespeare's plays in England and America has been very similar in recent years, an intermittent flow of successful revivals in the great cities where star actors and actresses have played the leading parts, and a continuous stream of experimental performances in summer theatre, universities, and group communities which appeal, it seems, to large audiences less sophisticated and wealthy than those who patronize the houses of London and New York.

Alas, poor Shakespeare. With no royalties to be paid, no author to interrupt at rehearsals, there is unlimited opportunity for his survival at the hands of any star, director, or group of actors who have the temerity to tackle his long-suffering creations. Blessed by scholars and professors, adored by star actors and actresses, every new young director itching to interpret him, audiences prepared to endure him for every kind of reason—educational, intellectual, snob, or popular appeal—it is small wonder he has worn so well, but a great wonder that no company has ever dedicated itself to perfecting themselves in the skill that alone may realize his glories to the full.

Many star players have attempted to train their own companies to support them in one or two Shakespeare plays, and, here and there, there have been periods of success—but no company, collected at random for a few short rehearsal weeks under the overwhelming personality of a star or director, however brilliant, can achieve unity and style, or hope to fill in the intricate canvas of a Shakespeare play and achieve the perfect symmetry which its composite structure and technical problems demand.

The speaking of the verse (and prose) is the root of the matter, and I know of no English-speaking theatre which attains to a really high standard in this respect. The plays should be read and worked on, for the speaking alone, for several weeks, by a company of players prepared to take patient note of breathing, tempo, rhythm, phrasing and correct diction, to understand the ebb and flow of the writing, which differs so enormously in every one of the plays. When that first hurdle has been passed, there is still the ordinary work to be done—characterization, balance, emphasis, and the particular quality of atmosphere which may be dictated by an original director, or the shifting of detail and perspective which inevitably occur in building the whole performance in support of the individual personalities who may enact the leading parts.

Some progress, however, has been made, though not, I think, the progress that one might have hoped for, considering the light that has been shed upon the theatre from so many contributory sources over the last fifty years.

Books, essays, critical and experimental treatises have poured into the presses from scholars, professors, experts and innovators of brilliant talent. Every kind of production has been attempted—modern-dress, theatre-in-the-round, fancy period, apron-stage, cyclorama, unlocalized permanent setting, archaeological realism—and directors have lavished experiment and effort in a hundred ways. The plays are more widely read, less drastically cut and remodeled, familiarized by radio and film adaptation, but there is still no outstanding record of sustained quality to create a standard for actors and audiences.

Directors and leading players desire nothing better than to interpret Shakespeare after their individual fashion, and those who have succeeded in a play of his seldom work in the plays of other authors without wishing to return to him and seal their reputations with a production of one of his most famous plays (though the lesser known masterpieces are apt to be relegated to the experimental theatres and universities). Shakespeare is always an honorable and honored stand-by when the new author fails to produce a likely script.

The interruption of the two wars may be blamed, among other things, for the inability of England and America to produce a first-class permanent company of Shakespearean players. The difference in age and experience between the older and younger actors is bound to be difficult to reconcile in a period during which tradition has been so severely and continually interrupted. The important men who led the way have been actors like Benson and Ben Greet, directors like Granville-Barker and William Poel—actor-managers, Irving, Booth, Barrymore, Ada Rehan. They are all now dead, and those of us who have tried to follow in their footsteps find ourselves trammeled by economic conditions, a fantastic rise in costs in every department of the theatre, and the ever-depleting influence of the cinema, radio, and television, whose blandishments lure the limited number of talented players and even compete with the theatre by seizing Shakespeare's texts from our jealous hands and trying to remold him in their own image—to popularize him, in forms that he would scarcely recognize himself, for the entertainment of millions who would never dream of crossing the street to see one of his plays acted in a theatre.

At the Old Vic in London and the Memorial Theatre at Stratford, permanent companies are, it is true, engaged each year to perform a series of four or five Shakespeare plays. I have had the honor to lead the company at both these theatres in different years—at the Vic in 1929 and 1930 and at Stratford in

1950—and they were perhaps the three happiest seasons of my career. But in both cases the company failed to achieve the standard which I feel, ideally, ought to be able to be attained, considering the effort and general good will which was engendered by everyone concerned.

Though we have at least half a dozen brilliant directors of Shakespeare in England and America, we have perhaps only about fifty players who are really expert at speaking and acting Shakespearean roles. This is hardly enough to satisfy the continual demand for adequate revivals of his plays. Also, the versatility of our directors demands an equal virtuosity from the players. An old-fashioned, declamatory style, however experienced, does not fit well into a modern, swift, vividly imagined presentation; while the careless, inelegant, natural delivery demanded by realistic modern authors fails to train young players in the elementary graces of distinction and clarity of speech and movement so essential to the playing of Shakespeare even upon the modern stage.

The successful leading players of today stand on an uneasy bridge between two extremes of theatrical development. Behind us lie the glories of tradition, the grand manner, the star system, and the slow-moving panoply of Shakespeare presentations that our fathers and grandfathers delighted in. Before us lie the fear of convention and imitation, the demand for novelty, the restless, impatient craving for easy success through strikingly original precocities and perversity of interpretation. I think we are perhaps a little more modest than some of our distinguished predecessors. We respect the text, try to balance our companies and encourage young talent, strive to give every part its full value. But the theatres are too big, the audiences, drawn from every class, are composed of amazingly contrasted types: those who know the plays too well or do not know them at all. They are not entirely to be trusted in their attitude toward Shakespeare, for they are apt to be easily bored, easily impressed, and often indiscriminately enthusiastic at an indifferent but sensational performance. The actors, working in their own curiously individual ways, are impelled by many different ambitions and theories, and can only be welded together by a respected leading player or an inspiring director to any kind of unified attempt at coherent solid harmony. The indifferent standard of ensemble playing in Shakespeare leads the critics to concentrate on the star performances and any showy novelties in direction that may or may not be faithful and helpful to a true interpretation of the text.

Given one fine company, playing half a dozen of the great plays in repertory, of a standard easily recognizable as of the very finest quality, I believe that the understanding of Shakespeare could be a wonderful influence in the theatre. Such a company should be able to appear in a dozen cities, improving in performances continually over several years, and serve as a model of its kind for actors and audiences everywhere. Requiring sacrifices on the part of every player in it—a dedication of energies and a unity of purpose not easy to achieve—it would be a company that would combine the best traditions of style and beautiful speaking with the vigor and thrust of the modern world. For the plays themselves still hold their own. Their timeless wisdom and beauty live on with greater certainty today than the works of any other poet or playwright, despite the fumbling efforts of so many lesser hands that, in all these hundreds of years, would surely have destroyed the work of any lesser man. Shakespeare has made the reputation of so many actors and actresses, directors, critics, and scenic designers. We should perhaps consider, for a change, how we can create a theatre capable of justifying his reputation before the English-speaking world—above all, by speaking him as he deserves.

65 Notes on film acting

Hume Cronyn

June 1949

Cronyn's film career was closely associated with Alfred Hitchcock's: he played the crime-addled neighbour in *Shadow of a Doubt* (1943) and a nervous radio operator in *Lifeboat* (1944). He also worked on the screenplays for *Rope* (1948) and *Under Capricorn* (1949). Owing perhaps to his slight physique and querulous features, he tended to be cast as cowards, traitors and sadists, most memorably as the collaborator in *The Seventh Cross* (1944), the slimy shyster in *The Postman Always Rings Twice* (1946) and the fascistic prison warden in *Brute Force* (1947). However, he did get to play hectic farce with Fannie Brice in the sketch "The Lottery Ticket" (*The Ziegfeld Follies*, 1946). From the sidelines, Cronyn, always a thoughtful actor, could observe the essentials of his craft.

GOOD actors usually act and don't talk. Whenever they may be prodded into discussing their approach to work, they're inclined to disagree on ways and means. Coquelin and Irving are an excellent example. Here the disagreement in approach was so fundamental as to result in a celebrated debate between the two actors. It is nonsense to expect, or to try to impose, a standard attack in the work of any category of creative artist—and an actor can be such. We may pick up a little here, a little there from the example or advice of other actors; but like everyone else, we learn chiefly from our own experience.

I went to Hollywood in 1942 to play a part in "Shadow of a Doubt," a picture directed by Alfred Hitchcock. Life was full of surprises. Nothing was as I thought it would be. Most of my preconceptions were to be confounded and I was to find little basis for the anti-Hollywood prejudice which is so carefully nurtured along Broadway.

A great part of "Shadow of a Doubt" was shot on location in Santa Rosa, California, a small town north of San Francisco in the heart of the vineyard country. I was required to report there. For the first few days I wandered around disconsolate on the edge of the crowd, watching the shooting. It was obvious that in theatre terms there was to be practically no rehearsal. My first scene was quite a long and important one, establishing the character. I grew nervous and depressed in anticipation of the moment when, like that figure in an actor's nightmare, someone would say to me "You're on!" and I would be totally unprepared. My script became grey with anxious fingering, and the wallpaper of my room at the Hotel Occidental took on a crazy pattern of dialogue à la Reginald Gardiner.

With the director's permission, I was allowed to choose from a second-hand store the clothes which I felt were right for the part. These and my hand props helped a little, giving me something to hide behind.

I now had words, wardrobe and as a result of study, a theoretical sense of "my" relationship to the other characters in the screenplay, as well as some detailed ideas on my own character's background and his action throughout the story. A feeling of complete inadequacy persisted. I remained outside the material without any sense of personal identification whatever. I tried an extension of the theatre's prop and dress-rehearsal routine—that time when you familiarize yourself with doors, drawers, steps, the furniture and light switches. I chose "my" house in the district in which we were shooting, "my" place of work and walked the routes between, absorbing whatever I could use. These locations were neither seen nor referred to in the picture. Nobody gave a damn about them except me, and had I discussed what I was attempting at the time, anyone bothering to listen would have justifiably thought me crazy. An actor's search for security is his own private affair, in which a successful end justifies almost any means that does not impose on the other players or waste the director's time.

I take what comfort I can from "things"—sometimes an idea, the reflection of a habit or an attitude which may fit the character, whatever stimulation or depression may be radiated by a particular individual's everyday surroundings. Picasso put it very well in a statement to be found in the Museum of Modern Art's "Picasso—50 Years of His Art," where he is quoted as remarking: "The artist is a receptacle for emotions that come from all over the place: from the sky, from the earth, from a scrap of paper, from a passing shape, from a spider's web. That is why we must not discriminate between *things*. Where things are concerned there are no class distinctions. We must pick out what is good for us where we can find it—except from our own works. I have a horror of copying myself. But when I am shown a portfolio of old drawings, for instance, I have no qualms about taking anything I want from them."

DOES this kind of procedure compensate for lack of rehearsal? No, but it helps. At least it helps me. Security and familiarity are so closely related that you can often reach one through developing the other. It's a very simple and unoriginal process, though in disrepute with those people who insist that all acting is instinctive and who shudder at the "intellectual approach" involved in the simple use of the imagination.

An actor's security cannot be achieved merely through familiarity with externals. What goes on within the character you play? What makes him tick? What motivates his actions and reactions? What are his values, his strengths, fears, obsessions? What does he want? What has he had? *What has been his experience?* I must have at least a nodding acquaintance with such a history. In the course of theatre rehearsals, under a good director I might reasonably expect to discover or create appropriate answers to all these questions. But without rehearsals, I needed a substitute activity. I began to keep a notebook. A notebook has certain practical and psychological uses. To start with, it provides a record of first impressions.

Picasso, again, has expressed the principle with admirable insight: "It would be very interesting to preserve photographically, not the stages, but the metamorphoses of a picture. Possibly one might then discover the path followed by the brain in materializing a dream. But there is one very odd thing—to notice that basically a picture doesn't change, that the first 'vision' remains almost intact, in spite of appearances. I often ponder on a light and a dark when I have put them into a picture; I try hard to break them up by interpolating a color that will create a different effect. When the work is photographed, I note that what I put in to correct my first vision has disappeared and that, after all, the photographic image corresponds with my first vision before the transformation I insisted on."

Secondly, a notebook gives the actor a point of reference if it becomes necessary to return to, and recheck, character fundamentals (weird things can happen in the logical development of a performance when the schedule requires you to shoot the middle of the picture first, the first scene last, and that big emotional scene out of relation to anything that comes either before or after it). Thirdly, it requires that you be specific in your study. Those blank sheets of paper must be filled with exact words, words that make sense when strung together and bear on a particular problem. No airy generalities are acceptable. No muddy thinking to the accompaniment of the bedroom radio will let you off the hook of a notebook's demand. Alternately, once done, once the digging is over, you have material proof that part of your book is accomplished. You have the security of knowing you know something about the character and the job in hand.

THE camera, the old saw notwithstanding, lies like hell and the actor must be prepared to aid in this deception. A move which would be utterly false on stage, which goes directly against every reasonable impulse, may be camerawise effective and necessary. In "Shadow of a Doubt," I had a scene in which I sat down to gossip with a neighbor while he and his family had dinner. During the meal, I said something upsetting to the character played by Teresa Wright. She turned on me with unexpected violence. I stood up in embarrassment and surprise and automatically took a step backward. However, at the point of the rise, the camera moved in to hold us in a close two-shot, and to accommodate it—that is, to stay in the frame—it became necessary for me to change the instinctive move so that when I got up from my chair, *I took a step toward the person from whom I was retreating*. Because of my inexperience and the falseness of the move, this made a hazard for me in the middle of an otherwise simple scene. I was convinced the action would look idiotic on the screen, but I was wrong. When I saw the rushes, I had to admit that the occasion passed almost unnoticed even by me.

You have to learn to adjust to such requirements easily and with a minimum of rehearsal. The problems of lighting, camera movement and sound are liable to get considerably more attention than the actors. This is unfortunate and indefensible, but it is not likely that you will be able to change the situation. So again, you must learn to adjust and to be so well prepared that you are secure in spite of it.

The difference between acting for the screen and acting for the stage is negligible and the latter is, despite the exceptions, the best possible training for the former. The screen brings the actor into front row range for an entire audience throughout most of the picture and occasionally it puts him into their laps. It is obviously unnecessary and irritating to speak or move as you would for the benefit of people in the back of a gallery. It may take a little time and some guidance for the stage actor to become accustomed to the degree of projection which will be most effective on the screen, but the technique of film acting is no unique or mystic formula.

Almost everything in picture-making stresses the importance of mechanical perfection. I think the actor does well to trust in the people who are experts in this field and paid to insure it. His business, as in the theatre, remains with the character he is to play and this will require his full powers of concentration.

In "closeup" very little becomes very much; a whole new range of expression is opened to the actor. He can register with a whisper, a glance, a contraction of a muscle, in a manner that would be lost on the stage. The camera will often reflect what a man thinks, without the degree of demonstration required in the theatre.

The profession of motion-picture director is an ulcerous one. Considering the harassment and pressure under which most of these men work, one finds a surprising degree of patience and understanding in their relationship to actors and actors' problems. There are, of course, exceptions. I've worked with a director who started the day off by thumbing through the script, grimacing with distaste, then muttering "Oh well, let's shoot it." That's a little hard to overcome. There's the director who bullies his cast and crew, especially its less important members. There's the pompous ham who looks on any suggestion—even though he may adopt it—as an assault on his dignity and his capability as a director. There's the "I wish they were puppets" school, and the condescending "Humor them, but for God's sake don't take them seriously" attitude. But by and large, one will be allowed the rights of his part, and an actor's skill and creativity will be respected.

There is little time for analytical discussion on the set, and none for doing what you should have done in your study. If you can *step before the camera with a clear and logical plan* of what you would like to do and how you would like to do it, the chances are that you will be far better off than if you had just learned the lines.

There are many scenes which an actor cannot study or conceive of playing without considering the character's movement in detail, so intermeshed are words and activity. What can you do when the director is not available for discussion of such a scene beforehand, when it's not even possible to familiarize yourself with the set because it won't be up, let alone dressed, until the day it's to be used? (This is an extreme situation, but it does occur.) I find it best to plan your own set at home, indicate the furniture, plant your own simulated props, imagine your fellow actors and *rehearse!* Walk through whatever pattern of activity seems logical to you, explore the possibilities, decide on a course, and turn up for work with an idea. It may have to be changed. Your timing will depend on the *actual* action and reaction of the other players, not on what you imagined; the set may turn out to be the reverse of the one you indicated for yourself; the whole thing may have to be altered, but the chances are that much of the work you have done will help you, and that your conception can be adapted to the director's to achieve a more successful result than if you offer him nothing other than memorized lines and sublime negativity in regard to the scene's execution.

Does continued motion picture acting ruin the stage actor? You mean like Charles Boyer, Spencer Tracy, Jessica Tandy, Madeleine Carroll, Paul Kelly, Joe E. Brown, Lee Cobb, Rex Harrison and Henry Fonda—each of whom spent from five to fifteen years in picture-making prior to their most recent appearances on the New York stage?

THERE's a line of Tennyson's in "Locksley Hall" about "a little hoard of maxims" being preached to someone's daughter. I think of it now because I am going to list a little hoard of maxims. They are offered without apology despite the fact that they're quite obvious—so obvious that it's surprising how often they're forgotten. I didn't make them up, although the way in which they're worded may be my own. They've been culled from various sources: The American Academy of Dramatic Art, Benno Schneider, Lee Strasberg, from some of the authorities I've read, or from an occasional director under whom I've worked. I've been asked repeatedly by students at either the Academy or the Actor's Lab in Hollywood about "rules" for acting. There may be none; at any rate, they are never precisely the same for any two actors. However, I've often been rescued on a set by returning to what I consider are first principles. All actors find themselves involved in difficult scenes where they can't see the woods for the trees and on such frightening occasions anything—maxim, platitude, rule, call it whatever you like—that will return you to security and the right path is worth remembering.

Establish the facts. It's surprising how much information is contained in the text, how many questions are answered by careful re-reading. Don't insist on doing work that has been done for you. Your own creative work should be based on the fact and suggestion supplied by the author, rather than on independent fancy.

Establish the relationships. Nobody, other than a bad actor, behaves in an identical manner toward all other persons—with the possible exception of behavior toward strangers of the same sex, size, age, appearance, manner, and so forth. A proper appreciation and understanding of all the other characters in the play is essential to understanding and performance of your own part.

Establish the surroundings. I hate actors who bump into the furniture, or stand where they seem to be goosed by a chair arm, or are frightened by tables, beds, lamps, doors and the surroundings in general. You can make an obvious liar of yourself and the character you play be pretending familiarity with props you've never bothered to consider. My references to "things" comes under this heading.

If. That word seems to be the key to the complexities of an actor's imaginative and creative processes. "If" provides an answer to innumerable questions, it's the equivalent of the algebraic X. *If* I were in this situation, what would *I* do? *If* I were *this kind of person* in this situation, what would I do? How would I feel, think, behave, react, etc.? "If" will often do for you what an author may have failed to do.

What is the action? (Purpose, intention) Neither you nor your character are ever without one. You may have to consult an analyst to understand your own, but if there is any mystery concerning the "action" of your character during any moment of his life on stage or before the camera—look out. The vacuum will be filled with either an actor's uncertainty or an actor's cliché.

What is the activity? (Physical business) You carry on some activity as long as you remain alive, even in absolute repose. "Activity" often contradicts action. For instance, the activity of sleep does not necessarily reflect the action "to rest." There are many examples. King Richard says quite accurately: "I can smile and murder whilst I smile."

The actor has great range and opportunity in the field of "activity" for, except in its broadest sense, it is rarely dictated by the author, being left, wisely, to the collaborative effort of actor and director. A good director will control "activity" but try to refrain from imposing it.

Correct "activity" on the part of a sensitive actor may provide a perfect reflection of, or delicate counterpoint to, the all important "action".

The Character's problem—never the actor's! Actor's problems are always intruding on the concentration which the actor should lend to the *character's* problems (that sounds like double talk, but I'm afraid I can't express it more simply). This is a constant difficulty in motion pictures and television, where much emphasis is laid on mechanical operation. Having attacked the actor's problem in study and rehearsal—sometimes only immediately prior to the "take"—awareness of it in performance must be sublimated by concentration on the character's problem (his action and activity).

In discomfort, look to the object. There is an object toward which every action or activity is directed. Have you ever watched a jeweler, glass in eye, probe the internals of a watch or a confectioner dipping chocolates or a cook flipping pancakes? (In each such case, the action and activity happen to complement rather than contradict one another.) There is a certain fascination in the simple concentration on the object involved.

An actor, playing the part of a man who wishes to please and impress another character to whom he is introduced, may not have such a theatrical activity in the business of a handshake as he would in flipping pancakes, but his concentration on the character, the—"object" of "to impress," will carry some of the same fascination.

When consistent with the text, create a mood opposite to the one you're going into. Clumsily expressed, but worth remembering. "Change" is the essence of "color," and in acting terms almost synonymous with "variety" and "development." *You must not manipulate the changes, but be aware of them.* Too many motion picture performances remain in one key. To risk a broad generalization, I would say that tears are usually more effective following laughter than as the logical result of lugubrious-ness. It's dangerous to talk about "effect" because of the temptation to substitute effect, a trick, for simple honest development. On the other hand, it is stupid not to recognize what is effective and not to try to come to it honestly.

An emotion always outlives its usefulness. That is, it will color an attitude long after the climax has passed and the incident provoking the emotion has been neutralized. This, too, is often overlooked in motion picture performances. Sometimes the reason for the oversight is understandable. If a scene is left uncompleted, in a state of emotional suspension, for a day or a week because the schedule or weather dictates that the company shoot something else, it may be difficult for the actor to recapture the exact emotional pitch when he returns to it. It is easier to match lighting or props than performance. The director's responsibility?—Yes, but also the actor's. However, this maxim is not meant to apply only in such emergencies. Emotional scenes, big scenes, which are not fully rehearsed are inclined to be contrived, with the result that the characters seem to run hot and cold at the same time. The leading lady suffers exquisitely in one moment and is picking her teeth in the next. This is "change" all right, but the wrong kind.

Sometimes both actor and director will prefer to shoot a big scene, usually a highly emotional one, with a minimum of any sort of rehearsal. They hope to capitalize on the spontaneity of the First Time. They are frightened that, with familiarity, the scene will go stale. They gamble on an *actual* first time rather than work toward a more complete *illusion* of the first time. The danger in this method is that the emotion evoked in the actor will be general rather than specific—belly emotion—having no object and being created out of equal parts of acting excitement and nervousness. Good readings are often based on this false stimulation which occurs in the initial run-through of playable material.

I can't list any more, although there are many. As I intimated in the beginning, the thing to do about acting is to act rather than read about it—or write about it.

66 The actor as thinker

Eric Bentley

April 1950

Eric Bentley (1916–) was at the start of a brilliant career when he published this piece. In his *annus mirabilis* 1950 he co-directed Brecht's *Mother Courage* in Munich, and staged the German-language premiere of *The Iceman Cometh* in Zurich, *The House of Bernarda Alba* at the Abbey Theatre, and a production of *him* with Kenneth Tynan in the lead. However, he was known in the U.S., if at all, as a translator and proponent of Brecht and the author of *The Playwright as Thinker* (1946). Two years later he would become Brander Matthews Professor of Dramatic Literature at Columbia and dramatic critic of the *New Republic*, and from those influential podiums could propagandize for new repertories and new approaches.

"In view of the bloody and dark period in which I am writing, a period when reason is misused and more and more mistrusted, I believe the plot of 'Hamlet' can be read this way. It is an age of warfare. Hamlet's father, king of Denmark, has slain the king of Norway in a victorious war of aggression. While the latter's son, Fortinbras, prepares for another war, the Danish king is also slain—by his brother. The brothers of the slain kings, now kings themselves, avoid war by having Norwegian troops cross Danish territory for a war of aggression against Poland. But at this point young Hamlet is called upon by the ghost of his warlike father to avenge the foul deed done to him. After some hesitation about repaying one bloody deed with another, almost deciding to go into exile, he meets young Fortinbras on the coast; the latter is on his way to Poland with his troops. Overwhelmed by the warlike example, Hamlet turns back and in a barbaric mêlée brings about the death of his uncle, his mother, and himself, leaving Denmark to the Norwegian. Throughout these events the young man—young but already corpulent—is seen making quite inadequate use of the new reason which he has learned at the University of Wittenberg. In the feudal enterprises to which he has returned, reason is at cross-purposes with him. Practice is unreasonable; his reason is unpractical. He falls: a tragic victim of the contradiction between such reason and such actions."

*   *   *   *   *

"He is the hero of the Renaissance. The hero of doubt, of a higher hesitation; he who is tired of mediocre life; he whom meanness tortures; he who is scrupulous, who brings all in question. He is chaste, pure, admirable, fascinating—Richard II, Henry VI and, last, Hamlet. . . . Paradise lost once again. The paradise of Faith is lost, Faith is exhausted. All is brought into question. It is the drama of belief; it is trial by doubt. But Shakespeare's hero preserves a chaste nature, a scrupulous intelligence, a noble heart; his soul remains pure. And, arriving at the brink of action, here he is, discussing the necessity of action, for manners are corrupt and one has come to an impasse. To act is to encourage mediocrity, greed, injustice. . . . How then can one continue to act and not stain one's soul? Thus the whole question is here: 'Howsoever thou pursuest this act, taint not thy mind.' Taint not thy mind. That's the problem. . . . Then appears the weariness with living, the tendency to suicide (individual or collective, the tendency is the same) the melancholy or furious acceptance of despair. . . . But, on the other side of the greatest despair the very depths of his soul re-emerge intact; it is then that the Shakespearian hero, though a temporal victim, wins his metaphysical victory. . . . His soul has remained pure. . . . Suicide itself has been impossible. True, he has let himself die with a sort of relief, but he has had a glimpse of grace, of the solution; he prophesies the advent of action in the new faith. The trial by doubt is over; one has passed by the void; one starts out again; one is truly reborn. He has sacrificed himself with the most lucid intelligence, perhaps the most complete that has ever existed, he has served as our martyr-guide in the most desolating labyrinths of doubt; in order to have us perceive in the end the renewed and primitive sensation of faith."

The first of the above passages is from Brecht's "Little Organum for the Theatre." The second is from Jean-Louis Barrault's "À Propos de Shakespeare et du théâtre." I quote them not to show that "Hamlet" is all things to all men, but to show that it is rather precisely opposite things to two types of modern men—the first type, materialist and collectivist; the second, religious and individualist. It will be noted that Brecht considers the events a challenge and the intellect of Hamlet inadequate to meet it, while Barrault considers the events disgusting and Hamlet too intellectual to lower himself to them. Brecht asks whether Hamlet can master the situation that confronts him. Barrault asks whether he can keep himself pure *despite* the situation that confronts him. Both, as interpreters of Shakespeare, are extremists. They pull Shakespeare in their own direction. They even do violence to facts. (It is not quite true that Hamlet turns back on seeing Fortinbras; he sets sail for England. It is not true that Richard II is chaste; it is intimated that he has homosexual relations with Bushy, Bagot, and Greene.) We live in a doctrinaire age.

From time to time I have set forward, as I understand them, the doctrines of Brecht insofar as they concern theatre. In trying to do the same by Jean-Louis Barrault I am faced with the difficulty, for which Barrault can hardly be blamed, that he is not primarily a writer. It is his performances and not his publications that claim our first attention, and one should judge the former independently of the latter. However, Barrault has now published two books—"À Propos de Shakespeare et du théâtre" (Editions de la Parade) and "Refléxions sur le théâtre" (Jacques Vautrain)—and is therefore asking us to judge him as a thinker as surely as a critic who played Hamlet would be asking us to judge him as an actor.

Barrault, we have seen already, is a thinker of the opposite camp from Brecht. As a theorist he adheres to that magical view of the theatre which I discussed last month. He finds theatre precisely where Brecht asks us not to find it. While Brecht tries to reduce the degree of illusion and "identification" by putting the action (as it were) in the third person and the past tense, Barrault sees the essence of theatre in its use of the first person and the present tense. The present tense: "In masterpieces," he writes, "the present is caught, and it is in this instant that the masterpiece disengages a magical presence." The first person: Barrault compares the actor to a child identifying himself with external nature (a tree, the wind). He finds this *animism* at the root of theatre, and is thus led away from the social conception of the art to a pantheistic, metaphysical, religious conception. Hence the language of Barrault's theatrical writing is romantic, magniloquent, in the manner of Gordon Craig. As a philosopher he hesitates, one might say, between estheticism and religion. In the passage on "Hamlet" quoted above, you are not sure if this is a religionist tactfully keeping his faith in the background or an esthete exploiting the vocabulary of religion. Barrault, as we are often told, is the heir of Jacques Copeau.

Brecht is an artist with a definite view of life; he knows it and is committed to it. Barrault's view of life is not so definite; he is not so sharply aware of its nature, and cannot therefore be very fully committed to it. Comparison between the two men should not therefore be pushed very far. It is better to see Barrault against his own background. You may judge what this is by reading him and by reading the men he quotes—by reading what one might call the French theatrical intelligentsia. This latter category, like all such, involves a simplification of the facts, yet we do find a surprising uniformity of tone on the higher levels of French writing about theatre—a tone, moreover, quite distinct from any other that is familiar to us (unless we are readers of Craig). A lofty tone, of a loftiness very deliberate and self-conscious. A ceremonious tone. A pretentious tone. Hear the French theatre-man linger on the long vowels of the words "pure" and "austère" and you catch the flavor of a whole outlook.

Pretentiousness is, I suppose, the price paid for having even legitimate pretensions. A certain public was prepared to accept the art of Copeau and his successors at a certain price. If it was to give up commercialism it must be repaid in kudos: as exchanges go, this was not a bad one. You pay the price, and in return Paris affords you more serious theatre than any other capital. You accept the bargain as a good one—except possibly when you review the books that stem from it. Here the achievements of the stage are not revealed; it is pretentious language that parades in the theatre of our minds.

The importance of my point here could not be fully driven home without an examination of modern French culture generally. For especially those of us who love France have to see some of the unfortunate positions into which the French intelligentsia, the whole educated class, has been led. This class suffers from a superiority complex. It is the "master race" of the cultural world. Your French intellectual does not need to know other languages, but he will consider you civilized in the degree to which you speak French. He need not go anywhere, because everybody else comes to him. Consequently, if provincialism is being cut off from the world, Paris is more provincial than Buenos Aires. Snobbery and superciliousness impose their limitations even on people who, personally, are far from snobbish and supercilious.

The background is relevant in considering the eccentricities of the critic Barrault. Glance at his books and you can hardly fail to note the symptoms of *haute couture*. Both books are limited editions on deluxe paper. The "Refléxions" contains illustrations by eleven artists, but, since all are of the same ambience, unity of tone is not impaired. It is a tone of good taste, charm, delicate wit, mannered melancholy. Barrault tells us that the late Christian Bérard is the very symbol of his whole theatrical enterprise. The remark is just. Bérard was a fine artist, but utterly one-sided. No one could dress a woman more handsomely than he, but he took every play and the stage itself for a woman. I should not like to align myself with stern Marxists condemning Bérard (and Barrault with him) for decadence, but I should see their point. In the theatre of Barrault, as he himself presents it in print, are apparent all the limitations of a certain period, a certain class, and a certain group.

As a critic Barrault is of course very limited—not because the words do not come, but because they come all too plentifully. Words, words, words. There is much in his books that should by all means have been written, but which should not have been published; it belongs to the private notebook of a charming person and a genius of another art. It is effervescence which has subsided before reaching the reader.

A large part of "À Propos de Shakespeare" is lecture material. The original audience was no doubt delighted simply to see and hear M. Barrault, to find that he can compose sentences, and sentences on a high level of discourse, to find that he reads the best of books and quotes Valéry; since Barrault concluded by reading a scene or two from "Hamlet," the performances must have been memorable. The mere text—now offered to us by his publishers—is the shell without the nut.

To an effusive manner and an affected style Barrault adds a couple of bad habits: the habit of meaningless eulogy and the habit of pointless classification. One searches in vain through the two volumes for insight into particular works of art. When Barrault dislikes something, he shies away from it. When he likes something, he bubbles over with joy and places it in a general category. Barrault's eulogies really say nothing but How Wonderful. Many pages of his commentary on Shakespeare and other authors down to Claudel really say no more than that. Even when a little more is being said, the style can be a kind of shadow-boxing, all waste motion. For example:

> "It is no less true that when we are too exhausted from seeking out the rare, Shakespeare is our great helper back to life: he helps us find our place, revives our heart, and makes us see the human again.
>
> But, you will say, you have in your patrimony another man in whom taste and genius agree, and in whom, as with Shakespeare, the scale comes down on the side of fecundity and force, on the side of life:

This is Molière.

Why do you prefer Shakespeare to him? I do not prefer Shakespeare to Molière. Molière is ourselves. From our birth . . ."

It might be said that Barrault starts a new paragraph every time he does not have a new idea, which, on occasion, is many times per page.

Then there are the classifications. They are often those of the schoolroom:

"It is no less true that in an international contest they would give to Racine the prize for taste and to Shakespeare the prize for abundance."

Not seldom Barrault exercises a playful, eccentric fancy in diagrams. He forms wings on the page with the titles of his five favorite books on theatre. In one chapter, encouraged by Artaud, he indulges in an orgy of columns and lists. Often starting a new paragraph with every sentence, underlining words as furiously as Queen Victoria, using block capitals and italics and dashes and exclamation marks for much more than they are worth, the actor as thinker helplessly tries to make shift with a mere book, where what he would prefer is the physical presence, the gesture, the vocal inflection.

None the less, when all these reservations have been made, Barrault is a man to read as well as see. If most actors should be warned away from writing, there are others—of whom Barrault is one—from whom we demand, sooner or later, a statement of policy, a confession of faith. These are the actor-directors, or at least those actor-directors who manage to stand for something. True, what they stand for has above all to be clear on the stage itself, but we also benefit from an attempt at verbal definition—Stanislavski's, Reinhardt's, or Copeau's. By his achievement onstage, Barrault has placed himself on the level of great predecessors; it is fair enough that he, like them, should try to explain himself.

If we do not find real criticism in his books, we do find autobiography and a surprising number of ideas. In the autobiography, probably the most revealing— as well as the amusing—portion consists of anecdotes. Justice can scarcely be done here to Barrault the raconteur. Suffice it that the "Refléxions" enable one to grasp Barrault's career from 1931 to 1949 pretty much as a whole—if one can read between the lines of such half-phoney diagrams as this:

Dullin	**Artaud**	**Granval**
THE EARTH	THE SUN	THE MOON
birth	trial by force	sentiment
body	spirit	soul
purity	truth	virtue
the pioneer	the prophet	the artist

The book makes it clear that just as important in Barrault's life as Dullin, Artaud, and Granval, was the mime Etienne Decroux, who doesn't happen to fit into the diagrammatic scheme. From Dullin, Barrault learnt the whole craft of theatre and acquired the right respect for his art. From Decroux, he learnt the art of pantomime, of which he has become the most celebrated exponent now living. Artaud gave him a lot of ideas (some of which seem to me untrue) and made him, so to speak, a member of the avant-garde. Granval, of the Comédie-Française, showed him that avant-garde ideas are not enough.

One of the most interesting things in Barrault's book is his awareness of the conflicting pressures of French culture and his determination to retain, if possible, what he has learnt both from the avant-garde and from the academic tradition. He does not despise the latter.

> "When I became a member of the Comédie-Française I noticed to what extent Granval was the representative of the illustrious house. This 'house,' as one calls it, which was born of the marriage of the traditional spirit coming from the Hôtel de Bourgogne and the modern spirit brought by Molière's troop. Granval was the very example of the great tradition in profound accord with the spirit of the avant-garde. Of these two apparently opposed tendencies, Granval managed to make a synthesis. My ambition henceforward was also directed towards this synthesis. . . ."

Which is something to remember when we hear Barrault condemned for not devoting himself wholly to avant-garde work. It is not a matter of compromise with commercialism. The academic tradition is not commercial. It is a matter of professional standards. Speaking of his production of "Le Soulier de Satin" at the Comédie, Barrault writes: "this admirable troop showed in the work a docility which one finds only in great professionals." Anyone who has worked with undocile amateurs or ungreat professionals will feel the force of the statement.

Barrault's sanity here is matched by the sanity of his conception of drama: an art in which the actor serves the author and in which the other theatre arts and artists serve the actor. It is not a startling view—but it is different from the fashionable one that drama is a combination of all the arts on an equal footing. In my opinion it is a true theory; and it is certainly the theory of Barrault's practice. That is why one can underline Barrault's written presentation of it and pass lightly over his more shocking avowals and revelations—such as: that he apparently has no means of discovering an important author (Cervantes, Hamsun, Faulkner) except when someone, usually a famous personage, puts the book in his hands; that he can profess general ignorance, yet roundly call Artaud's book "incontestably the most important thing written on theatre in the twentieth century"; that he places Artaud and Craig on the level of Aristotle and Corneille.

In addition to being a self-portrait, the "Refléxions" is strewn with ideas, not all of which are of the platitudinous sort cited above. The idea of Poetic Realism, as defined by Barrault, is well worth taking issue with. Barrault follows Artaud in believing that the theatre may be extremely physical, provided that at some point the physical take a fantastic leap into the metaphysical. He praises Laurence Olivier for painting blood on his feet in "Lear," because thus the actor is released from all further obligations to reality: he can just play the poetry:

> "This realistic note enables the actor precisely not to play the realism of the situation and liberates him poetically. In pushing realism to its extreme poetry frees itself."

The conception of poetry here implied is the dubious one of popular parlance, and, indeed, Barrault defines the poetic world as "the world of the waking dream."

Another idea to quarrel with is that of modern mime as against the older pantomime. The latter we know from the silent movies: the actors consciously use gesture as a substitute for words, a sort of deaf-and-dumb language. The technique, as Barrault observes, is appropriate to comedy. He adds that modern mime is to be gesture *without language*—*i.e.* having no reference to language—and that its destiny is the exploration of the tragic. Is this convincing? Barrault is ready of course with definitions of the tragic. But what can be done about it with mime alone? Such efforts in this direction as I have seen in various parts of France and Italy lose themselves—as one would expect—in a miasma of false poetry. Barrault, I should say, must either be content to incorporate mime in the drama or must return to the comic pantomime which he regards as old-fashioned. The fact is that most of the tragic (*i.e.* romantic) mime that one sees is old-fashioned at the first appearance, whereas Chaplin's "Shoulder Arms" is still as fresh as the day it was made.

Many ideas remain to be discussed. There is Diderot's paradox from which Barrault proceeds to the double nature of the actor and of man. There is "drama as the art of justice"; an idea by which Barrault brings himself a little closer to a "social" theatre (though why he thinks other writers less interested in justice than playwrights are is not made clear). There is the idea of *éloignement* or *dépaysement*, in which Barrault approaches from the individualist side the Brechtian idea of alienation. Many ideas: and one does not know if they come together into a coherent philosophy of theatre. But if my comments leave an unfavorable impression of the critic Barrault, let me repeat that he has to be read. Most writing by actors is the merest rubbish in comparison. Barrault must be taken seriously—even as a thinker.

Glossary of proper names

A.A. Alcoholics Anonymous, American self-help organization founded in 1935. Influenced by ideas of Carl Jung and William James, it offers its members a personal sponsor and a twelve-step program.

Abbey Theatre. See headnote to Chapter 34, "Between curtains: The acting of the Abbey Theatre".

Abravanel, Maurice (1903–93), Greek-born Swiss conductor and pianist. A student of Kurt Weill in Berlin, he eventually became guest conductor at the Berlin Philharmonic, but with the rise of the Nazis moved to Australia and then New York, where he directed Weill's musicals on Broadway. He was the permanent conductor of the Utah Symphony Orchestra (1947–79), and made the first complete recording of all of Mahler's symphonies.

Ackland, Rodney (1908–91), English playwright. His off-beat dramas *Strange Orchestra* (1931) and *The Old Ladies* (1935) were unexpectedly successful, but *The Pink Room* (1952), about a gay London club during the Blitz, was banned by the Lord Chamberlain (it was finally staged in 1987 as *Absolute Hell*). An admirer of Russian drama, he adapted a play of Ostrovsky's as *The Diary of a Scoundrel* and dramatized *Crime and Punishment* for John Gielgud.

An Actor Prepares. See headnote to Chapter 40, "Perspective in character building".

Actor's Laboratory. See headnote to Chapter 45, "The Actor's Lab".

Actors Studio. See headnote to Chapter 48, "A study of the Actors Studio".

Adams, Bown. See headnote to Chapter 8, "Seven interviews in search of good acting".

Adler, Luther (Lutha, 1903–84), American actor, born into the first family of the New York Yiddish theatre. Member of the Group Theatre (1932–7), he played lead roles in *Men in White* (1933), *Awake and Sing!* (1935), and *Golden Boy* (1937) (a would-be violinist like his first Broadway role in *Humoresque*, 1923). He appeared as Shylock in 1953 and replaced Zero Mostel in *Fiddler on the Roof*.

Adler, Stella. See headnote to Chapter 8, "Seven interviews in search of good acting".

Adrienne Lecouvreur, French drama by Eugène Scribe and Ernest Legouvé (1849), based on historical persons. Set in 1730 Paris, it concerns the love of Maurice, Comte de Saxe, for the actress Adrienne Lecouvreur. Intrigues lead to her death by poison. The play was a popular vehicle for Rachel and Bernhardt played her own version of it.

Advise and Consent, American novel by Allen Drury (1959). Congressional intrigues ferment when a former member of the Communist Party is nominated as Secretary of State. The character based on Richard Nixon dredges up a homosexual incident to blackmail a senator to cast a negative vote. Otto Preminger made it into a film with an all-star cast in 1962.

After the Ball (*Posle bala*), Russian play by Nikolay Pogodin (1934). On the night of a community dance, the members of a collective farm deal with social problems.

Agate, James (1877–1947), English dramatic critic, on the *Manchester Guardian* and the *Saturday Review*. His views, set forth in numerous collections and his journal *Ego*, were strongly opinionated, with a preference for French and popular theatre, but juicily phrased and compulsively readable.

Agave, mother of Pentheus, King of Thebes, in Euripides' *The Bacchae*. In a Dionysian delirium she thinks her son is a lion, slays him and mounts his head on a thyrsus.

The Ages of Man, English platform entertainment (1957). When John Gielgud found himself unemployed during the New Wave period of English drama, he put together a chrestomathy of Shakespearean excerpts, and unveiled it at the 1958 Edinburgh Festival. He toured this one-man show for years, and it supported him until he was seen as employable once more.

Aguglia, Mimi (1884–1970), Sicilian actress-manageress. On stage from childhood, she was "discovered" by Giovanni Grasso, and managed her own company which played *verismo* dramas by Verga and Pirandello, touring to North, South and Central Americas. The first actress to bob her hair, she became a U.S. citizen in 1945 and acted in Hollywood films (Assunta in *The Rose Tattoo*, 1955).

L'Aiglon, French verse drama by Edmond Rostand (1900), about Napoleon's son, the adolescent Duc of Reichstadt, who hopes to repeat his father's victories, but is captured at the Battle of Wagram and dies. It was written for Sarah Bernhardt as a grandiose breeches role, and was played in the U.S. by Maude Adams and Eva Le Gallienne (in her own abridgement).

Alcott, Louisa May (1832–88), American writer. Daughter of the Utopian thinker Bronson Alcott, she served as a nurse in a Union hospital during the Civil War. Her first and most abiding literary success was *Little Women* (1868), followed by a sequel *Good Wives* (1869), *Little Men* (1871) and *Jo's Boys* (1886).

Alias Jimmy Valentine, American melodrama by Paul Armstrong (1909), based on an O. Henry story. Lee Randall, a safe-cracker gone straight, is put in a quandary when the boss's daughter is locked in a safe. Should he save her and thus reveal his past?

Alice in Wonderland, correctly *Alice's Adventures in Wonderland*, children's book by Lewis Carroll (1865); the shortened title has become axiomatic for topsy-turvydom. It was frequently dramatized from the late nineteenth century. The most famous adaptation in the U.S. was that by Eva Le Gallienne and Florida Friebus for the Civic Repertory Company (1932) which incorporated episodes from *Through the Looking Glass*.

Alice Sit-By-The-Fire, English comedy by James M. Barrie (1905), written in his typically whimsical style. Amy Grey knows nothing of life except what she has learned at the theatre, and consequently misreads the behaviour of her "mutton-dressed-as-lamb" mother Alice.

All for Love, or The World Well Lost, English blank verse tragedy by John Dryden (1678). A concise reduction of Shakespeare's *Antony and Cleopatra*, it is focused on the siege of Alexandria and Antony's wavering between love and duty.

All God's Chillun Got Wings, American drama by Eugene O'Neill (1924). A tragedy of miscegenation, in which black Jim adores white Ella, who marries him only to protect her illegitimate child. Her prejudice poisons the marriage: she goes mad and destroys his prospects, but he continues to care for her. The Kamerny Theatre in Moscow staged it in 1929 under the title *Negroes*.

Allentuck, Max (1911–95), American manager. Out of vaudeville, he served as assistant to several successful producers. His Broadway debut was as company manager for *Jacobowsky and the Colonel* (1944); he then became an associate of Kermit Bloomgarten, managing *Death of a Salesman* (1949), *A View from the Bridge* (1955), *The Diary of Anne Frank* (1955), and *The Music Man* (1957). The first husband of Maureen Stapleton, he retired in 1986.

Allgood, Sara (1883–1950), Irish actress. A member of both the Irish National Theatre Society (1903) and the Abbey Theatre, Dublin, from 1904, she created Cathleen in *Riders from the Sea*, Deirdre in *Deirdre of the Sorrows* and Widow Quin in *Playboy of the Western World*. The summit of her Abbey career was Juno Boyle in *Juno and the Paycock* (1925) and Bessie Burgess in *The Plough and the Stars* (1924). On the US stage, she played more trivial roles (Jemima in *Shadow and Substance*) and in 1940 settled permanently in Hollywood.

Alving, Mrs Helena, in Ibsen's *Ghosts*, well-meaning widow of licentious Captain Alving and mother of the doomed artist Oswald. Her past decisions, always for the right reasons, are what bring on the catastrophe.

American Academy of Dramatic Arts, founded in New York in 1884 as the Lyceum Theatre School of Acting with a curriculum based on Delsarte. It later based its acting courses on Stanislavsky. A Los Angeles campus opened in 1974. Of uneven reputation, it graduated many of the leading American actors of the 1950s and 1960s.

American Gothic, American play by Martin Wolfson (1953). Directed by José Quintero at the Circle in the Square Theatre, with Jason Robards in the lead, it managed to survive for 77 performances.

American Laboratory Theatre, New York (1923–29). A school founded by Richard Boleslavsky and Maria Ouspenskaya to train an ensemble for three years in body, voice, imagination and intellect, in preparation for public performance. In practice, it concentrated on acting through improvisation and elements of the Stanislavsky system. Among its students were Stella Adler, Harold Clurman, Lee Strasberg and the critic Francis Fergusson.

American Shakespeare Festival Theatre, founded by Lawrence Langner in 1951 in Stratford, Conn.; it remained in full operation to 1979. Its stage was a rough equivalent of an Elizabethan playhouse. It offered summer seasons of plays by Shakespeare and a select few others, mainly as showcases for already established stars, but never gained regular critical acclaim or widespread audience popularity.

American Theatre Wing, New York. Founded as part of the Allied Relief Fund in the Second World War, it is devoted to "supporting excellence and education in theatre." It annually presents the Antoinette Perry or "Tony" awards for distinction in live theatre, and makes grants to not-for-profit theatre companies.

Ames, Winthrop (1871–1937), American producer and director, who gained experience managing the Castle Square Opera House, Boston (1904–8) and the New and Booth Theatres, New York. There he introduced the "New Stagecraft" by importing Reinhardt's orientalist pantomime *Sumurûn* in 1912, but was best known for his Gilbert and Sullivan revivals. His adaptation of *Snow White* (1913) inspired Walt Disney's first full-length animated feature film.

Amphitryon 38. See headnote to Chapter 52, "A play in the making".

Anatomy of a Murder, American film directed by Otto Preminger from the novel by Robert Traver (1959). A courtroom drama set in a small Wisconsin town, it is accompanied by a Duke Ellington score. In a less than crystal-clear moral climate, lawyers James Stewart and George C. Scott contest the guilt of an army sergeant (Ben Gazzara) who murdered his wife's (Lee Remick) alleged rapist.

Anderson, John (1896–1943), American dramatic critic on the New York *Post* (1918–24), the *Evening Journal* (1928–37) and the *Journal-American* (1937–43).

Anderson, John Murray (1886–1954), American producer and director, inspired by Gordon Craig in his mounting of sumptuous pageants. He masterfully staged dance-heavy and ingenious revues, such as the *Greenwich Village Follies* (1919) and *Murray Anderson's Almanac* (1929, 1953).

Anderson, Judith (Frances Margaret Anderson-Anderson, 1898–1992), Australian actress, translated to the U.S., who excelled as sinister, hawk-eyed matrons. Her best roles include Lavinia in *Mourning Becomes Electra* (1932), Gertrude to Gielgud's Hamlet (1936), Lady Macbeth to Maurice Evans' Macbeth (1941), and, most memorably, Robinson Jeffers's Medea (1947, 1974). Late in life she appeared as Hamlet, a miscalculation.

Anderson, Maxwell (1888–1959), American playwright, whose high reputation has not survived his death. Though he began with a lively, foul-mouthed chronicle of the First World War, *What Price Glory* (with Laurence Stallings, 1924), he aspired to orotund verse drama: *Elizabeth the Queen* (1930), *Winterset* (1935), *Joan of Lorraine* (1947). At the end of an illustrious career, his last produced play was the Grand Guignol exercise, *The Bad Seed* (1954).

The Andersonville Trial, American play by Saul Levitt (1959). A courtroom drama drawn from documentation of the post-Civil War trial of Henry Wirtz, commandant of an appalling Confederate P.O.W. camp, it raised questions about the moral neutrality of following orders. George C. Scott made a meal of the role of Judge Advocate.

Anderssen, Karl Ernst Adolf (1818–79), Silesian chess master. Coming to prominence late, he won international tournaments in 1851, 1862 and 1870. His technique was noted for careful timing of his moves.

Andreev, Leonid Nikolaevich (1871–1919). The most fashionable Russian playwright before the First World War, he ranged from naturalism to symbolism, his works permeated with a morbid pessimism. *The Life of Man*, staged by Stanislavsky in Moscow and by Meyerhold in St Petersburg (1907), expressed the absurdity of human existence. His best known play outside of Russia is *He Who Gets Slapped* (1915), in which the lost illusions theme is played out in a European circus.

Androcles and the Lion, comedy by G. B. Shaw (1916). The fable of the early Christian who pulls a thorn from a lion, who later refrained from eating him in the arena, is given a Shavian veneer.

Andromache (*Andromaque*), French verse tragedy by Jean Racine (1667). In the aftermath of the Trojan war, Hector's widow Andromache is the captive of Pyrrhus, who loves her and cold-shoulders his fiancée Hermione. A series of intrigues and broken promises leads to the death or insanity of the leading characters.

Angels in the Wings, American revue (1947). It is remembered solely for Elaine Stritch's performance of "Civilization" ("Bongo, Bongo, Bongo, I don't want to leave the jungle").

Anglin, Margaret (1876–1958), Canadian actress whose first outstanding role was Roxane in *Cyrano de Bergerac* (1898). She devoted much of her career to classical drama, staged according to the ideas of Gordon Craig. *Antigone, Electra* and *Medea* were produced in the Hearst Amphitheater at the University of California, Berkeley, (1910–15) with designs by Livingston Platt.

Anne of Green Gables (1919), Lucie Maude Montgomery's children's book about a childless couple on Prince Edward Island who order a male orphan and are sent a girl. It was filmed from a screenplay by Kenneth Macgowan in 1934, and its featured performer, Dawn O'Day, became so popular she changed her name to that of her character, Anne Shirley.

ANTA, the American National Theatre and Academy, incorporated by an Act of Congress in 1935 as a non-profit, non-sectarian "people's theatre". It later staged poetic drama and revivals of past hits at the former Guild Theatre and then the Washington Square Theatre.

Antoine, André (1858–1943), French director and actor, labelled "the father of stage naturalism". His amateur Théâtre Libre in Paris inaugurated new plays in realistic settings, and later introduced Ibsen, Strindberg, and Brieux. As director of the Odéon, he innovated with staging Molière and presented the first uncut *King Lear* in French.

Antony and Cleopatra, blank verse tragedy by William Shakespeare, from Plutarch (1606). With more locations than any other Shakespearean play, it shuttles back and forth between Europe and Africa, to chronicle the last phase of Antony and Cleopatra's passion, ending in their deaths.

At various times in the twentieth century, Cleopatra was undertaken by Katharine Cornell, Tallulah Bankhead, Edith Evans, Vivien Leigh and Peggy Ashcroft.

The Apple Cart, political extravaganza by G. B. Shaw (1930). Some time in the future, glib King Magnus locks horns with his progressive Cabinet over the surrender of his veto; he threatens to abdicate and run for Parliament, a threat which makes his ministers capitulate.

Apple Blossoms, American operetta by William Le Baron, Victor Jacobi and Fritz Kreisler (1919). A trifle about a husband and wife who try to maintain an open marriage, it is significant for promoting the careers of Fred and Adele Astaire, who danced specialities in it.

Arabella, German/Austrian opera by Richard Strauss and Hugo von Hofmannsthal, their last collaboration (1933). A sentimental and comic plot set to serious music, it has a hysterical girl from an indigent family looking for Mr Right in Franz Joseph's Vienna.

Archer, William (1856–1924), Scottish dramatic critic and playwright. His reviews appeared in many journals, including *Figaro*, *The World*, *The Nation* and *The Star*, and in the 1890s were collected annually. He argued for a national theatre, and was the U.K.'s leading proponent of Ibsen, translating all his prose and some of his poetic plays. His one successful play, the retrograde melodrama *The Green Goddess*, is immortalized in a salad dressing.

Aristotle (384–322 B.C.E.), Greek philosopher. His *Poetics*, a collection of lecture notes on the drama, offered the concepts of catharsis, reversal, recognition, but in such cryptic and fragmentary form that they have been regularly reinterpreted over the centuries. In the sixteenth and seventeenth centuries, a series of rigid neo-Aristotelian rules and unities were formulated.

Arliss, George (Arliss-Andrews, 1868–1946), English actor, who came to the U.S. in 1901. His ferret-like face, graced by a monocle, was usually seen as Oriental villains (Zakkuri in *The Darling of the Gods*, 1902; the Rajah in *The Green Goddess*, 1921), benevolent codgers (*Old English*, 1924) and, most frequently, his perennial *Disraeli* (1911, filmed 1929).

The Armored Train (*Bronepoezd* 14–69), Russian play by Vsevolod Ivanov (1927). A propaganda piece about Siberian partisans demolishing a train crucial to a White Russian victory, it introduced the character of the levelheaded Bolshevik activist. Its success at the Moscow Art Theatre gave that company credibility with the Soviet government.

Arms and the Man, comedy by G. B. Shaw (1904). Ideas about war and pacifism give a grounding to this otherwise slight but well-constructed romantic comedy, set in the Balkans. It inspired, very loosely, the operetta *The Chocolate Soldier*.

Armstrong, Louis Daniel (1900–71), American jazz musician, known as "Satchmo". From the mid-1920s he established a reputation as a virtuoso improvisational soloist on the trumpet. He also introduced "scat" singing, orally mimicking instrumental sounds with his gravelly voice. At 63, he recorded his biggest hit "Hello, Dolly!".

Arnold, Benedict (1741–1801), American general whose name is synonymous with treason. A trusted aide of George Washington during the Revolutionary War, he hearkened to his Tory wife and nursed a grudge about being overlooked. With British Major André, he brewed a plot to betray his command of West Point. When it failed, André was hanged and Arnold fled to England. He has often been the subject of plays such as James A. Culpepper's *Treason at West Point* (1965).

Aronson, Boris (1898–1980), Russian-born designer, who introduced his constructivist approach at the New York Yiddish Art Theatre and the Group Theatre. He provided settings for *Awake and Sing!* (1935) and a host of other productions, culminating in the Chagallesque *Fiddler on the Roof.* He invented Projected Scenery, throwing coloured light on to neutral gray scrim.

Around the World in Eighty Days (*Le Tour du monde dans 80 journées*), Jules Verne's novel about an eccentric Englishman's bet (1873), was frequently staged as an excuse for spectacle and extravaganza. Verne was first in the field (1875) and his adaptation was translated for New York by the Kiralfy brothers. Orson Welles concocted a new version (1945) to feature magic tricks, Cole Porter tunes and a train wreck. Mike Todd's lavishly cast film (1968) gave it a new lease on life.

Arsenic and Old Lace, a macabre American comedy by Joseph Kesselring (1941), which had a run of 1,444 performances. In it two sweet old ladies of Brooklyn who poison and bury single gentlemen for altruistic reasons clash with their nephew, a genuine homicidal maniac.

The Art of the Theatre, essay by Edward Gordon Craig (1904), containing a Dialogue between a Playgoer and a Stage Director. In it, the future of the theatre is put in the hands of a director who can be "faithful" to a text by finding out its rhythm, movement, and color. It was expanded as *On the Art of the Theatre* (1911).

Artaud, Antonin (1896–1948), French actor and writer. A classmate of Barrault at Dullin's Paris studio, sometime surrealist, co-founder of the Théâtre Alfred-Jarry, he is best known as the theorist of the "Theatre of Cruelty" (1932–3). Impressed by the physicality of Balinese dance and his own paranoia, he posited the theatre as an arena of psychic therapy, where audiences would be lobotomized by the intensity of the performance. His own experiment, staging *The Cenci* (1935), was inconclusive, but his influence, especially in the 1960s and 1970s, was unavoidable.

Arts Theatre Club, London, founded in 1927 to stage experimental drama. Many of its productions were transferred to the West End, aiding the careers of young actors (Edith Evans in *The Lady with a Lamp*, 1929; John Gielgud in *Richard of Bordeaux*, 1932). Under Alec Clunes (1942–52), it introduced *The Lady's Not for Burning* (1948), and under Campbell Williams (1953–62) *Waiting for Godot* (1955). It then passed to the Royal Shakespeare Company and miscellaneous uses.

The Art Student League, New York, was founded in 1875 by Richard Watson Gilder, father of *Theatre Arts'* editor Rosamund Gilder. Primarily a school for painters and sculptors, based on the French studio system, it also offered lectures and exhibitions. Its faculty boasted Thomas Eakins, Childe Hassam and Augustus Saint Gaudens, and its alumni include Winslow Homer, Thomas Hart Benton, Georgia O'Keeffe, Reginald Marsh and John Sloan. It is still in operation.

As You Like It, blank verse comedy by William Shakespeare (1599). This pastoral romance of a lady in danger disguised as a boy wooing a youth in danger has never lost its popularity. The cross-dressed role of Rosalind has proven irresistible to actresses as different as Edith Evans and Katherine Hepburn. The return to all-male casts began in the 1970s.

Asquith, Raymond (1878–1916), English lawyer and literary man. Son of the Prime Minister H. H. Asquith, he died seeing active service during the First World War. A good friend of the novelist John Buchan, he was also a member of the Coterie, a supercilious group of wealthy intellectuals.

Atkins, Sir Robert (1886–1972), English actor and director. After touring with Martin-Harvey, Forbes-Robertson and Frank Benson, he worked at the Old Vic from 1915 to 1925, devoting himself almost exclusively to Shakespeare. He resuscitated *Troilus and Cressida* and *Titus Andronicus*, and staged the first English *Peer Gynt*. He was a pioneer of reviving Elizabethan stage conditions and presenting open-air productions.

Atkinson, Brooks (1894–1984), American dramatic critic. Leading reviewer for the New York *Times* off and on from 1926 to 1960, he was admired for his evenhandedness and appeal to the taste of the common man. His middle-of-the-road opinions were couched in well-formed sentences.

Auden, W[ystan] H[ugh], English poet and playwright (1907–73). His plays, written in collaboration with Christopher Isherwood and first staged by the London Group Theatre, are mildly allegorical comments on the state of the world: *The Dog Beneath the Skin* (1935), *The Ascent of F.6* (1936) and *On the Frontier* (1938). In the 1950s, he began, in collaboration with his life partner Chester Kallman, to compose new opera libretti (*The Rake's Progress*, 1951) and translate old ones (*The Magic Flute*).

Aufricht, Ernst, German actor and producer. It was his commission of Bertolt Brecht to create a work for the Theater am Schiffbauerdamm in Berlin in 1928 that led to *Die Dreigroschenoper*. He subsequently produced the original cast album, as well as Brecht and Weill's *Happy End*, *Mahagonny* and *Der Kuhhandel*.

Aurthur, Robert Alan (1922–78), American screenwriter and director. Most of his work was done for television in the 1950s and 1960s. His best known film, which he both wrote and produced, is *All That Jazz* (1979).

Averardi, Franco-Bruno. See headnote to Chapter 31, "Eleonora Duse".

Awake and Sing!, the best play of Clifford Odets, staged effectively by Harold Clurman for the Group Theatre in 1935. The vicissitudes of an ordinary Jewish family in the Bronx stand for the oppression of the spirit under capitalism. An ensemble piece, it is distinguished by a snappy use of slang and newly minted colloquialisms.

Awakening of Spring (*Frühlingserwachen*), German tragedy of sex by Frank Wedekind (1891). A group of pubescent adolescents comes to various sticky ends, because of social conventions and lack of sex education.

Ayliff, H[enry] K[iell]. (1871–1949), South African actor and director. From 1922 most of his work was done for the Birmingham Repertory Theatre, where he staged modern-dress productions of Shakespeare, among them *Macbeth* and *The Taming of the Shrew* (1927), as well as Shaw's *Caesar and Cleopatra* (1925). His productions of *Yellow Sands* (1927) and *Payment Deferred* (1931) were seen on Broadway.

Aymé, Marcel (1902–67), French writer. Known chiefly as a prose stylist, whose short story of a man who walks through walls, *Le Passe-muraille* (1943), is now a classic, he also had success as a playwright and screenwriter. *Clérambard* (1950), his farce about small-town prostitution, was an Off-Broadway hit in a watered-down version, and *Tête des autres* attacked capital punishment. He also shaped French adaptations of *The Crucible* (1954) and *Night of the Iguana* (1965).

Ayrton, Michael (1921–75), English painter and designer. Considered one of the Neo-Romantic school, influenced by Eugene Berman, John Piper and Graham Sutherland, he designed John Gielgud's *Macbeth* (1940). He continued as a stage designer and illustrator, as well as a radio quiz contestant.

Babanova, Mariya Ivanovna (1900–83). Russian actress, female lead in Meyerhold's early biomechanical experiments in the 1920s. A new lease on her creative life came with Aleksey Arbuzov's *Tanya* (1939), which allowed her to show the dilemmas of a contemporary woman. Essentially a miniaturist, she excelled in details, her early agit-prop style developing into a more refined psychology.

Babes in Arms, American musical comedy by Richard Rodgers and Lorenz Hart (1937), in which the young scions of showbiz families put on a show to maintain their independence. It featured George Balachine's choreography and the numbers "My Funny Valentine", "Johnny One Note" and "The Lady Is a Tramp".

Babes in the Wood. An English folk tale, found in print no earlier than 1595, it tells of two small children abandoned to die in the forest by their wicked uncle, so he might inherit the estate. From the 1860s, given a happy ending, it was a popular plot for British pantomime, with comic cut-throats and fairy choruses.

The Bacchanals, more commonly known as *The Bacchae*, tragedy by Euripides (406 B.C.). Dionysos comes to Thebes to wreak revenge on the house of Cadmus.

Bacon, Frank (1864–1922), American stock actor who specialized in rube parts, shot to fame in *Lightnin'* (1918), his own comedy, written with Winchell Smith. It ran for three years and broke all records with 1,291 performances. Will Rogers played it in the movies.

Badel, Alan (1923–82), English actor. Although he had leading-man qualities, particularly a throbbing voice, he was usually cast as villains. His best film role was as John the Baptist opposite Rita Hayworth in *Salome* and for years he played the Sheriff of Nottingham in a television series of *Robin Hood*.

Baker, George Pierce (1866–1935), American educator, whose Workshop 47 course at Harvard offered a laboratory to such embryonic playwrights as Eugene O'Neill, Edward Sheldon, Sidney Howard, S. N. Behrman and Philip Barry. When Harvard's anti-theatrical prejudice refused him a fully accredited program, he moved to Yale to found its Department of Drama in 1925.

Bakst, Léon (Lev Samoilovich Rozenberg, 1866–1924). Russian designer, co-founder in 1898 of the World of Art, and in 1904, with Sergey Diaghilev and Aleksandr Benois, the Ballets Russes, for which he designed revolutionary costumes and sets, especially after the company moved to Paris in 1909. With his exotic, ornamental style, he greatly influenced the next generation in haute couture and interior decoration as well as the theatre.

Bald Iggle, a mythological bird created by Al Capp in his comic strip *Li'l Abner*. The Iggle had the dire quality of forcing people to tell the naked truth.

Ballet Russe de Monte Carlo, a name adopted by several companies descended from Diaghilev's Ballets Russes. Using that name the René Blum and Col. de Basil Ballet Russes de Monte Carlo, with Georges Balanchine and Leonide Massine as choreographers, toured the U.S. annually from 1933 under Sol Hurok's management. Blum left in 1936 to form his own company, joined in 1938 by Massine. The two companies eventually resolved into the Ballet Russes de Monte Carlo (Blum and Massine), with the U.S. as its turf, and the Original Ballet Russes (de Basil) claiming Europe.

Ballets Russes, Russian ballet company, created in 1910 by Sergey Diaghilev, as part of the Russian seasons of opera and dance in Paris. Its troupe was drawn from the Imperial Ballet of St Petersburg, and included Vatslav Nizhinsky, Tamara Karsavina, Leonid Myassin and Mikhail Fokin. Diaghilev promoted inventive designers (Bakst, Benois, Picasso) and composers (Debussy, Stravinsky, Prokofiev, Satie) to create surprising synthesis of sound, movement and colour in such works as *Scheherazade* (1910), *Petrushka* (1911), *L'Après-midi d'un faune* (1912) and *The Rite of Spring* (1913).

The Band Wagon, American revue by George S. Kaufman and Howard Dietz, with music by Arthur Schwartz (1931). It applied New Stagecraft principles to light entertainment by installing a revolving stage and lighting the show from the balcony. Fred Astaire appeared in "A Beggar Waltz" and a take-off on feuds "The Last of the Claghornes".

Bankhead, Tallulah (1902–68), American actress, who established herself as a star in London before appearing on Broadway as Regina in *The Little Foxes* (1939) and Sabrina in *The Skin of Our Teeth* (1942). Her celebrity was based in part on her husky voice, temperamental rehearsal habits and unabashed sexuality.

Bardot, Brigitte (Camille Javal, 1934–), French actress. At 18, she married the film-maker Roger Vadim who promoted her as a pouting, blonde, bikini-clad "sex kitten" in *And God Created Woman* ... (1952). Her film career was undistinguished, and as she aged she turned to political activism. In 1986 she founded the Brigitte Bardot Foundation to promote animal rights.

Barrault, Jean-Louis. See headnote to Chapter 36, "Child of Silence".

Barrett, Wilson (1846–1904), English actor-manager. A matinee idol of imposing profile and stentorian voice, he managed the Princess's Theatre, London from 1881. There he made several fortunes with his perdurable hits, the melodramas *The Lights o' London, The Sign of the Cross* (a proto-DeMillian epic of Romans and Christians, which he coauthored) and *The Silver King*.

The Barretts of Wimpole Street, English historical drama by Rudolph Besier (1930). This conventional account of the romance between ailing and cloistered Elizabeth Barrett and the poet Robert Browning had its villain in the person of her monstrous father. It premiered at the Malvern Festival, ran in London for a year and a half with Cedric Hardwicke as the "cruel pari-ent", and another two years in New York and on the road with Katharine Cornell as the interesting invalid.

Barrie, Sir James Matthew (1860–1937), Scottish playwright. His many plays, shot through with whimsy and carpentered with great expertise, are, for the most part, too twee and disingenuous to stand revival. Only *Peter Pan* (1904), the story of the boy who wouldn't grow up, has survived in multiple avatars.

Barry, Philip (1896–1949), American playwright. A student of George Pierce Baker, he confected urbane comedies about the mores of high society: *Paris Bound* (1927), *Holiday* (1928), *Hotel Universe* (1930), *The Animal Kingdom* (1932) and *The Philadelphia Story* (1939), which gave a boost to Katherine Hepburn's career. By the 1940s he was considered a back number.

Barrymore, Ethel (1879–1959), American actress, daughter of Maurice, sister of John. Her first success was in *Captain Jinks of the Horse Marines* (1901) and she became society's darling, playing in Barrie, Ibsen, Shakespeare and drawing-room comedy. As Miss Moffat in *The Corn Is Green* (1940), she capped her stage career and retired to make movies in Hollywood.

Barrymore, John (1882–1943), American actor. With his clear-cut profile, resonant voice and personal magnetism, he was considered the great white hope of the U.S. stage. This seemed to be insured by his performances in *Justice* (1916), *Redemption* (1918), *Richard III* (1920) and *Hamlet* (1922). Indolence, alcohol and womanizing led him to fritter away his talents in Hollywood, returning to the stage as a self-parody in *My Dear Children* (1939).

Barrymore, Maurice (Herbert Blythe, 1847–1905), Anglo-American actor. A handsome leading man, he partnered Helena Modjeska in *As You Like It* and made a career of his own swashbuckling *Captain Swift* (1888). He married into the Drew theatrical dynasty, sired three children and died of syphilitic paresis.

Barter Theatre was named for the barter system of admission used when it was founded in Depression-era Abingdon, Virginia in 1933. It became known for the high quality of its ensemble and was appointed State Theatre of Virginia.

Bassermann, Albert (1867–1952), German actor. He worked with the

Meiningen company and under Otto Brahm, especially in Ibsen. Max Reinhardt cast him in a wide variety of roles, from Othello to farceurs in Nestroy, but the rise of the Nazis forced him to emigrate to the U.S., where he worked in film for Hitchcock (*Foreign Correspondent*), among others, playing benevolent codgers.

La Bataille de la Marne (*The Battle of the Marne*), French play by André Obey (1931). Written for the Compagnie des Quinze, it uses a bare stage, a Messenger narrator and a chorus of women to depict a heartening French victory during the First World War.

Batalov, Nikolai Petrovich (1899–1937), Russian actor. At the Moscow Art Theatre, his razor-sharp Figaro (1927) put him in the first rank of actors, a Russian answer to Rudolph Valentino. He was *de facto* head of the acting company from 1925.

Battleship Gertie, American play by Frederick Hazlitt Brennan (1935), which sank without a trace. A naval farce meant to capitalize on the success of *Hello, Sailor*, it had a huge cast which included Burgess Meredith in one of his first Broadway roles as Seaman Jones. When it was remade as a film, *Miss Pacific Fleet*, Allen Jenkins played his part.

Baylis, Lilian (1874–1937), English manageress. Her aunt, Emma Cons, offered her the management of the Royal Victoria Coffee Music Hall in London, and she converted it to a cheap-admission theatre for drama, later adapting Sadler's Wells to ballet and opera. From 1914 to 1923, she produced the entire Shakespearean canon at the Vic. She was mocked for her cheese-paring economies and eccentricities, but honored for her devotion to the legitimate theatre.

Be Good, Sweet Maid!, English play (1957) by C. E. Webber. The rest of the quotation, from Charles Kingsley, goes "and let who will be clever".

The Bear (*Medved*), one-act Russian "joke" by Anton Chekhov (1888). A rude and ungainly landowner intrudes on a grieving widow to collect a debt. In best farce tradition, they hate one other, fight a duel and fall in love. The plot updates Petronius's ancient Roman tale of the Widow of Ephesus, which Christopher Fry later turned into the one-act play *A Phoenix Too Frequent*.

Becket, ou l'honneur de Dieu (*Becket, or The Honor of God*), French play by Jean Anouilh (1958). A historically inaccurate examination of the friendship and falling-out of King Henry II and Thomas à Becket. Laurence Olivier played Becket to Anthony Quinn's Henry for the Broadway production of 1960, only to discover that the warm-hearted King was the better part; he switched to it on Quinn's departure. A successful film (1963) starred Peter O'Toole and Richard Burton.

Beckett, Samuel (1906–89), Irish writer, for a time James Joyce's secretary. Settling permanently in Paris in 1937, he wrote a number of essays and novels before embarking on drama. His first play, *Waiting for Godot* (1954), appeared in French, then in his English translation, a process continued with *Endgame* (1960) and *Happy Days* (1961). His later plays made even fewer concessions to conventional dramaturgy. At first scorned as wilfully cryptic and incomprehensible, he has become a classic byword for salient minimalism.

Beerbohm, Max (1872–1956), English humorist and critic, half-brother of the actor-manager Herbert Beerbohm-Tree. As dramatic critic for the London *Saturday Review* (1898–1910), he trained his wry wit at all manner of performances. He teased stars of the legit while praising the vitality of the music hall.

Beethoven, Ludwig von, German composer (1770–1827). His chief contributions to the lyric stage are his only opera *Fidelio* (1805–14) and a number of overtures (to *Egmont*, etc.). He himself appeared as the protagonist of several plays, among them René Fauchois's of 1909, later made into a film with Harry Bauer.

The Beggar's Opera, English ballad opera by John Gay (1728). A satire both of Italian *opera seria* and political corruption, it introduced the enduring characters of the highwayman Macheath, the fence Peachum, and his daughter Polly. Elisabeth Hauptmann recommended it to Brecht and it served as the basis for his *Threepenny Opera*.

Behrman, S[amuel] N[athaniel] (1893–1973), American playwright, specializing in comedies of manners about the privileged and sophisticated. Usually produced by the Theatre Guild, they include *Biography* (1932), *End of Summer* (1936) and *No Time for Comedy* (1939), and provided gratifying roles for such actors as Ina Claire and Katharine Cornell.

Bein, Albert (1902–90), American playwright and producer. A product of a reform school who lost a leg trying to escape, this "proletarian playwright" exposed abuses at reformatories in *Little Ol' Boy* (1933) and created an agit-prop about a strike at a Carolina cotton mill in *Let Freedom Ring* (1935). His screenplay *Boy Slaves* (1938) was a harrowing depiction of a juvenile prison farm. He then moved to fantasy with *Heavenly Express* (1940).

Belasco Theatre, New York, was opened in 1907 as the Stuyvesant Theatre by the impresario and director David Belasco, with a penthouse for himself on top (the name changed in 1910). It housed his lavish productions of *The Return of Peter Grimm* (1911), *The Governor's Lady* (1912) and *The Merchant of Venice* (1925). It eventually became a Shubert property and housed the National Players repertory company in the 1990s.

A Bell for Adano, American play by Paul Osborne, from the novel by John Hersey (1944). Italian-American Major Joppolo, put in charge of a captured Sicilian town, works to preserve a 700-year-old bell, as he falls in love with a fisherman's daughter. This love *vs* duty plot starred Fredric March as Joppolo. When it was made into a film in 1945, the recalcitrant Major was played by John Hodiak.

Benavente y Martínez, Jacinto (1866–1954), the most popular Spanish playwright of the early twentieth century. His oeuvre comprises 168 plays, aimed at the middle-class playgoer, but only *The Bonds of Interest* (1907), which uses *commedia dell'arte* characters in a modernist way, found popularity in English.

Bennett, Constance Campbell (1904–65), American actress. Daughter of Richard and sister of Barbara and Joan, she entered silent pictures in 1924 and by 1931 was one of Hollywood's highest paid stars. Her vivacious presence enlivened *What Price Hollywood?* (1932, the model for *A Star in Born*), *Our Betters* (1933), *Topper* (1937, as the ghostly Marian Kirby) and *Two-Faced Woman* (1941) out-facing Garbo.

Benson, Sir Frank (1858–1939), English actor-manager. Oxford-educated, he trouped his Shakespeare company through the English provinces from 1883, playing all the leads himself. His aquiline looks and athletic physique made up for less than subtle acting. The young actors in the troupe, often chosen for their skill at cricket, received invaluable training and plumed themselves on being Old Bensonians.

Benson, Lady (Constance Featherstonhaugh, 1860–1946), English actress. She played opposite her husband in leading roles.

Bentley, Eric. See Chapter 66, "The actor as thinker".

Bérard, Christian (1902–49), French designer. His earliest work was done for Diaghilev and he continued to serve the ballet. For the theatre, he worked most with Jean Cocteau (*La voix humaine*, 1930; *La machine infernale*, 1934; *L'Aigle à deux têtes*, 1946), Louis Jouvet and Jean-Louis Barrault, for whom he remodelled the look of Molière comedies. His style was both precious and audacious, colourful and delicate, and always surprising.

Bérénice, verse tragedy by Jean Racine (1670). The intrigue is based on another love *vs* duty situation: should Titus, Emperor of Rome, consummate his affair with Berenice, granddaughter of Herod the Great?

Berghof, Herbert. See Chapter 8, "Seven interviews in search of good acting".

Berlin Stories, English fiction by Christopher Isherwood (1946), a conflation of *Mr Norris Changes Trains* and *Goodbye to Berlin*. A dispassionate fictional treatment of Isherwood's experiences in Weimar Germany, the stories mute the homosexual element as they introduce the reader to the sprightly Sally Bowles. They served as inspirations for the play *I Am a Camera* and the musical *Cabaret*.

Berliner Ensemble. See **Brecht, Bertolt** and **Weigel, Helene**.

Bernhardt, Sarah (Rosine Bernard, 1845–1923), eidolon of the actress from the late nineteenth century to today, famous for her golden voice, unfashionable svelteness, love affairs with men and women, publicity stunts, payment in gold, extravagant on-stage deaths, indomitable touring, and, after an amputation, her wooden leg. She could dazzle as Hamlet and Phèdre, but many of her vehicles were tailored by Sardou to a unvarying pattern, allowing her to smile, snarl, rhapsodize and do violence by turns.

Bernstein, Leonard (1918–90), American composer and conductor. His activities were unequally divided between the world of classical music and that of musical comedy. For Broadway, he composed the scores of *On the Town* (1944), *Wonderful Town* (1953), *Candide* (1956) and *West Side Story* (1974), often collaborating with choreographer Jerome Robbins.

The Best Man, American play by Gore Vidal (1960) about the seamy side of Presidential politics (if that's not redundant). An upstanding liberal refuses to use the threat of homosexual blackmail to force a sleazy senator, based on Richard Nixon, out of the race for the nomination. Vidal also wrote the screenplay for the 1964 film with Henry Fonda as the Adlai Stevenson type, and Cliff Robertson as his unscrupulous opponent.

Big Fish, Little Fish, American play by Hugh Wheeler (1961). Originally this was a witty tale of a man whose career had been harmed by a homosexual slander and who was trying to find himself amidst a circle of self-serving friends. Before its Broadway opening, the homosexual element was omitted, and, despite a strong cast, it played only 101 performances.

A Bill of Divorcement, English play by Clemence Dane (1921). It was a protest against a law allowing a wife to divorce her husband on the grounds of insanity. After 15 years in an asylum, a shell-shocked veteran discovers that his wife has sued for divorce and his daughter does not know him. It was filmed by George Cukor in 1932 with John Barrymore as father and Katherine Hepburn as daughter.

Billy Liar, English play by Keith Waterhouse and Willis Hall from Waterhouse's novel (1960). In a northern industrial town, an undertaker's clerk dreams fantasies of a more exciting life. On stage the action was limited to the house of the protagonist, played by Albert Finney. It was filmed by John Schlesinger in 1963, with Tom Courtenay as the dreamer.

The Bird Cage, American play by Arthur Laurents (1950). A backstage drama set in a nightclub based on Leon and Eddie's, it was described by its author as structurally "schizophrenic". The large cast, directed by Harold Clurman, included Maureen Stapleton, badly miscast in her first Broadway role as a sophisticated socialite.

The Bird of Paradise, American play by Richard Walton Tully (1912). One of the archetypical South Seas melodramas, it posits a marriage between the native princess Luana (Laurette Taylor) and an American scientist, which ends in disaster. The catalytic gimmick is a long dormant volcano in which Luana (shades of Fenella in the opera *Masaniello*) tosses herself.

Birmingham Repertory Theatre was developed by wealthy Barry Jackson from domestic theatricals. These evolved into the amateur Pilgrim Players (1907–13). His playhouse, devoted to non-commercial drama, opened in 1913, premiered many novelties (*Abraham Lincoln; Back to Methuselah*; modern-dress Shakespeare), and apprenticed many outstanding actors (Richardson, Olivier, later Scofield and Finney). When Jackson, angered by the city's seeming indifference, threatened to close the theatre in 1924, the financial slack was picked up by the Birmingham Civic Society, and the commercial success of *The Barretts of Wimpole Street* enabled him to found the Malvern Festival, staffed by the Rep company.

Black Fury, American film, directed by Michael Curtiz (1934). In a coal-mining company town, a Slovak miner, played by Paul Muni, is deceived into betraying his fellow strikers and spends the rest of the picture putting things right. The gritty Warner Brothers film was based on an actual case of a murdered agitator and banned in Pennsylvania as incendiary.

Blair House. Built on Pennsylvania Avenue in Washington, D.C. in 1824, it stands opposite the West Wing of the White House, and, after purchase by the government in 1942, became the official guest house for visiting dignitaries and heads of state.

Blake, William (1757–1827), English poet, draughtsman and visionary. One of the great originals of English literature, Blake is more familiar from his *Songs of Innocence and Experience* than from his epic allegories. His politics were anti-establishment, his religion antinomian and his aesthetics anti-classical.

Blitzstein, Marc, American composer (1905–64). He shot to celebrity with *The Cradle Will Rock* (1937), a Federal Theatre project closed down by the government and performed in the audience of New York's Venice Theatre on two hours' notice. A colleague of Orson Welles, he wrote the music to accompany *Julius Caesar* (1937) and turned *The Little Foxes* into an opera (1953). His most famous work is *The Threepenny Opera* (1954), a bowdlerized version of Brecht and Weill's *Dreigroschenoper*.

Blockade, American film, directed by William Dieterle from a screenplay by John Howard Lawson (1938). Henry Fonda is badly miscast as a Spanish peasant caught up in the Civil War, who makes a full-frontal appeal to the audience to stop the conflict.

Bloomgarten, Kermit (1904–76), American producer. After apprenticeship under Albert Bein, he struck it lucky with *Deep Are the Roots* (1945). He was the regular producer of Lillian Hellman and Arthur Miller, as well as a number of successful musical comedies. By the late 1960s he was seldom a player.

The Blue Bird (*L'Oiseau bleu*), Belgian symbolist fantasy by Maurice Maeterlinck (1908). Two children seeking the Blue Bird of Happiness travel through various realms, returning home to begin the quest once more. Its first successful production, by Stanislavsky at the Moscow Art Theatre, was copied in Paris and London.

Bogolyubov, Nikolay Ivanovich (1899–1980), Russian actor. He worked with Meyerhold from 1923, and found his calling in patriotic military roles, such as the partisan leader in *The Command* and the Sergeant-Major in *The Final Conflict* (1938). At the Moscow Art Theatre (1938–58) he specialized in Soviet heroes.

Bohnen (or Bonen), Roman (1901–49). Became a fully fledged member of the Group Theatre in 1934, playing roles in *Waiting for Lefty*, *Golden Boy*, *Awake and Sing!* and *The Gentle People*. An arrangement with Walter Wanger in 1937 to turn the Group into a resident film-making company fell through, but Bohnen stayed in Hollywood as a character actor (Candy in *Of Mice and Men*) and playwright. There he co-founded the Actor's Laboratory Theatre.

Boleslavsky, Richard. See headnote to Chapter 41, "Fundamentals of acting".

Bonstelle, Jessie (Laura Justine Bonesteele, 1872?–1932), American director and actress, nicknamed "The Star Maker". After an apprenticeship under Augustin Daly and the Shuberts, she founded a repertory theatre in Detroit (1910–24), in imitation of the Theatre Guild, and later ran the Detroit Civic Theatre. Katharine Cornell and William Powell were among the actors she nurtured.

Booth, Edwin (1833–93), American actor. Son of Junius Brutus, brother of John Wilkes, he was Victorian America's leading tragedian, with dark good looks and a voice of liquid mahogany. For 30 years, he was everyone's exemplary Hamlet, Iago, Benedick, Petruchio, Shylock and Cardinal Richelieu. His Booth's Theatre, devoted to Shakespeare (1868–74), reduced him to bankruptcy and forced him to tour for the rest of his life.

Boston Museum Company. The Boston Museum, founded in 1841 with a name meant to reassure those for whom the theatre was the Devil's Chapel, was famous for its ensemble acting company in the 1860s and 1870s, many of whose members the audience knew as neighbors. It included William Warren the Younger, Mrs Vincent and Kate Reignolds. The company was disbanded in 1894.

Botticelli, Sandro (Alessandro di Mariano di Vanni Filipepi, 1445–1510), Florentine painter. Under the patronage of Lorenzo di Medici, he created both religious works (*The Adoration of the Magi*) and the graceful fantasies *Primavera* (1478) and *The Birth of Venus* ("Venus on the Half-shell", 1486), overly familiar from calendars and posters.

Boy Meets Girl, American farce by Sam and Bella Spewack (1935), an uproarious lampoon of Hollywood studios, featuring an irreverent team of screenwriters who greatly resemble Ben Hecht and Charles MacArthur. Their activities combine finding a vehicle for a cowboy star and getting a pregnant waitress out of a jam.

Boyer, Charles (1899–1978), French actor. He played romantic leads on the French stage and the title character in Fritz Lang's film of *Liliom*, before becoming a Hollywood star. His deep, accented voice and hooded eyes prompted affectionate parody ("Come wiz me to ze Casbah!"). After the war, he returned to the stage as Don Juan in *Don Juan in Hell* (1951) and in sophisticated roles in high comedy. The last of these was the unsavory art dealer Antonescu, who tries to use his son as a homosexual lure in *Man and Boy* (1963).

Boyle, Captain "Jack", a feckless, unemployed working man, forever promising to dig out his moleskin trousers and find a job, is the "paycock" of Sean O'Casey's tragicomedy *Juno and the Paycock* (1924). He is always in the company of his drinking companion Joxer Daly. The role was played by Barry Fitzgerald when the Abbey Theatre toured the U.S.

Brand, Phoebe (1907–2004), American actress. Active in Winthrop Ames' Gilbert and Sullivan company, she was, with her husband Morris Carnovsky, a charter member of the Group Theatre, for whom she played Hennie Berger in *Awake and Sing!* (1935) and Anne in *Golden Boy* (1937). When the Group dissolved, they acted in Hollywood films until 1951, when a denunciation by Elia Kazan to the House Committee on Un-American Activities led to their being blacklisted. When the ban was broken in 1956, Brand founded Theater in the Street, offering free performances in poor neighbourhoods.

Brando, Marlon (1924–2004), American actor. Trained by both Stella Adler and the Actors Studio, he was already a Broadway veteran when he stunned audiences as Stanley Kowalski in *A Streetcar Named Desire* (1947). The role brought him to Hollywood, ended his stage career and made a torn T-shirt and mumbled lines the signs of a Method actor.

Bread (*Khleb*), Russian play by Vladimir Kirshon (1931). Although it attacked private hoarding on collective farms and praised duty to the Communist cause over love, the authorities disliked it for its faulty ideology. The Moscow Art Theatre staged it to validate its credentials as a Soviet institution.

The Breadwinner, English play by W. Somerset Maugham (1930). A London stockbroker, having undergone a financial crisis, decides to give up his conventional life and abandon his parasitic family.

Brecht, Bertolt (1898–1956), German poet and playwright. His earliest works are expressionistic, influenced by popular culture, and culminate in the wildly successful *Dreigroschenoper* (1928). The didactic plays that followed were infused with Marxism. Brecht lived abroad during the Nazi regime and when he returned, ran the Berliner Ensemble in East Berlin (1948–56), where he experimented with theories of Epic acting and theatrical distanciation in such works as *Galileo* (1938), *Mother Courage* (1941), *The Good Person of Sichuan* (1943) and *The Caucasian Chalk Circle* (1949).

Brecht on Brecht, American "theatrical collage" by George Tabori from Bertolt Brecht (1961). Intended by the Hungarian playwright as a one-night tribute produced at ANTA, this melange of songs, scenes and speeches enjoyed a long run. The female contingent of the original cast was distinguished: Lotte Lenya, Martha Schlamme and Viveca Lindfors.

"Bredon Hill", English poem by A. E. Housman. One of the poems in *A Shropshire Lad* (1896), it tells of a fiancée's untimely death. It was set as a rhapsody by Julius Harrison in 1942.

Bridges, Lloyd (1913–98), American actor, father of Jeff and Beau. After work in stock in California, he joined the leftist Actor's Lab, and made his Broadway debut in a modern-dress *Othello* (1939). Throughout the 1940s and early 1950s, he played innumerable tough-guy roles in film and television until briefly blacklisted by the House Committee on Un-American Activities. His career recovered in 1957 when he starred in the television series *Sea Hunt* which ran to 1961.

Brigadoon, American musical by Alan Jay Lerner and Frederick Loewe (1947), about an eighteenth-century Scottish village which is held in suspended animation until its reappearance once a century. Its tunes include "Go Home with Bonnie Jean" and "Almost Like Being in Love".

Broadhurst farces. A reference to the mechanical comedies churned out by American playwright George Broadhurst (1866–1952), such as *The Wrong Mr Wright*, *What Happened to Jones* (both 1897) and *Why Smith Left Home* (1899). They proved to be extremely popular on the West End stage as well.

Broadway, American play by Philip Dunning and George Abbott (1926), a backstage melodrama about hoofers and gangsters, set in a night club. Its dialogue crackles with the latest slang. The novelty remarked on at the time was a love scene between a dancer and a comedian while he has his pants off during a costume change. It was filmed in 1942 as a musical vehicle for George Raft.

The Broken Heart, English blank verse tragedy by John Ford (1633). Thwarted loves lead to multiple murders and suicides in the kingdom of Laconia.

Bromberg, J[oseph] Edward (1903–51), Austrian-born American actor. After study with the Moscow Art Theatre veteran Leo Bulgakov, he became a much-used character actor in New York, appearing with the Civic Repertory Theatre (1928–30) and the Group Theatre, most memorably as Uncle Morty in *Awake and Sing!* He also had a thriving Hollywood career, before he was blacklisted by the House Committee on Un-American Activities for non-cooperation. He died of a heart attack shortly after trying to establish himself on the London stage.

Brother Rat, American comedy by John Monks, Jr., and Fred F. Finkelhoffe (1936). A varsity farce about an illicitly married baseball player about to become a father. A cadre of room-mates devise schemes to extricate him from his difficulties. José Ferrer was first noticed in this unlikely imbroglio.

The Brothers Karamazov (*Bratya Karamazovy*), Russian novel by Fyodor Dostoevsky (1880). This philosophical novel which sets speculations about God's intentions in the midst of a lurid murder story has been frequently dramatized. Vladimir Nemirovich-Danchenko adapted it for the Moscow Art Theatre (1910), as two evenings of tableaux played against black draperies. A French version was confected by Jacques Copeau and Jacques Croué (1913) with Charles Dullin as Smerdyakov; translated into English, it was produced in New York by the Theatre Guild with Alfred Lunt (1927). A later adaptation was made by Alec Guinness, who played Mitya (1946). Hollywood wrought its own alterations in a film with Yul Brynner as Mitya and Maria Schell as Grushenka (1958).

Brown, Ivor (1891–1974), English dramatic critic, who served on many publications, including the *Manchester Guardian*, the *Observer* and the *Saturday Review*. His perceptive and appreciative reviews rarely revealed an animus, but his chief interest was Shakespeare.

Brown, Joe E. (in full, Joseph Evans, 1892–1973), American comedian. Famous for his pocket mouth and tiny eyes, he worked in the circus from childhood, moving into vaudeville and then revue (*Greenwich Village Follies*, 1921). The movies were his true medium (Snout the Tinker in Reinhardt's *Midsummer Night's Dream*), but he returned to the stage as Elwood P. Dowd in a road company *Harvey* (1946).

Brown, John (1800–59), American abolitionist. His intemperate actions shocked North and South alike: first a massacre of slave owners at Pottawatomie (1856), then a failed raid on the Federal Armory at Harpers Ferry (1859), which led to his execution by hanging. His exploits inspired the song "John Brown's Body" and Stephen Vincent Benet's epic poem.

Brown, Phil (1916–2006), American actor. A member of the Group Theatre, he moved to Hollywood when it disbanded and helped found the Actor's Laboratory. Its radicalism brought it under the scrutiny of the House

Committee on Un-American Activities and, blacklisted after an accusation from Ronald Reagan, he moved to England, where he continued to act and direct. In old age, he won new fans as Luke Skywalker's uncle in *Star Wars* (1977).

Bruce, Nigel (1895–1953), English actor. From a military family, he worked as a stage manager and supporting actor before he moved to Hollywood in 1934. There he played the same role over and over, that of a "silly ass" Brit, in 78 films: his Dr Watson in the Sherlock Holmes series featuring Basil Rathbone was their epitome. He was also a valued cricketer in the British colony.

Brustein, Robert (1927–), American critic and director. He made his reputation with *The Theatre of Revolt* (1964) and regular reviewing for *The New Republic*, leading him to be made Dean of the Yale Drama School. When dismissed from that position, he shifted his activities to Harvard and founded the American Repertory Theatre in 1979.

Brynner, Yul (in full, Yuly Borisovich, 1920–85), Siberian-born actor. He sang Russian folksongs in European nightclubs and gained employment as a model in New York (photographed nude by George Platt Lynes). Perhaps owing to his alleged Mongol ancestry, he was best in pseudo-Oriental roles: the Chinese husband in *Lute Song* (1946) and Siamese autocrat of *The King and I* (1951, 1977; film 1956), but his only non-film role thereafter was Odysseus in the musical *Home Sweet Homer* (1976), which folded after one performance.

Buchanan, Jack (1891–1957), Scottish entertainer. In London he made his name in the revue *Tonight's the Night* (1912) and *Charlot's A–Z Revue* (1921). A suave, lanky song-and-dance man, he appeared in early Hollywood sound films, then returned to England to build the Leicester Square Theatre (1933) and star in British movies. He was brought back to Hollywood to hoof it with Fred Astaire in *The Band Wagon* (1953).

Buckingham Palace, irreverently known as "Buck House", is the official residence of the British monarch when in London. A residence of royalty from 1762, it became the official royal palace in 1837. It is used for state banquets, exhibitions of the royal collections, and a Changing of the Guard, immortalized in A. A. Milne's verse.

The Bunch and Judy, American musical comedy by Jerome Kern, Anne Caldwell and Hugh Ford (1922). It is memorable for the musical-comedy debuts of Ray Dooley and Fred Astaire, but was otherwise a flop.

Bunthorne, Reginald, the "idyllic poet" of Gilbert and Sullivan's *Patience* (1881), a hybrid caricature of Oscar Wilde, Algernon Charles Swinburne, J. M. Whistler, and Du Maurier's *Punch* cartoons of aesthetes.

Die Burgschaft (*The Pledge*), German opera by Kurt Weill and Caspar Neher from a story by Herder (1931). In this parable about the corrupting power of gold, the farmer Mattes and the merchant Orth quarrel over a sack filled with money, until their country is invaded. A series of ups and downs enables Orth to sacrifice Mattes to save his own life. It was first staged in 1932 at the Berlin Civic Opera.

Busch, Ernst (1900–80), German actor and singer. A Berlin cabaret performer interpreting the songs of Kurt Tucholsky, he created the Ballad-singer in *Der Dreigroschenoper* (1920), a role he repeated in the 1931 film. He fled Germany in 1933, and fought as a Communist in the Spanish Civil War. Brecht enrolled him in the Berliner Ensemble in 1945, and he became world-famous for his sardonic, pithy performances as Galileo, the Cook in *Mother Courage* and Azdak in *The Caucasian Chalk Circle*.

Busoni, Federico (1866–1924), Italo-German composer and pianist. Labelled an anti-romantic, he composed operas on familiar romantic themes: *Arlecchino, Turandot* (both 1917), *Doktor Faust* (1925).

Caesar and Christ, history by Will Durant (1944). Volume 3 of Durant's best-selling "integral history" of the world, it deals with the Roman Empire.

Campbell, Mrs Patrick (Beatrice Stella Tanner, 1865–1940), English actress. Tall, dark and eccentric, she made a sensation as Paula, *The Second Mrs Tanqueray* (1893), followed by Juliet, Ophelia, Lady Macbeth and Mélisande (in French, opposite Sarah Bernhardt as Pelléas). Shaw, an on-again-off-again admirer, wrote Eliza Doolittle in *Pygmalion* for her. Their entertaining correspondence was dramatized by Jerome Kilty as *Dear Liar* (1959).

Candida, comedy by G. B. Shaw (1897). A triangle, in which the insightful wife Candida abandons her pastor husband for a young poet, because he needs her more. Unless the leading role is played by a woman of immense magnetism, the play comes across as Ibsen revised by Barrie. Luckily, the best American revival featured Katharine Cornell (1924).

Caniff, Milton (1907–88), American cartoonist. He became famous for his adventure strip, set in Southern China, *Terry and the Pirates* (1934–46): it was Tintin with sex appeal, for its female characters included the sultry Dragon Lady and the lesbian Sanjak. During the Second World War, he drew *Male Call*, starring the curvaceous Miss Lace, exclusively for military publications. Wishing to own his own work, in 1946 he introduced tight-jawed airforce commander *Steve Canyon*, which ran till his death.

Capp, Al (1909–79), American cartoonist. His long-running strip *L'il Abner* (1937–77), set in the hillbilly town of Dogpatch, eventually reached 60 million readers. Its characters entered the national mythology, along with such beasts as the Shmoo, the Kigmy and the Bald Iggle, and such inventions as Kickapoo Joy Juice and Sadie Hawkins Day. In later years, Capp became a hardbitten political reactionary and used his strip to parody war protestors and reformers.

Carew, James (1876–1938), American actor. An occasional player on Broadway, in 1907 he met and married Ellen Terry, who was 30 years his senior. They appeared together in *The Good Hope, Captain Brassbound's Conversion* and *Henry of Lancaster*. Although never formally dissolved, the marriage lasted in reality only two years.

Carnegie, Hattie (Henriette Kanengeiser, 1889–1956), Austrian-born American designer. She rose from being a downtown New York milliner to a leader in fashion design with a famous dress shop on the Upper West Side. She was particularly renowned for her costume jewellery, and counted Joan Crawford and the Duchess of Windsor among her clientele.

Carnovsky, Morris (1897–1992), American actor, chiefly associated with the Group Theatre which he joined in 1921. His best roles were the Jewish grandfather in *Awake and Sing!* (1935) and the Italian father in *Golden Boy* (1937). He was blacklisted in 1951, when he was named as a Communist sympathizer by Elia Kazan, but turned to the classics, in 1956, when John Houseman invited him to the American Shakespeare Festival, where he portrayed Lear, Prospero and Shylock.

Carousel, a musical by Richard Rodgers and Oscar Hammerstein II (1945), based on Molnár's *Liliom*. The action takes place in a New England fishing village (and Heaven), and contains such numbers as "If I Loved You" and "June Is Bustin' Out All Over".

Carroll, Lewis (Charles Lutwidge Dodgson, 1832–98), English nonsense writer, clergyman and mathematician. He was fond of theatre-going, but scandalized by what he regarded as immorality on stage. His *Alice* books were dramatized in his lifetime, with his advice and consent.

Carroll, Madeleine (1906–87), English film actress. A sophisticated blonde, she was a favorite of Alfred Hitchcock, who paired her with Robert Donat in *The 39 Steps* (1935) and with John Gielgud in *Secret Agent* (1936). Her Hollywood career languished after successes in *The General Died at Dawn* and *The Prisoner of Zenda* (both 1937), but revived on American radio.

Carroll, Paul Vincent (1900–68), Irish playwright with a Scottish education. Influenced by the Abbey Theatre, his plays, usually about the lives of priests, combine observed realism with spiritual messages: *Things That Are Caesar's* (1932), *Shadow and Substance* (1938), *The Wayward Saint* (1955). He also founded the Curtain Theatre, Glasgow.

Caruso, Enrico (1873–1921), Italian tenor. Perhaps the most famous opera singer of the early twentieth century, owing to the wide distribution of his phonograph records, he excelled in French and Italian opera, especially Verdi and Puccini. His rendition of George M. Cohan's "Over There" was an effective recruiting tool when the U.S. entered the First World War.

The Case of Clyde Griffiths, German play by Erwin Piscator and Lena Goldschmidt from a novel by Theodore Dreiser (1936). This adaptation of *An American Tragedy* was translated and produced by the Group Theatre: the critics approved of Lee Strasberg's spare direction, but found the narrative device of the Speaker, played by "cello-voiced" Morris Carnovsky, tendentious.

Casey Jones, American play by Robert Ardrey (1938). Uncertain in tone, this stage version of a folk ballad about a legendary train engineer who died in a crash was directed by Elia Kazan and designed by Mordecai Gorelik. Despite a cast that included Charles Bickford and Van Heflin, the on-stage locomotive was judged more impressive than anything else.

Cassandra, mythical princess of Troy, daughter of King Priam and Queen

Hecuba. She was enslaved by Agamemnon and murdered by his wife Clytaemnestra. Her burden was to be able to see and foretell future events but have no one believe her.

Casson, Sir Lewis (1875–1969), English actor. He played Shakespeare and Shaw during the Vedrenne-Barker season at the Court Theatre, London (1904–7), and then directed the Gaiety, Manchester (1911–14). With his wife Sybil Thorndike, he managed a season of Greek tragedy at the Holborn Empire and one of Grand Guignol at the Little Theatre. They toured widely both in plays and recitals. One of his last roles was Waffles in the Chichester Festival revival of *Uncle Vanya*.

Castle Square Theatre, Boston (1894–1932). Located in the South End, it was small but well-appointed, with a rococo interior and an up-to-date lighting board. It housed touring, opera, and, from 1908 to 1916, its own stock companies. Alfred Lunt was a young, disgruntled member of the company for three seasons (1912–14).

Cat on a Hot Tin Roof, a drama by Tennessee Williams (1955) about the repressed homosexuality of a former football star festering on a Texas plantation. The director Elia Kazan persuaded Williams to rewrite the third act to make it less bleak. In that form, it won the Pulitzer Prize.

Cervantes Saavedra, Miguel de (1547–1616), Spanish writer. Best known as the author of *Don Quixote* (much adapted for the stage in various genres), he also penned a number of plays, including *The Siege of Numantia* (*El cerco de Numancia*), revived by Barrault at the Théâtre Marigny, Paris, and comic interludes (*entremeses*) revived by Evreinov at the Antique Theatre, St Petersburg. His own suffering as a galley-slave in Algiers is portrayed in *El trato de Argel*.

Chaliapin, Feodor (correctly Fyodor Ivanovich Shalyapin, 1873–1938), Russian bass. Imposing in stature, with a cavernous voice, he played a wide variety of roles with Stanislavskian conviction. He is best known for his Boris Godunov, but also for his concert performances of art and folk songs. Murnau filmed him as Don Quixote.

Chaplin, Charlie (in full, Sir Charles Spencer, 1889–1977), English actor. A youth spent in the music hall prepared him for his invention of the Little Tramp in the movies, a shrewd blend of physical comedy and heart-tugging sentiment. He was driven from the U.S. by the anti-Communist witchhunts of the 1950s, and settled in Switzerland with his third wife, Eugene O'Neill's daughter Oona.

Charlot's Revue, English revue (1924). André Charlot put together the A-list material from his London revues for his first U.S. appearance. It introduced Jack Buchanan, Gertrude Lawrence and Beatrice Lillie to New York, in such songs as "Limehouse Blues" and "March with Me". Its popularity was due in part to its intimacy, in contrast to the lavish gigantism of the "Follies".

Chase, Mary (1907–81), American playwright, who began under the Federal Theatre Project. Her one-hit wonder *Harvey* (1944), about a man whose best friend is an invisible rabbit, settled in for a long run.

Chatterton, English one-act play by Henry Arthur Jones and Henry Herman (1884).

Chayefsky, Paddy (1923–81), American playwright, whose first works were produced on television and film (*Marty*, 1953; *The Catered Affair*, 1955). His Broadway career was checkered, ranging from naturalistic soap opera (*Middle of the Night*, 1956) to fantastic realism (*The Tenth Man*, 1959) to Biblical rant (*Gideon*, 1961) to over-the-top comedy (*The Latent Heterosexual*, 1968).

Cheep, English revue by Harry Grattan (1917). Produced by André Charlot, it featured Beatrice Lillie in several roles, including a Canadian soldier and a highbrow drawing-room soprano.

Chekhov, Anton Pavlovich (1860–1904), Russian writer and physician. The 1880s was the era of most of his lucrative short farces, often written at the request of performers. *The Wood Goblin* (1889–90) was transformed into *Uncle Vanya* (produced 1899), contemporary with *The Seagull*, which flopped in St Petersburg in 1896, and had a triumphant revival at the Moscow Art Theatre two years later. *Three Sisters* (1900–01) and *The Cherry Orchard* (1904) were written for the Art Theatre. Chekhov's writing was innovative: the banality of situations and dialogue seem to reproduce social reality even as they conceal an inner life which surfaces in subtle correspondences of gestures, behaviour, sounds, the framework of the humdrum.

Chekhov, Michael. See headnote to Chapter 47 "An actor must have three selves".

Chekhov Theatre Studio. At the invitation of the millionaire Elmhirsts, in turn inspired by Beatrice Straight who had seen him act in New York, Michael Chekhov established a school of acting at Dartington Hall in Devon. With a faculty of eight, it served as a laboratory for physical expression and improvisation, often drawing on Yogic techniques and meditation (1936–38). In 1939, it moved to a large estate in Ridgefield, Conn., training American students until 1942.

The Cherry Orchard (*Vishnyovy sad*), Russian comedy by Anton Chekhov (1903). Facing eviction and the auction of their estate, Ranevskaya and her brother Gaev, landowning gentry, cling to the past and hope for a miracle. Their land is sold to the peasant millionaire Lopakhin, and the family disperses to new lives. The play was written for the Moscow Art Theatre, and opened there on 17 January 1904, directed by Stanislavsky and Nemirovich-Danchenko. Eva Le Gallienne staged it for the Civic Repertory Theatre in 1928, with Nazimova as guest Ranevskaya.

Chevalier, Albert, English actor (1861–1923). He came from the legitimate stage to the music hall, where, from 1891, he perfected the type of the "coster", smartened up and sentimentalized for public consumption. Among his best-loved songs were "My Old Dutch", "Knocked 'Em in the Old Kent Road" and "Never Introduce Your Donah to a Pal". His wife published a book of his conversations from beyond the grave.

The Children of Darkness, American play by Edwin Justus Mayer (1930). This pastiche of Fielding and Gay, set in an eighteenth-century London prison, failed at its first production. A 1959 revival at Circle in the Square, directed by José Quintero, brought George C. Scott into prominence.

Chinoy, Helen Krich (1922–), American scholar and educator. An influential teacher of drama at Smith College from 1953, she researched the Group Theatre and the presence of women in theatre. Her enduring anthologies, edited with her sister-in-law Toby Cole, are *Actors on Acting* (1949) and *Directors on Directing* (1953), and, with Linda Walsh Jenkins, *Women in American Theatre* (1981).

The Chosen People, the American title of *Jews* (*Evrei*), Russian play by Evgeny Chirikov (1904). This "ripped-from-the-headlines" drama depicts life in a ghetto in a Southern Russian town disrupted by a pogrom in which the heroine is raped and killed. Pavel Orlenev and Alla Nazimova brought it to New York in 1905, when Hamlin Garland described it as "a bloody page torn out of Russian history, done with quiet art and intense earnestness".

Christians, Mady (in full Marguerita Maria, 1900–51), Austrian actress. After a distinguished career in Vienna, she returned to the U.S., where she had acted as a child. Soft-spoken and matronly, she played Gertrude to Maurice Evans's *Hamlet* (1938) and Sara Mueller in *Watch on the Rhine* (1941), but is lovingly recalled as Marlon Brando's Norwegian mother in *I Remember Mama* (1944).

Christy Mahon, hero of Synge's *Playboy of the Western World*, who is made much of by the inhabitants of a West Ireland village for killing his da with a loy, until they discover he didn't.

Chrysalis, American play by Rose Albert Porter (1932). Produced by the Theatre Guild, this short-lived underworld play, with Margaret Sullavan, featured Humphrey Bogart and Elisha Cook, Jr., both of whom were later to appear in John Huston's film of *The Maltese Falcon*.

Churchill, Marguerite (1910–2000), American actress. A child actress on Broadway, she entered motion pictures in 1929, co-starring with Paul Muni in *The Valiant* (1929) but returned to the stage in *Dinner at Eight* (1933). Married to George O'Brien, she settled in Hollywood, playing mainly in Westerns, an exception being as a victim of *Dracula's Daughter* (1936).

Circle in the Square, a New York theatre company in Sheridan Square, founded in 1951 by José Quintero and Theodore Mann, named for its "round" arena. Opening with a revival of *Summer and Smoke*, it specialized in Tennessee Williams and Eugene O'Neill, and fostered outstanding performances by George C. Scott, Jason Robards Jr., and James Earl Jones.

La Città morta. See *The Dead City*.

Claire, Ina (Inez Fagan, 1892?–1985), American actress, mistress of the elegant epigram and cocktail-shaker manner, which concealed her early beginnings in vaudeville. Her best opportunities came in the comedies of S. N. Behrman, but she was also effective in Maugham and T. S. Eliot.

Clairon, Mlle (Claire-Josèphe-Hippolyte Léris de la Tude, 1723–1803), French actress, who shot to the top of the Comédie Française with a stunning performance as Phèdre. She excelled in the tragedies of Voltaire, many of them written with her in mind. Although she strove for naturalness, her carefully studied effects were contrasted with the more spontaneous approach of Dumesnil and championed by Diderot.

Claudel, Paul (1868–1955), French poet and diplomat. Claudel's early plays, *L'Echange* (1893) *L'Annonce faite à Marie* (1912), and *L'Otage* (1919), steeped in devotional Catholicism, were embraced by little theatres in Europe and the U.S. His later, more grandiose, works, *Le Soulier de Satin* (1919–24), *Partage de Midi* and *Christophe Colomb* were promoted as total theatre by Barrault both at the Comédie-Française and his own company.

Clift, Montgomery (1920–66), American actor. When very young, he played mixed-up adolescents on the Broadway stage: Henry in *The Skin of Our Teeth* (1942) and Samuel in *The Searching Wind* (1944). His Konstantin in *The Seagull* (Phoenix Theatre, 1954), to paraphrase Hamlet, made the unskilful swoon and the judicious grieve, but he was on the brink of a splendid film career, owing to his sensitivity and personal beauty.

Clurman, Harold. See Chapter 43 "An actor prepares: Comments on Stanislavsky's Method".

Cobb, Lee J. (Leo Jacoby, 1911–76), American actor, a veteran of the Group Theatre. A hulking presence, he created Willy Loman in *Death of a Salesman* (1949), despite the author's preference for a mousier man. Most of his work was done in film, but he played King Lear on Broadway in 1968.

Cohan, George Michael (Keohane, 1878–1942), American performer and playwright. Emerging from the Four Cohans of vaudeville, he became a byword for musical comedy and Tin Pan Alley hits, the "Yankee Doodle Dandy". He starred in his own musicals *Little Johnny Jones* (1904) and *Forty-five Minutes from Broadway*, and had great success with a comic thriller *Seven Keys to Baldpate* (1913). He surprised audiences with his understated performance as the father in *Ah, Wilderness!* (1933).

Colbert, Claudette (1903–96), French-born American actress. On Broadway 1925–9 she broke out of the ingenue mold as a snake charmer in *The Barker* (1927) and in O'Neill's *Dynamo* (1929). Talkies brought her to Hollywood, where she was usually cast as rich women, first sexy (Poppaea in a milk-bath in *Sign of the Cross*, 1932; *Cleopatra*, 1934), then screwball (*It Happened One Night*, 1934; *Tovarich*, 1937). Hollywood's highest paid actress in 1938, she insisted that her right profile never be photographed.

The Cold Wind and the Warm, American play by S. N. Behrman (1958). Drawing on his own past, Behrman presented a Jewish family in Worcester, Mass. in the years before the First World War. The characters played by Morris Carnovsky, Maureen Stapleton and Sanford Meisner were familiar clichés, and did not prepare the audience for the suicide of the son, portrayed by Eli Wallach.

Cole, Toby (Marion Cholodenko, 1916–), American agent and producer. She worked on theatre with many socially engaged groups (1938–56), among them the Federal Theatre Project, and then as producer's assistant on Broadway. In 1957 she set up as an agent for actors, playwrights and translators, representing Zero Mostel, Sam Shepard, and the American rights of

Brecht and Pirandello. With her sister-in-law Helen Crich Chinoy, she edited the useful anthologies *Actors on Acting* (1953), *Directors on Directing* (1953), and, on her own, *Playwrights on Playwriting* (1961).

Colman, Ronald (1891–1958), English actor. A wounded veteran of the First World War, he went on the West End stage and was brought to Broadway in *La Tendresse* (1922). He broke into silent films in *The White Sister*, opposite Lillian Gish (1923), and, when talkies came in, his velvety voice was at a premium, usually in costume pictures (*A Tale of Two Cities*, 1935; *The Prisoner of Zenda*, 1937; *If I Were King*, 1938). His homicidal tragedian in *A Double Life* (1948) won him an Oscar.

Comédie-Française, the national French theatre, created in 1680 when Molière's company and the Théâtre du Marais joined with the Comédiens du roi of the Hôtel de Bourgogne. An actors' cooperative, it maintained a monopoly on legitimate drama until the Revolution, and was regarded, usually correctly, as a bastion of tradition. Over the years it has recruited directors from the most progressive theatres (Copeau, Barrault, Planchon), but they rarely stayed for long.

Comes a Day, American drama by Speed Lamkin from his own short story (1958). Despite a strong cast, which included Judith Anderson, George C. Scott, Brandon De Wilde, with the debuts of Larry Hagman and Michael J. Pollard, and good reviews, this tale of a dysfunctional family did not last a month. (Joseph Papp was stage manager.)

Commedia dell'arte (Italian for "professional theatre"). In the late Middle Ages, itinerant acting troupes began presenting partly improvised farces featuring masked characters which became conventional by the fifteenth century: Arlecchino the doltish servant from Bergamo, Pantaleont the old Venetian merchant, il Dottore, the longwinded lawyer, and so on. They larded the sketches with *lazzi* or joke routines. Research into the *commedia* inspired a good deal of modernist theatre at the beginning of the twentieth century.

Compagnie des Quinze, an offshoot of Jacques Copeau's Vieux Colombier troupe, 15 young actors led by Michel Saint-Denis, who sought inspiration from rural surroundings and village life. Their house dramatist was André Obey, whose *Noé* became their show piece.

Congreve, William (1670–1729), English playwright, although he preferred to be known as a gentleman. Transitional works, halfway between licentious Restoration comedy and sentimental comedy, his plays are polished exercises in wit and urbanity: *The Old Bachelor* (1693), *Love for Love* (1695), the intricate *Way of the World* (1700). He locked horns with Jeremy Collier, attempting to disprove the immorality of the theatre, but failed.

Connell, Leigh, American producer. Having served as assistant to José Quintero on *Portrait of a* Lady (1954), he became co-producer of some of Circle in the Square's biggest hits: *A Long Day's Journey into Night* (1956), *The Iceman Cometh* and *Children of Darkness*.

Connolly, Cyril (1903–74), English critic. Co-editor of *Horizon* (1939–50), he also contributed his witty and coruscating prose to the *New Statesman, The Observer* and the *Sunday Times*. He wrote his uncommon commonplace book *The Unquiet Grave* (1944) under the pseudonym Palinurus.

The Constant Nymph, English play by Margaret Kennedy and Basil Dean, from Kennedy's novel (1926). The title character is Teresa, an impossibly mercurial adolescent, brought up in a bohemian musical household. She is loved by a man who marries another woman, then returns to her, but Teresa dies just before their affair is consummated. This soap-operatic balderdash had a great success in London and even enjoyed a French adaptation by Giraudoux, but cut no ice in New York.

Conte, Richard (actually Nicholas, 1910–75), American actor. Under his real name, he was discovered as a singing waiter at the Connecticut resort by Elia Kazan and John Garfield and won a scholarship to the Neighborhood Playhouse. He had a brief stage career, before moving to Hollywood in 1939. He was a rugged standby in war films and then in *film noir* B pictures.

Conti, Itala (1874–1946), English actress and pedagogue. After a decade of acting in the U.K. and Australia, she was hired to train the children in *Where the Rainbow Ends* (1911). She founded a theatre school, whose illustrious alumni included Gertrude Lawrence, Noël Coward and Anton Dolin. In 1918 the Ministry of Education sought her advice on a licensing code for juvenile actors.

Cooke, George Frederick (1756–1812), Irish tragedian, who established himself at Covent Garden in 1800 in a handful of villainous roles, among them Shylock, Richard III and Sir Giles Overreach. His acting was forceful if raw. He was the first foreign star to tour to North America (1810–12), where he died, done in by his drinking.

Cooper, Gary (actually Frank, 1901–61), American actor. Exclusively employed in films, he made over 100 in the course of his career. Lean, long, handsome, he alternated action roles with high comedy, and was turned by Frank Capra into a metonym for small-town American decency (*Mr Deeds Goes to Town*, 1936; *Meet John Doe*, 1941). He won an Oscar for *Sergeant York* (1941), but is best remembered as the abandoned sheriff in *High Noon* (1952), thought to be a protest against the blacklist.

Cooper, Melville (1896–1973), English actor. He made his stage debut in Stratford-upon-Avon in 1920, and on Broadway played Bernard Baxley in *Laburnum Grove* (1934) and, opposite Sophie Tucker, the King in *Jubilee* (1935). He was a much-employed character actor in films, usually cast as stuffy or dim-witted types, such as the Sheriff of Nottingham in *The Adventures of Robin Hood* (1938) and Mr Collins in *Pride and Prejudice* (1940).

Copeau, Jacques (1878–1949), French director, actor and critic. At his Paris theatre, the Vieux Colombier, he experimented with a stripped-down, athletic acting style and a unit set, breathing fresh life into Molière and Shakespeare comedies. He also preached going back to the land, where the actor could learn from all fields of knowledge. His influence was immense, particularly on Louis Jouvet, Michel Saint-Denis and, later, Giorgio Strehler.

Copeland, Charles Townsend (1860–1952), American academic. Dramatic critic on Boston newspapers and author of a biography of Edwin Booth, he became the much-loved Boylston Professor of Rhetoric and Oratory at Harvard, renowned for his literary readings. Among the undergraduates "Copey" mentored were Heywood Broun, Robert Benchley, T. S. Eliot, Robert E. Sherwood and Alan Seeger.

The Copperhead, a melodrama of the American Civil War by Augustus Thomas (1918). It dealt with the schizoid activities of a loyalist farmer pretending to be a Confederate sympathizer, and featured John and Lionel Barrymore.

Coquelin, Benoît Constant (1841–1909), French actor. A leading comedian at the Comédie Française (1860–86, 1890–92), snub-nosed and pocket-mouthed, he excelled at Molière, particularly as the pretentious valet Mascarille in *Les Précieuses ridicules*. At the Porte St Martin, he created Cyrano de Bergerac (1897) and toured America with Sarah Bernhardt. He died while rehearsing the cock of the walk in Rostand's *Chantecler*.

Coriolanus, English blank verse tragedy by William Shakespeare, from Plutarch (1607). During a power struggle with the tribunes, Coriolanus, a Roman military hero, is banished. He joins forces with his enemy Aufidius to march on Rome, but gives in to his mother's pleadings, saves Rome, but is killed by Aufidius. The play was rarely produced in the late nineteenth century, but enjoyed an exceptional revival by Laurence Olivier.

The Corn Is Green, English play by Emlyn Williams (1938), based on his own experiences. Miss L. C. Moffat, a spinster schoolmistress, inherits a house in a Welsh mining town and sets out to prepare the young miner Morgan Evans (Williams himself) for university, despite a number of obstacles. This inspirational tale benefitted from Ethel Barrymore in the New York premiere; Bette Davis was out of her element in the 1945 film, which added a hidden passion to Miss Moffat's motivations.

Corneille, Pierre (1606–84), French playwright, whose baroque tendencies were held in check by his loyal adherence to the neo-classic unities. *Le Cid* (1636) raised a controversy, adjudicated by the Académie Française, which disallowed several of his innovations. The most durable of his plays, *Horace* (1640), *Cinna* (1641) and *Polyeucte* (1642), are drawn from classical myth and Christian history; but his comedies *L'Illusion comique* (1636) and *Le Menteur* (1644) have greater audience appeal.

Cornell, Katharine. See headnote to Chapter 54 "The actor attacks his part: Katharine Cornell".

Corot, Jean-Baptiste Camille (1796–1875), French painter. Although he produced many figure studies, he is known for his evocative, atmospheric and often mystical landscapes. Honoured leader of the Barbizon school, he influenced Monet, Degas and Picasso.

Cort Theatre, New York. Named after a Seattle producer, it opened in 1912 with Laurette Taylor in *Peg o' My Heart*. Managed by and starring Charles Coburn, it put on revivals of the pseudo-Chinese play *The Yellow Jacket* and the comedy of the trenches *The Better 'Ole*. It housed a number of long-running hits (*Abraham Lincoln; Boy Meets Girl; Room Service*) and premiered *The Diary of Anne Frank* (1955).

Coué, Émile, French psychologist (1857–1926). His self-help method of psychotherapy was popular worldwide in the 1920s through his books and personal appearances. The dapper, goateed doctor was famous for his catchphrase "Every day in every way I am getting better and better".

Counsellor-at-Law, American drama by Elmer Rice (1931). A New York Jewish attorney with a thriving practice is bedevilled by an unfaithful wife and disbarment proceedings based on earlier malfeasance. On the brink of suicide he is pulled back by his loyal, loving secretary. Paul Muni consolidated his reputation on the English-language stage in this; John Barrymore played it in the movies.

The Country Wife, English comedy by William Wycherley (1675). One of the most frequently revived of the Restoration comedies of manners, it presents the lecherous Horner masquerading as impotent to improve his chances with the ladies, among them a naive young bride. The play's sexual frankness and the innuendo of the famous "china" scene kept it off the stage between 1753 and 1924. A revival with Ruth Gordon brought it back into favor.

Court Theatre. See **Royal Court Theatre**.

Courtney, Tom (Sir Thomas, 1937–), English actor. He joined the Old Vic company in 1960 and was acclaimed for his Hamlet at the Edinburgh Festival (1968). His career veered from Shakespeare to the grittier Angry Young school, when he starred in the film versions of *The Loneliness of the Long Distance Runner* (1962) and *Billy Liar* (1963). His outstanding stage and film role of the 1980s was the title role in *The Dresser*.

Coward, Noël (1899–1973), English actor, composer and playwright. A byword for wit, sophistication and virtuosity, Coward worked in a number of genres, from sensational dramas to romantic tearjerkers to light comedy to operetta to national pageant. The comedies of bad manners, among them, *Hay Fever* (1925), *Private Lives* (1930), *Design for Living* (1932) and *Blithe Spirit* (1941), have survived the best.

Cowl, Jane (1884–1950), American actress, noted for her vivacity and grace. After playing the victimized heroine of *Within the Law* (1912), she wrote most of her vehicles, and in 1923 had a great success as Juliet. From 1927 to 1935, she was seen mostly in comedies of manners, and appeared in Thornton Wilder's *Merchant of Yonkers* (1939), forerunner to *The Matchmaker*.

Crabtree, Paul (1918–79), American actor and director. A member of the Theatre Guild, he appeared in the original production of *Oklahoma!* and was hand-picked by Eugene O'Neill to play Don Parritt in *The Iceman Cometh*. He also worked in film and television. In 1964, he founded the Cumberland County Playhouse in Tennessee.

Craig, Edith or Ailsa (1869–1947), English actress and director, daughter of Ellen Terry, sister of Gordon Craig. She served as her mother's stage manager on an American tour of 1907, and from 1911 directed and designed for the Pioneer Players, which staged, among others, the medieval plays of Hroswitha of Gandesheim. In 1929 she began giving annual Shakespearean performances at her mother's home in Small Hythe, now the Ellen Terry Museum.

Craig, Edward Gordon (1872–1966), English designer and theorist. An actor under Henry Irving whom he considered a second father, he dabbled in illustration and design before moving to the Continent. His concepts and opinions were disseminated under many pseudonyms in his journal *The Mask*, founded in 1908. He worked for Eleonora Duse and conceived a *Hamlet* for the Moscow Art Theatre (1909–12), but spent most of his time at his school at the Arena Goldoni in Florence. His ideas about the use of screens as movable scenery and lighting from above had been adopted by many designers, but he was scorned by Bernard Shaw and Lee Simonson for not getting his hands dirty in the living theatre. In 1928 he designed a New York production of *Macbeth* which proved to be a disaster and was his last realized design for the theatre.

Craig's Wife, an American drama by George Kelly (1925) about a woman obsessed with the home beautiful and insuring her place in it. Her obsession with isolating her husband from his friends eventually isolates her. Chrystal Herne played her in the original production.

Crawford, Ann (Street, 1734–1801), English actress. Against her family's wishes she went on the stage, first in Dublin, then in London, resident at Drury Lane 1767–74, playing all the heroines in Shakespeare and comedies of manners. Critics considered her equal to Garrick in her versatility, but noted a tendency to overdo emotions.

Crawford, Cheryl (1902–86), American producer. A ubiquitous presence in leading theatre companies, as executive or co-founder, she had a hand in the Theatre Guild, the Group Theatre, the American Repertory Theatre and the Actors Studio. Hard-headed, diplomatic, shrewd, she eventually became a canny independent producer and made a fortune with *Brigadoon* (1947).

Crawford, Joan (Lucille Fay Lesueur, 1904–77), American actress. In the flapper era, her dancing skills, honed as a chorus girl, made her an emblem of flaming youth in silent pictures. After starring as a glamour girl for MGM, she moved to Warner Brothers in 1943 and created a series of hard-edged, ambitious career women, most famously *Mildred Pierce* (1945). Her film career ended in Grand Guignol: *What Ever Happened to Baby Jane* (1962) and *Hush . . . Hush Sweet Charlotte* (1964), teamed with her long-time rival Bette Davis.

Crime and Punishment (*Prestuplenie i nakazanie*), Russian novel by Fyodor Dostoevsky (1866). This novel of a murderer-by-theory was much dramatized in Russia in the late nineteenth century, usually as a duo for the criminal student Raskolnikov and the police inspector Porfiry Petrovich. A version by Laurence Irving, *The Fool Hath Said in His Heart "There Is No God"*, played New York in 1908 and, retitled *The Unwritten Law*, London in 1910. Rodney Ackland's dramatization, with John Gielgud as Raskolnikov and Edith Evans as Katerina Ivanovna, was a hit in both those cities (1946).

Cronyn, Hume. See headnote to Chapter 15, 'Dear Diary . . .'

The Cross of Lorraine, American film directed by Tay Garnett from a novel by Hans Habe (1943). A prison camp drama about French soldiers who obeyed Marshall Pétain's order to surrender to the Germans and wound up as P.O.W.s, it plays with the moral dilemmas they face. The cast is very strong, with fine performances from Jean-Pierre Aumont, Gene Kelly, Cedric Hardwicke, Richard Whorf, Peter Lorre, and especially Hume Cronyn as the *collabo*.

The Crucible, American play by Arthur Miller (1953). Ostensibly a re-creation of the Salem witch trials, it cast aspersions on the House Committee on Un-American Activities and its anti-Communist pursuits. Caught up in a hysteria of accusations, upright John Proctor goes to his unjust death, refusing to compromise with his judges and their prejudices. It remains Miller's most produced play, particularly outside the U.S.

Crummles, Vincent. The magniloquent manager of a touring company encountered by Nicholas Nickleby in Dickens's novel (1838–9). He is the father of the "infant phenomenon" and persuades Nicholas to join the company while they are in Portsmouth. He was based on the actor-manager T. D. Davenport (1792–1851).

Cummings, Vicki (1914–69), American actress. She appeared on Broadway from 1934 to 1961, usually in secondary roles in flops. Her one association with a success came when she got to play Olive Lashbrooke in *The Voice of the Turtle* (1948).

Cyrano de Bergerac, French poetic drama by Edmond Rostand (1897). The most lasting international success of the neo-Romantic upsurge at the *fin de siècle*, this exploit-packed comedy-drama drew on the life of the seventeenth-century author, endowing him with expert swordsmanship, literary virtuosity and an enormous nose. He was created by Constant Coquelin in 1897, and played in the U.S. by Richard Mansfield, Walter Hampden, and José Ferrer, usually in the blank verse translation by operetta-librettist Brian Hooker.

Dalcroze. See **Jaques-Dalcroze, Émile**.

Daly's Theatre, New York. Originally built as a museum in 1867, its heyday came when producer and playwright Augustin Daly transformed it in 1879 into the home for his stock company, headed by John Drew and Ada Rehan, who starred in a series of Shakespearean revivals. After his death in 1899, its decline was swift, dwindling into a burlesque house and ultimately demolished in 1920.

Damala, Jacques (Aristides Damalas, 1855–89), Greek actor. A former diplomat and notorious womanizer, he took up with Sarah Bernhardt. Infatuated, she made him her acting partner on her tours and married the swarthy leading man in 1882. The marriage was short-lived, owing to his philandering.

Dancing Lady, American musical film directed by Robert Z. Leonard (1933). Noteworthy as the cinematic acting premiere of Fred Astaire who plays himself, partnered with Joan Crawford. The burlesque-to-Broadway-stardom story is larded with a strong cast and the song "Everything I Have Is Yours".

Daniell, Henry (1894–1963), English actor. Frequently employed as icy, unsmiling villains in American films (he plays Propaganda Minister Herring in Chaplin's *The Great Dictator* in the same manner), he exercised his malign suavity on Broadway in *Kind Lady* (1935). Such stylish hauteur was in demand for revivals of Ibsen, Shakespeare and Wilde.

D'Annunzio, Gabriele (Rapagnetta, 1863–1938), Dalmatian poet, dramatist and politician. Opposed to the Italian *verismo* movement, he indulged in lush, sensuous but dramatically inert evocations of the past, often performed by his sometime mistress Eleonora Duse: *The Dead City* (1898), *La Gioconda* (1898), *Francesca da Rimini* (1902), *The Daughter of Jorio* (1904). During the First World War, he had a swashbuckling episode, occupying and governing the city of Fiume. This was a preliminary to his later flirtation with fascism in the person of Mussolini.

Dante Alighieri (1265–1321), Italian poet. Motivated by his love for Beatrice Portinari, he wrote the autobiographical *Vita nuova* (*New life*, *c.*1293). His most famous work is *The Divine Comedy*, tracing a journey through Hell, Purgatory and Paradise (1307–21).

Danton's Death, German drama by Georg Büchner (1835). This vigorous, quasi-Shakespeare play written by the 21-year-old radical as a tract for the times covers the bloody episode in the French Revolution when Georges Danton and his allies succumbed to Robespierre and the Reign of Terror. It was produced only posthumously, several times by Max Reinhardt, and first in English by Orson Welles.

Dark Victory, American film directed by Edmund Goulding, with a score by Max Steiner (1939). In this undying tear-jerker Bette Davis plays a spoiled heiress who learns she has a short time to live, becomes a better person and finds love just in time for a deathbed scene. This was the first, but not the last, time Davis assumed a role created on stage by Tallulah Bankhead.

Dartington Hall, Totnes, Devon, England, a derelict medieval hall purchased by the wealthy Americans Leonard and Dorothy Elmhirst in 1925, to house a programme of progressive education. Activities at the co-educational school, founded in 1926, included tending the estate grounds. Michael Chekhov established his Theatre Studio there in 1936, but in 1938 relocated to Ridgefield, Conn. It is now a conference centre.

Darwin, Charles Robert (1809–82), English naturalist. His *Origin of Species by Means of Natural Selection* (1859) and *The Descent of Man and Selection in Relation to Sex* (1871) argued that plants and animals evolved through sexual selection and that human beings descended from an ancestor common to the great apes. Although ultimately accepted by the scientific and humanistic establishments, his ideas remain controversial among religious fundamentalists.

Dassin, Jules (Julius, 1911–), American actor and director. He acted with the Yiddish Proletarian Theatre troupe ARTEF, but launched a successful film career directing gritty urban dramas such as *Brute Force* (1947) and *Naked City*

(1948). Blacklisted by the House Committee on Un-American Activities, he found that even work in Europe was denied him, until he had a huge success with the French "caper" film *Rififi* (*Du rififi chez les hommes*, 1955). He later married Melina Mercouri, whom he featured in the immensely popular *Never on Sunday* (1960).

Daviot, Gordon, pseudonym of Elizabeth Macintosh (1896–1952), Scottish novelist and playwright. A former games mistress, she is best known under the name Josephine Tey for her thrillers. Her history play about Richard II, *Richard of Bordeaux* (1932), provided a vehicle which brought celebrity to John Gielgud and its costume designers Motley.

Davis, Bette. See headnote to Chapter 58, "Great roles reborn".

The Days of the Turbins (*Dni Turbinykh*, also known as *The White Guard*), Russian play by Mikhail Bulgakov from his novel (1924). A family of land-owners is caught in Kiev in 1918–19 between advancing Bolshevik armies and Ukrainian nationalists; after the crisis, they try to decide whether to emigrate or face the future in Russia. The production by the Moscow Art Theatre (1926) played to full houses, but Communist Party organs attacked it as bourgeois and pro-White. It was banned in 1928, but four years later Stalin had it revived, as "proof of the invincible truth of Bolshevism".

The Dead City (*La Città morta*), Italian play by Gabriele D'Annunzio (1899). Near the ruins of Mycenae, an incestuous love between brother and sister is complicated by their relations with another couple, ending in murder and accidental death in an antique tomb. Eleonora Duse's personal magnetism made this overheated nonsense acceptable for a while.

Dean, Basil (1888–1978), English actor, director and playwright. In partnership with Alec Rea as ReandeaN (1919–26), he became the leading manager and director on the commercial London stage, making hits of *A Bill of Divorcement* (1921), *The Constant Nymph* (1926), *Young Woodley* (1928) and *Johnson over Jordan* (1931). As a lighting designer he was ingenious and imaginative; as a director, peremptory and inflexible, allegedly reducing an actress to tears at each rehearsal.

Dear Brutus, English comedy by James M. Barrie (1917). A variation on *Mid-summer Night's Dream*, it has a country house party wander into a mysterious wood that appears once a year. Although they are given a second chance at life, very little changes.

Deception, American film directed by Irving Rapper, with a score by Erich Wolfgang Korngold (1946). An overwrought emotional triangle is com-posed of musician Bette Davis, her Svengaliesque tutor Claude Rains, and cellist Paul Lukas. The title refers to the tangle of lies Davis uses to organize her life.

Decroux, Étienne (1898–1991), French mime and pedagogue, extremely influential in the teaching of modern physical expression. Associated with Charles Dullin to 1934, he founded his own mime school in Paris in the late 1930s, where he inducted Jean-Louis Barrault into the rudiments of an abstract, non-representational pantomime performed almost naked. Barrault cast him as Deburau père in *Les Enfants du Paradis* (1945) and brought him to the Comédie Française (1947–51).

Dekker, Albert (Ecke, 1905–68), American actor. An undistinguished Broadway career, initiated with the Theatre Guild in 1928, brought him to Hollywood in 1937. He was in demand as master criminals (*Dr Cyclops*, 1940; *The Killers*, 1946) and solid businessmen (*East of Eden*, 1955). He returned to the stage as Lee J. Cobb's replacement in *Death of a Salesman* (1949) and the Duke of Norfolk in *A Man for All Seasons* (1961). He died in a bizarre auto-erotic scenario.

Delaney, Shelagh (1939–), English playwright. A working-class 19-year-old, she sprang to fame in 1958 with *A Taste of Honey*. This bitter comedy about an abandoned, unmarried mother who sets up housekeeping with a rejected homosexual had been licked into shape by Joan Littlewood at her Theater Workshop. Delaney wrote the screenplay with Tony Richardson (1961), but her next play *The Lion in Love* (1960) sank without a trace.

Delmar, Viña (Croter, 1903–90), American writer. Well-known for hard-boiled novels of the jazz age – *Bad Girl* (1928), *Loose Ladies* (1929), *Kept Woman* (1930) and *Marriage Racket* (1933) – she wrote the screenplay for *The Awful Truth* (1937). Her play *The Rich, Full Life* (1945) failed on Broadway but was made into the film *Cynthia* (1947) with Elizabeth Taylor.

Desiderio da Settignano (1428–64), Florentine sculptor, a follower of Donatello and Della Robbia. His tombs and friezes are masterpieces of serene grace.

Design for Living, English comedy by Noël Coward, written to feature himself and the Lunts (1932). Three bohemian types, Gilda, Otto and Leo, live as an ever-shifting *ménage à trois*, always unfaithful and always sufficient unto themselves. The knowing were alert to the fact that the bisexuality of the characters was mirrored in the actors. A tame version was filmed in 1933 by Ernst Lubitsch with the misconceived trio of Gary Cooper, Fredric March and Miriam Hopkins.

Desire Under the Elms, an American play by Eugene O'Neill (1924), a twisted interplay of quasi-incestuous emotions in a New England farm family. It was O'Neill's most successful play to date, owing partly to the scene design by Robert Edmond Jones and a sexual emanation that prompted an attempt at censorship by New York's District Attorney.

Detective Story, an American police procedural play by Sidney Kingsley (1949), designed by Boris Aronson. It offered a day in the life of a New York precinct, with criminals and victims interwoven through one detective's marital miseries. One outdated aspect is that the vilest villain is an abortionist.

The Devil's Advocate, American play by Dore Schary from the novel by Morris L. West (1961). The Vatican sends a dying priest to determine whether a dead Italian patriot is a candidate for sainthood or not. Leo Genn acted the ailing Monsignor and Sam Levene played Dr Aldo Meyer, a Jewish physician, one of the consultants, in settings designed by Jo Mielziner.

Diderot's Paradox. Denis Diderot (1713–84), French writer, encyclopedist and art critic, began writing *Le Paradoxe sur le comédien* in 1770, but it was published only posthumously. Citing Mlle. Clairon as his paragon, he argued that actors are most convincing when they are least impassioned. Acting must be under control at all times, carefully rehearsed and never subject to outbursts of real emotion.

Dietrich, Marlene (Maria Magdalene von Losch, 1904–92), German actress and singer. She was already a star on the Berlin musical stage when she became internationally renowned for her legs and musky voice as the siren Lola-Lola in the film *The Blue Angel* (1930). In the hands of her Svengali, Joseph von Sternberg, she was constructed as an enigmatic sex symbol, but when that image faded in 1937, she reinvented herself to regain popularity. During the Second World War, she entertained the Allied troops, and continued in the chanteuse role thereafter.

Digges, Dudley (1879–1947), Irish character actor, who started with the Abbey Theatre. He came to New York in 1904 and stage-managed for George Arliss. From 1919, he was one of the stalwarts of the Theatre Guild in such roles as Boss Mangan in *Heartbreak House*, the Sparrow in *Liliom*, and Volpone. His last stage appearance was as Harry Hope in *The Iceman Cometh* (1946).

Dikki, or **Diky, Aleksey Denisovich** (1889–1955), Russian actor and director, a member of the Moscow Art Theatre and its First Studio (1910–28). He infused his roles with virile energy. His most remarkable staging was the rollicking *Flea* (1925) at the Second Art Theatre, where he frequently came into conflict with Michael Chekhov. He was also responsible for the first, rapidly banned production of Shostakovich's *Lady Macbeth of the Mtsensk District*.

Dinner at Eight, American drama by George S. Kaufman and Edna Ferber (1932). This episodic play traces the fates of the guests at a dinner party from the time they receive their invitations to the actual event a week later. Some are tragic, some comic, but the roles are plums for actors, and MGM turned it into an all-star feature film in 1933.

The Disenchanted, American play by Budd Schulberg and Harvey Breit, from Schulberg's novel (1958). Concerning a young screenwriter in the period from the silents to the late 1930s, it featured the cream of young American actors: Rosemary Harris, Jason Roberts Jr., George Grizzard and Salome Jens.

Dishonored Lady, American play by Margaret Ayer Barnes and Edward Sheldon (1930). Katharine Cornell starred in this melodrama of a sexually promiscuous society woman who cannot find happiness. A laundered film version was made in 1947 for Hedy Lamarr.

Disraeli, Benjamin, 1st Earl of Beaconsfield (1804–81), British statesman and novelist. A colourful Tory politician of Jewish ancestry, he served as Prime Minister (1868, 1874–80), won Suez for Britain (1875) and made Queen Victoria Empress of India (1876). He features prominently in a great many plays and films, his wit and monocle proving irresistible to character actors.

Dix, Dorothy (Elizabeth Meriwether Gilmer, 1870–1951), American journalist. While editing the woman's pages of the New Orleans *Picayune* (1896–1901), she developed the first "agony aunt" column of advice to the lovelorn. It was perpetuated at the New York *Journal* (1901), and by the Wheeler (1917) and Ledger (1923) syndicates. She also authored self-help manuals such as *How to Win and Hold a Husband* (1939).

Dobbs, Mattiwilda (1925–), African-American coloratura soprano. After winning the International Music Competition in Geneva (1951), she performed throughout Europe, the first black woman to sing at La Scala (1953). Following her debut as Gilda in *Rigoletto* at the Met (1956), she was offered a long-term contract, another first, singing six roles over eight seasons. She refused to sing in segregated venues, preferring churches and colleges to civic auditoria.

Dobrolyubov, error for **Dobronravov**.

Dobronravov, Boris Georgievich (1896–1949), Russian actor. In 1915 he entered the Moscow Art Theatre, where he stayed all his life, dying in the wings during a performance of *Tsar Feodor*. Though usually cast in leads (Vaska Pepel, *Lower Depths*, 1924; Voynitsky, *Uncle Vanya*, 1947), he was a true ensemble player, much appreciated by Stanislavsky. His Soviet heroes offered a positive, utopian paragon.

The Doctor's Dilemma, comedy-drama by G. B. Shaw (1906). A representative group of physicians, each with his own speciality, is called in by Jennifer Dubedat to treat her husband, a dying painter. With only one dose of a cure available, the dilemma of Sir Colenso Ridgeon is whether to heal that immoral fraud or a decent man; Ridgeon's love for Jennifer complicates the issue.

Don Juan (*Dom Juan, ou Le Festin de pierre*), French comedy by Molière (1691). The successor to *Tartuffe*, this play shows the legendary seducer as an atheist and blasphemer as well. It was rarely produced before the twentieth century when Louis Jouvet revealed its power and relevance.

Dorsch, Käte (Katherina, 1890–1957), German actress. Beginning as an operetta soubrette, she moved into legitimate theatre, helped to popularity by her Bavarian charm in such roles as Eliza Doolittle (1922) and Nora (1923). A favorite of Hermann Goering, she received exorbitant salaries during the Nazi period, but tried to help colleagues in danger. After the war, she continued to work, often with fellow collaborator Gustaf Gründgens (Mrs Alving in *Ghosts*, 1946; Clare Zachanassian in *The Visit*, 1956).

Dostoevsky, Fyodor Mikhailovich (1821–81), Russian novelist, none of whose attempts at drama came to fruition. In recompense, his novels have been frequently dramatized. *Crime and Punishment* was popular on the stage from the 1890s. The Moscow Art Theatre staged *The Brothers Karamazov* (1910), *The Devils* (as *Nikolay Stavrogin*, 1913), *The Village of Stepanchikovo* (1917) and *Uncle's Dream* (1929). *The Idiot* was a sensation of the post-Stalinist stage (1957) with Innokenty Smoktunovsky as Prince Myshkin.

A Double Life, American film directed by George Cukor from a screenplay by Garson Kanin and Ruth Gordon (1947). The role of Othello begins to take over the mind of a popular tragedian (Ronald Colman), leading him to strangle his waitress mistress (Shelley Winters).

Down in the Valley, American opera by Kurt Weill and Arnold Sungaard

(1945). A short piece devised for the radio, it was later expanded and produced at Indiana University in 1948. Its folksy plot concerns a country boy who accidentally kills the scoundrel who is after his girl and is hanged for it.

D'Oyly Carte Company, founded by Richard D'Oyly Carte, in 1880, to perform the comic operas of Gilbert and Sullivan. It came to be housed in the Savoy Theatre, London, Run subsequently by Carte's descendants and partly supported by government subsidy, it preserved the staging traditions and disseminated them through frequent tours. It was disbanded in 1982, but revived six years later.

Dramatists Guild, The. It was created in 1920 to protect U.S. playwrights from piracy and exploitation, and provided boiler-plate contracts. It is still active.

Die Dreigroschenoper (*The Threepenny Opera*), musical comedy by Bertolt Brecht, Elisabeth Hauptmann and Kurt Weill (1928). An adaptation of John Gay's *The Beggar's Opera*, transferred to Victorian London, it was a runaway sensation, despite Brecht's social messages and because of Weill's jazz-inflected score. The remarkable cast included Lotte Lenya, Carola Neher, Kurt Gerron and Ernst Busch, some of whom reappeared in the film directed by G. W. Pabst in 1931. Brecht detested the film and sued.

Drinkwater, John (1882–1937), English poet and dramatist. A charter member of Barry Jackson's Pilgrim Players in Birmingham, he started playwriting in the Pre-Raphaelite vein with the verse legend *Cophetua* (1911). The success of his *Abraham Lincoln* (1919), in which he played the Chronicler, led him to try and repeat the same mixture as before with *Mary Stuart* (1922), *Oliver Cromwell* and *Robert E. Lee* (both 1923).

Drury Lane, Theatre Royal, London. When the 1663 edifice burned down, it was rebuilt by Christopher Wren in 1674. It became David Garrick's playhouse, as manager and star, from 1747 to 1776. Rebuilt and enlarged in 1794, it burned down in 1809, and was reconstructed in 1812 on its present site, making it the oldest extant playhouse still in use in London. Audiences flocked to it to see Edmund Kean. A succession of managers tried to make a go of it before Augustus Harris took the reins and in the 1880s filled the house with spectacle and pantomime. Since the Second World War, it has been chiefly a showplace for American musicals.

Dryden, John (1631–1700), English poet and playwright. His plays run from heroic tragedies written in rhymed couplets (*The Indian Queen*, 1664; *Aurengzebe*, 1675) to comedies of manners (*Sir Martin Mar-all*, 1667; *Marriage a la Mode*, 1672), usually prefaced with rationales for his practice. Although he argued for rhymed dialogue in the *Essay of Dramatick Poesie* (1668), he turned to blank verse in *All for Love*, his Antony-and-Cleopatra variant (1678).

Du Maurier, Sir Gerald (1873–1934), English actor and director, son of the caricaturist George, and father of novelist Daphne. A past master at playing Barrie (*The Admirable Crichton*, the first Captain Hook in *Peter Pan*, Harry Dearth in *Dear Brutus*), he won greatest popularity as the safe-cracker

Raffles (1906). He was said to be able to underact any other player off the stage.

Duccio di Buoninsegna (1255?–?1319), Sienese painter. Late representative of the Italo-Byzantine style, he created the altarpiece for the Cathedral of Siena, with its large panel of the "Madonna Enthroned with Angels and Saints" and scenes from the life of Christ and the Virgin Mary.

The Duchess of Malfi, English blank verse tragedy by John Webster, from Bandello, Painter and Spenser (*c.*1614). One of the characteristic revenge plays of the Jacobean era, it demonstrates the punishment inflicted on the Duchess by her brothers, a Cardinal and the Duke of Calabria, for marrying beneath her. It is a poetic chamber of horrors, lingering on madness, incestuous feelings, murder and lycanthropy. Brecht and W. H. Auden attempted an adaptation in 1946 for Elisabeth Bergner, with the actor of color Canada Lee in whiteface as the bravo Bosola.

Dukes, Ashley. See headnote to Chapter 20, "The Gielgud *Macbeth*".

Dullin, Charles (1885–1949), French actor, director and pedagogue. Work with Firmin Gémier and Jacques Copeau was followed by the establishment of the Théâtre de l'Atelier, Paris, which offered audiences Aristophanes, Shakespeare, Ben Jonson (by way of Zweig and Romains), Balzac and Pirandello. Hunchbacked and wizened, he was unparalleled in the roles of Richard III, Volpone and Molière's Miser. Among the students he nurtured were Jean-Louis Barrault, Antonine Artaud and Jean Marais.

Duncan, Augustin (1873–1954), American actor, brother of Isadora. After work with Richard Mansfield, William Gillette and Charles Coburn, he joined the new Theatre Guild in 1919, and played the lead in their first hit *John Ferguson*. He was a much-employed actor (his best part probably Capt. Boyle in *Juno and the Paycock*), and director for the Guild. When he went blind, Maurice Evans cast him as John of Gaunt in *Richard II* and the Ghost in *Hamlet* (1938).

Duncan, Isadora, American dancer (1878–1927). Despite her ungainliness, Duncan disseminated her *faux*-Grecian idea of dance widely throughout Europe, Russia and eventually America. It involved bare feet, much manipulation of draperies, and a free interpretation of emotions. Duncan schools, their lawns speckled with girls in garlands and flowing robes, were a phenomenon of the 1910s and 1920s.

Durant, Will (in full, William James, 1885–1961), American historian. With his wife Ariel, he set out to write a history of civilization. The venture was subsidized by the phenomenal sales of *The Story of Philosophy* (1926), and eventually they turned out *The Story of Civilization*, eleven readable volumes of "synthetic history", covering cultural and scientific developments as well as the usual political events.

The Dybbuk, Yiddish play by Shlomo Ansky (1914). Drawn from Jewish folklore and religious ritual, this fantastic tale of a bride possessed by a dead Talmudic scholar and exorcised to death was first staged in Yiddish in Vilna in 1917. It made its most effective mark when directed for Habima by Evgeny

Vakhtangov in Moscow (1920) in a Hebrew translation by Chaim Nachman Bialik. The grotesque style of acting and design influenced the Neighborhood Playhouse production in New York (1926).

Dynamo, American tragedy by Eugene O'Neill (1929). Proclaiming the Expressionist distrust of the machine, O'Neill makes the dynamo an everpresent backdrop for a schematic and overheated drama of passion. The son of a fundamentalist Christian, in love with the daughter of an atheist, grows disillusioned and worships Electricity as his one god. A second disillusionment leads him to kill the girl and electrocute himself on the dynamo.

E. E. Clive Stock Company, American acting troupe out of Boston in the late 1910s, managed by the British character actor E. E. Clive (1879–1940). It moved to Hollywood in the 1920s, and many of its members, including Clive and Rosalind Russell, transferred their activities to the movies.

Eames, Claire (1896–1930), American actress. Her first outstanding part was in the lead of Drinkwater's *Mary Stuart* (1921), followed by a variety of roles from flighty Mrs Tiffany in *Fashion* to Lady Macbeth (opposite James K. Hackett) and Hedda Gabler. Her husband, Sidney Howard, wrote *Lucky Sam McCarver* (1925) and *Ned McCobb's Daughter* (1926) for her.

Ebert, Carl (1887–1980), German actor and director. He studied under Max Reinhardt (1909–14) and acted under Leopold Jessner (1914–18), and although he began as a director of modernist drama, took an interest in musical theatre. During the Nazi period (1933–46), he worked in Buenos Aires and Ankara. In 1947 he founded and ran the Glyndeborne Festival, where he created new directions in staging opera. He taught at UCLA (1954–62).

Edward VII (1841–1910), King of Great Britain and Ireland from 1901. Eldest son of Queen Victoria, he filled the many years before his coronation with high living, innumerable mistresses and regular visits to European spas. A frequenter of Parisian night-spots as Prince of Wales, he was often greeted familiarly by the cancan dancers.

Edwards, Ben (1916–99), American set designer. After work with the Federal Theatre Project in New York, he became one of Broadway's most prolific designers, providing evocative interiors for Eugene O'Neill and William Inge, as well as monumental exteriors (*Medea*, 1947) and more abstract spaces (Richard Burton's rehearsal-room *Hamlet*, 1964). He also worked for the Guthrie Theatre in Minneapolis and the American Shakespeare Festival.

Eglevsky, André (1917–77), Russian-born American ballet dancer. Following much training in France with Russian dancers, from the age of 14 he appeared with both de Basil's Ballet Russe and René Blum's homonymous troupe. He became the *premier danseur* in Balanchine's New York City Ballet (1937–8), but returned to Europe, rarely staying in any troupe for more than four years. His longest stint was again with Balanchine (1951–8).

Eisler, Hanns (1898–1962), German composer. A pupil of Schönberg, he created a scandal with his "musical cartoons" and saw his published music destroyed when the Nazis came to power. He lived in New York and Hollywood from 1937, and, deported back to Europe in 1948, wrote incidental music for many of Brecht's works, especially *Mother Courage* and *Die Verurteilung des Lukullus*.

El Greco. See **Greco, El**.

Electra, Greek poetic tragedies by Sophocles (*c.*450 B.C.E.) and Euripides (*c.*414 BC). In Sophocles' version, Electra welcomes the return of her brother Orestes and persuades him to murder their mother Clytaemnestra and her lover; then she marries Orestes' bosom friend Pylades. In Euripides, Orestes and Electra flee, remorsefully, after the murder and are condemned by the gods. Later versions were written by Hofmannsthal, Giraudoux and O'Neill.

Eliot, T[homas] S[tearns] (1888–1965), Anglo-American poet and playwright, who redirected attention to the Senecan origins of Elizabethan drama. Working with E. Martin Browne, he began to experiment with verse plays: *The Rock* (1934) and *Murder in the Cathedral* (1935). His later dramas – *The Family Reunion* (1939), *The Cocktail Party* (1949), *The Confidential Clerk* (1953) and *The Elder Statesman* (1958) – with themes drawn from Ibsen and Sophocles, were in a taut and rarefied style that discouraged imitation.

Elizabeth the Queen, a verse history play, by Maxwell Anderson (1930). It is conceived as the love story of Good Queen Bess and the Earl of Essex (portrayed by the Lunts). Much admired in its time when produced by the Theatre Guild, it now comes across as fustian. It served as a model for the film *The Private Lives of Elizabeth and Essex* (1939), starring Bette Davis and Errol Flynn.

Ellida Wangel. See *The Lady from the Sea*.

Empire Theatre, New York. Built in 1893, further uptown than the regular theatre district, it was headquarters for producer Charles Frohman, and after his death in 1917, Alf Hayman and Gilbert Miller to 1931. Owing to its bijou size, actors and audiences loved it, and Katharine Cornell preferred it. The six-year run of *Life with Father* in 1939 confirmed its popularity. It was razed in 1953.

Enemies (*Vragi*), Russian scenes in three acts by Maksim Gorky (1906). The play represents a conflict between factory owners and militant workers. As a "missing link between Chekhov and the Russian Revolution" (Ronald Bryden), the play was banned, and received its first staging at the Kleines Theater, Berlin. In 1933, Gorky revised the text, particularly the last act, and this version was widely produced, most memorably at the Moscow Art Theatre in 1935.

The Entertainer, English play by John Osborne (1957). Three generations of music-hall performers face extinction in a diminished England during the Suez Crisis of 1956. The scenes alternate overlapping domestic chatter with Archie Rice's on-stage routines. Laurence Olivier gave a jolt to his career as Archie and repeated his performance in the film directed by Tony Richardson (1960).

Épinal, Image d', a French term for a rose-coloured, naïve view of things. It is based on the crudely coloured lithographs of saints, battles and *commedia* figures produced by Jean-Charles Pellerin in the town of Épinal in the nineteenth century.

Equity Players, an American acting company founded in 1922 by Actor's Equity members, to present non-commercial drama and classic revivals. Two years later, faced with dwindling audiences, it renamed itself the Actors' Theatre. It was amalgamated with Kenneth Macgowan's Greenwich Village troupe in 1927.

Ethel Barrymore Theatre, New York. The Shuberts wooed Ethel Barrymore with the promise of building a theatre with her name on it, which they did in 1928. Despite its alluring intimacy, it rarely housed runaway hits, so the few that did appear there, such as *The Women* (1936), *Pal Joey* (1940) and *A Streetcar Named Desire* (1947), deserve mention.

Euripides (486–407 B.C.E.), Greek tragedian. Eighteen of his reputed 90 plays survive, allowing us to gauge how experimental and revolutionary were his psychologized treatments of standard myths. He invented Medea's murder of her children and shifted sympathy from Hippolytos to Phaedra. Although he rarely won first prize and was ridiculed by Aristophanes, he was respected and at his death the Athenians performed a tribute in the theatre.

Evans, Dame Edith (1888–1976), English actress. She developed her precise style in Restoration roles for the Phoenix Society, especially Millamant in *The Way of the World* (Lyric Hammersmith, 1924), and was trusted with Shakespearean leads at the Old Vic (1925–6). Her Lady Bracknell in *The Importance of Being Earnest* (1939), with its octave shift on "A ha-a-and bag!", set the bar for that part. She shuttled between classic and modern roles throughout her long career, with exceptional performances in St John Ervine (*Robert's Wife*), Chekhov and Fry.

Evans, Maurice (1901–89), English actor and director. He came to the U.S. to play Romeo and the Dauphin in *St Joan* opposite Katharine Cornell (1934), and, becoming a citizen, developed into America's best-known Shakespearean and Shavian player. He was acclaimed for his Richard II (1937), Malvolio (1940), Macbeth (1941) and "G.I. Hamlet", cut down to an hour and a half to amuse the troops. His performances were technically competent, but rarely exciting.

Evreinoff or **Evreinov, Nikolay Nikolaevich** (1879–1953), Russian play-wright, director and theorist. His theory of monodrama, which views reality through a single consciousness, is exemplified in *Backstage at the Soul* (1912), which shows the psyche divided into its rational, emotional and subliminal entities. His best play *The Main Thing* (1921) explores his favorite notion of theatre as life, an art "for oneself", shape-shifting to overcome chaos.

Ewell, Tom (S. Yewell Tompkins, 1909–94), American actor. After years of study at Actors Studio and efficient comedy performances in undistinguished plays, he gained celebrity as the grass widower in *The Seven Year Itch* (1952). Brought to Hollywood to recreate it opposite Marilyn Monroe, he stayed there, but thought film acting uncreative. He played opposite Bert Lahr in the disastrous U.S. debut of *Waiting for Godot* in Miami (1956).

Ewing, Marjorie, American producer. In tandem with her husband Sherman Ewing, she produced four shows on Broadway, including the musicals *Angel in the Wings* (1947) and *The Rape of Lucretia* (1948) and a revival of Shaw's *Getting Married* (1951). She also worked Off-Broadway (*A Certain Young Man*, 1967).

The Exemplary Theatre, English treatise by Harley Granville-Barker (1922). This was Granville-Barker's reasoned plea for a national theatre which would be educational for audiences and inspiring for actors. His ideas were praised for their highmindedness, but criticized for their neglect of reality.

Fagan, James Bernard (1873–1933), Irish playwright and director. After work with Benson and Beerbohm Tree, he staged *The Merchant of Venice* with the Yiddish actor Maurice Moskovitch (Court Theatre, 1919). His first repertory theatre was founded in a Big Game Museum in Oxford in 1923, and included John Gielgud, Tyrone Guthrie, Flora Robson and Raymond Massey; it put on a memorable *Cherry Orchard*. He then directed the Festival Theatre, Cambridge, and the Irish Players.

Fanny's First Play, comedy by George Bernard Shaw (1911). On Fanny's birthday, her father Count O'Dowda has her play staged anonymously and invites leading critics to appraise it. It is a melodrama in which a suffragette falls in love with a footman (actually a duke's younger son) and her fiancé becomes engaged to a prostitute. Of the critics, only the one based on A. B. Walkley of the *Times* guesses that Fanny wrote it about her own experiences.

Farmer, Frances (1914–70), American actress. Unable to get a foothold on the New York stage, she went into film and rapidly became a star in *Come and Get It* (1936). Her appearance in the Group Theatre's *Golden Boy* made the play a hit (1937), despite her own mixed notices. Back in Hollywood, her erratic behavior and backstage recalcitrance relegated her to B pictures and, from 1942 on, her life was a revolving door of arrests for drunk driving, nervous breakdowns, incarceration in mental hospitals, and sporadic public appearances.

Farren, William Percival (1853–1937), English actor and playwright. Scion of a long line of actors, he joined Henry Irving's company in 1896. He created the roles of Dr Patrick Cullen in *The Doctor's Diemma* (1906) and Gaffer Tyl in *The Blue Bird* (1909), and was seen as Dr Drury in *Ned Kean of Old Drury* (1932).

Fata Morgana, Hungarian comedy by Ernest Vajda (1924). An experienced coquette casts her spell over an 18-year-old schoolboy, who believes they are engaged. When it appears she is married, he reluctantly renounces her and accepts disillusionment as the price of adulthood.

Faulkner, William (1897–1962), American novelist, famous for his stream-of-consciousness depictions of Southern decadence in fictional Yoknapatawpha County. *As I Lay Dying*, a polyphonic tale of transporting a coffin to its final resting place (1930), was made into a mime piece by Jean-Louis Barrault.

Sanctuary (1931) was dramatized and filmed as *The Story of Temple Drake*. Faulkner did a brief and sterile stint as a Hollywood screenwriter.

Faust, German poetic drama in two parts by Johann Wolfgang von Goethe (1808, 1831). Goethe's version of the legend of the scholar who sells his soul to the devil is enriched by a good deal of crisp verse, shrewd philosophy and cosmic symbolism. In performance it is usually reduced to the plot of the seduction and execution of Margarethe (Gretchen).

Fay, Frank (1897–1961), American actor. He began as a child actor, and became a popular headliner in revue and vaudeville, his easy manner and shaggy-dog stories making him a sought-after master of ceremonies. His waning career was given a boost when he played the pixilated Elwood P. Dowd in the long-running comedy *Harvey* (1944–6).

Fay, Frank J. (1870–1931) and **William George** (1872–1947), Irish actor-managers. Their Ormonde Dramatic Society, Dublin (1898–4), which included Dudley Digges and Sara Allgood and put on works by Yeats, was an important springboard for the Abbey Theatre. There they developed a restrained style with harmonized voices and acted in most of the repertoire. Later work was carried on in London and the U.S.

Ferdinand the Bull, American children's book by Munro Leaf, illustrated by Robert Lawson (1936). Ferdinand, a Spanish bull, would rather doze under a cork tree than fight in the arena. Taken by fascists as a pacifist tract, it was banned in Nazi Germany. Walt Disney made it into an animated short (1938) and it was adapted as a puppet play by the Federal Theatre Project.

Ferdinandov, Boris Alekseevich (1889–1959), Russian actor and director. After a stint at the Moscow Art Theatre (1911–12), he joined the Kamerny Theatre (1917–25, with interruptions), where he directed a few shows and played physically active roles (Tybalt in *Romeo and Juliet*, Young Syrian in *Salome*, *King Harlequin*). In 1921–23 he ran the Experimental Heroic Theatre, with rhythm as the basis of the acting.

Ferrer, José (1912–92), Puerto-Rican actor and director, came to fame in *Brother Rat* (1936), and as Charley's Aunt (1940), Iago to Paul Robeson's Othello (1943), and Cyrano de Bergerac. He was noted for his resonant voice and energized performances. He later directed classic revivals for the New York Theatre Company.

The Fervent Years (1945) is Harold Clurman's account of the rise and fall of the Group Theatre.

Ffrangcon-Davies, Gwen (1891–1992), English actress. Her stage debut was in 1911, and soon she became a favorite leading lady for effete leading men: Juliet, the Queen in *Richard of Bordeaux*, Lady Macbeth opposite Gielgud (1924, 1933, 1942), Princess Katherine in *Henry V* opposite Ivor Novello (1938). She was also the first Mrs Manningham in *Gaslight* (1938). She retired in 1970.

Fidelio, or Conjugal Love (*Fidelio, oder Die eheliche Liebe*, 1805–14), German opera by Ludwig von Beethoven. A failure at its first showing, it was rewritten several times (with four separate overtures). Fidelio is the assumed male persona of Leonora, who is seeking to free her husband from a Spanish political prison.

Fielding, Henry (1707–54), English novelist and playwright. He adapted Molière's *The Mock Doctor* (1732) and *The Miser* (1733), but his own comedies and farces were even more popular. Some, like *The Tragedy of Tragedies, or Tom Thumb* (1730) were burlesques of current genres, but others, such as *The Historical Registry for 1736* (1736) were such pungent critiques of the political scene that they brought about the Licensing Act of 1737, which restricted performances.

The Final Conflict (*Posledny Reshitelny*), Russian play by Vsevolod Vishnevsky (1931) (the title is a quotation from "The Internationale"). Depicting the heroic death of Baltic Fleet sailors defending the Soviet Union against invasion, it was staged by Meyerhold with the gimmicks of machine guns, searchlights, plants in the house, and direct address to the audience.

The Firebrand of Florence, American musical comedy by Ira Gershwin and Kurt Weill (1945). It was based on Edwin Justus Mayer's romance comedy *The Firebrand* (1924), flamboyant foolery about the love affairs of Benevenuto Cellini, also made into a film with Douglas Fairbanks, Jr. It failed badly despite the presence of Lotte Lenya and Melville Cooper.

Five Finger Exercise, English play by Peter Shaffer (1958). A charismatic German tutor involuntarily weaves a powerful spell over a nasty middle-class English family in this well-tailored precursor to Pasolini's *Teorema*. It was filmed in 1962 by Daniel Mann with Maximilian Schell as the irresistible outsider.

Flowers of the Forest, American play by John Van Druten (1935). Produced by and starring Katharine Cornell, it is a flashback account of a woman who wasted her life in a loveless marriage by forsaking the dead poet she thought had abandoned her. Burgess Meredith played the ventriloqual and consumptive young genius who speaks for the war dead. The critics turned thumbs down on it.

Flying Down to Rio, American musical film directed by Thornton Freeland with songs by Vincent Youmans and Gus Kahn (1933). Fred Astaire and Ginger Rogers were teamed for the first time (though not as the stars) in the "Carioca" number, and Busby Berkeley choreographed a camp aerial ballet.

Fogerty, Elsie (1866–1945), English actress and pedagogue. Her lectures on diction and elocution laid the foundation for the Central School of Speech Training and Dramatic Art, London, in 1906, housed in the Albert Hall until 1957. Its alumni include Laurence Olivier and Peggy Ashcroft. She published several textbooks and adaptations of Greek drama.

Follow the Fleet, American musical film directed by Mark Sandrich with songs by Irving Berlin (1936). Fred Astaire, a hoofer turned able seaman, woos showgirl Ginger Rogers in such spectacular numbers as "Let Yourself Go" and "Let's Face the Music and Dance".

Fonda, Henry (1905–82), American actor, known mainly for his screen performances. The role which brought him to critical notice, *The Farmer Takes a*

Wife (1934), established him as a personification of American folk decency. As the tolerant naval officer in *Mr. Roberts* (1948) he won a Tony award, and later made occasional stage appearances, especially in a one-man show about Clarence Darrow (1974).

Fontanne, Lynn. See headnote to Chapter 51 "The Actor Attacks His Part: Lynn Fontanne and Alfred Lunt".

For Goodness Sake, American musical comedy by Fred and Arthur Jackson, with music by William Daly and Paul Lannin and additional songs by George and Ira Gershwin and Arthur Francis (1922). This show was noteworthy as the first encounter of Fred and Adele Astaire with the Gershwins, who contributed "Someone", "Tra-la-la" and "French Pastry Walk" to it.

Forbes-Robertson, Jean (1905–62), English actress, daughter of Sir Johnstone. Distinguished in Chekhov (Sonya in *Uncle Vanya* for Komisarjevsky, 1926), Ibsen (Rebecca West, Hedda Gabler), Shakespeare (Juliet, Viola, Puck, Oberon), she was her generation's inevitable Peter Pan (1927–34).

Forbes-Robertson, Sir Johnstone (1853–1927), English actor-manager. Having established a reputation as a handsome juvenile in Henry Irving's Lyceum productions, he set up as a manager, playing Romeo to the Juliet of Mrs Patrick Campbell (1895). He was considered the definitive Hamlet of his day, albeit somewhat stiff and dry. With his noble profile, he created the great Julius in Shaw's *Caesar and Cleopatra*, but won more popularity as the mysterious do-gooder in *The Passing of the Third Floor Back* (1908).

Ford, John (1586–1639), English playwright. With Dekker and Rowley he wrote about domestic wickedness in *The Witch of Edmonton* (1621?), but on his own pursued evil in an imaginary Italy. His non-collaborative works, *'Tis Pity She's a Whore* (1626) and *The Broken Heart* (1629), are sanguinary pageants of self-consuming passion.

Foregger, Nikolay Mikhailovich (Foregger von Greifenturn, 1892–1939), Russian director. Out of his belief that human movement must be modelled on machinery he created the Foregger Workshop (Mastfor), Moscow (1922–4), which put on episodic plays inhabited by recurring characters or "social masks". *Kind Treatment of Horses*, a parody of the music hall, had costumes by Sergey Eisenstein. After his death, his name became synonymous with "inveterate formalism".

Four Walls, American play by George Abbott and Dana Burnet from Burnet's story (1927). Paul Muni made a hit as ex-convict Benny Horowitz who wants to go straight but has to commit a crime for the sake of his girlfriend. It was filmed in 1928 with John Gilbert and Joan Crawford, and again in 1934 with a miscast Franchot Tone.

The Foxes of Harrow, American film directed by John M. Stahl from the novel by Frank Yerby (1947). Set on a Louisiana plantation, it revolves around the card-sharp planter Stephen Fox and the three women in his life. The movie, with Rex Harrison, Maureen O'Hara and Victor McLaglen, omits the miscegenation theme which was central to the novel.

France, C[harles] V[ernon] (1868–1949), English actor. He first appeared in film in 1910 as Time in *The Blue Bird*, and continued through the sound era to 1944 in roles of priests, lawyers and officers.

Franz Joseph I, Emperor of Austria and King of Hungary (1830–1916), almost the last of the Habsburgs. His attempt to consolidate his empire by imposing a centralized bureaucracy resulted in the loss of Lombardy (1859) and Venetia (1866) and forced him to loosen his hold on constituent populations. The latter part of his life was scarred by personal tragedies: the assassination of his wife, the suicide of his son, and the murder of his heir which led to the First World War. In drama and comic opera, he is invariably portrayed as a bewhiskered, grandfatherly old gaffer.

Freud, Sigmund (1856–1939), Austrian neurologist. As the founder of psycho-analysis, he launched the idea that neuroses and dreams derive from repressed sexual desire. His theories of an unconscious mind divided into the Id, Ego and Super-Ego, of the Oedipus complex and penis envy, entered the popular imagination and language.

Fry, Christopher (Harris, 1907–2005), English playwright. His plays were praised as part of a new poetic, religious-inspired drama, inaugurated by T. S. Eliot, but the best have much more humour and stage savvy than Eliot's: *A Phoenix Too Frequent* (1946), *The Lady's Not for Burning* (1948), *Venus Observed* (1950). He also forged successful adaptations of plays by Anouilh and Girau-doux. His *Curtmantle* (1961) comes across as a critricism of Anouilh's *Becket*.

Funny Face, American musical film directed by Stanley Donen (1956), with songs by George and Ira Gershwin. Paris is the scene for this romance between Fred Astaire and Audrey Hepburn, against a background of the fashion industry. It contains a typical Hollywood take on the beatnik scene in the number "Clap Yo' Hands."

G.I. Bill of Rights. The Serviceman's Readjustment Act of 1944 aimed to aid veterans in adjusting to civilian life. The U.S. federal government pledged to subsidize college tuition and contingent living expenses. Within seven years, 8 million servicemen received the educational benefits at a cost of $14 billion.

Gabel, Martin (1912–86), American actor. Short and stocky, with a clarion voice, he was a member of the Mercury Theatre (Danton in *Danton's Death*). Old inhabitants remember him as the narrator of Norman Corwin's epic radio poem *On a Note of Triumph*, to celebrate the defeat of the Nazis (1945). In the dramatization of the Lincoln–Douglas debates *The Rivalry*, he was Douglas, and played Professor Moriarty in the Sherlock Holmes musical *Baker Street*.

Gable, Clark (1901–60), American film actor, known as "The King". After a checkered career as an oil-field roughneck, lumberjack and male hustler, he broke into films and, in *Red Dust* (1932) and *It Happened One Night* (1934), found his niche as a hard-boiled, cynical "man's man". He was everyone's first choice for Rhett Butler in *Gone with the Wind* (1939).

Gainsborough, Thomas (1727–88), English painter. Influenced by Hogarth and Francis Hayman, he began as a landscape painter and interior decorator, but after his marriage to an heiress, devoted himself to portraits, preferably of royalty and socialites. Ironically, it is the anonymous *Blue Boy* (1770) which has become iconic.

Gardiner, Reginald (1903–80), English actor. A graduate of RADA, he made his stage debut as a walk-on in *The Prisoner of Zenda* and his film debut in Hitchcock's *The Lodger* (1926). Typed as a light comedian, in Hollywood movies (1931–65) he clowned with Laurel and Hardy in *Flying Deuces* (1939), Charlie Chaplin in *The Great Dictator* (1940) and Jack Benny in *A Horn Blows at Midnight* (1945).

Garfield, John (Julius Garfinkle, 1913–52), American actor. Following study with Maria Ouspenskaya and small parts under Eva Le Gallienne, he joined the Group Theatre, where his pugnacious style was at a premium. He created the son in *Awake and Sing!* (1935), but left when he was not cast in the lead of *Golden Boy* (1937), which he finally played the year of his death. He made a wry comment on his successful Hollywood career when he rejoined Odets to appear as the blackmailed star in *The Big Knife* (1949).

Garrick, David (1717–79), English actor and playwright. Equally successful in tragedy and comedy, he was credited with bringing a new realism to the London stage. His best parts, testifying to his range, were Lear, Hamlet, Richard III, Abel Drugger in *The Alchemist*, Archer in *The Beaux' Stratagem*, Sir John Brute in *The Provok'd Wife* and Don Felix in *The Wonder*. He campaigned for Shakespeare's reputation, banned spectators from the stage, reformed lighting and scene design, and raised the status of actor from vagabond to solid citizen.

Gate Theatre, London, opened in 1925 as a club meant to present plays rejected by the commercial managements. The premiere drama was *Bernice* by Susan Glaspell, and Ernst Toller's *From Morn to Midnight* confirmed its success. Norman Marshall was its most effective director, whose productions often had strong sexual content. It was bombed out of existence during the Blitz.

Gay Divorcee, American musical film, directed by Mark Sandrich with songs by Cole Porter et al. (1941). It provides a lavish setting for the dance numbers of Fred Astaire and Ginger Rogers, who trip to "Night and Day" and "The Continental".

Gay, John (1685–1732), English poet and playwright. *The Beggar's Opera*, studded with sardonic lyrics set to popular ballads, made him rich, and he supplied a sequel, *Polly* (1729), which was debarred the stage until 1777. His *Achilles*, another ballad opera, shows the Grecian hero in drag most of the time. His last stage work was a libretto for Handel's *Acis and Galatea*, itself a reformation of Italian opera.

Gazzara, Ben (accurately Biagio Anthony, 1930–), American actor and film-maker. Work with Erwin Piscator and at the Actors Studio preceded a number of intensely emotional roles: Jocko de Paris in *End as a Man* (1953), Brick in *Cat on a Hot Tin Roof* (1955), the drug addict Johnny Pope in *A Hatful of Rain* (1955), along with revivals of Eugene O'Neill. As a film-maker, he has taken a *cinéma-verité* approach, grainy in technique and subject matter.

Genée, Adeline (Anina Kirstina Margarete Petra Jensen, 1878–1970), Danish dancer. She is credited with raising the artistic level of ballet when she appeared in London (1897–1907) in music hall and musical comedy (*The Little Michus*, 1905). Ziegfeld brought her to New York in 1907. After a period of retirement, she toured Australia (1913–16) and then took an active part in dance teaching in London.

The Gentle People, American drama by Irwin Shaw (1939). One of the Group Theatre's lesser efforts, it extols the resilience of the "little man". Two fishermen, a Jew and a Greek, save their neighbourhood and their own plans for retirement by drowning an extortionist gangster.

Gentlewoman, American play by John Howard Lawson (1934). A Group Theatre production, it charts the mismatched romance of a left-wing agitator and a Park Avenue widow. It ends with her predicting that her unborn, illegitimate child will scan "a red horizon". Stella Adler has so much trouble with the lead role that she went to Europe to consult Stanislavsky about it.

George V (1865–1936), King of Great Britain. A devoted stamp collector, he changed the family name from Saxe-Coburg-Gotha to Windsor owing to anti-German sentiment during the First World War. The greatest innovation of his reign was to address his subjects via Christmas Day radio broadcasts, beginning in 1932.

Gerron, Kurt (Gerson, 1887–1944), German actor. His vast paunch and moon-face were familiar features of the Weimar German musical revue and cabaret, especially at Berlin's Wild Stage to 1924. He created the role of Tiger Brown in *Die Dreigroschenoper* (1928) and the m.c. in the film *The Blue Angel* (1930). Deported by the Nazis to the Theresienstadt concentration camp, he was compelled to direct the propaganda film *The Führer Bestows a City on the Jews*.

Gershwin, Ira (Israel Gershvin, 1896–1983), American lyricist. For his brother George and many other songwriters, he provided scores of lyrics, witty and banal, but always upbeat. After his brother's death in 1937, he collaborated with Kurt Weill on *Lady in the Dark* (1941).

Gest, Morris (1881–1942), Russian-born impresario, who, in partnership with F. Ray Comstock, imported to New York the Ballets Russes, the Chauve-Souris revue, the Moscow Art Theatre (1923–4), Max Reinhardt's *The Miracle* (1924), the Art Theatre Musical Studio (1925) and the Freiburg Passion Players (1929). He married David Belasco's daughter, but lost his fortune in the Depression and was reduced to sponsoring midgets.

Ghosts (*Gengængere*), Norwegian drama by Henrik Ibsen (1884). A tightly constructed tragedy of fate, unraveling all the wrong decisions made in the past in an upper-middle-class family in rural Norway. Because hereditary syphilis plays a role, the play was slow to be performed, the premiere taking place in Chicago in Norwegian. Its first English production was met with vituperation and contumely.

Gibbs, Wolcott (1902–58), American dramatic critic, associated with the *New Yorker* (1940–58). His mousy looks belied a poison pen, used to skewer mediocre plays and performers, and his parodies of celebrated writers were right on the mark.

Giehse, Therese (1989–1975), German actress. She and Erika Mann founded an anti-Nazi cabaret, The Peppermill (1933), which took them to Zurich, where she settled. After the war, she was the first to play Brecht's *Mother Courage* (1941) and acted with the Berliner Ensemble (1949, 1952). Short and dumpy, she became the leading character actress on the German-speaking stage, especially as Dürrenmatt's Claire Zachanassian in *The Visit* (1956) and Matilde von Zahnd in *The Physicists* (1962), as well as Pelagaya Vlasova in the Brecht/Gorky *The Mother* (1970).

Gielgud, Sir John. See headnote to Chapter 19, "An Artist's Apprenticeship".

Gielgud, Val Henry (1900–81), English radio and television innovator. Head of Productions at the BBC (1929–49), he honed the techniques of radio drama, and in 1930 transmitted the first television play: Pirandello's *The Man with a Flower in His Mouth*. In 1946 he became Head of Television Drama (to 1952), after which he directed his brother John as Sherlock Holmes in a series of radio adaptations.

Giraudoux, Jean (1882–1944), French dramatist. His highly rhetorical and fantastical plays were championed and produced by Louis Jouvet, and in their time enjoyed worldwide success. *Amphitryon 38* (1929), *The Enchanted* (*Intermezzo*, 1933), *Tiger at the Gates* (*La guerre de Troie n'aura pas lieu*, 1937) and *Ondine* (1939) were translated to Broadway, usually in heavily abridged and edulcorated versions.

The Girl in Waiting, American play by J. Hartley Manners (1910), yet another comedy written to show off his wife Laurette Taylor.

Gleason, Jackie (in full, Herbert John, 1916–87), American comedian. Corpulent, boozy and loud-mouthed, he was one of great comic talents of early U.S. television, with a wide palette of characters, often created in mime. He had first been noticed in the revue *Follow the Girls* (1944) and returned to Broadway as Uncle Sid in *Take Me Along*, the musical version of *Ah, Wilderness!* (1959).

Glebov, Anatoly Glebovich (Kotelnikov, 1899–1964), one of the first Russian dramatists to write specifically Soviet plays: *Zagmuk* (1925), about a slave revolt in ancient Babylon, and *Power* (1927) about the October Revolution. *Inga* (1929) is an interesting treatment of women juggling family life with factory work.

Glizer, Iudif Samoilovna (1904–68), Russian actress. Trained at the Moscow Proletkult First Worker's Theatre, she acted there (1921–28), appearing in Sergey Eisenstein's *The Mexican*. Then she moved her high-spirited physicality and mastery of make-up to the Moscow Theatre of Revolution. Glizer was the first Russian Mother Courage.

Gobel, George (1919–91), American comedian, known as "Lonesome George". Identifiable by short stature, crewcut and tagline "Well, I'll be a dirty bird", the former country-music singer won inexplicable popularity for his NBC television show (from 1954).

Goddard, Paulette (Marion Pauline Levy, 1910–90), American actress. From a Ziegfeld girl on stage (1926), she became a Goldwyn girl in films. Charlie Chaplin starred her in *Modern Times* (1936) and *The Great Dictator* (1940); their marriage ended in divorce, and she later wed Burgess Meredith, followed by Erich Maria Remarque. In such films as *The Women* (1939) and *Kitty* (1945), she maintained her star status, but by the 1950s was reduced to playing in stock and on television. She retired to a comfortable life in Switzerland.

Godfrey, Arthur (1903–83), American radio and television host. He was exalted from amateur ukelele player to breakfast-show host after he wept during his coverage of President Roosevelt's funeral (1945). His laidback ad-libbing and soapy personality became improbably popular, leading to radio and television stardom in *Arthur Godfrey's Talent Scouts* (1946–55) and *Arthur Godfrey and His Friends* (1949–72). He fell from grace when he peremptorily fired the young tenor Julius LaRosa.

Goethe, Johann Wolgang von (1749–1832), German poet and thinker. His dramatic activity began with "Storm and Stress" dramas, inspired by Shakespeare: *Götz von Berlichungen*. After a trip to Italy (1786–8), he adopted a neoclassical approach in *Iphigenie auf Tauris* (1787), *Egmont* (1977) and *Torquato Tasso* (1790). He applied this style to stage practice when he was the dictatorial Intendant of the court theatre in Weimar. For much of his later life, he worked on an epic treatment of Faust.

Gold Eagle Guy, American play by Melvin Levy (1934). A Group Theatre production, it charts the rise and fall of a San Francisco shipping tycoon from 1862 to his death in the 1906 earthquake. J. Edward Bromberg played the protagonist, a blend of Ibsen's Consul Bernick and Boss Tweed, Stella Adler appeared as the "naked" Adah Isaacs Menken, and Donald Oenschlager designed the sets.

Golden, John (1874–1953), American producer. After stints as a writer and composer for vaudeville, from 1918 he produced over 150 plays before striking gold with the record-breaking *Lightnin'* (1918). He prided himself on providing wholesome fare and promoting family values.

Golden Boy, a play by Clifford Odets (1937), about a second-generation Italian-American who gives up the violin for the material rewards of prize-fighting. Its popularity shored up the Group Theatre financially and it was filmed in 1939. Joe Bonaparte was played by Luther Adler in the original production, by John Garfield in the movies.

The Golden Treasury of English Songs and Lyrics, English anthology of poetry edited by Francis Turner Palgrave (1861). The influential compilation covered poets from the Elizabethan period to early nineteenth century, omitting those who were still alive. It was later brought up to date by Laurence Binyon (1891), C. Day Lewis (1954) and Christopher Ricks (1991).

Gone with the Wind, American film directed by Victor Fleming and George Cukor, from the novel by Margaret Mitchell (1939). A romantic saga of the war between the States and the ensuing reconstruction, seen from the viewpoint of the defeated South, it reduces all the important issues to whether temperamental Scarlett O'Hara will get her man. After a long series of screen tests, Vivien Leigh won the role and was partnered with suave Clark Gable as the profiteer Rhett Butler.

The Good Earth, American film directed by Sidney Franklin, Victor Fleming and Gustav Machaty (1937). Pearl Buck's novel of the epic struggle of Chinese farmers (1931) was first dramatized by Owen Davis and Donald Davis for the Theatre Guild (1932), with Claude Rains as Wang Lung and Alla Nazimova as Olan. It was made into a blockbuster film in 1937 with Paul Muni and Elisabeth Bergner in the leads, and a locust attack added for good measure.

The Good Soldier Schweik is an English translation of a German translation of *Osudy dobrého vojáka Švejk za světové války, The Exploits of the Good Soldier Švejk in the World War*, an unfinished Czech novel by Jaroslav Hašek (1921–22). Švejk, a volunteer on the Austro-Hungarian side, manages to survive (whatever the situation) due to an obtuse stupidity, which may or may not be intentional. Erwin Piscator staged a dramatization in Berlin (1928) with Max Pallenberg as "Schweik" and an early use of film clips; Bertolt Brecht updated it as *Schweyk in the Second World War* (1943).

Goolden, Richard (1895–1981), English actor. The diminutive, plangent-voiced actor was a member of the Oxford Playhouse company and acted the Fool to Donald Wolfit's King Lear. He was never out of work (Nagg in *Endgame*, 1958; Noël Coward's *Look After Lulu*, 1959; *Lock Up Your Daughters*, 1963), and was considered the definitive Mole in *Toad of Toad Hall* (1974). A new generation heard him on BBC Radio as Zaphod Beeblebrox IV in *The Hitchhiker's Guide to the Galaxy* (1978–80).

Gordon, Max (Mechel Salpeter, 1892–1978), American agent and producer, whose record as a picker of winners was enviable. In 1934, he had four hits running simultaneously on Broadway. His productions include such long-running comedies as *The Women* (1936), *My Sister Eileen* (1940), and *Born Yesterday* (1945).

Gorelik, Mordecai (1899–1990), Russian-born American designer, whose expressionist-inspired work first appeared at the Provincetown Playhouse in 1920. He was designer-in-chief for the Group Theatre in the 1930s, and later propagandized for Brecht and the Epic Theatre in his book *New Theatres for Old* (1940).

Gorky, Maksim (Aleksei Maksimovich Peshkov, 1868–1936), Russian writer. With a reputation as a popular spokesman for the dispossessed in his fiction, he began to write plays at the instigation of Anton Chekhov and the Moscow Art Theatre. His best known play is *The Lower Depths* (1902), set in a Moscow flophouse. The pseudo-Chekhovian *Summer Folk* (1904), *Children of the Sun* (1904), *Barbarians* (1905) and *Enemies* (1906) attempt to depict the intelligentsia at grips with popular uprisings. He kept aloof from the Revolution, but returned to the U.S.S.R. in 1929 and wrote a trilogy showing the reverberations of the Revolution on reactionary society. He died in 1936 under mysterious circumstances, probably poisoned.

The Government Inspector. See ***Revizor***.

Goya y Lucientes, Francisco José de (1746–1848), Spanish artist. As court painter to Charles IV (1799), he refrained from flattering his royal subjects, and in his etchings *Los Caprichos* commented bitterly on human folly. The Napoleonic invasion led to the savage series *The Disasters of War*. Increasingly deaf and reclusive, he withdraws to France in 1824.

Graf, Herbert (1903–73), Austrian director. As a child in Vienna, he was a patient of Sigmund Freud, "Little Hans", diagnosed with acute castration anxiety, Oedipal complex and fear of horses. Peter Shaffer dramatized this in *Equus* (1973). At age 19 he was considered cured, and became a major opera director in German-speaking Europe. In 1936, he emigrated to the U.S. and staged many successful productions at the Metropolitan Opera (1936–60). He eventually settled in Switzerland, working in Zurich (1960–3) and Geneva (1965–73).

Grant, Mary (1917–2002), American costume designer. After serving as assistant to Raoul Pène du Bois and Miles White, she designed the costumes for *Carmen Jones* (1943), *Mexican Hayride* (1944), and *Big Fish, Little Fish* (1961). In Hollywood, her credits include *The Vagabond King* (1956), *Sweet Smell of Success* (1957) and *The Devil's Disciple* (1959). Married to Vincent Price for 24 years, she designed his *An Evening with Edgar Allan Poe* (1972).

Granval, Charles (1882–1943), French actor and director. At the Comédie Française (1904–34), he staged *Hamlet* in a new translation (1932) and *Hedda Gabler*. An anarchist, he was regularly hissed by the subscription audience. He married and helped train Madeleine Renaud, 18 years his junior, but willingly ceded her to Jean-Louis Barrault. Filmgoers know him as the portly, altruistic bookseller in *Boudu Sauvé des Eaux* (1932) and Maxime in *Pépé le Moko* (1937).

Granville-Barker, Harley (1877–1946). English playwright, actor and director. His co-management of the Court Theatre, London (1904–7) introduced the New Stagecraft in productions of *A Winter's Tale* and *A Midsummer Night's Dream*. He also staged many of Shaw's early plays, creating Cusins in *Major Barbara*. His own dramas, including *The Voysey Inheritance* (1905), *Waste* (1907) and *The Madras House* (1910), are insightful explorations of social abuses. His *Prefaces to Shakespeare* are among the shrewdest available introductions to the plays as theatre pieces.

The Great John Ganton, American play by J. Hartley Manners from the novel by Arthur J. Eddy (1909). Although it was intended to feature the star player George Fawcett in the title role, the play served as the debut of Laurette Taylor as May Keating and introduced her to its author, her future husband and purveyor of vehicles.

Greco, El ("The Greek"; Domenico Theotocopoulos, 1541–1614), Cretan painter. He settled in Toledo *c*.1577 and became Spain's most eminent portraitist and painter of religious subjects. His works are readily identified by their dramatic Mannerist lighting and elongated figures.

The Green Bay Tree, English drama by Mordaunt Shairp (1932). One of the earliest treatments of homosexuality on the English commercial stage, it allusively depicted the deleterious effects of an aesthete on a young man he has adopted from the lower classes. The New York production introduced Laurence Olivier to the American audience.

The Green Cockatoo (*Das grüne Kakadu*), one-act drama by Arthur Schnitzler (1899). While the Bastille is being stormed, an actor convinces a group of aristocrats that he has killed a duke who abducted his bride. When it turns out the abduction is genuine, the player kills the duke for real.

The Green Hat, English drama by Michael Arlen from his novel (1925). The plot, far too intricate to describe briefly, centers on the ill-starred Iris Fenwick, née Marsh, scorned by her father and brother, disappointed in her marriage and love affairs, and conveniently accidental in her death. Somehow Katharine Cornell managed to turn this turbulent soap opera into a personal triumph.

Green Mansions: A Romance of the Tropical Forest, English novel by William Henry Hudson (1904). This adventure of a Venezuelan traveller in the Guyana jungle who comes upon the exotic Rima the Bird Girl was made into a film in 1959. Mel Ferrer directed it for his wife Audrey Hepburn as Rima, with Anthony Perkins as Abel the traveller, to a score by Heitor Villa-Lobos. It was an unredeemed flop.

The Green Sash, English play by Sylvestre Debonnaire and T. P. Wood (1935). This is usually cited as Vivien Leigh's first stage appearance, although she had had a line in an Ivor Novello show the previous year. According to rumor, she heard at a party that the part called for nothing but beauty and auditioned. The role was of Giusta, a Florentine soldier's wife widowed during the plague.

Green, Paul (1894–1981), white American playwright, whose plays mirror the life of the Deep South and its African-American religiosity. His musical *Johnny Johnson* (1936) is a paean to pacifism, in a Brechtian vein. He founded the national pageant with *The Lost Colony* (1937), an annually performed outdoor drama about the settlement of Virginia.

Greenstreet, Sydney Hughes (1879–1954), English actor. On stage from 1902, he toured in Ben Greet's Shakespeare company and came to New York in 1905. The portly actor was a member of the Theatre Guild, often appearing with the Lunts (Baptista in *Taming of the Shrew*, the Herald in *Amphitryon 39*, Sorin in *The Seagull*). Brought to Hollywood to play Caspar Gutman in *The Maltese Falcon* (1941), he became a favourite heavy (in every sense) at Warner Brothers, usually partnered with Peter Lorre.

Greet, Sir Philip Ben (Barling, 1856–1936), English actor-manager, who trouped Shakespeare through Great Britain and North America (1902–14). After some seasons at the Old Vic during the First World War, he returned to the U.S. and toured regularly, often performing in the open air, for schools and community centers. He also inaugurated the alfresco Shakespeare performances in Regent's Park, London (1933–34).

Gregory, Lady Augusta (1859–1932), Irish playwright. An Anglo-Protestant landowner, she researched Irish folklore and peasant traditions, co-founding the Abbey Theatre with W. B. Yeats. Her own plays were tragedies based on legends and short comedies, and she also rendered three plays of Molière into the "Kiltartan" dialect.

Grein, J[acob] T[homas] (1862–1935), Dutch-born English critic and producer. While serving as drama critic on the *Sunday Times* (1897–1918), he founded the Independent Theatre, to produce works either considered uncommercial or banned by the Lord Chamberlain, among them the first English *Ghosts* and Shaw's *Widowers' Houses*.

Grimes, Tammy (1934–), American actress, whose spirited comic performances were much aided by her raspy voice. She was much lauded as *The Unsinkable Molly Brown* (1960), Elvira in *High Spirits* (1964) and Amanda in *Private Lives* (1969). The role most savoured by connoisseurs, however, was the promiscuous pussy in the 1960 television production of *Shinbone Alley*, based on *archie and mehitabel*.

Grizzard, George (1928–2007), American actor. One of the most frequently employed leading men in New York theatre from the 1940s to 1960s, he seems to have derived his versatility from his colorlessness. His outstanding roles were Hamlet (1963) and George in the original production of *Who's Afraid of Virginia Woolf?* (1962).

Group Theatre. See headnote to Chapter 44, "The Group Theatre in its tenth year".

The Guardsman, Hungarian comedy by Ferenc Molnár (1911). When an actress wearies of her actor husband, he disguises himself as a Russian guardsman, but unmasks when she grows amorous. She says she knew him all the time, but did she? This trifle provided a splendid vehicle for the Lunts at the Theatre Guild, and the film adaptation was their only movie.

Guitry, Lucien-Germain (1860–1925), French actor-manager, father of Sacha. Massive in build, he became a star at the Théâtre de la Renaissance, Paris (1902–9), especially in such proletarian roles as the victimized old costermonger in *Crainquebille* and the alcoholic roofer Coupeau in *L'Assommoir*. He was also a sinister Tartuffe.

Guthrie, Sir Tyrone (1900–71), English director. He became celebrated for his physically busy, often modern-dress Shakespeare, especially at the Old Vic and the Stratford Memorial Theatre. He later was founding director of the Stratford Festival Theatre in Ontario (1953–7), of the thrust-stage Minneapolis (later, Guthrie) Theatre (1963). He occasionally descended to directing on Broadway (*The Matchmaker, Candide*).

Guys and Dolls, an American musical comedy by Jo Swerling, Abe Burrows and Frank Loesser (1950), based on the Broadway stories of Damon Runyon. Set in a milieu of gangsters, gamblers and Salvation Army lassies, its witty score includes "Adelaide's Lament", "Sit Down, You're Rocking the Boat" and "Luck, Be a Lady Tonight".

Haas, Hugo (1901–68), Czech actor and film director. On the Prague stage he was acclaimed as a tragicomic Panisse in *Fanny* (1931) and Malvolio in *Twelfth Night* (1934) and was one of the most creative early Czech filmmakers. Self-exiled to Los Angeles during the Second World War, he created the role of the Pope in the Laughton/Brecht *Galileo* (1947), directed by Joseph Losey. He returned to directing films in Vienna (1952–61).

Habima ("The Rostrum"), a Hebrew-language acting company founded in Moscow in 1917 with a Zionist agenda. It became famous in 1922 for *The Dybbuk*, directed by Evgeny Vakhtangov with designs by Natan Altman. The supernatural was transformed into the supertheatrical, and a similar style infused *The Eternal Jew* (1923), *Jacob's Dream* and *The Golem* (both 1925). A theatre of the past in its religious themes and Biblical language could not expect Soviet support, so it settled in Palestine in 1931, becoming the State Theatre of Israel in 1945.

Hagen, Uta (1919–2004), American actress and pedagogue. First seen in New York as Nina in *The Seagull* (1938), she made rare appearances as Desdemona in the Paul Robeson *Othello* (1945), the title role in *The Country Girl* (1950) and, most memorably, as the shrill shrew Martha in *Who's Afraid of Virginia Woolf?* (1963). With her husband Herbert Berghof, she was an inspiring teacher at the HB Studio (1947–2004), offering her own acerbic critique of the Stanislavsky system.

The Hairy Ape, "a comedy of ancient and modern life" by Eugene O'Neill (1922). Strongly influenced by European Expressionism, it is a "station play", tracing the descent of the brutish stoker Yank. His elemental powers are foiled by the dehumanizing forces of the modern city, represented by actors in masks, and he ends up in a gorilla cage at the zoo. It was designed by Robert Edmond Jones for the Provincetown Players.

Hale, Frank J., American producer. His Broadway activity was slight: *Midsummer* (1953) was followed over a decade later by *The Girl in the Freudian Slip* (1967). He was also the designer for a Spanish musical-comedy version of the ballet *Coppélia, Dr Coppelius* (1968).

Hammond, Percy (1873–1936), American dramatic critic, famed for his vitriolic and dismissive reviews which spared only his favorites. He wrote for the *Chicago Tribune* (1908–21) before moving to the influential *New York Tribune* (1921–36). Broadway legend holds that his death was due to the spells of a Haitian witch doctor, after Hammond delivered a damning review of the voodoo *Macbeth*.

Hampden, Walter (1879–1953), American actor. Last of the romantic school, trained under Frank Benson, from 1918 well into the 1940s he toured his Hamlet, Julius Caesar, Cyrano, Richelieu and Dr. Stockman in *An Enemy of the People*. His imposing presence and hawklike profile enhanced the role of Rev. Danforth in *The Crucible* (1953).

Hamsun, Knut (1859–1952), Norwegian playwright and novelist. His Ivan Kareno trilogy, *Ved rigets port* (*At the Gates of the Kingdom*, 1895), *Livets spil* (*The Game of Life*, 1896) and *Livet i vold* (*In the Grip of Life*, 1911), were staged by the Moscow Art Theatre. At the time, the comic treatment of Nietzschean ideas was found attractive. His novel *Sult* (*Hunger*, 1890) was dramatized by Jean-Louis Barrault.

The Hanging Tree, American Western film directed by Delmer Daves from the novel by Dorothy M. Johnson (1959). This tale of an enigmatic doctor who saves a youth from a lynch mob, only to mould him to his own ends, was one of Gary Cooper's last films. It was electrified by the New York actors Karl Malden and George C. Scott.

Happiness, American play by J. Hartley Manners (1914). Another of Manners' showcases for his wife Laurette Taylor, it deals with a Broadway errand girl who is invited to live with a rich family (the template of *Peg O' My Heart*). Taylor also starred in the 1924 film.

Happy End, German musical play by Bertolt Brecht, Elisabeth Hauptmann and Kurt Weill (1929). A Salvation Army lassie tries to convert a gang of crooks, one of whom falls in love with her. When the gang's boss, the Lady in Gray, attacks the Sally Army, she discovers one of its lieutenants is her missing husband. The two factions unite to found a bank.

Happy Landing, American comedy by John B. Hymer and William E. Barry (1932). Based on the exploits of Charles Lindbergh, it displays a young aviator who becomes a celebrity as the result of a transatlantic flight, and has to choose between a glamorous rich lion-hunter and his hometown sweetheart. Margaret Sullavan played the heroine. The 1938 musical film of the same name is entirely unrelated.

Harding, Ann (Dorothy Walton Gatley, 1901–81), American actress. Charming the New York critics in *The Trial of Mary Dugan* (1927), she then became a luminous film presence, excelling in so-called "women's pictures" as self-sacrificing daughters and wives (*Her Private Affair*, 1929; *The Animal Kingdom*, 1932; *Peter Ibbetson*, 1935). Retirement in 1937 on her marriage to the conductor Werner Janssen was frequently rescinded, and she was lured by George C. Scott to Broadway (*General Seeger*, 1962).

Hardwicke, Sir Cedric. See headnote to Chapter 27, "An actor stakes his claim".

The Harp of Life, American play by J. Hartley Manners (1916). Yet another vehicle for Laurette Taylor, it is noteworthy as the American debut of Lynn Fontanne.

Harpagon, the title character in Molière's *L'Avare* (*The Miser*, 1668). He makes his middle-class household miserable with his avarice, and drives himself frantic when his beloved cashbox is stolen. It was one of the best roles of Charles Dullin and Jean Vilar.

Harper's Bazaar, American fashion magazine. Founded in 1867 as the weekly *Harper's Bazar* [*sic*], it became a monthly in 1901. It is now famous for its photography and graphics as much as for its launching of fashions.

Harris, Julie. See headnote to Chapter 16, "Julie Harris".

Harris, Sam H. (1872–1941), American producer. He partnered George M. Cohan from 1904 to 1920, and then, on his own, produced some of the key plays of the age: *Rain* (1925), *The Jazz Singer* (1925), the comedies of Kaufman and Hart, and, later, the innovative musical *Lady in the Dark* (1941).

Harrison, Rex. See headnote to Chapter 26, "Shaw and the actor".

Hart, Moss (1904–61), American playwright, best known as writing partner of George S. Kaufman on a number of hit comedies: *Once in a Lifetime* (1930), *You Can't Take It with You* (1936), *The Man Who Came to Dinner* (1939). He also created the librettos for the musicals *Lady in the Dark* (1941) and *Light Up the Sky* (1948), and directed *My Fair Lady* (1956).

Harvey, American comedy by Mary Chase (1944), which set a record by running for 1,775 performances. It is a slight, Thurberesque fable of a sweet-natured alcoholic, Elwood P. Dowd, whose best friend is a tall, invisible rabbit named Harvey. His relatives' attempt to have him institutionalized is thwarted by the contagion of whimsy.

A Hatful of Rain, American domestic drama by Michael Gazzo (1955), dealing with drug addiction among the genteel poor. The overwrought style exemplified American naturalism at this period, and its performers – Ben Gazzara, Shelley Winters, Anthony Franciosa and Steve McQueen – were all exemplars of the Actors Studio school.

Havilland, Olivia de (1916–), Tokyo-born American actress, sister of Joan Fontaine. After playing Hermia in Max Reinhardt's *Midsummer Night's Dream* at the Hollywood Bowl (1935), she reprised the role on film, and found herself as Errol Flynn's leading lady in *Captain Blood* (1936) and *The Adventures of Robin Hood* (1938). Her mild-mannered Melanie in *Gone with the Wind* (1939) was followed by a lawsuit against Warner Bros which essentially vitiated the contractual power of studios over actors. She went on to star in the emotional melodramas *The Snake Pit* (1948) and *The Heiress* (1949).

Hay Fever, English comedy by Noël Coward (1925). When too many guests descend on the bohemian Bliss household one weekend, the family keeps changing partners and finally drives them away. Always popular but underestimated for its apparent flimsiness, this play was the first modern comedy to be produced by the National Theatre, under Coward's direction.

Hayes, Helen (1900–93), American actress. Prominent in the theatre from childhood, she was often described as "first lady of the American stage", but possessed a remarkably limited range and rarely appeared in the classics. After a flapper phase, she ascended to royalty (*Mary of Scotland*, 1933; *Victoria Regina*, 1934) and, as she aged, wallowed in whimsy (*Happy Birthday, Ring Round the Moon*, 1950; *Mrs McThing*, 1952). Her last period was devoted to tart-tongued crones (*The Show-off*, 1967).

Heartbreak House, drama by George Bernard Shaw (1916). On the eve of war, a variegated group of friends and relations gather at the country house of venerable Captain Shotover. A young girl tries to decide whether to marry a coarse capitalist, but a bombardment kills him. Shaw regarded this apocalyptic talkfest as Chekhovian, and it was first staged in 1919, after England had indeed been bombed. The Theatre Guild brought it to New York.

Hedda Gabler, Norwegian drama by Henrik Ibsen (1891). The daughter of a general, Hedda has married beneath her to a mild-mannered scholar and hates her marriage, her unborn child and her suburban surroundings. When her endeavour to create some excitement blows up in her face and she is confronted by a unpalatable future, she commits suicide.

Helburn, Theresa (1887–1959), American director and producer. Another product of George Pierce Baker's Harvard class, she served a brief stint as a reviewer for *The Nation*. Eventually, she became the iron-willed administrative director of the Theatre Guild, inviting the Lunts, and producing the musical *Oklahoma!* and Paul Robeson's *Othello* (both 1943).

Hellman, Lillian (1906–84), American playwright. For three decades, she supplied the stage with a succession of high-strung melodramas disguised as problem plays: among others, *The Children's Hour* (1934), *The Little Foxes* (1939), *Watch on the Rhine* (1941), *The Autumn Garden* (1951) and *Toys in the Attic* (1960). Her appearance on Hollywood's blacklist did nothing to reduce her popularity on Broadway.

Henry IV, two-part English history play by William Shakespeare from Holinshed and an earlier play (1598). Three sets of characters are interwoven: King Henry assailed by bad conscience and state cares, his dissolute heir Prince Hal and his tavern friends, led by the ribald Falstaff, and the rebel lords, headed by Henry Percy (Hotspur). In Part I, the three strands are drawn together at the Battle of Shrewsbury. In Part II, the King dies and Hal succeeds to the throne, disowning his former friends.

Henry V, English history play by William Shakespeare from Holinshed and an earlier play (1599). This bit of jingoism chronicles Henry V's campaign to win back the French throne on the battlefield. Despite a number of discreditable actions, the king is portrayed as a paladin.

Henry VIII, English history play by William Shakespeare and John Fletcher (1613). It dramatizes Henry's repudiation of his wife Catherine of Aragon in order to wed Anne Boleyn. The play views this as a Good Thing, since it results in the birth of Good Queen Bess.

Henson, Leslie (1891–1957), English actor and director. He made his name as a comedian in musical comedy (*Funny Face*, 1928), farce (*It's a Boy*, 1930) and pantomime in the dame role. During the Second World War, he was assiduous in entertaining the troops all over the map. He assumed Sid Field's part of Elwood P. Dowd in the London run of *Harvey* (1950).

Hepburn, Audrey (Rushton, 1929–93), Belgian-born American actress. The doe-eyed ballerina had become an actress in London and was discovered by Colette, who insisted she play the lead in *Gigi* (1951) on Broadway. Her waif-like presence buoyed up lighthearted films: *Roman Holiday* (1953), *Sabrina* (1954), *Funny Face* (1957), *Breakfast at Tiffany's* (1963), *My Fair Lady* (1964). With her husband Mel Ferrer, she played *Ondine* (1954) on stage, directed by Alfred Lunt.

Hepburn, Katherine (1907–2003), American actress. Her stage career was a limited one, until the role of an Amazon in *The Warrior's Husband* brought her to Hollywood, where she had a glorious career. Her clipped, disingenuous manner was seen to best advantage in screwball comedies. When she was qualified as "box-office poison" she returned to the stage as the heiress Tracy Lord in *The Philadelphia Story* (1939), which resuscitated her movie career. Later, in the theatre she played Rosalind in *As You Like It* (1950), Epifania in *The Millionairess* (1952), and a non-Gallic Chanel in the musical *Coco* (1971).

Hesterberg, Trude (Gertrud, 1892–1967), German actress and singer. She began in the Berlin theatre and silent film in 1912, and soon became famous as a *diseuse* and vocalist in Wintergarten revues (from 1915) and cabarets (from 1919), with material by Kurt Tucholsky and Friedrich Hollaneder. In 1923 she founded the literary-political cabaret the Wild Stage, where she introduced Bertolt Brecht. After the war she worked mainly in film and was cast as Mrs Peachum in the first full-score recording of *Die Dreigroschenoper*.

Hewitt, Alan (1915–86), American actor. He appeared in most of the Lunts' productions, usually in tiny roles (the best was Lucentio in *Taming of the Shrew*, 1935), and remained devoted to them, compiling a chronology of their careers for the American National Theatre Academy (1972). He was also seen as Howard Wagner in the original *Death of a Salesman* (1949). He served as Actors' Equity Association's unofficial archivist.

Heywood, Thomas (1574?–1641), English playwright. An actor in Henslowe's troupe in 1598 and then the King's Company, he claimed to have had a hand "or at least a main finger" in 220 plays. The best remembered of these is the domestic tragedy *A Woman Killed with Kindness* (1603), which Copeau staged in his first Vieux Colombier season.

Hicks, Sir Edward Seymour (1871–1949), English actor-manager and play-wright. With his wife Ellaline Terriss, he was a prominent star of Edwardian musical comedy, opening his Aldwych Theatre with *Blue Bell in Fairyland* (1905) and the Hicks Theatre with *The Beauty of Bath* (1906). In later years, he frequently appeared as Scrooge in his own dramatization of *A Christmas Carol*.

High Tor, American comedy by Maxwell Anderson (1937). Van Dorn, descend-ant of the settlers of Nieuw Amsterdam, is under pressure to sell his Hudson River mountain top to developers. A confrontation with a phantom crew of Dutch sailors and a beautiful ghost evaporates into distasteful reality.

Hilda Wangel. As the snotty pubescent daughter of Dr. Wangel, she makes her bow in *The Lady from the Sea* (1888), and then returns, in a more dangerous guise, to put risky ideas in the head of Halvard Solness in *The Master Builder* (1892). Ibsen based her on Emilie Bardach, a young fan with whom he failed to have an affair.

Hindemith, Paul (1895–1963), German composer. His first operas, *Cardillac* (1926) and *Neues vom Tag* (1929), contravened the conventions of the form and attracted Nazi disapproval, which led to the banning of his *Mathis der Maler* (1938). He promoted *Gebrauchsmusik* ("applied music") for social uses. After time in Turkey and England, he settled in the U.S. (1939), teaching at Yale.

Hippodrome Theatre, New York, opened in 1905 to be the world's largest playhouse, with seating for 5,300 and installation of the most up-to-date technology. Despite (or because of) lavish extravaganzas, it proved to be a bigger white elephant than its attractions and was turned into a sports arena. Its last gasp was Billy Rose's *Jumbo* (1935) and it was demolished in 1939.

Hitchcock, Sir Alfred (1899–1980), English film director. During his British period, he gravitated to thrillers (*The Thirty-Nine Steps*, 1935; *The Lady Vanishes*, 1938) heightened with wry comedy. Brought to Hollywood to direct sub-Gothic gush (*Rebecca*, 1946), he shaped his own genre of suspense (*Rear Window*, 1955; *Psycho*, 1960). The plots were often propelled by what he called a "mcguffin" or trivial premise.

Hitler, Adolf (Schicklgruber, 1889–1945), Austrian-born chancellor of Germany. The evil genius of the twentieth century, he led the National Socialist Party to victory in Germany, and then set out to create a Thousand Year Reich by exterminating "sub-humans" and subjugating the rest of Europe. Chaplin mocked him to little avail in *The Great Dictator* (1940).

Hobart, Rose (Kefer, 1906–2000), American actress. Lead roles on Broadway in *The Vortex* and *Death Takes a Holiday* brought her to Hollywood, where she played opposite Fredric March (*Dr Jekyll and Mr Hyde*, 1931), Lionel Barrymore (*Lady Be Good*, 1941) and Humphrey Bogart (*Conflict*, 1945). In 1949, on the basis of forged documents, the House Committee on Un-American Activities accused her of being a Communist and she was blacklisted. She found work in television.

Höflich, Lucie (Helene Lucie von Holwede, 1882–1956), German actress-manageress. Under Reinhardt's direction (1902–32), her natural emotionalism blossomed as Faust's Gretchen and in Ibsen and Hauptmann. She was also exceptional in classical drama: Luise in *Love and Intrigue*, Viola in *Twelfth Night*, Cordelia in *King Lear*. Married to Emil Jannings, she thrived under the Nazis, managing a dramatic school and opening her own film studio.

Hokinson, Helen Elna (1893–1949), American cartoonist. From its inception in 1925, *The New Yorker* carried her drawings of well-upholstered club women, bargain-hunters and dowagers, accompanied with captions by James Reid Parker or Richard McAllister. She died in a plane crash.

Hokusai, Katsushika (1760–1849), Japanese artist, known as "Old Man Mad about Painting". A master of woodblock printing, he turned his hand to all manner of subjects, from laughable monsters to the much-admired "Great Wave off Kanagawa". His most famous series is *Thirty-six Views of Mount Fuji* (*c.*1831).

Holcroft, Thomas (1745–1809), English dramatist. A prompter and an actor, he made a translation of Beaumarchais' *Marriage of Figaro* from memory. He is credited with introducing melodrama to England with an adaptation of Pixérécourt, *A Tale of Mystery* (1802). The only one of his own plays to have a shelf life was *The Road to Ruin* (1792), with its catchphrase "What will Mrs Grundy say?".

Holman, Joseph George (1764–1817), English actor. He made his amateur debut as Hamlet, and his professional debut as Romeo in London (1784). His parts included Orestes in *The Distressed Mother* and Elvirus in *Such Things Are*. He came to the U.S. in 1812 and died two days after his second marriage.

Home of the Brave, American play by Arthur Laurents (1945), was one of the first wartime plays to deal with post-traumatic stress syndrome and anti-Semitism in the ranks, but ran barely two months. Its cinematic version (1949) made the victim of prejudice black rather than Jewish.

Homolka, Oscar (1898–1978), Austrian actor. Frequently cast in the early Berlin productions of Bertolt Brecht who esteemed him highly (Mortimer in *Edward II*, 1924; *Baal*, 1926; Bill Cracker in *Happy End*, 1929), he emigrated to London where he played the anarchist cinema owner in Hitchcock's *Sabotage* (1936). He had a long career in Hollywood films (Uncle Chris in *I Remember Mama*, 1948; Kutuzov in *War and Peace*, 1956), but after the war also took on classic stage roles in New York, Vienna and Zurich.

Hopkins, Arthur (1878–1950), American producer and director, who studied European innovation, subscribed to the New Stagecraft and promoted the stage pictures of Robert Edmond Jones. His first major successes featured John and Lionel Barrymore in costume melodrama and Shakespeare, Nazimova in Ibsen. His directing ranged successfully from O'Neill to Philip Barry to the classics, and often relied on a revolving stage.

Hopkins, Miriam (1904–72), American actress. Georgia-born, she never shed her southern accent which was out of place in *Lysistrata* (1930), but stood her in good stead in *Jezebel* (1933). She never forgave Bette Davis for replacing her in the film version of that play, even when they were thrown together as a star team in *Old Acquaintance* and *The Old Maid*.

Horner, Harry (1910–94), Bohemian art director. He was an assistant to Max Reinhardt in Salzburg and emigrated with him to the U.S., where he soon found work as a designer at MGM Studios. He was particularly successful collaborating with George Cukor (*A Double Life*, 1947; *Born Yesterday*, 1950) and William Wyler (*The Heiress*, 1949). He retired in 1980.

The House of Connelly, American drama by Paul Green (1931), about the degeneration of a Southern family in 1905, saved by the love of its heir for a "white trash" girl, who helps him to restore the plantation. The Theatre Guild farmed out the play to its filial, the Group Theatre, which applied the Stanislavsky system in its rehearsals. Artistic differences caused the Group to break away from the Guild and make a critical success of the play.

Houseman, John. See headnote to Chapter 10, "Shakespeare and the American actor".

Howard, Leslie (1893–1943), English actor. He had established a successful British career when he came to New York in 1920. He became a popular matinee idol in *Outward Bound* (1924), *The Green Hat* (1924), *Berkeley Square* (1929) and *The Petrified Forest* (1935). His popularity continued in films from 1930. In 1936 he made the mistake of assuming Hamlet in New York just as Gielgud appeared in it, to Howard's disadvantage.

Howard, Sidney (1891–1939), American playwright. He developed a line of domestic comedy which dealt with such ticklish subjects as smothering mother love (*The Silver Cord*, 1926) and the New Woman (*Ned McCobb's*

Daughter, 1927). He was also a deft adapter (*The Late Christopher Bean*, 1932; *Dodsworth*, 1934). A prolific career was cut short by a tractor accident.

Huckleberry Finn, American novel by Mark Twain (1884). The classic tale of a runaway urchin and a fugitive slave floating down the Mississippi was frequently dramatized and filmed from 1919, but there is no definitive version, chiefly because producers prefer to emphasize the picaresque over the satiric.

Hughes, Hatcher (1883–1945), American playwright. A product of the regional literature movement, he wrote a number of plays, but is known chiefly for *Hell-bent for Heaven* (1924), a high-pitched melodrama about the old-time religion and hillbilly feuds in the Carolina mountains. When it was awarded the Pulitzer Prize, protests were lodged by the critical establishment.

Hull, Henry (1890–1977), American actor. Most of his roles on Broadway were of well-mannered losers or spineless aristocrats. The moral infirmity, if not the polished manners, recurred in his most enduring role, the sharecropper Jeeter Lester, in the long-running red-dirt comedy *Tobacco Road* (1933). His career never recovered from it.

Humoresque, American film, directed by Jean Negulesco from a screenplay by Clifford Odets from the novel by Fanny Hurst (1946). A boy from the wrong side of the tracks (John Garfield) is taken in hand, for transparent motives, by Joan Crawford and turned into a virtuoso violinist. Odet's art *vs* Mammon theme here fades into art *vs* hormones.

Humperdinck, Engelbert (1854–1925), German composer. Assistant to Wagner, he composed a number of fairy-tale operas, including the holiday favorite *Hänsel und Gretel* (1893), which made him famous. His name was usurped by a pop singer.

Hurst, Fanny (1889–1968), American novelist. Despite the neglect of critics and the scorn of colleagues, she remained a regular best-seller for decades. She is now known by the films that were made and remade from such tearjerkers as *Back Street* (1931) and *Imitation of Life* (1933).

Huston, Walter (1884–1950), Canadian actor, whose lanky presence, prairie accent and dry delivery became bywords for the American character. After years of touring, he finally caught the New York critics' attention as gnarled Ephraim Cabot in *Desire Under the Elms* (1924), followed up by a sadistic trader in *Kongo* (1926) and a sympathetic *Dodsworth* (1934). As one-legged Pieter Stuyvesant in *Knickerbocker Holiday* (1938), he introduced "September Song".

I Am a Camera, American drama by John Van Druten (1951), based on Christopher Isherwood's *Berlin Stories*. It introduced a Broadway audience to the devil-may-care Sally Bowles, in the person of Julie Harris, but suppressed the original's homosexual content. In this diluted form, it served as a model for the musical *Cabaret* (1966).

I Am a Fugitive from a Chain Gang, American film directed by Mervyn Leroy from a *Saturday Evening Post* series (1932). One of the best of the Warner Brothers social-purpose dramas, it exposes the inhumane prison system in the rural South. War veteran Paul Muni is condemned unjustly to a chain gang, escapes, makes a career as a civil engineer up North, is exposed, agrees to return to finish his sentence, and must escape again to a life of crime. Although the narrative gets lumpy towards the end, it remains a chilling indictment.

I Have Been Here Before, English play by J. B. Priestley (1937). Another of his explorations of the circularity of time, it brings six characters together in a Yorkshire inn where they are overwhelmed with a sense of *déjà vu* and *déjà vécu*. A German exile reveals a good deal about the others, before he realizes that he is in the wrong year.

Ibsen, Henrik (1828–1906), Norwegian poet and playwright, invariably labelled "the father of modern drama". His first plays were verse dramas drawn from history; they culminate in works reflecting Kierkegaardian questions of choice and identity, *Brand* (1864) and *Peer Gynt* (1867). The next phase was in prose, plays of modern life, superficially dealing with social problems, but still basically concerned with questions of personal integrity, e.g. *A Doll's House* (1878–9), *Ghosts* (1881), *The Wild Duck* (1883–4), *Rosmersholm* (1885–6), *Hedda Gabler* (1890). The last phase is almost Wagnerian in its use of grandiose symbols: *The Master Builder* (1891–2), *John Gabriel Borkman* (1895–6), *When We Dead Awake* (1897–9).

Icebound, American drama by Owen Davis (1923). Very much in the comic tradition of legacy-hunting (e.g. *Volpone*), it concerns the fate of the Jordan family on a hardscrabble farm in rural Maine. A housekeeper from outside the family is left the whole estate, reforms them and marries the now-reclaimed black sheep.

The Iceman Cometh, American play by Eugene O'Neill (1946). A variation on Gorky's *Lower Depths*, it brings together in Harry Hope's gin mill a convocation of losers, who are galvanized into salvatory "pipe dreams" by the voluble salesman Hickey. When he reveals he murdered his wife, they relapse into their alcoholic comas.

Idiot's Delight, American play by Robert E. Sherwood (1936). An anti-war polemic, set in a hotel in the Italian Alps, it convenes a miscellaneous group of types, headed by an American hoofer and a phoney White Russian countess. Muddled in its message, it provided an entertaining vehicle for the Lunts.

If Love Were All, American comedy by Cutler Hatch (1931). It is significant chiefly for the debut of Margaret Sullavan. Noël Coward introduced a song of that name in *Bittersweet*.

Ilinsky, Igor Vladimirovich (1901–87), Russian actor and director. In 1920, he became one of Meyerhold's most reliable comedians, playing the jealous miller Bruno (*The Magnanimous Cuckold*), the barnstormer Arkashka (*The Forest*), and the vulgarian Prisypkin (*The Bedbug*), red letters in the history of Soviet acting. In 1938 he was transferred to the Moscow Maly Theatre, where he played both Khlestakov and the Mayor in *The Government Inspector*. In 1958 he staged an outstanding adaptation of Thackeray's *Vanity Fair*.

The Importance of Being Earnest, English comedy by Oscar Wilde (1895). This comedy of manners infused with Gilbertian nonsense has never lost its popularity. The characters spar verbally in epigrams and polite insults, while composure is rarely lost. Artifice has never been more brittle.

L'Impromptu de Versailles (*The Versailles Improvisation*), one-act play by Molière (1663). A response to criticisms aimed at *The School for Wives*, the play uses the device of Molière and his actors rehearsing for a court entertainment to ridicule their rivals and answer both personal and professional assaults. The conclusion is that satire should be drawn from observation but directed not at individuals, but at types.

In a Garden, American play by Philip Barry (1925). In this comedy, a strong-willed young woman frees herself from her husband and her lover.

Infant Phenomenon, Miss Ninetta Crummles, exhibitionist under-aged daughter of the manager of a touring company, in Dickens' *Nicholas Nickleby* (1838–9). She has been 10 years old for at least five years; her parents keep her up late drinking gin to stunt her growth.

Inga, Russian play by Fyodor Gladkov (1928). Set in a clothing factory during the First Five-Year Plan, it represents a gallery of women, trying to reconcile their personal lives with the needs of Soviet industry.

The Insect Play (*Ze zivota hmyzu*), Czech comedy by Karel and Josef Čapek (1922). This transparent allegory in which all human activities are equated with the lives of insects is cast as the dream of a drunken bum. Owen Davis adapted it as *The World We Live In* (1922).

Intermezzo, Austrian opera by Richard Strauss (1924). Fed up with his long absences and convinced that he is carrying on an affair, the wife of a conductor decides to divorce him. A notary works out the confusion and the couple is reconciled. This is Strauss's only opera to be set in contemporary Austria and was based on an incident in his own life, when a love letter from an unknown admirer caused marital strife.

International Revue, American revue produced by Lew Leslie (1930). This show is memorable chiefly because it introduced the song "On the Sunny Side of the Street" by Dorothy Fields and Jimmy McHugh.

Ionesco, Eugène (Eugen Ionescu, 1912–94), Romanian-born French playwright. Categorized as a prime examples of "Absurdism", his early one-acts, the long-running *The Bald Soprano* (1950), *The Lesson* (1951) and *The Chairs* (1952), toy with the arbitrary nature of language. The later, longer plays, including *Rhinoceros* (1960) and *Exit the King* (1963), engage long-windedly with questions of conformity and mortality. The last plays, *Jeux de Massacre* (1971) and *Macbett* (1972), portray random violence.

Iphigenia, daughter of Agamemnon and Clytemnestra, who had to be sacrificed in Aulis to allow the Greek ships to proceed to Troy. One variant on the legend has her whisked by the goddess Diana to Tauris, where, 20 years later, she is discovered by her brother Orestes. *Iphigenia in Aulis* by Euripides (407 B.C.), and Goethe's *Iphigenie auf Tauris* deal with the latter episode.

Irving, Sir Henry (John Henry Brodribb, 1838–1905), English actor-manager. The first actor to be knighted, Irving was the leading Shakespearean tragedian of the late Victorian period. Despite a number of handicaps (odd pronunciation, a loping walk, a gaunt physique), he lorded it over the Lyceum Theatre, revising plays for optimal pictorial effect and focus on his role. Having made his name in melodrama (*The Bells*) and grotesque comedy (*Jingle*), he introduced elements of them into Hamlet, Shylock, Faust, Macbeth and Richard III.

Isherwood, Christopher (1904–86), English writer. His plays were written in collaboration with W. H. Auden (*The Dog Beneath the Skin*, 1936; *The Ascent of F6*, 1937; *On the Frontier*, 1938). Living in Hollywood and practising Vedantic Hinduism, he became a U.S. citizen in 1945. His collection *Berlin Stories* was the source for *I Am a Camera* (1951) and the musical *Cabaret*.

It's a Gift, American film, directed by Norman McLeod (1934). This field day for W. C. Fields presents him as the long-suffering butt of small-town aggravations. The plot, such as it is, is studded with many of Field's *Ziegfeld Follies* routines, including the golf game.

Iturbi, José (1895–1880), Spanish conductor and pianist. A specialist in Spanish and French repertoire, he possessed a technique that was flashy and audience-pleasing. Consequently, he was in demand in Hollywood movies of the 1940s as a lightweight musical accompaniment to Gene Kelly, Deanna Durbin and Frank Sinatra.

Jackson, Sir Barry (1879–1961), English impresario. Creator and promoter first of the Pilgrim Players, then the Birmingham Repertory Theatre (1913–38), he maintained a quality repertory and strong production values in the face of community indifference and public funding. He innovated with modern-dress Shakespeare and championed Shaw, making him the central feature of the Malvern Festival, founded in 1929.

James I of England and VI of Scotland (1567–1625), son of Mary Queen of Scots. He succeeded to the English throne in 1603, and pursued peace at any price. His severity and rudeness to non-Conformists led to the Gunpowder Plot (1606). He wrote a treatise on witches and an attack on tobacco-smoking, and sponsored the Authorized Version of the Bible (1611).

Jaques-Dalcroze, Émile (1865–1950), Swiss musician and educator. His system of eurhythmics trained practitioners to experience music through movement. The body is treated as a musical instrument to be played by a virtuoso. In 1910, he founded a school in Hellerau, Germany, where, with the aid of the theorist Adolphe Appia, he staged a number of movement concerts.

Der Jasager (*The Yea-sayer*), German didactic play by Bertolt Brecht from the Japanese play *Taniko* (1930). Devised for a speaker and chorus, it is a parable about a teacher leading a team of students up a mountain to get medicine for victims of an epidemic. One boy falls ill and agrees to be left behind, according to the custom. He is flung into the valley below. A counterpart, *The Nay-Sayer*, has the boy refusing and insisting that custom be renovated.

Jealousy (*Revnost*), Russian play by Mikhail Artsybashev (1913). In tune with Artsybashev's misogyny and pessimism about relations between the sexes, this deals with a jealous husband and a promiscuous wife, and ends in him strangling her.

Jefferson, Joseph, III (1829–1905), American actor. Scion of a clan of players, he established a reputation as a popular comedian before he played Rip Van Winkle in 1865. This became his signature role, loved for its warmth and pathos, and he toured it for decades. He was also an hilarious Bob Acres in *The Rivals* and a pitiful Caleb Plummer in *Dot*.

Jerger, Alfred (1889–1976), Austrian bass-baritone. He created the role of the band-leader Jonny in the jazz opera *Jonny Spielt Auf* (1928) in blackface, causing riots in the German audiences who thought he was black. He also was the first Mandryka in Strauss's *Arabella* (1933).

Jeritza, Maria (Jedličková, 1887–1982), Moravian soprano. A favorite of Richard Strauss, the blonde diva created Ariadne in *Ariadne auf Naxos* (1912), the Empress in *Die Frau ohne Schatten* (1919) and (at the Met) Helena in *Die Ägyptische Helena* (1928). In *Tosca*, she caused a stir by singing "Vissi d'arte" recumbent on the floor.

Jessie Bonstelle Stock Company. See **Bonstelle, Jessie**.

Jessner, Leopold, German director (1878–1945). When he became director of the Berlin State Theatre (1919–25), he was famous for using symbolic steps as his basic stage construction in *Wilhelm Tell* (1919) and *Richard III* (1920). He also staged a modern dress *Hamlet* with his favorite actor Fritz Kortner.

Jezebel, American film directed by William Wyler from the play by Owen Davis (1938). This melodrama of a selfish Southern belle in antebellum New Orleans who learns self-sacrifice in a yellow-fever epidemic was a huge success. The play had featured two real Southerners, Miriam Hopkins and Tallulah Bankhead, but the star role was offered to Bette Davis as compensation for not being cast as Scarlett O'Hara in *Gone with the Wind*.

Jilinsky, Andrius (Golyak, 1893–1948), Lithuanian actor and teacher. A member of the Moscow Art Theatre (1915–22) and its 1st Studio, where he met his wife Vera Soloviova; he emigrated with her to Lithuania in 1929. There he invited Michael Chekhov to play Hamlet. Chekhov returned the favor by bringing the couple to New York in 1935. Jilinsky founded an acting school in Mount Kisco, where he taught his own version of Stanislavsky's system, and in 1940 he and Soloviova opened the Actors Workshop at the Sutton Hotel.

Jitney Players, American acting troupe (1923–39). Founded by Richard Aldrich, this was one of the first itinerant summer stock companies, travelling throughout New England in two trucks which could be combined into a stage. Staffed by college graduates, headed by Bushnell Cheney of Yale and his wife Alice Keating, it once contained Hume Cronyn, seen as Charles Marlowe in *She Stoops to Conquer* (1935). When it played New York in 1929, it was regarded as amateurish.

Jocasta. In Greek mythology, the wife of Laius, king of Thebes, and mother (and wife) of Oedipus, by whom she had Antigone, Eteocles, Polyneices and Ismene. When she discovered her incestuous situation, she committed suicide, in some versions by hanging, in others by stabbing.

Jodin, Marie-Madeleine (1741–90), French actress, who acted at the Comédie Française and on tour throughout Europe. A protegée of Denis Diderot, who advised her to turn her back on the audience at salient moments, she was once imprisoned for blasphemy. During the French Revolution, she addressed a pamphlet to the National Assembly (1790) calling for an independent legislative code for women and the suppression of prostitution.

Johann, Zita (1904–93), Hungarian actress. Brought to the U.S. in 1911, she made her Broadway debut in 1924 in *Man and the Masses* and continued in expressionistic drama (*The Goat Song*, 1926; the Young Woman in *Machinal*, 1928). D. W. Griffith cast her in *The Struggle* (1931), but she is best remembered as Boris Karloff's posthumous love interest in *The Mummy* (1932). She married John Houseman.

John Ferguson, English play by St John Ervine (1914). An Irish farm family marries off its daughter to a man she loathes in order to save themselves from eviction. The second production of the Theatre Guild, it was its first real success and insured its continuity.

Johnny Johnson, American musical by Paul Green and Kurt Weill (1936), staged by Lee Strasburg for the Group Theatre. Strongly influenced by Weimar German revue and agit-prop, it related the mishaps of a pacifist who joins up in the First World War and has his life destroyed in the process.

Jones, Robert Edmond (1887–1954), American designer, taken to be the pioneer of the New Stagecraft in the U.S. Influenced by Max Reinhardt's stagings, he simplified settings in the hopes of liberating the spectator's imagination. He did much of his work for Arthur Hopkins: *Richard III*, *Hamlet* and *Macbeth*, as well as for Eugene O'Neill's early plays at the Provincetown Players. His book *The Dramatic Imagination* (1941) prescribed a visionary theatre.

Jonny Spielt Auf (*Johnny Strikes Up*), German jazz opera by Ernst Křenek (1927). An atonal, jazz-inflected account of a black band leader who steals a violin, it was translated into 18 languages and played all over Europe. The Nazis denounced it as "decadent music", but it lent its name to a brand of cigarettes.

The Journey, American film directed by Anatole Litvak from a screenplay by George Tabori (1959). When the 1956 Hungarian revolt breaks out, foreigners caught in Budapest must take a bus to get to Vienna; a Soviet commandant at the border is looking among them for a Hungarian dissident. Meant as a post-*King and I* vehicle for Deborah Kerr and Yul Brynner, it marks the film debut of Jason Robards Jr. as Paul the dissident.

Journey's End, English drama by R. C. Sherriff (1928). The most powerful of the plays about military life in the trenches during the First World War, it launched the careers of Colin Clive as the conscientious Col. Stanhope and James Whale as its director. For all its air of authenticity (its author had seen service), its understated, "stiff-upper-lip" quality made it a butt of parody.

Jouvet, Louis. See headnote to Chapter 37, "Louis Jouvet: The triumph of deceit".

Joy Street (*Ulitsa radosti*), Russian play by N. A. Zarkhi (1932). A satirical depiction of a London slum and its reaction to news of the Soviet Union.

Juarez, American film directed by William Dieterle from the novel *The Phantom Crown* by Bertita Harding and Franz Werfel's play *Juarez and Maximilian* (1939). With Paul Muni cast as the Mexican patriot Benito Juarez, the focus shifted to him and away from Maximilian and Carlotta (Brian Aherne and Bette Davis). John Garfield played Porfirio Diaz (badly), Claude Rains Napoleon III (farcically), and Vladimir Sokoloff a generic peasant (Slavicly).

Julius Caesar, American film directed by Joseph Mankiewicz from the play by William Shakespeare (1953). A sober account of the play which mixes English actors (John Gielgud as Cassius, James Mason as Brutus) with Americans (Louis Calhern as Caesar, Edmond O'Brien as Casca). The revelation is Marlon Brando's Mark Antony, whose polished delivery is infused with psychological intensity.

Kabbala, the Orthodox Jewish source of occult knowledge. Long immersion in and interpretation of its texts is supposed to achieve spiritual insight and a deep knowledge of Creation. The canon includes works from the first century to the thirteenth century (the Zohar).

Kachalov, Vasily Ivanovich (Shverubovich, 1875–1948), Russian actor. He joined the Moscow Art Theatre in 1910 as a character actor (Julius Caesar, a falsetto Baron in *The Lower Depths*, a pock-marked Tusenbach in *Three Sisters*, and an absent-minded Trofimov in *The Cherry Orchard*), and soon became a favorite leading man. Of high intelligence, urbanity, good looks and a velvety voice of remarkable timbre, he became a kind of matinee idol for the intelligentsia. He was also noted for platform readings of lyric poetry and dramatic works.

Kaiser, Georg (1878–1945), German playwright, leading exponent of Expressionism. Often based on historical characters and events, his innumerable plays are satires directed against the trends of an increasing dehumanized modern world. *From Morn to Midnight* (1916), a "station drama" of a lowly bank clerk dissipating embezzled money, won international popularity, as did the anti-industrial *Gas* trilogy (1920), staged by Eisenstein in Moscow in an actual gasworks.

Kamerny Theatre (Moscow State Chamber Theatre). Founded in 1914 by the director Aleksandr Tairov, it exemplified modernist currents in Russian art until the mid-1930s. The Kamerny strove to be a "synthetic theatre" with a high level of theatrical expression, powerful passions and sophisticated acting techniques. The collaboration of cubist and constructivist painters put the Kamerny in the first rank of experimental design. Savagely criticized for its apoliticism and "aestheticism", eventually the theatre was put under the control of a committee and finally obliterated in 1950.

Katerina Ivanovna, Russian play by Leonid Andreev (1912). A highly strung young wife is falsely accused of infidelity by her husband, who tries to shoot her. She leaves him, and has a brief affair with a man she detests. When her husband pleads for forgiveness, she returns but abandons herself to sexual depravity. Nemirovich-Danchenko staged it at the Moscow Art Theatre and it was produced in New York by the Theatre Guild.

Kaufman, George S. (1889–1961), American playwright. Master of the wise-crack and member of the Algonquin Round Table, he was happiest as a collaborator, with Marc Connelly (*Beggar on Horseback*, 1924), Morrie Ryskind (*Animal Crackers*, 1928), Edna Ferber (*Stage Door*, 1936), Moss Hart (*Once in a Lifetime*, 1930; *You Can't Take It with You*, 1936; *The Man Who Came to Dinner*, 1939). Kaufman's contribution was the snappy dialogue and the satiric shafts at current abuses. His fast-paced directing style was also effective.

Kazan, Elia (1909–2003), American director and actor. As a member of the Group Theatre, he came in contact with Stanislavsky's ideas which influenced his intimately emotional approach to actors. This paid off in his stagings of *A Streetcar Named Desire* (1947), *Death of a Salesman* (1949), *Cat on a Hot Tin Roof* (1955) and *Sweet Bird of Youth* (1959). The limitations of his intensely intimate method were seen when he was co-directed the repertory of the new Lincoln Center Theatre, which he left in 1964.

Kean, Edmund (1778–1833), English actor. Considered the epitome of a romantic tragedian, the diminutive Kean had played Harlequin in fairbooths before gaining fame as a fulminous Shylock at Drury Lane in 1814. Coleridge's remark that seeing him was like reading Shakespeare by lightning referred to his notorious unevenness, due in part to a dissipated way of life. He was the subject of a play by Alexandre Dumas *père*, revised by Jean-Paul Sartre.

Keane, Doris (1881–1945), American actress. She was celebrated for a single role, the ill-fated operatic soprano Margherita Cavallini in Edward Sheldon's *Romance* (1913), which she played for nearly three decades in the U.S. and England.

Keats, John (1795–1821), English poet. In his short life, cut off by tuberculosis, he produced some of the most beautiful lyric poems in English, among them "Endymion", "Lamia", "The Eve of St Agnes", "Ode to a Nightingle" and "Ode on a Grecian Urn". In a letter he enunciated the concept of "negative capability".

Kelly, Paul (1899–1956), American actor. Active as a dashing leading man in the 1920s, he saw his career take a tumble in the 1930s, so moved to Hollywood. His best movie role was as the alcoholic actor Frank Elgin in *The Country Girl* (1950).

Kemble, Fanny (Frances Anne, 1809–93), English actress. Eldest daughter of Charles Kemble, she made her debut as Juliet to her father's Mercutio in 1829. Her successes recouped his managerial losses, leading to an American tour in 1832. She married a Southern slave-owner and led a wretched life, returning to the stage in 1847 as a Shakespearean reader.

Kemble, John Philip (1757–1823), English actor-manager. Most illustrious of the theatrical Kemble clan, he was a frigid but imposing tragedian. His Hamlet, Coriolanus, Brutus and Addison's Cato, often teamed with his sister

Mrs Siddons, set the benchmark for formal neoclassicism in acting. His raising the prices at Covent Garden to cover his losses from the 1808 fire caused the disruptive O.P. ("Old Prices") riots.

Kerr, Deborah (Kerr-Trimmer, 1921–2007), Scottish actress. She appeared in ballet at Sadler's Wells and in rep in Oxford, before becoming a major film actress in *The Life and Death of Colonel Blimp* (1943) and *Black Narcissus* (1947). Her genteel, lady-like presence made her desirable in Hollywood playing ladies, although she was allowed a sex life in *From Here to Eternity* (1953).

Kerr, Jean (Collins, 1923–2003), American playwright, wife of Walter Kerr. Her slight comedies of suburban life found audiences from the late 1940s to the 1980s. The most successful was *Mary, Mary* (1961) which ran for 1,572 performances.

Kerr, Walter (1913–96), American dramatic critic and playwright. He came to reviewing in 1950 after many years of teaching and playwriting, and served at the New York *Herald Tribune* (1951–66) and the New York *Times* (1967–83). His own keen mind distrusted intelligence in the theatre, and he disliked Beckett's later plays, preferring the common touch. His most famous judgment is that on *Gypsy*: "Best damned musical I've seen in years."

Key Largo, American play by Maxwell Anderson (1939). On the eve of a hurricane, a criminal gang threatened with deportation seeks refuge in a Florida Keys hotel, which houses a Spanish Civil-War veteran. Anderson's real concern is how old-fashioned wickedness is being supplanted by a more pervasive evil. It was filmed in 1948 by John Huston with a sterling cast, including Humphrey Bogart, Edward G. Robinson, Lionel Barrymore and Lauren Bacall.

Khmelyov, Nikolay Pavlovich (1901–45), Russian actor and director. From 1919, he was considered one of most interesting of the "second generation" at the Moscow Act Theatre, creating a series of psychologically complex figures. His multi-faceted Peklevanov (*Armored Train 14–69*, 1927) changed the theatrical portrayal of Communist Party members. At the death of Nemirovich-Danchenko in 1943, he assumed the artistic directorship of the Art Theatre, where he died during a dress rehearsal, playing Ivan the Terrible.

King John, English history play by William Shakespeare from an earlier play and Holinshed (1596). The play concentrates on the ongoing war with France, its brief cessation, and the fate of Prince Arthur. John, with his machinations and bet-hedging, never attains the stature of a tragic hero.

King Lear, English blank-verse tragedy by William Shakespeare from an earlier play and Holinshed (1605). Existing in two distinct versions, what begins as a fairy tale ("Once upon a time there was a king with three daughters") devolves in a tragedy of cosmic dimensions. The play's intensity of cruelty and compassion gives it an existential resonance difficult to achieve in performance. In the twentieth century, the central role was attempted in England by Gielgud, Olivier, Laughton, Scofield; in the U.S. by a lesser breed: Louis Calhern, Lee J. Cobb, Morris Carnovsky.

King, Edith (Keck, 1896–1973), American actress. A long stage career (1916–64) saw her age from ingenues to matrons. She was a regular partner of the Lunts (Leda in *Amphytrion 38*, 1937; Polina in *The Seagull*, 1938; Curtis and the Widow, *Taming of the Shrew*, 1940).

King McCloud, the Spanish Civil-war veteran in *Key Largo* (1939), who gives his life to save a family menaced by gangsters. The role was created by Paul Muni. When Humphrey Bogart played it in the 1948 film, he was updated to be a veteran of the Second World War.

Kingsley, Sidney (1906–95), American playwright. His hospital play *Men in White* (1933) ran for more than 300 performances and made money for the Group Theatre. His first Broadway success was the superficially naturalistic *Dead End* (1935), which gave him a cheaply won reputation for social concern. The best of his later plays is the police procedural melodrama *Detective Story* (1949).

Kipling, Rudyard (1865–1936), English writer. Although he is usually dismissed as a jingoistic champion of the British Empire, he was a master of many genres, including the school novel, the animal tale and the travel essay. His novel *The Light That Failed* (1890), about a painter who goes blind, was dramatized successfully as a vehicle for Johnstone Forbes-Robertson.

A Kiss for Cinderella, English play by J. M. Barrie (1916). During the First World War, "Miss Thing", a young cleaner in a studio building is discovered by a policeman to be supporting four war orphans. She dreams of being Cinderella with the policeman as prince, and when she awakes, ill from exposure, he marries her.

Kittredge, George Lyman (1860–1941), American scholar. His bearded eminence lorded it over the Harvard English Department, although he lacked formal degrees. His utterances on Shakespeare and his contemporaries were taken as gospel by American theatre people.

Klöpfer, Eugen, German actor and director (1886–1950). After appearances in many German theatres (for Reinhardt he played Woyzeck and for Jessner Hauptmann leads), the stocky actor became director of the Berlin Volkbühne (1936–44) and in 1933 a member of the Reichsfilmkammer. An immensely vital player, prone to explosive outbursts, he put his talents at the disposal of the Nazi culture machine.

Knickerbocker Holiday, American musical comedy by Maxwell Anderson and Kurt Weill (1938). Roughly based on Washington Irving's comic history of Nieuw Amsterdam, it featured Walter Huston as hot-tempered Governor Stuyvesant and is best remembered for "September Song".

Komisarjevsky, Fyodor or **Theodore**, correctly Fyodor Fyodorovich Kommissarzhevsky (1882–1954), Russian director. Venice-born brother of Vera Kommissarzhevskaya, in 1914 he founded his own theatre in Moscow, staging the symbolists, then the first Russian productions of *The Middle-class Gentleman*, *Princess Turandot*, Goethe's *Faust* and Offenbach's *Tales of Hoffmann*. He preached a "synthetic theatre" in which the appropriate atmospheric style for each playwright would be sought. He emigrated in 1919, becoming a

British subject in 1932. He anglicized many modernist innovations, even at the Shakespeare Memorial Theatre, Stratford, and popularized Anton Chekhov by adapting him to the romantic taste of the matinee goer. He settled in the U. S. in 1939, directing Gielgud in *Crime and Punishment* (1947).

Komisarzhevsky, Vera, correctly Vera Fyodorovna Kommissarzhevskaya (1864–1910), Russian actress and manageress, sister of Fyodor. Considered the Russian Duse, with her remarkable sincerity and deep passion she excelled in Ibsen and Sudermann, as well as Nina in the premiere of *The Seagull* (1896). In 1904 she opened the Theatre in the Passage in St Petersburg, and, attracted to the Symbolists, invited the young director Meyerhold to take over; he persuaded her to become highly stylized, hieratic in gesture. After her failure in *Pelléas and Mélisande*, she dismissed him in 1907. She died of smallpox while on tour.

Koonen, Alisa Georgievna (1889–1974), Russian actress. She began at the Moscow Art Theatre and offended Stanislavsky by joining the Free Theatre in 1913, where she met and married Aleksandr Tairov. The next year they opened the Kamerny Theatre. Of dusky beauty, throbbing voice and a gracility influenced by Isadora Duncan, she was the ideal leading lady, both in comedy and tragedy, in such parts as Salome (1917), Adrienne Lecouvreur (1919), Juliet, Phèdre and Giroflé-Girofla (both 1922), Saint Joan, Abbie Putnam (*Desire Under the Elms*), and the Commissar (*An Optimistic Tragedy*, 1934).

Kortner, Fritz (F. Nathan Kohn, 1892–1970), Austrian actor and director. The very model of the expressionist performer, he was Leopold Jessner's tempestuous leading man, playing Gessler in *Wilhelm Tell* (1919, 1923), Richard III (1921) and a modern-dress Hamlet (1926), as well as Shlink in Brecht's *Jungle of Cities* (1924). After the defeat of the Nazis, he was rated as Germany's most powerful classic actor, especially for Shakespeare. As a director, he insisted on getting the spectator emotionally and politically involved.

Krauss, Werner (1884–1959), German actor. At Reinhardt's Deutsches Theater (1913–24, 1926–31), he became one of the most Protean character actors of his day as Julius Caesar (in both Shakespeare and Shaw, 1920), Shylock (1921), Falstaff (1929). He was also outstanding in expressionist silent film as the original Caligari. Under the Nazis, he played the lead in the anti-Semitic propaganda film *Jud Süss*, which did not prevent him from a continuous career on the West German stage once Hitler was defeated.

Kreisler, Fritz (1875–1962), Austrian violinist. Considered the greatest touring virtuoso of his generation, he stuck to a very limited repertoire of classics and his own compositions which he passed off as "arrangements" of minor baroque composers.

Křenek, Ernst (1900–94), Austrian composer. Over an eclectic career, he never composed anything more popular than his jazz opera *Jonny spiel auf* (1926). Denounced by the Nazis for his electronic and 12-tone experiments, he and his wife (Gustav Mahler's daughter) came to the U.S. where he taught at colleges and settled in Hollywood in 1947.

Kudriavtsev, Ivan Mikhailovich (1898–1966), Russian actor. After study with Michael Chekhov (1918–22), in 1924 he joined the Moscow Art Theatre where he played 46 roles. His gentle charm infused parts of decent men of conviction, such as young Nikolka in *Days of the Turbins* and Tyatin in *Yegor Bulychyov and Others*. His last part was Father Zosima in *The Brothers Karamazov* (1960).

Kurnitz, Harry (1908–68), American novelist and playwright. His foothold in Hollywood came in 1938 when he was commissioned, as Marco Page, to write the screenplay for one of his many detective stories. His output (1940–57) includes the Errol Flynn *Adventures of Don Juan* (1948), the Danny Kaye *Inspector General* (1949) and the Billy Wilder *Witness for the Prosecution* (1957). Affected by the blacklist, he moved to Europe (1946–56), and, on return to New York, wrote for the stage *A Shot in The Dark* (1961), the seed of all the *Pink Panther* movies.

Laboratory Theatre. See **American Laboratory Theatre**.

Lackaye, Wilton (1862–1932), American actor. Much employed in the 1880s and 1890s, he is best known as Svengali in the first U.S. production of *Trilby* (1895) and as Jean Valjean in his own adaptation of *Les Misérables, The Law and the Man* (1906). Although a devout Catholic, he was also effective as the Rabbi in *Children of the Ghetto* (1899).

Ladies in Love, American film directed by Edward H. Griffith (1936). To impress their boyfriends, three working girls in Budapest rent a posh apartment. In a fine cast, Janet Gaynor, Loretta Young and Constance Bennett were the hard-pressed trio, supported by Simone Simon, Don Ameche, Paul Lukas, Tyrone Power, J. Edward Bromberg and Wilfrid Lawson.

Lady, Be Good!, American musical comedy by Guy Bolton, Fred Thompson, and George and Ira Gershwin (1924). The first successful Broadway collaboration of the Gershwin brothers, this slender comedy about a real estate dispute initiated a jazz-based score for musicals. Fred and Adele Astaire, playing brother and sister, mounted another rung in their fame.

The Lady from the Sea, Norwegian play by Henrik Ibsen (1888). Ellida Wangel, living on the edge of a fjord, is torn between her attraction to the sea, represented by a mysterious Stranger, and her physician husband. When Dr. Wangel grants her freedom to choose, she stays with him. Owing to its delicate blend of symbolism and realism, it is a difficult work to pull off, needing an actress of subtle power as Ellida.

Lady in the Dark, American musical comedy by Kurt Weill, Ira Gershwin and Moss Hart (1941). The first avowedly Freudian musical, it used dream sequences to plot the inner life of fashion magazine editor Liza Elliott, played by Gertrude Lawrence. The score includes "My Ship Has Sails" and "Poor Jenny", and introduced Danny Kaye in the number "Tchaikowsky".

The Lady with a Lamp, English play by Reginald Berkeley (1929). A biography of Florence Nightingale, it featured Edith Evans when it opened in London, and served for her Broadway debut in 1931 in a very brief run. The film, starring Anna Neagle (1951) was much more popular.

Lahr, Bert (Irving Lahrheim, 1895–1967), American comedian. A veteran of burlesque and vaudeville with a store of grimaces and gurgles, he was an antic presence in many musicals, including *Hold Everything* (1928), *Flying High* (1930) and *Du Barry Was a Lady* (1939). After he created Estragon in the first American productions of *Waiting for Godot* (1956), he was cast as Bottom. He is immortalized as the Cowardly Lion in the MGM film of *The Wizard of Oz* (1938).

Langer, Lawrence (1890–1962), Welsh-born American producer, who was a guiding genius of the Washington Square Players (1914) and the Theatre Guild (1918), which he chronicled in *The Magic Curtain* (1951). He argued for a largely foreign repertory, heavy on Shaw and the Central Europeans, but championed O'Neill as well. He then founded the American Shakespeare Festival.

Langtry, Lillie (Emilie Charlotte Le Breton, Lady de Bathe, 1853–1929), English actress. A society beauty known as the "Jersey Lily", much painted and photographed, she created a stir by going on the professional stage, although her talent was slight. Her looks won her audiences in the U.K. and North America in such roles as Kate Hardcastle (*She Stoops to Conquer*, 1881) and Rosalind (*As You Like It*).

The Lark, American play by Lillian Hellman, based on *L'Alouette* by Jean Anouilh (1953). The life of Joan of Arc is presented in flashbacks, in the course of her trial. Although it follows Anouilh's basic pattern of a central character hemmed in by caricatural vice figures, Hellman, in shaping it for Julie Harris, reduced the cynicism and increased the sentimentality.

Laughton, Charles (1899–1962), English actor. Corpulent and moody, he became a West End star in the late 1920s and played Shakespearean leads at the Old Vic (1933–4). He was also the first Englishman to act Molière at the Comédie Française (1936). Following a successful Hollywood career, he launched Brecht's *Galileo* in Los Angeles (1947), and returned to the stage with readings from the Bible and the Bard. He directed and played the Devil in *Don Juan in Hell*, adapted *John Brown's Body* for the stage (1953), acted Undershaft in *Major Barbara* (1956), and at Stratford-upon-Avon took on Bottom and Lear (1959).

Laurents, Arthur (1918–), American director and playwright. His serious plays, dwelling on severe psychic crises (*Home of the Brave*, 1945; *The Time of the Cuckoo*, 1952; *The Bird Cage*, 1950) were treated respectfully, but were far less popular than his libretti for musicals: *West Side Story* (1957) and *Gypsy* (1959). His tell-all memoirs are an entertaining account of a gay man on the make.

Law, Andrew Bonar (1858–1923), Canadian-born Scottish statesman. A Unionist, he was a member of Parliament (1900–15), served in the War Cabinet and from 1916 led the House of Commons. He was Prime Minister briefly (1922–3), dying in office.

The Law and the Man, American play by Wilton Lackaye from *Les Misérables* by

Victor Hugo (1906). Lackaye toured this adaptation for years, but it was usually panned by more discriminating critics for its turgid banality and lack of dramatic excitement.

Lawrence, Marc (Max Goldsmith, 1910–2005), American actor. He and his friend John Garfield acted together until Lawrence got a film contract in 1931. He was invariably cast as gangsters (*Key Largo*, 1948; *The Asphalt Jungle*, 1950). Blacklisted by the House Committee on Un-American Activities for Communist associations, he emigrated to Europe, but returned to the U.S. in the 1970s, and carried on as heavies in movies until 1996.

Lawson, John Howard (1895–1977), American playwright, who co-founded the New Playwright's Theatre. His leftist leanings led him to create "political vaudeville" such as *Processional* (1925), a revue-style treatment of a coal strike. In the 1930s he wrote marginally more realistic accounts of the working class, as in *Success Story* (1932) and *Gentlewoman* (1934). He was imprisoned for a year (1948) for contempt of Congress in his opposition to the House Committee on Un-American Activities.

Lawson, Wilfrid. See headnote to Chapter 22, "The Actor as Biographer".

Le Gallienne, Eva (1899–1991), Anglo-American actress and director. A torchbearer for high art, influenced by Duse and the Moscow Art Theatre, she created the Civic Repertory Theatre (1926–33) and the American Repertory Company (1946–7), which spread the gospel of Ibsen, Chekhov, Shakespeare, Rostand and Schiller. In a lighter vein, she was the first actress to fly in *Peter Pan* and played an exquisitely distracted White Queen in *Alice in Wonderland*.

Lee, Auriol (1880–1941), English actress and director. She came to the U.S. in 1903, but did not become a fixture of the New York stage, usually in drawing-room comedy, until 1917. Starting in 1930, she was one of the few women to direct on Broadway: *Flowers of the Forest* (1936), *Leave Her to Heaven, Old Acquaintance* (both 1940). She died in an auto accident.

Lee, Will (1908–82), American actor and director. A member of the Group Theatre (replacement lead in *Golden Boy*; *Johnny Johnson*) and the Federal Theatre Project, he directed shows for the troops in the Pacific during the Second World War. A film career was blocked by House Committee on Un-American Activities blacklisting, but he continued to act on Broadway, teach (American Theatre Wing, New School, HB Studio), and eventually to create the much-loved role of the grocer Mr. Hooper in television's *Sesame Street* (1969–82).

Leeds, Nina, central character of Eugene O'Neill's *Strange Interlude*. After conducting a number of affairs with other men, she marries a complaisant boob, only to discover that insanity runs in his family. She aborts her pregnancy and conceives another child with her doctor. They fall in love and preserve the secret for 20 years.

Lehmann, Lotte. See headnote to Chapter 57, "The singing actress attacks her part".

Leigh, Vivien. See headnote to Chapter 24, "The Oliviers".

Lekain, Henri Louis (1729–78). French actor. A protegé of Voltaire, who built him a private theatre, he joined the Comédie-Française in 1750. Despite his ugliness, he became a popular tragedian, especially in Voltaire, often partnered with Mlle. Clairon. This popularity did not obtain with his colleagues, whose intrigues got him thrice jailed. His reforms included thorough preparation of roles and historical costuming.

Lely, Sir Peter (1618–80), Dutch painter. Arriving in England in 1641, he served Charles I, Oliver Cromwell ("warts and all") and Charles II in turn, becoming the Merry Monarch's Principal Painter in Ordinary (1661). His portraits, turned out in abundance with much help from his pupils, include the Windsor Beauties, ten portraits of court ladies, with ringlets, arched eyebrows, perfect complexions and oval faces.

Lemaitre, Frédérick (1800–76). French actor. After a stint as a mime in Deburau's Théâtre des Funambules, he gained celebrity by sending up a melodrama *L'Auberge des Adrets* (1820), in the process birthing the legendary figure of the cynical criminal Robert Macaire. He became the most powerful romantic actor of his time, creating Dumas' Antony, Hugo's Ruy Blas and Balzac's Vautrin, as well as *The Rag-picker of Paris* and the gambling addict in *Thirty Years* (1827).

Lerner, Alan Jay (1918–86), American lyricist, who, in collaboration with Viennese-born composer Frederick Loewe (1904–88), created a string of hit musicals that continue to be revived: *Brigadoon* (1947), *Paint Your Wagon* (1951), *My Fair Lady* (1956), *Camelot* (1960) and the film *Gigi* (1958; remade for Broadway, 1973). When Loewe retired, Lerner took Burton Lane as his partner, creating the reasonably successful *On a Clear Day You Can See Forever* (1965) and the dismal flop *Carmelina* (1979).

The Letter, English play by W. Somerset Maugham (1927), a cynical take on colonial hypocrisy and miscegenation set in Southern Asia. The film version, directed by William Wyler (1940) with a "poetic justice" ending, provided parts to tear a cat in for Bette Davis and Gale Sondergaard.

Levene, Sam (Levine, 1905–80), American actor. Small and wiry, he drew on his New York Jewish sarcasm as Patsy in *Three Men on a Horse* (1935), Gordon Miller in *Room Service* (1937), Nathan Detroit in *Guys and Dolls* (1950) and Al Lewis in *The Sunshine Boys* (1972).

Levitt, Saul (1913–77), American playwright. Wounded in a jeep accident in Germany in 1943, he was assigned to *Yank* magazine, where he developed his reporter's skills. His plays are all documentary in nature: *The Andersonville Trial* (1959), *The Trial of the Catonsville Nine* (1971) and a musical work for children about the Native American football player, *Jim Thorpe, All-American*.

Lewes, George Henry (1817–78), English dramatic critic, life partner of George Eliot. A member of Dickens' amateur troupe, he essayed an interpretation of a noble Shylock in Manchester (1849). His reviews for *The Leader* (1850–4), often of his own plays, were insightful. His *On Actors and the Art of Acting* (1875) remains a canny analysis of how a player achieves his effects.

Lewis, Robert. See headnote to Chapter 49, "A point of view and a place to practice it".

Lewisohn Stadium, New York. A gift of the philanthropist Adolph Lewisohn, it is an athletic field *cum* amphitheater, seating 6,000. It opened in 1915 with *The Trojan Women*, and, under the supervision of Minnie Guggenheimer, became a summer venue for music of all kinds. Marian Anderson and George Gershwin were among its early favourites.

Libel!, English courtroom drama by Edward Wooll (1934). A baronet brings a libel suit against a newspaper for claiming he is a fraud who exchanged identities with another Englishman in a German P.O.W. camp. It was a great hit on Broadway (1935), directed by Otto Preminger, and marking the return of Colin Clive to the stage. It was not filmed until 1959 by Anthony Asquith, with Dirk Bogarde and Olivia de Havilland, updated to the post-Second World War period.

Lieberson, Goddard (1911–77), English producer. As president of Columbia Records, he followed up Jack Kapp's invention of the "original cast album" by recreating complete scores of Broadway musicals in the recording studio. Often his re-creations inspired revivals.

Lied von Hoboken, Das, the German title of *Hoboken Blues*, a musical mime piece by Michael Gold, meant to decry injustice visited on African Americans. Its first production by the New Playwrights' Theatre in 1927 was attacked for racism, because it was performed by white actors in blackface. It was adapted by Günther Weisenborn from a translation by Hermynia zur Mühlen, and performed at the Theater an Bülowplatz, Berlin, in 1930, with Dolly Haas in the cast.

Liliom, Hungarian drama by Ferenc Molnár (1908). Liliom, a carnival barker, seduces the innocent Julie, and when she gets pregnant, is killed during a theft intended to get money to take them to America. For his lack of repentance, he is sentenced to 16 years in Hell. In the one day given him to return to earth to expiate his sins, he fails to reform. Eva Le Gallienne made a success of Julie in the Theatre Guild production (1920), and, in a much sweetened form, the play served as the basis for the musical *Carousel*.

Lillie, Beatrice, Lady Peel (1894–1989), Canadian comedienne. Success in London revues brought her to the U.S., where she became a byword for sophisticated slapstick in *This Year of Grace* (1929), *The Show Is On* (1936) and *Inside U.S.A.* (1948). Her air of bemused condescension made hilarious her renderings of "There's Are Fairies at the Bottom of My Garden" and "I've Been to a Ma-ahvelous Party".

Lincoln, Abraham. Although the 16th president of the U.S. was assassinated while in a theatre watching a play, he has constantly appeared as a dramatic hero. John Drinkwater's *Abraham Lincoln* (1919) was the first commercial success for both the Theatre Guild and the Birmingham Repertory Theatre. Robert E. Sherwood's *Abe Lincoln in Illinois* (1938) made a star of Raymond Massey. E. P. Conkle's *Prologue to Glory* (1938) covered the years in New Salem. The Lincoln–Douglas debates were re-created in *The Rivalry* (1959). Lincoln

Kirstein's *White House Happening* (1968) was one of the great fiascos of the American stage.

Lincoln Center Theatre, more accurately Vivian Beaumont and Mitzi E. Newhouse Theatres, New York. The repertory theatre and a smaller experimental house, designed by Eero Saarinen and Jo Mielziner, opened in 1964. The first season, led by Elia Kazan and Robert Whitehead, was a failure, and they were replaced by Herbert Blau and Jules Irving, in turn succeeded by Joseph Papp (1973–7).

Lindsay, Howard (1889–1968), American playwright, actor, director and producer. His quadruple coup was to co-author (with Russell Crouse), produce, direct and play autocratic Father Day in *Life with Father* (1946–7), which enjoyed a run of 3,216 performances. He also collaborated on libretti for the musicals *Anything Goes* (1934), *Call Me Madam* (1950) and *The Sound of Music* (1962).

Linklater, Eric (1899–1974), Scottish novelist. Hugely prolific in a wide array of genres, from history to children's books, from picaresque adventures to memoirs, he also had a second career as a broadcaster.

The List of Benefits, more accurately *A List of Assets* (*Spisok blagodeyaniya*), Russian play by Yury Olesha (1931). It shows a Soviet actress (based on Michael Chekhov) who keeps a diary listing the pros and cons of life in Soviet Russia. When she goes to Paris, she discovers the squalor of capitalist society (she is asked to play a recorder through her rectum) and sacrifices herself for a Communist workers' movement. Meyerhold's Moscow production featured his wife Zinaida Raikh.

Lister, Francis (1899–1951), English actor. This polished leading man shuttled between the West End and Broadway in the 1920s and 30s, usually featured in sex comedies (*Uneasy Virtue*, 1931; a double role in *The Red Cat*, 1934). He and his wife Margot Grahame were utility players in Hollywood (*Clive of India; Mutiny on the Bounty*, both 1935) until the Second World War broke out, when he returned to England.

The Little Foxes, American melodrama by Lillian Hellman (1939), about the conniving machinations in a genteel Southern family at the turn of the nineteenth century, for whom ties of affection are weaker than power-grabs. Tallulah Bankhead made a strong impression as the grasping Regina.

Little Man, What Now?, American film directed by Frank Borzage from the novel by Hans Fallada (1934). The source, *Kleiner Mann, was nun?* (1933), was a deeply felt record of the last days of the Weimar Republic. The film turns it into an account of the tribulations of a young couple, played by Margaret Sullavan and Douglass Montgomery.

The Little Michus (*Les P'tites Michus*), French operetta by Albert Vanloo and Georges Duval with music by André Messager (1897). Even with a plot about two baby girls switched at birth who fall in love with the same man, it was a hit worldwide. Adaptations had long runs in London (1905, with Adeline Genée) and New York (1907).

Little Moon of Alban, American play by James Costigan (1960). Taking place during the Time of Troubles in Dublin (1919–22), it tells of the love between an Irish nurse (Julie Harris) and a wounded British officer (John Justin). Robert Redford was also in the original cast. The title comes from Synge's *Deirdre of the Sorrows*.

Little Ol' Boy, American play by Albert Bein (1933). A variegated group of youths in a mid-western reform school is catalyzed by the arrival of Red Barry (Burgess Meredith). Ploys to save his brother on Death Row lead to a mass flogging and escape, and end with Red on the way to the penitentiary after his brother's execution. The Group Theatre was convinced by this play to take an interest in Bein.

Little Women, American play by Marion de Forst, based on Louisa May Alcott (1912). Alcott's famous novel about the New England March sisters at the time of the American Civil War was successfully dramatized, with emphasis on their relations with Lawrie, Professor Bhaer and John Brooks. It served as the framework for the film versions.

Livanov, Boris Nikolaevich (1904–72), Russian actor and director. A stalwart of the Moscow Art Theatre from 1924, he had a strong line in heroic proletarians. In the 1940 revision of *Three Sisters* his interpretation of Solyony as a flamboyant bully became the model for the role. Rude and highhanded in private life, he fully expected to become the head of the MAT and when he was passed over in 1970, he withdrew and soon died.

Lloyd, Marie (Matilda Alice Victoria Wood, 1870–1922), English music-hall singer. Beloved for her saucy innuendo and warm heart, she became a symbol of the late Victorian music hall. Beginning as a soubrette, she became a fashion plate and ended as a game old bird. Such songs as "Oh, Mr Porter!" ("She'd never had her ticket punched before"), "The Old Cock Linnet" and "I'm One of the Ruins that Cromwell Knocked Abaht a Bit") became folkloric.

Lloyd George, David (1863–1945), Welsh statesman. An outspoken Liberal who opposed the Boer War, he proved himself a belligerent when war-time Prime Minister (1916–22). He revealed a genuine talent for diplomacy during the peace negotiations. He was voted out of office when he conceded the Irish Free State.

Locksley Hall, English poem by Alfred Lord Tennyson (1842). The interior monologue of an officer halting to pay a sentimental visit to his old home, musing on past disappointments and future utopias. Winston Churchill named it "the most wonderful of modern prophecies".

Loewe, Frederick. See **Lerner, Alan Jay**.

Logan, Joshua (1908–88), American director, producer and playwright. His sure instinct for what the public liked is evinced by his many successes: *Knickerbocker Holiday* (director, 1938), *Annie Get Your Gun* (director, 1946), *Mister Roberts* (co-author, director, 1948), *South Pacific* (co-author, 1949), *Fanny* (librettist, 1954), *Picnic* (director, co-producer, 1953). His approach to directing was no-nonsense "let's get on with it".

Lola-Lola, the Tingel-Tangel singer and *femme fatale* in Heinrich Mann's novel *Professor Unrath* (1905). When it was about to made into a film in 1929, the role was slated for Leni Riefenstahl, when the director Josef von Sternberg decided on Marlene Dietrich. Her smoky voice, heavy-lidded gaze and unending legs became iconic in *The Blue Angel* (1930), along with Friedrich Hollaender's song "Ich bin von Kopf bis Fuss" ("Falling in Love Again").

London Calling, English revue by Noël Coward and Ronald Jeans (1923). A small-scale show produced by André Charlot, it contained Coward's first hit song, "Parisian Pierrot", sung by Gertrude Lawrence.

The Loneliness of the Long Distance Runner, English film, directed by Tony Richardson, from a short story by Alan Sillitoe (1962). An angry young delinquent (Tom Courtenay) finds his only joy in running, against a background of unmitigated industrial grime and proletarian desperation.

Long, John Luther (1861–1927), American playwright. Inspired by *Madame Butterfly*, he collaborated with David Belasco on the melodramatic *japonoiserie The Darling of the Gods* (1902), followed by *Adrea* (1904), a fifth-century European intrigue concocted for Mrs Leslie Carter. Plays he wrote on his own were vehicles for her and Mrs Fiske.

Lonsdale, Frederick (Lionel Frederick Leonard, 1881–1954), English playwright. After a successful career as a librettist of Ruritanian operettas, he settled into writing epigrammatic drawing-room comedies, portraying the vagaries of the huntin', shootin', fishin' class: *Aren't We All?* (1923), *Spring Cleaning, The Last of Mrs Cheyney* (both 1925), *On Approval* (1927).

Loraine, Robert (1876–1935), English actor-manager. In life and art, he was essentially a heroic swashbuckler, playing D'Artagnan, Cyrano and Rudolf Rassendyl (*The Prisoner of Zenda*), and winning honors as an aviator in the First World War. He was a polished player of Shaw (John Tanner, Don Juan, Bluntschli). He also introduced Strindberg to the English stage, as the Captain in *The Father*.

Lord, Pauline (1890–1950), American actress. She came into her own in the 1920s as the original *Anna Christie* (1921), Amy in *They Knew What They Wanted* (1924) and Nina in *Strange Interlude* (1928). Her peculiar charm was then muted in the roles of mousy women in *The Late Christopher Bean* (1932) and *Ethan Frome* (1936).

Lorre, Peter (Laszlo Löwenstein, 1904–64), Hungarian actor. A favourite of Bertolt Brecht in Weimar Berlin, he created the role of Galy Gay in *Mann ist Mann* and became the national bogeyman as the pudgy child-murderer in the film *M* (1931). Hitchcock perpetuated his *emploi* as a villain in *The Man Who Knew Too Much*. In Hollywood, the pop-eyed, nasal actor became typed as psychopaths, poltroons, and crooks.

Losey, Joseph (1909–84), American director. He was a working Broadway stage manager and director (*Galileo Galilei*, 1947), before going into film, addressing social problems. Blacklisted by the anti-Communist witchhunt, he moved to England (1952) and directed under a pseudonym until 1957. He came into his own in the 1960s, often collaborating with Dirk Bogarde and Harold Pinter, on such enigmatic films of modern morality as *The Servant* (1963), *The Accident* (1967) and *The Go-Between* (1971).

Lost in the Stars, American "musical tragedy" by Maxwell Anderson and Kurt Weill (1949). Adapted from Alan Paton's *Cry the Beloved Country*, it confronted problems of apartheid in South Africa. A black minister discovers that his son has murdered a white reformer, and seeks reconciliation with the murdered man's father.

Love, Elizabeth, American actress. She made sporadic appearances on Broadway from 1931 to 1939.

Love for Love, English comedy by William Congreve (1695). Valentine, deeply in debt, tries to avoid signing over his inheritance by feigning madness. He is saved by Angelica, who, by a ruse, secures the bond and destroys it. On this plot is hung a number of lesser ones and highly amusing characters. John Gielgud revived it in a very stylish production in 1947.

The Lower Depths (***Na dne***), drama by Maksim Gorky (1902). It consists wholly of interactions among a group of down-and-outers in a Moscow flophouse. A vagrant named Luka offers many of them illusory visions of hope, but ultimately these end in death from disease, violence and suicide. The first production by the Moscow Art Theatre was a revelation, the educated cast slumming as derelicts. It had an enormous success all over the world, not least in Japan.

Luce, Claire Boothe (1905–87), American actress and playwright, married to Henry Luce, founder of *Time* magazine. She was the first American to be invited to perform at the Shakespeare Memorial Theatre in Stratford. Her most durable play is *The Women* (1936), a catty all-female cartoon of New York society. She attacked fascism in *Kiss the Boys Goodbye* (1938) and *Margin for Error* (1939), but eventually embraced ultra-rightist causes.

Lucrece (*Le viol de Lucrèce*), French play by André Obey (1931). Written for the Compagnie des Quinze, this was a poetic tragedy drawn from Shakespeare's *Rape of Lucrece*. As actors mime the action, two narrators, a man and a woman, describe the Roman legend and Lucretia's state of mind. A New York production starred Katharine Cornell as Lucretia and Brian Aherne as Tarquin.

Luka. See **The Lower Depths**.

Lukas, Paul (Pal Lukasz, 1895–1971), Hungarian actor. After stage and screen work in Hungary, Austria and Germany (with Max Reinhardt), he learned English to work in Hollywood from 1928. His heavy accent relegated him to suave romantic leads and continental villains (Prof. Bhaer in *Little Women*, 1933; Dr. Hartz in *The Lady Vanishes*, 1938). His best part was the anti-Nazi fugitive Karl Mueller in *Watch on the Rhine* (stage 1941, film 1943).

Lunt, Alfred. See headnote to Chapter 51, "The actor attacks his part: Lynn Fontanne and Alfred Lunt".

Lyric Theatre, Hammersmith, London, opened in 1888. Its glory days began in 1918 when Nigel Playfair took it over, drawing audiences with *Abraham Lincoln* (1919), acclaimed revivals of *The Beggar's Opera* (1920), Congreve and Farquhar, Chekhov and Wilde, and a host of revues and operettas. John Gielgud brought in Peter Brook as director for a repertory season in

1952–3. In the 1990s, it had a resurgence as a house for artistic innovation under Neil Bartlett.

Macbeth, English blank-verse tragedy by William Shakespeare from Holinshed (1606). Although swathed in an atmosphere of supernatural evil, the play carefully traces the human devastation caused by overweening ambition. The valiant warrior Macbeth and his enterprising spouse are destroyed by their acceptance that the end justifies the means. Owing to a history of accidents and failures, the tragedy has a cursed reputation and must be named in the theatre only as "the Scottish play".

MacDonald, Ramsay (1866–1937), Scottish politician. A leader of the Labour Party (1893–1930), he became the first prime minister from that faction (1924, 1929–31). Although many of his party denounced him for serving as head of the National Coalition Cabinet (1931–5) under the Conservatives during the Depression, he remained active in politics till his death.

Macgowan, Kenneth (1888–1963), American producer and critic. A regular contributor to the New York *Globe* and *Theatre Arts*, he founded the Experimental Theatre with Robert Edmond Jones and Eugene O'Neill (1924), where he produced six of O'Neill's plays and first New York production of Strindberg's *Spook Sonata* (*sic*, 1924). His books propagandized for the New Stagecraft and particularly the use of masks.

Machinal (pronounced Machine-al), American drama by Sophie Treadwell (1928). Influenced both by German expressionism and a sensational murder case, it features The Young Woman who, despite a brief interlude with a dashing Young Man, is so dehumanized by her environment that she murders her husband and is sentenced to the electric chair. It was successfully revived in Moscow in 1933.

Mackeben, Theo (1897–1953), German musician. After a career as a concert pianist, he came to Berlin to play piano at Rosa Valetti's Café Großenwahn. He then became conductor at the Volksbühne and the Muncipal Schauspielhaus. In 1928 he conducted the premiere of *Die Dreigroschenoper* and updated Millöcker's operetta *Die Dubarry*. After the Second World War, he conducted at the Berlin Metropol-Theater.

MacKenna, Kenneth (Leo Mielziner, 1899–1962), American actor, brother of designer Jo Mielziner. In 1920s and 1930s he alternated leading roles between stage and screen, rarely in outstanding scripts: exceptions were Richard Niles in *Merrily We Roll Along* (1934), and Macduff and Iago (1935). He became a script editor and in the 1960s a character performer in film.

Mackenzie, Ronald (d.1934), English playwright. A former schoolmate of John Gielgud, he sent him unsolicited his play *Musical Chairs* (1932), which was produced and well received. He also wrote *The Maitlands* (1934) before his untimely death.

Macklin, Charles (McLaughlin) (1697?–1797), Irish actor and playwright. A leading player at Drury Lane, the Haymarket and Covent Garden, London, he is credited with the first serious interpretation of Shylock. Testy and quarrelsome, he distilled those qualities into his performances of Macbeth and Sir Archy MacSarcasm in his own play *The Man of the World* (1781). He acted well into his 90s.

Maclaine, Shirley (Beatty, 1934–), American actress and writer, sister of Warren Beatty. Her Broadway debut was in the chorus of *Me and Juliet* (1953), where she was discovered by producer Hal B. Wallis and transferred to film usually playing a good-time girl (*Can-Can*, 1959; *The Apartment*, 1959; *Irma La Douce*, 1963). She was a protester against the Vietnam war, and then a propagandist for reincarnation.

Macready, William (1755–1829), Irish actor-manager. An expert at playing coxcombs, he was well employed at Covent Garden, London (1786–96). When he ran the Theatre Royal, Birmingham, he improved scenery and lighting, but went bankrupt, forcing his son William Charles to leave Rugby and go on the stage.

Macready, William Charles (1793–1873), English actor-manager. The leading London tragedian of the early Victorian period, as manager of Covent Garden (1827–39) and Drury Lane (1841–3), he promoted the plays of Edward Bulwer-Lytton and restored the Fool and an unhappy ending to *King Lear*. Against his will, he was embroiled in a feud with the American tragedian Edwin Forrest, which led to the Astor Place Riot, New York (1849).

Mademoiselle Colombe (*Colombe*), French play by Jean Anouilh (1941). When the moralizing Julien goes off to military service, he leaves his innocent wife in the care of his mother, a calculating stage star. Two years later he returns to find Colombe an actress adored by stage-door Johnnies and the mistress of his brother. She insists on pursuing the chimeras of career and romance, while his ideals are blasted. Harold Clurman directed the New York premiere.

Maeterlinck, Maurice (1862–1949), Belgian playwright. His mystical and symbolist dramas were very popular at the *fin de siècle*, especially *Pelléas et Mélisande* (1892) and *Monna Vanna* (1902). The tense atmosphere works best in his one-acts, *L'Intruse* (1890) and *Les Aveugles* (1891). *The Blue Bird* (1909), with its fairy-tale plot, had great appeal for juvenile audiences, especially in productions based on the Moscow Art Theatre staging.

Magnani, Anna (1908–73), Egyptian-born Italian actress. From the deepest poverty she became an actress and music-hall performer, before Roberto Rossellini cast her as the fiery tenement dweller in the film *Open City* (1945). A sulphurous earth mother, she asked too much money when Tennessee Williams wanted her for the lead in *The Rose Tattoo*, but she played it in the film (1955).

The Magnanimous Cuckold (*Le Cocu magnifique*), Belgian play by Ferdinand Crommelynck (1920). An effort to revive the ancient Greek *comus*, this grotesque farce concerns Bruno who is so enamoured of his wife Stella that he becomes monstrously jealous of her, and, to confirm his worst fears, forces her to have sex with the whole village. Nothing allays his suspicions, which continue to consume him. It was first staged by the Théâtre de l'Oeuvre and then in a groundbreaking constructivist production by Meyerhold.

Magnolia Alley, American comedy by George Batson (1949). Marking the stage debut of Jackie Cooper in a cast that also included Julie Harris and Anne Jackson, this mess of a play concerns the slatternly women who live in a Southern rooming house and the men who take an interest in them. It ran a week.

Major Barbara, comedy by George Bernard Shaw (1907). Of an aristocratic family, Barbara Undershaft is a devoted major in the Salvation Army. Her father, an arms dealer, illustrates to her the futility of alleviating a rotten system, and persuades her to aid in the brave new world of his factory town. The society-comedy first act and the cockney-comedy second act make the play popular, despite an overly didactic third act.

Malden, Karl (Mladen George Sekulović, 1912–), American actor. Recognizable by a bulbous nose, resulting from basketball injuries, he joined the Group Theatre, where he met Elia Kazan who cast him in his productions of *All My Sons* and as Mitch in *A Streetcar Named Desire* (film 1951), and his films *On the Waterfront* (1954) and *Baby Doll* (1956). From 1957 to 1972, he played in dozens of films, and then transferred his activities to television.

Maly (Little) Theatre, Moscow, the oldest extant theatre in Russia, unofficially dating from 1755 when an amateur public theatre was opened in Moscow University. In 1806, it became an Imperial theatre, the only such edifice to house dramatic, ballet and operatic performances. Between 1854 and 1888 the Maly introduced and popularized the works of Aleksandr Ostrovsky, leading to its designation "The House of Ostrovsky". In 1919, the Maly was named a state-supported "academic theatre", and the auditorium was remodelled to prevent class distinctions. It had difficulty adapting to the new regime and the theatre languished under a parade of undistinguished artistic directors during the war and post-war years. Even now it plays the classics in a traditional style which rarely sends the pulse of theatre buffs racing.

Mamoulian, Rouben (1897–1987), Russian-born American director, inspired by Vakhtangov. His Broadway debut for the Theatre Guild directing *Porgy* (1923) established him as a master of co-ordinating music, dance and drama. Most of his later New York stagings were of musicals: *Porgy and Bess* (1933), *Oklahoma!* (1943), *Carousel* (1945) and *Lost in the Stars* (1949). His considerable film work includes the first all-color dramatic movie *Becky Sharp*.

The Man and the Law. See **The Law and the Man**.

The Man Outside, English film directed by George A. Cooper from a story by Donald Stuart (1933). A "crook" drama set in a country house, it concerns a jewel heist effected by a police official. Henry Kendall played the detective who cracks the case.

The Man Who Came Back (English title of *Swamp Water*), American film directed by Jean Renoir (1941) from a screenplay by Dudley Nichols. Shot on location in the Georgia marshes, it tells of an escaped convict (Walter Brennan) who erupts into the life of the hero (Dana Andrews).

The Man Who Came to Dinner, an American comedy by George S. Kaufman and Moss Hart (1939). The personality of the outrageous journalist and commentator Alexander Woollcott is grafted on to the impossible Sheridan Whiteside, who camps out in the living room of a Midwestern family. A *pièce à clef* with caricatures of Harpo Marx, Noël Coward and Gertrude Lawrence, it has been a perennial favorite with schools and community theatres.

Mann, Daniel (Chugerman, 1912–91), American director. Once a child actor, on Broadway he staged *Come Back, Little Sheba* (1950, film 1952), *The Rose Tattoo* (1951, film 1955), *Paint Your Wagon* (1951) and the musical revue *Pins and Needles*. As a film director, he concentrated on adaptations of plays and novels (*The Teahouse of the August Moon*, 1956; *Butterfield 8*, 1960; *Five Finger Exercise*, 1962). He also had a distinguished career as a television director (*Playing for Time*, 1980).

Mann, Theodore (Goldman, 1924–), American producer and director. A co-founder of Circle in the Square, New York (1951), he served as its artistic director with a speciality in staging O'Neill. In 1961 he established a school there to train actors.

Mann Ist Mann (*A Man's A Man* or *Man Equals Man*), German play by Bertolt Brecht (1926). Based on Kipling's *Barrack Room Ballads*, it has four British tommies loot a temple and try to free their comrade Jeriah Jip. They implicate the mild-mannered market porter Galy Gay in a crime, "kill" him with blanks and turn him into Jeriah, a mindless fighting machine, i.e., the perfect soldier. Peter Lorre played Galy Gay in the original production

Manners, John Hartley (1870–1928), Anglo-American playwright and director. Crafting a play for Lillie Langtry gave him the knack of showcasing an actress. So his career was devoted to providing vehicles for his wife Laurette Taylor and then directing them to her advantage. These included the phenomenally popular *Peg o' My Heart* (1912), as well as *The Harp of Life* (1916) and *Happiness* (1917).

Mansurova, Tsetsiliya Lvovna (Vollershtein, 1897–1976). Russian actress. She was a student in Moscow of Evgeny Vakhtangov who cast her in the title role of *Princess Turandot* (1922). She preserved the principles of his teachings throughout her career as leading lady at the Vakhtangov Theatre. In 1942–5 she entertained at the front.

Marceau, Marcel (Mangel, 1923–2007), French actor, the icon of the white-faced mime. Having played Arlequin to Barrault's *Baptiste* (1945), he concentrated on developing his Pierrot-like Bip and the form of mimodrama. He introduced them at the Théâtre de Poche in 1946, and travelled all over the world with his troupe, offering simple scenarios as well as the more elaborate *The Mask Maker* and his adaptation of Gogol, *The Overcoat*.

March, Fredric (Frederick McIntyre Bickell, 1897–1975). American actor. A long period as juvenile leads led to a marriage with actress Florence Eldridge and prime roles in Hollywood films. He returned to the stage occasionally, creating Mr Antrobus in *The Skin of Our Teeth* (1942), Major Joppolo in *A Bell for Adano* (1944) and, most significantly, James Tyrone in *Long Day's Journey into Night* (1956). In every role, one could sense a mind conscientiously at work.

Marco Millions, American comedy by Eugene O'Neill (1927). The central conceit is to portray Marco Polo and his Venetian kinfolk as typical Midwestern Babbitts, go-getters who completely miss the romance and adventure that surrounds them. While pursuing the main chance, Marco abandons Princess Kukachin who dies of a broken heart. Alfred Lunt played Marco for the Theatre Guild in the first production.

Marlowe, Julia (Sarah Frances Frost, 1866–1950), Anglo-American actress. Partnered with her husband E. H. Sothern, she was America's leading Shakespearean actress in the first decades of the twentieth century, especially noted as Ophelia, Juliet and Beatrice. She also appeared on Broadway in more than 70 productions.

Marsh, Reginald (1898–1954), American artist. After study at the Art Students League of New York, he became associated with the Ashcan School of social realism. His favourite subjects were vaudeville, burlesque and life on Coney Island and the Bowery streets, his drawings often published in the New York *Daily News* and the *New Yorker*. Many were worked up as egg-tempera paintings.

Marshall, E[dda] G[unnar] (1910/14–98). American actor. Nondescript in appearance but constantly employed, he was seen as Willie Oban in *The Iceman Cometh* (1946), John Proctor in *The Crucible* (1953) and as a bland Vladimir opposite Bert Lahr's scene-stealing Estragon in *Waiting for Godot* (1956).

Martin, Mary (1913–90), American singer and actress. Beginning as a siren singing "My Heart Belongs to Daddy" (*Leave It to Me*, 1938) and as a statue of Aphrodite (*One Touch of Venus*, 1943), she gradually turned more wholesome in *Annie Get Your Gun* (1947), *South Pacific* (1949), *Peter Pan* (1954), and was practically sainted in *The Sound of Music* (1959). The saccharine climax came in a two-character musical about a 50-year marriage, *I Do! I Do!* (1966).

Martin Beck Theatre, New York. Named for its owner, a vaudeville producer, it opened in 1924 and was constantly in demand. Katharine Cornell preferred it above all others. It housed at various times the Theatre Guild, the Abbey Players and the D'Oyly Carte Company.

Martin-Harvey, Sir John (1863–1944), English actor-manager. He apprenticed as a juvenile lead with Henry Irving at the Lyceum, London (1882–96), which he took over in 1899. His perennial vehicle was *The Only Way* (1899), a version of *A Tale of Two Cities* in which he played Sydney Carton. With his wife Nina da Silva he toured a repertory of Victorian melodrama and Edwardian romance through the U.K., the U.S. and Canada, where his presence is registered in the novels of Robertson Davies.

Martinson, Sergey Aleksandrovich (1899–1984), Russian actor. After cabaret work, he developed a strong line in grotesque characters, especially caricatural Americans, under Meyerhold (*Roar China*; Khlestakov in *The Inspector General*, both 1926); and at the Theatre of Revolution (1925–40; *The Final Conflict*, 1931). At the Moscow Music Hall he played clowns: Skid in *Burlesque* (1933) and Skameikin in *Under the Big Top* (1934).

Marvell, Andrew (1621–78), English poet. Part of the Puritan cultural establishment (Cromwell's ward's tutor, Milton's assistant) and an active politician during the Interregnum, he made his peace with the Restoration for a while, but eventually worked against the Stuarts.

Mary, Mary, American comedy by Jean Kerr (1961). Written for Barbara Bel Geddes, it was a wisecracking account of a married couple breaking up and coming together again. Its basic appeal was such that it became the fifth longest-running play in Broadway's history.

The Mask of Virtue (*Die Marquise von Arcis*), German play by Carl Sternheim (1918). An eighteenth-century pastiche, drawn from Diderot and Prévost's *Manon Lescaut*, it was adapted by Ashley Dukes and served as the true London debut of Vivien Leigh (1935).

Massary, Fritzi (Friederike Massarik, 1882–1969), Austrian actress and singer. Seasoned in Viennese revue, she became the glittering star of musical comedy and operetta at Berlin's Metropol-Theater, and set the styles. In 1916 she married the comedian Max Pallenberg, who worked with her in Reinhardt's productions of *Die Fledermaus* and *La Belle Hélène*. In 1933 she left Germany and came to the U.S. in 1938, settling into the German colony in Los Angeles.

Massey, Raymond (1896–1983), Canadian actor and director. The gaunt, cavernous-voiced actor made his Broadway debut in Norman Bel Geddes' *Hamlet*, and was used primarily in classics, although he was also seen as *Ethan Frome* (1936), Harry Van in *Idiot's Delight* (1938), and his most memorable role, *Abe Lincoln in Illinois* (1938). After several Shavian roles, he played God, i.e. Mr. Zuss in *J.B.* (1958).

The Master Builder (*Bygmester Solness*), Norwegian drama by Henrik Ibsen (1892). Master builder Solness, who has made a successful career of building homes, suffers a guilty conscience and fears the younger generation. A teen-aged girl Hilde Wangel inspires him to higher things, quite literally, and he dies attempting to put a garland on the tower of his new edifice.

Maugham, William Somerset (1874–1965), English playwright. He was already a successful novelist when his first play came to the stage in 1904, and by 1908 he had four hits running in the West End of London. The audacious society comedies include *Our Betters* (1917), *The Circle* (1921), and *The Constant Wife* (1927). But he was also a dab hand at melodrama set in the exotic East: *Rain* (1921), *East of Suez* (1922) and *The Letter* (1927).

Maxtone-Graham, John (1929–), American stage manager, son of Joyce Maxtone-Graham, author of *Mrs Miniver*.

Mayr, Richard (1877–1935), Austrian bass-baritone. He made his debut as Hagen at the Bayreuth Festival in 1902, and was with the Vienna Opera from 1907. His outstanding performances ranged from portentous (Sarastro in *The Magic Flute*; Gurnemanz in *Parsifal*) to rakish (Leoporello in *Don Giovanni*). For Strauss, he created Barak in *Die Frau ohne Schatten* and was a Falstaffian Baron Ochs in *Der Rosenkavalier*.

McClintic, Guthrie (1893–1961), American director. Although he received plaudits for his staging of *The Old Maid* (1935) and *Winterset* (1935), his career is inextricably bound with that of Katharine Cornell, whom he married in 1921. He carefully staged and promoted all the plays in which she appeared, making sure that, while surrounded by strong casts, she was the audience's focus at all times.

McCormick, Myron (Walter, 1907–62), American actor. A Princeton graduate, who toured with a medicine show, he made his Broadway debut in 1932. With a barking voice and a face like a beagle's, he was in demand in military roles on stage (*South Pacific*) and in films (Sgt. King in *No Time for Sergeants*, 1958). He was constantly active in radio and television.

McCullers, Carson (Smith, 1917–67), American playwright. Primarily a novelist in the Southern Gothic vein, she came to Broadway with the dramatization of *The Member of the Wedding* (1950), which launched Julie Harris's career.

McGuire, Dorothy (1916–2001), American actress. She became a star as the selfish child bride in *Claudia*, first on Broadway (1943) and then on film (1945), which bred a sequel *Claudia and David*. She was most often seen in melodrama (*The Spiral Staircase*, 1946) and comedy (*Mister 880*, 1950), but was best as the harrassed mother in *A Tree Grows in Brooklyn* (1945). Mothers then became her line of business.

McKenna, Siobhán. See the headnote to Chapter 26, "Shaw and the actor".

Meader, George (1888–1963), American tenor. He made his operatic debut as the Steersman *The Flying Dutchman* (Leipzig, 1910), and at the Stuttgart Opera troupe (1912–19), he created Scaramouche in the world premiere of *Ariadne auf Naxos*. He joined the New York Metropolitan in 1921, singing Max in *Der Freischütz*, Mercutio in *Roméo et Juliette*, Loge in *Das Rheingold* and Tamino in *The Magic Flute*. A big success in *Boccaccio* (1931) with Maria Jeritza convinced him to move to musicals and operettas. In the 1940s and 50s, he played character roles in film and television.

Measure for Measure, English comedy by William Shakespeare from Cinthio and Whetstone (pub. 1623). While the Duke of Vienna pretends to be on vacation, Angelo, his puritanical deputy, institutes moral reform legislation to clean up the dissolute city. When novice Isabella comes pleading for the life of her brother, condemned to death for lechery, Angelo's lust overcomes his prudence. This requires the disguised Duke to set things aright. Dark in its humor and scamped in its denouement, it is a rich panoply of bad behaviour.

Medea, American tragedy by Robinson Jeffers from a play by Euripides (1947). Cleaving closely to Euripides' original, Jeffers provided a sinuous English that sounded right in the mouths of modern actors. Judith Anderson, who created the part (opposite John Gielgud as Jason) made Medea her signature role, and revived it on several occasions. In old age, she played the Nurse to Zoë Caldwell's Medea.

Mei Lan-fang. See headnote to Chapter 33, "Mei Lan-Fang".

Meisner, Sanford. See headnote to Chapter 8, "Seven interviews in search of good acting".

The Member of the Wedding, play by Carson McCullers from her novel

(1950). The title character is the adolescent Frankie (Julie Harris), who daydreams about going with her soldier brother on his honeymoon. Set in a small Southern town during a steamy summer, its other main characters are the one-eyed cook Bernice (a brilliant performance by Ethel Waters) and a prissy little boy (Brandon De Wilde). Its tone is one of strained nerves in a heat wave.

Men in White, play by Sidney Kingsley (1933). An idealistic medical intern is torn between surgical research and a lucrative practice. This modern take on the love *vs* duty theme won popularity because of its choreographed scenes set in an operating room. It got the Group Theatre out of debt, and convinced many that Lee Strasberg's version of the Method worked.

Mendl, Gregor (1822–84), German geneticist. The abbot of an Augustinian monastery, he investigated hybridity and heredity in plants, especially peas. His Laws of Heredity coined the terms "recessiveness" and "dominance".

Mendl, Lady (Elsie de Wolfe, 1865?–1950), American interior decorator. She made her stage debut in 1890, acted with the Empire Stock Company and founded her own troupe. In 1903, she retired to recreate herself as "the inventor of interior decoration", promoting bright colors and Louis XV furnishings. In 1926 she broke off a long lesbian relationship with the powerful theatrical agent Elizabeth Marbury to marry Sir Charles Mendl.

Menken, Helen (1901–66), American actress. A versatile player much in demand, she had roles in 1926 that touched on the outré: the 300 year-old heroine of *The Makropoulous Secret* and the married lesbian Irene in *The Captive*. She is best remembered for her Queen Elizabeth to Helen Hayes' *Mary of Scotland* (1933) and as the married sister, opposite Judith Anderson, in *The Old Maid* (1935). She produced the Stage Door Canteen series for the American Theatre Wing during the Second World War.

Mephisto, short for Mephistopheles, the satanic emissary in the various versions of the Faust legend, from Marlowe to Gounod. Although Goethe gave him stature as "the spirit that negates", in later avatars he is usually nothing more than a wise-cracking bravo with a cock's feather in his cap.

The Merchant of Venice, English comedy by William Shakespeare from Boccaccio and Fiorentine (1597). Two plot lines are advanced: the Jew Shylock demands a pound of flesh from the merchant Antonio if he defaults on his loan; and the heiress Portia of Belmont will choose her husband from the suitor who chooses the correct casket. As Antonio's friend and Portia's lucky wooer, Bassanio straddles both plots, and Portia extricates the merchant from his peril. From the eighteenth century on, star performances of Shylock dominated the play, upsetting its artistic balance.

Mercury Theatre, New York. A repertory company founded by Orson Welles and John Houseman in 1937 when they were let down by the Federal Theatre Project. A remarkable acting company – which included Joseph Cotten, Martin Gabel, Norman Lloyd and Geraldine Fitzgerald – performed a ribald *Shoemaker's Holiday*, *Heartbreak House*, a modern dress *Julius Caesar* which pointed up parallels with fascism, and *Danton's Death*, against a wall of heads. It folded in 1938, just as Welles was launching a conflation of Shakespearean history plays called *Five Kings*.

Merivale, Philip (1886–1946), India-born English actor. He arrived in the U.S. with Mrs Patrick Campbell in *Pygmalion* (1905) and later toured with George Arliss in *The Merchant of Venice* (1922) and *The Swan* (1923). He was a reliable leading man, especially in costume drama, for which he had the legs.

The Merry Wives of Windsor, English comedy by William Shakespeare (pub. 1602). Allegedly written because Good Queen Bess wanted to see Falstaff in love, it rather reduces the fat knight. However, as the Bard's only comedy set on his home territory, it offers delightful glimpses of middle-class Elizabethan life. Mrs Ford and Mrs Page were often cast from two equally famous actresses of a certain age.

Mexican Hayride, American musical comedy by Herbert and Dorothy Fields and Cole Porter (1944). Set in a synthetic Mexico, this inflated revue offered opportunities for the comic Bobby Clark. It was filmed in 1948 as a vehicle for Abbott and Costello.

Meyerhold Theatre, Moscow. As the RSFSR Theatre 1, under the guidance of Vsevolod Meyerhold, it opened in November 1920 in the massive Zon Playhouse on Triumphal Square to house "revolutionary tragedy and revolutionary clown shows". As the herald of "Theatrical October", it suffused entertainment with propaganda, and exchanged the usual elegant theatre décor for bare platforms and unpainted wood, while the actors performed without wigs or make-up, as in *The Magnanimous Cuckold* and *Tarelkin's Death* (both 1922). In 1923 it was renamed the Meyerhold Theatre. Artistic differences led to Meyerhold creating the Meyerhold Studio, which developed into an autonomous theatre.

Meyerhold, Vsevolod Emilievich (1874–1940), Russian actor and director. A charter member of the Moscow Art Theatre, he played two Chekhov roles before touring Russia with his own company (1902–5). At Vera Kommissarzhevskaya's theatre, he experimented with highly stylized symbolistic forms and theorized about a "theatrical theatre". The first director to become a Bolshevik, after the Revolution he was the most powerful and influential stage worker, promoting constructivist design and biomechanical acting. When Socialist Realism became the official style, he fell from grace, was accused of treason and shot.

Michelangelo (correctly, Michelagniolo di Lodovico Buonarroti, 1475–1564), Italian artist and poet. For Lorenzo di Medici, he created his *Battle of the Centaurs*, for Cardinal San Giorgio the *Pietà*. The *David* was carved from a single block of marble. Pope Julius II commissioned him to paint the ceiling of the Sistine Chapel; Pope Leo X rehired him to finish it. His sonnets were dedicated to a noble youth.

Miller, Arthur (1915–2005), American playwright, whose work breathes a spirit of revolt against injustice and the stifling of human potential. Two of his plays – *Death of a Salesman* (1949) and *The Crucible* (1953) – are accepted as indisputable masterpieces. A handful of others – *All My Sons* (1947), *A View* *from the Bridge* (1955), *After the Fall* (1964) and *The Price* (1968) – are considered stageworthy and interesting. The rest have rarely been revived after their premieres.

Millstein, Gilbert. See headnote to Chapter 14, "Maureen Stapleton".

Milton, Ernest (1880–1974), American actor. A Shakespearean, noted for his King John, he performed largely in England, and was admired by Olivier. He was extremely mannered, causing James Agate to say his Allmers in *Little Eyolf* recalled Bunthorne. He created the role of Rupert Cadell in Patrick Hamilton's *Rope*.

Milton, John (1608–47), English poet. Milton's connection to the theatre is to be found in his courtly masque *Comus* and in his chamber play *Samson Agonistes*, whose preface advises that tragedy be written along ancient Greek lines.

Mino da Fiesole (*c*.1429–84), Florentine sculptor. A comrade of Desiderio da Settignano, he ornamented tombs and altar pieces with his delicate portraits and decorative moldings.

The Miracle (*Das Mirakel*), German spectacle by Karl Voelmoeller with music by Engelbert Humperdinck (1910). Based on the same legend as Maeterlinck's *Soeur Béatrice* of a nun who runs away to the world and whose place in taken by a statue of the Virgin Mary, it was a pretext for a lavish production by Max Reinhardt. To house it and its seething crowds, he converted the London Olympia to a Gothic cathedral and did the same in New York in 1924 with the help of Norman Bel Geddes. It became traditional to cast the Madonna with a society beauty, such as Lady Diana Manners, rather than an actress.

The Miracle of St Anthony, Belgian one-act play by Maurice Maeterlinck (1903). In this satire on middle-class morality, the saint arrives to bring to life the dead Hortensia. He is ridiculed by her relatives and the priest, and believed only by the maid. When he does succeed in reviving Hortensia, she insults him and he is declared insane. Vakhtangov staged a memorable production with his students in Moscow (1921).

Les Misérables (*The Scum of the Earth*), novel by Victor Hugo (1862). This massive epic of the spiritual and material progress of the escaped convict Jean Valjean is embellished with disquisitions on everything from the Battle of Waterloo to urban sewage removal. It was frequently dramatized in the 19th century, and then made as silent films (1909, 1912, 1918, 1924). In the sound era Valjean has been interpreted by Harry Bauer (1933), Fredric March (directed by Boleslavsky, 1935), Michael Rennie (1952), Jean Gabin (1957), and Jean Paul Belmondo (modernized, 1995).

Mister Roberts, an American comedy by Thomas Heggen and Joshua Logan, based on Heggen's short stories (1948). A loose-knit account of a U.S. naval vessel cruising through the Pacific as the war goes on somewhere else, it proved to be hugely popular. Part of this was due to the public's conviction that the U.S. military was a benign institution, partly to Henry Fonda's appealing performance as the easy-going lieutenant.

Moby Dick, American novel by Herman Melville (1851). The saga of Captain Ahab's quest to kill the great White Whale would seem to resist adaptation to the stage, but it was attempted by P. Oettly in 1949 and by Orson Welles in 1955. Welles wrote his own sermon when he appeared as Father Marple in John Huston's 1956 film.

A Modern Virgin, American play by Elmer Blaney Harris (1931). Notable as the debut of Margaret Sullavan, this mildly distasteful comedy concerns a spoiled 16-year-old girl whose older fiancé decides she needs to be "educated" (read "deflowered") by a worldly novelist. The "morning after" scene was considered shocking at the time.

Molière (Jean Baptiste Poquelin, 1622–73), French actor and playwright. Provincial touring prepared him to bring his troupe to Paris, where it eventually set up at the Palais Royal. Despite court intrigue and religious intolerance, he enjoyed the protection of King Louis XIV. His plays range from *commedia*-inspired farces (*Sganarelle*, 1660) to prose comedies (*The Miser*, 1668; *The Would-be Gentleman*, 1671) to brilliant verse satires (*The School for Wives*, 1663; *The Misanthropist*, 1666; *Tartuffe*, 1667) to musical extravaganzas (*Psyché*, 1671).

Molyneux, Captain Edward Henry (1891–1974), English fashion designer. After study with the London designer Lucile and losing an eye in the First World War, he opened his own house in Paris in 1916. His "New Look" was distinguished by elegantly tailored suits, pleated skirts and evening gowns. His clientele ranged from royalty and high society to Hollywood stars such as Greta Garbo and Vivien Leigh, and he formed Christian Dior and Pierre Balmain.

Monterey, Carlotta (Hazel Neilson Taasinge, 1898–1970), American actress. With European training, she auditioned in New York under a stage name that reflected her swarthy, exotic looks and played a few roles in forgettable plays (1915–24). When she met and married Eugene O'Neill, she became his muse and manager, moving him to California for his health. After his death, she was keeper of the flame, releasing unperformed plays to favored directors.

Montserrat, American play by Lillian Hellman from a French play by Emmanuel Roblès (1948). In 1812 Venezuela, the young Spanish officer Montserrat is hiding the rebel Bolivar. To get him to talk, his colonel threatens to shoot six innocent townspeople. A talky melodrama, it was directed by Hellman herself with Emlyn Williams as the villainous officer.

Moore, Erin O'Brien (1902–79), American actress. She made her New York debut at 15, and played the daughter in *Street Scene* (1929) 800 times on Broadway and the West End. Brought to Hollywood in 1934 to re-create the role, she was replaced by Sylvia Sidney. Her most memorable movie role was Nana in *The Life of Emile Zola* (1937). Following plastic surgery to correct burns from a restaurant fire, she continued as a character actress on stage and television.

Morgan, Frank (Francis Philip Wupperman, 1890–1949), American actor. His roles ranged from elegant boulevardiers to confused businessmen, usually found in comedy, musical or not. After appearing in the revue *The Band Wagon* (1931), he became a much-used character actor at MGM, best remembered as *The Wizard of Oz* (1938).

Morgan, Henry "Harry" (Henry Bratsburg, 1915–), American actor. After he performed with Frances Farmer in Mt Kisco summer stock, she got him an audition with the Group Theatre, and he played two years as Pepper White in *Golden Boy*. He also was cast in Saroyan: *My Heart's In the Highlands* and *Hello, Out There!* An unreleased film of the latter led to a movie contract, playing wise-cracking comic relief or thugs, eventually moving to military men and sheriffs. He later had featured roles in twelve successful television series (1954–85).

Morley, Robert (1908–92), English actor and playwright. After time with J. B. Fagan's Oxford company, he made a West End hit as Oscar Wilde (1936), and was the London Sheridan Whiteside in *The Man Who Came to Dinner* (1941), which capitalized on his girth and his fruity delivery. Other commercial successes were his own domestic tragedy *Edward, My Son* (1947) and the French comedy *The Little Hut* (1954). His stage career pales in comparison to his more varied film appearances.

Morphy, Paul Charles (1837–84), American chess master. A child prodigy, he was internationally famous by the age of 21 and retired in 1859. His technique was versatile, but often used the open position and the sacrifice of the Queen to achieve checkmate.

The Mortal Storm, American film directed by Victor Saville but credited to Frank Borzage (1940). The title refers to the looming Nazi peril. James Stewart and Margaret Sullavan carry on their love affair in a small German town, inhabited by such Teutonic types as Frank Morgan, Maria Ouspenskaya and Ward Bond.

Moscow Art Theatre. See headnote to Chapter 39, "Stanislavsky to his players".

Moscow Art Theatre 2 (*Moskovskii Khudozhestvennii Teatr Vtoroi*). In 1924, the Art Theatre First Studio was reopened under this name, reviving some earlier productions. Its first new show, *Hamlet*, with Mikhail Chekhov the artistic director (1924–28) in the lead, was hailed by the public and the profession. It maintained an exciting repertory, although the Communist press regularly attacked it for "aestheticism" and "eclecticism". In 1928 internal dissension led to Chekhov's emigration. The theatre became a pedestrian showcase for Soviet hackwork and was liquidated in 1936.

Moscow Art Theatre Musical Studio. Vladimir Nemirovich-Danchenko founded it in 1919–20, to apply Art Theatre methods to the production of opera and musical comedy; he insisted on the psychological truth of the acting and the historical accuracy of the designs. Its first productions (1920–25), which all toured abroad, were *The Daughter of Mme Angot*, *La Périchole*, *Lysistrata*, *Carmencita and the Soldier*, and an Aleksandr Pushkin evening. In 1926 it became the Nemirovich-Danchenko Musical Theatre, and moved to darker works, with *La Traviata* (1934) and the controversial premiere of Dmitry Shostakovich's *Lady Macbeth of the Mtsensk District* (1936).

Moser, Hans (Johann, 1880–1964), Austrian actor. With a background in circus, variety and cabaret, he entered the Theater in der Josefstadt, Vienna, in the mid-1920s, and was promoted by Max Reinhardt as the ideal of Austrian comedy. His mixture of farce, sentimentality and irony was featured in Impertinence in *The Great Salzburg World Theater* (1924), Tartaglia in *Princess Turandot* (1926), Bottom in *A Midsummer Night's Dream* (1927), and the jailer Frosch in *Die Fledermaus* (1929). After the war, he was in demand as a character actor.

Moskvin, Ivan Mikhailovich (1874–1946), Russian actor. A charter member of the Moscow Art Theatre from 1898, he created the title role in *Tsar Feodor*, an engimatic Luka (*The Lower Depths*, 1902), the child-like Rodé (*Three Sisters*), a ludicrous Epikhodov (*The Cherry Orchard*, 1904), and a pathetic Captain Snegirëv (*The Brothers Karamazov*, 1910). When he toured the U.S. (1923–4), the impresario Morris Gest and Max Reinhardt tried to get him to defect, to no avail.

Mounet-Sully, Jean (1841–1916), French actor. With his symmetrical physique and leonine hair and beard, he was the ideal classical tragedian at the Odéon, Paris (1872–4) and the Comédie-Française from 1874. He was noted for his intense concentration and musical voice. Once he had played Racine's Oreste, Oedipus, Othello or Hamlet (with Sarah Bernhardt as Ophelia), no other French actor tried to compete.

Mourning Becomes Electra, an American trilogy based on Aeschylus's *Oresteia* by Eugene O'Neill (1931). The House of Atreus becomes the New England Mannon family at the end of the U.S. Civil War. Playing for five hours, with an interval for dinner, it was produced by the Theatre Guild with Alla Nazimova as Christine/Clytemnestra, Alice Brady as Lavinia/Electra, and Earl Larrimore as Orin/Orestes.

Much Ado about Nothing, English comedy by William Shakespeare from Bandello (1598). Set in Messina, the intrigue plot, marring the romance of Claudio and Hero, is less important than the characters. Beatrice and Benedick are the best of Shakespeare's bantering lovers, and Dogberry a fruity portrait of idiocy in office. In performance the play is almost foolproof.

Murder in the Cathedral, English poetic drama by T. S. Eliot (1935). Thomas à Becket, saintly archbishop of Canterbury, knows that King Henry II is sending knights to kill him. Despite the enticements of Tempters, Becket goes to his martyrdom. In an epilogue inspired by Shaw's *St Joan*, the four knights explain to the audience their reasons. The first production was directed by E. Martin Browne, with Robert Speaight as Becket.

Murnau, F[riedrich] W[ilhelm] (Plumpe, 1888–1931), German film director. A dominant presence in Weimar movie-making, he created the classic vampire film *Nosferatu* (1922), the intertitle-less *Der letzte Mann* (*The Last Laugh*, 1925), and a sumptuous *Faust* (1926). He came to Hollywood, but achieved only the exquisitely atmospheric *Sunrise* (1926), the acrobatic *Four Devils* (1928), the naturalistic *City Girl* (1930) and the South-Seas semi-documentary *Tabu* (1931), before dying in an auto accident.

Murray, Gilbert (1866–1957), English classicist. One of the first great popularizers of Greek drama in English, he provided translations of Euripides for the Barker-Vedrenne management of the Court Theatre (1904–7). It was his version of Sophocles' *Oedipus the King* that Max Reinhardt staged in London. He was a friend of Bernard Shaw, who is supposed to have modelled Adolphus Cusin in *Major Barbara* on him.

Museum of Modern Art, New York. Conceived by a trio of wealthy women, it opened in 1929 and finally won the favour of the public with a Van Gogh exhibition in 1935, followed by a Picasso retrospective in 1939–40, having moved to its present location on West 53rd Street. It was the first art museum to institute a film department and is also famous for its photographic holdings.

Musical Chairs, English play by Ronald Mackenzie (1932). Produced by John Gielgud and directed by Theodore Komisarjevsky, this "tragic farce" was called by James Agate "the best first play by any English playwright during the last 40 years". With Roger Livesey and Margaret Webster in the cast, it contained some of the most conspicuous gay characters of the time.

My Fair Lady, American musical comedy by Alan Jay Lerner and Frederick Loewe, based on G. B. Shaw's *Pygmalion* (1956). The familiar tale of the Cockney flower girl transformed into a well-spoken "lydy" got a radical makeover. Ornamented by Rex Harrison's *Sprechstimme*, Cecil Beaton's costumes, Stanley Holloway's music-hall delivery and Hanya Holm's carefully integrated choreography, it broke records by running for 2,717 performances.

My Life in Art (*Moya zhizn v iskusstve*). Konstantin Stanislavsky's autobiography was cobbled together under daunting circumstances during the Moscow Art Theatre's tours to the U.S. in 1923–4. It was first published in English by Little, Brown, in 1924. Stanislavsky, aided by the critic Lyubov Gurevich, then rewrote it thoroughly to address a Soviet Russian audience (1926).

My Heart's in the Highlands, American play by William Saroyan (1939). Directed by Robert Lewis for the Off-Broadway Group Theatre, it was a fantastic allegory of the victimization of artists by their communities. Despite this contrarian theme, it enjoyed a reasonable success.

Myerberg, Michael, American producer, noted for his outrageous promotions. His productions of *The Skin of Our Teeth* (1942) and *Lute Song* (1946) were respected, but his play *Dear Judas* was threatened with a Boston ban (1947). He booked the first U.S. production of *Waiting for Godot* (1956) into a Miami theatre as "the laugh riot of two continents", fired Alan Schneider as its director, and later staged an all-black version (1957). His production of *Compulsion* (1957) was bedevilled with lawsuits and counter-suits. He conceived the first New York discothèque but failed to secure Andy Warhol as its nightly attraction.

Napoleon I (Bonaparte, 1769–1821), French general and emperor. His career, beginning as a Corsican officer at the siege of Toulon, moving through his romance with a Creole widow, European victories, assumption of an imperial title, retreat from Moscow, exile, return and re-exile, was irresistible to playwrights and screenwriters. Shaw wrote *The Man of Destiny* as a riposte to

Sardou's *Madame Sans-Gêne*. The actors who have played Napoleon are a mixed bag, as varied as Richard Mansfield, Henry Irving, Charles Boyer and Marlon Brando.

Nash, Ogden (1902–71), American poet. Popular for his audacious rhymes and run-on lines, he contributed the lyrics to *One Touch of Venus* (1943), *Two's Company* (1952) and *The Littlest Revue* (1956). He also appeared as a quiz-show panelist on U.S. television.

Nathan, George Jean (1882–1958), American critic, whose reviews and essays appeared in a wide variety of publications. Outspoken and colourful in his language, he began with a highbrow stance, campaigning for European modernists and deploring the American theatre's crudeness. As the American drama matured with playwrights he approved of such as O'Neill and Saroyan, he began to praise popular entertainment at the expense of pretentious sophistication.

National Anthem, American play by J. Hartley Manners (1922). In this attack on the debauchery of modern youth, jazz, denounced as "the modern man's Saturnalia" and a threat to civilization, is called the "new national anthem". His wife Laurette Taylor starred, and Manners himself appeared as a waiter.

Native Son, play by Paul Green and Richard Wright from Wright's novel (1941). Bigger Thomas is an African-American delinquent, at odds with the white world; the murder of his boss's daughter brings him to the electric chair. Orson Welles directed Canada Lee in the leading role, but audiences were not ready for this confrontational production.

Natwick, Mildred (1908–94), American actress. Even as a young woman, she was cast as matrons and eccentrics, from Queen Elizabeth to the befuddled spirit medium Madame Arcati in *Blithe Spirit* (1941). Her last major role was the winded Mrs Banks in *Barefoot in the Park* (1963).

Nazimova, Alla. See the headnote to Chapter 53, "The actor attacks his part: Nazimova".

Ned McCobb's Daughter, American comedy by Sidney Howard (1926). Carrie McCobb, proprietor of a small New England diner, falls in with a gang of rum-runners, but outwits them and comes out on top.

Neher, Carola (1900–42), German actress, sister of Caspar. In the 1920s she played in many Berlin venues, but is most closely associated with Brecht, as Polly in *Der Dreigroschenoper* (1928), Hallelujah-Lillian in *Happy End* (1929), and Johanna in *St Joan of the Stockyards* (1932). Athletic, sunny, unsentimental, she emigrated when the Nazis came to power, and joined the German colony Engelsk in the Soviet Union (1933–7). With her compatriots she was branded a Trotskyite (1937) and was exiled to a camp in Siberia where she died.

Neher, Caspar (1897–1962), German scene designer. From childhood, a close friend and collaborator of Bertolt Brecht, who called him "the greatest scenographer of our time"; he designed Brecht's *In the Jungle of Cities* (1923), *Edward II* (1924), *Baal, Mann Ist Mann* (both 1926), *Mahagonny* (1927) and *Die Dreigroschenoper* (1929). After the war, he was house artist for the Berliner Ensemble. He was also an outstanding designer of opera. His stage was anti-illusionistic, using sets and costumes to accompany, not to illustrate; his scenery was therefore relatively uncluttered and schematic.

Neilson, Julia (1868–1957), English actress. She made her name in W. S. Gilbert's plays *Broken Hearts* and *The Wicked World* and with Beerbohm Tree at the Haymarket, where she met Fred Terry, whom she married. As a team they toured (1900–30) in such warhorses as *The Scarlet Pimpernel*, *Sweet Nell of Old Drury* and *Henry of Navarre*.

Neilson-Terry, Phyllis (1892–1977), English actress, daughter of Julia and Fred Terry. She came on stage under her father's management, achieving success as Viola in *Twelfth Night*. After starring in New York in a new production of *Trilby* (1915) and acting in many Shakespearean revivals, she went on the vaudeville stage and played Principal Boy in pantomimes.

Nelson, Ruth (1905–92), American actress. A charter member of the Group Theatre, she acted in many of its most important productions: Essie in *The House of Connelly* (1931), Edna in *Waiting for Lefty* (1935), Sister in *Johnny Johnson* (1936), Belle Stark in *Rocket to the Moon* (1938) and Miss Kirby in *Thunder Rock* (1939). She appeared in a few films (*Of Human Bondage*, 1934; *The North Star*, 1943), but after she married director John Cromwell (1946), her stage and screen appearances became rarer.

Nemirovich-Danchenko, Vladimir Ivanovich (1858–1943), Russian playwright, director and pedagogue. A prize-winning dramatist at the time he co-founded the Moscow Art Theatre in 1898 with Stanislavsky, he was in charge of the theatre's literary side and promoted Chekhov and Gorky as house authors. In an attempt to remain topical, he championed the plays of Andreev and adapted Dostoevsky's novels. After the Revolution, he founded a musical studio (1919), which toured the U.S. and whose most important creation was Shostakovich's *Lady Macbeth of Mtsensk* (1934). For a year he was on salary for MGM in Hollywood, with nothing to show for it, and worked in Italy and Germany (1931–3). In 1940 he revived *Three Sisters* as socialist optimism.

The New School for Social Research, New York, a university founded in 1919 as "a progressive institution of learning for adults", under the leadership of the historian Charles Beard, the economist Thorsten Veblen and the philosopher John Dewey. In 1933 the University in Exile and the École Libre des Hautes Études were opened to house émigré scholars fleeing persecution in Europe. The Frankfurt School of critical theory had a strong influence, and Erwin Piscator taught and directed there for many years, introducing ideas of political theatre developed in Weimar Germany.

The New Yorker, American weekly magazine, founded in 1925 by Harold Ross, who announced that "it is not edited for the old lady in Dubuque". It soon became known for its lively cartoons (Peter Arno, Helen Hokinson, Charles Addams), acerbic reviewing (Robert Benchley, Dorothy Parker), and colourful reportage of local and foreign phenomena (Joseph Mitchell, A. J. Liebling, Janet Flanner). Its fiction, occasionally innovative (James Thurber, John Hersey, J. D. Salinger, Donald Barthleme), usually tended to the safely suburban.

Newsweek, American weekly news magazine, the rival and runner-up to *Time*. It was founded as *News-Week* in 1933, and provides reportage, commentary and reviews. It is thought to be more liberal in its politics than its competition.

Nickleby, Nicholas, the stalwart hero of Dickens' eponymous novel (1838–9) does a stint as romantic lead in a barnstorming acting troupe, run by Vincent Crummles.

Night Music, American play by Clifford Odets (1940). Uncharacteristic of its author, it was an optimistic account of a Hollywood messenger boy's trip to New York. The Group Theatre did not produce it, but the Broadway premiere featured Group actors: Morris Carnovsky, Elia Kazan and Jane Wyatt.

No Time for Comedy, American comedy by S. N. Behrman (1939). Self-referential to a degree, it concerns a comic playwright trying to write a serious play at the behest of a flighty socialite. In the original production, Katharine Cornell and a young Laurence Olivier made an engaging couple.

Noé (*Noah*), French play by André Obey (1931). Written for the Compagnie des Quinze, this is an updated, slangy version of the Genesis story of the Flood. Noah follows divine directives, builds an ark, fills it with his sons and their wives, and survives the deluge. However, he is continually undermined by his children, especially his sarcastic son Ham, and berated by his demented wife. At the end, as he tries to build a house, a rainbow appears. An English translation directed by Michel Saint-Denis was one of John Gielgud's earliest successes (1939).

Nosferatu, eine Symphonie des Grauens, German film directed by F. W. Murnau from Bram Stoker's *Dracula* (1922). Murnau reset this, a founding movie of the horror genre, in early nineteenth-century Bremen, and drew close physical parallels between the master vampire and his attendant rats. It was superfluously remade by Werner Herzog as *Nosferatu: Phantom der Nacht* (1979).

Nugent, Elliott (1899–1980), American actor and playwright. A long record of ups and downs in playwriting culminated in a hit collaboration with James Thurber, *The Male Animal* (1940). He played the embattled professor himself, and followed up this success as the soldier on leave in *The Voice of the Turtle* (1943).

Ober, George (1849–1912), American actor. A seasoned player of old men, he appeared as Ebenezer Goody in the Broadhurst farce *What Happened to Jones* (1897) and in two roles in *A Temperance Town* (1900). In 1901 he played vaudeville as Rip Van Winkle, with projected scenes of Joseph Jefferson's interpretation behind him. He also appeared in early silent film comedy (1912).

Oberon, Merle (Estelle Marie O'Brien Thompson, 1911–79), India-born English actress, who went to great lengths to conceal her mixed-race heritage. Her career took off in British film, under the aegis of Alexander Korda, and then with Samuel Goldwyn (*The Dark Angel*, 1935). Despite damage to her face from an auto accident and cosmetic poisoning, she enjoyed success as

Cathy in *Wuthering Heights* (1939) and George Sand in *A Song to Remember* (1945).

Obey, André (1892–1975), French playwright. House dramatist for the Compagnie des Quinze (1929–31), he wrote for them the folk parable *Noé* with its anthropomorphic beasts, and *Le Viol de Lucrèce* and *La Bataille de la Marne*, which modernized the Greek chorus (all 1931).

O'Casey, Sean (1880–1964), Irish playwright. Half-blind, from a working-class background, he drew on the streets of Dublin and their political uprisings for material in his successes at the Abbey Theatre, *Shadow of a Gunman* (1922), *Juno and the Paycock* (1925) and *The Plough and the Stars* (1926). He then began to dabble in expressionism, symbolism and more strident anti-establishment sentiments in *The Silver Tassie* (1929); *Within the Gates* (1934) and *Cock-a-doodle Dandy* (1949). *Purple Dust* (1945) enjoyed a long run in New York.

Odets, Clifford (1906–63), American actor and playwright. When he had a hit with the labour agitation one-act *Waiting for Lefty* (1935), the Group Theatre, previously uninterested, adopted him as their house dramatist. He provided them with effective ensemble and propaganda plays, couched in an artificial language that sounded as if it came from the streets: *Awake and Sing!* (1935), *Golden Boy* (1937), *Rocket to the Moon* (1938). When Hollywood came calling and he answered the call, his friends complained he had sold out, a feeling he shared and expressed in *The Big Knife* (1949).

Oedipus Rex, Latin title of *Oidipus tyrannos* (*Oedipus the King*), tragedy by Sophocles (*c*.450 B.C.E.) The people of Thebes call on their king, Oedipus, to rid them of the plague. When Oedipus investigates the cause – the murderer of the previous king has gone unpunished – he discovers that fate has led him to kill his father and wed his mother. He puts out his eyes and banishes himself. Tightly structured, with taut suspense and language full of significant puns, this play served as Aristotle's example as the perfect tragedy.

Of Human Bondage, English novel by W. Somerset Maugham (1915). Partially autobiographical, it traces the early career of an orphaned, handicapped artist and physician, who has a tempestuous relationship with a venal Cockney waitress Mildred. The moral is that only gradually does a life reveal a pattern as intricate as that of a Turkish rug. The novel was filmed in 1934 with Leslie Howard as the hero and Bette Davis as the ravening bitch, and, rather irrelevantly, in 1946 (Paul Henreid, Eleanor Parker) and 1964 (Laurence Harvey, Kim Novak).

Offenbach, Jacques (1819–80), German-born French composer and cellist. As manager of the Bouffes Parisiens from 1855, he experimented with minor forms which culminated in the satiric, scintillating *opéra bouffe*. His masterpieces – *Orpheus in the Underworld* (1858), *La Belle Hélène* (1864), *Blue Beard, La Vie Parisienne* (both 1866), *The Grand Duchess of Gerolstein* (1867) – were the world's most popular shows for three decades. His opera *The Tales of Hoffmann* (1880) was left unfinished and produced posthumously.

Oh, Kay!, American musical comedy by Guy Bolton, P. G. Wodehouse, and George and Ira Geshwin (1926). Written to promote Gertrude Lawrence as a star, it enabled her to sing "Someone to Watch Over Me", "Clap Yo' Hands" and "Do, Do, Do". The story was topical, shaped around rum-runners and their federal nemeses.

Oklahoma, American musical comedy by Richard Rodgers and Oscar Hammerstein II from a play by Lynn Riggs (1943). Despite doubts and fears, this upbeat version of *Green Grow the Lilacs* proved to be a profitable and durable classic. Those unfamiliar with *Show Boat* claim it as the first integrated musical because song and dance all contributed to the story; it also laid down the matrix for later Rodgers and Hammerstein works. It was not filmed until 1955.

Old Acquaintance, American film directed by Vincent Sherman from a screenplay by John Van Druten et al. from his play (1943). Two novelists, played by Bette Davis (noble and idealistic) and Miriam Hopkins (meretricious and commercial), spend 20 years fencing in their writing careers and their love lives. It was remade pointlessly by George Cukor in 1981 as *Rich and Famous*.

The Old Maid, American play by Zoë Akins, based on Edith Wharton's novel (1935). Set in the nineteenth century, it concerns an unmarried woman who allows her illegitimate daughter to be raised by her married cousin as her own. The critics were outraged when this tearjerker won the Pulitzer Prize and founded the Drama Critics' Circle Award to prevent future abuses. As a film it provided a vehicle for Bette Davis and Miriam Hopkins.

Old Vic, London, short for the Royal Victoria Theatre, the name bestowed on the Coburg in 1833. Originally a minor theatre specializing in bloody melodramas, it went through a period as a music hall, both wet and temperance, before Emma Cons and her niece Lillian Baylis took it over. Under Baylis, it became a Shakespearean theatre: its compact size made it a favourite with actors. Its most memorable seasons were 1944–6 when Laurence Olivier and Ralph Richardson produced *Richard III*, *Cyrano de Bergerac*, *Oedipus Rex*, *The Critic*, *Henry IV*, *Peer Gynt* and *Uncle Vanya*. The Vic housed the National Theatre company, under Olivier, before its permanent house was built.

Olesen, Oscar E. (1916–), American manager. From 1952 to 1981, he served as general manager on a host of Broadway productions, both revivals and premieres, with a remarkable number of hits, including *Bus Stop* (1955), *Separate Tables* (1956), *The Visit* (1958), *A Man for All Seasons* (1961) and *A Texas Trilogy* (1976).

Olivier, Laurence. See headnote to Chapter 24, "The Oliviers" and Chapter 25 "Sir Laurence and Larry".

Olympia, Hungarian comedy by Ferenc Molnár (1928). In the pre-war days of the Habsburg empire, a Hussar is insulted by a young widowed princess. He takes revenge by making her think him a confidence man and she offers him a night of love to avoid a scandal. The New York production, considerably less scabrous, featured Fay Compton and Laura Hope Crews as the princess and her cigar-smoking mother. Filmed as *His Glorious Night* in 1929, it damaged John Gilbert's career by revealing his high-pitched voice.

On the Evils of Tobacco (*O vrede tabaka*), Russian monologue by Anton Chekhov (1886, 1898, 1901, 1902). A henpecked but pompous husband attempts to deliver an anti-smoking harangue, but in the process exposes his appalling private life. Six distinct variants exist of this monologue, the more serious changes concomitant with the greater depth of psychology of Chekhov's works throughout the 1890s. It was first performed by the writer Aleksandr Kuprin at a private club in Moscow in September 1901.

One Night in Rome, American play by J. Hartley Manners (1919). One of his less successful vehicles for his wife Laurette Taylor, it has a faintly Jamesian theme of American innocence abroad. Taylor also starred as "L'Enigme" in the silent-film version (1924).

One Touch of Venus, American musical comedy by Kurt Weill, Ogden Nash and S. J. Perelman from a novel by F. Anstey (1943). A barber inadvertently brings a statue of Venus to life, and has to live with the consequences. Of its songs, only "Speak Low" has had a shelf life, but it perpetuated Agnes De Mille dream ballets as integral to musicals. It was filmed in 1948 with Ava Gardner as the goddess.

O'Neil or **O'Neill, Barbara** (1909–80), American actress. She began acting with the University Players on Cape Cod, founded by Joshua Logan, who married her. After time on Broadway in the 1930s, she came to Hollywood to appear in *Stella Dallas* (1937). After a series of forgettable roles, she was cast as Scarlett O'Hara's mother in *Gone with the Wind* (1939) and was then stylishly murdered by Charles Boyer in *All This and Heaven Too* (1940). Further Broadway appearances include *Little Moon of Albans*.

O'Neill, Eugene (1888–1953), American playwright. Owing to his prolific output, perfervid emotionalism and experimentation in a wide variety of styles, O'Neill is accepted as America's greatest playwright. He is infuriating in his contradictions: turgid but eloquent, overwrought but sincere, awkward but effective. He was associated with the Provincetown Players, the Greenwich Village Theatre, and the Theatre Guild, which assured his plays strong first productions. The plays drawn from his own life, published only posthumously, are among his most powerful: *Long Day's Journey into Night* (1956) and *A Moon for the Misbegotten* (1956). Abroad, he was an acquired taste, much produced in Soviet Russia and Sweden.

O'Rear, James (1914–2000), American actor. After an apprenticeship at the Westport, Conn., Playhouse and a brief stint with Orson Welles' Mercury Theatre (*The Shoemakers' Holiday, Julius Caesar*, 1938), he joined the Group Theatre to play Rufe Apley in *My Heart's in the Highlands* (1939). He served in the army during the war, and afterwards played mainly in film and television (1947–75), with an appearances in *Chinatown* (1974).

Oregon Shakespeare Festival, founded in Ashland in 1935 to produce the Bard in an Elizabethan playhouse. It later added an indoor theatre for modern plays and an experimental stage. It has managed to work its way through the Shakespearean canon twice, in 1958 and in 1978.

Orff, Carl (1895–1982), German composer. His clamorous settings of the medieval poems of roving monks, the trilogy *Carmina Burana* (1937), *Catulli Carmina* and *Trionfo di Afrodite* are now staples of the concert hall. The Nazis condemned them as "decadent art", but he worked for them, replacing Mendelssohn's music to accompany *Midsummer Night's Dream* with his own.

Orpheus Descending, American play by Tennessee Williams (1957). A reworking of his *Battle of Angels*, it has a modern-day Orpheus, the guitarist Val, descending into the underworld of a Southern small town, where he clashes with the corrupting Lady and is befriended by the reformer Carol.

Osborne, John (1929–94), English dramatist. *Look Back in Anger* (1956) is taken to be the opening salvo of the "Angry Young Man" attack on the British establishment, and was followed by another lament for England in decline, *The Entertainer* (1957). After *Luther* (1961), *Inadmissible Evidence* (1964), and the unlicensed *A Patriot for Me* (1965), his many plays devolved into distasteful displays of misogyny and ill temper.

Othello, English tragedy by William Shakespeare from Cinthio (1604). Othello, a Moorish general in the pay of Venice, secretly marries a senator's daughter Desdemona. On the isle of Cyprus, his jealousy is aroused by his villainous ensign Iago, and he murders Desdemona and, disabused, himself. This most compact of the Bard's tragedies has a misunderstanding plot most common to comedy. With the exception of Ira Aldridge, the role of Othello was a white man's preserve until Paul Robeson assumed it. Now it is almost totally the province of actors of color.

O'Toole, Peter (1932–), Irish actor. A graduate of RADA (1952–4), he was gaining a reputation as one of England's best and sexiest Shakespearean actors at the Bristol Old Vic and the English Stage Co. when he was cast as T. E. Lawrence in the film *Lawrence of Arabia* (1962). Despite his movie stardom, he continued to perform on stage: Hamlet under Olivier's direction for the National Theatre (1963), *Waiting for Godot* at the Abbey (1970), a disastrous Macbeth (1980), Shaw's John Tanner and Professor Higgins.

O.U.D.S., Oxford University Dramatic Society, an amateur group founded in 1885 by Arthur Bourchier, who later became a professional character actor. A guiding genius from 1940 on was the Chaucerian Nevill Coghill, succeeded by Glynne Wickham, who introduced college women in lieu of professional actresses. Peter Brook is one of many who gained his earliest experience there.

Our Town, American drama by Thornton Wilder (1938). This paean to everyday life was considered revolutionary for it was first staged with no scenery and a Stage Manager as narrator. The last act, set in a cemetery, points out the wide gap between the living and the dead, the former hasty and careless, the latter indifferent. The play's profundity is usually masked by the sentimentality of its productions.

Ouspenskaya, Maria (correctly Mariya Alekseevna Uspenskaya, 1876–1949), Russian actress and pedagogue. On tour with the Moscow Art Theatre in 1922–4, she stayed in New York and played on Broadway to 1936, but made her deepest mark as a teacher, co-founding the American Laboratory

Theatre in 1928. She settled in Los Angeles and had a secure film career, although her thick accent and wizened appearance relegated her to roles of hags, the best-remembered being the gypsy Maleva in the horror movie *The Wolfman* (1941). Among her students were John Garfield, Anne Baxter and Franchot Tone. A chain smoker, she died after a lit cigarette set fire to her bed.

Out There, American play by J. Hartley Manners (1918). Ostensibly the patriotic story of a Cockney girl who gets to do her part in the war as a nurse, a role Taylored for Laurette, this was an all-star benefit for the Red Cross. So the second-act hospital scene contained a mass of types played by George M. Cohan, Chauncey Olcott, James T. Powers and George Arliss. It ran a week on Broadway, before touring for three weeks.

Outward Bound, English drama by Sutton Vane (1923). A representative miscellany of types is trapped on a fogbound ship. Gradually, they realize that they are all dead and headed for eternity. One young couple is allowed to return to life. The play is one of many post-First World War fantasies which treat the possibility of cheating death. It was filmed in 1930 with Leslie Howard.

Over the Top, American revue by Philip Bartholomae and Harold Atteridge, with music by Sigmund Romberg at al. (1917). A Shubert extravaganza staged at the 44th Street Roof Garden, it headlined Fred and Adele Astaire.

Oxford Playhouse, last provincial English theatre to be built before the Second World War, opened in 1938 with J. B. Fagan's adaptation of Pepys' diaries, *And So to Bed*, and housed his outstanding company of actors. About to close in 1956, because of dwindling audiences, it was resuscitated briefly by the Meadow Players and was totally refurbished in 1963.

Paar, Jack (1918–2004), American television host. Experience as a radio announcer in Cleveland, an entertainer for the USO in the Pacific, and the host of daytime TV shows equipped him to be the temperamental, improvising compère of the late-night *Tonight Show* (1957–62), quickly renamed *The Jack Paar Show*. Flanked by such favourite guests as "dumb Dora" Dody Goodman and the artist Alexander King, he was prone to fits of weeping, anger and uncontrollable laughter.

Pabst, Georg Wilhelm (1885–1967), German film director. He began as an actor and did not turn to film until after the First World War. The silent films of his Weimar period were masterpieces of both social commentary (*Streets of Sorrow*, 1925) and expressionist psychosis (*Pandora's Box*, 1928). The Nazi ascent to power drove him to France, where he directed *Don Quixote* with Fyodor Chaliapin, but he returned to Germany in 1939 to make two films under the Nazis, and after the war filmed an exposé of anti-Semitism, *The Trial* (1948).

Pal Joey, musical comedy by Alan Jay Lerner and Frederick Loewe (1951). Considered an anomaly because of its protagonist's amorality, it chronicles the exploits of a heel with several kinds of woman. Its memorable numbers include "I Could Write a Book" and "Bewitched, Bothered, and Bewildered".

Palgrave, Francis Turner (1824–97), English poet and critic. He is remembered less for his own works than for his ground-breaking anthologies, *The Golden Treasury of Lyrical Poetry* (1875) and *Sonnets and Songs of Shakespeare* (1877).

Pallenberg, Max (1877–1934), German comedian. He was Max Reinhardt's favourite comic actor and for him played many roles at the Deutsches Theater, Berlin, from 1914, especially a pathetic Menelaus in *La Belle Hélène* and Argan in The *Imaginary Invalid*. Married to the operetta diva Fritzi Massary, he also starred in comic opera (Koko in *The Mikado*). He was the lead in Erwin Piscator's *Good Soldier Schweik* and created *Liliom* on the German stage.

Papp, Joseph (Papirofsky, 1921–92), American producer. After serving as managing director of the Actor's Laboratory in Hollywood (1948–50) and stage-managing the road company of *Death of a Salesman*, he set up as a director in New York. His Shakespearean Theatre Workshop (1952) grew into the New Shakespeare Festival (1960), which spun off the Public Theatre (1967), dedicated to new American plays. He was the most daring and enterprising producer in New York, nurturing musicals (*Hair*), experimental work and multicultural art, whose occasional successes subsidized the rest.

Paradise Lost, American play by Clifford Odets (1935). The effects of the Depression on a lower middle-class family and their circle are traced through the responses of a variety of characters. This domestic drama was written with the actors of the Group Theatre in mind, and thus works best as an ensemble exercise for an established company.

Parks, Larry (Samuel Klusman Parks, 1914–75), American actor. After a few years in stock companies, he signed a contract with Columbia Pictures in 1941 and was cast in the lead of *The Jolson Story* (1946), followed by *Jolson Sings Again* (1949). The curse of this role was exacerbated by his being forced to testify before the House Committee on Un-American Activities, the only actor of the original 19 to be called. He was blacklisted, and he and his wife Betty Garrett had to return to the stage (*Teahouse of the August Moon*, *Any Wednesday*).

Parrish, Maxfield (1870–1966), American artist. The highest-paid illustrator of his time, he proliferated advertisements, hotel murals, children's books, magazine covers. His highly saturated cobalt blues were a trademark feature of his fanciful medieval scenes and pastoral landscapes.

Partisan Review, American magazine (1934–2003). This literary-political quarterly was progressive but anti-Communist in sympathies, issued by the John Reed Club to supplant the Communist *New Masses*. It was an organ of the Jewish intelligentsia (Philip Rahv, Saul Bellow, Leslie Fiedler, Delmore Schwartz, Isaac Bashevis Singer, Susan Sontag) and exercised considerable influence in the 1950s and 1960s.

The Party, English play by Jane Arden (1958). Described as "sex-drenched", it concerns people who dissipate their considerable energies and talents in exercising their libidos. Albert Finney had one of his first West-End leads in it, with support from Charles Laughton and Elsa Lanchester.

The Passing Show, an American revue which pioneered the form. The first edition opened in 1894, and in 1912 the Shuberts revived the name to compete with Ziegfeld. They presented one annually till 1924 (barring 1920). Featured players included the comedians Willie and Eugene Howard and Ed Wynn, and Fred and Adele Astaire.

Pasteur, Louis (1822–95), French bacteriologist. His experiments in preventing the toxic effects of micro-organisms eventuated in a treatment for hydrophobia. The Warner Brothers film *The Life of Louis Pasteur* was one in a series of biopics to feature Paul Muni in the roles of great humanitarians.

Paulsen, Harald (1895–1954), German actor. Best known for creating the role of Mack the Knife in the original production of *Die Dreigroschenoper* (1928), he also played in 20 silents and 90 sound films.

Pavlova, Anna (1885–1931), Russian dancer. After some time in Diaghilev's Ballets Russes, featured in the choreography of Michel Fokine, she established her own touring company. There she limited herself to a handful of balletic showcases, especially *The Dying Swan* (1907). Her iconic status as prima ballerina provoked unending parody from Fannie Brice to Imogene Coca down to the Gloxinia Ballet in our own day.

Paxinou, Katina (Ekaterina Konstantopoulo, 1900–73), Greek actress. A member of the Greek National Theatre, often directed by her husband Alexis Minotis, she perpetuated a tradition of impassioned and almost chanted Greek tragedy, especially as Electra. Her classical qualities shone through such modern roles as Mrs Alving in *Ghosts* and Christine Mannon in *Mourning Becomes Electra*.

Payne, Ben Iden (1881–1976), English actor and director. After work with Frank Benson, he came to the U.S. in 1913 to direct for Charles Frohman. He moved to educational theatre, heading the drama school of the Carnegie Institute of Technology, the Goodman Theatre in Chicago, and the Department of Drama at the University of Texas. Shakespeare in a quasi-Elizabethan setting was his speciality and he directed at several American Shakespeare festivals.

Peg o' My Heart, comedy by J. Hartley Manners (1912). Written by Manners to demonstrate the talents of his wife Laurette Taylor, it tells of a simple Irish girl trying to adapt to the expectations of her aristocratic relations. The play chalked up 6,000 performances by 1918, and Taylor wound up playing it over 1,000 times herself.

Percy, Esmé (1887–1957), English actor. After work with Benson and Granville-Barker, he staged 140 plays for the troops during the First World War, and then became part of the ReandeaN team. He was the pre-eminent Shavian actor of his time, playing John Tanner, Androcles, Dubedat, Higgins and King Magnus, and, despite an aura of preciosity, had a remarkable range, from Hamlet to Humpty Dumpty.

Perkins, Anthony (1932–92), American actor. Slender, boyish son of the actor Osgood Perkins, he was typed as sensitive youths: Tom Lee in *Tea and Sympathy*, Eugene Gant in *Look Homeward, Angel* (1957) and the hero of the Amish musical *Greenwillow* (1960). Most of his later New York stage work was trivial compared to his busy Hollywood career. He could never live down being Norman Bates in *Psycho*, so embraced it and specialized in troubled, indeed mentally unbalanced, protagonists.

Peter Pan, English fantasy by James M. Barrie (1904). Peter, "the boy who would not grow up", lives in Never Land with the Lost Boys and the fairy Tinker Bell, always at daggers drawn with the pirate Captain Hook. An episode with Wendy as his "mother" remains inconclusive. It was originally meant as a Christmas pantomime, and producer Charles Frohman imposed the idea of a girl as Peter. It has undergone so many adaptations and reinterpretations over the years – musical comedy, animated cartoon, sequels, prequels – that its main features have become ingrained in English-language folklore.

The Petrified Forest, American play by Robert Sherwood (1933). Set in a gas station *cum* diner in Arizona near the Mexican border, it brings together a variety of sensibilities and uses the eruption of fugitive gangsters as the catalyst. Leslie Howard as the poet *manqué* and Humphrey Bogart as the killer on the run played to their strengths.

Phèdre, French verse tragedy by Jean Racine (1677). This adaptation of Euripides' *Hippolytos* is Racine's most intense play, packing all manner of passion into the tight constraints of neoclassic unities and the rhymed alexandrine. Phaedra is the testing role for French actresses, passed with flying colours by Rachel, Bernhardt and Marie Bell.

Phidias (fifth century B.C.E.), Athenian sculptor. Superintendent of public works under Pericles, he designed and commissioned the Propylaea and the Parthenon, and may have sculpted the gold and ivory Athena. Accused of stealing the gold and carving his own head on it, he was banished from Athens.

Phoebus, Latin spelling of Greek *phoibos*, "the resplendent", a metonym for the sun god Apollo. Later mythologies make a distinction between Phoebus the sungod and Phoebus Apollo, the god of music and poetry.

Picasso, Pablo (1881–1973), Spanish artist. After a blue period (1902–4) depicting gaunt paupers and a pink period (1904–6) portraying circus performers, he became the universal metonym for Cubist with *Les Demoiselles d'Avignon* (1906–7). Partnered with Jean Cocteau, he designed sets and costumes for Diaghilev's Ballets Russes (1917–24) and wrote a couple of avant-garde plays (*Desire Caught by the Tail*). *Guernica* (1937) went beyond his leftist sympathies to express outrage at all wars.

Pinero, Sir Arthur Wing (1855–1934), English playwright. He gave up careers as a lawyer and an actor to become a highly popular and prolific dramatist. His farces – *Dandy Dick* (1887), *The Schoolmistress* (1886), *The Magistrate* (1888) and *The Gay Lord Quex* (1899) – are full of fun. Shaw scorned his attempts at the Ibsene problem play *The Second Mrs Tanqueray* (1893) and *The Notorious Mrs Ebbsmith* (1895). However, the nostalgic *Trelawney of the "Wells"* (1898), the social comedy *The Thunderbolt* (1908) and the proto-Proustian *The Princess and the Butterfly* still deserve a hearing.

Pioneers in Ingolstadt (*Pionere in Ingolstadt*), German comedy by Marieluise Fleisser (1928). In a small town in Bavaria, the presence of the militia, come to repair a bridge, wreaks havoc on the stolid lives of the citizens. Heavily rewritten by Bertolt Brecht, the play emphasizes the selfishness and sexism of both soldiers and civilians, and the scene of a deflowering created a scandal. Peter Lorre was featured in the first production which was attacked by the Nazis.

Pirandello, Luigi (1867–1936), Italian writer. Although his early fiction was naturalistic depictions of Sicilian life, he is best known for teasing the contrast between truth and illusion in his plays. The very titles: *Right You Are! (If You Think So)* (1918), *Six Characters in Search of an Author* (1921) and *Each in His Own Way* (1924) proclaim the provisional nature of reality. The tenuousness of identity is fully explored in *Henry IV* (1922), whose modern-day protagonist cannot determine whether or not he is a Holy Roman Emperor.

Piscator, Erwin. See headnote to Chapter 8, "Seven interviews in search of good acting".

Pitts, ZaSu (in full Eliza Susan, 1894–1963), American actress. In silent film from 1914, she was discovered by Erich von Stroheim, who crafted her into a brilliantly sensitive character actress in *Greed* (1924), *The Wedding March* (1928) and *Walking Down Broadway* (1933). Others saw her primarily as a comedienne and capitalized on her staring eyes and fluttering hands; partnered with Thelma Todd, she won great popularity in the 1930s.

A Place in the Sun, American film directed by George Stevens from the novel *An American Tragedy* by Theodore Dreiser (1951). Following the original story, it depicts a working-class youth embroiled with a socialite and a factory-girl, whose accidental but willed death puts him in the dock for murder. Montgomery Clift, Elizabeth Taylor and Shelley Winters were outstanding as the central triangle.

Platt, Livingston (1885–1933/9?), American designer. Artistic director of the Toy Theatre of Boston, he introduced ideas of the New Stagecraft. Much of his work, in the style of Gordon Craig, was done for Margaret Anglin's classical revivals. He was also capable of providing realistic settings for such Broadway fare as *Rain* (1922), *Grand Hotel* (1930) and *Dinner at Eight* (1933). His death-date is uncertain, because he disappeared after an arrest on a morals charge.

The Playboy of the Western World, Irish comedy by J. M. Synge (1907). Coming to a village in County Mayo, farmboy Christie Mahon claims to have killed his father. This makes him a hero with the locals, especially its eligible women, but the arrival of the far-from-dead father alters the situation. The less-than-flattering portrait of Irish character and filthy words like "shift" caused riots during the first production at the Abbey Theatre, Dublin, and they were repeated when the Abbey toured America in the 1920s.

Playfair, Sir Nigel (1874–1934), English actor-manager. Experience with Benson, Tree and Harley Granville-Barker prepared him to make the Lyric Theatre, Hammersmith, into one of the most popular playhouses in London

(1918–32). A revival of *The Beggar's Opera* won a devoted following, and was succeeded by other comedies of manners, revues and even *The Insect Play*.

Plummer, Christopher (1929–), Canadian actor, father of Amanda. Had he been born in England, he might have been knighted, for his career resembled that of the leading British Shakespeareans. He played the leading classical roles throughout the English-speaking world.

Poel, William (1852–1920), English actor-manager. After professional ventures managing the Old Vic and stage-managing for Frank Benson, he founded the Elizabethan Stage Society, to revive not only Shakespeare but also other Tudor and Stuart playwrights. Poel staged them in halls relatively uncut, with amateur actors, minimal to no scenery, Elizabethan costume, and occasional attempts at period pronunciation. Shaw was an admirer.

Point Valaine, English melodrama by Noël Coward (1935). The owner of a hotel in the British West Indies is in thrall to a brute of a head waiter, who, when she falls in love with a young aviator, spits in her face, slashes his wrists and throws himself to the sharks. Lynn Fontanne and Alfred Lunt were stuck playing these impossible parts, while Osgood Perkins enjoyed the Cowardly role of a know-it-all novelist.

Polyeucte, French verse tragedy by Pierre Corneille (1643). Polyeucte, a convert to Christianity in third-century Armenia, aspires to martyrdom and manages to win over his wife Pauline and her father, the Roman governor Félix, to his faith. He even persuades his wife's former lover Sévère to cease the persecutions.

Ponto, Erich (1884–1957), German actor. He was a seasoned player of Shakespeare, Hauptmann and Strindberg when he created Peachum in *Die Dreigroschenoper* (1928). A humanistic comedian, he was also famous for his Mephisto (1928) and Willy Loman (1950). He had a serious film career from 1930, often playing physicians and scientists, and appears in *The Third Man* (1949) and *Lola Montez* (1955).

Porgy and Bess, American "folk opera" by Dubose Heyward and George and Ira Gershwin from a play by Dubose and Dorothy Heyward (1935). The Theatre Guild, which produced the original play in 1937, took a chance on this original combination of ambitious music and folk vernacular, with an all-black cast. Received coolly at the time, it is a fixture in the operatic repertoire.

Portman, Eric (1903–69), English actor. In 1924 he joined Henry Baynton's touring company, and by 1928 was playing Romeo at the Old Vic. He had great success in the West End and on Broadway, but after he entered films in 1933 he was best known for his performances of damaged souls and disturbed personalities, especially in the films of Michael Powell and Emeric Pressburger. He returned to the stage as the disreputable major in *Separate Tables* (1954).

Poston Tom (in full, Thomas Gordon, 1921–2007), American actor. After becoming an airforce captain, he studied acting in New York and had a quiet career until he became known as the terrified, dim-witted "Man in the Street" on the Steve Allen television show in the 1950s. He appeared in a number of Broadway shows (*Will Success Spoil Rock Hunter*, 1955; *The Golden Fleecing*, 1959; *Mary, Mary*, 1961; *A Funny Thing Happened on the Way to the Forum*, 1971), but was most at home on television game shows and situation comedies.

Pound on Demand, A Irish one-act farce by Sean O'Casey (1947). A drunken Dubliner attempts to withdraw a pound from his postal savings account.

Price, Vincent (1911–93), American actor. While studying art at the Courtauld Institute in London, he auditioned for a part at the Gate Theatre and was cast in *Chicago* (1935). As Prince Albert in *Victoria Regina*, first in the West End, then on Broadway (1935–7), he gained a reputation and joined Orson Welles' Mercury Theatre (1938). A stab at movie stardom was interrupted for three years while he played the villainous husband in *Angel Street* (1941–44). On his return to Hollywood, he became typed as a heavy, which continued in a series of camp horror movies from the 1950s through the 1980s.

Priestley, J[ohn] B[oynton] (1894–1984), English novelist and playwright. His plays frame questions of the relativity of time and space within the conventions of the drawing-room comedy and the thriller: *Dangerous Corner* (1932), *Time and the Conways*, *I Have Been Here Before* (both 1937), *Johnson Over Jordan* (1939), *An Inspector Calls* (1946).

Princess Turandot. See *Turandot*.

Pritchard, Hannah (1711–68), English actress, who came to Drury Lane from fairground theatres as a comedienne. She partnered Garrick when he joined the company, and became his Lady Macbeth and Gertrude. Corpulent and staid, she was admired for her exquisite diction.

Private Lives, English comedy by Noël Coward (1931). A divorced couple meet during their honeymoon with others and run off together. This slimmest of premises, decked out in staccato dialogue, has proved to be more durable than its original audiences might have thought. Devised for Coward and Gertrude Lawrence, it is regularly revived for other star couples.

Der Protagonist, a German one-act play by Georg Kaiser, with music by Kurt Weill (1920).

Proust, Marcel (1871–1922), French novelist. Snob, valetudinarian and mamma's boy, he endures because of his 13-volume meditation on the passage of time and its effect on human relations, *A la recherche du temps perdu* (1913–22). Moving through the upper echelons of French society, it subtly analyzes both outward manners and inward motivations, in sentences of slithering sinuosity.

Puente, Tito (Ernesto Antonio, 1923–2000), American musician, nicknamed "El Rey", The King. Born in Spanish Harlem of Puerto Rican parents and trained at the Juilliard School, he channelled these influences into Latin jazz and mambo. From 1948, when he formed his first band, he made more than 100 recordings, including the all-time best-selling salsa LP *Dance Mania* (1958).

Pushkin, Aleksandr Sergeevich (1789–1837), Russian poet and playwright. While in exile on his father's estate, Pushkin immersed himself in Shakespeare and composed the chronicle play *Boris Godunov* (1824–25), but it was forbidden full publication or performance in his lifetime. He made plans in 1826–27 for a number of plays, but the only ones realized were the so-called *Little Tragedies*, poetic one-act character studies of dominant emotions, *The Miser Knight*, *Mozart and Salieri*, *The Stone Guest*, a treatment of the Don Juan story; and *A Feast in Plaguetime*, allegedly based on a play by Barry Cornwall (1830). He also worked on *The Rusalka* (1832), an attempt at a folk drama.

Pygmalion, English comedy by George Bernard Shaw (1914). Henry Higgins, a professor of phonology, turns a cockney flower girl Eliza Doolittle into a fake duchess by correcting her speech. At the premiere, Herbert Beerbohm Tree played Higgins and Mrs Patrick Campbell Eliza. A minor scandal was created by the utterance of the epithet "Bloody" from the stage. The play has been somewhat eclipsed by the musical version *My Fair Lady*.

Quartermaine, Leon (1876–1967), English actor. Work with Granville-Barker helped him to become an excellent Shakespearean, who often appeared at the Stratford Memorial Theatre in mature and regal roles: Banquo, John of Gaunt, Duke of Buckingham, Cymbeline. He married the actress Fay Compton.

Quinault-Dufresne, Abraham-Aléxis (1693–1767), French actor. Member of a family of actors, he entered the Comédie-Française and soon made his mark in tragedy. Handsome, well-spoken and understated in his acting, he was also impossibly arrogant. He created Voltaire's Oedipus (1718).

Quinn, Anthony (Antonio Rudolfo Oaxaca Quinn, 1915–2001), Mexican-born American actor. In film from 1936, he had a desultory career, cast as heavies of various nationalities, so went on stage to replace Marlon Brando as Stanley Kowalski in *A Streetcar Named Desire* which he played for two years (1947–9). His film career revived when cast by Elia Kazan (*Viva Zapata!*, 1952) and Federico Fellini (*La Strada*, 1954), and reached its apogee with the has-been pugilist in *Requiem for a Heavyweight* and the Falstaffian *Zorba the Greek* (both 1962). In 1960 he played Henry II opposite Olivier's *Becket* on Broadway.

Quintero, José (1924–99), Panamian-American director, who co-founded the Circle in the Square in 1951. He concentrated on O'Neill with powerful productions of *The Iceman Cometh* (1956), *Long Day's Journey into Night* (1956), *Moon for the Misbegotten* (1973), *Strange Interlude* (1963) and *A Touch of the Poet* (1977). Disappointed by the poor reception of Tennessee Williams' *Clothes for a Summer Hotel* (1980), he abandoned New York.

Quintilian (Marcus Fabius Quintilianus, *c.*33–*c.*100), Roman rhetorician. The summation of his oratorical teachings, *Istitutio Oratoria*, 12 books of rhetorical techniques, prescribed gestures and tones of voice. It became a kind of text for actors during the Renaissance.

Racine, Jean (1639–99), French playwright. Although he wrote only a dozen plays, he is ranked as the epitome of neoclassic tragedy, compressing intense emotions into claustrophobic formats. *Andromaque* (1667), *Britannicus* (1669), *Bérénice* (1670) and *Phèdre* (1677) are masterful variations on classic themes. For the girls' school at St. Cyr, he composed the Biblical dramas *Esther* (1689) and *Athalie* (1691). He also wrote one comedy, about litigation, *Les Plaideurs* (1668).

Raffles, the Amateur Cracksman, English play by E. W. Hornung and Eugene Presbrey (1903). The novelty was having an elegant and well-behaved burglar as its hero, and it set the style for a series of "crook dramas". Gerald Du Maurier played Raffles in London, Kyrle Bellew in New York.

Rain, American drama by John Colton and Clemence Randolph, from Somerset Maugham (1922). During a monsoon on Pago Pago the puritanical Rev. Davidson manages to persuade the prostitute Sadie Thompson to repent and face a prison sentence. When he succumbs to her sex appeal, he kills himself and she and her marine boyfriend depart for Sydney. This sensational melodrama was created by Jeanne Eagels, and Joan Crawford played Sadie on film.

Rains, Claude (1889–1967), English actor. Much of his early career was spent as stage manager, and in that capacity he came to the U.S. in 1913 with Granville-Barker's company. He had an active Broadway career, then spent 20 years in Hollywood as a versatile character actor, often opposite Bette Davis, and returned to the stage in *Darkness at Noon* (1951) and *The Confidential Clerk* (1953).

Red Rust, American adaptation by Virginia and Frank Vernon (1929) of *Konstantin Terekhin* by Vladimir Kirshon and Aleksandr Uspensky (1926). Kirshon's first play, a Soviet melodrama about adolescents having trouble adjusting to the new way of life, it was offered by the Theatre Guild. The cast was full of outstanding young talents: Luther Adler, Gale Sondergaard, Lionel Stander, Lee Strasberg and Franchot Tone.

Redgrave, Sir Michael (1908–85), English actor, father of Vanessa, Lynn and Corin. Critics considered him more versatile than Gielgud, more attractive than Richardson and more introspective than Olivier. He played much the same Shakespearean roster as they, at the Old Vic and Stratford: a queeny Richard II, a sexy Antony, a cerebral Hamlet, Shylock, Prospero, Lear. A temperate believer in the Stanislavsky system, he was a superb Uncle Vanya (Chichester Festival, 1962).

Regent Theatre, London. Originally the Euston music hall, it became a legitimate playhouse in 1922. *The Insect Play* with John Gielgud as a Poet Butterfly appeared there in 1923. It eventually was turned into a cinema.

Rehan, Ada (Crehan, 1860–1916), Irish-born American actress. As a leading player in Augustin Daly's company she played over 200 comedy roles. She excelled in Shakespeare, especially as Kate in *Taming of the Shrew* and Rosalind in *As You Like It*, with a melodious voice and bell-like delivery. Lady Teazle in *The School for Scandal* was another of her triumphs.

Reignolds, Kate (in full Katherine Mary, 1836–1911), American actress. After a checkered acting career, she joined the Boston Museum company (1860–5), playing Desdemona, Juliet, Lydia Languish in *The Rivals* and leading roles in Dion Boucicault's Irish plays. She then starred in her own touring company and was instrumental in introducing Ibsen, Sudermann and Echegaray to the U.S. public.

Reinhardt, Max (Goldmann, 1873–1943), Austrian director. From 1902 to 1933, he was the very model of a modern stage director, dominating the German-speaking stage, in intimate houses, open-air arenas and vast circuses. His repertory ranged from high tragedy to comic opera, and he used every possible means – sonorous voices, gorgeous costumes, musical accompaniment, three-dimensional scenery – to provide the audience a synaesthetic experience. He emigrated to the U.S. in 1934, but, except for *A Midsummer Night's Dream*, in Hollywood, was unable to recreate his success.

Requiem for a Heavyweight, American film directed by Ralph Nelson from a teleplay by Rod Serling (1962). A punch-drunk boxer may die if he takes on another fight, but he resists the alternative of phony wrestling and decides to train younger men instead. The original version on television's *Playhouse 90* (1957) had Jack Palance as the pugilist, Keenan Wynn as his manager and Ed Wynn as his trainer. The film version had Anthony Quinn, Jackie Gleason and Mickie Rooney in those roles, with Cassius Clay in an opening fight sequence.

Reunion in Vienna, American play by Robert E. Sherwood (1931), a romantic confection about the one-night reunion of a Habsburg prince with his former mistress, now the wife of a famous psychiatrist. It served as a vehicle for the Lunts.

Revizor (known in English as *The Inspector General* and *The Government Inspector*), Russian comedy by Nikolay Gogol (1836, revised 1842). Warned that a government inspector is arriving incognito, the corrupt city fathers of a backwater town assume that a visiting penpusher from St. Petersburg is that feared official. Khlestakov, a vapid fop and braggart, is wined, dined, bribed and romanced. Gogol's comedy eschewed conventional love interest, gloried in bloated hyperbole, and organized its micro-society around non-existent entities. It was first produced in the U.S. by the Yale Dramatic Society, John Anderson wrote a version for Broadway and Michael Chekhov brought it to New York in 1935.

Rhinoceros (*Le Rhinocéros*), French play by Eugéne Ionesco (1960). Béranger, an average man in a provincial town, watches as the entire community turns into rhinoceroses. He withstands the metamorphosis and ends up alone. This transparent parable of conformity gave Zero Mostel an opportunity, as Béranger's friend Jean, for a virtuoso transformation scene in the New York production, but Olivier failed to make it work as well in the London premiere.

Rice, Elmer (Reizenstein, 1892–1967), American playwright. His first success was an almost documentary courtroom drama *On Trial* (1914) and he dabbled in Expressionism with *The Adding Machine* (1923). However, his forte was the realistic treatment of ordinary lives touched by social injustice: *Street*

Scene (1929), *Counsellor-at-Law* (1931), *We, the People* (1933). He was a regional director for the Federal Theatre Project.

Richard II, English history play by William Shakespeare from Holinshed (1595). The usurper Bolingbroke overthrows weak, narcissistic Richard II to become Henry IV. It was long believed that the play was revived in 1601 to support Essex's rebellion, but this has recently come into question. Maurice Evans successfully revived it on the U.S. stage in 1937; its best English exponents were Michael Redgrave, John Gielgud and Irish actress Fiona Shaw.

Richard of Bordeaux, English play by Gordon Daviot (1933). Written specifically for John Gielgud and covering some of the same ground as *Richard II*, it brought him to stardom during a 14-month run. The costume designers Motley also became famous. Alec Guinness saw it over a dozen times to hear Gielgud's "fabulous voice [. . .] like a silver trumpet muffled in silk".

Richardson, Sir Ralph (1902–83), English actor. With Gielgud and Olivier, one of the dominant triumvirate of the British stage in mid-twentieth century, and the best comedian of the three. Besides his toothsome Shakespearean acting (Bottom, Falstaff, Prospero, Timon of Athens), he excelled in Ibsen (Peer Gynt, John Gabriel Borkman), Rostand (Cyrano), and Priestley (*Johnson over Jordan*, 1938). He was partnered with Olivier when they ran a season at the Old Vic in the late 1940s, and with Gielgud in *The School for Scandal* (1963), *Home* (1970) and *No Man's Land* (1975).

Richardson, Tony (Cecil Antonio, 1928–91), English director. He was seasoned at the BBC before taking up directing, with a strong line in working-class angst: *Look Back in Anger* (1956; film 1959), *The Entertainer* (1957; film 1960), *A Taste of Honey* (1960; film 1961) and *Loneliness of the Long Distance Runner* (film 1962). He broke out of the gritty mould with *Tom Jones* (1963).

Richman, Harry (Harold Reichman, 1895–1972), American entertainer. He ascended from a vaudeville piano accompanist at age 18 to be a star of *George White's Scandals* and the *Ziegfeld Follies* (1931), with singing, dancing and snappy patter. His natural milieu was the nightclub, where his expansive personality had full rein.

Ricketts, Charles de Sousy (1866–1931), English designer. In reaction against realism, he insisted on pictorial allure and lush colour, evident in his earliest work for Wilde's *Salome* and *A Florentine Tragedy* (1906). He designed Shaw plays at the Court Theatre (*Don Juan in Hell*, 1907; *A Man of Destiny*; *Saint Joan*, 1924) as well as Shakespeare (*Henry VIII, Macbeth*). The public knew him best from his recostuming of *The Mikado* for the D'Oyly Carte Company.

Rin Tin Tin, German Shepherd actor (1918–32). Rescued from a bombed-out kennel in Germany, he was brought to the U.S., where he starred in 26 adventure films for Warner Brothers. One of the best is *Clash of the Wolves* (1925), in which he plays a vulpine half-breed who learns to become man's best friend. In the 1950s a new generation of "Rinties" was seen on television Westerns.

Rise and Fall of the City of Mahagonny (*Aufstieg und Fall der Stadt Mahagonny*), German "epic opera" by Bertolt Brecht and Kurt Weill (1927, revised 1929).

A band of thieves on the run founds a city to cheat gold prospectors of their gains. In the face of an oncoming hurricane, which spares the city, they abolish all restrictions. Everyone is ruined in a year and the city burns. Moral: society is based on getting and spending. The first version of Baden-Baden was thoroughly revised and staged two years later in Leipzig.

Ritt, Martin (1914–90), American actor and director. On receiving good reviews for a blackface role, Crown in *Porgy and Bess*, he joined the Federal Theatre Project as a playwright and the Group Theatre as an actor. He was a successful television director when he was blacklisted in 1951 for donating money to China. He returned to the stage, and eventually was able to make 25 films including *Hud* (1963), *The Great White Hope* and a comedy about the blacklist *The Front* (1976).

Robards, Jason, Sr. (1892–1963), American actor. Much less illustrious than his son, he made few Broadway appearances, most notably in the musical *Turn to the Right* (1917) and as John Marvin in *Lightnin'* (1918–21), whose long run blighted his future chances. He and his son worked together only once, in *The Disenchanted*, a play drawn from the life of F. Scott Fitzgerald (1958). His film career was more productive (1921–61).

Robards, Jason, Jr. See headnote to Chapter 12, "Jason Robards, Jr.".

Robert E. Lee, English play by John Drinkwater (1920). It covers the period from Lee's taking command of the Confederate army to the surrender at Appomatox. A series of tableaux rather than a dynamic drama, it has all the appeal of a waxworks.

Roberta, American musical comedy, by Otto Harbach and Jerome Kern from a novel by Alice Duerr Miller (1933). An American football player inherits his aunt's Parisian fashion house, Roberta, and falls in love with its forewoman, who turns out to be a Russian princess. Its enduring number is "Smoke Gets in Your Eyes". It was filmed in 1935 with Fred Astaire and Ginger Rogers.

Robinson, Lennox (1886–1958), Irish actor and playwright. Closely associated with the Abbey Theatre as dramatist and director, he was equally deft at tragedy (*Patriots*, 1912; *The Dreamers*, 1916) and comedy (*The White-Headed Boy*, 1916; *Drama at Inish*, 1933). More than Yeats or Lady Gregory, he had a finger on the pulse of change in Irish life, and reflected it in his work.

Robson, Dame Flora (1902–84), English actress. In her early years, she was cast as sexually driven women: Abbie Putnam in *Desire Under the Elms* (1931), Mary Paterson in *The Anatomist* (also 1931) and Ella in *All God's Chillun* (with Paul Robeson, 1933). As she aged, she thrived in character parts, as sympathetic spinsters (*The Corn Is Green*, 1938) or formidable matrons (Paulina in *The Winter's Tale*, 1951).

Rocco and His Brothers (*Rocco i suoi fratelli*), Italian film directed by Luchino Visconti (1960). A late entry in the neo-realism stakes, it charts the decline and fall of a peasant family transported to the big city. Typically, Visconti pumps up the emotional quotient until it reaches operatic proportions.

Rock Me Julie, American play by Kenneth Raisbeck (1931). The title comes from an African-American folk song, and the play's own folksy qualities failed to help it run more than a week, despite performances from Helen Menken and Paul Muni.

Rocket to the Moon, American play by Clifford Odets (1938). Another Group Theatre effort, directed by Harold Clurman, it was focused tightly on the marital woes of a dentist.

Roger Bloomer, American play by John Howard Lawson (1923). His first experiment in jazz-vaudeville, it is an expressionistic chronicle of a young man's life, fraught with adolescent anxiety. In depicting the inhumanity of urban capitalism, there was a scene in an office with waxwork-like clerks in cubicles and a final dream sequence in a jail cell. Henry Hull played the title role and John Dos Passos praised it strongly.

Rogers, Ginger (Virginia Katherine McMath, 1911–95), American actress and dancer. She had a brief vaudeville and comedy career as a hoofer before she made her Hollywood acting debut as Anytime Anny, a wise-cracking chorus girl in *42nd Street* (1933: "The only time she said no was when she didn't hear the question"). Her strictly professional partnership with Fred Astaire (1933–9) made "Fred and Ginger" metaphoric for smooth teamwork.

Romains, Jules (Louis-Henri-Jean Farigoule, 1885–1972), French playwright and novelist. As staged and played by Louis Jouvet, his *Knock* (1924) became a perennial hit. It satirizes national hypochondria as a road to fascism. His later plays, also championed by Jouvet, were less popular, although *M. de Trouhadec saisi par la débauche* (1925) found an audience in Soviet Russia. His adaptation of Stefan Zweig's adaptation of *Volpone* (1928) was produced worldwide.

The Roman Spring of Mrs Stone, American film directed by José Quintero from Tennessee Williams' novella (1961). A widowed actress, adrift in decadent Rome, takes up with a gigolo, loses her head and eventually her life. Compensation for the soap-operatics comes from the casting: Vivien Leigh as the foolish lady, Warren Beatty as the toy boy and Lotte Lenya as a pandering parasite.

Romeo and Juliet, English verse tragedy by William Shakespare from Bandello and Brooke (*c*.1595). The tale of star-crossed lovers from the feuding clans of Montague and Capulet had a brief period of neglect in the seventeenth century, but thereafter never left the stage, even with an ending rewritten by David Garrick. The balcony scene is proverbial even to those who never read or saw the play.

Room Service, American farce by John Murray and Allen Boretz (1937). Set entirely in a hotel room, it depicts the frantic attempts of a producer and his colleagues to get a play subsidized and opened before they are evicted.

Roscius Quintus (126?–62 B.C.), Roman actor. A slave who managed to become a freeman and a citizen through the phenomenal success of his performances, he was alleged to make the equivalent of ten million dollars a year. Excellent at both comedy and tragedy, he trained Cicero in elocution. His name became equivalent to "superb actor", so that Master Betty was deemed "the young Roscius" and Edwin Forrest "the Bowery Roscius".

The Rose Tattoo, American play by Tennessee Williams (1951). Serafina, a full-figured, full-blooded Sicilian, carries a torch for her dead husband, but it is extinguished by the lusty truck-driver Alvaro Mangiacavallo. The play's insistent muskiness is muffled by its blatant symbolism. Williams wanted Anna Magnani for Serafina, but settled for Maureen Stapleton (Magnani played it on film).

Rossellino, Antonio (1427–*c*.1479), Florentine sculptor, brother of the architect Bernardo. His portrait busts and reliefs were much in demand, but he also produced more monumental pieces, such as tomb of the Cardinal of Portugal (1466).

Der Rosenkavalier (*The Knight of the Rose*), Austrian "comedy for music" by Richard Strauss and Hugo von Hofmannsthal (1911). In the Vienna of Maria Theresa, the mature Marschallin is having an affair with young Octavian, but knows she must give him up to a younger fiancée. With exquisite words set exquisitely and a famous anachronistic waltz, the opera features three sopranos as its leading voices, one of them in a breeches role.

Rostand, Edmond (1868–1918), French playwright, whose lush poetic dramas were always received with acclaim. His first success, the short comedy *Les Romanesques* (1894) was later adapted as the musical *The Fantasticks. La Princesse Lointaine* (1895), a Maeterlinckian fairy tale, starred Sarah Bernhardt, but his enduring masterpiece was *Cyrano de Bergerac* (1897), created by Coquelin. Bernhardt made an international hit out of *L'Aiglon*, about Napoleon's son (1900) and Coquelin impersonated the lead in the barnyard fable *Chantecler* (1910).

Rowe, Nicholas (1674–1718), English playwright. His tragedies – *The Fair Penitent* (1703) and *Jane Shore* (1714) – achieved popularity, because his blend of the heroic and the pathetic appealed to a new bourgeois audience. His lachrymose heroines were always more sinned against than sinning.

The Royal Family, American comedy by George S. Kaufman and Edna Ferber (1927). This play about the acting family of the Cavendishes is a loosely veiled take-off of the Barrymores: Fanny (Mrs John Drew and Georgiana), Julie (Ethel) and Tony (John). Stripped of this topical element, it is pretty thin fooling.

Royal Academy of Dramatic Arts (RADA), London, founded by Sir Herbert Beerbohm Tree in 1904. Its premises in Gower Street contain a full-scale stage, rebuilt in 1952. It is largely subsidized by the royalties from *My Fair Lady*, since Shaw had bequeathed part of his estate to it.

Royal Court Theatre, Sloane Square, London. Opened in 1888 by the comedienne Mrs John Wood, it earned its popularity with Pinero farces and Martin-Harvey's novelettish *A Cigarette-maker's Romance* (1901). J. E. Vedrenne and Harley Granville-Barker made it a byword for innovative productions of Shakespeare and Shaw (1904–07). Later, it housed Barry Jackson's Birmingham Repertory. In 1959 the English Stage Society managed by George Devine opened it to the "Angry Young Man" movement, with the plays of John Osborne and John Arden. It has remained a home for cutting-edge drama ever since.

Royde-Smith, Naomi (1875–1964), English novelist. The wife of the actor Ernest Milton, she wrote the play *The Private Room* (1934).

Rudolph of Habsburg (1858–89), Crown Prince of Austro-Hungary. Son and heir of Emperor Franz Joseph, he and his mistress carried out a suicide pact at a hunting lodge. This was the so-called Mayerling tragedy.

Rutherston, Albert Daniel (Rothenstein, 1884–1954), English painter and stage designer. For Harley Granville-Barker, he provided a series of simplified sets for *The Winter's Tale* and *Androcles and the Lion* (1913).

Russian Ballet. See **Ballets Russes**.

Ryder, Alfred Pinkham (1847–1917), American painter, member of the Society of American Artists with whom he exhibited his oneiric landscapes (1878–87). His *Death on a Pale Horse*, executed in jaundiced yellows, is one of the spookiest paintings of the nineteenth century.

Saint Joan, drama by George Bernard Shaw (1923). Shaw's revisionist view of Joan of Arc as a flawed human being (and proto-Protestant), exploited by Church and State, a gifted amateur threatened by the professional establishment. Sybil Thorndike created the role in London, and Alisa Koonen appeared in the constructivist production by the Kamerny Theatre in Moscow. Siobhán McKenna made a personal triumph of it in 1953–7.

Saint-Denis, Michel (1897–1974), French director and pedagogue. A nephew of Jacques Copeau, he helped form the Compagnie des Quinze and direct *Noé*. An English version with Gielgud in 1935 established his career in London, where he staged *Three Sisters* and *Oedipus* with Olivier, and founded the Theatre Studio. He came to North America in 1957 as an expert on theatrical training and was later recruited to head the Juilliard School at Lincoln Center. His Copeauian principles include developing the actor as a well-rounded human being.

Salomé, drama by Oscar Wilde (1892). This lapidary version of the Biblical episode of Salome dancing to obtain the head of John the Baptist from Herod was written in French for Sarah Bernhardt. Banned in England until 1931, it was first performed in France in 1896; Richard Strauss set it as an opera and Salome dances became popular in vaudeville. Alisa Koonen played it at the Kamerny Theatre.

Salvini, Tommaso (1829–1916), Italian actor. Regarded by many, including Shaw and Stanislavsky, as the greatest actor of the nineteenth century, he did not make his reputation until he began touring outside of Italy. His tempestuous, almost bestial Othello was his standby role, but he also played Hamlet (with a soup-strainer moustache), Lear, Macbeth, Alfieri's Saul, and Corrado the wretched outlaw in Giacometti's *La morte civile* (1861).

Saroyan, William (1908–81), American playwright. Supported by the Group Theatre and the Theatre Guild, his first play *My Heart's In the Highlands* (1939) set the tone for his future works: realism tempered with fantasy and an indomitable optimism about the goodness of the average guy. *The Time of*

Your Life (1939), with its colourful assortment of bar-room denizens, has been frequently revived, which was not the case with his later plays.

Saturday Night and Sunday Morning, English film directed by Karel Reisz from a screenplay by Alan Sillitoe (1960). A prime example of the cinematic New Wave in the U.K., set as usual in a factory town (Nottingham here), this offers Albert Finney as the Angry Young prole, fed up with the options his drab life offers. Having made the most of his weekend, he prepares to settle into petty-bourgeois limbo.

Scarface, American film directed by Howard Hawks from a screenplay by Ben Hecht et al. (1932). A great gangster picture, based on the career of Al Capone, it offered Paul Muni one of his best roles as the amoral, instinctual Chicago bootlegger. The film reaches Jacobean heights by its suggestion of incest between the brute and his sensitive sister. The drug-fuelled remake with Al Pacino (1983) heightened the sadism, with no perceptible improvement.

Scarpia, the head of the Roman secret police in Sardou's *La Tosca*. He tortures the diva's lover Mario to gain information and is killed by her. In Puccini's opera, *Tosca*, the role is composed for a bass.

Schalk, Franz (1863–1931), Austrian conductor. A student of Anton Bruckner, he popularized his teacher's music. He was music director of the Vienna State Opera (1918–29), often in collaboration with Richard Strauss, whose *Die Frau ohne Schatten* he premiered (1919). Instrumental in establishing the Salzburg Festival, he is quoted as saying: "Every theatre is a madhouse, but an opera theatre is an incurable ward."

Schildkraut, Rudolph (1862–1930), Rumanian-born Austrian actor, father of Josef. A leading member of Reinhardt's team in Berlin, he was considered the finest Shylock on the German-speaking stage (1905, 1913), terrifying in his anger and anguish. His King Lear (1908) and Mephisto (1909) were also exceptional. In New York he founded his own Yiddish theatre (1925) and played in English from 1922.

Schiller, Johann Christoph Friedrich von (1759–1805), German poet and playwright, an immoveable fixture in German culture, whatever the regime. His early plays – *The Robbers* (1781), *Fiesco* (1783) and *Love and Intrigue* (1784) – are fiery, fervent attacks on tyranny and pleas for freedom both personal and political. Influenced by Goethe at the court of Weimar, his later works, drawn from history and often in verse, show more artistic restraint: *Don Carlos* (1782), *Wallenstein* (1799), *Maria Stuart* (1800), *The Maid of Orleans* (1801) and *Wilhelm Tell* (1804).

Schmidt, Willi (1910–94), German director and designer. His career was shared among many theatres in Berlin, Hamburg and Düsseldorf before, during and after the Second World War (when he specialized in Giraudoux). As a director, he was highly literary, his productions cool, precise and distanced but located in a theatrical ambience.

Schnabel, Artur (1882–1951), Carinthian pianist. An expert at Beethoven, he was the first to record all his sonatas.

Schneider, Benno (d.1977), Yiddish director. Considered the most innovative director of the ARTEF Theatre, he combined aesthetic excellence with revolutionary ideology in stylized ensembles, as in *The Dybbuk* (1926), *Aristocrats*, a version of Sholem Aleichem's *Menschn* and *200000* (*The Jackpot*). He was lured to Broadway where he staged *Liliom* (1940) with Ingrid Bergman and *Strange Bedfellows* (1948).

The School for Scandal, English comedy by Richard Brinsley Sheridan (1777). A satire of English polite society, it pits a fashionable coterie of scandal-mongers and hypocrites against the sincerity of Sir Peter Teazle and Charles Surface. An excellent ensemble piece, it enjoyed a large number of all-star revivals in England and the U.S. in the nineteenth and twentieth centuries, and was one of the few English plays staged by the Moscow Art Theatre.

Schweik, Good Soldier. See *The Good Soldier Schweik*.

Scofield, Sir Paul (1922–), English actor. His throaty voice and liquid eyes give a bittersweet tinge to his interpretations. He was closely connected with Peter Brook who directed him as Don Armado (*Love's Labours Lost*, 1948), Hamlet in Victorian dress, Pierre in *Venice Preserved* (1953) and a militaristic *King Lear* (1962). His Thomas More in *A Man for All Seasons* (1960) was preserved on film.

Scott, Sir Walter (1771–1832), Scottish novelist and poet. Although he did not himself write plays, he translated Goethe's *Götz von Berlichingen*, and his Waverley novels were repeatedly turned into plays and operas. Dramatizations of *Guy Mannering* (1815) and *Heart of Midlothian* (1818) were popular on the stage, and opera audiences hearkened to sung versions of *The Bride of Lammermoor* (1819), *The Talisman* (1825), *Ivanhoe* and *The Fair Maid of Perth* (1828).

The Seagull (*Chaika*), Russian comedy by Anton Chekhov (1895–96). Conflicts on a provincial estate occur between an established actress, her lover a celebrated novelist, her son, a would-be writer, and Nina, a country girl who longs to be a star. The opening night at the Alexandra Theatre, St Petersburg (17 October 1896), is a legendary fiasco. It was triumphantly restaged at the Moscow Art Theatre (1898). Its first English-language production was in Glasgow (1909).

Seale, Douglas (1913–99), English actor and director. His acting career began in 1934, with seasons at Stratford (1946–8). He began directing with a season of Shaw plays (1949) and became chief director at the Birmingham Rep (1950) and the Old Vic (1958–9). In the U.S. from 1961 he served as director at regional theatres in Cincinnati, Baltimore, Chicago, Philadelphia et al. and acted frequently on television.

Second Art Theatre. See **Moscow Art Theatre 2**.

Selznick, David O[liver] (1902–65), American film producer. He worked at MGM and Paramount before being named vice-president in charge of production at RKO Studios, where he micromanaged *A Bill of Divorcement* (1932) and *King Kong* (1933). As head of his own production company, he issued innumerable memos to control the details of such blockbusters as *A Star Is Born* (1937), *Gone with the Wind* (1939), *Rebecca* (1940) for which he brought Alfred Hitchcock to Hollywood and *Farewell to Arms* (1957).

Serao, Matilde (1856–1927), Greek-born Italian writer. A popular novelist of Roman life, she founded and edited several newspapers, among them *Il Corriere di Roma* and *Il Giorno*. Her novels are naturalistic in style, with close attention to vernacular speech, but infused with a nebulous idealism.

The Seven Deadly Sins (*Die sieben Todsünden der Kleinbürger*), German ballet cantata in verse by Bertolt Brecht with music by Kurt Weill (1933). Two sisters, Anna I (singer) and Anna II (dancer), make their way in the world to earn money to build their family a house in Louisiana. In each city they visit Anna II is tempted by a sin considered deadly by the bourgeoisie but which proves to be a basic human virtue. She avoids temptations and comes home wealthy.

Shadow and Substance, Irish drama by Paul Vincent Carroll (1937). Essentially a debate about Roman Catholicism, it pits a devout young girl against a cynical bishop.

Shadow of a Doubt, American film directed by Alfred Hitchcock (1943). To the sleepy California town of Santa Clara comes the "Merry Widow" murderer (Joseph Cotton), to visit his typical American family. Only gradually does his niece (Teresa Wright) come to realize his identity and the danger he poses. Thornton Wilder had a hand in the screenplay.

Shall We Dance?, American musical film, directed by Mark Sandrich, with songs by George and Ira Gershwin (1937). One of the lesser Fred Astaire–Ginger Rogers showcases, it is enlivened by such songs as "Let's Call the Whole Thing Off" and "They Can't Take That Away from Me".

Shaw, George Bernard (1856–1950), Irish playwright and critic. While employed as a music and theatre critic on several London periodicals, promoting Wagner and Ibsen, he began to write plays to promulgate his ideas on social, political and artistic questions. The first of these, *Widowers' Houses*, was produced by the Independent Theatre in 1892; the last was *Buoyant Billions* (1948). In between, his more than 50 comedies juggled controversial and contrarian ideas in dialogue of exhausting volubility.

Shaw, Irwin (1913–84), American playwright. Reversing the usual trend, he began as a radio play- and screenwriter. His first play, the grimly anti-war *Bury the Dead*, was written for a competition (1936) and remains his most successful. *The Gentle People* (1939) was one of the lesser efforts of the Group Theatre.

Shchukin, Boris Vasilevich (1894–1939), Russian actor. He worked under Vakhtangov at the Moscow Art Theatre 3rd Studio from 1920. A pillar of the Vakhtangov Theatre (1926–1938), expert at showing the psychic convolutions of a character, he was at his best in the title role of *Yegor Bulychyov and Others* (1932). Owing in part to his baldness, Shchukin was the first actor chosen to impersonate Lenin, in *Man with a Gun* (1937).

She Loves Me Not, American comedy by Howard Lindsay from a novel by Edward Hope (1933). A nightclub dancer, witness to a gangland murder, is disguised as a boy by Princeton undergrads; this entails bringing in a disruptive film crew. In a "hero's best friend" role, Burgess Meredith had his first success.

Sheridan, Richard Brinsley (1751–1816), Irish playwright and politician. It was while he managed the Drury Lane Theatre, London, that he began to write plays. *The Rivals* (1775) and *The School for Scandal* (1777) remain the two most frequently revived English comedies of the eighteenth century. In 1799 he wrote the theatrical satire *The Critic* and *Pizarro*, an adaptation of Kotzebue, set in Peru, which was a great favorite on the Regency stage.

The Shewing-Up of Blanco Posnet, "a Sermon in Crude Melodrama" by George Bernard Shaw (1909). In the American West, the alleged horse-thief Blanco cannot be convicted without a witness, but there is confusion in the testimony of two women, and he is hanged. It was first played by the Abbey Theatre.

Shor, Toots (correctly, Bernard, 1903–77), American restaurateur. After work as a nightclub bouncer in New York, he opened Toots Shors Restaurant on West 51st Street, which became wildly popular as a gathering-place for macho, hard-drinking celebrities in sports, show business and journalism.

A Shot in the Dark, American comedy by Harry Kurnitz (1961), from a play *L'Idiot* by Marcel Achard. A parody of the Agatha Christie murder mystery, it was directed by Harold Clurman with a cast that included Julie Harris, Walter Matthau and William Shatner. Filmed in 1964, it served as the first *Pink Panther* sequel, with Peter Sellers as the accident-prone Inspector Clouzot, an interpolated character expanded to become the lead.

Shoulder Arms, American film comedy by Charlie Chaplin (1918). Chaplin's most popular film until then, it presents the Little Tramp as a doughboy in the French trenches during the First World War. It was his second film for First National Pictures, and had a cast of his regulars: Edna Purviance, Syd Chaplin and Henry Bergman.

Shuberts, American producers. The Shubert brothers, Sam S. (1877?–1905), Lee (1875?–1953) and Jacob J. (1879?–1963) rose from managing road companies to become the most powerful producers in the U.S. Bucking the monopoly of the Theatrical Syndicate, they eventually controlled an "empire" of over 100 theatres, with booking privileges at another thousand. Musicals and revues were their speciality, although they would occasionally branch out into sponsoring a commercially safe drama. Their legacy is the Shubert Organization.

The Shy and the Lonely, American one-act comedy by Irwin Shaw (1941). It was written for the Group Theatre as a curtain-riser for Saroyan's *My Heart's in the Highlands*. About a young man's first attempt at seduction, it became popular with college theatres.

Siddons, Sarah (1755–1831), English actress. A member of the Kemble dynasty of actors, she was viewed in her time not only as the leading tragedienne, but also as a quasi-divinity, the "Muse of Tragedy". Her aquiline beauty was matched by a forceful delivery that ran the gamut from heart-rending pathos to terrifying menace. The former was seen in Isabella in *The Fatal Marriage* and Queen Katherine in *Henry VIII*, the latter in Lady Macbeth, her signature role.

Sierra, American film, directed by Alfred E. Green from the novel *Mountains Are My Kingdom* by Stuart Hardy (1950). This standard Western boasted a very strong cast, many of them from the legitimate stage: Audie Murphy, Burl Ives, Dean Jagger, Tony (still Anthony) Curtis, Houseley Stevenson, Sara Allgood and Erskine Sanford.

The Silver Lake (*Der Silbersee*), German "winter's fairy tale" by Georg Kaiser and Kurt Weill (1932). Written for actors rather than singers, it is a parable about hope. A policeman enriched by the lottery takes into his castle a man he unjustly crippled; his housekeeper manages to usurp the property and evict both of them. As they approach a lake to drown themselves, it freezes over, giving them a path to a new life. Just as the Nazis were coming to power, this optimism proved popular. It was first produced in New York in 1980, in a very loose adaptation by Hugh Wheeler.

Simonov, Ruben Nikolaevich (1899–1968), Russian actor and director. He joined the Moscow Art Theatre 3rd Studio in 1920, and under Vakhtangov developed a belief in improvisational, celebratory theatre. When the Studio became the Vakhtangov Theatre in 1924, Simonov was its leading actor, with a bent for comedy. When students he had trained had an outstanding success in 1931, he turned to directing, becoming chief director of the Vakhtangov (1939–68).

Simonson, Lee (1888–1967), American designer. He began working for the Washington Square Players and moved to the Theatre Guild. He was a hard-bitten opponent of Gordon Craig's theories, laid out in his opinionated book *The Stage Is Set* (1932).

Sims, George Robert (1847–1922), English journalist and playwright. Under the name "Dagonet" he wrote a regular column in the sporting journal *The Referee*. His many popular melodramas include *The Lights o' London, Harbour Lights, Two Little Vagabonds*, and *The Romany Rye*. His sentimental narrative poems, such as "'Ostler Joe", were favourites with platform reciters.

Sircom, Arthur (1899–1980), American actor and director. A classmate of Humphrey Bogart at Andover Academy and a student at the American Laboratory Theatre, he acted in New York (*They Knew What They Wanted*, 1924; *Processional*, 1925) and with the Boston Repertory Theatre (1928). He was a frequently employed Broadway director of minor comedies, best known for *Springtime for Henry* (1931) and *Sailor, Beware!* (1933). He was the director of the Cape Dennis Playhouse on Cape Cod for many years.

The Skin of Our Teeth, American dramatic parable by Thornton Wilder (1942). Inspired by Joyce's *Finnegans Wake*, it presents a pageant of human progress or lack thereof. Mankind, in the persons of the Antrobus family and their irreverent maid Sabina, live through the Ice Age, the Flood and a world war. Asides, the eruption of the stage crew into the action, and similar devices regularly break the frame. The first production, directed by Elia Kazan, almost failed to open, owing to the disruptive behaviour of Tallulah Bank-head in rehearsals.

Skylark, American comedy by Samson Raphaelson (1939). A needlessly entangled plot about an estranged couple and the results of a dinner party enabled Gertrude Lawrence to shine.

The Sleeping Prince, English "occasional fairy tale" by Terence Rattigan (1953). Written to celebrate the coronation of Elizabeth II, this comedy takes place during the coronation ceremonies for Edward VII. The regent of a Balkan kingdom has a brief affair with an American chorus girl. Filmed as *The Prince and the Showgirl* (1957), it paired a supercilious Laurence Olivier with Marilyn Monroe.

Slezak, Walter (1902–83), Austrian actor, son of the Czech baritone Leo Slezak. His first roles in European film were as tall, sylph-like young men adored by other men in *Sodom und Gomorra* (1922) and *Michael* (1924). Growing stout, he usually was cast in American films as the villain (*Lifeboat*, 1944), but was at ease playing comedy. His musical abilities were heard in the musical *Fanny* (1954).

Smilin' Through, American play by Jane Cowl and Jane Murfin (1919). A vehicle for Cowl herself, the play is a romantic weepy about a man whose fiancée died tragically and who tries to prevent her daughter from marrying the son of her murderer. It made a hit with audiences, and was refashioned as a silent film (1922) and two sound films (1932; and as a musical, 1941).

Smith, Art (1899–1973), American actor. A member of the Group Theatre who appeared in most of their productions between 1931 and 1939 (Myron in *Awake and Sing!*, Tokio in *Golden Boy*), on its dissolution went to Hollywood and, gray-haired and sad eyed, played detectives and doctors in B movies. He was blacklisted in the late 1940s and returned to the stage as Chris in *Anna Christie* (1952) and Doc in *West Side Story* (1957).

Smith, Clay (1877–1930), American arranger, composer and conductor. Located in Chicago, he was married to Lee White, and played with her as a vaudeville team.

Smith, Kent (1907–85), American actor. On Broadway from 1932, after a good role in *Dodsworth* (1934), he partnered Katharine Cornell in *Saint Joan*, *The Wingless Victory* (both 1936) and *Candida* (1937). In the 1940s he played stalwart heroes and their best friends in B pictures and thrillers (*The Curse of the Cat People*, 1944; *The Spiral Staircase*, 1946).

Sokoloff, Vladimir (Sokolov, 1889–1962), Russian actor. A member of the Moscow Art Theatre Studio, he emigrated to Germany in 1923 and worked with Max Reinhardt (Wurm in *Love and Intrigue*). He came to the U.S. in 1937, and his saggy face and thick accent became familiar in character parts. He was rarely cast as a Russian, but played Paul Cézanne in *The Life of Emile Zola* (1937), a Mexican peasant in *Juarez* (1939) and the Spanish partisan Anselmo in *For Whom the Bell Tolls* (1943) – 35 nationalities in all.

Soloviova, Vera. See headnote to Chapter 8, "Seven interviews in search of good acting".

Sophocles (496–406 B.C.E.), Greek playwright. Although he was a frequent prize-winner at the festival of Dionysos, only seven of his more than one hundred plays survive. The so-called Theban trilogy (not composed as such)

– *Oedipus the King*, *Oedipus at Colonnus* – and *Antigone*, was the best known. He is said to have introduced the third actor and invented scene painting.

Le Soulier de Satin, ou Le pire n'est pas toujours sûr (*The Satin Slipper*), French play in "four days" by Paul Claudel (1925). "The play takes place in the world," the author says, and is so long, so full of characters and so spread over the globe that it is rarely performed. A drama of sin and redemption, it revolves around the love of Dona Prouhèze and Don Rodrigue in the age of conquistadors. Barrault staged an abridged version in 1943 and then complete in 1980.

A Sound of Hunting, American play by Harry Brown (1945). As weary G.I.s are about to pull out of Monte Cassino, they linger to rescue their least popular fellow from a dangerous position. The play succeeded on the basis of its hard-bitten, cynical dialogue, but even that could not save the turgid film version *Eight Iron Men* (1953), directed by Stanley Kramer.

Soyer, Raphael (1899–1987), Russian-born American painter. A disciple of the Ashcan School, he devoted himself to recording the life of New York City in representational style. His "social realism" was widely exhibited, and he won golden opinions as a teacher.

Spewack, Sam (1899–1971) and **Bella** (1899–1990), American press agents turned playwrights, whose teamwork produced well-carpentered farces. *Boy Meets Girl* (1948) and the Shakespearean musical *Kiss Me, Kate* (1948) are still viable; their adaptation of a play by Albert Housson, *My Three Angels* (1953), reveals its mechanism too baldly.

Staatstheater, Berlin. Originally, the Königliche Schauspielhaus (Royal Playhouse), opened in 1821, it was renamed the Preußiches Staatstheater Berlin (Prussian State Theatre) in 1919. Its intendants included the artistically controversial Leopold Jessner (1919–30) and the politically controversial Gustaf Gründgens (1934–45). It was bombed to smithereens in 1945, and then rebuilt to house musical concerts (1979–84). After the Wall divided the city, the Deutsches Theater was deemed the East Berlin Staatstheater from 1949.

Stage Door, American drama by Edna Ferber and George S. Kaufman (1936). With a huge cast typical of Depression Era plays, it presents the Footlights Club, a rooming house for actresses. The fates, happy and unhappy, of the residents and their various boyfriends and protectors, are tracked. The film version with Katherine Hepburn was so altered that Kaufman said it should be called *Screen Door*.

Stanislavsky, Konstantin Alekseevich (Alekseev, 1863–1938), Russian actor, director and pedagogue. His fingerprints are all over the modern theatre for two main reasons. First, as co-founder and leading actor of the Moscow Art Theatre, he demonstrated the effectiveness of a disciplined, educated ensemble with a literary repertory, an integrated *mise-en-scène*, and an almost religious devotion to work. Then, as the inventor of the "System", he attempted to discover ways to trigger an actor's creativity, avoid routine and inspire original performances.

Stanley, Kim (Patricia Kimberly Reid, 1925–2001), American actress. One of the conspicuous products of the Actors Studio, she excelled in what passed for realism on the Broadway stage, as Millie in *Picnic* (1953) and Cherie in *Bus Stop* (1955). She also played an overwrought Masha in Strasberg's staging of *Three Sisters* and Maggie in the London run of *Cat on a Hot Tin Roof* (1958).

Stapleton, Maureen. See headnote to Chapter 14, "Maureen Stapleton".

Steiner, Rudolf (1861–1925), Austrian philosopher. An eminent Goethe scholar, he established the Goethaneum near Basel, to promulgate a "spiritual science" influenced by Theosophy. His own doctrine, anthroposophy, a sort of spiritual therapy, made use of Dalcroze eurhythmics and other theatrical techniques. Michael Chekhov was deeply committed to it in his pursuit of an acting method.

Sternheim, Carl (1881–1943), German playwright. With Molière as their model, his comic works skewer the Wilhelmine middle-class in its prejudices and inhibitions, as in *The Underpants* (1911), *Burgher Schippel* and *The Snob* (both 1913). He also wrote one of the earliest plays about Oscar Wilde (1924).

Stevens, George (1904–75), American film director. His first assignments were broad farce, but he broke through with Katherine Hepburn in *Alice Adams* (1935). He moved from Fred Astaire–Ginger Rogers vehicles to Second World War documentaries to domestic dramas (*I Remember Mama*, 1948) to blockbusters (*A Place in the Sun*, 1951; *Shane*, 1953; *Giant*, 1956; *The Diary of Anne Frank*, 1959).

Stevens, Mark (actually Richard, 1916–1994), American actor. After work as a radio announcer, he became a contract actor at Warner Brothers, and then moved to 20th Century Fox, where he was employed as a rough-and-ready leading man in *film noir* (*Within These Walls*, 1945; *The Dark Corner*, 1946; *The Street with No Name*, 1948). He occasionally appeared in comedies and musicals, and was very active in television.

Stevenson, Houseley (1879–1953), English actor. Frequently cast as doctors and professors in Hollywood films from 1936 to 1952, he is best remembered as the demented plastic surgeon who alters Humphrey Bogart's face in *Dark Passage* (1947).

Stewart, James (1908–97), American actor. The rangy, drawling Princeton alumnus made his Broadway debut in 1932, but soon drifted to Hollywood, where he became a model of ingenuousness in *Mr Smith Goes to Washington* (1939). He also created the role of Elwood P. Dowd in *Harvey* (1940), which he repeated on the screen (1950). Other nuanced performances came in *The Philadelphia Story* (1940), and Alfred Hitchcock's *Rear Window* (1954) and *Vertigo* (1958).

Stoska, Polyna, Polish soprano. A student of Marcella Sembrich, she sang at the Deutsche Oper (1939–41), before emigrating to the U.S. where she joined the New York City Opera (1944–46). During the war, she also toured the Pacific with a UFO concert unit. 1947 was her *annus mirabilis*: she created Anna Maurrant in the operatic version of *Street Scene*, made a Metropolitan

Opera debut in *Die Meistersinger*, and sang in *Three Musketeers* with the Los Angeles Light Opera. She returned to Europe in 1953.

Strange Interlude, American drama by Eugene O'Neill (1928). Stretched over nine acts and two generations, this treats the problems of the *femme fatale* Nina Leeds in her failed marriage, love affairs and maternity. At certain points the characters step forward and reveal their innermost thoughts. This device was parodied by Groucho Marx in *Animal Crackers* (1928, film 1930).

Strasberg, Lee. See headnote to Chapter 8, "Seven interviews in search of good acting".

Stratford Memorial Theatre. The first modern Shakespeare festival was held in Stratford-upon-Avon in 1879 and became an annual event. It was housed in a Gothic building which burned in 1926, and was replaced in 1932. The 1,500-seat building was renamed the Royal Shakespeare Theatre in 1961, and in 2007 was remodelled to accommodate modern ideas of Elizabethan performance.

Strauss, Richard (1864–1949), German composer. Most original of the disciples of Wagner, he made his name with symphonic poems based on literary themes. He also wrote 15 operas, shocking with his earliest works *Salome* (1905) and *Elektra* (1909), charming with *Der Rosenkavalier* (1911) and *Arabella* (1933). *Ariadne auf Naxos* (1912) and *Capriccio* (1942) dramatize issues of art *vs* life, while *Die Frau ohne Schatten* (1919) is a murky fable redeemed by the lyricism of the music.

Stravinsky, Igor Fyodorovich (1882–1971), Russian composer. He was given his first big chance by Diaghilev and composed striking scores for the Ballets Russes: *The Firebird* (1910), *Petrouchka* (1911), *The Rite of Spring* (1913, which caused a riot) and several others. He later wrote other works for the stage, among them *The Soldier's Tale* (1918) and *Les Noces* (1923). His one opera, composed to a libretto by W. H. Auden, is the Hogarthian *The Rake's Progress* (1951).

Street Scene, American drama by Elmer Rice (1929). Against the background of a New York tenement, a day in the life of 50 characters – Swedes, Jews, Italians, Irish – is unfolded. The catalyst for the various plot lines is a milkman shooting his wife and her lover. The daily reviewers were impressed, but Stark Young found it trashy. It was made into an opera by Kurt Weill and Langston Hughes in 1947.

Strictly Dishonorable, American play by Preston Sturges (1929). A Southern belle is deserted by her fiancé in a New York speakeasy and so spends a blameless night in the apartment of an operatic divo with a reputation as a Lothario. It launched Sturges' career as a screenwriter and film director.

Strindberg, August (1849–1912), Swedish playwright. Although in his early phase he longed to be considered a naturalist, his plays are too personal and too beholden to his idiosyncratic scientific and social concepts to qualify. Later, they became more blatantly symbolic and even expressionistic, with a strong mystical element. His late chamber plays were produced by the Intimate Theatre in Stockholm (1907).

Stritch, Elaine (1925–), American actress. She gained renown singing the strip-tease parody "Zip" in *Pal Joey* (1952), as the lead in Noël Coward's *Sail Away* (1955), and Martha in matinees of *Who's Afraid of Virginia Woolf?* Her hoarse rendition of "The Ladies Who Lunch" in *Company* (1970) became legendary, and she repeated it in her one-woman show *At Liberty* (2002).

Stuyvesant, Pieter (1592–1672), Dutch administrator. He lost a leg while governor of Curaçao, which did nothing to improve a peppery temper. As governor of Nieuw Amsterdam, he was arbitrary and intolerant, but a shrewd negotiator. He is one of the comic heroes of Washington Irving's Diedrich Knickerbocker's *History of New York* (1805), itself the inspiration for the Weill and Anderson musical *Knickerbocker Holiday*.

Sullavan, Margaret. See headnote to Chapter 5, "Margaret Sullavan".

Sullivan, Ed (in full Edward Vincent, 1902–74), American reporter and television host. His column about Broadway, "Little Old New York", appeared in the New York *Daily News* from 1933 to 1974. Almost as long-lived was his Sunday-night television variety show *Ed Sullivan Presents* (1948–71), in which his unsmiling presence introduced to the viewing public Dean Martin and Jerry Lewis, Elvis Presley, the Beatles, Carol Burnett and the ineffable ventriloquist Señor Wences.

Summer and Smoke, American play by Tennessee Williams (1947). In small town Mississippi Miss Alma, a minister's daughter, is all delicate spirit, while her beloved Dr. Buchanan is all fleshly hedonism, but matters are reversed by play's end. Reasonably well received when it was first produced, it got more attention in a 1952 revival as *Eccentricities of a Nightingale*, with Geraldine Page as Alma.

The Summing Up, autobiography by W. Somerset Maugham (1938). This opinionated, conversational memoir, in which he characterizes himself as first among second-raters, describes prose drama as a minor and ephemeral art-form.

Sundown Beach, American play by Bessie Breuer (1948). An intense drama about Second World War pilots being treated for post-traumatic stress syndrome at an air force hospital in Florida, it was the Actors Studio's first production, directed by Elia Kazan. The cast included Julie Harris, Martin Balsam and Cloris Leachman, but ran for only a week.

Susan and God, American play by Rachel Crothers (1937). Gertrude Lawrence made a personal success of the role of Susan Trexel, a religious zealot whose proselytizing of others devolves into reforming her own personal life.

Swing Time, American musical film directed by George Stevens from a screenplay by Howard Lindsay et al., with songs by Jerome Kern and Dorothy Fields (1936). In traditional style, Fred Astaire and Ginger Rogers are at each other's throats at the start, at each other's lips by the end. The stirring numbers include "A Fine Romance", "The Way You Look Tonight" and "Pick Yourself Up".

Symons, Arthur (1865–1945), Welsh critic and poet. A propagandist for European symbolism through his critical writings and translations of D'Annunzio and Baudelaire, he also drew on popular culture, particularly the music hall, for inspiration.

Synge, John Millington (1871–1909), Irish playwright. He followed the French symbolists, until W. B. Yeats suggested he study the remote Irish peasantry. Time spent in Wicklow, Connemara and the Aran Islands was exploited in his plays, among others *The Shadow of the Glen* (1903), the one-act tragedy *Riders to the Sea* (1904), the dark comedy *Playboy of the Western World* (1907) and *Deirdre of the Sorrows* (1910), all performed by the Abbey Theatre.

Tabs, English revue (1918). Produced by André Charlot, it is noteworthy for introducing Gertrude Lawrence as understudy to Beatrice Lillie.

Tairov, Aleksandr Yakovlevich (Kornblit, 1885–1950), Russian director. In 1914, he created the Kamerny (Chamber) Theatre, Moscow. Opposed to the tradition of Russian realism, exalting the "truth of art" over the "truth of life", his synthetic theatre was organized around mystery and harlequinade; the theatrical spectacle was to rely on the actors, masters of their external (voice, elocution, body) and internal (mastery and expression of emotions) techniques. He incurred increasingly harsh criticism for maintaining that politics has no part in theatrical art, was made to denounce his theatre for its "deviation from naturalism" and was dismissed from it in 1949.

Talma, François Joseph (1763–1826), French actor. His notes of fervour instilled into neoclassic drama were much to the taste of French Revolutionaries. The favorite tragedian of Napoleon, who reinvented the Comédie-Française on the basis of Talma's Théâtre de la République, he also reformed costuming, replacing court dress with togas for Roman characters.

Tamerlane, English historical tragedy in verse by Nicholas Rowe (1701). It is less an imitation of Marlowe's *Tamburlaine* than a political commentary on the present, in which the Scythian warrior stands for William III, the Prince of Orange who had saved Protestantism in Great Britain, and the sultan Bajazet for Louis XIV of France.

The Taming of the Shrew, English comedy by William Shakespeare (*c.*1594). The farce of the fortune-hunter Petruchio taming Katherine into a docile wife by means of physical and mental abuse is staged for the benefit of the drunken tinker Christopher Sly. David Garrick rewrote it to showcase his own abilities, and it earned fresh popularity in the Victorian age. The Lunts turned it into a rollicking jokefest.

Tandy, Jessica (1909–94), Anglo-American actress. She had caught the critics' eye, playing Ophelia to Gielgud's Hamlet (1934) before shooting to stardom as the first Blanche Du Bois in *A Streetcar Named Desire* (1947). Most of her later appearances were in tandem with her husband Hume Cronyn, notably in classic roles in the first seasons of the Guthrie Theatre. *A Delicate Balance* (1966) and *The Gin Game* (1974) were outstanding performances of her later career.

Tannhäuser und der Sängerkrieg auf Wartburg (*Tannhaeuser and the Wartburg Song Competition*), German opera by Richard Wagner (1845). Tannhaeuser, a late medieval troubadour, must choose between erotic love, represented by

Venus, and spiritual love, represented by Lady Elisabeth. A pilgrimage to Rome sets him straight and he proceeds to win the contest. It was parodied devastatingly by the Austrian comic Johann Nestroy.

Tarcai, Mary (1906–79), American actress and pedagogue. After a few Broadway roles in the 1930s, she was made the permanent head of the workshop at the Actor's Lab in Hollywood. Later, she ran her own acting studio in New York, counting among her students Charlotte Rae and Valerie Harper.

Tartuffe (*Tartuffe, ou L'Imposteur*), French comedy by Molière (1664, 1669). A satire on religious hypocrisy, it was banned on its first appearance, owing to pressure from the *dévots*, but, heavily rewritten, it was staged with Louis XIV's permission. Hence the fulsome compliment to the king in the last act denouement. In the twentieth century it received radical reinterpretations from Louis Jouvet, Roger Planchon and Antoine Vitez.

A Taste of Honey, English play by Shelagh Delaney (1958). In the North of England, a working-class girl finds herself pregnant by a black sailor. Neglected by her slatternly mother, she cohabits with a gay male art student, until the mother returns and takes over. Kitchen-sink in style, it was first produced by Joan Littlewood's Theatre Royal Stratford, and filmed in 1961 with Rita Tushingham.

Taylor, Robert (Spangler Arlington Brugh, 1911–69), American film actor. His chiselled features and lush eyelashes made him one of MGM's most popular leading men in the 1930s, despite his wooden acting (Armand opposite Garbo in *Camille*, 1936). Although he continued to star in sword-and-sandal epics (*Quo Vadis?*, 1951; *Ivanhoe*, 1952), as his features thickened, he found a new niche in *film noir*. Classified a friendly witness before the House Committee on Un-American Activities, he played out his later career on TV.

Taylor, Valerie (Velma Nacella Young, 1913–97), American poet and novelist. A prolific author of novels under various pseudonyms, she is best known for the lesbian pulp fiction she produced from the late 1940s. She was also a conspicuous activist in various protest movements.

Tellegen, Lou (Isidor Louis Bernard van Dammeler, 1881–1934), Dutch actor. Tall, dark and handsome, he partnered Sarah Bernhardt on her 1910 tour of the U.S., and settled there in 1914. He wrote several plays in which he appeared as a matinee idol, and then had a brief career as a film star. When he felt he was washed up both as an actor and a lady's man, he committed homespun hara-kiri with a pair of scissors.

The Tempest, English comedy by William Shakespeare (1611). Often erroneously cited as Shakespeare's farewell to the stage, it is a magical pageant of revenge and reconciliation. Duke Prospero, exiled on a spirit-infested island, uses his magic to cause a shipwreck, put his enemies in peril and then forgive them.

Tennyson, Alfred, Lord (1809–92). English poet. His verse dramas held some appeal for actors, but rarely for audiences. The Kendals played *The Falcon* (1979) and Ada Rehan was Maid Marian in his Robin Hood play *The Foresters*

(1892). Henry Irving lavished sumptuous resources on productions of *Queen Mary* (1875) and *Becket* (1884).

Terry, Dame Ellen Alice (1848–1928), English actress, member of a stage clan, mother of Edward Gordon and Edith Craig. Icon of Victorian womanhood, immortalized in the paintings of her husband G. F. Watts, she was Henry Irving's leading woman at the Lyceum (1878–1902). She was better at charm, sparkle and pathos (Beatrice, Lady Teazle, Portia) than at grand tragedy (Lady Macbeth, Gretchen in *Faust*). Shaw admired her and wrote Lady Cicely in *Captain Brassbound's Conversion* for her (1906).

Terry, Fred (1863–1933), Ellen's younger brother. A specialist in swashbuckling, he made a perennial favorite out of Sir Percy Blakeney in *The Scarlet Pimpernel*. Married to Julia Neilson, they toured widely in *Sweet Nell of Old Drury, Matt o' Merrymount* and *Henry of Navarre*.

Terry, Kate (1844–1924), Ellen's elder sister, grandmother of John Gielgud. On stage from childhood, playing Prince Arthur to Charles Kean's King John and Ophelia to Fechter's Hamlet, she retired on marrying in 1867.

Terry, Marion (1852–1930), Ellen's younger sister. She also played Ophelia, but was beloved for her wholesome heroines in T. W. Robertson's modern-dress comedies. She also appeared in the plays of Wilde (the first Mrs Erlynne in *Lady Windermere's Fan*), Henry Arthur Jones and J. M. Barrie.

Théâtre Français. See **Comédie Française**.

Theatre Guild, New York, grew out of the Washington Square Players (1914–18), and continued its policy of producing non-commercial and European drama. Led by Lawrence Langner and Theresa Helburn, it opened with Benavente's *Bonds of Interest* (1919), but had its first box-office success with *John Ferguson*. It had a fondness for Central European historical dramas and comedies (*Goat Song, Juarez and Maximilian, The Guardsman*), but also promoted Shaw (*Arms and the Man, Heartbreak House*) and O'Neill (*Mourning Becomes Electra*). Among its regular actors were the Lunts, Dudley Digges and Helen Westley, with occasional appearances by Nazimova and Helen Hayes.

Theatre Magazine, an American periodical which first appeared in 1917, was a glossy, large format journal, lavishly illustrated and packed with advertisements for luxury products. Edited by Arthur Hornblow, it ended in 1931, by which time it was devoting much of its coverage to the movies.

Theatre of Dionysos, Athenian amphitheatre cut into the southern cliff face of the Acropolis. Originally of wood and earth, it was rebuilt in stone (342–326 B.C.E.) to seat 17,000 in 64 rows of seats. It is considered the cradle of ancient Greek drama, for the plays were performed there during the dramatic competitions of the City Dionysia. The Romans converted it to a gladiatorial arena.

The Theatre of Tomorrow, American book by Kenneth Macgowan (1921). A manifesto of the New Stagecraft, it argued against mere realism and for the theatre as a means to a higher spiritual state. To this end, scenery and lighting should conduce to a more abstract mood, the sort of psychological states popularized by Freud and Jung. Macgowan cited *Rosmersholm* and *Beyond the*

Horizon as model plays, Robert Edmond Jones as a model designer, and America as the theatre's future.

Theatre Wing. See **American Theatre Wing**.

Thesiger, Ernest (1879–1961). A favorite actor of G. B. Shaw, he created the Dauphin in *St Joan* (1924), Sir Orpheus Midlander in *Geneva* (1938) and Charles II in *Good King Charles's Golden Days* (1939). His fey, gaunt presence enlivened James Whales' *The Old Dark House* (1932) and *The Bride of Franken-stein* (1937) and several Alec Guinness comedies.

This One Man, American play by Sidney R. Buchman (1930). Two burglar brothers are opposed in character: Marvin is the weak, sensitive one, Saul the tough guy. So Marvin commits a murder with the intention that, at his execution, he will convey his soul into Saul. Paul Muni, still billed as Muni Weisenfreund, played Saul.

Thorndike, Dame Sybil (1882–1976), English actress. After repertory experience in Manchester, she became leading lady at the Old Vic (1914–18), working her way through the standard roles. Often partnered with her husband Lewis Casson, she managed the New Theatre, excelled in Greek tragedy and as St. John Irvine's *Jane Clegg*, and created Shaw's St. Joan. She also played a season of British Grand Guignol. As she aged, she had a strong line in dowagers, nannies and harridans.

Three Men on a Horse, American comedy by John Cecil Holm and George Abbott (1935). The hero, a feckless greeting-card versifier, has a knack for picking horses, which embroils him with Damon Runyonesque characters from the underworld. His hobby saves his marriage.

Three Sisters (*Tri sestry*), drama in four acts by Anton Chekhov (1900). The daughters of deceased General Prozorov, Olga, Masha and Irina, and their brother Andrei live in a remote county town and dream of returning to Moscow. Their chief diversion is the officers of a battalion stationed nearby. Andrei becomes a cuckold and a gambler; his wife Natasha gradually evicts the sisters from their rooms and then from the house; Olga and Irina fail to marry or find productive work; Masha's affair with Colonel Vershinin ends. First produced at the Moscow Art Theatre (1901), it became one of its signature productions and audiences spoke of "visiting the Prozorovs".

The Threepenny Opera, American musical by Marc Blitzstein, from Bertolt Brecht and Kurt Weill (1954). Stripped of much of the original's political and social commentary, as well as its more sardonic jokes, this adaptation of *Die Dreigroschenoper* proved so popular it ran at New York's Theatre de Lys for 2,611 performances, an Off-Broadway record. The cast included Lotte Lenya as Jenny, the role she had created in Berlin, and Beatrice Arthur as Lucy. Blitzstein's lyrics to "Mack the Knife" had a remarkable afterlife, as sung by Louis Armstrong, Sammy Davis Jr., Frankie Laine and many unlikely others.

Thunder Rock, American play by Robert Ardrey (1939). A journalist has become a hermit in a lighthouse off the Great Lakes, disappointed that he cannot convince others of a fascist threat; a visit by ghosts from a shipwreck persuades him to return to life. This topical variation on *A Christmas Carol* was directed by Elia Kazan for the Group Theatre with Luther Adler and Lee J. Cobb, but closed after 23 performances. A 1942 British film version with Michael Redgrave and James Mason was more popular and it became a standby with college theatres.

Tiger Cats, American comedy by Karen Bramson from *Les Félines* by Michael Orme (1924). David Belasco produced and directed it, with Katharine Cornell and Robert Loraine in the lead roles.

Tilley, Vesta (Matilda Alice Powles, 1864–1952), English music-hall performer. The favourite male impersonator of the late Victorian and Edwardian periods, she was celebrated for her natty masculine outfits and cocky air. Her popular numbers include "Burlington Bertie" and "Following in Father's Footsteps". During the First World War, she lent her talents to recruiting for the army.

Time, American weekly news magazine. Founded in 1923 by Briton Hadden and Henry Luce, as the first such periodical in the U.S. it soon became famous for its flippant tone, capsule character sketches and "Timese" of inverted syntax and hyphenated descriptive adjectives. After Hadden's death in 1929, it grew more sober and more conservative in its politics, although, after Luce's death in 1967, it did call for Richard Nixon's resignation in 1974.

The Times, London, English daily newspaper. Published since 1788, it was long considered the most influential organ of opinion in the British Empire. Its offputting format, with advertisements on the first page, its long opposition to illustrations, and its lively correspondence section ("I shall write to *The Times*" was a regular expression of outrage) bespoke its conservative bent. It has now bowed to the demands of a pop-culture market with a compact format and color pictures.

Tolstoy, Aleksey Nikolaevich (1882–1945), Russian dramatist After self-exile to Paris (1917–21), he returned to Russia and won popularity with his science fictions, *Aelita* (1924), in which a Red soldier visits Mars and leads a workers' rebellion, and *The Revolt of the Machines* (1924), an adaptation of Čapek's robot play *R.U.R.* He found favour with the Soviet regime and became known as "the Red Count", and his plays offer positive views of Peter the Great and Ivan the Terrible as precedents for Stalin.

Tolstoy, Lev Nikolaevich (1828–1910), Russian writer and titan. Although he disliked the theatre, he wrote several plays aimed at a mass audience. *The Power of Darkness* (1886), a somber drama of peasant crime and rapacity, was long suppressed by the censor. *The Fruits of Enlightenment* (begun 1886; published 1891), a comedy satirizing upper-class superstition, was first staged by amateurs. At his death, he left three plays dealing with moral issues: *The Living Corpse* (1900), the highly personal *The Light That Shines in Darkness* (1900) and *The Cause of It All* (1921), a temperance tract meant for amateurs. In *What Is Art?* he stated his belief that the theatre must tell the truth about the human soul to aid in its purification.

Tom Jones, English film directed by Tony Richardson from the novel by Henry Fielding (1963). Eighteenth-century bawdry released the New Wave of British filmmaking from its grit and grime. This is a high-spirited romp, its narrative disingenuousness and camera tricks redeemed by a superb cast: Albert Finney as Tom, Edith Evans as Miss Weston, Hugh Griffith as Squire Weston, Joyce Redman as Mrs Waters, down to Wilfrid Lawson in the tiny role of the gamekeeper.

Tone, Franchot (1905–68), American actor. A leading man of polished demeanour, for the Theatre Guild he played Tom Ames in *Hotel Universe* (1930) and Curly in *Green Grow the Lilacs* (1931). He was briefly with the Group Theatre, and, in the interstices of a thriving Hollywood career, continued to appear on and off Broadway in revivals.

Tonight at 8:30, nine English one-act plays by Noël Coward (1935–6). Divided into three groups, these modern comedies were performed by Coward and Gertrude Lawrence as displays of virtuosity, with different sequences on different nights of the week. The best are *Red Peppers*, about a husband-and-wife music-hall team, and *Fumed Oak*, in which the worm turns in a ghastly suburban family. *Still Life* was expanded into the weepy film *Brief Encounter* (1946).

Top Hat, American film directed by Mark Sandrich, with songs by Irving Berlin (1935). Fred Astaire and Ginger Rogers in one of their best pairings dance to the choreography of Hermes Pan. Although it is almost a carbon-copy of *Gay Divorcee*, it boasts such songs as "Isn't This a Lovely Day?", "Top Hat, White Tie and Tails" and "Cheek to Cheek".

Tosca, an Italian diva, heroine of a French drama by Victorien Sardou (1887). This vehicle for Sarah Bernhardt is set in Rome in Napoleon's time: to save her lover, the rebel painter Mario Cavaradossi, she offers herself to the secret police chief Scarpia, but stabs him instead. When Mario is shot by firing squad, she throws herself from the parapet of the Castel St. Angelo. The play was renovated as an opera by Puccini (1900), and is now a warhorse for sopranos.

Toscanini, Arturo (1867–1957), Italian conductor. He began as a cellist, but soon became an orchestral and operatic conductor of European renown, rigorous in cleaving to the tempi in Verdi and Wagner. He defied Mussolini and emigrated to the U.S. to become leader of the NBC Symphony Orchestra (1937–54), created for him. A strict taskmaster, he used his phenomenal memory to conduct without a score.

Toulouse-Lautrec, Henri Marie Raymond de (1864–1901), French artist. Dwarfish scion of a noble family, he became a denizen of bohemian Montmartre, whose dance-halls and brothels he immortalized in his lithographs and paintings. Cabaret stars such as Yvette Guilbert and Aristide Bruant sought him out to design their advertising posters. In John Huston's film *Moulin Rouge* (1952) José Ferrer played him as a lovelorn loner.

Toys in the Attic, American play by Lillian Hellman (1960), her last to enjoy critical favour. She returned to her theme of decaying Southern families. This time the repressed incestuous feelings of two spinster sisters surface when their brother brings home a bride.

Tracy, Spencer (1900–67), American actor. He made his Broadway debut in 1923, and was praised as the hard-boiled convict in *The Last Mile*

(1930). Typed as a tough guy when he came to Hollywood in 1930, he eventually found roles that softened the contours (the Portuguese fisherman in *Captains Courageous*, 1937; Father Flanagan in *Boy's Town*, 1938). Partnered professionally and personally with Katherine Hepburn, he made a number of enduring comedies, from *Woman of the Year* (1942) to *Guess Who's Coming to Dinner* (1967).

Treasure Girl, American musical comedy by Fred Thompson, Vincent Lawrence, and George and Ira Gershwin (1929). Starring Gertrude Lawrence, assisted by Walter Catlett, Clifton Webb and Constance Cummings, it offered a feeble plot about an heiress who marries a realtor and is threatened by hijackers.

Trenk-Trebitsch, Willi (1902–83), Austrian actor. After a debut in Prague, he came to Berlin where he worked with Max Reinhardt and Leopold Jessner, but had his greatest successes with Brecht and Weill, as the original Mack the Knife in *Die Dreigroschenoper* (1928) and in *The Rise and Fall of the City of Mahagonny*. The Nazi takeover drove him abroad. In Hollywood as William Trenk he founded My L.A. Ltd, an acting company for unemployed emigrés. After the war he returned to Germany.

Tsar Fyodor Ivanovitch (*Tsar Feodor Ioannovich*), Russian history play by Aleksey K. Tolstoy (1864). Feodor, heir of Ivan the Terrible, is spiritually pure, incapable of ruling with a firm hand. Various factions drive him from pillar to post, while the people seethe under his feeble sway. The second play of a blank-verse trilogy, it was forbidden the stage for 30 years. The Moscow Art Theatre production (1898), with its rich costumes, choral singing and picturesque groupings, remained a showpiece for decades.

Tudor, Antony (William Cook, 1908–87), English dancer and choreographer. A member of the Ballet Rambert in London, he choreographed several popular pieces (1931–7), before forming a breakaway group Dance Theatre (later the London Ballet, 1938–40). He moved to New York to lead the American Ballet Theatre (1940–50), staging *Pillar of Fire* and *Romeo and Juliet*. He continued to teach and make ballets throughout the 1970s.

Turandot, Italian fable by Carlo Gozzi (1762). In a legendary China, the cruel Princess Turandot poses each suitor three riddles and if he fails to answer them he is executed. Only Prince Calaf manages, by guile, to learn the answers. Schiller adapted it in 1802, and it was revived in Russia, first by Fyodor Kommissarzhevsky, then in a famously exuberant production by Evgeny Vakhtangov (1921). Puccini turned it into an opera in 1926, and Maria Jeritza created the role at the Metropolitan Opera, New York.

Turgenieff, more correctly **Turgenev, Ivan Sergeevich** (1818–83), Russian novelist and playwright. He wrote plays primarily to serve specific actors; their strongest aspect is his dialogue between two characters. A number of distinctive comedies (1843–52) were based in part on Alfred de Musset's *proverbes*. His best known play outside Russia, *A Month in the Country* (1849), was kept off the stage by censorship until 1872. Psychologically acute, it is an examination of the limits of individual freedom within social norms.

Turleigh, Veronica (1903–71), Irish actress. After work in William Poel's Shakespearean experiments, she had a long career on the West End stage playing aristocratic young women. At the Stratford Festival in 1947 she appeared in *Love's Labour's Lost* and had success in the comedy *The Rape of the Belt* (1958). Her most memorable film role was Lady Beeder in *The Horse's Mouth*, being gulled by Gully Jimpson (Alec Guinness).

Twain, Mark (Samuel Langhorne Clemens, 1835–1910), American writer. His ventures into playwriting, which included the collaborative comedies *Colonel Sellers* (based on his novel *The Gilded Age*) and *Two Men of Sandy Bar*, found little favour with the public. However, adaptations of such works as *The Prince and the Pauper*, *Puddinhead Wilson* and *A Connecticut Yankee* were constantly successful.

Twelfth Night, or What You Will, English comedy by William Shakespeare from Bandello, Cinthio and Riche (1599). One of the most frequently revived of his plays, using a girl-disguised-as-boy plot, it has a bittersweet quality that modulates the farcical aspects. Viola, the transvestite heroine, is irresistible to actresses of a certain size, and Malvolio the uppity steward offers rich comic opportunities. Helen Hayes and Maurice Evans played them on U.S. tour in 1940.

Two Corpses at Breakfast. This obscure Yiddish play makes a regular appearance in interviews with Paul Muni. Depending on the reporter, he was 11 (or 13) in 1907 (or 1908), when he was thrust on stage as a last-minute replacement, playing an elderly lodge president, and pulling it off.

The Two Mrs Carrolls, American play by Martin Vale (i.e., Marguerite Veiller, 1943). A thriller, in which a twisted artist attempts to poison his second wife in the same manner in which he did away with her predecessor, was successful in New York only after it had been heavily rewritten seven years after its original failure in London. As the villain, Victor Jory confirmed his knack at playing sinister heavies.

Tynan, Kenneth Peacock (1927–80), English critic. His criticism in the London *Evening Standard* and *The Observer* championed in witty, erudite prose heroic acting, Brecht, Beckett, and the Angry Young school. This led to his being appointed literary adviser to the new National Theatre in 1963, where he constantly butted heads with officialdom. Poster boy for sexual licence, he was the first to utter "fuck" on BBC television and authored the phenomenally successful erotic revue *Oh! Calcutta!* (1969).

Uncle Vanya (*Dyadya Vanya*), Russian "Scenes from Country Life in four acts" by Anton Chekhov (1890–6). A retired professor of fine art and his beautiful young wife Elena come from St. Petersburg to live on his late wife's estate. His brother-in-law, the estate manager Ivan Voynitsky, and the country doctor Astrov, become infatuated with Elena, but all the romances remain frustrated or abortive, including that of Sonya, the professor's daughter, for Astrov. At the play's end, Voynitsky and Sonya are abandoned by the others to face a life of empty drudgery. It was first staged by the Rostov-on-Don Dramatic

Society (1897) and revived frequently in the provinces, where audiences saw it as a mirror of their dismal lives.

Urban, Joseph (1871–1933), Vienna-born American designer. After much work in Europe designing expositions, operas and plays, he was brought to the U.S. in 1912 by the Boston Opera. Florenz Ziegfeld recruited him to design the *Follies*, as well as the Ziegfeld Theatre (1927). He also provided sets and costumes for James K. Hackett's Shakespearian revivals. His ingenious use of scene painting and colored lights, platforms and portals, strongly influenced Robert Edmond Jones and Lee Simonson.

Vakhtangov, Evgeny Bagrationovich (1883–1922), Armenian-born Russian actor and director. At the Moscow Art Theatre First Studio, he imbibed Stanislavsky's new system of acting and in 1913 founded his own studio. His umbrella term "fantastic realism" covered an amalgam of emotional and psychological truth with theatrical outward expression. His most influential productions were *The Dybbuk* (1922) for the Hebrew troupe Habima and *Princess Turandot* (1922), which employed *commedia dell'arte* and improvisational techniques to offer a highly coloured fantasia.

Vakhtangov Theatre, Moscow, the name given to the Moscow Art Theatre 3rd Studio in 1926. The music, rhythm and physicality of a young troupe were to characterize the productions that followed Vakhtangov's death, and imbue its comedies and farces. Later the theatre found it difficult to reconcile Vakhtangov's principles with socialist realism.

Valetti, Rosa (Vallentin, 1878–1937), German actress. Stocky, with the face of a bull-dog, she was one of the great stars of Weimar Berlin cabaret, especially as an interpreter of the work of Kurt Tucholsky. She founded the Café Grossenwahn (Megalomania) in 1920, and played Mrs Peachum in the first production of *Die Dreigroschenoper* (1928). In film she is recognizable as Marlene Dietrich's stage mother in *The Blue Angel* (1930). With the coming of the Nazis, she emigrated, ending up in Palestine.

The Valiant, American play by Holworthy Hall and Robert Middlemass (1925). The identity of a condemned man on death row is a mystery, until the night before his execution when a young woman asks to see him. The 1929 film gave Paul Muni one of his first starring roles (it was remade in 1940 as *The Man Who Couldn't Talk*).

Vanderbilt Theatre, New York, opened in 1921 with Pauline Lord in *Anna Christie*. It had one burst of glory with an all-star revival of *The Importance of Being Earnest*, before it was turned into a broadcasting studio, and then demolished in 1954.

Variety, a weekly trade paper of show business published in New York from 1905. It covers every genre of performances and devised a lingo that added a great many words and phrases to the American language. Because it prints weekly box-office grosses and attendance figures, it is read religiously by agents and producers, less so by performers.

Verdi, Giuseppe (1813–1901), Italian composer. Given the length of his productive career, his early operas bear traces of the *bel canto* tradition, while the later ones display the influence of Wagner. Intensely (melo)dramatic, *Rigoletto* (1851), *La Traviata* (1853), *Il Trovatore* (1853), *Aida* (1871), *Othello* (1887) and *Falstaff* (1893) have become imbedded in Western culture's memory bank.

Vernon, Frank (1875–1940), English actor. He made his debut in 1894, and was a member of Edmund Tearle's Shakespearean troupe and W. J. Holloway's South African tour (1898). He played with Martin-Harvey in *The Breed of Treshams* and as Capulet in *Romeo and Juliet* (1904). Under his own management, he staged *Cymbeline, The Winter's Tale* (1908) and *King Lear* (1909).

Victoria, Queen of Great Britain and Ireland (1819–1901). Her long reign (1838–1901) comprised so many revolutionary changes that it is known as the Victorian age, although she herself was formed by Regency attitudes. Episodes from her life were published as a series of one-act plays by Laurence Housman, eventually boiled down to *Victoria Regina* (1935). Helen Hayes gave an illusion of great acting by impersonating Victoria from a young woman to her jubilee.

La Vie Parisienne (*Parisian High Life*), French opéra bouffe by Jacques Offenbach (1866). Set during the Parisian Exhibition of 1865, it represents tourists falling prey to both the high spirits and the low intrigues of the residents. The first version was in five acts; the fourth act was dropped at the revival in 1873. The London premiere came in 1872, the New York in 1876.

Vieux Colombier, Théâtre du, Paris (1913–24). Jacques Copeau opened it in the old Athénée-Saint-Germain with an enlarged stage and proscenium, intending to simplify and modernize stage production. There he directed Claudel, Molière and Shakespeare. After a wartime hiatus, it was reopened in 1920, but four years later was turned over to Georges Pitoëff, while Copeau's troupe decamped to the countryside.

Village Wooing, "a comedietta in two voices, three conversations" by George Bernard Shaw (1933). Author A is pursued by female Passenger Z on shipboard during a cruise. He runs into her again running her village shop, and is persuaded to assist and then marry her. In performance, Author A is often made up to look like Shaw.

Villon, François (François de Montcorbier, 1431 – after 1463), French poet. While a student in Paris, he wounded a priest in a brawl and joined a criminal gang. Regularly sentenced for felonies and then pardoned, he was ultimately banished in 1463. His poems, often written in underworld slang, appeared in 1489. He was the picaresque hero of Justin Huntley McCarthy's play *If I Were King*, which was then turned into Rudolf Friml's comic opera *The Vagabond King*.

Vincent, Mary Ann (Farlow, 1818–87), Anglo-American actress. She and her actor husband came to Boston in 1846 and after his death she joined the Boston Museum Company in 1852, remaining there for 35 years in 444 roles. Plump, rosy, homely, she was a darling of the public in old lady parts.

Le Viol de Lucrèce. See ***Lucrece***.

Virgil (Publius Vergilius, 70–19 B.C.E.), Roman poet. His pastoral poems – the *Eclogues* and the *Georgics* – established him as the leading poet of his day, so that the emperor Augustus commissioned him to write a national epic about the founding of Rome. This turned out to be the *Aeneid* (*c*.18 B.C.E.). His poems were regarded as sacred works, often used for bibliomancy, and he himself was appointed as Dante's guide in the afterlife in the *Divine Comedy*.

Vogue, American fashion magazine. First published in England in 1892, it passed into the ownership of the American Condé Nast and achieved a reputation for elegant reportage of fashion and society news. It gained popularity during the Depression, probably because it supported wishful thinking, and became extremely influential in the 1960s under the editorship of Diana Vreeland, who promoted the idea of the supermodel.

Volksbühne, a generic term for people's theatre, current in Germany from 1889. The Berlin Volksbühne, built in 1913–14, grew out of the Freie Volks-bühne, created in 1890 to express working-class concerns at popular prices. It was managed by Max Reinhardt (1915–18) and later Erwin Piscator (1923–8), who moved it farther to the left. During the Second World War, it was bombed into rubble, and then rebuilt in what was then East Berlin (1950–4).

Volpone, or The Fox, English comedy by Ben Jonson (1606). In Venice a group of legacy-hunters swarm around the bed of the rich and childless Volpone, bearing him gifts; his "creature" Mosca aids the deception that his master is dying. Everyone comes to a bad end in Jonson, which may be why the twentieth century preferred Stefan Zweig's happy-ending version. It was produced by the Theatre Guild in 1928, and a French adaptation by Jules Romains was a vehicle for Charles Dullin for years.

Von Sternberg, Joseph (Jo Sternberg, 1894–1969), Austrian-born American film director. His first successful film was the atmospheric silent gangster picture *Underworld* (1927), but *The Blue Angel* (1930), filmed in Germany, became legendary. Dictatorial, impatient, self-centered, he devoted his energies to turning his star Marlene Dietrich into an international sex-symbol, through lighting, costume and ridiculous plots, as in *Morocco* (1930), *Blonde Venus* (1932) and *The Scarlet Empress* (1934). When she left him, so did his inspiration.

The Vortex, an English drama by Noël Coward (1925). This heady cocktail, one part Ibsen's *Ghosts* to two parts Somerset Maugham, created a sensation when first produced, with Coward as the male lead. An older woman who behaves far too young for her age has her lover stolen by her son's fiancée and then discovers that her son is a drug addict.

Wagner, Fritz Arno (1894–1958), German cinematographer. Collaborating with G. W. Pabst, Fritz Lang and F. W. Murnau, he provided the moody, beautifully composed images of *Nosferatu* (1922), *M* and *Die Dreigroschenoper* (both 1931). His compositions could be poetically evocative (*Die müde Tod*, 1921) or documentary (*Kameradschaft*, 1931). He worked on 143 films before his death in an automobile accident.

Wagner, Richard (1813–83), German tone-poet and impresario. At the Festival Theatre in Bayreuth, which opened in 1876, he could carry out his theories of the *Gesamtkunstwerk* or total work of art. Besides composing, libretto-writing, designing, and staging his epic works, *Tristan und Isolde* (1854), *Die Meistersinger* (1862) and *Der Ring des Nibelungen* (1876), it allowed him to innovate in stagecraft as well as orchestration. Once Bayreuth was turned into a place of pilgrimage, *Parsifal* came in 1882.

Waiting for Godot (*En Attendant Godot*), French/English play by Samuel Beckett (1952, 1954), in which "nothing happens twice" (Vivian Mercer). First produced in Paris, then in London, it was greeted with confusion and hostility, but is now routinely used as a set text for schools. After a Miami fiasco, billed as "the laugh riot of two continents", it was revived in New York with Bert Lahr and E. G. Marshall (1956) and had a success with the critics, if not the public.

Walker, June (1899?–1966), American actress. She excelled at dumb blondes, particularly Lorelei Lee in *Gentlemen Prefer Blondes* (1926), and ingenues, such as Laurey in *Green Grow the Lilacs* (1931). She played opposite Henry Fonda in *The Farmer Takes a Wife* (1934).

Walkley, A[lfred] B[ingham] (1855–1926), English dramatic critic. Writing for *The Star* and other papers, he analyzed the literary merits of a play more than its performance. Shaw continually teased him and made him a character in *Fanny's First Play*.

Die Walküre (*The Valkyries*), German opera by Richard Wagner (1870). The second part of *Der Ring des Nibelungen* (but the first "festival play" if *Das Rheingold* is taken to be a prologue), it introduces the incestuous union of Siegmund and Sieglinde. For interfering in their fates, the Valkyrie Brünnhilde is condemned by her father-god Wotan to sleep within a ring of magic fire. "The Ride of the Valkyries" has become one of the most hard-working themes in musical history.

Wallace, Edgar Horatio (1875–1932), English novelist and playwright. A prolific purveyor of crime fiction, he boasted of finishing one of his plays in four days. He had three West-End hits in the 1929/30 season, and several of his plays appeared on Broadway. *The Terror* (1927) was frequently remade as a film, in English and German. Shortly before his death he became a script doctor in Hollywood.

Wallach, Eli (1915–), American actor. Acquaintance with Elia Kazan at Actors Studio led to a small role in the original *A Streetcar Named Desire*, leading in turn to the gaudy part of Alvaro Mangiacavallo in *The Rose Tattoo* (1951). With his wife Anne Jackson he made a hit in the bill of one-acts *The Typists and The Tiger* (1963) and again in *Luv* (1964). His multi-faceted character acting is chiefly seen in the movies.

Walter, Bruno (Schlesinger, 1876–1962), German conductor and pianist. A friend of Gustav Mahler and an enthusiast for Bruckner, he promoted their music throughout Europe. He was the chief conductor at the Vienna Opera House (1901–12) and the Munich Opera House (1913–22). He adopted

French citizenship in 1938, and emigrated the following year to the U.S., where he perpetuated the romantic tradition.

Walton, Sir William Turner (1902–83), English composer. A protegé of the literary Sitwells, he won a reputation as a modernist for his setting of Edith Sitwell's poems, *Façade* (1923); Osbert Sitwell compiled the texts for his oratorio *Belshazzar's Feast* (1931). His scores for Laurence Olivier's Shakespeare films – *Henry V* (1944), *Hamlet* (1945) and *Richard III* (1955) – became popular programme music. He also turned *Troilus and Cressida* into an opera (1954).

Waram, Percy (1881–1961), English actor. He had a long career on the U.S. stage beginning in 1902 in *Everyman* and Shakespearean comedy. He acted for the Theatre Guild (1922, 1930), and aged into the parts of elderly gentlemen. He was the original Horace Vandergelder in *The Merchant of Yonkers* (1938), Roger Newcombe in *The Late George Apley* (1944, filmed 1947), Marcus Hubbard in *Another Part of the Forest* (1946) and Cardinal Wolsey in *Anne of the Thousand Days* (1948).

Warm Peninsula, American comedy by Joe Masteroff (1959). Described by *Time* as "something for the slightly retarded matinee trade", it contrasts a plain girl with glasses (Julie Harris) and an unemployed show girl (June Havoc) who fall for the wrong man (Farley Granger and Larry Hagman, respectively) while confiding in the audience. Set in a Miami Beach apartment, it had an afterlife in regional theatres.

Washington Square Players, an amateur group co-founded by Lawrence Langner in 1915, to improve the quality of the dramatic repertoire. In a 40-seat theatre, they staged a wide variety of one-acts and the first American production of *The Seagull*, which failed. In a larger house, the Comedy, they succeeded with O'Neill's *In the Zone*, and in 1919 reconstituted themselves as the Theatre Guild.

Watch on the Rhine, an American play by Lillian Hellman (1941). Topical in intent, it tried to compel Americans to shake off their torpor and take Fascism seriously. A well-carpentered domestic melodrama, it was rendered irrelevant by the entrance of the U.S. into the Second World War, so that the film version (1943) comes across as alternately wooden and overwrought.

Watts, Richard, Jr. (1898–1981), American dramatic critic. When Percy Hammond of the New York *Herald* died suddenly, he took over the drama desk (1936–42) and later moved to the New York *Post* (1946–74). He kept an open mind about experimental theatre, but could be vitriolic.

The Way of the World, English comedy by William Congreve (1700). Called by Swinburne the "unapproached masterpiece of English comedy", it is burdened with an incomprehensible plot. Fortunately, the sparkle of the dialogue and the richness of the characters have kept this comedy of manners viable in the theatre. Edith Evans first played Millamant in 1924, and then Lady Wishfort in 1948. A revival with John Gielgud, Paul Scofield and Margaret Rutherford in 1953 added to its lustre.

Wayne, David (Wayne James McMeekan, 1914–95), American actor. In the post-war period, he had a remarkable streak of hits, as the leprechaun Og in *Finian's Rainbow* (1947), Ensign Pulver in *Mr Roberts* (1948) and Sakini in *The Teahouse of the August Moon* (1953), among others. His best film role was as Kip, the effete neighbour of Spencer Tracy and Katherine Hepburn in *Adam's Rib* (1949). He was a member of the first Lincoln Center Repertory company (1964).

We Americans, American play by Milton Herbert Gropper and Max Siegel (1926). A melting-pot story of Jewish immigrants attending a night school to improve their chances at success in the Golden Land, it offered Paul Muni his first English-speaking role. Luther Adler also appeared. It was filmed in 1928 with an entirely different cast.

We Are Not Alone, American film directed by Edmund Goulding from a story by James Hilton (1939). Paul Muni's favourite among his pictures, it casts him as a deferential Edwardian Englishman married to domineering Flora Robson and in love with their governess (Jane Bryan). He is accused of his wife's murder and undergoes agonies of conscience.

We Love a Lassie, American comedy by Marcel Wallenstein and Kathleen Kennedy (1947). Staged by Melville Cooper, with Julie Harris in the cast, this play tried out in Boston and Washington, but failed to make it to New York.

Webster, John (1580?-1625), English playwright. A leading exponent of the revenge tragedy, set in Italy and replete with blood-letting and gruesome conceits, he collaborated with most of the working dramatists of his time. The plays from his hand alone include *The Devil's Law Case*, *The White Devil* and *The Duchess of Malfi*, tragedies streaked with black comedy.

Wedding Breakfast, American comedy by Theodore Reeves (1954). The romantic difficulties of two Jewish sisters who share a New York apartment were acted out by a quartet of Anthony Franciosa, Lee Grant, Harvey Lembeck and Virginia Vincent. Sniffed at by the critics, it still enjoyed a decent run.

Wedekind, Frank (1864–1918), American-born German playwright. After work in circus and cabaret, he outraged his fellow countrymen with his "tragedies of sex", *The Awakening of Spring* (1891) and the "Lulu" plays, *Earth Spirit* (1895) and *Pandora's Box* (1902). He wrote prolifically and saw his works staged, but by the First World War, he seemed less shocking.

Weep for the Virgins, American play by Nellise Child (Lillian Gerard, 1935). One of the Group Theatre's biggest mistakes, despite direction by Cheryl Crawford, sets by Boris Aronson, a cast that included John Garfield, Phoebe Brand and J. Edward Bromberg, and a subsidy from Warner Brothers. Three sisters who work in a fish cannery have been raised to know nothing of sex and to dream of Hollywood stardom. It ran nine performances.

Weigel, Helene (1900–71) was already an experienced actress on the Berlin stage when she met Bertolt Brecht in 1923, had his son the next year and married him in 1928. She became his leading actress in *The Mother* (1932) and *Señora Carrer's Rifles* (1937). She accompanied him during his emigration and kept a frugal house in the Hollywood hills. Once Brecht returned to

Germany and founded the Berliner Ensemble, Weigel's deeply seamed features and sinewy physique composed the iconic face of epic acting, especially as the hardbitten war profiteer Mother Courage. She ran the company and, after Brecht's death in 1956, helped it to international fame by touring it to London.

Weill, Kurt (1900–50), German composer. His career breaks easily into two parts, the European and the American. A student of Busoni and a proponent of *Gebrauchsmusik* ("applied music"), he collaborated with Bertolt Brecht on a number of theatre pieces, including *The Protagonist* (1926), *Rise and Fall of the City of Mahagonny* (1927–9) and the immensely popular *Dreigroschenoper* (1928). With the advent of the Nazis, he and his wife Lotte Lenya emigrated to the U.S. (1935), where he wrote successfully for the Broadway stage: *Knickerbocker Holiday*, *Lady in the Dark*, *Lost in the Stars* et al.

Weill-Davis, Karoline, daughter of Kurt Weill and Lotte Lenya, wife of George Davis.

Wenham, Jane (Figgins, 1927–), English actress. Briefly married to Albert Finney (1957–61), she had her best film role as Eva in *An Inspector Calls* (1954). The rest of her career was played out on British television well into the 1990s.

West Side Story, American musical by Leonard Bernstein, Arthur Laurents and Stephen Sondheim (1957). The feuding families of *Romeo and Juliet* are transformed into white and Puerto Rican gangs in Manhattan. Given a dynamic staging by choreographer Jerome Robbins, it opened up a new vein in musical comedy, less appreciated at the time than since. Its songs include "Tonight", "Officer Krupke" and "Somewhere".

Westminster Theatre, London. First opened in 1876 as an adjunct to the Royal Aquarium under the management of Henry Labouchère, it was rebuilt as a showplace for Lillie Langtry in 1902. The building was eventually moved to Canning Town where it functioned as a music hall.

Whale, James (1889–1957), English director. His service in the First World War and as a P.O.W. was of value when he directed *Journey's End* (1928), discovering Laurence Olivier along the way. Brought to Hollywood to film the play, he found his metier was horror movies, filmed with great mastery of the moving camera: *Frankenstein* (1931), *The Old Dark House* (1932), *The Invisible Man* (1933) and *Bride of Frankenstein* (1934). He is also responsible for the best film version of *Show Boat* (1936). He has been fictionalized in Christopher Bram's novel *Father of Frankenstein* (1995), itself made into the film *Gods and Monsters* (1998).

The Wheel, English play by J. B. Fagan (1922). The original cast for this fantasy was a mixture of veterans and such beginners as Edith Evans and John Gielgud. He described it as "fearfully difficult but fine and most interesting to be in" and predicted its success among artistic types.

Wheeler, Hugh (1912–87), English writer, who emigrated to the U.S. in 1934. After turning out several mystery novels under a variety of pseudonyms, he launched into playwriting with *Big Fish, Little Fish* (1961). His greatest theatrical successes were as librettist to Stephen Sondheim, with whom he created *A Little Night Music* (1973), *Pacific Overtures* (1976) and *Sweeney Todd* (1979).

White, Lee (1886–1927), American actress and singer. Teamed with her husband Clay Smith, she was a great hit at the London Coliseum (1918).

White, Ruth (1914–69), American actress. After studying acting with Maria Ouspenskaya, she launched a career in 1949, which she cut short to nurse her mother. She returned to the stage in 1956 as a homely character woman, and soon was in demand for avant-garde drama, appearing off and on Broadway in *Happy Days, Malcolm* (1966), *Little Murders* (1967), *The Birthday Party* and *Box Mao Box* (both 1968).

The White Devil, English revenge tragedy by John Webster (1612). Grounded on the actual murder of Vittoria Accoramboni in Padua, the play uses Italian corruption to comment on contemporary English court intrigues. A 1925 revival of a heavily cut version, featuring Cedric Hardwicke, at the Renaissance Theatre, London, was poorly received, but it was successfully staged at the Phoenix Theatre in 1955.

Who's Who in the Theatre, a dictionary of the English-speaking stage, first published in 1912. In addition to biographical entries, it included dates of long runs, statistics, and genealogical charts. A comprehensive four-volume conflation of all previous editions was published in 1978.

Whorf, Richard (1906–66), American actor and designer. He played with the Lunts throughout the 1930s and 1940s, in such roles as Mercury in *Amphitryon 38* and Konstantin in *The Seagull* (both 1938). After playing and designing *Richard III* (1949), he moved more exclusively to very chi-chi set and costume design (*Ondine*, 1954) and directing (*Seventeen*, 1951).

Widowers' Houses, play by George Bernard Shaw (1892). Shaw's first play to be produced, it is typically paradoxical in making a slum landlady his heroine. By the end the idealistic hero has yielded to economic necessity and joined the system.

Wilde, Oscar (1856–1900), Irish poet and playwright. The success of Wilde's society comedies – *Lady Windermere's Fan* (1892), *A Woman of No Importance* (1893), and *An Ideal Husband* (1894) – owed a lot to their coruscating epigrams, but more to their resemblance to familiar dramas of high life. Only *The Importance of Being Earnest* (1895) rises to the level of sublime nonsense. When he was condemned for sodomy, his plays remained on stage but his name was removed from the bills.

Wilder, Thornton (1897–1975), American novelist and playwright. The closest thing to an avant-garde dramatist America had in the 1930s, he experimented with starkness in *Our Town* (1938), period nostalgia in *The Merchant of Yonkers* (1938; revised as *The Matchmaker*, 1954), and allegory in *The Skin of Our Teeth* (1942). A proposal from Max Reinhardt for a film of *The Tales of Hoffmann* came to nothing, but he did work with Alfred Hitchcock on *Shadow of a Doubt*.

Wilkinson, Norman (1892–1934), English designer. He designed the sets for Harley Granville-Barker's *Twelfth Night* and *Iphigenia in Tauris* (both 1912).

Williams, Harcourt (1880–1957), English actor and director. His early career was spent with Benson, Ellen Terry, H. B. Irving and George Alexander, in a wide array of plays. A beautiful Romeo and the Player King to John Barrymore's Hamlet, he concentrated on Shakespeare as artistic director of the Old Vic (1929–34), where his reforms were drawn from Granville-Barker. Olivier cast him as the King of France in his film of *Henry V*.

Williams, Rhys (1897–1969), Welsh actor. A member of a number of Shakespearean companies in England, he came to the U.S. touring in stock. He settled in Hollywood, and was hired as adviser on Wales to *How Green Was My Valley* (1941). The only real Welshman in the cast, he was thereafter never out of work as a character actor in film and television.

Williams, Tennessee (actually Thomas, 1911–83), American playwright. The juicy dialogue and dramatic confrontations of characters in his plays compensate for their often hysterical and self-loathing tone. *The Glass Menagerie* (1945), *A Streetcar Named Desire* (1947) and *Cat on A Hot Tin Roof* (1955) have become tried-and-true classics. *Summer and Smoke* (1948), *The Rose Tattoo* (1951), *Camino Real* (1953), *Sweet Bird of Youth* (1959) and *Night of the Iguana* (1961) have qualities that bring them back to the repertory. The considerable remainder of his work is a freak show of emotional over-indulgence and technical miscalculation.

Windust, Bretaigne (1906–60), American director and actor. Seasoned by work with the Theatre Guild, staging the London premiere of *Strange Interlude*, he became associated with the Lunts, playing Tranio in *Taming of the Shrew* (1935), directing them in *Idiot's Delight* (1936), *Amphitryon 38* (1937) and *The Great Sebastians* (1956). He excelled at comedy, staging *Life with Father* (1939), *Arsenic and Old Lace* (1945) and *Finian's Rainbow* (1947).

Winfred and Mills. Henry Winfred (1871–1931) and Billy (William R.) Mills (d.1971) were an African-American vaudeville team. Winfred played a Chinese laundryman and Mills, his face blackened with burnt cork, a Negro customer.

Wingless Victory, American play by Maxwell Anderson (1936). The tale of Medea is transferred to New England (shades of O'Neill!). A Yankee skipper brings home a Malaysian princess as his bride, but when she finds herself rejected by his family and community she kills herself and their children. The part allowed Katharine Cornell to wear dusky make-up and little else.

Winslow, Mrs Erving. See **Reignolds, Kate**.

The Winslow Boy, English play by Terence Rattigan (1946). Based on the Archer–Shee case, it concerns a 13-year-old boy expelled from the Royal Naval College for having stolen a 5-shilling postal order. His father stakes everything on hiring the coolly rational Sir Robert Morton to defend his son and wins an acquittal. It was first filmed by Anthony Asquith in 1948, with Robert Donat as the Q.C., and remade claustrophobically by David Mamet in 1998 with Jeremy Northam as the Holmesian barrister.

Winterset, a blank verse play by Maxwell Anderson (1935). An attempt to elevate current events, the Sacco and Vanzetti trial and bootlegging, to poetic drama, it was highly thought-of in its time, but now comes across as windily pretentious. Setting it in the shadow of the Brooklyn Bridge did give it a certain specious grandeur.

The Wizard of Oz is a musical-comedy adaptation by L. Frank Baum, Paul Tietjens and A. Baldwin Sloane (1903) of Baum's children's book *The Wonderful Wizard of Oz*. The book and its sequels entered American folklore, and were even more widely promulgated by the MGM movie of 1938.

A Woman Killed with Kindness, English domestic tragedy by Thomas Heywood (1603). In Yorkshire a gentleman finds his wife in the arms of his friend. Although she pleads for death, he banishes her to another house to live out her life in comfort, but she wastes away from the considerate treatment. Jacques Copeau offered this in his first season at the Vieux Colombier.

Woollcott, Alexander (1887–1943), American dramatic critic. Obese, bespectacled, tart-tongued, he was less an analyst than a rhapsodist, distributing superlatives to his darlings (Charlie Chaplin, Harpo Marx, Mrs Fiske, Thornton Wilder) and brickbats to his *bêtes noires* (O'Neill). He won a nationwide audience as a radio commentator, and in this guise is caricatured as the insufferable Sheridan Whiteside in *The Man Who Came to Dinner*, a role he played in the Los Angeles company.

Wuthering Heights, American film directed by William Wyler, from the novel by Emily Brontë (1939). Half of the novel is jettisoned in order to concentrate on the other-worldly passion of Cathy (Merle Oberon) and Heathcliff (Laurence Olivier), framed by narration by Flora Robson. Severely studio-bound, the film lacks true atmosphere, either Gothic or period, but established Olivier as a pattern of a romantic lover.

Wyatt, Jane (1910–2006), American actress. A fresh-faced ingenue, she was dropped from the New York Social Register when she understudied Rose Hobart in *Trade Winds* (1931). For a while, she successfully alternated Broadway (*Night Music*, 1940), with Hollywood (*Lost Horizons*: stage 1934, screen 1937). Falling foul of anti-Communist Senator Joseph McCarthy (she had attended a performance of the Bolshoi Ballet), she found her film career blighted and acted on stage exclusively (*The Autumn Garden*, 1951). A new generation welcomed her as the submissive mother in the television series *Father Knows Best* (1954–60).

Wynyard, Diana (Dorothy Isobel Cox, 1906–64), English actress. She became a star as Charlotte Brontë in *Wild Decembers* (1933) and created Gilda in the London company of *Design for Living* (1939). Her delicate beauty and melodious voice were bestowed on a number of Shakespearean roles at Stratford (Desdemona, Beatrice, Queen Katharine, Hermione, Lady Macbeth) and she played Gertrude to Paul Scofield's Hamlet on a tour to Moscow.

Yanshin, Mikhail Mikhailovich (1902–76), Russian actor and director. In 1924 he was accepted into the Moscow Art Theatre. The short, tubby actor played secondary roles until he won over audiences in 1926 as the sprightly Lariosik in *Days of the Turbins*, which suited his temperament exactly. Of his

50 roles, only a few were original creations As a director, he professionalized the gypsy theatre Romén (1937–1941), where he staged Lorca's *Blood Wedding*.

Yeats, William Butler (1865–1939), Irish poet and playwright. With Lady Gregory, he founded the Irish Literary Theatre (1899) which developed into the Abbey Theatre (1904). To his disappointment, the public taste was not for poetic drama (*On Baile's Strand*, 1904; *Deirdre*, 1907), so he turned to prose (*Cathleen Ni Houlihan*, 1902; *The Hour Glass*, 1903). He was so disgusted by audiences' rejection of Synge's *Playboy of the Western World* that he turned his back on them and dreamed of a Western version of the elitest Noh play (*The Cat and the Moon; Four Plays for Dancers*, both 1924).

Yegor Bulichov and Others (*Egor Bulychyov i drugie*). Russian tragedy in three acts by Maksim Gorky (1931–2). On the eve of the Russian Revolution, Bulychyov, a rich merchant dying of cancer, tries to be a war profiteer, while his house fills up with greedy relatives, quack healers and religious hypocrites. It opened on 25 September 1932 simultaneously at the Vakhtangov Theatre, Moscow, and at the Bolshoi Dramatic Theatre, Leningrad, and was eventually staged by almost every theatre in the U.S.S.R.

You Can't Take It with You, American comedy by George S. Kaufman and Moss Hart (1936). As the Depression was ending, there was great appeal to this tale of the Sycamore family who care nothing for money and everything for doing what they choose. With a love interest devoid of sex, it is a regular favorite with high schools and community theatres.

Young, Stark. See the headnote to Chapter 3, "Billets doux".

The Young and the Fair, American play by N. Richard Nash (1948). This play about a Boston girl's school featured Julie Harris, but had a short run on Broadway. It was revived on television in 1953 with Mildred Dunnock and Joanne Woodward.

Zacconi, Ermete (1856–1948), Italian actor-manager. Along with plays by Tolstoy, Hauptmann and Strindberg, he introduced *Ghosts* to the Italian stage with himself as Oswald and Duse as Mrs Alving. In Shakespeare, he was outstanding as Hamlet and Othello, and toured widely.

Zanuck, Daryl Francis (1902–79), American film producer. Beginning as a scenarist at Warner Brothers (for Mack Sennett and Rin Tin Tin), in 1933 he co-founded Twentieth Century Pictures, which two years later became Twentieth Century-Fox. He was more or less in control there until 1971, defying the competition from television with sumptuous and expensive productions.

Zarkhi, Natan Abramovich (1900–35), Russian playwright. He provided the scenarios for two of the most important Soviet silent films: *Mother* (1925) and *The End of St Petersburg* (1926). His only stage play of significance is *Joy Street* (1932).

Zavadsky Theatre, actually Zavadsky Studio, Moscow, founded by the actor Yury Zavadsky in 1924 as a training school for the Vakhtangov Theatre.

Its lack of space lent a miniature quality to its staging of plays by Shaw, Ostrovsky and Sheridan, with close attention to texts and surprising transformations of characters. Zavadsky fell out of favour and it was transferred to Rostov in 1936, to make up the core of the Gorky Theatre.

Ziegfeld "Follies", a New York revue, conceived by Florenz Ziegfeld. It ran for 24 editions (1907–31). Its main purpose was to "glorify the American girl", but in the process it featured brilliant comedians (W. C. Fields, Bert Williams, Fanny Brice, Eddie Cantor, Will Rogers) and innovative design by Joseph Urban.

Ziegfeld Theatre, New York. Opened by Florenz Ziegfeld in 1927 to house his lavish spectacles, it had an ovoid auditorium. It underwent the customary changes: a cinema from 1914, then a theatre from 1944, a television studio 1955–63, and a theatre again until it was razed in 1966.

Zoffany, Johann (Zauffelij, 1733–1810), German painter. Much in demand for his "conversation pieces" showing families and friends in their natural habitats, he also painted portraits of actors in and out of their roles. David Garrick, as Hamlet, King Lear or at his Thames-side property, was a recurrent model.

Zola, Émile (1840–1902), French novelist and playwright. He theorized about naturalism in the theatre, but few of his plays exemplify his tenets or appeal to audiences. *Thérèse Raquin* (1873), his manifesto play, is more a psychological thriller than a documentary dossier. His most successful dramas were collaborative adaptations of his novels: *L'Assommoir* (1878) with its cat-fight in a laundry, *Le Ventre de Paris*, with its on-stage sausage-making, etc.